Wissenschaftliche Untersuchungen
zum Neuen Testament · 2. Reihe

Herausgeber / Editor
Jörg Frey (Zürich)

Mitherausgeber/Associate Editors
Markus Bockmuehl (Oxford) · James A. Kelhoffer (Uppsala)
Tobias Nicklas (Regensburg) · Janet Spittler (Charlottesville, VA)
J. Ross Wagner (Durham, NC)

485

Giuseppe G. Scollo

The Strength Needed to Enter the Kingdom of God

An Exegetical and Theological Study
of Luke 16,16 in Context

Mohr Siebeck

GIUSEPPE G. SCOLLO, born 1978; 2000 Bachelor of Catholic Thought from St. Philip's Seminary (Toronto); 2007 M.Div. from St. Augustine's Seminary (Toronto); 2013 S.S.L. from the Pontifical Biblical Institute (Rome); 2018 S.T.D. from the Pontifical Gregorian University (Rome); currently vice-rector of the Redemptoris Mater Missionary Seminary of Toronto and assistant professor at St. Augustine's Academic Faculty.

ISBN 978-3-16-156859-6 / eISBN 978-3-16-156860-2
DOI 10.1628/978-3-16-156860-2

ISSN 0340-9570 / eISSN 2568-7484 (Wissenschaftliche Untersuchungen zum Neuen Testament, 2. Reihe)

The Deutsche Nationalbibliothek lists this publication in the Deutsche Nationalbibliographie; detailed bibliographic data are available on the Internet at *http://dnb.dnb.de*.

The book was printed by Laupp & Göbel in Gomaringen on non-aging paper and bound by Buchbinderei Nädele in Nehren. BWLexs, Bwgrkn, Bwheba, and Bwhebb are fonts from BibleWorks, LLC.

Printed in Germany.

To my Guardian Angel

(למלאך השומר שלי)

Preface

In the Gospel of Luke, what does Jesus say about the strength needed to enter the kingdom of God? The present study of Luke 16,16 represents the full revised version of my Ph.D. dissertation of the same title, presented in part to the Theological Faculty of the Pontifical Gregorian University of Rome, in May 2018. As such, it is the result of intuitions, reflections, research and investigations on the fascinating subject of how we should all go about tackling the paradox between love and violence for the sake of securing an eternal abode in Heaven. The choice and inspiration of the topic flowed from an initial question that came to me in 2013, while silently praying before the Blessed Sacrament, in the chapel of the Pontifical Canadian College in Rome. I was looking for a dissertation topic and I suddenly remembered a question which I had left unanswered in a footnote of my previous thesis for the Licentiate, at the Pontifical Biblical Institute: considering the targumic interpretation of Deut 6,5 and the evangelist's emphasis on the word "mammon" (μαμωνᾶς), within the unique immediate context in which the "violence saying" occurs as against that of Matthew's Gospel (cf. Matt 6,24; 11,12; and Luke 16,9.11.13. 16), could the heavenly kingdom be acquired by one who loves the Lord God with all one's strength or possessions, by means of a violent detachment of the self from material goods, through almsgiving? The examination of the material, the development of the research, and rumination on its findings have both strengthened that original perception and gradually substantiated it. I am pleased to share here the research, documentation and conclusions of my work in the hope that it will contribute to the better understanding of this verse, and so broaden the scope of Lucan studies and theology.

Acknowledgements

First of all, I would like to thank the Lord for the gift and privilege of dedicating years of study to his holy Word. Likewise, the completion of the project and its achievements would not have been possible without the support and collaboration of several key people and institutions. I would thus like to express my most sincere gratitude to His Eminence, Thomas Cardinal Collins, Archbishop of Toronto and my current Ordinary, as well as to Msgr. Héctor Vila, former Rector at my Seminary and today Bishop of Whitehorse: their inspiration, trust, and encouragement have been and are a tremendous help to me. I thank also Msgr. Robert Nusca, former Rector at St. Augustine's Seminary, for supporting me at the beginning of this long journey, as well as the Dean of St. Philip's Seminary, Fr. Paul Pearson, for his faithful guidance and his personal accompaniment over many years.

God has then granted me an abundance of graces and blessings through my attendance at the meetings and celebrations of the Neocatechumenal Way: to its founders (Mr. Kiko Argüello, the late Ms. Carmen Hernández and Fr. Mario Pezzi) and to my catechists (Fr. Isidoro Tomasoni and Ms. Donatella Viozzi) I owe not only my formation as a priest, but also my very life, faith, and Christian vocation. I also want to express many thanks to all the lay brothers and sisters of my communities, whether in Rosolini, Toronto or Rome, as well as the seminarians, priests, and religious, who in one way or another have patiently accompanied me during all these years, providing me with both material and moral support, especially those at the Redemptoris Mater and St. Augustine Seminaries in Toronto, the Pontifical Biblical Institute, Gregorian University, and Canadian College in Rome, as well as the Benedictine Monasteries of "Santa Maria delle Rose" and "San Ruggero", in Sant'Angelo in Pontano and Barletta, respectively.

A heart-felt word of thanks goes then to all my professors, particularly those who have taught me the languages and passed on to me a love for the Sacred Scriptures: Profs. Jean-Noël Aletti, S.J., Gianguerrino Barbiero, S.D.B., Pino Di Luccio, S.J., Maurice Gilbert, S.J., Craig E. Morrison, O. Carm., and Reinhard Neudecker, S.J., of the Pontifical Biblical Institute in Rome; Profs. Bruna Costacurta, Mario López Barrio, S.J., and Piero Stefani, of the Pontifical Gregorian University; Profs. Eugenio M. Alliata, O.F.M., Alfio M. Buscemi, O.F.M., Frédéric Manns, O.F.M., and Massimo Pazzini,

O.F.M., of the Studium Biblicum Franciscanum of Jerusalem; Prof. Étienne Nodet, O.P., of the École Biblique de Jérusalem; and Prof. Francesco G. Voltaggio, of the Studium Theologicum Galilaeae.

Likewise, I wish to acknowledge and thank all those individual friends and benefactors who at various levels and stages of the drafting process have been particularly helpful and greatly supportive. Father Dean Béchard, S.J., Associate Professor of New Testament Exegesis at the Pontifical Biblical Institute in Rome and moderator of this doctoral thesis, has been a very kind, careful and wise mentor; his tireless work, scholarly expertise, and constructive critical remarks have contributed invaluable insights and guidance for the topics covered in it and their arrangements. Father Edmond Gendron, professor emeritus of philosophy and present pastor at Assomption de Notre-Dame Parish in Oshawa, has carefully read over the entire manuscript and made many valuable suggestions and corrections. Sister Federica, a Benedictine nun and fellow-sister of my youngest sibling in the Cloister of Sant'Angelo in Pontano, has been of great help to me in translating some texts from German. Other brother priests (e.g., Fr. Tomasz Skibinski and Fr. Grzegorz Nowicki) and lay people (e.g., Aleksander Kowalski and Anna Rogala) have done the same with regard to Polish.

Finally, one last word of special thanks goes to my parents, Giovanni and Graziella, and my three sisters, Carmen, Stefania and Sr. Emanuela, for their love, encouragement and unfaltering support, as well as to my two brothers-in-law, my seven nieces and nephews, and all who have prayed for me over the past few years, making a number of beneficial observations and sustaining me in a variety of ways, whether directly or indirectly, as friends and colleagues. To them and countless other precious contributors, I would like to extend my deepest and heartfelt gratitude.

Toronto, October 18, 2018
Feast of St. Luke, Evangelist   Fr. Giuseppe G. Scollo

Foreword

From the early days of Christianity, disciples have been puzzled and disturbed because of the Gospel references to the kingdom being taken by force, or violence, in Luke 16,16, and in the parallel passage, Matt 11,12. What can this mean? What can violence have to do with the kingdom of God? In the inspired text there seem to be very few indications of the meaning of these paradoxical and mysterious scriptural verses.

Down through the centuries the Fathers of the Church, and later exegetes, have proposed numerous solutions. In *The Strength Needed to Enter the Kingdom of God: An Exegetical and Theological Study of Luke 16,16 in Context*, Fr. Giuseppe G. Scollo seeks to explicate these puzzling verses, and to set them within the context not only of the portion of the Gospel in which they are found, but also of the wider biblical perspective, and that of the ancient world, so that we might understand them more fully, and thus be helped to become better disciples of Jesus.

Fr. Scollo's work is a model of meticulous scholarship, as he examines the history of interpretation of theses verses, and offers a multi-faceted analysis of the scriptural text. He reflects upon the whole of Luke 16, and helps us to understand not only the verse upon which he focuses, but also the two parables on either side of it: The Shrewd Steward, and The Rich Man and Lazarus. He reveals how these two parables help us to interpret the meaning of the whole of Luke 16. We must act wisely, and think clearly about the end in view, and for a Christian that is the last judgement and the fulfilment of the kingdom of Heaven in the presence of God. Everything in this life must be focused on that, and not in some complacent, or half-hearted way, for we are to love the Lord in this world with all our strength. That love, offered abundantly, not sparingly, is the force that will allow us to break through to the kingdom. That violence of love, that forceful living of Christian discipleship to the full, with wild abandon, is the only path for the disciple who will learn from the two parables of Luke 16, and from the mysterious saying in Luke 16,16 which is the object of study in this dissertation.

The thorough and penetrating scholarly analysis of the Gospel text by Fr. Scollo has most fruitful practical implications, which come to my mind as a bishop of the Church. Too often Christians, laity and clerics, can become complacent, and worldly, and half-hearted – too enamoured of the earthly kingdom. That disposition inhibits our evangelical effectiveness in fulfilling our mission to win the world for Christ, and prevents us from reaching salvation ourselves. It is also the foundation for the grievous scandals of all kinds that plague the Church. We must never forget that Vatican II speaks not of the universal call to mediocrity, but of the universal call to holiness: nothing less than holiness. God does not play with us, holding out an admirable but unattainable ideal in the Gospel. Christianity is not some elite enterprise; we are all sinners, in constant need of repentance and forgiveness, but every single Christian each day is expected to actually live the call of the Gospel, with heart and mind and soul and strength, and by God's grace, and not without the cross, can actually do so. Millions do so every day. The faith need not be watered down to be livable.

As I finished reading this dissertation a story from the desert Fathers came to mind. A young monk approaches his spiritual father and complains that although he has fulfilled every rule and obligation of the Christian life, he feels unsatisfied. The wise old desert father stretches out his hands and flames shoot out of his fingers, and he tells the young monk: "You must become fire".

+ Thomas Cardinal Collins
Archbishop of Toronto

Table of Contents

Chapter 4: The Linguistic Spectrum
of the "βία-based" Lexemes 165

List of Symbols and Abbreviations[*]

#	number(s)
*	Unattested/reconstructed word or phrase
/	or
=	parallel text(s)/passage(s)
§(§)	section(s)
AAS	*Acta Apostolicae sedis. Commentarium Officiale*
ABD	*The Anchor Bible Dictionary*, D.N. FREEDMAN – *al.*, ed., London / Toronto / New York NY, 1992.
Abr.	PHILO, *De Abrahamo*
ABRL	The Anchor Bible Reference Library
ACav	*Australian Caver*
Ach.	ARISTOPHANES, *Acharnes*
ACW	Ancient Christian Writers
Adrados	F.R. ADRADOS, ed., *Diccionario Griego-Español*, I–VII, CSIC.IF, Madrid 1980–2009.
AestP	Aesthetica Preprint
Aet.	PHILO, *De aeternitate mundi*
Ag.	AESCHYLUS, *Agamemnon*
AgBer	Aggadat Bereshit
AGJU	Arbeiten zur Geschichte des antiken Judentums und des Urchristentums
AGLB	Aus der Geschichte der lateinischen Bibel
Aia.	SOPHOCLES, *Aiace*
A.J.	Flavius Josephus, Antiquitates judaicae
AJBI	*Annual of the Japanese Biblical Institute*
al.	(*et*) *alii* = (and) others
Alb. Matt	ANSELM OF LUCCA, *Albinus in libro secundo super Matthaeum*
Alexander	P.H. ALEXANDER – *al.*, ed., *The SBL Handbook of Style. For Ancient Near Eastern, Biblical, and Early Christian Studies*, Peabody MA, 1999.
Althann	R. ALTHANN, *Elenchus of Biblica 1995–2005*, EBB 11–21, Roma 1998–2008.
Amat.	PLUTARCH, *Amatorius*
Amh.	*Amherst*
Anab.	XENOPHON, *Anabasis*
AnBib	Analecta Biblica

---

[*] The following symbols and/or abbreviations are used in accordance with the rules laid down in "Instructions for Contributors", *Bib.* 70 (1989) 577–594, Schwertner, Althann, Lampe, BiPa, Alexander, and Bazyliński, 115–119, 139–142, 147–150, 222–232.

AncB	The Anchor Bible
AncYB	The Anchor Yale Bible
Anderson	W.C. ANDERSON, *A Dictionary of Law. Consisting of Judicial Definitions and Explanations of Words, Phrases, and Maxims, and an Exposition of the Principles of Law. Comprising a Dictionary and Compendium of American and English Jurisprudence*, Chicago IL, 1889.
Andr.	EURIPIDES, *Andromache*
A–N Fathers	*The Ante-Nicene Fathers. Translations of the Writings of the Fathers down to A.D. 325. American Reprint of the Edinburg Edition. Revised and Chronologically Arranged, with Brief Prefaces and Occasional Notes, by A. Cleveland Coxe, I–X, A. ROBERTS – J. DONALDSON, ed., Grand Rapids MI, 1978–1985.*
Ant.	HESYCHIUS OF JERUSALEM, *In sanctum patrem nostrum Antonium*
AnTard	*Antiquité Tardive*
ANTC	Abingdon New Testament Commentaries
Anth.	EURIPIDES, PAULUS SILENTIARIUS, *Anthologia Palatina*
AntiB	The Antioch Bible
ANTJ	Arbeiten zum Neuen Testament und zum Judentum
AOTC	Abingdon Old Testament Commentaries
Ap.	FLAVIUS JOSEPHUS, *Contra Apionem*
ApMos	The Apocalypse of Moses
1 *Apol.*	JUSTIN MARTYR, *Apologia I*
Apoll.	ISAEUS, *De ereditate Apollodori*
Apoph. C.G.S.	*Apophthegmata Patrum. Collectio Graeca Systematica*
Apoph. Lac.	PLUTARCH, *Apophthegmata Laconica*
Apoph. Reg.	PLUTARCH, *Regum et imperatorum apophthegmata*
Apoph. Rom.	PLUTARCH, *Apophthegmata Romanorum*
Aram.	Aramaic
ArBib	The Aramaic Bible. The Targums
ArcR	*Architectural Review*
Aris	Letter of Aristeas
Arist.	DEMOSTHENES, *Contra Aristocrates*
ASeign	*Assemblées du Seigneur*
ASEs	Annali di storia dell'esegesi
ASNP	*Annali della Scuola Normale di Pisa*
ASNU	Acta Seminarii Neotestamentici Upsaliensis
ASPub	All Student Publications
ASTI	*Annual of the Swedish Theological Institute (in Jerusalem)*
ATh	*L'année théologique*
Ath.	ARISTOTLE, *Athenaion Politeia*
AThANT	Abhandlungen zur Theologie des Alten und Neuen Testaments
Athen.	PROCLUS, *Eis Athenan Polymetin*
AThI	*American Theological Inquiry*
AThR	*Anglican Theological Review*
Aug.	*Augustinianum*
AULy	Annales de l'Université de Lyon. Troisième Série
AusBR	*Australian Biblical Review*
BAC.EE	Biblioteca de Autores Cristianos – Estudios y Ensayos

Bailly	M. BREAL – A. BAILLY, *Dictionnaire étymologique Latin*, LMCS, Paris 1885.
Bapt.	AUGUSTINE OF HIPPO, *De Baptismo contra Donatistas*
2Bar	2 Baruch (Syriac Apocalypse)
Barl.	GREGORY PALAMAS, *Contra Barlaam et Acindynum*
Barn.	PSEUDO-BARNABAS, *Barnabae Epistula*
Barthélemy	D. BARTHÉLEMY, ed., *Critique textuelle de L'Ancien Testament*, I–III, OBO 50.1–4, Fribourg / Göttingen 1982–2005.
bAZ	Babylonian Talmud (*Talmud Bavli*), Tractate *'Avoda Zara*
Bazyliński	S. BAZYLIŃSKI, *A Guide to Biblical Research*, SubBi 36, Rome 2009.
bBB	Babylonian Talmud (*Talmud Bavli*), Tractate *Baba Batra*
bBer	Babylonian Talmud (*Talmud Bavli*), Tractate *Berakhot*
BBR	*Bulletin for Biblical Research*
BCBC	Believers Church Bible Commentary
BCE	Before the Common Era = BC
BCILL	Bibliothèque des Cahiers de l'Institut de Linguistique de Louvain
BCL	Bohn's Classical Library
BCPE	*Bulletin du Centre Protestant d'Études*
BCRe	Blackwell Companions to Religion
BDAG	W. BAUER – F.W. DANKER – W.F. ARNDT – F.W. GINGRICH, ed., *A Greek-English Lexicon of the New Testament and Other Early Christian Literature*, Chicago IL / London 1957, 2000³; Ger. orig., W. BAUER – B. ALAND – K. ALAND, ed., *Griechisch-deutsches Wörterbuch zu den Schriften des Neuen Testaments und der frühchristlichen Literatur*, Berlin / New York NY, 1988⁶.
BDB	F. BROWN – S.R. DRIVER – C.A. BRIGGS, *The New Brown – Driver – Briggs – Gesenius Hebrew and English Lexicon with an Appendix containing the Biblical Aramaic*, Peabody MA, 1979.
BDF	F.W. BLASS – A. DEBRUNNER – R.W. FUNK, *A Greek Grammar of the New Testament and Other Early Christian Literature*, Cambridge / Chicago IL, 1896, 1961¹⁰.
BECNT	Baker Exegetical Commentary on the New Testament
BemR	*Bemidbar Rabba* (Midrash on Numbers)
BerR	*Bereshit Rabba* (Midrash on Genesis)
BET	Beiträge zur biblischen Exegese und Theologie
BEThL	Bibliotheca Ephemeridum theologicarum Lovaniensium
BFCT	*Beiträge zur Förderung christlicher Theologie*
BGU	*Aegyptische Urkunden aus den königlichen Museen zu Berlin. Greschiche Urkunden*, I–XX, Berlin 1895–2014.
BH	Bibliothèque historique
BHer.SE	Biblioteca Herder – Sección de sagrada escritura
BHJS	Baltimore Studies in the History of Judaism
BHM	Bet HaMidrash
BHS	*Biblia Hebraica Stuttgartensia*, K. ELLIGER – W. RUDOLPH, ed., Stuttgart 1967–1977.
BHTh	Beiträge zur historischen Theologie
Bib.	*Biblica*
BiBi(B)	Biblioteca biblica

Bibl.	PSEUDO-APOLLODORUS, *Bibliotheca*
Bib.TS	Biblica – Testi e studi
BiMi	Biblioteca Midrásica
BInterp	*Biblical Interpretation*
BiPa	J. ALLENBACH – *al.*, ed., *Biblia Patristica: index des citations et allusions bibliques dans la littérature patristique*, I–VI, Paris 1975–1995.
BIS	Biblical Interpretation Series
BiScP	Bibliotèque Scientifique Payot
BiTS	Biblical Tools and Studies
BiWo	*The Biblical World*
B.J.	FLAVIUS JOSEPHUS, *Bellum judaicum*
BJS	Brown Judaic Studies
bKet	Babylonian Talmud (*Talmud Bavli*), Tractate *Ketubbot*
BNP	Brill's New Pauly. Encyclpedia of the Ancient World. Antiquity
BNTC	Black's New Testament Commentaries
Boisacq	É. BOISACQ, *Dictionnaire étymologique de la langue grecque étudiée dans ses rapports avec les autres langues indo-européennes*, Heidelberg 1916, 1938³.
Bonino	S. BONINO, ed., *Dizionario di psicologia dello sviluppo*, Torino 1994.
bQid	Babylonian Talmud (*Talmud Bavli*), Tractate *Qiddushin*
BR	*Biblical Research*
BRab	Bibliotheca Rabbinica. Eine Sammlung alter Midraschim
Brev. Ps.	PSEUDO-JEROME, *Breviarium in Psalmos*
bRHSh	Babylonian Talmud (*Talmud Bavli*), Tractate *Rosh HaShana*
BrJP	The Brill Josephus Project
Brugmann	K. BRUGMANN, *Griechische Grammatik*, in I. MÜLLER, ed., *Handbuch der klassischen Altertumswissenschaft*, II, Munchen 1890².
bSan	Babylonian Talmud (*Talmud Bavli*), Tractate *Sanhedrin*
BSGRT	Bibliotheca scriptorum Graecorum et Romanorum Teubneriana
bShab	Babylonian Talmud (*Talmud Bavli*), Tractate *Shabbat*
bSuk	Babylonian Talmud (*Talmud Bavli*), Tractate *Sukka*
BT	Biblioteca teologica
BTB	*Biblical Theology Bulletin*
BT(N)	Bibliothèque théologique (Neuchâtel)
Buck	C.D. BUCK, *A Dictionary of Selected Synonyms in the Principal Indo-European Languages. A Contribution to the History of Ideas*, Chicago IL, 1949, repr. 1988.
Burton	E.W. BURTON, *Syntax of the Moods and Tenses in the New Testament Greek*, Chicago IL, 1892, 1898³.
BWANT	Beiträge zur Wissenschaft vom Alten und Neuen Testament
bYev	Babylonian Talmud (*Talmud Bavli*), Tractate *Yevamot*
bYom	Babylonian Talmud (*Talmud Bavli*), Tractate *Yoma*
BZ	*Biblische Zeitschrift*
BZAW	Beihefte zur Zeitschrift für die alttestamentliche Wissenschaft
BZNW	Beihefte zur Zeitschrift für die neutestamentliche Wissenschaft und die Kunde der älteren Kirche
c(s).	century(-ies)
CAHS	Clarendon Ancient History Series

Cap. car.	Maximus the Confessor, *Capita de caritate quattuor centuriae*
Carn.	Plutarch, *De esu carnium*
CBG	*Collationes Brugenses et Gandavenses*
CBi	Collana biblica
CBQ	*Catholic Biblical Quarterly*
CBRA	Collectanea biblica et religiosa antiqua
CBRe	*Currents in Biblical Research*
CCC	United States Catholic Conference, *Catechism of the Catholic Church*, Washington DC, 1994, 2000[2].
CCCB	Canadian Conference of Catholic Bishops
CCen	*Christian Century*
CChr.CM	Corpus Christianorum – Continuatio medievalis
CChr.SL	Corpus Christianorum – Series Latina
CCLEE	*A Copious and Critical Latin-English Lexicon. Founded on the Larger Latin-German Lexicon of Dr. William Freund: with Additions and Corrections from the Lexicons of Gesner, Facciolati, Scheller, Georges, etc.*, E.A. Andrews, New York NY, 1851.
CCS	Calvin's Commentaries Series
CD	Cairo (Geniza text of the) Damascus (Documents)
CE	Common Era = AD
CEA	Collection d'études anciennes
CEJL	Commentaries on Early Jewish Literature
CEv	Cahiers évangile
cf.	confer(endum)
CFHB.B	Corpus fontium historiae Byzantinae – Series Berolinensis
CFi	Cogitatio fidei
CFTL	Clark's Foreign Theological Library
C. gent.	Thomas Aquinas, *Summa contra gentiles*
Chantraine	P. Chantraine, *Dictionnaire étymologique de la langue Grecque. Histoire des mots*, Paris 1968.
chap(s).	chapter(s)
ChEth	Le champ éthique
ChiStHJ	Chicago Studies in the History of Judaism
Choeph.	Aeschylus, *Choephori Perseus*
Choisir	*Choisir. Revue culturelle*
Chron.	George the Monk, *Chronicon*
ChrTo	*Christianity Today*
CIG	A. Böckh – *al.*, ed., *Corpus inscriptionum graecarum. Aucoritate et impensis Academiae Litterarum Regiae Borussicae*, I–IV, Berolini 1828–1877.
Ciron.	Isaeus, *De ereditate Cironis*
CistSS	Cistercian Studies Series
Civ.	Augustine of Hippo, *De civitate Dei*
1–2 Clem.	Clement of Rome, *Epistula prima-secunda Clementis ad Christianos urbis Corinthi directae*
C. litt. Petil.	Augustine of Hippo, *Contra litteras Petiliani*
CLPB	Collana Lettura pastorale della bibbia
ClS	Classical Series
CN	Codex Neofiti

CNT	Commentaire du Nouveau Testament
CNTTS	The Center for New Testament Textual Studies
CoBC	Cornerstone Biblical Commentary
Coel.	ARISTOTLE, *De coelo*
col(s).	column(s)
Coll.	*Colloquium*
Collat.	JOHN CASSIAN, *Collationes*
ComBib	Commenti biblici
Comm. Dan.	HIPPOLYTUS OF ROME, *Commentarium in Danielem*
Comm. Jo.	ORIGEN OF ALEXANDRIA, *Commentarii in Evangelium Johannis*
Comm. Luc.	BRUNO OF SEGNIS, CYRIL OF ALEXANDRIA, ORIGEN OF ALEXANDRIA, *Commentarii in Lucam*
Comm. Matt	HILARY OF POITIERS, ORIGEN OF ALEXANDRIA, *Commentarium in Evangelium Matthaei*
Comm. quat. Luc.	EUTHYMIUS ZIGABENUS, *Commentarius in Quatuor Evangelia. Evangelium secundum Lucam*
Comm. quat. Matt	EUTHYMIUS ZIGABENUS, *Commentarius in Quatuor Evangelia. Evangelium secundum Matthaeum*
Commen. Matt	JEROME OF STRIDON, *Commentarium in Matthaeum*
Comment. Matt	BRUNO OF SEGNIS, RABANUS OF MAINZ, *Commentaria in Matthaeum*
Conc. Evang.	ZACHARY OF BESANÇON, *In unum ex quator sive de Concordia Evangelistarum*
ConCom	Concordia Commentary
Conf.	AUGUSTINE OF HIPPO, *Confessiones*
Conf. reg.	BERNARD OF CLAIRVAUX, *Parabola II. De conflictu duorum regum*
Const.	BASIL THE GREAT, *Constitutiones asceticae*
Corteggiani	J.-P. CORTEGGIANI, *L'Égypte ancienne et ses dieux. Dictionnaire illustré*, Paris 2007.
CPS.G	Corona patrum Salesiana – Series Graeca
CR	Corpus Reformatorum
CRI	Compendia rerum Iudaicarum ad Novum Testamentum
Cri.	PLATO, *Crito*
CritR	*The Critical Review of Theological and Philosophical Literature*
CrTR	*Criswell Theological Review*
CSCO.Ae	Corpus scriptorum Christianorum orientalium – Scriptores Aethiopici
CSCO.Ar	Corpus scriptorum Christianorum orientalium – Scriptores Armeniaci
CSEL	Corpus scriptorum ecclesiasticorum Latinorum
CSIC.IF	Consejo Superior de Investigaciones Científicas – Instituto de Filología
CSIC.TE	Consejo Superior de Investigaciones Científicas – Seminario Filológico 'Cardinal Cisneros'. Textos y estudios
CSPac	Col·lectània Sant Pacià
CTan	Corpus Tannaiticum
CTePa	Collana di testi patristici
CThL	Crown Theological Library
CTM	*Concordia Theological Monthly*
CUFr	Collection des universités de France
CuTe(BA)	*Cuadernos de teología. Buenos Aires*
CwH	Calwer Hefte
Cyrop.	XENOPHON, *Cyropaedia*

DAD	*Drug and Alcohol Dependence*
D&Q	*Diritto & questioni pubbliche*
30Days	*30Days. In the Church and in the World*
DBY	*The "Holy Scriptures". A New Translation from the Original Languages*, J.N. DARBY, ed., Lancing 1890, repr. 1961.
DCLS	Deuterocanonical and Cognate Literature Studies
Decal.	PHILO, *De decalogo*
Def.	PSEUDO-PLATO, *Definitiones*
Deipn.	ATHENAEUS, *Deipnosophistai*
Deus	PHILO, *Quod Deus sit immutabilis*
DevR	*Devarim Rabba* (Midrash on Deuteronomy)
Dial.	JUSTIN MARTYR, *Dialogus cum Tryphone*
Dialex.	ANONYMOUS, *Dialexeis* (or *Dissoi logoi*)
Diatr.	EPICTETUS, *Diatribae*
Did.	*Didache*
Diogn.	*Diognetus*
Direction	*Direction. A Mennonite Brethren Forum*
diss.	dissertation, unpublished thesis for the degree of Doctor
DJD	Discoveries in the Judean Desert
DJPA	*A Dictionary of Jewish Palestinian Aramaic of the Byzantine Period*, M. SOKOLOFF, DTMT 2, Ramat-Gan 1990, 1992[2].
Doc.	DOROTHEUS OF GAZA, *Expositiones et doctrinae diversae*
Doctr. Ant.	PSEUDO-ATHANASIUS, *Doctrina ad Antiochum ducem*
DSBP	*Dizionario di spiritualità biblico-patristica. I grandi temi della S. Scrittura per la "Lectio divina"*
DSBS	The Daily Study Bible Series
DSp	*Dictionnaire de spiritualité ascétique et mystique*
DTMT	Dictionaries of Talmud, Midrash and Targum
DTU	*Dio Trinità, unità degli uomini. Il monoteismo Cristiano contro la violenza*, COMMISSIONE TEOLOGICA INTERNAZIONALE [On-line edition: access 08.05.2017], Città del Vaticano 2014, http://www.vatican.va/roman_curia/congregations/cfaith/cti_documents/rc_cti_20140117_monoteismo-cristiano_it.html.
DUP.S	Dublin University Press – Series
DV	VATICAN COUNCIL II, *Dei Verbum, Dogmatic Constitution on Divine Revelation* (November 18, 1965), in A. FLANNERY – *al.*, ed., *Vatican Council II. The Conciliar and Postconciliar Documents*, I, Collegeville MN, 1992.
EBB	Elenchus bibliographicus biblicus
Ebr.	PHILO, *De ebrietate*
ECL	early Christian literature
EChSt	Eastern Christian Studies
ed.	*edidit, editerunt* = editor(s), edited by
EDNT	*Exegetical Dictionary of the New Testament*, I–III, H. BALZ – G. SCHNEIDER, ed., Grand Rapids MI, 1990–1992; Ger. orig., *Exegetisches Wörterbuch zum Neuen Testament*, I–III, Stuttgart 1980–1983.
EDP	Epifania della parola
EeT	*Église et théologie*

e.g.	*exempli gratia* = for example
EHS.T	Europäische Hochschulschriften – Reihe 23, Theologie
EiPB	Einaudi Paperbacks
EJ	*Encyclopaedia Judaica*, I–XXII, F. SKOLNIK – M. BERENBAUM, ed., Jerusalem 1971, Farmington Hills MI, 2007².
EKK	Evangelisch-katholischer Kommentar zum Neuen Testament
El.	THEOGNIS, *Elegies*
Eleem.	JOHN CHRYSOSTOM, *De eleemosyna*
Eleemos.	CYPRIAN OF CARTHAGE, *De opere et eleemosynis*
Eloc.	DEMETRIUS, *De elocutione*
1En	1 Enoch (Ethiopic Apocalypse)
Enarrat. Matt	THEOPHYLACT OF BULGARIA, *Enarratio in Evangelium Matthaei*
Enarrat. Ps.	AUGUSTINE OF HIPPO, *Enarrationes in Psalmos*
Eng.	English
Ep.	AMBROSE OF MILAN, ANSELM OF CANTERBURY, BASIL THE GREAT, BERNARD OF CLAIRVAUX, GREGORY OF NAZIANZUS, JEROME OF STRIDON, PETER DAMIAN, THEODORE THE STUDITE, *Epistulae*
Ep. ab.	JOHN CHRYSOSTOM, *Epistula ad abbatem*
Ep. div.	DOROTHEUS OF GAZA, *Epistulae ad diversos*
Ep. vigil.	JOHN CHRYSOSTOM, *Epistula ad monachos utilitatis et vigilantiae plena*
Ep. Tib. Pil.	*Epistula Tiberii ad Pilatum*
EPh	*Les études philosophiques*
Erat.	LYSIAS, *De Eratosthenis nece*
Erga	HESIOD, *Erga kai Hēmerai*
Ernesti	J.C.G. ERNESTI, *Lexicon Technologiae Graecorum Rhetoricae*, Lipsiae 1795, repr. Hildesheim 1983.
ESEC	Emory Studies in Early Christianity
esp.	Especially
EstBib	*Estudios Bíblicos*
ESV	*The Holy Bible. English Standard Version. Containing the Old and New Testaments*, J.I. PACKER, ed., Wheaton IL, 2001.
ET	*Expository Times*
EtB	Études Bibliques
etc.	*et cetera* = and so on
EThL	*Ephemerides theologicae Lovanienses*
EtPap	*Études de papyrologie*
ETR	*Études théologiques et religieuses*
EtT	Études Théologiques
Eur.	HERMOGENES, *Peri Eureseos*
EV	Enchiridion Vaticanum
Ev. Naz.	*Evangelium Nazarenorum*
Ev. Nic.	*Evangelium Nicodemi*
Ev. Phil.	*Evangelium Philippi*
EvQ	*The Evangelical Quarterly*
Ev. Thom.	*Evangelium Thomae Graece A*
Exp.	*The Expositor*
Exp. Act.	BEDE THE VENERABLE, *Expositio Actuum Apostolorum*
Exp. Apoc.	PSEUDO-AMBROSE, *Expositio super septem visiones libri Apocalypsis*

Exp. Luc.	AMBROSE OF MILAN, *Expositio Euangelii secundum Lucam*
Exp. Matt	JEROME OF STRIDON, *Expositio quatuor Evangeliorum, de brevi Proverbio edita. In Evangelium secundum Matthaeum*
Exp. Poen.	GREGORY THE GREAT, *Expositio Psalmi Sexti Poenitentialis*
Exp. Ps.	JOHN CHRYSOSTOM, *Expositiones in Psalmos*
EzNT	Erläuterungen zum Neuen Testament
f(f).	and following verse(s), or chapter(s), or page(s), etc.
Fab.	AESOP, *Fabulae*
FaCh	The Fathers of the Church. A New Translation
FD	Fuentes Documentales
Fid. op.	AUGUSTINE OF HIPPO, *De fide et operibus*
fig.	Figure
FiTh	*First Things*
Fr.	ALCAEUS, ANAXAGORAS, ANONYMUS IAMBLICHUS, ANTIPHON, CLEMENT OF ALEXANDRIA, CLEOBULUS, CRITIAS, DEMOCRITUS, GORGIAS, HERACLITUS, MOSCHION, PINDAR, SOLON, *Fragmenta*
Fract.	HIPPOCRATES, *De fracturis*
frag.	Fragment
FrE	Frühgeschichte des Evangeliums
Friberg	T. FRIBERG – B. FRIBERG – N. MILLER, ed., *Analytical Lexicon of the Greek New Testament*, Grand Rapids MI, 2000.
FRLANT	Forschungen zur Religion und Literatur des Alten und Neuen Testaments
Fr. Matt	PHOTIUS OF CONSTANTINOPLE, *Fragmenta in Matthaeum*
FRSEP	Fonti e ricerche di storia ecclesiastica Padovana
Fug.	PHILO, *De fuga et inventione*
FV	*Foi et vie*
FzB	Forschung zur Bibel
GAP	*Guides to Apocrypha and Pseudepigrapha*
Garr.	PLUTARCH, *De garrulitate*
GCS	*Die griechischen christlichen Schriftsteller der ersten drei Jahrhunderte*
Geo.	STRABO, *Geographia*
Ger.	German
Già	Già e non ancora
Gk.	Greek
Glaph. Gen.	CYRIL OF ALEXANDRIA, *Glaphyra in Genesim*
GNS	Good News Studies
GNT[4]	*The Greek New Testament*, B. & K. ALAND – J. KARAVIDOPOULOS – C.M. MARTINI – B.M. METZGER, ed., Stuttgart 2001[4].
Gorg.	PLATO, *Gorgias*
Gr.	*Gregorianum*
Graec.	PAUSANIAS, *Graece descriptio*
GRBS	*Greek, Roman, and Byzantine Studies*
GSCS	Greek Series for Colleges and Schools
GTJ	*Grace Theological Journal*
Haer.	IRENAEUS OF LYONS, *Adversus haereses*
Hal.	*Halensis*

HALOT	*The Hebrew and Aramaic Lexicon of the Old Testament. Study Edition*, I–II, L. KOEHLER – W. BAUMGARTNER, Leiden / Köln / Boston MA, 2001; Ger. orig., *Hebräisches und Aramäisches Lexikon zum Alten Testament*, I–II, Leiden / New York NY, 1995.
HAW	Handbuch der Altertumswissenschaft
HC	Hand-Commentar zum Neuen Testament
Hel.	EURIPIDES, *Helena*
Henoch	*Henoch. Studi storicofilologici sull'ebraismo*
Hermeneia	Hermeneia. A Critical and Historical Commentary on the Bible
HeyJ	*The Heythrop Journal*
Hist.	HERODOTUS, THUCYDIDES, POLYBIUS, *Historiae*
Hist. Eccl.	EUSEBIUS OF CAESAREA, *Historia Ecclesiastica*
Histor.	DIODORUS OF SICILY, *Bibliotheca historica*
HistRech	History of the Rechabites
Hist. scrib.	LUCIAN OF SAMOSATA, *Quomodo historia scribenda sit*
HNT	Handbuch zum Neuen Testament
Hom.	BASIL THE GREAT, *Homiliae variae*
Hom. Act.	JOHN CHRYSOSTOM, *Homiliae in Acta apostolorum*
Hom. 1–2 Cor.	JOHN CHRYSOSTOM, *Homiliae in epistulam i–ii ad Corinthios*
Hom. div.	MAXIMUS OF TURIN, *Homiliae de diversis*
Hom. eleem.	JOHN CHRYSOSTOM, *In homiliam de jejunio et eleemosyna monitum*
Hom. Eutrop.	JOHN CHRYSOSTOM, *Homilia de capto Eutropio*
Hom. Evang.	GREGORY THE GREAT, *Homiliae in Evangelia*
Hom. Jo.	JOHN CHRYSOSTOM, *Homiliae in Johannem*
Hom. Lev.	ORIGEN OF ALEXANDRIA, *Homiliae in Leviticum*
Hom. Matt	JOHN CHRYSOSTOM, *Homiliae in Matthaeum*
Hom. Pasc.	CYRIL OF ALEXANDRIA, *Homiliae Paschales*
Hom. Prov.	BASIL THE GREAT, *Homilia in principium Proverbiorum*
Hom. sp.	PSEUDO-MACARIUS, *Homiliae spirituales*
Hom. 2 Tim.	JOHN CHRYSOSTOM, *Homiliae in epistulam ii ad Timotheum*
HRh	A History of Rhetoric
HThK	Herders theologischer Kommentar zum Neuen Testament
HThR	*Harvard Theological Review*
HTS	*Hervormde Teologiese Studies*
HUCA	*Hebrew Union College Annual*
HUTh	Hermeneutische Untersuchungen zur Theologie
Hypn.	*Hypnos (Sao Paulo)*
Hypoth.	PHILO, *Hypothetica*
Ibid.	*Ibidem* = in the same work
ICC	The International Critical Commentary on the Holy Scriptures of the Old and New Testaments
ID.	*Idem* = in the same author
Idet.	Idetica
i.e.	*id est* = that is, in other words
Ily.	HOMER, *Ilyades*
IMJP	*Issues. A Messianic Jewish Perspective*
InEsB	Instrumentos para el estudio de la Biblia
inf.	Infinitive
Instit.	GREGORY OF NYSSA, *De instituto Christiano*

Interp.	*Interpretation.* Richmond VA
InTr	Introduzioni e trattati
Ion	EURIPIDES, *Ion*
Ios.	PHILO, *De Iosepho*
IPS	INSTITUTUM PESHITTONIANUM LEIDENSE, ed., *Vetus Testamentum Syriace. Iuxta simplice Syrorum versionem*, I–V, Lugduni Batavorum 1966–2013.
IPUL	Institut Papyrologique de l'Université de Lille
Iren.	*Irénikon*
Is.	PLUTARCH, *De Iside et Osiride*
ISCH	Institutum Pro Studiis Classicis Harvardianum
It.	Italian
ITC	International Theological Commentary
JAAR	*Journal of the American Academy of Religion*
JAEd	*Journal of Architectural Education*
JAHe	*Journal of Adolescent Health*
JAJud	*Journal of Ancient Judaism*
Jastrow	M. JASTROW, *A Dictionary of the Targumim, the Talmud Babli and Yerushalmi, and the Midrashic Literature*, I–II, London / New York NY, 1886–1903.
JBL	*Journal of Biblical Literature*
JBPR	*Journal of Biblical and Pneumatological Research*
JCTC	Jewish and Christian Texts in Context and Related Studies
Jejun.	TERTULLIAN, *De jejunio adversus psychicos*
JETS	*Journal of the Evangelical Theological Society*
JGeo	*The Journal of Geology*
JHScr	*Journal of Hebrew Scriptures*
JJS	*Journal of Jewish Studies*
JosAs	Joseph and Aseneth
Jov.	JEROME OF STRIDON, *Adversus Jovinianum*
JPe	The Jewish People. History, Religion, Literature
JPSTC	Jewish Publication Society – The JPS Torah Commentary
JQR	*Jewish Quarterly Review*
Jr.	Junior
JSJ	*Journal for the Study of Judaism in the Persian, Hellenistic and Roman Period*
JSJ.S	Supplements to the Journal for the Study of Judaism
JSNT	*Journal for the Study of the New Testament*
JSNT.S	Journal for the Study of the New Testament – Supplement Series
JSOT.S	Journal for the Study of the Old Testament – Supplement Series
JSPE	*Journal for the Study of the Pseudepigrapha*
JSPE.S	Journal for the Study of the Pseudepigrapha – Supplement Series
JSSt	*Journal of Semitic Studies*
JTAK	*Journal of Theta Alpha Kappa*
JThS	*Journal of Theological Studies*
JThS.NS	*Journal of Theological Studies – New Series*
JTSA	*Journal of Theology for Southern Africa*
Jub	Jubilees
KBANT	Kommentare und Beiträge zum Alten und Neuen Testament

KEHNT	Kurzgefasstes exegetisches Handbuch zum Neuen Testament
KEK	Kritisch-exegetischer Kommentar über das Neue Testament
KIT	Kleine Texte für theologische Vorlesungen und Übungen
KNT	Kommentar zum Neuen Testament
l(s).	line(s)
L	Luke's proper source material
Lacr.	DEMOSTHENES, *Contra Lacritum*
Lampe	G.W.H. LAMPE, ed., *A Patristic Greek Lexicon*, Oxford 1961.
Lat.	Latin
Laud. mil.	BERNARD OF CLAIRVAUX, *Liber ad milites temple. De laude novae militiae*
Lausberg	H. LAUSBERG, *Handbook of Literary Rhetoric. A Foundation for Literary Study*, Leiden 1998; Ger. orig., *Handbuch der literarischen Rhetorik. Eine Grundlegung der Literaturwissenschaft*, München 1960, 1973².
LCHS	J.P. Lange's Commentary on the Holy Scriptures. Critical, Doctrinal, and Homiletical, with Special Reference to Ministers and Students
LCL	Loeb Classical Library
Lect.	*Lectionary. The Roman Missal. Revised by decree of the Second Vatican Council and published by authority of Pope Paul VI. I. Sundays and Solemnities. II. Weekday A. III. Weekday B*, CCCB, Ottawa 1992–1994.
LeDiv	Lectio Divina
Leg.	PLATO, *Leges*; PHILO, *Legum allegoriae*
LEH	J. LUST – E. EYNIKEL – K. HAUSPIE, ed., *Greek-English Lexicon of the Septuagint. Revised Edition*, Stuttgart 2003.
LeqT	Midrash *Leqaḥ Ṭob*
Lib. cor.	PSEUDO-MACARIUS, *Liber de custodia cordis*
LiBi	Lire la Bible
Lib. ment.	PSEUDO-MACARIUS, *Liber de libertate mentis*
LIMC	Lexicon iconographicum mythologiae classicae
LipM	*Lippincott's Monthly Magazine*
lit.	Literally
Lit.	*The Divine Office. The Liturgy of the Hours. According to the Roman Rite*, I–IV, New York NY, 1970, repr. 1975.
LJeS	Lives of Jesus Series
LMCS	Leçons de mots. Cours supérieur
LMGL	*Lexicon manuale Graeco-Latinum in libros Novi Testamenti*, I–II, C.G. BRETSCHNEIDER, Lipsiae 1824, 1829².
LNTS	Library of New Testament Studies
Lond.	*Londinensis*
LSJ	H.G. LIDDEL – R. SCOTT – H.S. JONES, ed., *A Greek-English Lexicon*, I–II, Oxford 1843, 1968⁹, repr. 1985.
LUÂ	Lund Universitets ársskrift
LXX	Septuagint(al) Greek Version
Macar.	DEMOSTHENES, *Contra Macartatum*
Magd.	*Magdolensis*
Magn.	ARISTOTLE, *Magna moralia*
Marc.	TERTULLIAN, *Adversus Marcionem*

mAv	Mishnah, Tractate *Avot*
mBB	Mishnah, Tractate *Baba Batra*
MBPF	Münchener Beiträge zur Papyrusforschung und antiken Rechts-geschichte
mBQ	Mishnah, Tractate *Baba Qamma*
MdN	Maria di Nazaret
mEd	Mishnah, Tractate *'Eduyot*
Med.	EURIPIDES, *Medea*
Meillet	A. ERNOUT – A. MEILLET, *Dictionnaire étymologique de la langue Latine. Histoire des mots*, Paris 1932, 1959[4].
MekhSh	*Mekhilta deRabbi Shim'on b. Yoḥai*
MekhY	*Mekhilta deRabbi Yishma'el*
Mem.	XENOPHON, *Memorabilia*
Merk[9]	A. MERK, ed., *Novum Testamentum. Graece et Latine*, Romae 1933, 1964[9].
Merriam[11]	*Merriam-Webster's Collegiate Dictionary*, F.C. MISH – al., ed., Springfield MA, 2003[11].
Met.	ARISTOTLE, *Metaphysica*
Metal.	JOHN OF SALISBURY, *Metalogicon*
Metzger[2]	B.M. METZGER, ed., *A Textual Commentary on the Greek New Testament. A Companion Volume to the UBS's GNT[4]*, Stuttgart 1971, 1994[2], repr. 2012.
mGit	Mishnah, Tractate *Giṭṭin*
Mid.	DEMOSTHENES, *Contra Midias*
Mind	*Mind. A Quarterly Review of Psychology and Philosophy*
mKet	Mishnah, Tractate *Ketubbot*
MNTC	Moffatt New Testament Commentary
MoBi	Le monde de la Bible
Monier	M. MONIER-WILLIAMS, *A Sanskṛit-English Dictionary, Etymologically and Philologically Arranged, with Special Reference to Cognate Indo-Europen Languages*, Oxford 1899, repr. 1974.
Mos.	PHILO, *De vita Mosis*
Moulton	J.H. MOULTON – G. MILLIGAN, *The Vocabulary of the Greek Testament. Illustrated from the Papyri and Other Non-Literary Sources*, London 1930.
mPea	Mishnah, Tractate *Pe'a*
mQid	Mishnah, Tractate *Qiddushin*
ms(s)	manuscript(s)
mSan	Mishnah, Tractate *Sanhedrin*
MT	Masoretic Text
MTann	*Midrash Tanna'im* (Mekhilta le-Sefer Davarim)
MThZ	*Münchener theologische Zeitschrift*
Muraoka	T. MURAOKA, *A Greek-English Lexicon of the Septuagint*, Louvain / Paris / Walpole MA, 2009.
Mut.	PHILO, *De mutatione nominum*
mYev	Mishnah, Tractate *Yevamot*
n(s).	(foot)note(s)

NA[27/28]	EB. & ER. NESTLE – B. & K. ALAND – J. KARAVIDOPOULOS – C.M. MARTINI – B.M. METZGER, ed., *Novum Testamentum Græce*, Stuttgart 1898, 1993[27], 2012[28].
NAC	The New American Commentary
Narr. Ios.	*Narratio Iosephi Arimathiensis*
NASB	*New American Standard Bible*, R.A. OLSON – *al.*, ed., La Habra CA, 1971, repr. 1995.
NBAg	Nuova biblioteca agostiniana
NCBC	The New Century Bible Commentary
NCR	*National Catholic Register*
NCWTM	*Neuhebräisches und Chaldäisches Wörterbuch über die Talmudim und Midraschim*, I–IV, J. LEVY, Leipzig 1876–89.
NDIEC	New Documents Illustrating Early Christianity
Neotest.	*Neotestamentica*
Nic.	ARISTOTLE, *Ethica Nicomachea*
NICNT	The New International Commentary on the New Testament
NICOT	The New International Commentary on the Old Testament
NIGTC	New International Greek Testament Commentary
NIV	*The Holy Bible. New International Version. Containing the Old Testament and the New Testament*, E.H. PALMER – *al.*, ed., Grand Rapids MI, 1978, 2011[3].
NIV.ASB	*The NIV Archeological Study Bible. An Illustrated Walk Through Biblical History and Culture. Genesis*, Grand Rapids MI, 2005.
NJB	*The New Jerusalem Bible*, H. WANSBROUGH, ed., Garden City NY, 1985.
NLT	*The Holy Bible. New Living Translation*, M.R. NORTON, ed., Carol Stream IL, 1996, repr. 2007.
NovT	*Novum Testamentum*
N-PN Fathers[1]	*A Select Library of Nicene and Post-Nicene Fathers of the Christian Church. First Series*, I–XIV, P. SCHAFF, ed., Grand Rapids MI, 1974–1975.
N-PN Fathers[2]	*A Select Library of Nicene and Post-Nicene Fathers of the Christian Church. Second Series. Translated into English with Prolegomena and Explanatory Notes*, I–XIV, P. SCHAFF – H. WACE, ed., Grand Rapids MI, 1979–1983.
NRTh	*Nouvelle revue théologique*
NSBT	New Studies in Biblical Theology
NT	New Testament, Nuovo Testamento
NTA.NF	Neutestamentliche Abhandlungen – Neue Folge
NTComm	Il Nuovo Testamento Commentato
NTD	Das Neue Testament Deutsch
NTLi	The New Testament Library
NTOA	Novum Testamentum et Orbis Antiquus
NT.S	Novum Testamentum – Supplements
NTS	*New Testament Studies*
NTTS	New Testament Tools and Studies
OBO	Orbis Biblicus et Orientalis
OBTh	Overtures to Biblical Theology

ODCC	*The Oxford Dictionary of the Christian Church*, F.L. CROSS – E.A. LIVINGSTONE, ed., New York NY, 1957, 2005³.
Ody.	HOMER, *Odyssea*
Oec.	PSEUDO-ARISTOTLE, *Oeconomica*
OiChr	Oi Christianoi
OJTh	*Ogbomoso Journal of Theology*
Ol.	PINDAR, *Olympionikai*
OL	*Opus Lucanum*
Op.	HESIOD, *Opera et diez*
Opif.	PHILO, *De opificio mundi*
Or.	TERTULLIAN, *De oratione liber*; DIO CHRYSOSTOM, GREGORY OF NAZIANZUS, *Orationes*
Or. bapt.	GREGORY OF NAZIANZUS, *Oratio in sactum baptisma*
Or. Dom.	CYPRIAN OF CARTHAGE, ORIGEN OF ALEXANDRIA, *De oratione Domini*
Orat.	SIMEON JUNIOR, *Orationes*
orig.	original
OSArb.	Old South Arabian
OSG	*The Old Syriac Gospels. Studies and Comparative Translations*, I–II, E.J. WILSON, ed., EChSt 1, Piscataway NJ, 2002.
OT	Old Testament
OTM	Oxford Theological Monographs
OTS	Oudtestamentische Studien
Oxy.	*Oxyrhynchus*
p(p).	page(s)
Pac.	ISOCRATES, *De pace*
Pand. hom.	ANTIOCHUS THE MONK, *Pandecta scripture sacrae. Homiliae*
Pap.	*Papyrus*
Par.	Paradosis. Études de littérature et de théologie anciennes
Par.	*Parinensis*
Parall.	JOHN DAMASCENE, *Sacra parallela*
Pauper.	GREGORY OF NYSSA, *De pauperibus amandi et benignitate complectendis*
PesK	*Pesiqta deRav Kahana*
PesR	*Pesiqta Rabbati*
PG	*Patrologiae cursus completus. Series Graeca*, I–CLXII, J.-P. MIGNE, ed., Parisiis / Turholti 1857–1904.
Ph.	SOPHOCLES, *Philoctetes*
Phae.	PLATO, *Phaedo*
PhAl.CS	Philo of Alexandria – Commentary Series
PhAnt	Philosophia antiqua
Phil.	DEMOSTHENES, *Ad Philippi epistolam*
Phili.	ISOCRATES, *Philippus*
Phys.	ARISTOTLE, *Physica*
PJC	Jews' College Publications
PL	*Patrologiae cursus completus. Series Latina*, I–CCXXI, J.-P. MIGNE, ed., Parisiis / Turholti 1855–1904.
PLB	Papyrologica Lugduno-Batava
PLO	Porta linguarum orientalium

PNTC	Pelican New Testament Commentaries
Pol.	La politica. Metodi, storie, teorie
Pol.	ARISTOTLE, *Politica*
Polit.	PLATO, *Politicus*
PPAf	*Philosophy and Public Affairs*
Praem.	PHILO, *De praemiis et poenis*
Prob.	PHILO, *Quod omnis probus liber sit*
Progym.	THEON, *Progymnasmata*
Prom.	AESCHYLUS, *Prometheus vinctus*
Prot.	PLATO, *Protagoras*
Prot. Iac.	*Protoevangelium Iacobi*
PRSt	*Perspectives in Religious Studies*
PsHec	Pseudo-Hecateus
Ps.-Mt.	*Pseudo-Matthaeus Evangelium*
PsPho	Pseudo-Phocylides
PSREP.T	Publications de la Société Royale Égyptienne de Papyrologie – Textes et documents
PsSol	Psalms of Solomon
Psych.	Psychismes
PTh.MS	Pittsburgh Theological – Monograph Series
PTS	Patristische Texte und Studien
Pud.	TERTULLIAN, *De pudicitia*
PulC	The Pulpit Commentary
PVTG	Pseudepigrapha Veteris Testamenti Graece
Pyr.	ISAEUS, *De ereditate Pyrrhi*
Q	*Quelle* (Ger.) = Luke's (hypothetical) source material shared with Matthew
QE.	PHILO, *Quaestiones et solutiones in Exodum*
1QH	*Hôdayôt* (Thanksgiving Hymns)
QKoin	Quaderni di Koinonia. Associazione di studi tardoantichi
1QM	*Milḥamah* (War Scroll)
QohR	*Qohelet Rabba* (Midrash on Ecclesiastes)
1QpHab	*Habakuk-Pešer* (Pesher on Habakkuk)
QS	Qumran Scrolls
1QS	*Serek hayyahad* (Rule of the Community, Manual of Discipline)
QT	Qumran Temple Scroll
Quaest. Ant.	PSEUDO-ATHANASIUS, *Quaestiones ad Antiochum ducem*
Quaest. Evang.	AUGUSTINE OF HIPPO, *Quaestiones Evangeliorum*
Quis div.	CLEMENT OF ALEXANDRIA, *Quis dives salvetur*
Rahlfs	RAHLFS, A., ed., *Septuaginta. Id est Vetus Testamentum graece iuxta LXX interpretes. Editio altera*, I–II, Stuttgart 2006.
RB	*Revue biblique*
RBS	Retorica biblica e semitica
RdQ	*Revue de Qumran*
REAug	*Revue des études augustiniennes*
Reg. fus.	BASIL THE GREAT, *Regulae fusius tractatae*
Reg. mon.	JEROME OF STRIDON, BENEDICT OF NURSIA, *Regula monachorum*

Rendich	F. RENDICH, *Dizionario etimologico comparato delle lingue classiche indoeuropee. Indoeuropeo. Sanscrito – Greco – Latino*, Roma 2010.
Resp.	PLATO, *De Respublica*
Respir.	ARISTOTLE, *De respiratione*
RestQ	*Restoration Quarterly*
RExp	*Review and Expositor*
RfR	*Review for Religious*
Rhet.	ARISTOTLE, *Ars Rhetorica*
RhG	Rhetores graeci
RhSem	Rhétorique sémitique
RIDA	*Revue internationale des droits de l'antiquité*
RivBib	*Rivista biblica. Organo dell'Associazione Biblica Italiana*
RNTS	Reading the New Testament Series
RoMo	Rowohlt's Monographien
Rosenthal	F. ROSENTHAL, *A Grammar of Biblical Aramaic*, PLO 5, Wiesbaden 1961, 2006[7].
RSAnt	*Rivista storica dell'Antichità*
RSR	*Recherches de science religieuse*
RTR	*Reformed Theological Review*
Sacr.	AMBROSE OF MILAN, *De sacramentis*
SAEp	Studia Amstelodamensia ad epigraphicam, ius antiquum et papyrologicam pertinentia
SAIS	Studies in the Aramaic Interpretation of Scripture
SAJ	*The Saint Anselm Journal*
Sal.	*Salesianum*
Satt	Shared Aggadic Targumic Traditions
SBFA	Studii Biblici Franciscani Analecta
SBFLA	*Studii Biblici Franciscani liber annuus*
SBL	Society of Biblical Literature. Studies in Biblical Literature
SBL.AB	Society of Biblical Literature – Academia Biblica
SBL.AS	Society of Biblical Literature – Aramaic Studies
SBL.DS	Society of Biblical Literature – Dissertation Series
SBL.MS	Society of Biblical Literature – Monograph Series
SBL.PS	Society of Biblical Literature – Texts and Translations: Pseudepigrapha Series
SBL.SPS	Society of Biblical Literature – Seminar Paper Series
SBL.W	Society of Biblical Literature – Writings from the Greco-Roman World
SBM	Stuttgarter Biblische Monographien
SBT	Studies in Biblical Theology
SC	Sources chrétiennes
Scal.	JOHN CLIMACUS, *Scala Paradisi*
ScBi.E	Sciences bibliques – Études
SCBO	Scriptorum classicorum bibliotheca Oxoniensis
ScEs	*Science et esprit*
Schwertner	S.M. SCHWERTNER, *IATG²*. *Internationales Abkürzungsverzeichnis für Theologie und Grenzgebiete / International Glossary of Abbreviations for Theology and Related Subjects*, Berlin / New York NY, 1992[2].
SciRep	*Scientific Reports*

SCJ	*Stone-Campbell Journal*
ScMon	*The Scientific Monthly*
SDan	*Studi Danteschi*
Sent.	BERNARD OF CLAIRVAUX, *Sententiae*
Sept.	AESCHYLUS, *Septem contra Thebas*
Ser.	PLUTARCH, *De sera numinis vindicta*
Serm.	AMBROSE OF MILAN, PETER CHRYSOLOGUS, CAESARIUS OF ARLES, *Sermones*
Serm. ascet.	BASIL THE GREAT, *Ejusdem sermo asceticus et exhortatio de renuntiatione saeculi, et de perfectione spirituali*
Serm. div.	BERNARD OF CLAIRVAUX, *Sermones de diversis*
Serm. Dom.	AUGUSTINE OF HIPPO, *De sermone Domini in monte*
Serm. jej.	JOHN CHRYSOSTOM, *In septem sermones de jejunio*
Serm. sanct.	AUGUSTINE OF HIPPO, *Sermones de sanctis*
Serm. Scr.	AUGUSTINE OF HIPPO, *Sermones de Scripturis*
Serm. temp.	MAXIMUS OF TURIN, *Sermones de tempore*
SFSHJ	South Florida Studies in the History of Judaism
SGEL	Scrittori Greci e Latini
ShemR	*Shemot Rabba* (Midrash on Exodus)
SHG	*Subsidia hagiographica*
ShirR	*Shir HaShirim Rabba* (Midrash on Song of Songs)
S.Hist	Collection SUP. L'Historien
Sib	Sibylline Oracles
SifDev	*Sifre Devarim*
Sim.	SHEPHERD OF HERMAS, *Similitude*
Simon.	LYSIAS, *In apologia contra Simonem*
SJRS	*Scottish Journal of Religious Studies*
SJTh	*Scottish Journal of Theology*
SMRT	Studies in Medieval and Reformation Thought
Smyth	H.W. SMYTH, *A Greek Grammar for Schools and Colleges*, GSCS, New York NY, 1916.
SNTS.MS	Society of New Testament Studies – Monograph Series
SNTU.B	Studien zum Neuen Testament und seiner Umwelt – Serie B
Sobr.	PHILO, *De sobrietate*
Sokoloff	M. SOKOLOFF, *A Syriac Lexicon. A translation from the Latin, Correction, Expansion, and Update of C. Brockelmann's Lexicon Syriacum*, Winona Lake IN / Piscataway NJ, 2009.
Somn.	PHILO, *De somniis*
SP	Sacra Pagina
Span.	Spanish
SPAW	*Sitzungsberichte der Preußischen Akademie der Wissenschaften*
SPCK	Society for Promoting Christian Knowledge
Spec.	PHILO, *De specialibus legibus*
Sperber	A. SPERBER, ed., *The Bible in Aramaic. Based on Old Manuscripts and Printed Texts*, Leiden / Boston MA, I–III, 2004; IV, 2013.
SPhA	*The Studia Philonica Annual. Studies in Hellenistic Judaism*
SPIB	Scripta Pontificii Instituti Biblici
SPJHS	*The Society for the Promotion of Hellenic Studies*
SSEJC	Studies in Scripture in Early Judaism and Christianity

SSNStT	Sola Scriptura. Nuovi Studi Teologici
ST	Studies in Theology
StBi	Studi Biblici
StBL	Studies in Biblical Literature
StGL	Studi grammaticali e linguistici
StMR	*St. Mark's Review. A Journal of Christian Thought and Opinion*
STP	Second Temple Period (538 BCE – 70 CE)
StPatr	Studia patristica. Études d'ancienne littérature Chrétienne
Str-B	H.L. STRACK – P. BILLERBECK, *Kommentar zum Neuen Testament aus Talmud und Midrasch*, I–IV, München 1922–1961.
StRic	Studi e ricerche
Strom.	CLEMENT OF ALEXANDRIA, *Stromata*
StTh	Studia Theologica. Scandinavian Journal of Theology
Stud.	*Studium. Rivista di vita e cultura*
SubBi	Subsidia biblica
Sup.	AESCHYLUS, *Supplices*
SVigChr	Supplements to Vigiliae Christianae
SVTG	Septuaginta: Vetus Testamentum Graecum
SVTP	Studia in Veteris Testamenti Pseudepigrapha
Swete	H.B. SWETE, ed., *The Old Testament in Greek According to the Septuagint*, I–III, Cambridge 1887–1894, 1912–1925⁴.
SWJT	*Source Southwestern Journal of Theology*
Syll.	*Sylloge*
Symp.	PLATO, *Symposium*
Sympl.	*Symplokē. A Journal for the Intermingling of Literary, Cultural and Theoretical Scholarship*
sy[p]	The Syriac Vulgate (or Peshitta) version
TaAp	Textes à l'appui
Tab.	Table
Tabu.	*Duodecim tabularum leges*
TanB	Midrash *Tanḥuma* (ed. S. BUBER)
TANZ	Texte und Arbeiten zum neutestamentlichen Zeitalter
TaS	Texts and Studies. Contributions to Biblical and Patristic Literature
Taur.	*Taurinensis*
tBQ	Tosefta, Tractate *Baba Qamma*
TDNT	*Theological Dictionary of the New Testament*, I–X, G. KITTEL – G.W. BROMILEY, ed., Grand Rapids MI, 1964–1976; Ger. orig., *Theologisches Wörterbuch zum Neuen Testament*, I–X, G. KITTEL, ed., Stuttgart 1933–1979.
TDOT	*Theological Dictionary of the Old Testament*, I–XV, J. BOTTERWECK – H. RINGGREN – H.-J. FABRY, ed., Grand Rapids MI / Cambridge 1977–2006; Ger. orig., *Theologisches Wörterbuch zum Alten Testament*, I–X, Stuttgart / Berlin / Köln / Mainz 1973–2000.
Tebt.	*Tebtunis*
TeCom	Testi e commenti / Texts and Commentaries
TED	Translations of Early Documents – Series II: Hellenistic-Jewish Texts
Tel.	*Telos. Critical Theory of the Contemporary*
TgCant	Targum Song of Songs (on the book of Song of Songs)
TgProv	Targum Proverbs (on the book of Proverbs)

TgPs	Targum Psalms (on the book of Psalms)
TG.ST	Tesi Gregoriana – Serie Teologia
Th.	HESIOD, *Theogonia*
Thayer	J.H. THAYER, ed., *A Greek-English Lexicon of the New Testament. Being Grimm's Wilke's Clavis Novi Testamenti*, New York NY, 1886, 1889[2].
THBW	Theologisch-homiletisches Bibelwerk
Thdr.	NECTARIUS OF CONSTANTINOPLE, *De festo S. Theodori*
Thea.	PSEUDO-PLATO, *Theages*
Thead.	*Theadelphiae*
Them.	PLUTARCH, *Vita Themistoclis*
Themelios	*Themelios. An International Journal for Theological Studies*
Theol.	*Theology*
Théophilyon	*Théophilyon. Revue des Facultés de théologie et philosophie de l'Université catholique de Lyon*
THEv	Traductions hébraïques des Evangiles rassemblées par Jean Carmignac
ThH	Théologie historique
ThHK	Theologischer Handkommentar zum Neuen Testament
ThHK.TP	Theologischer Handkommentar zum Neuen Testament – mit Text und Paraphrase
ThLZ	*Theologische Literaturzeitung*
ThStKr	*Theologische Studien und Kritiken*
Thurber	S. THURBER, *Vocabulary of the First Six Books of Homer's Iliad*, Boston MA, 1890.
ThZ	*Theologische Zeitschrift*
Tischendorf	C. VON TISCHENDORF, ed., *Novum Testamentum Graece. Ad antiquissimos testes denuo recensuit apparatum criticum omnii studio perfectum*, I, Lipsiae 1869[8].
TJ	Targum Jonathan
TJI	Targum Yerushalmi I (or Targum Pseudo-Jonathan)
TJII	Targum Yerushalmi II (or Fragmenten-Targum)
TJos	Testament of Joseph
TLevi	Testament of Levi
TLNT	*Theological Lexicon of the New Testament*, I–III, C. SPICQ, Peabody MA, 1994; Fr. orig., *Notes de lexicographie néo-testamentaire*, I–III, OBO 22, Fribourg / Göttingen 1978, repr. 1982 = *Lexique théologique du Nouveau Testament*, Paris / Fribourg 1991[2].
TNTC	Tyndale New Testament Commentaries
TO	Targum Onqelos
tPe	Tosefta, Tractate *Pe'a*
Tract. Ev. Jo.	AUGUSTINE OF HIPPO, *In Evangelium Johannis tractatus*
Tract. Ps.	HILARY OF POITIERS, *Tractatus super Psalmos*
Trad.	*Tradition*
trans.	Translation
TReu	Testament of Reuben
TrinJ	*Trinity Journal*
TS	*Theological Studies*
TSol	Testament of Solomon
tSot	Tosefta, Tractate *Soṭa*

TThS	Tilburg Theological Studies
TU	Texte und Untersuchungen zur Geschichte der altchristlichen Literatur
TUAT.NF	*Texte aus der Umwelt des Alten Testaments – Neue Folge*
Turner	C.R. COULTER – P. TURNER, *Encyclopedia of Ancient Deities*, Chicago IL, 2000.
TWOT	*Theological Wordbook of the Old Testament*, I–II, R.L. HARRIS – G.L. ARCHER, Jr. – B.K. WALTKE, Chicago IL, 1980.
tx.	Text
TynB	*Tyndale Bulletin*
UBS	United Bible Societies
UCP.GRA	University of California Publications – Graeco-Roman Archeology
UFHM	University of Florida Humanities Monograph
UnCAT	Università di Catania. Pubblicazioni della facoltà di giurisprudenza
UniSt	UniTrel Studieserie
UnSa	Unam sanctam
UNT	Untersuchungen zum Neuen Testament
USQR	*Union Seminary Quarterly Review*
v(v).	verse(s)
V.	FLAVIUS JOSEPHUS, *Vita*
Vg.	Latin Vulgate
Virg.	PSEUDO-ATHANASIUS, *De virginitate, sive de ascesi*
Virginit.	GREGORY OF NYSSA, *De Virginitate, Epistola exhortatoria ad frugi vitam*
Vir. ill.	JEROME OF STRIDON, *Liber de viris illustribus*
Virt.	PHILO, *De virtutibus*
Vit. Const.	EUSEBIUS OF CAESAREA, *Vita Constantini*
Vit. Hyp.	CALLINICUS THE MONK, *Vita sancti Hypatii*
Vit. Sync.	PSEUDO-ATHANASIUS, *Vita et gesta sanctae beataeque magistrae Syncleticae*
vs.	Versus, as opposed to
VSen	Verba seniorum. Collana di testi e studi patristici
VT	*Vetus Testamentum*
VTB	*Vocabulaire de théologie biblique*, X. LÉON-DUFOUR – *al.*, ed., Paris 1962, 1970[2]; Eng. trans., *Dictionary of Biblical Theology*, New York NY, 1967, 1973[2].
VTM	Vetus Testamentum Miscellanea
VT.S	Vetus Testamentum – Supplements
Wallace	D.B. WALLACE, *Greek Grammar Beyond the Basics. An Exegetical Syntax of the New Testament. With Scripture, Subject, and Greek Word Indexes*, Grand Rapids MI, 1996.
WaR	*Wayiqra Rabba* (Midrash on Leviticus)
WBC	Word Biblical Commentary
WEAL	*West's Encyclopedia of American Law*, J. LEHMAN – S. PHELPS, ed., Farmington Hills MI, 2008[2].
Weber	R. WEBER – R. GRYSON, ed., *Biblia sacra iuxta vulgatam versionem*, Stuttgart 1969, 2007[5].
WHO	World Health Organization

Windekens	A.J. VAN WINDEKENS, *Dictionnaire étymologique complémentaire de la langue Grecque. Nouvelles contributions à l'interprétation historique et comparée du vocabulaire*, Leuven 1986.
Wisc.	*Wisconsin*
WST	*Warszawskie Studia Teologiczne*
WThJ	*The Westminster Theological Journal*
WUNT	Wissenschaftliche Untersuchungen zum Neuen Testament
x	times (attested)
Yalq	*Yalquṭ Shim'oni*
YJS	Yale Judaica Series
ySan	Jerusalem Talmud (*Talmud Yerushalmi*), Tractate *Sanhedrin*
Zaphiris	G. ZAPHIRIS, *Le Texte de l'Évangile selon saint Matthieu d'après les citations de Clément d'Alexandrie comparées aux citations des Pères et des Théologiens grecs du IIe au XVe siècle*, Gembloux 1970.
ZAW	*Zeitschrift für die Alttestamentliche Wissenschaft*
Zerwick	M. ZERWICK, *Biblical Greek. Illustrated by Examples*, SPIB 114, Rome 1963, repr. 2005; Lat. orig., *Graecitas biblica Novi Testamenti exemplis illustratur*, SPIB 92, Romae 1963[4].
ZNW	*Zeitschrift für die Neutestamentliche Wissenschaft und die Kunde der älteren Kirche*
ZPE	*Zeitschrift für Papyrologie und Epigraphik*
ZThK	Zeitschrift für Theologie und Kirche
ZS.NT	Zacchaeus Studies – New Testament

Chapter 1

Introduction

The sayings of Jesus, with their powerful and, often times, puzzling messages, have irresistibly drawn the attention of countless hearers and readers in the course of almost two thousand years of interpretation. At times, the brevity of these Gospel pearls, which causes perplexity over their significance, has led not a few researchers to the intuition that something more is involved than what meets the eye, some deeper meaning, which calls for a better understanding. The following study proceeds according to this perception, as it intends to draw its readers beyond the insights of current exegesis into new scholarly appreciation of one of these "obscure and [...] altogether incomprehensible"[1] NT sayings, that of the so-called "violence passage"[2], as recorded in Luke 16,16.

Considering the importance which the context is to play in this research, this introductory chapter shall open our investigation by placing the reader before the actual text and its challenges. For that reason, we shall first of all offer only a neutral translation of the saying, as it is currently found in Luke 16,16. Such an initial translation, based on a textual analysis of the Greek verse, shall both suggest and respect its hermeneutic issues, allowing nevertheless a tentative grasp of its meaning. After an analogous treatment of the similar saying, as it occurs in Matt 11,12–13, and immediately following a concise summary of the different Lucan and Matthean literary contexts, we shall briefly identify the general issues that continue to be discussed by exegetes, with no clear resolution. Finally, we shall provide a foretaste of the major suggestions which justify the need for a new interpretation of the saying, eventually concluding with a general summary of the arrangement and methodology of our proposal.

---

[1] E. TROCME, *Jésus*, 47. Unless otherwise noted, all English translations provided in this study are the author's.

[2] W. STENGER, "βιάζομαι, βιαστής", *EDNT*, I, 216.

A. Luke 16,16: A Preliminary Critical Analysis and Translation

A clear symptom of the difficulty this saying presents in modern scholarship is detectable in the diversity of the current translations[3]. However, as we will see in the following pages, the real challenge in translating Luke 16,16 is not on the textual level, but on that of its interpretation.

From the perspective of textual criticism, the verse presents no major problems[4]. Although a significant number of manuscripts have the synonymous preposition, "up to" (ἕως)[5], in place of "until" (μέχρι)[6], or the indefinite pronoun, "someone" (τις)[7], as opposed to the pronominal adjective, "everyone" (πᾶς)[8], the latter two readings are to be preferred on the grounds of both external and internal evidence: they actually occur in the oldest and most reliable witnesses and are supported by the vast majority of critical editions as a *lectio difficilior*[9]. In fact, as J.B. Cortés and F.M. Gatti remark, μέχρι would be the only occurrence in Luke's Gospel, without, however, being really foreign to Luke's style (see Acts 10,30; and 20,7)[10]. As to the pronominal adjective πᾶς, "as a substantive and without the article"[11], the problem would

---

[3] For an overview of the major modern translations of Luke 16,16, see J.B. CORTÉS – F.M. GATTI, "On the Meaning", 248–251; I.L.E. RAMELLI, "Luke 16,16", 737–738; W. LINKE, "'Gwałt'", 92; and M.W. BATES, "Cryptic Codes", 77, n. 11.

[4] The biblical Committee of the GNT[4] (Metzger[2], 140) does not even consider it in its commentary. Its insignificant variants include a shortened form of the sacred name (i.e., θυ for θεοῦ) and some orthographic differences (e.g., προφη, τε, εὐαγγελίζετε, εὐαγγελείζετε, εὐαγγελίζονται, etc.). See the critical apparatus in Merk[9], 265; Tischendorf, I, 624; NA[27], 214; NA[28], 253; the CNTTS database, on Luke 16,16; and M. KLINGHARDT, *Das älteste Evangelium*, II, 868.1254. Unless otherwise specified, the Greek text of all NT citations in this study is that of the NA[28] critical edition.

[5] A D E F G H K M N P S U W Y Γ Δ Θ Λ Π Ψ Ω 28 565 700 1424 etc.

[6] 𝔓[75] ℵ B L *f*[1.13] 13 69 124 346 579 788 892 1241 and 2542.

[7] 1 13 69 118 209 346 1582 *f*[1.13] etc.

[8] 𝔓[75] ℵ[c] A B D E F H K L N P S U W Δ Θ Ψ W 28 124 565 579 etc.

[9] See J.B. CORTÉS – F.M. GATTI, "On the Meaning", 248, n. 3; and D.A. CARSON, "Do the Prophets", 190.

[10] See J.B. CORTÉS – F.M. GATTI, "On the Meaning", 248. "Up to" (ἕως) occurs 27x in Luke and 22x in Acts, and could simply be a harmonization with Matt 11,13. Note that, along with the traditional claim and the scholarly consensus, the exegesis presented in the course of this study will presuppose Luke-Acts as two parts of a single literary composition, combined by the same author to form one coherent narrative unity, with a precise theological project in mind. See, e.g., H.J. CADBURY, *The Making*, 8–9; R. MORGENTHALER, *Die lukanische Geschichtsschreibung*, I, 159–194; *Ibid.*, II, 96–111; W. RADL, *Paulus*, 39–67; R.C. TANNEHILL, *The Narrative Unity*, I, 1–12; D.L. BOCK, *A Theology*, 55–61.134–148; and D. MARGUERAT – A. WÉNIN, *Sapori*, 51.

[11] J.B. CORTÉS – F.M. GATTI, "On the Meaning", 251.

allegedly consist in explaining "how only *one* sense, either positive or negative, would be true of 'everyone'"[12], as opposed to "someone" (τις). As accurately observed by M.W. Bates, however, the stylistic use of πᾶς in Luke-Acts is often hyperbolic (see, e.g., Luke 3,15; 4,15; and Acts 1,1), and, as can be inferred from its proximate context, this seems to be the case also in Luke 16,16[13].

Other textual variants obviously to be rejected are those which supply a supposedly missing verb in the first clause (Luke 16,16a), adding "arrived" (*pervenerunt*)[14] or "prophesied" (whether ἐπροφήτευσαν or προεφήτευσαν)[15], right after "John" (Ἰωάννου), as appropriate explanatory emendations meant to smooth the text or harmonize it with Matt 11,13. Analogously, in Luke 16,16c, a further clarifying gloss and another harmonization (see Matt 11,12) are visible in the additions, respectively, of the verb, "to enter" (εἰσελθεῖν)[16], and the whole final sentence, "and the *biastái* seize it" (καὶ βιασταί ἁρπάζουσιν αὐτήν)[17]. Although semantically more interesting, the Latin readings of *a quo* or *ex eo* (ἐξ οὗ), instead of ἀπὸ τότε, and *adnuntiatur* (ἀπαγγελίζεται), instead of εὐαγγελίζεται, are also to be refused, mainly on the basis of the scant external evidence[18]. Finally, the omission of the whole last clause, "and everyone *biázetai eis* it" (καὶ πᾶς εἰς αὐτὴν βιάζεται)[19], in just a few geographically widespread manuscripts of different text-types, such as, the early hand of Codex Sinaiticus, Codex Seidelianus, and a couple of later minuscules of the

---

[12] J.B. CORTÉS – F.M. GATTI, "On the Meaning", 251, n. 11. According to the BDAG Lexicon ("πᾶς", 783, §2bα), in fact, πᾶς would mean here: *"everyone without exception"*. See also P.H. MENOUD, "Le sens", 209–210.

[13] M.W. BATES, "Cryptic Codes", 84. According to the author (*Ibid.*, 84–85), "the immediate context of Luke 16,16 both in its Matthean parallel (11,11: 'among those born of women, *nobody* has arisen who is greater than John the Baptist') and its Lucan form (16,17: 'it is easier for heaven and earth to pass away *than for one* stroke [of a letter] of the law to fall') suggest[s] that hyperbole is operative here". See also G. SCHRENK, "βιάζομαι, βιαστής", *TDNT*, I, 612; C.J.A. HICKLING, "A Tract", 256, n. 2; and P.S. CAMERON, *Violence*, 134.191, n. 4. For the rhetorical force of such a use of πᾶς, see T. BEDNARZ, "Status Disputes", 380–381.

[14] See the Sahidic (sah) translation, according to Tischendorf, I, 624.

[15] D Θ vg^ms and sy^c.

[16] Thus, e.g., the *Pešiṭtâ* (sy^p), which explicitly supplies the verb "to enter" (ﺟﺎﺴﻦ). See, e.g., J. NOLLAND, *Luke*, II, 813; G.L. CARREGA, *La Vetus Syra*, 356–360; and J.W. CHILDERS – G.A. KIRAZ, ed., *Luke*, 134–135.

[17] See the later correctors of Codex Sinaiticus (א^c).

[18] Tert a aur b c d e ff² gat i l and r¹. Such variants seem to suggest a reading of the text, wherein the starting point "by", "from" or "out of which/whom" the *basiléia* of God is announced is not so much the temporal dimension of the first phrase (Luke 16,16a), but rather its messenger or contents.

[19] Luke 16,16c.

Byzantine type, can presumably be dismissed as a simple scribal homoiote-leuton[20].

Overall, then, the evaluation of the extant variants poses no real problem in the establishment and translation of the critical text, and yet the textual level itself seems to indicate some kind of hermeneutic perplexity with regard to the Lucan verse. As recently noted by I.L.E. Ramelli, the very omission of the "*biázetai*-sentence", as well as the aforementioned scribal attempts to read Luke 16,16 in the light of Matt 11,12–13[21], "may be a sign of a certain difficulty with these words and their meaning"[22]. As a result of this introductory critical analysis, we present here a preliminary translation of the Greek text, which we shall henceforth use in our study of this verse.

The Greek text of Luke 16,16, now established, can therefore be translated as follows:

"[(a)] The Law and the Prophets until John; [(b)] since then the *basiléia* of God is preached [as good news], [(c)] and everyone *biázetai eis* it"[23].

Such a translation does not make clear the hermeneutic route which we shall eventually undertake in this dissertation. However, it is an adequate basis from which to begin our investigation.

B. Matt 11,12–13: A Similar Saying but in a Different Context

As the former analysis has pointed out, and as is evident in most modern synopses, Luke 16,16 regularly tends to be associated with a very similar saying recorded in Matt 11,12–13[24]. Both sets of Gospel texts, in fact, mention

---

[20] ℵ* G[(011)] 716, 788 and 2358. In fact, the copyist of the earliest and most important Alexandrian witness, and those of later mss. as well, may either have accidentally jumped from the end of v. 16b (εὐαγγελίζεται) to the like ending in v. 16c (βιάζεται), thus skipping the entire clause, or even deliberately wished to resolve the semantic obscurity of the text. See P.S. CAMERON, *Violence*, 183, n. 69.

[21] Namely, the harmonizing additions of ἐπροφήτευσαν after Ἰωάννου, εἰσελθεῖν or καὶ βιασταὶ ἁρπάζουσιν αὐτήν after βιάζεται, and, perhaps, even the variant readings of ἕως in place of μέχρι.

[22] I.L.E. RAMELLI, "Luke 16,16", 737.

[23] "[(a)] Ὁ νόμος καὶ οἱ προφῆται μέχρι Ἰωάννου· [(b)] ἀπὸ τότε ἡ βασιλεία τοῦ θεοῦ εὐαγγελίζεται [(c)] καὶ πᾶς εἰς αὐτὴν βιάζεται" (Luke 16,16). The current threefold subdivision ([abc]) is ours.

[24] See, e.g., J. SCHMID, ed., *Sinossi*, 133; M.E. BOISMARD – A. LAMOUILLE, ed., *Synopsis*, 248; J. CERVANTES GABARRÓN, ed., *Sinopsis*, 128–129; A. POPPI, ed., *Nuova Sinossi*, I, 222–223; and K. ALAND, ed., *Synopsis*, 197. Additionally, M.E. Boismard and

"John" (Ἰωάννης) the Baptist, the "Law" (νόμος) and the "Prophets" (προφῆται), and, most importantly, contain these same interesting words; *pās*, *basiléia* and *biázetai*.

From a critical point of view, when compared to Luke 16,16, this other Greek text (Matt 11,12–13) is less ambiguous than the previous one, being attested in the vast majority of the original manuscripts and followed by all critical editions[25]. Its quite insignificant variants, in fact, are mostly a matter of orthographic errors, different spellings, nominal abbreviations or verbal forms[26], with only a couple of sporadic explanatory emendations, which either add or omit some short textual segments[27]. Perhaps, the only substantially attested dubious reading concerns the possibly different spelling of "prophesied" (ἐπροφήτευσαν)[28], which, notwithstanding its oldest and most reliable textual support, would in any case leave the meaning of the text unaffected.

Just as it is with Luke 16,16, then, the difficulty in translating this related text pertains not to its textual level, but to the meaning and interpretation of its words, and, specifically, those recorded in Matt 11,12[29]. Consequently, we wish momentarily to delay the subsequent elucidation of these semantic and hermeneutical issues and likewise offer here only a preliminary and impartial translation of the accepted Greek text of Matt 11,12–13, as follows:

"[12] [(a)] So from the days of John the Baptist up to now [(b)] the *basiléia* of Heaven *biázetai*, [(c)] and the *biastái* seize it. [13] For all the Prophets and the Law up to John prophesied"[30].

A. Lamouille (*Synopsis*, 248, n. on Matt 11,12–13) also mention JUSTIN MARTYR, *Dial.* LI.3. For the Greek text, see P. BOBICHON, ed., *Justin Martyr*, I, 314–315.

[25] ℵ B C D E F G K L M N S U W Y Δ Θ Π Ω 1 2 13 28 33 35 118 124 157 346 565 579 700 788 1071 1424 1582 2358 *f*[1.13] 𝔐 etc. As to its textual variants, see the critical apparatus in Merk[9], 33; Tischendorf, I, 56; NA[27], 27; NA[28], 31; and the CNTTS database, on Matt 11,12–13.

[26] See, e.g., ἱμερῶν (N), Ἰω (1071), Ἰωάνου (B), Ἰάννου (C E 124 565), Ἰωάννους (D* Clem), ἕω ἄρτι (K), βασιλία (ℵ*), οὐνῶν (E F G K L M U Y Δ Π Ω 1 13 28 124 157 565 *f*[1.13] etc.), βιάζεται (L), βιάζετε (ℵ* 346), βιαζοτέ (ℵ*), βιαστέ (ℵᶜ 1071), διαρπάζεται (Εν. Naz.), προφήτε (2*), προφήτευσαν (Δ), and ἐπροεφήτευσαν (346).

[27] See, e.g., the additions of the article οἱ to βιασταί (D* Clem) or τὸ βαπτιστοῦ to the second occurrence of Ἰωάννου (1071), in Matt 11,13, and the omissions of δέ (D* Taᵛ syˢ copᵐᵉ Amb), ἕως ἄρτι (28 1071), and καὶ ὁ νόμος (syˢ boᵐˢ). See also D.A. CARSON, "Do the Prophets", 190.

[28] ℵ B* C D 1 13 33 124 579 1582* *f*[1.13] etc., as opposed to, προεφήτευσαν (Bᶜ E G K L M N S U W Y Q P W 2 28 35 118 157 565 700 1071 1424 1582ᶜ etc.). For a grammatical explanation on this different NT "handling" of the verb, see BDF, 38, § 69.

[29] For a concise survey of some of the major recent translations of Matt 11,12, see M.W. BATES, "Cryptic Codes", 77, n. 12.

[30] "[12] [(a)] ἀπὸ δὲ τῶν ἡμερῶν Ἰωάννου τοῦ βαπτιστοῦ ἕως ἄρτι [(b)] ἡ βασιλεία τῶν οὐρανῶν βιάζεται [(c)] καὶ βιασταὶ ἁρπάζουσιν αὐτήν. [13] πάντες γὰρ οἱ προφῆται καὶ ὁ νόμος

As is evident from this translation, and as the aforementioned synoptic works also indicate, however, this comparable saying in Matt 11,12–13 differs from that in Luke 16,16, in two essential ways. Structurally, it basically reverses the sequential order of the "law-prophets" and "kingdom-violence" clauses[31], with *biázetai* in lieu of "is preached" (εὐαγγελίζεται), *biastái* in lieu of "everyone" (πᾶς), and "seize" (ἁρπάζουσιν) in lieu of *biázetai eis*[32]. Contextually, Matt 11,12–13 differs also in its literary location within the Gospel narrative. In fact, while Luke 16,16 is surrounded by an enveloping concern with the use of wealth and material possessions (see Luke 16,1–15.19–31), the Matthean text is well integrated within a framework wholly focused on the figures of John the Baptist and Jesus (see Matt 11,2–11.14–19; and Luke 7,18–35)[33].

More precisely, Luke 16,16 belongs to the central section (Luke 15–16) of Luke's Travel Narrative (Luke 9,51–19,44)[34] and is immediately tied to two other sayings of Jesus (Luke 16,17–18), which respectively affirm his teaching on the permanent value of the "Law" (νόμος)[35] and on "dismissing one's wife" (ἀπολῦσαι τὴν γυναῖκα)[36]. In the slightly broader narrative setting, this threefold collection of "seemingly disparate dicta"[37] (Luke 16,16–18), concerning the "violent" entry into God's kingdom, Torah, and divorce, is directly addressed by Jesus to the Pharisees (Luke 16,14–15), precisely insofar

---

ἕως 'Ιωάννου ἐπροφήτευσαν" (Matt 11,12–13). Also for this text, the subdivision is ours and the reasons for this "open" translation shall gradually become obvious.

[31] Namely, Luke 16,16a = Matt 11,13; and Luke 16,16b–c = Matt 11,12ab–c.

[32] See P.S. CAMERON, *Violence*, 1.

[33] See D.R. CATCHPOLE, "On Doing Violence", 51.

[34] Note that, along with the scholarly claim that the next section of the Gospel cannot begin without the goal of the journey (i.e., Jerusalem) having first been reached, and consistent with the well-known Lucan pattern of introducing major sections of the narrative (e.g., "The Galilean Ministry": Luke 4,14–9,50; "The Travel Narrative": Luke 9,51–19,44; and "The Jerusalem Ministry": Luke 19,45–21,38) by means of some rejection scene (see Luke 4,14–30; 9,52–55; and 19,45–20,18), the present study shall assume Luke 19,44 as the cut-off point of the Travel Narrative. A full discussion of the major issues related to the subject of its proper ending, in fact, lies beyond the scope of this thesis. For a survey of the various solutions and arguments proposed thus far, see F. Ó FEARGHAIL, *The Introduction*, 48–60; D.J. IRELAND, *Stewardship*, 139–156; F. NOËL, *The Travel Narrative*, 1–206; A. DENAUX, "Het lucaanse reisverhaal", (1968) 214–242; (1969) 464–501; ID., "The Delineation", 359–392; and ID., ed., *Studies*, 3–37.

[35] Luke 16,17 actually reads: "But it is easier for Heaven and earth to pass by than for one stroke of a letter of the Law to fall" (εὐκοπώτερον δέ ἐστιν τὸν οὐρανὸν καὶ τὴν γῆν παρελθεῖν ἢ τοῦ νόμου μίαν κεραίαν πεσεῖν).

[36] Luke 16,18 actually reads: "Anyone who dismisses his wife and marries another commits adultery, and he who marries one [who has been and still is] dismissed by [her] husband commits adultery" (πᾶς ὁ ἀπολύων τὴν γυναῖκα αὐτοῦ καὶ γαμῶν ἑτέραν μοιχεύει, καὶ ὁ ἀπολελυμένην ἀπὸ ἀνδρὸς γαμῶν μοιχεύει).

[37] T. BEDNARZ, "Status Disputes", 403.

as they are "money lovers" (φιλάργυροι)[38], and inserted between two peculiarly Lucan (*L*) parables dealing with the proper use of riches: that of "The Shrewd Steward" (Luke 16,1–8a), with its attached amplifying verses (Luke 16,8b–13) on the "mammon of unrighteousness" (μαμωνᾶ τῆς ἀδικίας)[39], and that of "The Rich Man and Lazarus" (Luke 16,19–31), with its focus on the care of the poor and its eschatological reach[40].

From a literary perspective, however, the text belongs to one of the six narrative units adjoining the five great discourses of Matthew's Gospel, and specifically the third one (Matt 11–12), which mainly relates the opposition that Jesus' preaching meets among his people[41]. Specifically, in its most immediate context, the saying seems to be part of a "soliloquy of Jesus [...] reflecting on his own mission and that of John"[42] (Matt 11,2–15), as well as on their rejection by the current generation (see Matt 11,16–19). More precisely, Matt 11,2–15 presents, on the one hand, the person of John the Baptist who, hearing from prison about Jesus' deeds, sends his disciples to ask him whether he is the stronger one who is to come (vv. 2–3; cf. Matt 3,11), and, on the other hand, Jesus himself, who, in mentioning his messianic works, points to his own identity (vv. 4–6). Then, turning to the crowds, Jesus draws the attention back to John and begins to praise him, at first, somewhat weakly: as a prophet and more than that, the greatest man on earth, and yet, as less than the least in the heavenly kingdom (vv. 7–11); but then, unambiguously: he is the Elijah destined to come (vv. 14–15; cf. Matt 17,12).

From these differences, a small number of scholars have even drawn the conclusion that Luke 16,16 and Matt 11,12–13 should not be considered parallels at all, thus arguing that their "forced harmonization [...] is [...] misleading"[43]. This assumption, however, is quite contested. Actually,

---

[38] Luke 16,14.

[39] Luke 16,9. See the repetition of the term "mammon" (μαμωνᾶς), in Luke 16,11.13.

[40] See, e.g., D.J. IRELAND, *Stewardship*, 48–49.116–160.

[41] As is generally accepted by scholars, Matthew builds his Gospel by successively alternating six segments of narrative (Matt 1–4.8–9.11–12.14–17.19–23.26–28) and five major discourses (Matt 5–7.10.13.18.24–25), which progressively move toward a climax in the passion and resurrection stories. These six narrative blocks are demarcated by a recurring formula (see Matt 7,28; 11,1; 13,53; 19,1; and 26,1), signaling the end of each discourse, namely, "And [it happened that] when Jesus had finished" (καὶ ἐγένετο ὅτε ἐτέλεσσεν ὁ Ἰησοῦς). See, e.g., J.P. MEIER, *The Vision*, 45–48.75–89; and D. MARGUERAT – A. WÉNIN, *Sapori*, 41–42.200. For the immediate context of Matt 11,12–13, see C.H. TALBERT, "Between Text and Sermon", 406–408.

[42] D. SENIOR, *Matthew*, 124. See also *Ibid.*, 124–135; and R.A. EDWARDS, "Matthew's Use", 273–275.

[43] I.L.E. RAMELLI, "Luke 16,16", 739. Likewise, e.g., see M. SCHNECKENBURGER, *Beiträge*, 50–51; A. SCHWEIZER, "Ob in der Stelle", 118–119; F.F. ZYRO, "Erklärung", 409–410; and ID., "Neue Auslegung", 663–704.

"contention" seems to be the only common ground uniting modern exegetes on the subject of these verses! We shall attempt to penetrate more deeply into the main reasons this specific NT saying and its translation still represent a "*crux interpretum*"[44] in modern scholarship.

C. The Present State of Research: A Bundle of Unresolved Issues

As we gradually move away from the level of textual criticism to that of semantic, source, and redaction-critical analyses, the "legion"[45] of questions, which continues to demand an explanation by modern-day exegetes, materializes before us along three main lines: semantic issues concerning the wording of the saying[46]; historical issues concerning its formation and transmission[47]; and redactional issues concerning the implications of its literary collocation[48].

Among the most significant semantic problems which this NT saying calls the reader to face, we find, first and foremost, the very meaning of "violence" (βία) contained in the verb βιάζομαι[49]. This lexeme occurs nowhere in the NT, except in Luke 16,16c and Matt 11,12b and, as underscored by P.H. Menoud, might even carry different meanings in each account[50]. The derivative plural noun, "violent ones" (βιασταί), in Matt 11,12c, further complicates the matter,

---

[44] W. STENGER, "βιάζομαι, βιαστής", *EDNT*, I, 216. See also R. BULTMANN, *The History*, 164; E. KÄSEMANN, "The Problem", 42; I.H. MARSHALL, *Luke*, 630; C. SPICQ, *Lexique*, 294; S.G. WILSON, *Luke*, 51; J.A. FITZMYER, *Luke*, II, 1117; and J.B. CORTÉS – F.M. GATTI, "On the Meaning", 247. For a survey of the varied hermeneutic solutions advanced thus far, see, e.g., G. BRAUMANN, "'Dem Himmelreich'", 104–109; G. SCHRENK, "βιάζομαι, βιαστής", *TDNT*, I, 609–614; R. SCHNACKENBURG, *Règne*, 109–113; P.H. MENOUD, "Le sens", 207–212; P.S. CAMERON, *Violence*; C. SPICQ, "βιάζομαι", *TLNT*, I, 287–291; G. HÄFNER, "Gewalt", 21–25; G. THEIßEN, "Jünger", 183–200; É. CUVILLIER, "Jésus", 339–341; S.F. KEHINDE, "'The Violent Kingdom'", 99–100; and M.W. BATES, "Cryptic Codes", 77–80.

[45] P.S. CAMERON, *Violence*, 1.

[46] As summed up by P.S. Cameron (*Violence*, 1), for instance, "The meaning of almost every word [...] is disputed".

[47] See, e.g., S. LLEWELYN, "The Traditionsgeschichte", 330–349; C.M. TUCKETT, *Q*, 135–137.404–409; C. HEIL, *Lukas*, 119–127.136–140; D. MARGUERAT, "Le règne", 113–127; H.T. FLEDDERMANN, *Q*, 781–792; J. VERHEYDEN, "The Violators", 397–415; and S.J. JOSEPH, "For Heaven", 169–188.

[48] See, e.g., D. KOSCH, *Die Gottesherrschaft*, 65–78.

[49] Because of the notorious difficulty in determining the meaning of the verb βιάζομαι, D.L. Bock (*Luke*, II, 1350) calls Luke 16,16, actually, "an exegetical minefield in Lucan studies".

[50] See P.H. MENOUD, "Le sens", 210–212.

being, as it is, a biblical *hapax legomenon*. This unique occurrence is also, as noted by P.S. Cameron, "a very uncommon word, unattested in classical literature, the LXX, Josephus, and the papyri"[51]. As a result, researchers generally wonder how these two "βία-based" Gospel terms should be interpreted, that is, whether "positively" (*in bonam partem*) or "negatively" (*in malam partem*), and whether, in this saying, they are actually meant to convey a literal, metaphorical, ironic, or cryptic message[52].

Moreover, as if that were not enough of a problem, by reason of the Greek verb's middle voice, the grammar equally allows the Lucan clause in v. 16c (πᾶς εἰς αὐτὴν βιάζεται) to be read *actively* ("everyone does violence to it")[53], *intransitively* ("everyone forces his way into it")[54], or even *passively* ("everyone is forced into it")[55]. Likewise, in Matt 11,12b, because of its different subject, the same verb could actually imply an action being either experienced ("suffers violence")[56] or carried out ("has been forcefully advancing")[57] by the heavenly "kingdom" (βασιλεία) itself.

Whatever answer one chooses to give to these questions, it will affect the identity of the alleged "violent" (βιασταί) *agents* in Matt 11,12c, which shall respectively be thought of as human, angelic, or divine. The solutions proposed are numerous. The *biastái*, in fact, have been identified with the

---

[51] P.S. CAMERON, *Violence*, 142.193, n. 44. See G. SCHRENK, "βιάζομαι, βιαστής", *TDNT*, I, 613–614.

[52] The cryptic interpretation, for instance, has lately been advanced by M.W. Bates ("Cryptic Codes", 74–93), who eventually argues (*Ibid.*, 75) that "Jesus [...] is deliberately speaking in code in these passages in his denouncement of Herod Antipas".

[53] P. ROSSANO, ed., *Vangelo*, 147. An *active* exertion, in fact, could be performed "towards", "against" or "for [the advantage of]" the kingdom of God. See, e.g., Luke's use of εἰς in Acts 24,17: "I came to do alms for [the advantage of] my people" (ἐλεημοσύνας ποιήσων εἰς τὸ ἔθνος μου παρεγενόμην).

[54] Thus, according to the *ESV* and *DBY* translations (see also *NIV* and *NASB*). In fact, when used absolutely, the middle voice of βιάζεσθαι can mean entry by force. See Moulton, "βιάζομαι", 109–110. Moreover, as noted by the BDAG Lexicon ("εἰς", 289, §2aα), the preposition εἰς can also be used to indicate an extension in time, as in: "εἰς Χριστόν *until the coming of the Messiah* Gal 3,24", or simply introduce the direct object, as a translation of the Hebrew preposition ל. See, e.g., M. BLACK, *An Aramaic Approach*, 80, n. 2; *Ibid.*, 116; and W.E. MOORE, "ΒΙΑΖΩ, ΑΡΠΑΖΩ", 520, n. 2.

[55] I.L.E. RAMELLI, "Luke 16,16", 738. A divine *passive* action, in fact, would here suggest God's pressing desire (see Luke 14,23; and Matt 22,9) to extend his salvation universally to "all" (πᾶς). By pointing to the "conceptual parallel [...] found in Luke 14,23 [...] which, in the active form, perfectly corresponds to the passive form in Luke 16,16", I.L.E. Ramelli (*Ibid.*, 739–740) argues that, "just as the master forces all to enter his house, God (for βιάζεται is clearly a theological passive) forces all to enter his kingdom".

[56] Thus, e.g., according to the *NASB*, the *ESV*, and several other translations.

[57] Thus, e.g., according to the *NTL* translation. See, e.g., Matt 4,23; 9,35; 10,7; 11,12b; 12,28; and 24,14.

Qumran's 'ārîṣîm (עריצים), Baptists, Zealots, Jewish religious authorities, Scribes and Pharisees, Herod Antipas, Satan, his demons and forces (with or without their human counterparts), tax-collectors and sinners, ascetic Christian believers and Gentiles, John the Baptist and Jesus, their disciples or their persecutors, the Pope or his clerics, and eventually, even God himself[58].

Linked to this initial, and *per se* "overflowing" question, two further semantic problems must likewise be mentioned. The first one concerns the exact meaning of the *basiléia* envisioned in this NT saying, and whether it is to be understood *spiritually* (God or the single believer's heart), *physically* (a concrete place, either in Heaven above or on earth below), or *historically* (the Church or the state, in their socio-political connotation)[59]. Several recent investigations have been conducted with regard to the concept of the divine kingdom held by Jesus and his contemporaries, analyzing whether their first-century Palestinian understanding was really the same as that of the early Church or that of the two synoptic evangelists[60]. Some authors have even noticed a substantial difference between the two expressions (see Luke 16,16b; Matt 11,12b), "kingdom of God" (βασιλεία τοῦ θεοῦ) and "kingdom of Heaven" (βασιλεία τῶν οὐρανῶν), whereas others consider the latter simply a stylistic variation or circumlocution for the divine name contained in the former[61].

The second issue relating to the meaning of the words pertains to the temporal adverbial expressions on John the Baptist and the kingdom of God, and whether they are to be regarded as inclusive or exclusive of the prophet[62]. As the aforementioned textual emendations indicate, and as P.S. Cameron remarks, the preposition "from" or "since" (ἀπό)[63] could mean "'since John was born', 'since John began to preach', 'since John was imprisoned', or 'since John was executed'"[64], whereas "until" (μέχρι) or "up to" (ἕως)[65] could entail

---

[58] See, e.g., D. HILL, *Matthew*, 200–201; P.W. BARNETT, "Who Were the 'Biastai'", 65–70; R. DOYLE, "Matthew 11,12", 20; and P.S. CAMERON, *Violence*, 1–2.131.

[59] For a review of the multiplicity of meanings, which the word has eventually taken up throughout the history of its interpretation, see B.T. VIVIANO, *The Kingdom of God*, 30–148.

[60] See, e.g., S.J. HULTGREN, "The Apostolic Church", 208–209.215; D.C. ALLISON, Jr., *Constructing Jesus*, 164–204; L. SEMBRANO, "Il Regno", 19–140; F. MANNS, "Il Regno", 141–162; and F. PANIMOLLE, "Il Regno", 163–224.

[61] See, e.g., F.F. ZYRO, "Neue Auslegung", 663–700; R. FOSTER, "Why on Earth", 487–499; J. RATZINGER, *Jesus*, I, 55–56; and J.T. PENNINGTON, *Heaven*, 1–76.339–348. Note that, in spite of the eventual differences, these terms shall be used interchangeably in this study, for purely stylistic reasons.

[62] See P.S. CAMERON, *Violence*, 178, n. 52; and J. RINDOŠ, "The Place", 269, n. 1.

[63] See Luke 16,16b; and Matt 11,12a.

[64] P.S. CAMERON, *Violence*, 1.

[65] See Luke 16,16a; and Matt 11,12a.13.

either "an extension of the period since John, or [...] an imminent third period"[66].

Finally, as to the other major exegetical questions occupying the scholarly mind even today, they apply mostly either to the historical development of the saying or to its redaction. In keeping with the hypothetical existence of a Matthean/Lucan common "source" (*Quelle*), the three *dicta*, in *Q* 16,16–18, could well be a coherent unit belonging to an original tradition, or an amalgamation of several autonomous and dispersed *logia* into one editorial arrangement (see Matt 5,18.32; 11,12–13)[67]. Generally, however, regarding its *Traditionsgeschichte*, exegetes continue to discuss the *logion*'s original form and context; whose is the earliest location, whether Luke's or Matthew's; and "to what situation or pattern in Jesus' activity [...] the saying [can] reasonably be attached"[68].

As to the possible redactional changes, attention is focused especially on how to interpret the different contexts and the peculiarly Lucan occurrences, "everyone" (πᾶς), and "is preached [as good news]" (εὐαγγελίζεται)[69]. Some authors neglect them, others see in them simply an "attempt by Luke to render what is either unintelligible or offensive to him"[70], and still others consider them as a redactional indication of something more profound[71].

---

[66] P.S. CAMERON, *Violence*, 1.

[67] See J. SCHLOSSER, "Le Règne", 509. Our study will presuppose the validity of the "Two Source Theory" (or 2DH: i.e., "Two Document Hypothesis"), which posits that, in composing his Gospel, Luke made use of two written sources, namely the Gospel of Mark and a collection of Jesus' teachings (the "*Q* Source", from Ger., *Quelle*, meaning "source"), together with a set of oral and/or written traditions (the "*L* Source"), known exclusively to Luke. See, e.g., D. MARGUERAT, "L'évangile", 92. For a reconstruction of *Q* 16,16–18, in keeping with the majority scholarly opinion, see J.M. ROBINSON – P. HOFFMANN – J.S. KLOPPENBORG, ed., *The Critical Edition*, 464–471; and D. MARGUERAT, "Le règne", 115–116.

[68] P.S. CAMERON, *Violence*, 1.

[69] In Luke 16,16b, in fact, as observed by G. Aichele ("Jesus' Violence", 74), "The proclamation of the good news of the kingdom (*hē basileia tou theou euaggelizetai*) [...] is associated with, or at least concurrent with, violence against the kingdom". Concerning πᾶς, instead, see J.B. CORTÉS – F.M. GATTI, "On the Meaning", 251; and P.H. MENOUD, "Le sens", 209–210.

[70] P.S. CAMERON, *Violence*, 42. For the author (*Ibid.*, 42), in fact, "it is clear that without Luke's εὐαγγελίζεται it would never occur to anyone to understand βιάζεται in Matt 11,12 as '*praedicatur*'". Similarly, see also E. KÄSEMANN, "The Problem", 42; G. BRAUMANN, "'Dem Himmelreich'", 106; and U. LUZ, *Matthew*, II, 143.

[71] T. Bednarz ("Status Disputes", 406), e.g., notes: "Throughout the Gospel, Luke stresses the good news of reversals for the [...] poor ones (4,18; 6,20; 7,22; 14,13.21; 16,20.22; 18,22; 19,8; 21,2–3)". Likewise, C. Spicq ("βιάζομαι", *TLNT*, I, 291) remarks: "we can understand Luke 16,16 in terms of the *dynamis* inherent in the apostolic preaching: the reign of God is announced with power". See also J. ERNST, *Luca*, II, 663.

D. The Scope of a New Proposal
and its Justification

Because of this bundle of unresolved exegetical questions, it becomes obvious that our preliminary "open" translation is capable of taking on innumerable colours. Different exegetes can have divergent perceptions of the same text. Even in our investigation, the reader shall find many specific hermeneutic choices and answers, of which we will now briefly display a small sample.

The aim of this dissertation is twofold. Firstly, by means of an in-depth study of Luke 16,16 and, only indirectly, of Matt 11,12–13, we intend to fill in the gaps of the work done thus far. The two most recent monographs written on the subject – those that we have been able to find in our research, namely, *Violence and the Kingdom* (1984), by P.S. Cameron, and *Die Gottesherrschaft im Zeichen des Widerspruchs* (1985), by D. Kosch – may well require updating. Several interesting articles have since then been published, over the past approximately thirty years of academic research. Some of the new discoveries and suggestions provide sufficient grounds to support the need for a different understanding of the question. So we intend to propose a "satisfactory explanation"[72] of this saying, which, through an original hermeneutic "pattern"[73], will offer our reader a new view of the biblical discussion, in full compliance with the context, language, and theology of the Lucan text.

Secondly, as the foregoing paragraphs have concisely exposed, one of the main difficulties emerging in the translation of these two texts, whether or not they are related, is the interpretation of their meaning. Meaning, however, is closely related to context and is often affected by it. Consequently, whereas most commentators seem to feel "at liberty to treat the saying in isolation"[74], the thesis propounded in this work agrees rather with those who view context as potentially significant. As we shall see, failure to recognize the significance of the connection between the Lucan verse and its narrative setting has generally resulted in a partial impoverishment of the interpretation of the saying and of its possible nuances. The contention of this study, then, is not only to prove that a specific text (v. 16) generally fits into its context, but also that there exists evidence that warrants a new look at the surrounding teachings on poverty, riches, and kingdom.

On an etymological level, we have reason to believe that the two forces (or phenomena) of "violence" (βία) and "life" (βίος) may be related implicitly in

---

[72] M.W. BATES, "Cryptic Codes", 74.
[73] P.S. CAMERON, *Violence*, 161.
[74] P.S. CAMERON, *Violence*, 157.

Luke 16,16's use of the verb βιάζομαι[75], and that the *biastái* may simply be "all" (πᾶς) those who "stand" or "come up"[76] (στῆναι) in God's kingdom, by way of *bía* (βία). Over and above these linguistic considerations, an appraisal of a number of legal papyri, dated to the 3rd and 2nd cs. BCE, in connection with an assessment of the concept of βία in ancient Greece, Athenian-Hellenistic and Jewish law, reveals that Luke may have actually drawn on these notions to refer to a not necessarily hostile "potential use of force"[77], which, consistent with the legal notion of "acquisition by *usucapio* or *ḥazaqah*"[78] (חזקה), is actually needed to take possession of the "immovable" (spatial) property of God's kingdom[79]. The term βία, in this sense, would concretely imply the "seizing" (Matt 11,12c) of such a divine space, "without the consent of God"[80] (its true lawful owner) and by means of almsgiving[81].

Finally, the novelty of this study and, consequently, the possibility of it bringing a new thrust to the theological research on the subject, consists in the original proposal that the "broad reference"[82] of our saying, hidden behind the binomial "kingdom of God" (βασιλεία τοῦ θεοῦ) and "violence" (βία), may be the *Šᵉmaʿ Yiśrāʾēl* of Deut 6,4–5, namely, the very commandment of life mentioned in Luke 10,25–28[83]. In the verses immediately preceding Luke 16,16,

---

[75] In contrast to the other term for "life" (ζωή), in fact, βίος signifies not only "life" but also those "possessions" and "riches" by which life itself is sustained, but in which it clearly does not consist (see, e.g., Luke 8,14.43; 12,15; 15,12.30; 21,4.34). Likewise, the kingdom of God (see Mark 9,1; and 1Cor 4,20) is somehow related to the concept of *ḥayil* (חיל), which, in a way akin to βία/βίος, can mean not only "power, force, strength" (see, e.g., Mark 12,30.33; Luke 10,27a; 21,26–27; Acts 1,8; and 4,7), but, as specified by Sokoloff ("ܚܝܠ", 447–448), also, "abundance [...] resources, possessions of a household", or even "wealth". Finally, in the OT, *ḥayil* is sometimes linked with the concepts of "cleverness" (תבונה; φρόνησις), "trade" (רכלה; ἐμπορία), "gold" (זהב; χρισίον), "silver" (כסף; ἀργύριον), "treasure" (אוצר; θησαυρός), "heart" (לבב; καρδία), "wife" (אשה; γυνή), and "sinful violence" or "lawlessness" (חמס; ἀνομία). See, e.g., Ru 3,11; Job 20,18–19; Ps 73(72),6.12–13; Prov 12,4; 31,10.29; Ezek 28,4–5.16; Luke 16,1.8–9.15–16.18; also, X. LÉON-DUFOUR, "Violence", *VTB*, 1360; BDB, "חַיִל", 298–299; H.-J. RITZ, "βίος, βιωτικός", *EDNT*, I, 219; *OSG*, II, 489; and J.-D. CAUSSE, "*La violenza*", 57.

[76] See BDAG, "ἵστημι", 482–483.

[77] S. LLEWELYN, "Forcible Acquisition", 152.

[78] S. LLEWELYN, "The Introduction", 156.

[79] See D.C. ALLISON, Jr., *Constructing Jesus*, 171–179.

[80] S. LLEWELYN, "The Traditionsgeschichte", 348.

[81] See, esp., F. D'AGOSTINO, *BIA*, 1–126; C. SPICQ, "βιάζομαι", *TLNT*, I, 288; S. LLEWELYN, "Forcible Acquisition", 130–162; ID., "The Introduction", 154–167; A. TOSATO, *Vangelo*, 307–457; G.A. ANDERSON, "Faith", 29–34; and N. EUBANK, "Storing up Treasure", 77–92.

[82] P.S. CAMERON, *Violence*, 133.

[83] Although some authors occasionally and in different ways draw close to a proposal such as ours, in fact, they never explicitly identify it or convincingly support it in their arguments. See, e.g., H. OLSHAUSEN, *Biblischer Commentar*, I, 658.666; and ID., *Biblical*

we find the threefold occurrence of the Aramaic word for "money" (μαμωνᾶς)[84], as opposed to the "love" of God (ἀγαπήσει[ς])[85], its assonance with the Semitic verb for faith *'āman* (אמן)[86], as well as the mention of one's "heart" (καρδία)[87]. All these indications point in this hermeneutic direction as a very good and reasonable possibility. Research into the Aramaic stratum of this text shows that its sincere recitation was generally "understood as taking [up] on one's shoulders the yoke of God's sovereign lordship"[88] (see Mark 12,34) and that its shared targumic interpretation of "all your 'muchness'"[89] (כל־מאדך) was equivalent to "all your money" (כל ממונכון)[90] or "all your properties" (כל נכסך)[91].

In the wake of the Dead Sea Scrolls' discovery (1947–1956) and the renewed Catholic-Jewish relationships fostered by the Vatican Council II (1962–1965), as well as in the light of the reassessment of Jewish apocryphal, pseudo-epigraphic, and targumic literature, the Holy See has challenged biblical scholars not to dismiss *a priori* the value of Jewish hermeneutic traditions and their historical context[92]. A growing number of authors agrees

---

Commentary, II, 55.62; C.E.B. CRANFIELD, "Riches", 309.313; A. POPPI, *Sinossi*, II, 363; D.J. IRELAND, *Stewardship*, 212, n. 260; D.L. BOCK, "The Parable", 63; M.-L. RIGATO, "'Mosè e i Profeti'", 163–165.177; G. GIURISATO, "Come Luca", 462.482; F. BOVON, *Luc*, III, 94; D.B. GOWLER, "'At His Gate'", 262; J.J. KILGALLEN, *Twenty Parables,* 131; A. MACLAREN, *Luke*, II, 83; and B.B. BRUEHLER, "Reweaving the Texture", 66.

[84] Luke 16,9.11.13.

[85] See Luke 7,42; 10,27; and 16,13. Within the *Opus Lucanum*, the indicative future active form of ἀγαπάω (reminiscent of Deut 6,5) occurs only in these three instances, which may be thus, somehow, related.

[86] See G.M. CAMPS – B.M. UBACH, "Un sentido", 75–82; F. HAUCK, "μαμωνᾶς", *TDNT*, IV, 388; G. ROSSÉ, *Luca*, 624, n. 20; F. BOVON, *Luc*, III, 73; A. TOSATO, *Vangelo*, 392, n. 129; and K.R. SNODGRASS, *Stories*, 412.

[87] Luke 10,27; and 16,15.

[88] J. RATZINGER, *Jesus*, I, 57. See also A. BÜCHLER, *Sin*, 150–154; J. NEUSNER, *The Theology*, 326–328; and A. BERLIN – M.Z. BRETTLER, ed., *The Jewish Study Bible*, 380.

[89] BDB, "מְאֹד", 547. See MT on Deut 6,5.

[90] See CN and TJI on Deut 6,5.

[91] See TO on Deut 6,5. Conversely, our common reading of the text ("with all your 'strength'"), comes rather from the Greek and Latin translations of *m^e'ōd* (מְאֹד), respectively, as δύναμις (LXX on Deut 6,5) or ἰσχύς (LXX on 2Kgs 23,25), and as *"fortitudine"* (*Vg.* on Deut 6,5) or *"virtute"* (*Vg.* on 2Kgs 23,25). See, e.g., Jastrow, "מָמוֹן", II, 794; ID., "נִכְסִין", II, 911; M. MCNAMARA, *Targum*, 99–100; and P. DI LUCCIO, *The Quelle*, 31–41.196–217.264–268.274–275.

[92] For instance, quoting Pope John Paul II, the Commission for Religious Relations with the Jews (*Notes on the Correct Way*, § I.3) points out that, to assess the common patrimony of the Church and Judaism, "with due awareness of the faith and religious life of the Jewish people *as they are professed and practised still today*, can greatly help us to understand better certain aspects of the life of the Church". Also, the Pontifical Biblical Commission (*The Jewish People*, §§ 22.85) remarks: "On the practical level of exegesis, Christians can, nonetheless, learn much from Jewish exegesis practiced for more than two thousand years,

with the observation that the NT can often remain incomprehensible without a deep acquaintance of the OT textual background, especially as it was interpreted by the Jewish liturgy and its oral tradition[93]. Although it is a genuine problem, and caution is justly recommended, the possibility of drawing from these sources should never be excluded scientifically, simply because of the challenges involved in the dating and attribution of these traditions[94].

As a matter of fact, quite a few testimonies (e.g., the Nash Papyrus, a few *tefillin* found at Qumran, the NT, Flavius Josephus, Justin Martyr, and the Mishnah) attest that Israel's profession of "faith" (אמונה)[95] was already recited in 1st c. Palestine, and its apparent synagogal paraphrases may have well been known also to early Christians[96]. It is this work's conviction that, such an ancient Jewish-Christian background, with its understanding of "force" in terms of "possessions", along with the just mentioned fresh understanding of Jesus' language, before and after v. 16, promises to shed light not only on the saying in question, but also on its very *Traditionsgeschichte*. The potential reference of the "violence passage"[97] to the love commandment could

---

and, in fact, they have learned much in the course of history. For their part, it is to be hoped that Jews themselves can derive profit from Christian exegetical research [...] to properly interpret the New Testament, knowledge of the Judaism of this period is often necessary". In the *Instrumentum Laboris* on the Word of God in the life and mission of the Church, the Synod of Bishops (§ 55) states likewise: "The Jewish understanding of the Bible can be of assistance in the Christian understanding and study of the Bible. In some cases, ways to study Sacred Scripture together are being developed – and can be further developed – providing occasion to learn from each other, while closely respecting each's differences". See also J.A. FITZMYER, *The Biblical Commission's Document*, 74–78, ns. 101–113.

[93] See, e.g., S. LYONNET, *Il Nuovo Testamento*, 16; R. PENNA, "Appunti", 102–104; and F.G. VOLTAGGIO, *La oración*, 39–42.

[94] On this point, see, e.g., D.I. BREWER, "Review Article", 281–298; and J.P. MEIER, *A Marginal Jew*, 309. For some methodological studies, see R. BLOCH, "Note méthodo-logique", 194–227; A.J. SALDARINI, "Form Criticism", 237–274; B.M. BOKSER, "Talmudic Form Criticism", 46–60; G. VERMES, "Jewish Literature", 362–376; and F. MANNS, *Le judéo-christianisme*, 323–333. In fact, extant rabbinic literature can occasionally serve as a historical source for NT study, and vice versa, the Gospels can at times be helpful in dating ancient rabbinic traditions. See, e.g., A.D. YORK, "The Dating", 49–62; P. SIGAL, "Early Christian", 63–90; D. FLUSSER, "'The Book of Mysteries'", 3–20; J. NEUSNER, "Comparing Sources", 119–135; and, esp., M. LAVEE, "Rabbinic Literature", 319–351.

[95] This term is also found in association with "money" (כסף), "wealth" (πλοῦτος), or "treasures" (θησαυροί), and in opposition to "malice of deceit" (בעולא דנעתר). See, e.g., MT on 2Kgs 12,16 and 22,7; LXX on Ps 36,3 (cf. MT on Ps 37,3); TgProv on Prov 28,20; and LXX on Isa 33,6.

[96] See, e.g., J. MANN, "Changes", 288; E. CORTÉS, *Los Discursos*, 338; E.P. SANDERS, *Judaism*, 196; M. MCNAMARA, *Targum*, 190–192; F. MANNS, *La Preghiera*, 140–143; and K.H. TAN, "The Shema", 181–206. Generally, liturgical (prayer) traditions tend to be very conservative, even when they are transmitted orally.

[97] W. STENGER, "βιάζομαι, βιαστής", *EDNT*, I, 216.

definitely illuminate modern-day exegetes' understanding of the motives for its close association, in Luke, with the concept of the "Law" (νόμος) and its validity (see Luke 10,26–27; and 16,16–17), a notion of which the *Q* community is generally considered quite supportive[98].

E. A Summary of the Methodological Arrangement of this Proposal

Therefore, the question to which this proposal shall provide an answer is actually whether and how "Kingdom of God" and "Violence" converge, in Luke 16,16 and Matt 11,12–13[99]. As remarked by I.H. Marshall, and based on what we have observed thus far, we are convinced that "the practical problem lies [really] in how to combine force and love"[100], and that its solution ultimately comes down to establishing not only which concept of "kingdom" (βασιλεία) is here at stake, but also which nuance of βία is referred to, in its specific Gospel context and theology[101].

As we have already acknowledged in our preliminary analysis, the very basis of this study shall primarily be the text of Luke 16,16 itself, as it appears in the 28th Nestle-Aland's Greek critical edition of the *Novum Testamentum Græce*. At its different stages, moreover, we shall take into account the MT, the LXX, the Targumim, the Syriac and Latin translations, and when deemed necessary, we shall further deal with questions related to textual criticism. However, since part of the challenge in understanding and translating Luke 16,16 lies on the level of its interpretation, to lay the foundations for the hermeneutical route suggested in this research, the first section of our proposal shall directly deal with the historical reception and explanation of the text.

In this early part of the study, we shall rely mostly on the first of the two already cited monographs, updating it, from time to time, as we go along. In fact, in his doctoral thesis presented at the University of Cambridge, in 1979, under the title, *Violence and the Kingdom. The Interpretation of Matthew 11,12*, the scholar, Peter Scott Cameron, already dedicated most of his efforts to describing in minute detail the long history of the discussion concerning this problematic verse[102]. Indeed, as reviewed by K.A. Barta:

---

[98] See P. DI LUCCIO, *The Quelle*, 23–43; and S.J. JOSEPH, "For Heaven", 169–188.

[99] See R. DEVILLE – P. GRELOT, "Royaume", *VTB*, cols. 1142–1150; and X. LÉON-DUFOUR, "Violence", *VTB*, cols. 1360–1366.

[100] I.H. MARSHALL, "The Hope", 230, n. 47.

[101] For the hermeneutic importance of the usage of a term in its context, see J.B. CORTÉS – F.M. GATTI, "On the Meaning", 257.

[102] In reality, the 1st published edition of his dissertation dates to 1984. The 2nd edition, corrected and enlarged, which we had at our disposal, was issued in 1988. As we read in its

this study of Matt 11,12 is primarily a history of its interpretation. Only one chapter, modestly titled "Towards a Solution" (chap. 6), is devoted to elucidating this enigmatic and troublesome saying of Jesus on the kingdom of God suffering violence. The bulk of the study, some two hundred pages, traces the history of its interpretation, beginning with the Greek Fathers and ending with redaction criticism in the twentieth century[103].

Although we shall be aiming strictly at the Lucan text (vs. Matt 11,12–13), there is no need for us to reinvent the wheel. On the contrary, wishing to build on Cameron's history of interpretation, we shall also take into account his ultimate methodological suggestions. As a matter of fact, P.S. Cameron argues that "results [...] may still be achieved if a more stringent method is used"[104], and remarks:

In the light of this strange mixture of collective confusion and individual confidence, it must be seriously asked whether any further attempt to interpret the saying is justified. So many scholars have been certain that their conflicting solutions were right that [it] is tempting to suggest that the saying ought to be accorded a status of its own, protected by the critical principle that a text of such proven uncertainty should not be exposed to the violence of the ingenious. But it is just possible that a more rigorous method, coupled with an awareness of the deficiencies of the previous attempts, may succeed in determining from the saying itself at least what its broad reference is, and on that basis some speculation on its *Sitz im Leben Jesu* may in turn suggest further implications[105].

As clarified by the same author, this more demanding method eventually implies a re-examination of both "context and language"[106] together. For that reason, following our first chapter, and faced with the general lack of consensus characterizing even the latest history of its interpretation, the second stage of our work shall then take a synchronic look at the context of Luke 16,16 and, with the help of narrative analysis, identify its literary delimitation and unfolding[107].

Preface (P.S. CAMERON, *Violence*, iii), whereas in the former release the author "took no account of anything published after 1979", the latter edition has been enriched with an *Epilogue* (see *Ibid.*, 161–169), which, as he himself defines it (*Ibid.*, iii), is but "a more or less haphazard dip into contemporary research", containing publications as far as the year 1986 (see *Ibid.*, 199). For a brief bibliographic overview on P.S. Cameron's life and writings, see, e.g., ID., "J'accuse", 107–112; ID., "The Making", 14; ID., *Necessary Heresies*; ID., *Heretic*; S. MACLEAN, "The 'Heretic'", 11; H.A. HARRIS, "Where love", 2–9; and W. DE MARIA, *Deadly Disclosures*, 74–87.

[103] K.A. BARTA, review of P.S. CAMERON, *Violence*, 133–134.

[104] P.S. CAMERON, *Violence*, 131.

[105] P.S. CAMERON, *Violence*, 133.

[106] P.S. CAMERON, *Violence*, 157. See also *Ibid.*, 134–154.

[107] For a distinction between synchronic and diachronic approaches to the text and the successfulness of their methodological cooperation in biblical exegesis, see D. MARGUERAT – A. WÉNIN, *Sapori*, 199–221.

On the basis of the thematic coherence around the proper use of wealth resulting from the context of the saying, the third stage of this study shall then broaden the analytic spectrum of the text, by a diachronic examination of the biblical (NT & OT) and extra-biblical (e.g., 4Macc 2,8, papyri, etc.) use of the verb βιάζεσθαι, taking into consideration its etymological family and its actual connections with the notions of wealth and property[108]. A careful look at the plurality of meanings of its occurrences, along with a fairly detailed examination of its contextual, philosophical, and legal implications, shall ultimately encourage us to view Luke 16,16 as fitting impeccably into its contextual whole.

Following the latter semantic and historical critical analysis of the terms, the fourth and concluding stage of our dissertation shall finally apply the ordinary tools of redactional and pragmatic analysis, as a springboard to the theological message conveyed by the evangelist, through a close study of the text and context of our problematic verse. Luke's redactional choices and possible narrative strategies shall eventually come to light as vehicles ordered towards the communication of a coherent message, intended, in the first place, for a particular community, but then, by extension, also for all subsequent Christian believers[109].

---

[108] Namely, ἡ βία, -ας; βίαιος, -α, -ον; βιαίως; ἡ βιαστής, -ου; καταβιάζομαι; παραβιάζομαι; ἀποβιάζομαι; and διαβιάζομαι. Some of these terms occur in the NT only in the *Opus Lucanum* (i.e., παραβιάζομαι: Luke 24,29; Acts 16,15; βία: Acts 5,26; 21,35; 27,41; and βίαιος: Acts 2,2).

[109] As rightly pointed out by E. Lupieri ("Mammona iniquitatis", 136), in the immediate context of the saying, the Lucan Jesus "turns also to the disciples, and therefore probably also to the believers of the time of Luke". However, since the Gospel verse, as we understand it, actually conveys a universal good news (see the Lucan πᾶς and εὐαγγελίζεται), it may well address itself to believers of all times. See A. BOLIN, *Du bon usage*, 46–47.

Chapter 2

A History of the Interpretation of an Enigmatic Saying

A. Introduction

Most recently, in the opening remarks of his article, M.W. Bates has stated:

The sayings in Matt 11,12 and Luke 16,16 are among the most enigmatic in the NT. Indeed, I do not believe any truly satisfactory explanation of these verses has ever been given in either ancient or modern scholarship[1].

Augustine of Hippo suggested that past hermeneutic errors can often prove very helpful in bringing the hidden meaning of Scriptures to light[2]. In keeping with his assertion and before proceeding with the fresh claim proposed in this study, we wish to review the very problematic and extensive history of the interpretation of the "violence passage"[3]. This will allow us to raise our own preliminary questions and present some initial assumptions that will lay the groundwork for the remainder of our study.

In our research and assessment of both "ancient and modern scholarship"[4], we shall follow the stages of classical historical analysis: a) starting with the patristic interpretation, we shall especially note the Fathers' positive, interwoven, profitmaking, and legal comprehension of the saying, as well as their earthly, heavenly, present, future, and spiritualized vision of the kingdom of God; b) the Middle Ages shall then give us the opportunity to observe a strikingly analogous and uncontested understanding, but with the further development of a political earthly idea of the kingdom, which shall probably set the stage for the subsequent polemical interpretation of the saying; c) with the advent of the Modern Age and modern scholarship, and as the emphasis is progressively laid on the kingdom's morality and eschatology, we shall note the rise of the first serious attempts to refute, on exegetical grounds, the previous and long-running traditional interpretation, as well as their final

---

[1] M.W. BATES, "Cryptic Codes", 74.

[2] See AUGUSTINE OF HIPPO, *Enarrat. Ps.* LIV.22 (ed. A. TRAPÈ – P.R. PICCOLOMINI, III.26.2, 114–115). For patristic abbreviations, see Lampe, xi–xlv; Zaphiris, 45–71; BiPa I, 18–45; II, 22–55; III, 13–31; IV, 15–28; V, 15–33; VI, 13–18; LSJ, I, xvi–xxxviii; and Alexander, 237–263.

[3] W. STENGER, "βιάζομαι, βιαστής", *EDNT*, I, 216.

[4] M.W. BATES, "Cryptic Codes", 74.

hermeneutic impasse, with A. Schweizer and A. von Harnack as the representative examples of the two outermost positions; d) finally, we shall summarize some of the major lines of inquiry taken up in recent decades, including the rise of "the secularist reinterpretation of the idea of the kingdom"[5]. An assessment of these first results will note the general lack of scholarly consensus in each of these approaches, and this will raise questions which shall set the stage for our next chapter.

B. An Uncontested Traditional Understanding in both East and West.

As we "representatively"[6] consider the *paleo*-reception of this saying among both Greek and Latin Church Fathers, we are immediately struck by a remarkable fact: since the earliest stages of all traceable references to the "violence passage"[7], and for a significant length of time, the verse is received and interpreted *in bonam partem*. Such a unanimously positive understanding characterizes not only the Fathers of the first five centuries, but carries on, uncontested, throughout the Middle Ages (5th–15th cs.)[8], even to the rise of modern scholarship, in both the East and the West. That is why we shall consider the former two historical periods together in this section.

I. The Positive Voice of the Fathers of the Church

1. The Greek Fathers

Beginning with the writings of the Apostolic Fathers (2nd c.), and up to the 5th c. and beyond, the concepts of "violence" (βία) and "violent ones" (βιασταί) contained in this enigmatic saying are viewed positively, to such an extent that the most recurrent paraphrase appearing among the Greek commentators is: "for [the] violent [ones'] is the kingdom of God [or Heaven]"[9]. Irenaeus

---

[5] J. RATZINGER, *Jesus*, I, 53.

[6] As P.S. Cameron (*Violence*, 2) points out, "The historical investigation cannot claim to be exhaustive – no such investigation can; but it is *representative* [emphasis added], in the sense that no line of interpretation which has had any influence in the history of the verse has been left out of account". However, while P.S. Cameron's "study of Matt 11,12 is primarily a history of its interpretation" (K.A. BARTA, review of P.S. CAMERON, *Violence*, 133–134), our study of Luke 16,16 shall limit itself in this first chapter to summarizing only those results of his that we consider particularly relevant for our thesis.

[7] W. STENGER, "βιάζομαι, βιαστής", *EDNT*, I, 216.

[8] All dates in this thesis are assumed to be of the Common Era (CE), unless specified as before the Common Era (BCE).

[9] "βιαστή [or βιαστῶν] γάρ ἐστιν ἡ βασιλεία τοῦ θεοῦ [or τῶν οὐρανῶν]": see CLEMENT OF ALEXANDRIA, *Strom.* IV, II.5.3 (ed. O. STÄHLIN, II, 250); *Ibid.*, VI, XVII.149.5

of Lyons uses an equivalent Latin formula when he states: "the Lord asserted that of [the] violent [ones] is the kingdom of Heaven"[10].

In view of this evidence, the first characteristic feature, which one detects in the most primitive history of the interpretation of the "violence passage"[11], consists precisely in the Greek Fathers' harmonious understanding of its "violent" terms. This interpretation is connected with a certain *positive ascetic force*, which anyone wishing to take hold of the kingdom of God must possess. As summarized by G. Häfner, we could say that, in their judgment, "the βιαστής is one who utterly puts his heart and soul into it and thus 'seizes' life from God"[12].

This specific type of violence is expressly valued as good, fair, useful, noble and commendable, the "only beautiful violence" (μόνη βία καλή)[13]. Contrary to P.S. Cameron's assertion – that the latter expression "shows that the words still retain [...] their pejorative meaning"[14] – this syntagm, in our opinion, makes plain the positive character of this violence and, as we shall also have occasion to ascertain, attests how βιάζομαι and βιασταί may actually carry both positive and negative meanings. As argued by G. Häfner, this would also

---

(ed. *Ibid.*, II, 509); BASIL THE GREAT, *Hom. Prov.* XIII (*PG* 31, 413a.1775d); ID., *Serm. ascet.* IX (*PG* 31, 645c); GREGORY OF NAZIANZUS, *Or. bapt.* XL (*PG* 36, 392c); JOHN CHRYSOSTOM, *Hom. Eutrop.* II, 6 (*PG* 52, 401z); ID., *Ep. vigil.* XXXIV (ed. P.G. NIKOLO-POULOS, 481–482); ID., *Ep. ab.* CXXXVI (ed. *Ibid.*, 464.471); CYRIL OF ALEXANDRIA, *Glaph. Gen.* V, 3 (*PG* 69, 269d); ID., *Comm. Luc.* XIII, 23 (*PG* 72, 777a); and HESYCHIUS OF JERUSALEM, *Ant.* VIII, 8 (ed. M. AUBINEAU, I, 286). See, likewise, CALLINICUS THE MONK, *Vit. Hyp.* XXX, 12.3–4 (ed. G.J.M. BARTELINK, 204); PSEUDO-ATHANASIUS, *Doctr. Ant.* II, 21 (ed. W. DINDORF, 38); ID., *Vit. Sync.* LXIX (*PG* 28, 1528b); ANTIOCHUS THE MONK, *Pand. hom.* CXXX (*PG* 89, 1841b); JOHN DAMASCENE, *Parall.* (*PG* 95, 1517a); THEODORE THE STUDITE, *Ep.* CCLXII, 10 (ed. G. FATOUROS, II, 549); and GEORGE THE MONK, *Chron.* (ed. C. DE BOOR, I, 136). See also Lampe, "βιαστής", 296; Zaphiris, 539–542; and BiPa I, 255.362–363; II, 262.316; III, 243.303; IV, 223.253; V, 266.298; VI, 192.236.

[10] "*Dominus violent[i]um dixit regnum coelorum*" (IRENAEUS OF LYONS, *Haer.* IV, 37.7 [ed. A. ROUSSEAU, II, 939]). See P.S. CAMERON, *Violence*, 4.170, n. 3.

[11] W. STENGER, "βιάζομαι, βιαστής", *EDNT*, I, 216.

[12] G. HÄFNER, "Gewalt", 33.

[13] CLEMENT OF ALEXANDRIA, *Quis div.* XXI (ed. G.W. BUTTERWORTH, 314); and JOHN DAMASCENE, *Parall.* (*PG* 95, 1264b; *PG* 96, 181a.401d). See, also, the different ms. reading "μόνον βία καλή", in CLEMENT OF ALEXANDRIA, *Ibid.*, XXI (*PG* 9, 625c), as well as Gregory of Nazianzus' expression, "he forced with gentleness" (ἐπιεικῶς ἐβιάζετο), in *Or.* IV.79 (*PG* 35, 695a). For a discussion of the latter, as a subtle way of making coercion, see M. MARCOS, "'He Forced'", 191–204.

[14] P.S. CAMERON, *Violence*, 5. According to the author (*Ibid.*, 22), "none of the Fathers, Greek or Latin, unequivocally take the vocabulary of the saying, the crucial words βιάζεται, βιασταί and ἁρπάζουσιν *in bonam partem*, although their interpretations of the saying are *in bonam partem*". See also *Ibid.*, 5.48.92.

explain why the Fathers may sometimes feel the need to spell out the difference, as in this case[15].

By the same token, even the apparently violent action signified by the verb ἁρπάζω ("to take, seize, snatch, steal")[16], though it might undoubtedly carry adverse meanings as well, is not perceived as imperatively negative, but can sometimes be performed "with a good intention" (in guter Absicht)[17] and "with zeal" (μετὰ σπουδῆς)[18]. Thus, commenting on the implications of the verb ἁρπάζω, John Chrysostom affirms: "Therefore, it is not with laziness that one attains it [i.e., the kingdom], but with zeal"[19].

Likewise, according to Origen of Alexandria, there obviously can be "bad thieves" (*mali raptores*)[20], meaning either ἅρπαγες or βιασταί but only when they "seize" or "snatch [something] away" (ἁρπάζουσιν)[21] from the poor. On the contrary, "those [...] who seize the kingdom of Heaven are, in fact, good" (*boni quidem illi [...] quia regnum coelorum diripiunt*)[22], and actually do so "laudably" (*laudabiliter*)[23].

The concept is best encapsulated, perhaps, by John Chrysostom, when he unequivocally declares: "It is good to seize, yet not the perishable things, but the kingdom of Heaven"[24].

Overall, however, in addition to the generally positive understanding of the saying, a few more distinctive features characterize the Greek Fathers' her-

---

[15] See G. HÄFNER, "Gewalt", 32–33.

[16] See Lampe, "ἁρπάζω", 228–229. See also Matt 11,12c; 12,29; and 13,19.

[17] G. HÄFNER, "Gewalt", 34. See, e.g., Acts 8,39; 23,10; 2Cor 12,2.4; 1Thess 4,17; Jude 1,23; and Rev 12,5.

[18] IRENAEUS OF LYONS, *Haer.* IV, 37.7 (ed. A. ROUSSEAU, II, 939). See P.S. CAMERON, *Violence*, 3.5.7.170, ns. 2.7. The term σπουδή can also mean "eagerness, haste, diligence", or even "effort". See, e.g., G. HARDER, "σπουδάζω, σπουδή, σπουδαῖος", *TDNT*, VII, 559–568; LSJ, II, "σπουδή", 1630–1631; and LEH, "σπουδή", 565. See also the expression διεσπουδακώς ("done diligently"), just a few words before the citation of the saying, in CLEMENT OF ALEXANDRIA, *Quis div.* XXI (ed. G.W. BUTTERWORTH, 312). In TSol III.4 (ed. C.C. McCOWN, 17*), even μετὰ βίας is translated as "with haste" by Lampe ("βία", 297), although, as evinced by A. Cosentino (*Testamento*, 32), it better retains here the meaning of a "forza violenta".

[19] "Οὐκ ἀρὰ μετὰ ῥαθυμίας ἐστιν ἐπιτυχεῖν αὐτῆς, ἀλλὰ μετὰ σπουδῆς" (JOHN CHRYSOSTOM, *Hom. Jo.* VIII [*PG* 59, 301δ]). See P.S. CAMERON, *Violence*, 9.171, n. 23.

[20] ORIGEN OF ALEXANDRIA, *Hom. Lev.* IV, 4 (ed. M. BORRET, I, 172).

[21] Matt 11,12c. See, e.g., Isa 3,14; and 1Cor 6,10.

[22] ORIGEN OF ALEXANDRIA, *Hom. Lev.* IV, 4 (ed. M. BORRET, I, 172).

[23] ORIGEN OF ALEXANDRIA, *Hom. Lev.* IV, 4 (ed. M. BORRET, I, 172).

[24] "Καλὸν τὸ ἁρπάζειν, ἀλλ᾽οὐχὶ τὰ ἀπολλύμενα, ἀλλὰ τὴν βασιλείαν τῶν οὐρανῶν" (JOHN CHRYSOSTOM, *Hom. Jo.* VIII [*PG* 59, 301δ]). Even among the Desert Fathers (*Apoph. C.G.S.* VII, 52.45–47 [ed. J.-C. GUY, I, 384.386]), one could occasionally find expressions such as this one: "It is thus good to do violence to oneself by the aid [or for the sake] of God" (Καλὸν οὖν τὸ βιάζεσθαι ἑαυτὸν διὰ τὸν Θεόν).

meneutic views on the "violence passage"[25]. They appear regularly, here and there, already from the most primitive Greek interpretations of these verses, and are thus worth mentioning here.

a) Two Interwoven Strands: Self and God

First of all, P.S. Cameron accurately observes, for the Greek Fathers:

There are *two interwoven strands* [emphasis added] [...] which must be distinguished [...] violence, that is, directed at God; and [...] violence [...] exercised not against God but against either [the βιαστής] himself [...] or those things he must renounce in order to enter the kingdom (Mark 10,28)[26].

Thus, in his recapitulation of Pseudo-Macarius' thought, P.S. Cameron affirms:

He who wants to come to God must βιάζεσθαι ἑαυτόν [...] to obey the commandments, to be meek and humble, to persevere in prayer [...] to do good, to be merciful, to thrust away doubt[27].

Coming to God, in fact, entails a kind of "violence" (βία), which itself implies a certain amount of "force" (ἰσχύς) directed at oneself. The Syrian monk, for instance, but other Fathers as well, persistently explains this exigency by connecting Luke 16,16 (= Matt 11,12–13) with Luke 13,24 (= Matt 7,14)[28]. The effect is clear: in order to enter the kingdom of God (see Luke 13,28), the believer needs to "undertake a fight" (ἀγωνίζεσθε) and pass as "through a narrow door" (διὰ τῆς στενῆς θύρας), "since many [...] shall seek to enter but will not be strong enough"[29].

---

[25] W. STENGER, "βιάζομαι, βιαστής", *EDNT*, I, 216.

[26] P.S. CAMERON, *Violence*, 5. See also Lampe, "βιάζω", 296.

[27] P.S. CAMERON, *Violence*, 6. See PSEUDO-MACARIUS, *Hom. sp.* XIX.1–7 (*PG* 34, 644a–648c); ID., *Lib. cor.* XIII–XIV (*PG* 34, 836c–840b–c). P.S. Cameron (*Violence*, 7.170, n. 15) also observes here that such a use of βιάζεσθαι is similar to that of 4Macc 2,8, a text which we consider particularly relevant to our study. See G. GIURISATO, "Come Luca", 462–466; and B.B. BRUEHLER, "Reweaving the Texture", 60–61.

[28] See, e.g., PSEUDO-MACARIUS, *Hom. sp.* XIX.2 (*PG* 34, 644b); ID., *Lib. cor.* XIII (*PG* 34, 837a); and ID., *Lib. men.* XVIII (*PG* 34, 949c). See also CLEMENT OF ALEXANDRIA, *Strom.* IV, II.5.3 (ed. O. STÄHLIN, II, 250); ORIGEN OF ALEXANDRIA, *Comm. Jo.* VI, XIX.105 (ed. C. BLANC, II, 208–209); and GREGORY OF NYSSA, *Instit.* (ed. W. JAEGER – al., VIII.1, 46).

[29] "ὅτι πολλοί [...] ζητήσουσιν εἰσελθεῖν καὶ οὐκ ἰσχύσουσιν" (Luke 13,24). This association shall come back, time and again, even in modern commentaries. See, e.g., A. RESCH, *Aussercanonische*, II, 439–442; B. RALPH, "The Kingdom", 427; C. SPICQ, *Théologie morale*, II, 529, n. 2; E.E. ELLIS, *Luke*, 187.200; and P.S. CAMERON, *Violence*, 134.

According to this first trend of thought, then, this fierce "struggle" (ἀγών) is to be fought precisely "against the natural inclinations of the heart"[30] and, especially, one's own sins. This is, for instance, what Pseudo-Macarius affirms in this respect:

"Those Christians who wish to advance and grow must do violence to themselves as far as every good [thing], so that they may be freed from the indwelling sin, and be filled with the Holy Spirit"[31].

However, the Greek Fathers speak also of a "violence" (βία) that is directly exercised either toward God's heavenly kingdom or God Himself. John Chrysostom expresses this concept by "concentrating on the violence implicit in ἀρπάζειν"[32]. He writes:

"Become violent there, become thievish, that which is seized is not diminished! For neither is virtue divided, nor is piety diminished, nor is the kingdom of Heaven. Then virtue will increase, whenever you seize; then the bodily things are diminished, whenever you seize"[33].

Clement of Alexandria further specifies how this kind of *simultaneously thievish and heavenly violence* implies "violating God" (θεὸν βιάσασθαι)[34] and "snatching life away from Him" (παρὰ θεοῦ ζωήν ἀρπάσαι)[35] by force, "for God delights in being vanquished in such things"[36] (χαίρει γὰρ ὁ θεὸς τὰ τοιαῦτα ἡττώμενος)[37].

---

[30] P.S. CAMERON, *Violence*, 6. See the Pseudo-Macarian recurrent phrase (12x) "being the heart unwilling" (μὴ θελούσης τῆς καρδίας), in PSEUDO-MACARIUS, *Lib. cor.* XIII (*PG* 34, 836c–841a); and in ID., *Hom. sp.* XIX.2 (*PG* 34, 644c–645a.c). See also the similar expression "our heart being unwilling" (οὐκ ἐθελούσης ἡμῶν τῆς καρδίας), in ID., *Lib. men.* XVIII (*PG* 34, 949c).

[31] "Οἱ Χριστιανοὶ προκόπτειν καὶ αὐξάνεσθαι βουλόμενοι ὀφείλουσιν ἑαυτοὺς βιάζεσθαι πρὸς πᾶν τὸ ἀγαθὸν, ὥστε λυτροῦσθαι αὐτοὺς ἀπὸ τῆς ἐνοικούσης ἁμαρτίας, καὶ Πνεύματος ἁγίου πληροῦσθαι" (PSEUDO-MACARIUS, *Hom. sp.* XIX.1 [*PG* 34, 642d]). See also ID., *Lib. cor.* XIII (*PG* 34, 836c). On the spiritual "combat" against one's own will, see, e.g., DOROTHEUS OF GAZA, *Doc.* I (ed. L. REGNAULT – J. DE PRÉVILLE, 182–183); *Ibid.*, X (ed. *Ibid.*, 336–339); *Ibid.*, XVII (ed. *Ibid.*, 484–487); and ID., *Ep. div.* II (ed. *Ibid.*, 500–505).

[32] P.S. CAMERON, *Violence*, 9. See JOHN CHRYSOSTOM, *Hom. 2 Tim.* X.4–5 (ed. J. BA-REILLE, XIX, 630–634).

[33] "Γενοῦ βίαιος ἐκεῖ, γενοῦ ἅρπαξ, οὐ μειοῦται τὸ ἁρπαζόμενον. Οὐδὲ γὰρ μερίζεται ἡ ἀρετή, οὐ μειοῦται οὐδὲ ἡ εὐσέβεια, οὐδὲ ἡ βασιλεία τῶν οὐρανῶν. Τότε αὔξεται ἡ ἀρετή, ὅταν ἁρπάσῃς· τότε τὰ σωματικὰ μειοῦται, ὅταν ἁρπάσῃς" (JOHN CHRYSOSTOM, *Hom. 2 Tim.* X.4 [ed. J. BAREILLE, XIX, 632]).

[34] CLEMENT OF ALEXANDRIA, *Quis div.* XXI (ed. G.W. BUTTERWORTH, 314).

[35] CLEMENT OF ALEXANDRIA, *Quis div.* XXI (ed. G.W. BUTTERWORTH, 314).

[36] *A-N Fathers*, II, 597.

[37] CLEMENT OF ALEXANDRIA, *Quis div.* XXI (ed. G.W. BUTTERWORTH, 314).

b) A Thievish and Heavenly Violence: Fasting, Prayer and Alms

Another distinctive trait of the Greek Fathers' interpretation of the saying is that, by associating Matt 11,12–13 (= Luke 16,16) with Matt 7,7–8 (= Luke 11,9–10), they argue that God may be thievishly violated, and his "life" (βίος or ζωή) conquered in any of the three following ways: a) by "seeking", through confident *fasting*; b) by "asking", through faith-filled *prayer*; and c) by "knocking", through generous *almsgiving*. Here, the aforementioned "two interwoven strands"[38] tend to mingle again.

In an ascetical discourse on spiritual perfection, Basil the Great, for instance, quotes Matt 11,12 in connection with Matt 7,13–14 and Matt 11,30, stating:

few [...] are they who enter the kingdom of Heaven [...] The kingdom of Heaven is the prize of the violent [...] If, then, you wish to bear the kingdom of God, become a man of violence; bow your neck to the yoke [...] rub it thin by labor [...] in fasting[39].

In the same vein, having mentioned the impossibility of offering one's mind to both God and mammon (see Matt 6,24), John Climacus draws attention to fasting by using the image of a door leading to Heaven:

"restrain the belly [...] How narrow is the door and arduous the way of fasting [...] the violence of fasting and toil [...] Fasting is violence of nature [...] door of compunction [...] door and joy of Paradise"[40].

However, as G.W.H. Lampe remarks, for the Fathers, the kingdom of God may be attained "especially by almsgiving, frequently emphasized as a necessary qualification for entry"[41].

---

[38] P.S. CAMERON, *Violence*, 5.

[39] M. WAGNER, *Saint Basil*, 29–30. "ὀλίγοι εἰσὶν οἱ εἰσερχόμενοι εἰς τὴν βασιλείαν τῶν οὐρανῶν [...] Βιαστῶν γάρ ἐστιν ἡ βασιλεία τῶν οὐρανῶν [...] Εἰ τοίνυν βούλει ἁρπάσαι τὴν βασιλείαν τοῦ θεοῦ, γενοῦ βιαστής· ὑπόζευξόν σου τὸν αὐχένα τῷ ζυγῷ [...] λέπτυνον αὐτὸν τῷ πόνῳ [...] ἐν νηστείαις" (BASIL THE GREAT, *Serm. ascet.* IX [*PG* 31, 645c–648a]). See also ID., *Hom.* I.3–4 (*PG* 31, 168b); and *Ibid.*, I.9 (*PG* 31, 180b).

[40] "στένωσον τὴν γαστέρα [...] Τί στενὴ πύλη καὶ τεθλιμμένη ὁδὸς τῆς νηστείας [...] ἡ τῆς νηστείας βία καὶ πόνος [...] Νηστεία ἐστὶ βία φύσεως [...] κατανύξεως θύρα [...] παραδείσου θύρα καὶ τρυφή" (JOHN CLIMACUS, *Scal.* XIV.96 [ed. P. TREVISAN, I, 346–351]). On fasting and the kingdom, see GREGORY OF NYSSA, *Instit.* (ed. W. JAEGER – *al.*, VIII.1, 89); JOHN CHRYSOSTOM, *Hom. eleem.* (*PG* 48, 1060); ID., *Hom. 2 Cor* I.7 (*PG* 51, 278); ID., *Hom. Eutrop.* XV (*PG* 52, 410ιε); ID., *Hom. Matt* LXXVII.5 (ed. J. BAREILLE, XIII, 85); ID., *Serm. jej.* VII (*PG* 60, 724); ID., *Eleem.* (*PG* 62, 770); PSEUDO-ATHANASIUS, *Virg.* VI (*PG* 28, 257b); and, much more recently, NECTARIUS OF CONSTANTINOPLE, *Thdr.* XXII (*PG* 39, 1837c). See also Lampe, "νηστεία", 909.

[41] Lampe, "βασιλεία", 290. Thus, almsgiving is often considered to give strength, efficacy and wings both to prayer and fasting. See, e.g., JOHN CHRYSOSTOM, *Hom. Matt* LXXVII.6 (ed. J. BAREILLE, XIII, 87).

Thus, Pseudo-Athanasius mentions βιάζεται in an attempt to encourage the reader to "always give eagerly" (εἰς τὸ πάντοτε προθύμως διδόναι)[42] and "practice almsgiving" (ποιῆσαι ἐλεημοσύνην)[43], "for God loves a cheerful giver" (ἱλαρὸν γὰρ δότεν ἀγαπᾷ ὁ θεός)[44], and because:

"It belongs to the perfect always to do good cheerfully; but also those who do violence to themselves, in relation to the command of the poor, are acceptable to the God who said: 'The violent seize the kingdom of Heaven'"[45].

Finally, already in the 2nd c., Clement of Alexandria mentions our "violence passage"[46] with particular reference to almsgiving and prayer in general[47], whereas, in the 4th c., John Chrysostom identifies this "violent" prayer with the unceasing prayer of the heart: "Lord Jesus Christ, Son of God, have mercy on us" (Κύριε Ἰησοῦ Χριστὲ, Υἱὲ τοῦ Θεοῦ, ἐλέησον ἡμᾶς)[48]. Elsewhere, however, the latter Church Father explicitly exhorts his hearers to open Heaven's doors by means of both prayer and almsgiving, after the example of the poor widow (see Luke 21,3), the friend at an untimely night hour (see Luke 11,5.9–10) and Cornelius (see Acts 10,4)[49].

c) A Profitmaking Relationship: Violence and Possessions

The last recurrent significant feature, which we wish to underline here, is more strictly related to almsgiving, and concerns the Fathers' awareness of a certain *profitmaking relationship* of "violence" (βία) and its cognates (βιάζω, βίαιος, βιαστής, βιαστός) with either "possessions" (κτήματα), "substances" (οὐσία), "wealth" (πλοῦτος), "goods" (ὑπάρχοντα), or other synonyms[50]. Such a relationship is usually inserted within the context of "giving to the poor" (διδόναι πτωχοῖς), and often compared to a "divine market" (θεία ἀγορά), a "beautiful trade" (καλή ἐμπορία) or a wise business, whereby, in exchange for

---

[42] PSEUDO-ATHANASIUS, *Quaest. Ant.* LXXXII (*PG* 28, 649a).

[43] PSEUDO-ATHANASIUS, *Quaest. Ant.* LXXXII (*PG* 28, 649a).

[44] 2Cor 9,7.

[45] "Τῶν τελείων ἐστὶ τὸ πάντοτε ἱλαρῶς ποιεῖν τὸ ἀγαθόν· καὶ οἱ βιαζόμενοι δὲ ἑαυτοὺς εἰς τὴν τοῦ πτωχοῦ ἐντολὴν εὐπρόσδεκτοί εἰσι παρὰ Θεῷ τῷ εἰπόντι· Βιασταὶ ἁρπάζουσι τὴν βασιλείαν τῶν οὐρανῶν" (PSEUDO-ATHANASIUS, *Quaest. Ant.* LXXXII [*PG* 28, 649a]).

[46] W. STENGER, "βιάζομαι, βιαστής", *EDNT*, I, 216.

[47] See, e.g., CLEMENT OF ALEXANDRIA, *Strom.* IV, II.5.3 (ed. O. STÄHLIN, II, 250); *Ibid.*, V, III.16.7 (ed. *Ibid.*, II, 336); and ID., *Quis div.* X (ed. G.W. BUTTERWORTH, 288–289).

[48] JOHN CHRYSOSTOM, *Ep. vigil.* XXXIV (ed. P.G. NIKOLOPOULOS, 481–482).

[49] See JOHN CHRYSOSTOM, *Hom. Act.* XXXVI.2–3 (*PG* 60, 260–261); ID., *Hom. Jo.* LXXXVIII.3 (ed. J. BAREILLE, XIV, 422–423); ID., *Exp. Ps.* CXVII.5 (*PG* 55, 335ε). See also BASIL THE GREAT, *Const.* I.4 (*PG* 31, 1333c).

[50] See, e.g., Lampe, "κτήμα", 781; *Ibid.*, "οὐσία", 980–985; *Ibid.*, "πλοῦτος", 1096–1097; *Ibid.*, "ὕπαρξις", 1434–1435; and *Ibid.*, "ὑπάρχω", 1435.

the perishing things of this world, one can "purchase" (ἀγοράζω) or "buy" (ὠνέομαι) an eternal abode in the kingdom of Heaven[51].

This is, for instance, what Gregory of Nyssa affirms concerning the poor:

"They are the treasurers of the good things we look for, the door-keepers of the kingdom, those who secretly open the gates to the benevolent and close them to the peevish and misanthropic"[52].

More specifically, according to the latter Father, the kind of violence by which one greedily longs for God is actually "to be praised" (ἐπαινετόν)[53]:

The love of gain, which is a large, incalculably large, element in every soul, when once applied to the desire for God, will bless the man who has it; for he will be violent where it is right to be violent[54].

In his commentary on Paul's Second Letter to Timothy, John Chrysostom explicitly ponders the question of trading one's material wealth for the kingdom of Heaven, and asks:

"Is it then [permitted], you might say, to buy life [by means] of possessions? Certainly, provided that we pay it down with our [money], and not with that of others!"[55].

And a few chapters later he unambiguously asserts:

---

[51] See, esp., CLEMENT OF ALEXANDRIA, *Quis div.* XXXII (ed. G.W. BUTTERWORTH, 336–339), but also, BASIL THE GREAT, *Hom.* VI.3 (ed. Y. COURTONNE, 20–23); *Ibid.*, VI.8 (ed. *Ibid.*, 34–37); *Ibid.*, VII.1 (ed. *Ibid.*, 38–43); *Ibid.*, VII.3 (ed. *Ibid.*, 46–51); and ID., *Reg. fus.* VIII.2 (*PG* 31, 937d.940a). For the Armenian critical version and translation of the latter work, see G. ULUHOGIAN, *Basilio*, XIX, 64; and *Ibid.*, XX, 45. Finally, see also GREGORY OF NAZIANZUS, *Or.* XIV.22 (*PG* 36, 885b–c); JOHN CHRYSOSTOM, *Hom. Matt* XLVII.4 (ed. J. BAREILLE, XII, 313–314); ID., *Hom. 2 Tim.* VI.4 (ed. *Ibid.*, XIX, 590–591); and Lampe, "βασιλεία", 290.

[52] "οὗτοί εἰσιν οἱ ταμίαι τῶν προσδοκωμένων ἀγαθῶν, οἱ θυρωροὶ τῆς βασιλέιας, οἱ ὑπανοίγοντες τὰς θύρας τοῖς χρηστοῖς καὶ κλείοντες τοῖς δυσκόλοις καὶ μισανθρώποις" (GREGORY OF NYSSA, *Pauper.* I [ed. A. VAN HECK, IX, 99.5–7]). A few paragraphs later, he (*Ibid.* II [ed. *Ibid.*, IX, 122.1–3.18–19]) adds: "the Lord himself becomes totally indebted to you because of the love of mankind [purposefully shown] for this [...] For whatever you do to them, bears fruit in the treasure houses of Heaven" (αὐτὸν τὸν τῶν ὅλων κύριον ὑπόχρεών σοι διὰ τῆς εἰς τοῦτον φιλανθρωπίας γενόμενον [...] ὅσα γὰρ ἂν τούτοις ποιήσῃς, τοῖς οὐρανίοις θησαυροῖς καρποφορεῖς). See also Prov 19,17; and Matt 6,20.

[53] GREGORY OF NYSSA, *Virginit.* XVIII.3 (ed. M. AUBINEAU, 472).

[54] *N-PN Fathers²*, V, 363. "Τὴν δὲ τοῦ πλείονος ἔφεσιν, ὃ πολύ τε καὶ ἀμέτρητον ἔγκειται τῇ ἑκάστου ψυχῇ, τῇ κατὰ θεὸν ἐπιθυμίᾳ προσθείς, μακαριστὸς ἔσται τῆς πλεονεξίας, ἐκεῖ βιαζόμενος, ὅπου ἐπαινετὸν τὸ βιάζεσθαι" (GREGORY OF NYSSA, *Virginit.* XVIII.3 [ed. M. AUBINEAU, 472]).

[55] "Ἔστιν οὖν ἀγοράσαι ζωὴν χρημάτων, φησί; Ναί, ὅταν τὰ ἑαυτῶν, καὶ μὴ τὰ ἀλλότρια καταβάλλωμεν" (JOHN CHRYSOSTOM, *Hom. 2 Tim.* VI.4 [ed. J. BAREILLE, XIX, 591]). See also *Ibid.* X.4–5 (ed. *Ibid.*, XIX, 630–633); and Lampe, "πλεονεκτέω", 1091.

"by being seized, the [heavenly] goods multiply [...] Increase his [God's] substances; now, you shall increase [them] if you seize, if you covet, if you violate [...] How? [...] 'the violent', it is said, 'seize the kingdom of Heaven'. There is need of violence and robbery [...] we shall certainly be able to keep hold of what we have seized"[56].

The best and earliest example of this "profitable" association can be found in Clement of Alexandria's teaching on worldly wealth, probably addressed to the rich Christians of this city, in the 2nd c., and entitled "Who is the rich man that shall be saved?" (ΤΙΣ Ο ΣΩΙΖΟΜΕΝΟΣ ΠΛΟΥΣΙΟΣ)[57]. As P.S. Cameron recognizes, Clement "uses Matt 11,12 as a kind of bridge between Mark 10,27 and 28"[58]. It is undoubtedly true that, for Clement, "man can achieve nothing by his own unaided efforts"[59] (καθ᾽ αὐτὸν [...] ἄνθρωπος οὐδὲν ἀνύει) and without the "addition of the power that comes from God"[60] (τῇ προσθήκῃ τῆς παρὰ θεοῦ δυνάμεως). However, as the basic context (Mark 10,17–31) surrounding the quotation of the saying in Clement's treatise confirms[61], the central idea at stake consists rather in how one is to "seize" (ἁρπάσαι) "eternal life" (ζωῆς αἰωνίου) from God, by means of that "beautiful violence" (βία καλή), which "alone" (μόνη) implies one's "leaving" (ἀφῆκεν) and "flinging away"[62] (ἀπορρίψαντες) "all of [one's] possessions" (πάντα [...] τὰ κτήματα) for the sake of the kingdom of Heaven[63].

The point of Clement of Alexandria's essay is that Christians can be saved, and thus enter the kingdom of God[64], by renouncing not only their material possessions[65], as Anaxagoras, Democritus, Crates, or other non-Christians

---

[56] "ἐν τῷ ἁρπάζεσθαι πλεονεκτεῖ μᾶλλον τὰ ἀγαθά [...] Αὔξησον αὐτοῦ τὴν οὐσίαν· αὐξήσεις δὲ, ἂν ἁρπάσῃς, ἂν πλεονεκτήσῃς, ἂν βιάσῃ [...] Πῶς; [...] βιασταὶ, φησίν, ἁρπάζουσι τὴν βασιλείαν τῶν οὐρανῶν. βίας χρεία καὶ ἁρπαγῆς [...] δυνησόμεθα τὰ ἁρπαγέντα κατέχειν μετὰ ἀσφαλείας" (JOHN CHRYSOSTOM, Hom. 2 Tim. X.5 [ed. J. BA-REILLE, XIX, 632–633]). See also Lampe, "πλεονεκτέω", 1091.

[57] See G.W. BUTTERWORTH, ed., Clement, 265–269.

[58] P.S. CAMERON, Violence, 4.

[59] P.S. CAMERON, Violence, 4–5. See CLEMENT OF ALEXANDRIA, Quis div. XXI (ed. G.W. BUTTERWORTH, 312).

[60] G.W. BUTTERWORTH, ed., Clement, 313. See CLEMENT OF ALEXANDRIA, Quis div. XXI (ed. G.W. BUTTERWORTH, 312).

[61] See CLEMENT OF ALEXANDRIA, Quis div. IV–V (ed. G.W. BUTTERWORTH, 278–282).

[62] G.W. BUTTERWORTH, ed., Clement, 315.

[63] See Mark 10,29. See also CLEMENT OF ALEXANDRIA, Quis div. XX–XXI (ed. G.W. BUTTERWORTH, 312–314).

[64] See, e.g., Matt 19,16.21.23–25; Mark 10,17.21.23–26; and Luke 10,25.27–28; 18,18. 22.24–26.

[65] See, e.g., the expression: "the substance belonging [to him or her]" (ὑπάρχουσαν οὐσίαν), in CLEMENT OF ALEXANDRIA, Quis div. XI (ed. G.W. BUTTERWORTH, 290). See also Ibid., XIX (ed. Ibid., 308–311).

have previously done[66], but even their inner "desire" (ἐπιθυμίαν) or "affection" (συμπάθειαν) for them[67], so as to love God and one's neighbor instead[68]. This is why, after Jesus' observation concerning the difficulty of entering the kingdom of God for those who have possessions (see Mark 10,23), "Peter began to say to him: 'Look, we have left everything and followed you!'"[69]. Commenting on this sentence, Clement of Alexandria eventually concludes: "the blessed Peter [...] quickly seized and comprehended the saying"[70]. In other words, as acknowledged by P.S. Cameron, "such a renunciation made Peter a βιαστής"[71].

2. The Latin Fathers

As one transfers one's attention from the Eastern to the Western hermeneutic world, one immediately notes how the aforementioned features, so generally recurrent in the Greek Fathers' reception of the "violence saying", reappear also among the Latin Fathers and throughout the first five centuries. However, far from being a mere repetition of the Easterners, the interpretation of the Westerners carries its own distinctive features and enhancements. We shall accordingly review here some of the equivalent, enriched and peculiar aspects of their interpretation.

a) Equivalent Features: Interwoven, Thievish and Profitable βία

Already in the 2nd c., one finds the "violence passage"[72] being cited by Tertullian in the context of "fasting" (*jejunium*)[73]. Then, in the 3rd c., Cyprian

---

[66] See, e.g., CLEMENT OF ALEXANDRIA, *Quis div.* XI–XII (ed. G.W. BUTTERWORTH, 290–295); *Ibid.*, XX (ed. *Ibid.*, 312–313); and *Ibid.*, XXIV (ed. *Ibid.*, 318–321).

[67] See CLEMENT OF ALEXANDRIA, *Quis div.* XI (ed. G.W. BUTTERWORTH, 292).

[68] See, e.g., CLEMENT OF ALEXANDRIA, *Quis div.* XXVII–XXXI (ed. G.W. BUTTER-WORTH, 326–337); and *Ibid.*, XXXVII–XXXVIII (ed. *Ibid.*, 346–351).

[69] "Ἤρξατο λέγειν ὁ Πέτρος αὐτῷ· ἰδοὺ ἡμεῖς ἀφήκαμεν πάντα καὶ ἠκολουθήκαμέν σοι" (Mark 10,28).

[70] *A-N Fathers*, II, 597. "ὁ μακάριος Πέτρος [...] ταχέως ἥρπασε καὶ συνέβαλε τὸν λόγον" (CLEMENT OF ALEXANDRIA, *Quis div.* XXI [ed. G.W. BUTTERWORTH, 314]).

[71] P.S. CAMERON, *Violence*, 5. See also G. HÄFNER, "Gewalt", 33.

[72] W. STENGER, "βιάζομαι, βιαστής", *EDNT*, I, 216.

[73] See, e.g., TERTULLIAN, *Jejun.* II.2 (ed. A. REIFFERSCHEID – G. WISSOWA, II.29, 1258); and *Ibid.*, XI.6 (ed. *Ibid.*, II.29, 1270). Elsewhere, after mentioning the impossibility of serving both God and mammon, Tertullian quotes Luke 16,16a (= Matt 11,13) in support of the fulfillment of the OT in the NT (vs. the Marcionite insistence on the break with Judaism), or the validity of "the Law and the Prophets" as fulfilled in Christ. See, e.g., ID., *Marc.* IV.33 (ed. C. MORESCHINI – R. BRAUN, IV, 406–409); ID., *Pud.* VI.2 (ed. C. MICAELLI – C. MUNIER, I, 168–169); and W.P. LE SAINT, *Tertullian*, 65.213, n.135. Finally, in his treatise on prayer, Tertullian (*Or.* XXIX.15 [E. EVANS, ed., *Tertullian's Tract*, 38–39]) remarks: "Prayer alone it is that conquers God" (*Sola est oratio quae Deum vincit*).

of Carthage directly quotes it in a work of his on "almsgiving" (*eleemosyna*)[74]. In the latter case, in particular, it is clear how the author considers giving alms to the poor as a way to "conceal" (*recondere*) a "heavenly treasure" (*caelestes the[n]sauros*), by "trading" (*negotiari*) one's "monetary property" (*patrimonium*) in exchange for "heavenly grace" (*gratia caelestis*), and as a valuable means by which to "buy" (*mercari*) one's entrance into the "heavenly kingdom" (*regnum caeleste*)[75].

In the 4[th] c., Jerome of Stridon significantly inserts in the quotation of Matt 11,12 the word, "one fasting" (*jejunatoris*)[76], as an extra trait characterizing John the Baptist. Elsewhere, he further states that, by despising worldly "riches" (*divitias*) and "selling everything" (*vendere omnia*), like a "trading man" (*homo negotians*), one can actually "buy the kingdom of Heaven" (*emere regnum coelorum*), just as one does that precious pearl in the Gospel (see Matt 13,46), explaining:

"Such a violence, which terrifies nobody and causes no damage, is pleasing to God. On this robbery, which is crimeless and grants salvation, lay your hands!"[77].

The "violence passage"[78] is also quoted by Augustine of Hippo, who mentions prayer, fasting, and almsgiving as means by which one can hasten towards Heaven[79], and additionally explains why, according to him, Luke 16,16 was in reality uttered:

"so that each one may despise these [earthly things] [...] Thus, having done such a violence [to oneself], one somehow invades the kingdom of Heaven, almost as a violent plunderer. For this reason, the evangelist added [this statement] when, having told about Jesus being derided by the Pharisees, he was speaking about the contempt of earthly riches"[80].

---

[74] See CYPRIAN OF CARTHAGE, *Eleemos.* VII (ed. M. POIRIER, 92–97).

[75] See the previous note. On the patristic use of the expression, "heavenly treasure", see, e.g., R. CACITTI, "'*Ad caelestes thesauros*'", (1991) 151–169; (1993) 129–171; and M. POIRIER, ed., *Cyprien*, 94, n. 3.

[76] JEROME OF STRIDON, *Jov.* II.16 (*PL* 23, 323c). See P.S. CAMERON, *Violence*, 15.

[77] "*Talis violentia Deo grata est, quae neminem concutit, nullius damno nititur. In hanc rapinam manus tuas mitte, quae crimen non habet, et confert salutem*" (JEROME OF STRIDON, *Reg. mon.* XVIII [*PL* 30, 376d]). See, also, *Ibid.* XVIII (*PL* 30, 376b–d); ID., *Exp. Matt* XIII.33–38 (*PL* 30, 570c); ID., *Ep.* XXII.31–40 (ed. I. HILBERG, I, 191–209); and F.A. WRIGHT, ed., *Select Letters*, 128–155.

[78] W. STENGER, "βιάζομαι, βιαστής", *EDNT*, I, 216.

[79] See, e.g., AUGUSTINE OF HIPPO, *Serm. sanct.* CXCVI.8 (*PL* 39, 2113); and *Ibid.* CCCXXVI.1 (ed. A. TRAPÉ – P.R. PICCOLOMINI, III.33.5, 796).

[80] "*ut quisque ista contemnat* [...] *Hac enim vi facta invadit quodammodo quasi praedator violentus regna* [cf. *PL* '*regnum*'] *caelorum. Hoc enim subiunxit evangelista, cum dixisset derisum fuisse Iesum a Phariseis, cum de contemnendis terrenis divitiis loqueretur*" (AUGUSTINE OF HIPPO, *Quaest. Evang.* II.37 [ed. A. TRAPÉ – P.R. PICCOLOMINI, I.10.2, 382]). Elsewhere, he (*Conf.* VIII.8.19 [ed. *Ibid.*, I.1, 236–239]) refers back to the "violence"

Elucidating the relationship between these three valuable means of entering Heaven, Peter Chrysologus further adds that, while the first one only "knocks" (*pulsat*) and the second one "asks" (*impetrat*), the third one actually "receives" (*accipit*)[81], and this is most probably so because:

> The treasure-house of heaven is the hand of the poor person [...] The hand of the poor person is Christ's treasury [...] Therefore, O man, give the earth to the poor, so that you may *receive* [emphasis added] Heaven! Give a coin, that you may *receive* [emphasis added] the kingdom[82]!

Even according to the Christian monk and theologian, John Cassian, the βιασταί are essentially "laudable" (*laudabiles*) and "egregious plunderers" (*egregii direptores*):

> Who, then, are these violent? They are the ones who truly exercise a noble violence [...] by a praiseworthy pillage [...] By the Lord's words they are declared excellent pillagers, and with a plundering of this sort they gain violent entrance into the kingdom of Heaven [...] These violent persons [...] are certainly praiseworthy[83].

After comparing those who know how to direct their property with a good helmsman[84], Ambrose of Milan quotes the saying to underline the immediate

---

of those who "rob Heaven" (*caelum rapiunt*) in connection with a conversation held with Ponticianus, concerning the conversion of St. Anthony of Egypt and his contempt of earthly riches. See ID., *Conf.* VIII.6.14–15 (ed. *Ibid.*, I.1, 232–235); and A. GUCCIONE, "Il cielo", 491–492. Finally, Augustine (*Quaest. Evang.* II.31 [ed. *Ibid.*, I.10.2, 364–367]) compares the renunciation of "all" (*omnibus*) one's possessions also with the "strength" (see *vires* [...] *fortia*) needed to build the tower and be a disciple of Christ (see Luke 14,28–33).

[81] See, e.g., Matt 7,7–8 (= Luke 11,9–10); and PETER CHRYSOLOGUS, *Serm.* XLIII.2 (ed. A. OLIVAR, I, 242).

[82] W.B. PALARDY, *Saint Peter Chrysologous*, II, 44–45. "*Thesaurus caeli est manus pauperis* [...] *Manus pauperis est gazophylacium Christi* [...] *Da ergo, homo, pauperi terram, ut accipias caelum; da nummum, ut accipias regnum*" (PETER CHRYSOLOGUS, *Serm.* VIII.4 [ed. A. OLIVAR, I, 61]). The idea of the poor's hand as the "treasure-house of Heaven" often recurs among both Latin and Greek Fathers. See, e.g., *PL* 52, 210b, n. *k*; and Lampe, "γαζοφυλάκιον", 306.

[83] B. RAMSEY, *John Cassian*, 850. "*Qui ergo hi violenti sunt? Nempe illi qui* [...] *praeclaram inferunt violentiam* [...] *direptione laudabili* [...] *voce dominica egregii direptores pronuntiantur et per huiuscemodi rapinam regnum caelorum violenter invadunt* [...] *Isti profecto sunt laudabiles violenti*" (JOHN CASSIAN, *Collat.* XXIV.26 [ed. E. PICHERY, III, 203–204]). Augustine of Hippo (*Serm. Scr.* CXXXI.2 [ed. A. TRAPÉ – P.R. PICCOLOMINI, III.31.1, 192]) and Gregory the Great (*Exp. Poen.* II [*PL* 79, 633c]) call this violence even "sweet [...] suave" (*dulcis* [...] *suavis*) and "glorious [...] good violence" (*gloriosus* [...] *Bona violentia*), respectively. See A. GUCCIONE, "Il cielo", 494–495.

[84] According to Ambrose (*Ep.* LXIII.92 [ed. M. ZELZER – O. FALLER, III, 285]), "one who does not know [how] to steer [well] one's property is [eventually] drowned by its load" (*qui autem nescit regere suum censum onere suo mergitur*). See also *Ibid.* LXIII.87 (ed. *Ibid.*, III, 282).

effects of almsgiving, and urges his audience not to procrastinate[85]. And, even more strikingly, in a sermon on the grace of the upcoming Christmas day, he "arrives at Matt 11,12 by way of Sirach 3,30"[86] (LXX = *Vg.* on Sir 3,33), thus implying that one can do violence precisely by doing almsgiving[87]. Here, "in words reminiscent of '*O felix culpa!*'"[88], he writes:

"Truly, there is no crime so grave that is not cleansed by abstinence, [or] extinguished by almsgiving [...] Let us therefore force [or collect] the kingdom of Heaven and, in a certain way, do violence [to it], as the Gospel reading says: 'And by doing violence they steal it away' [...] Oh happy violence!"[89].

Moreover, albeit in the context of the Gentiles stealing it away from the Jews, the Western commentators restate even God's own "delight" (*delectatio*) in seeing his kingdom being stolen from him, by means of fervent and insistent prayer[90]. The believer is here actually encouraged to do violence, as Gregory the Great affirms:

"Almighty God wants to endure such a violence from us. For the kingdom of God wants to be snatched [...] Consider, therefore, [and] ponder how incomprehensible are, in the almighty God, the entrails of mercy [...] Who could [ever] tell the goodness of God, [or] who could adequately appraise it?"[91].

---

[85] See AMBROSE OF MILAN, *Ep.* LXIII.97 (ed. M. ZELZER – O. FALLER, III, 288); and M.M. BEYENKA, *Saint Ambrose*, 353–358. While encouraging his clerics to enter heaven through humility and poverty, Maximus of Turin (*Hom. div.* LXXXV [*PL* 57, 447b–c]) compares the rich man to a clumsy and overburdened colt: swollen because of honors and the burden of riches, they are incapable of passing through the narrow door of the kingdom of Heaven (see Matt 7,14; 19,44).

[86] P.S. CAMERON, *Violence*, 13.

[87] See AMBROSE OF MILAN, *Serm.* II.2 (*PL* 17, 626d–627a). Thus, in a sermon on divine and human mercy, Caesarius of Arles (*Serm.* XXV.2.27 [ed. G. MORIN, I, 113]) also quotes Sir 3,33 in the context of almsgiving, stating: "*Das pauperi nummum, et a Christo recipis regnum*". See M.M. MUELLER, *Saint Caesarius*, 127–130.

[88] P.S. CAMERON, *Violence*, 14.

[89] "*Nullum enim tam gravem delictum est, quod non purgetur abstinentia, eleemosynis extinguatur* [...] *Cogimus ergo regnum coelorum et vim quodammodo facimus, sicut ait evangelica lectio: 'Et vim facientes diripiunt illud'* [...] *O beata violentia!*" (AMBROSE OF MILAN, *Serm.* II.2–3 [*PL* 17, 626d–627c]). See also MAXIMUS OF TURIN, *Serm. temp.* LXI.1–4 (ed. A. MUTZENBECHER, 244–247; and *PL* 57, 531a–534c). As evinced by our translation, Ambrose may here be deliberately playing also with the "polysemic value" of the verb *cōgere* (i.e., "to collect, to bring together" or "to force, to compel"). See, e.g., *CCLEE*, "*cōgo*", 299–300; and D. MARGUERAT – Y. BOURQUIN, *How to Read*, 116–118.

[90] See, e.g., HILARY OF POITIERS, *Tract. Ps.* II.46 (ed. P. DESCOURTIEUX, I, 292–293; CSEL 22, 72; *PL* 9, 289c.). See also *Ibid.* CXXXIV.6 (ed. A. ZINGERLE, 697–298); ID., *Comm. Matt* XI.7 (ed. J. DOIGNON, I, 258–261); GREGORY THE GREAT, *Exp. Poen.* II (*PL* 79, 633c–d); and A. GUCCIONE, "Il cielo", 494.

[91] "*Vult a nobis omnipotens Deus talem violentiam perpeti. Nam regnum caelorum rapi vult* [...] *Cogitate ergo, cogitate quam sint incomprehensibilia in omnipotenti Deo*"

Finally, in a Pseudo-Hieronymian work of unclear origin (probably drawing from Jerome of Stridon or Augustine of Hippo), the author compares "violence" (*vis*)[92] to the "strength" (*fortitudo*) of the prayer coming from the heart, and describes it as a "violence of listening" (*vis auditionis*), a "shout" (*clamor*), which forcibly enters God's ears[93]. Likewise, both Ambrose of Milan and Pseudo-Ambrose identify "the manner in which the heavenly kingdom can [actually] be stolen" (*quemadmodum regnum caeleste rapiatur*)[94], with the repentant sinner's action of knocking on the doors of Paradise, by means of persistent and faith-filled prayers[95], and after the example of the Gospel widow and the patriarch Jacob (see, e.g., Gen 32,26; Matt 9,18–26; 15,28; and Luke 18,5)[96].

As the first apostle, Peter, among the Greeks, so also the latter patriarch, Jacob, among the Latins, is a model of the ideal "violent" (*violentus*), who "knocks importunately" (*pulsat importune*) and directly against God and his kingdom, mainly by means of his audacious prayers and perseverant trust in God's providence[97]. As P.S. Cameron comments:

indeed Jacob is the archetypal βιαστής. He strove with God and God allowed him to prevail [...] similarly the believer only really takes possession of the kingdom if he struggles for it[98].

b) A Western Enhancement: Faith and Love

Thus, as we have so far observed, both Latin and Greek commentators keep the positive sense of the "violence saying" and mention prayer, fasting, and almsgiving, as three distinct ways in which one can do violence and enter the kingdom of Heaven. Perhaps, along with P.S. Cameron, we could say that,

---

misericordiae viscera [...] *Quis tantam bonitatem Dei dicere, quis aestimare sufficiat?*" (GREGORY THE GREAT, *Hom. Evang.* XX.15 [ed. R. ÉTAIX, 169]).

[92] See, e.g., *CCLEE* , "*vis*", 1638.

[93] See PSEUDO-JEROME, *Brev. Ps.* XVII.7 (ed. H. BOESE, I, 73). Cf., also, *PL* 26, 916a; G. MORIN, ed., *Commentarioli*, 195–196; and E. DEKKERS, *Clavis*, 218.

[94] AMBROSE OF MILAN, *Exp. Luc.* V.114 (ed. G. TISSOT, I, 226).

[95] Pseudo-Ambrose (*Exp. Apoc.* VI [*PL* 17, 903b]), e.g., writes: "they knock on Paradise's door by [their] prayers" (*januam paradisi precibus pulsant*).

[96] See, e.g., AMBROSE OF MILAN, *Exp. Luc.* V.114–117 (ed. G. TISSOT, I, 226–227); and PSEUDO-AMBROSE, *Exp. Apoc.* VI (*PL* 17, 903a–b).

[97] See, e.g., JEROME OF STRIDON, *Ep.* XXII.29–40 (ed. I. HILBERG, I, 186–209); and AUGUSTINE OF HIPPO, *Enarrat. Ps.* CXLVII.27 (ed. A. TRAPÉ – P.R. PICCOLOMINI, III.28.4, 858–861). In this regard, the Latin Fathers combine references to passages such as: Gen 28,20–21; 29,20; 32,22–33; *Vg.* Pss 36,25; 147,8; Matt 6,33; 11,12; Luke 11,5–8; 1Pet 4,17–18; etc.

[98] P.S. CAMERON, *Violence*, 16. See also *Ibid.*, 16.171, n. 37.

in general, "it is clear that there is no rigid dividing-line between West and East"[99].

However, the Latin Fathers also tend to elaborate and be more explicit about the specific association of the kind of violence, which God or his kingdom can be said to suffer, with the particular theological virtues of *faith and love*. Commenting on Augustine of Hippo, P.S. Cameron accurately summarizes: "The violence […] is that of faith. '*Hoc enim diripiunt qui vim faciunt credendo...*' […] The βιασταί do violence by believing"[100].

However, faith alone is not enough. Augustine insists that the violent one must also obtain "the Spirit of love" (*Spiritum caritatis*)[101], "for to Him who is everywhere, one comes by loving" (*Ad illum enim qui ubique est, amando venitur*)[102], and associates "violence" (*violentia*) with the "force" (*vis*) needed to "love one's enemies" (*diligere inimicos*) and hate one's father, mother, wife, sons and brothers (see Luke 6,27.35; 14,26), just as Jacob himself has done[103].

Commenting on the latter patriarch and his violence, Pseudo-Ambrose compares Jacob's vision of the ladder (Gen 28,12) with a staircase to Heaven, in which the two greater vertical axes stand for the two precepts of love, and the smaller horizontal ones represent the other virtues, specifying the following:

"just as the different steps, unless they are inserted, on both sides, into the two greater wooden poles, cannot provide any ascent to men, so the other virtues, unless they proceed from the love of God and the love of neighbor, cannot provide any ascent to those who want to go up to Heaven"[104].

---

[99] P.S. CAMERON, *Violence*, 21.

[100] P.S. CAMERON, *Violence*, 17. See, e.g., AUGUSTINE OF HIPPO, *Fid. op.* XXI.39 (ed. A. TRAPÉ – P.R. PICCOLOMINI, I.6.2, 758–759); ID., *Enarrat. Ps.* LXXXVI.6 (ed. *Ibid.*, III.27.3, 14–17); and ID., *Serm. Scr.* CXXXI.2 (ed. *Ibid.*, III.31.1, 192). Apropos of violence and faith, see HILARY OF POITIERS, *Tract. Ps.* II.46 (ed. P. DESCOURTIEUX, I, 292–293); AMBROSE OF MILAN, *Exp. Luc.* V.114 (ed. G. TISSOT, I, 226); ID., *Ep.* LXIII.87 (ed. M. ZELZER – O. FALLER, III, 282); *Ibid.* LXIII.97 (ed. *Ibid.*, III, 288); and JEROME OF STRIDON, *Ep.* XXII.31–32.40 (ed. I. HILBERG, I, 191–195.207–209). The idea that one enters the kingdom of Heaven through faith is, nonetheless, already present also in the East. See, e.g., ORIGEN OF ALEXANDRIA, *Comm. Matt* XIV (ed. G. BENDINELLI, I, 156–157).

[101] AUGUSTINE OF HIPPO, *Fid. op.* XXI.39 (ed. A. TRAPÉ – P.R. PICCOLOMINI, I.6.2, 758). See also JEROME OF STRIDON, *Ep.* XXII.40 (ed. I. HILBERG, I, 207–209).

[102] AUGUSTINE OF HIPPO, *Serm. Scr.* CXXXI.2 (ed. A. TRAPÉ – P.R. PICCOLOMINI, III.31.1, 192–193). See A. GUCCIONE, "Il cielo", 496.

[103] See, e.g., AUGUSTINE OF HIPPO, *Serm. Dom.* I.15.40 (ed. A. TRAPÉ – P.R. PICCOLOMINI, I.10.2, 130); ID., *Serm. Scr.* V.6 (ed. *Ibid.*, III.29.1, 90–91); and A. GUCCIONE, "Il cielo", 493–494.

[104] "*quemadmodum diversi gradus, nisi in duobus lignis majoribus et utraque parte inserantur, ascensum hominibus praebere non possunt: ita et caeterae virtutes, nisi ex dilectione Dei et dilectione proximi nascantur, ad coelom ire volentibus ascensum praebere*

c) A Western Peculiarity: Legal Categories and Concepts

A second and most distinctive Western feature, characterizing the Latin Fathers' own interpretation of the "violence passage"[105], concerns their attention to *legal categories and concepts* and their consequent application of these latter to our saying, primarily "in terms of property rights and inheritance"[106]. For instance, commenting on Hilary of Poitiers, P.S. Cameron points out:

Hilary understands the saying in terms of the legal concept of inheritance – βιάζεται describes the usurpation of an *ex facie* legal right and the βιασταί are the usurpers. The kingdom is said to suffer violence because it is snatched by the Gentiles from its apparently rightful owners, the Jews [...] the violence being the illegal wresting of the inheritance from the legal heirs[107].

Adopting a similar legal language, Ambrose of Milan explains why and how, by occupying what the Jews have neglected, "we are therefore the thieves" (*raptores igitur sumus*)[108]:

"Consequently, the Church has seized the Synagogue's kingdom [...] Therefore, the kingdom of Heaven is seized [...] when it is not claimed by inheritance, [but] is acquired by adoption"[109].

Finally, whereas Jerome of Stridon mentions the violent ones' entrance into what "was the rightful place of angels"[110], Gregory the Great speaks rather of

---

non possunt" (PSEUDO-AMBROSE, *Exp. Apoc.* VI [*PL* 17, 902c]). A similar connection between "violence" and "love of God and neighbor" is, nevertheless, present among the Greek Fathers. See, e.g., CLEMENT OF ALEXANDRIA, *Quis div.* XXVII–XXXI (ed. G.W. BUTTERWORTH, 326–337); and *Ibid.*, XXXVII–XXXVIII (ed. *Ibid.*, 346–351).

[105] W. STENGER, "βιάζομαι, βιαστής", *EDNT*, I, 216.

[106] P.S. CAMERON, *Violence*, 21. See also *Ibid.*, 155.

[107] P.S. CAMERON, *Violence*, 11–12. See, e.g., HILARY OF POITIERS, *Tract. Ps.* II.46 (ed. P. DESCOURTIEUX, I, 292–293); *Ibid.* CXXXIV.6 (ed. A. ZINGERLE, 697–298); and ID., *Comm. Matt* XI.7 (ed. J. DOIGNON, I, 258–261).

[108] AMBROSE OF MILAN, *Serm.* II.4 (*PL* 17, 628b).

[109] "*Rapuit igitur Ecclesia Synagogae regnum* [...] *Rapitur ergo regnum coelorum* [...] *cum per haereditatem non agnoscitur, per adoptionem acquiritur*" (AMBROSE OF MILAN, *Exp. Luc.* V.115–117 [ed. G. TISSOT, I, 226–227]). See also ID., *Ep.* LXIII.97 (ed. M. ZELZER – O. FALLER, III, 288); ID., *Serm.* II.3–4 (*PL* 17, 627b–628c); and P.S. CAMERON, *Violence*, 13.

[110] P.S. CAMERON, *Violence*, 25. See, e.g., what Jerome of Stridon (*Ep.* XXII.40 [ed. I. HILBERG, I, 209]) writes in one of his letters, as translated by F.A. Wright (ed., *Select Letters*, 155): "Does it not seem to you to be truly violence when the flesh desires to be as God and to ascend to the place whence angels fell that it may judge angels?" (*An non tibi videtur esse violenti* [cf. '*violentia*'], *cum caro cupit esse, quod deus est, et illuc, unde angeli corruerunt, angelos judicatura conscendere?*). See also ID., *Exp. Matt* XIII–XIV (*PL* 30, 570a–771a); ID., *Jov.* II.16 (*PL* 23, 323b–324c); and P.S. CAMERON, *Violence*, 15.

"the violent breaking into what is the rightful place of the just"[111], as he wonders:

"What is, then, the kingdom of Heaven, if not the place of the righteous? [...] When someone [...] after [his] faults, truly returns to repentance and seizes eternal life, [then, it is as if] a sinner enters a place which belongs to another person [...] Let us [then] snatch, through repentance, the inheritance of the righteous, which we have not kept by [our way of] life!"[112].

3. The Patristic Vision of the Kingdom of God

The latter quotation of Gregory the Great is particularly significant, not only because of its legal language, but also because it actually expresses the Fathers' particular vision of what the kingdom of God is like. In the same way, most of the other patristic citations reproduced thus far show an understanding of the heavenly kingdom that somehow combines the heavenly life with a physical place. Indeed, the kingdom of God is oftentimes conceived as some distant *locus*, occupied by and prepared for angels, Jews and Gentiles, poor and righteous, a place which must be entered and pillaged by people of violence. Yet, this kingdom is simultaneously linked with an inner state of the soul, which needs to be freed from all passions and greed, mainly by means of prayer, fasting and almsgiving.

Such an understanding perfectly matches that which we have seen as to the subject of "violence" (βία). Also, as far as the "kingdom" (βασιλεία) is concerned, the Fathers' interpretations consist of interwoven strands, which are for them neither opposed nor incompatible with each other. Spiritual concepts (e.g., eschaton and soul) actually coexist with more socially material ones (e.g., inhabited world and Church), without causing any tension or apprehension in the minds of the same authors, who easily switch from one to the other. On the whole, then, no clashes exist between the poles of either space or time. On the contrary, earth and Heaven, as well as present and future, often touch each other and proceed hand in hand.

a) An Earthly or Heavenly Spiritual Dimension

The principal questions arising from the Fathers' commentaries, as to the nature of the "kingdom" (βασιλεία) of God, concern precisely the constraints of both space and time. Where is the kingdom of God to be found, and when will it be fully visible? The answers can be classified into four main currents

---

[111] P.S. CAMERON, *Violence*, 25.

[112] "*Quid est autem regnum caelorum, nisi locus iustorum?* [...] *Cum vero quis* [...] *post culpas ad paenitentiam redit, et vitam aeternam percipit, quasi in locum peccator intrat alienum* [...] *Hereditatem iustorum, quam non tenuimus per vitam, rapiamus per paenitentiam*" (GREGORY THE GREAT, *Hom. Evang.* XX.14–15 [ed. R. ÉTAIX, 168–169]). See P.S. CAMERON, *Violence*, 19.

of interpretation, according to whether one sees the realization of the kingdom of God happening eschatologically, spiritually, politically, or ecclesiastically[113].

The earliest interpretations of the Fathers tend to be closer to the Judeo-Christian and Apostolic understanding, insofar as they reflect the more Semitic and biblical concept of God's visible and active involvement in human affairs, already here, on earth. According to the OT vision, God's sovereignty resides, even now, amid his people (see, e.g., 2Sam 7,8–16; Luke 17,21), in the concrete events of their history, which God himself directs and whereby he also reigns[114]. The earliest biblical eschatology, rather than waiting for some future accomplishment of God's promises at the end of the world, thinks more in terms of the end of the actual state of affairs, and corresponds to the expectation that God shall soon "visit" (פקד) the here and now of his people's lives, to rescue and save them, by changing their actual conditions and destiny[115].

Thus, Clement of Rome, already in the 1st c., affirms that the Apostles "went forth with the glad tidings that the kingdom of God should come"[116] and, in keeping with the aforementioned Jewish biblical concept, mentions even the "visitation" (ἐπισκοπή) of the kingdom of Christ (see, e.g., Luke 1,68.78; 7,16; 19,44; 1Pet 2,12)[117]. In turn, in the 2nd c., Justin Martyr sees God's kingdom already present, here on earth, although in a more spiritual way: it is not a human but a divine kingdom, one "with God" (μετὰ θεοῦ)[118], and it implies Christ reigning over human history through the power of his cross, namely, the sign of his sovereignty upon his shoulders (see, e.g., Ps 95,10; Isa 9,5; and Dan 7,13)[119]. At the same time, however, after Christ's first kingly Parousia, a

---

[113] See B.T. VIVIANO, *The Kingdom*, 30–56.

[114] For an overview of the use of the expression "kingdom of God" in the OT, see, e.g., L. SEMBRANO, "Il Regno", 19–140 (esp. 137–139).

[115] See, e.g., Gen 21,1; 50,24–25; Exod 3,16–17; 4,31; Pss 8,5; and 65,10. See also B.T. VIVIANO, *The Kingdom*, 33; D.C. ALLISON, Jr., *Constructing Jesus*, 184; and A. BONATO, "Il regno", 206. As L. Sembrano ("Il Regno", 84) remarks, "la fede nel 'già', alla luce delle esperienze storiche dell'esodo e del ritorno dall'esilio, è così forte da rendere meno importante il 'non ancora' che verrà".

[116] J.B. LIGHTFOOT, ed., *The Apostolic Fathers*, I.2, 293. "εὐαγγελιζόμενοι τὴν βασιλείαν τοῦ θεοῦ μέλλειν ἔρχεσθαι" (CLEMENT OF ROME, *1 Clem.* XLII.3 [ed. A. JAUBERT, 168]). See also B.T. VIVIANO, *The Kingdom*, 32.

[117] See CLEMENT OF ROME, *1 Clem.* L.3 (ed. A. JAUBERT, 182); and B.T. VIVIANO, *The Kingdom*, 33.

[118] JUSTIN MARTYR, *1 Apol.* XI.1 (ed. M. MARCOVICH, 47). See L.W. BARNARD, *St. Justin*, 29.114.

[119] See, e.g., JUSTIN MARTYR, *Dial.* XXXI–XXXII (ed. P. BOBICHON, I, 256–264); *Ibid.*, XXXV (ed. *Ibid.*, I, 82–83); *Ibid.*, LI–LII (ed. *Ibid.*, I, 314–317); *Ibid.*, LXXIII–LXXIV (ed. *Ibid.*, I, 382–387); L.W. BARNARD, *St. Justin*, 43–46.47–48.58–60.145–149.151–152.162–163.203–215; and P. BOBICHON, ed., *Justin Martyr*, II, 667–672.677–680.722–726.770–773. For a similar approach, see PSEUDO-BARNABAS, *Barn.* VIII.5 (ed. K. LAKE, I, 368–371).

second and more glorious coming will follow, at the end of times, thus allowing the number of the elect to grow and access God's eternal heavenly kingdom[120].

A similar interaction between the "now" and "not yet", as well as the "down here" and "up there", can be seen in the rest of the Fathers, up to approximately the 4th c.[121]. However, the concept of the kingdom of God does go through a certain historical process of spiritualization. On the one hand, it seems to recede from a divine presence, already here on earth, to a future time and place in Heaven[122]. In order to reject chiliastic or millenaristic exegesis (see Rev 20,2.4)[123], the Church Fathers increasingly tend to identify the divine kingdom with eternal life and, accordingly, conceive it celestially or angelically[124]. On the other hand, this does not necessarily mean that the earthly dimension of God's kingdom is forgotten. It simply implies that, as a consequence of this opposite materialistic tension, even the earthly dimension tends to assume more spiritual or mystical interpretations, so that the actual realization of the heavenly kingdom is considered as happening, not so much in the outer history of this earth, but rather within the heart of the believer.

Such an "intangible" understanding can be seen, for instance, in Irenaeus of Lyons. In fact, according to the 2nd c. theologian, "the kingdom of Heaven resides within those who believe in Him, who is the Emmanuel born of the Virgin"[125].

This spiritual dimension is shared by other Fathers as well. Commenting on the second petition of the Lord's Prayer (see Matt 6,10a), for instance, Cyprian of Carthage sees the soul of the baptized Christian as the actual *locus* where

---

[120] See, e.g., J. LECLERCQ, "L'idée", 84–95; B.T. VIVIANO, *The Kingdom*, 35–37; E. DAL COVOLO, "Il Regno", 314–318; ID., "'Regno di Dio'", 111–123; ID., "Escatologia", 627–637 (esp. 631); and S. ZINCONE, "Regno di Dio", 30–31.

[121] See, e.g., IRENAEUS OF LYONS, *Haer.* V, 9.3 (ed. A. ROUSSEAU, II, 112–117); *Ibid.*, V, 33.3 (ed. A. ROUSSEAU, II, 410–417); E. BELLINI – G. MASCHIO, ed., *Ireneo*, 426.474–475; and S. ZINCONE, "Regno di Dio", 32–33.

[122] See B.T. VIVIANO, *The Kingdom*, 38–45; and D.C. ALLISON, Jr., *Constructing Jesus*, 184–185.

[123] See, e.g., BASIL THE GREAT, *Ep.* CCLXIII.4 (ed. Y. COURTONNE, III, 124–125); *Ibid.*, CCLXV.2 (ed. *Ibid.*, III, 128–131); GREGORY OF NAZIANZUS, *Ep.* CI.63–65 (ed. P. GALLAY, 64–65); *Ibid.*, CII.14 (ed. *Ibid.*, 76–79); B.T. VIVIANO, *The Kingdom*, 34–38; and E. PRINZIVALLI, "Il millenarismo", 138–151.

[124] See, e.g., CLEMENT OF ROME, *2 Clem.* V (ed. J.B. LIGHTFOOT, I, 193–194; II, 382); EUSEBIUS OF CAESAREA, *Hist. Eccl.* III, 20.4 (ed. G. BARDY, I, 123–124); AMBROSE OF MILAN, *Exp. Luc.* V.111 (ed. G. TISSOT, I, 224; cf. n. 2); G. PELAND, "Le thème", 639–674; P.S. CAMERON, *Violence*, 47; and D.C. ALLISON, Jr., *Constructing Jesus*, 174–175.

[125] "*regnum caelorum* [...] *inhabitare intra homines credentes in eum qui ex Virgine natus est Emmanuel*", "βασιλείαν τῶν οὐρανῶν [...] ἐνοικεῖν ἐντὸς ἀνθρώπων τῶν πιστευόντων εἰς τὸν ἐκ τῆς παρθένου γεννηθέντα Ἐμμανουήλ" (IRENAEUS OF LYONS, *Haer.* III, 21.4 [ed. A. ROUSSEAU, II, 410–411]). See A. BOLAND, "Royaume", 1045.

God historically begins to reign[126]. According to both Ambrose of Milan and Jerome of Stridon, the kingdom of God is essentially God's grace within a mortal body (see Luke 17,21) and entails victory over Satan and sin[127]. Finally, Maximus the Confessor argues that, by the Spirit of charity, man is conformed to Christ and carries within himself an imprint of his king; by the same Spirit, he also gains knowledge of God, which eventually introduces him into his kingdom[128].

The propagation of such a hermeneutic trend is mainly attributed to Origen of Alexandria[129]. As J. Ratzinger comments:

In his treatise *On Prayer*, he [i.e., Origen] says that "those who pray for the coming of the kingdom of God pray without any doubt for the kingdom of God that they contain in themselves [...]" (*Patrologia Graeca* II, pp. 495f.). The basic idea is clear: The "kingdom of God" is not to be found on any map. It is not a kingdom after the fashion of worldly kingdoms; it is located in man's inner being. It grows and radiates outward from that inner space[130].

In other words, by reigning within the individual, God's kingdom extends itself also into the inhabited world. Even when the kingdom of God is not something physical or spatial, or when it is ultimately identified with Christ himself and his person – e.g., as "the kingdom itself" (αὐτο-βασιλεία)[131] – in the measure that Christians allow their king to come and reign within themselves spiritually, the divine kingdom reveals itself also outside of and around them, in the here and now of their history and world, and, for that reason, it actually upholds them[132].

---

[126] See CYPRIAN OF CARTHAGE, *Or. Dom.* XIII.218 (ed. M. SIMONETTI – *al.*, III.2, 97).

[127] See, e.g., AMBROSE OF MILAN, *Exp. Luc.* V.111–117 (ed. G. TISSOT, I, 224–227); ID., *Sacr.* V.22 (ed. B. BOTTE, 130–131); JEROME OF STRIDON, *Commen. Matt* I.6.10 (ed. I.É. BONNARD, I, 130–131); and A. BONATO, "Il regno", 236–239.

[128] See MAXIMUS THE CONFESSOR, *Cap. car.* II.29–35 (ed. A. CERESA GASTALDO, 104–111); and A. BOLAND, "Royaume", 1054.

[129] See, e.g., ORIGEN OF ALEXANDRIA, *Or. Dom.* XXV.3 (ed. C.H.E. LOMMATZSCH – *al.*, XVII, 190–191); J. RATZINGER, *Jesus*, I, 49–50.59–60; and S. ZINCONE, "Regno di Dio", 39.

[130] J. RATZINGER, *Jesus*, I, 50. See, e.g., ORIGEN OF ALEXANDRIA, *Comm. Luc.* XXXVI.2–3 (ed. H. CROUZEL – F. FOURNIER – P. PÉRICHON, 432–435); and ID., *Comm. Jo.* VI.302–303 (ed. C. BLANC, II, 360–365).

[131] ORIGEN OF ALEXANDRIA, *Comm. Matt* XIV.7 (ed. E. BENZ – E. KLOSTERMANN, 289). See also *Ibid.*, XIII–XIV (ed. G. BENDINELLI, I, 152–159); CYPRIAN OF CARTHAGE, *Or. Dom.* XIII.220–227 (ed. M. SIMONETTI – *al.*, III.2, 97); M.I. DANIELI, ed., *Origene*, II, 120, n. 7; and J. RATZINGER, *Jesus*, I, 49.

[132] In this sense, H.U. von Balthasar speaks of Origen's extraordinary "cosmic conscience". See, e.g., H.U. VON BALTHASAR, *Origène*, I, 36.

b) A Political or Ecclesial Earthly Power

In conjunction with and, perhaps, as a result of this general process of spiritualization, the Patristic Age sees another development in the direction of a divinization of either the state, with its political power, or the earthly Church, with her ecclesial authority.

The former trend, on the one hand, is especially evident in the East and, more precisely, after Constantine embraces the Christian faith and the later Edict of Thessalonica (380)[133]. After the end of the persecutions, the kingdom of God tends to be connected with the temporal and political sphere, in what B.T. Viviano calls "a 'happy confusion'"[134], so much so that, commenting on the festivity held by Constantine on the occasion of his anniversary as emperor, Eusebius of Caesarea writes: "It might have been supposed that it was an imaginary representation of the kingdom of Christ"[135].

On the other hand, the kingdom of God on earth tends to be identified with the militant Church, as against all other earthly powers[136]. This kind of interpretation can already be traced back to the 2nd c. The Christian document *Shepherd of Hermas*, for instance, compares the kingdom of God with the building of a tower, which ultimately symbolizes the Church[137]. Similar associations can be found even in the *Didache* (Διδαχή) and other early literary works[138].

c) Ultimately: Eternal Life with God in Heaven

All the hermeneutic dimensions mentioned thus far can be said to find a true balance, eventually, in Augustine of Hippo's *City of God*. Although open to confusion, for Augustine the kingdom is neither the state, nor the Church, or their earthly history[139]. As A. Trapé writes in his introduction to this work:

---

[133] See B.T. VIVIANO, *The Kingdom*, 45–47.

[134] B.T. VIVIANO, *The Kingdom*, 46.

[135] A. CAMERON – S.G. HALL, *Eusebius*, 127. "Χριστοῦ βασιλείας ἔδοξεν ἄν τις φαντασιοῦσθαι εἰκόνα" (EUSEBIUS OF CAESAREA, *Vit. Const.* III.15.2 [ed. I.A. HEIKEL, I, 84]). See also *Ibid.*, III.10 (ed. *Ibid.*, I, 81–82); and L. TARTAGLIA, ed., *Eusebio*, 127–128, ns. 41–44.

[136] See, e.g., HIPPOLYTUS OF ROME, *Comm. Dan.* IV.9 (ed. G. BARDY – F.G. LEFÈVRE, 278–281); B.T. VIVIANO, *The Kingdom*, 51–52; and J. RATZINGER, *Jesus*, I, 50.

[137] See HERMAS, *Sim.* IX.12–13 (ed. R. JOLY, 316–323).

[138] See, e.g., *Did.* IX.4 (ed. W. RORDORF – A. TUILIER, 176–177); M. VAN PARYS, "L'Église", 51–62; and S. ZINCONE, "Regno di Dio", 25–29.

[139] See, e.g., AUGUSTINE OF HIPPO, *Civ.* XIV.28 (ed. A. TRAPÉ – P.R. PICCOLOMINI, I.5.2, 360–363); *Ibid.*, XIX.21.1–2 (ed. *Ibid.*, I.5.3, 66–71); ID., *Enarrat. Ps.* LV.2 (ed. *Ibid.*, III.26.2, 124–129); *Ibid.*, LXI.6 (ed. *Ibid.*, III.26.2, 348–351); and *Ibid.*, CXXIV.7 (ed. *Ibid.*, III.28.4, 98–101). See also B.T. VIVIANO, *The Kingdom*, 52–54; and A. BONATO, "Il regno", 280–289.

"the notion of the two cities is not institutional or political, but spiritual [...] mystical [...] allegorical explanation [...] of Scriptures. The two cities, spiritually understood, represent the forces of good and evil at work in history"[140].

Because Christ is always with his saints (see Matt 28,20), and in contrast to a millenaristic expectation of a visible kingdom here on earth, Augustine states:

the Church even now is the kingdom of Christ, and the kingdom of Heaven [...] they reign with Him who are so in His kingdom that they themselves are His kingdom[141].

In other words, by carrying the kingdom of God within themselves, and being spiritually united with Christ their king, the multitude of baptized Christians makes up the kingdom of God, that is, the Church[142]. However, according to Augustine, these two cities, namely, God's and the earthly one, are so much "entangled together in this world, and intermixed until the last judgment"[143], that neither the former can be properly confused with the Church, nor the latter with human society: someone outside the Church, in fact, can still be saved, just as any baptized member of the Church can eventually be lost[144]. The Augustinian city of God, then, is not a temporal state, nor a purely ecclesiastical institution, but the people of the elect, whose end and supreme good is eternal life (see, e.g., Ps 147,12–14; and Rom 6,22)[145]. The latter is yet to be found "ultimately [...] with God in heaven"[146].

II. The Positive Echo of the Middle Ages

As one moves from patristic to medieval history, one notes how the interpretation of the Fathers, with regard to our saying, has laid the foundations for what the following ten centuries shall write after them. In both the Eastern and the Western world, the former positive, intertwined, thievish, and

---

[140] A. TRAPÈ – P.R. PICCOLOMINI, ed., *Opera*, I.5.1, xxix.

[141] *N-PN Fathers¹*, II, 430. "*nunc Ecclesia regnum Christi est regnumque caelorum [...] regnant cum illo, qui eo modo sunt in regno eius, ut sint etiam ipsi regnum eius*" (AUGUSTINE OF HIPPO, *Civ.* XX.9.1 [ed. A. TRAPÈ – P.R. PICCOLOMINI, I.5.3, 126–128]). See also A. TRAPÈ – P.R. PICCOLOMINI, ed., *Opera*, I.5.1, lxxxv–lxxxvi.

[142] See also ORIGEN OF ALEXANDRIA, *Comm. Luc.* XXXVI.2–3 (ed. H. CROUZEL – F. FOURNIER – P. PÉRICHON, 432–435); and S. ZINCONE, "Regno di Dio", 29.

[143] *N-PN Fathers¹*, II, 21. "*Perplexae [...] in hoc saeculo invicemque permixtae, donec ultimo iudicio*" (AUGUSTINE OF HIPPO, *Civ.* I.35 [ed. A. TRAPÈ – P.R. PICCOLOMINI, I.5.1, 84]).

[144] See, e.g., AUGUSTINE OF HIPPO, *Bapt.* VI.39–40 (*PL* 43, 221–222); and B.T. VIVIANO, *The Kingdom*, 53–54.

[145] See, e.g., AUGUSTINE OF HIPPO, *Civ.* XIX.11 (ed. A. TRAPÈ – P.R. PICCOLOMINI, I.5.3, 42–45); *Ibid.*, XIX.13.1 (ed. *Ibid.*, I.5.3, 50–51); and *Ibid.*, XXII.30.1–2 (ed. *Ibid.*, I.5.3, 414–417). See also A. TRAPÈ – P.R. PICCOLOMINI, ed., *Opera*, I.5.1, xcii–xciii; and A. BOLAND, "Royaume", 1056–1057.

[146] B.T. VIVIANO, *The Kingdom*, 53.

profitable understanding of the "violence passage"[147] remains essentially unchallenged and the new historical period echoes and consolidates the previous traditional hermeneutic features. This is why, in this second section, we shall review these features briefly, concentrating especially on their "organic development [...], a [characteristic] process [...] of the Latin-Christian culture and the Western tradition"[148].

1. In the Eastern World

In the centuries which followed the Fathers' commentaries, throughout the Byzantine era, and up to the Protestant Reformation, Greek interpreters write in a manner analogous to that of the Fathers.

Thus, among the "carnal faults from which the βιαστής must strive to be free"[149], the 7th c. monk of St. Saba's monastery (near Jerusalem), Antiochus the Monk, mentions "greed, which is idolatry; love of money, the root of all evils"[150] (see, e.g., Col 3,5; and 1Tim 6,10), and interprets such violence as being concurrently inflicted both on oneself and on the kingdom. Likewise, the 9th c. Patriarch, Photius of Constantinople, conceives the "theft" (ἁρπαγή) of the kingdom as being performed, among others, by "those who despise wealth" (καταφρονήσαντες πλούτου)[151], whereas, according to the 11th c. Archbishop of Achrida (modern Ohrid), Theophylact of Bulgaria, the "much violence [...] needed" (βίας [...] χρεία πολλῆς) to enter Heaven implies that sort of "faith" (πίστιν) by which one is "to let go of father and mother, and disdain one's own life" (ἀφεῖναι πατέρα καὶ μητέρα, καὶ τῆς ψυχῆς αὐτῆς καταφρονῆσαι)[152].

Finally, the saying is cited also by Euthymius Zigabenus and Gregory Palamas, two other Greek monks of the 12th and 14th cs., who respectively lived in the monasteries of the Virgin Mary, near Constantinople, and Mount Athos. The former, commenting on Matt 11,12 and Luke 16,16, speaks separately of a "laudable violence" (ἐπαινετὴν βίαν)[153] and a "down payment of the kingdom of Heaven" (ἀρραβῶνα τῆς βασιλείας τῶν οὐρανῶν)[154], while the latter, writing in defence of Hesychasm, interprets the saying as an encouragement to pray

---

[147] W. STENGER, "βιάζομαι, βιαστής", *EDNT*, I, 216.

[148] C. DAWSON, ed., *Medieval Essays*, 87.

[149] P.S. CAMERON, *Violence*, 23.

[150] "πλεονεξία, ἥτις ἐστὶν εἰδωλολατρεία· φιλαργυρία, ἡ ῥίζα πάντων τῶν κακῶν" (ANTIOCHUS THE MONK, *Pand. hom.* CXXX [*PG* 89, 1841d]).

[151] PHOTIUS OF CONSTANTINOPLE, *Fr. Matt* XI.11 (*PG* 101, 1200c). For further readings on this author, see D.S. WHITE, *Patriarch*.

[152] THEOPHYLACT OF BULGARIA, *Enarrat. Matt* XI.12 (*PG* 123, 252b).

[153] P.S. CAMERON, *Violence*, 24. See EUTHYMIUS ZIGABENUS, *Comm. quat. Matt* XX (*PG* 129, 352c).

[154] EUTHYMIUS ZIGABENUS, *Comm. quat. Luc.* LVIII (*PG* 129, 1036d).

always, night and day, by means of the renowned prayer of the heart, even "until death" (ἕως θανάτου)[155].

One could certainly mention other analogous instances; however, we prefer to conclude here, that these and other Greek Medieval authors quote our verse in a manner analogous to that of their patristic predecessors, and often, in the context of either the narrow door (see Matt 7,14; Luke 13,24), the episode of the rich man – whom Jesus called to leave everything and follow him, since he wished to be perfect (see Mark 10,17.21.28) – or even against the negative example given by Ananias and his wife, Sapphira (see Acts 5,1–11)[156].

2. In the Western World

As observed by P.S. Cameron, the "influence of the classic interpretations of the Fathers"[157], and their typical lack of hermeneutic conflicts, is surely felt not only in the East, but also in the West.

Among the medieval commentators of the West, we hear again expressions concerning the grandeur and praiseworthiness of the violence spoken of in this enigmatic saying. Such is the case, for example, of Rabanus of Mainz, who, after citing the verse, in the proximate context of Agabus' prophecy and the collection sent to Judea (see Acts 11,27–30), exclaims: "Truly great is [such] violence!" (*Grandis est enim violentia!*)[158].

Other authors (e.g., Anselm of Canterbury) strikingly affirm that God has put the kingdom of Heaven and its merchandise nothing less than "on sale" (*venale*)[159], and that one way, by which one can "seize it entirely" (*percipere*)[160], is to "despise earthly goods for the sake of heaven and receive the goods of heaven in exchange for earthly ones"[161]. Anselm of Canterbury even insists that the only "price" (*pretium*), at which the kingdom of Heaven can be bought, is loving both God and one's neighbor, together:

"God [...] does not give such a [valuable] thing at no cost, because he does not give it to the one who does not love [...] nor does he have to give such a [great] thing to the one who

---

[155] GREGORY PALAMAS, *Barl.* I.48 (*PG* 151, 689d).

[156] See, e.g., SIMEON JUNIOR, *Orat.* XXVIII (*PG* 120, 458b–459a); GREGORY PALAMAS, *Barl.* I.48 (*PG* 151, 689d); etc. See also P.S. CAMERON, *Violence*, 23–24.

[157] P.S. CAMERON, *Violence*, 29.

[158] RABANUS OF MAINZ, *Comment. Matt* IV.11 (*PL* 107, 912a). See also ZACHARY OF BESANÇON, *Conc. Evang.* II.64 (*PL* 186, 208b–c); and P.S. CAMERON, *Violence*, 24–29.

[159] See ANSELM OF CANTERBURY, *Ep.* CXII.21 (ed. F.S. SCHMITT, III, 244); and *Ibid.*, CXII.34 (ed. *Ibid.*, III, 245).

[160] *CCLEE*, "*percĭpĭo*", 1107. See also *Ibid.*, "*accĭpĭo*", 14; and *Ibid.*, "*ēmo*", 529–530.

[161] J.R. FORTIN, "Saint Anselm", 9. "*pro caelestibus terrena despicere, pro terrenis caelestia percipere*" (ANSELM OF CANTERBURY, *Ep.* XLIV.2–3 [ed. F.S. SCHMITT, III, 156]). See also *Ibid.* CXII.69–70 (ed. *Ibid.*, III, 246); and W. FRÖHLICH, ed., *The Letters*, I, 268–270.

disdains to love it: he does not ask for anything but love [...] Therefore, give love and receive the kingdom! Love and you will have it! [...] that love [...] by which the kingdom of Heaven is bought"[162].

Another interesting commentary is that by Bernard of Clairvaux, who exhorts, first of all, never to offer a poverty, which can still be sold, crying out: "Woe to us, if we shall offer a sellable poverty!"[163]. Then, a few paragraphs later, he urges his audience to "violate" the kingdom by means of a truly humble prayer, after the example of the Gospel's tax-collector (see Luke 18,13)[164]. And, eventually, in one of his letters, he compares helping one's brothers in need with knocking on Heaven's door, linguistically alluding to images drawn from the military battlefield[165].

By way of recapitulation, we can take Bernard of Clairvaux's portrayal of who can enter and violently take possession of the heavenly kingdom:

"Four are the kinds of people who possess the kingdom of Heaven. Some snatch [it] violently, others trade [for it], [some] others steal [it], and [still] others are urged to-wards it"[166].

More precisely, and as explained by the author himself, the "violent snatchers", making up the first category, are the poor in spirit, namely, those "who despise everything and follow Christ"[167]. The "merchants" of the second category are the friends of the poor, namely, those who, by means of their "mammon of unrighteousness" (i.e., their worldly wealth), "give to the poor the temporal goods which they possess in the present, so that [in exchange] they may receive

---

[162] "*Nec* [...] *dat deus tantam rem sine omni pretio, quia non dat illam non amanti* [...] *nec dare debet tantam rem contemnenti amare illam: non quaerit nisi amorem* [...] *Da ergo amorem et accipe regnum; ama et habe* [...] *illum amorem* [...] *quo regnum caelorum emitur*" (ANSELM OF CANTERBURY, *Ep.* CXII.37–70 [ed. F.S. SCHMITT, III, 245–246]).

[163] "*Vae nobis, si vendibilem obtulerimus paupertatem!*" (BERNARD OF CLAIRVAUX, *Serm. div.* XXI.3 [ed. J. LECLERCQ – H. ROCHAIS, VI.1, 170; cf. *PL* 183, 595b]).

[164] See BERNARD OF CLAIRVAUX, *Serm. div.* XXV.2 (ed. J. LECLERCQ – H. ROCHAIS, VI.1, 188).

[165] See BERNARD OF CLAIRVAUX, *Ep.* II.12 (ed. J. LECLERCQ – H. ROCHAIS, VII, 22). As P.S. Cameron (*Violence*, 39) notes, a few centuries later, T. Beza (*Annotationes*, I, 71) shall again make use of "a metaphor drawn from the realm of camps and citadels" and explain ἁρπάζουσιν as signifying that which "is plundered by intruding enemies" (*irrumpentibus hostibus diripitur*). Other interpreters as well (e.g., T. Cajetan, C. Lapide, etc.) shall likewise refer, for instance, to the military metaphor of Israel's conquest of the promised land of Canaan. See, e.g., P.S. CAMERON, *Violence*, 37.39.

[166] "*Quattuor sunt genera hominum regnum caelorum possidentium. Alii violenter rapiunt, alii mercantur, alii furantur, alii ad illud compelluntur*" (BERNARD OF CLAIRVAUX, *Serm. div.* XCIX [ed. J. LECLERCQ – H. ROCHAIS, VI.1, 365]). Likewise, see ID., *Sent.* II.87 (ed. *Ibid.*, VI.2, 42).

[167] "*qui omnia contemnunt et sequuntur Christum*" (BERNARD OF CLAIRVAUX, *Serm. div.* XCIX [ed. J. LECLERCQ – H. ROCHAIS, VI.1, 365]).

from them eternal ones in the future"[168]. The "thieves" constituting the third category are those who, after the example of the hemorrhaging woman (see Matt 9,20–21), "shunning [all] human praise, are content only with God's testimony"[169]. Finally, the "urged ones", part of the fourth and last category, are "the poor of [this] age" (*pauperes saeculi*)[170], namely, those whom God's providence puts to the test with the fire of poverty while they are here on earth, but who eventually "attain eternal life" (*vitam consequuntur aeternam*)[171]. Of these latter ones, Bernard of Clairvaux concludes: "it is written: 'Urge them to enter, so that my house may be filled'"[172].

3. The Medieval Vision of a Political Earthly Kingdom

With regard to their vision of the kingdom of God, the medieval authors generally tend to conceive such an entity mostly as an earthly reality, by politically reinterpreting Augustine's teaching and advocating the submission of temporal rulers to ecclesiastical authority[173].

The spiritual and inner understanding, on the one hand, is still present in Bernard of Clairvaux and others. However, starting with Charlemagne and pope Gregory IV, and followed especially by the teachings of pope Gregory VII and Innocent III, the Middle Ages tend to believe in a kingdom which is mostly to be built *hic et nunc*, as a "*Sancta res publica christiana*"[174]. As a direct consequence of this interpretation, both Christian monarchs and crusaders shall eventually be conceived as divine instruments, chosen by God

---

[168] "*dant in praesenti pauperibus temporalia quae possident, ut in futuro recipiant ab eis aeterna*" (BERNARD OF CLAIRVAUX, *Serm. div.* XCIX [ed. J. LECLERCQ – H. ROCHAIS, VI.1, 365–366]).

[169] "*laudem humanam vitantes, solo divino testimonio contenti sunt*" (BERNARD OF CLAIRVAUX, *Serm. div.* XCIX [ed. J. LECLERCQ – H. ROCHAIS, VI.1, 366]).

[170] BERNARD OF CLAIRVAUX, *Sent.* II.87 (ed. J. LECLERCQ – H. ROCHAIS, VI.2, 42).

[171] BERNARD OF CLAIRVAUX, *Serm. div.* XCIX (ed. J. LECLERCQ – H. ROCHAIS, VI.1, 366).

[172] "*de quibus scriptum est: 'Compelle intrare, ut impleatur domus mea'*" (BERNARD OF CLAIRVAUX, *Serm. div.* XCIX [ed. J. LECLERCQ – H. ROCHAIS, VI.1, 366]). See Luke 14,21.23: "Go out quickly [...] the poor [...] bring [them] in here [...] urge [them] to enter, so that my house may be filled" (ἔξελθε ταχέως [...] τοὺς πτωκοὺς [...] εἰσάγαγε ὧ δε [...] ἀνάγκασον εἰσελθεῖν, ἵνα γεμισθῇ μου ὁ οἶκος).

[173] See, e.g., H. DE LUBAC, *Exégèse Médiévale*, III, 437–558; *Ibid.*, IV, 325–344; A. VAUCHES, *La spiritualité*; F. MARTELLI, "Reazione", 217–239; and B.T. VIVIANO, *The Kingdom*, 57–80.

[174] A. VAUCHES, *La spiritualité*, 67. See, e.g, BERNARD OF CLAIRVAUX, *Conf. reg.* (ed. J. LECLERCQ – H. ROCHAIS, VI.2, 267–273); C. DAWSON, ed., *Medieval Essays*, 67–83; and J. LECLERCQ, *L'idée*.

to bring about the kingdom of God on earth, not only spiritually, but also politically[175].

It is probably against this kind of interpretation that, as we are soon to see, someone like A. Karlstadt shall fervently react in his tractate[176]. As U. Luz explains, the German reformed theologian, in his intention "to comfort churches of the Reformation that were persecuted and under attack"[177], shall eventually manage to include among the βιασταί both "ecclesiastical rulers" (geistlich Regenten) and "the most high *pontifex*" (der aller hochste *pontifex*)[178].

C. The Rise of Modern Scholarship: First Attempts and Final Impasse

As we now consider the ages which followed the first 1500 years of continuous positive understanding of the "violence passage"[179], we are once again struck by this outstanding truth: not only does the *in bonam partem* interpretation, which defines the first five centuries of the Fathers' reception of the saying, survive throughout the Middle Ages (5th–15th cs.), but it is also generally maintained and kept uninterrupted, with the exception of a few instances, all through the Reformation (15th–16th cs.) and the Enlightenment (17th–18th cs.), up to the Romantic period (19th c.).

Only in the 20th c. does the number of *in malam partem* interpretations significantly increase, "particularly among Protestant scholars in Germany"[180], and new lines of inquiry are taken up, to the point that the major proposals of the latter period require an altogether separate assessment, which shall be dealt with in the next section of this chapter. Before turning to that, however, we wish to highlight the evidence and arguments presented in support of the two main positions, which progressively arise in modern scholarship, as the emphasis is gradually placed on the morality and eschatology of God's

---

[175] See, e.g., BERNARD OF CLAIRVAUX, *Laud. mil.* I–XIII (ed. J. LECLERCQ – H. ROCHAIS, III, 214–239); ID., *Ep.* CCCLXIII.1–8 (ed. *Ibid.*, VIII, 311–317); J. LECLERCQ, *L'idée*, 58–63; A. BOLAND, "Royaume", 1069–1070; and P.-Y. EMERY, *Bernard*, 19–47.50–133.

[176] See A. KARLSTADT, *Berichtung*; and P.S. CAMERON, *Violence*, 31–35.

[177] U. LUZ, *Matthew*, II, 144.

[178] See A. KARLSTADT, *Berichtung*, Cii.V; and P.S. CAMERON, *Violence*, 33.

[179] W. STENGER, "βιάζομαι, βιαστής", *EDNT*, I, 216.

[180] P.S. CAMERON, *Violence*, 131. Thus, the author (*Ibid.*, 2) remarks: "until the second half of the 19th century, those who supported an *in malam partem* interpretation were a small minority".

kingdom. These arguments are significant also because they prepare the ground for the 20th c. reading of this enigmatic verse.

More precisely, after a brief summary of the first rare attempts to consider alternative interpretations of the saying, we shall review here, on the one hand, the proposal of A. Schweizer, as the first substantial endeavor to refute, on exegetical grounds, the previous and long-running traditional interpretation, and, on the other hand, the study of A. von Harnack, as a representative example of those who, objecting to Schweizer's conclusions, find further reasons to sustain anew the traditional interpretation.

I. A Gradual Swing Towards the In Malam Partem Solution

The foremost novelty, which can be said to timidly and gradually mark the last five or six centuries of the interpretation of the "violence saying", concerns the advent of irregular thrusts that slightly but effectively set in motion a progression from the positive to the negative side of its hermeneutic scale.

According to P.S. Cameron, the first barely perceptible sense of inquietude over the saying, "of an admission of the *prima facie* offensiveness of the concept of the kingdom suffering violence"[181], occurs sometime between 1446 and 1449, with A. Tostatus de Madrigal[182]. His commentary, however, basically follows the Fathers' traditionally positive and interwoven strands[183], and the first true *in malam partem* interpretation of the saying occurs only in 1521, with the work of the aforementioned A. Karlstadt[184]. He is apparently "the first to challenge the interpretations of the Fathers"[185] and is "for two centuries the only person to interpret force [i.e., βία] as evil and hostile to God"[186]. His interpretation is, however, too "polemically inspired and [...]

---

[181] P.S. CAMERON, *Violence*, 30.

[182] See A. TOSTATUS, *Commentariorum* XXXVIII, 282; P.S. CAMERON, *Violence*, 28–29; and J.M. SÁNCHEZ CARO – R.M. HERRERA GARCÍA – M.I. DELGADO JARA, ed., *Alfonso de Madrigal*, 11–58.118–121.124–125.

[183] See, e.g., GREGORY THE GREAT, *Hom. Evang.* XX.14–15 (ed. R. ÉTAIX, 168–169); ANTIOCHUS THE MONK, *Pand. hom.* CXXX (*PG* 89, 1841b); and P.S. CAMERON, *Violence*, 19.23.28–29.

[184] See A. KARLSTADT, *Berichtung*; and P.S. CAMERON, *Violence*, 31–35. On A. Karlstadt's life and thought, see *ODCC*, "Carlstadt", 290–291; G. RUPP, "Andrew", 308–326; ID., *Patterns*, 49–153; R.J. SIDER, *Andreas*; and C.A. PATER, *Karlstadt*.

[185] P.S. CAMERON, *Violence*, 34.

[186] U. LUZ, *Matthew*, II, 144. A. Karlstadt (*Berichtung*, Bii.R) maintains that the kingdom of God "ist Christus, und alle, so Christo eingeleibt sein mit glawben", while he considers (*Ibid.*, Ci.R) a βιαστής to be a "sinner" (Sünder), who can only "Schaden und Leiden zufügen" to that kingdom. See also R.J. SIDER, *Andreas*, 135–136; and P.S. CAMERON, *Violence*, 31–33.

oriented"[187], so much "informed [...] by his effort to refute neo-Pelagians"[188] that it eventually plunges into oblivion and thus remains only a slightly stronger, but still isolated foray into the *in malam partem* hermeneutic trend[189]. In 1715, the French Benedictine monk, A. Calmet, proposes a less extensive and anti-Pharisaic explanation, which is "more historically sensitive than Karlstadt's [...] and less polemical"[190], but does not really add much to it.

Only in the early 1800s – albeit still quite gradually and almost reluctantly – the hermeneutic pendulum begins to swing over the saying. In 1806, in fact, J.C.R. Eckermann briefly identifies the "violent ones" (βιασταί) with the Zealots, as those "misguided supporters"[191] who, aroused by John's preaching, wish to accelerate the coming of the kingdom of God in their own forceful way[192]. In 1824, in keeping with A. Calmet's view, C.G. Bretschneider in turn considers Matt 11,12 and Luke 16,16 as referring, respectively, to the incarceration of the Baptist and the resistance of the Pharisees[193]. In 1832, M. Schneckenburger proposes an *in malam partem* solution, yet, only in so far as the Matthean version of the saying is concerned[194]. Solely in the Matthean context, βιάζεται refers to a "hostile" (feindselig)[195] violence, which implies not only the "Jewish conviction that the time of the Messiah can be delayed by sin"[196], but also a direct Pharisaic opposition against Jesus, which causes his "flight from Judea (John 4,1)"[197] and recalls "the behaviour of the Scribes and Pharisees denounced at Matt 23,13–15"[198].

Overall, however, as evinced by P.S. Cameron's assessment and his detailed history of the discussion:

> The *in malam partem* interpretations which appear sporadically throughout the period – those of Karlstadt, Calmet, Eckermann, Bretschneider and Schneckenburger – consist largely of assertions based on instinct[199].

---

[187] P.S. CAMERON, *Violence*, 33.

[188] K.A. BARTA, review of P.S. CAMERON, *Violence*, 134. See P.S. CAMERON, *Violence*, 46.

[189] See P.S. CAMERON, *Violence*, 35.46.

[190] P.S. CAMERON, *Violence*, 41. See A. CALMET, *Commentaire*, XV, 258; and *Ibid.*, XVI.2, 257–258.

[191] P.S. CAMERON, *Violence*, 44.

[192] See J.C.R. ECKERMANN, *Erklärung*, I, 61.

[193] See C.G. BRETSCHNEIDER, "βιάζω", *LMGL*, I, 212; ID., "βιαστής", *LMGL*, I, 213; and P.S. CAMERON, *Violence*, 44–45.

[194] See M. SCHNECKENBURGER, *Beiträge*, 48–52. See also P.S. CAMERON, *Violence*, 45.

[195] M. SCHNECKENBURGER, *Beiträge*, 49.

[196] P.S. CAMERON, *Violence*, 45. See M. SCHNECKENBURGER, *Beiträge*, 49.

[197] M. SCHNECKENBURGER, *Beiträge*, 49.

[198] P.S. CAMERON, *Violence*, 45. See M. SCHNECKENBURGER, *Beiträge*, 49.

[199] P.S. CAMERON, *Violence*, 48.

They are, indeed, "both infrequent and largely unsubstantiated"[200], and only occasionally derive from exegetical implications based on the Matthean and Lucan contexts[201]. Moreover, they appear to concur with the rise of another "innovative understanding"[202], which gradually tends to underscore a moralistic, individualistic and, eventually, eschatological idea of the kingdom of God. In other words, as the focus of the discussion on the entrance into the kingdom is progressively placed on the decisiveness of the individual's charitable works and ethical achievements (e.g., I. Kant)[203], and confronted with the consideration of our human frailty – subsequently witnessed to especially by the atrocities perpetrated during the First World War – such a realization shall become more and more only a future possibility and the idea of a positive violence shall gradually give way to that of a negatively "physical" one[204].

II. A. Schweizer and his Interpretation of βία as "Physical Violence"

As P.S. Cameron says, "the first properly argued attempt to discredit the traditional solutions"[205] occurs only in 1836, with Alexander Schweizer's extensive article – according to Cameron, "the most thorough and critical treatment the saying has so far received"[206]. With Schweizer, thus, the hermeneutic pendulum reaches the outermost negative side of its swing, for the first time, and it shall henceforth revert to it, over and over again. His philological arguments "will later so often be repeated"[207] that they merit here some more detailed consideration.

Right from the start, Alexander Schweizer directly confronts the fundamental difficulty of the saying, dedicating almost 32 pages of commentary to it, under the following fitting title: "Is the passage Matt 11,12 to be taken as praise or rebuke?" (*Ob in der Stelle Matth. 11,12 ein Lob oder ein Tadel erhalten sei?*)[208].

---

[200] P.S. CAMERON, *Violence*, 81.

[201] See P.S. CAMERON, *Violence*, 34.41.44–45.48.175, n. 48.

[202] J. RATZINGER, *Jesus*, I, 50.

[203] See, e.g., I. KANT, *Religion*, 127.

[204] See, e.g., N. PERRIN, *The Kingdom*, 12–206; B.T. VIVIANO, *The Kingdom*, 81–151; and J. RATZINGER, *Jesus*, I, 50–52.

[205] P.S. CAMERON, *Violence*, 48.

[206] P.S. CAMERON, *Violence*, 49. See A. SCHWEIZER, "Ob in der Stelle", 90–122.

[207] P.S. CAMERON, *Violence*, 49. See, e.g., G. SCHRENK, "βιάζομαι, βιαστής", *TDNT*, I, 609–614; M. DIBELIUS, *Die urchristliche Überlieferung*, 23–32; and W. MICHAELIS, *Der Herr*, 66–70.

[208] Note how, in reporting the full title, P.S. Cameron (*Violence*, 49) accidentally omits the word "to be given, receive" (erhalten).

After identifying four types of proposed solutions (two positive and two negative)[209], and on the basis of philological data, Schweizer reduces these four types to two,

by excluding the *in bonam partem* interpretation which takes βιάζεται as middle, and the *in malam partem* interpretation which sees the βιασταί as deliberately hostile [enemies][210].

The former is very often used in the passive and would be "a tautology" (eine Tautologie)[211], whereas Jesus could not possibly and successfully have allowed the latter group of people to preclude others from coming into the kingdom[212].

Secondly, the author turns to discuss the implications of the main terms as to the subject of violence, and deduces that they generally imply negative meanings. Concerning βία, for instance, his conclusion is that it "has [...] absolutely acquired the notion of violence" (hat [...] überhaupt den Begriff aneignender Gewalt)[213]. As to ἁρπάζειν, he notes: "either this word means 'to seize for oneself', hence ἅρπαξ, usually in a violent or unlawful way [...] or 'to tear apart' [...] טרף"[214].

However, he is fair in admitting that, sometimes, the latter can be used "also in a good sense" (auch in gutem Sinne)[215], but only "if such can be derived from the context"[216]. As regards βιάζεσθαι, and as P.S. Cameron summarizes, "the first thought is of physical violence, and the use of the word *in bonam partem* is, he says, never unequivocally attested"[217].

As far as a βιαστής is concerned, the latter "is actually quite a violent person" (ist recht eigentlich ein Gewalttätiger)[218], as opposed to "one who strives enthusiastically"[219] for the kingdom of God.

Thirdly, on the basis of these linguistic implications, Schweizer finally draws his first conclusions. If the term βία does evoke "always" (immer) and "first of all" (zunächst) the concept of "physical violence" (physische Ge-

---

[209] See A. SCHWEIZER, "Ob in der Stelle", 90–91.

[210] P.S. CAMERON, *Violence*, 49.

[211] A. SCHWEIZER, "Ob in der Stelle", 97. This argument shall likewise be used later, by other scholars. See, e.g., M.J. BIRKS, "St. Matthew 11,12", 425; and P.S. CAMERON, *Violence*, 100.

[212] See A. SCHWEIZER, "Ob in der Stelle", 92–96.

[213] A. SCHWEIZER, "Ob in der Stelle", 96.

[214] A. SCHWEIZER, "Ob in der Stelle", 98–99.

[215] A. SCHWEIZER, "Ob in der Stelle", 98.

[216] P.S. CAMERON, *Violence*, 50. See A. SCHWEIZER, "Ob in der Stelle", 98–99.

[217] P.S. CAMERON, *Violence*, 50. See A. SCHWEIZER, "Ob in der Stelle", 99. Moreover, as A. Schweizer (*Ibid.*, 100) remarks: "wenn auch der Begriff von physischer Gewalt mehr zurücktritt, als anderwärts, so bleibt doch immer, dass der, gegen welchen einer βιάζεται, eben ein βιασθείς sei und ἄκων, nur gezwungen wozu vermocht wird βία τινός".

[218] A. SCHWEIZER, "Ob in der Stelle", 101.

[219] P.S. CAMERON, *Violence*, 51.

walt)[220], "then Christ's assertion is not to be interpreted as praise"[221]. The Fathers' positive example of the narrow door (see Matt 7,14; and Luke 13,24) does not really apply, because "this image is not indicated in our text"[222]. If the *in bonam partem* interpretation has thus far prevailed, it is simply because of "an ascetic interest" (einem ascetischen Interesse)[223]. To conceive such a saying as "praise" (Lob) "does violence to the words of Christ himself" (den Worten Christi selbst Gewalt anzuthun)[224], and neglects their linguistic significance.

A. Schweizer looks also at the Matthean context and its historical *Sitz im Leben*, and along the lines of A. Karlstadt's and J.C.R. Eckermann's assumptions – as noted by P.S. Cameron – he autonomously argues:

> Jesus can never have meant that the kingdom should be brought on with physical violence, unwillingly [...] Indeed it is impossible to see how the general "Lob" implicit in an *in bonam partem* interpretation of [Matt] 11,12 could harmonize with the general "Tadel" expressed in [Matt] 11,16ff. [225].

The "violence passage"[226] must rather be connected to some historically hostile movement, such as that of the Zealots, which must have begun "from the days of John the Baptist" (Matt 11,12a), that is to say, after John's own "prompting" (veranlassende)[227], in a time "when mere prophecy gave place to the real initiation of the kingdom"[228]. Delving into the historical data of the census under Quirinus, Flavius Josephus' references to the Zealot party, Judas the Galilean's uprising, and all the pressure that these must have implied in those days for the Jews and their messianic hopes of liberation from the Romans, A. Schweizer eventually sees in Matt 11,12 a rather *indirect* "rebuke" (Tadel) and "a warning on Zealotism"[229], which is addressed by Jesus to those who are impatiently and forcefully trying to accelerate the, otherwise, naturally slow unfolding of the kingdom of God[230]. For fear of provoking a further Zealotic insurrection, "he could not say, 'since the days of Judas the Galilean...'"[231].

Finally, the article reaches its conclusion with the following closing considerations concerning Luke 16,16. As previously claimed even by M. Schneck-

---

[220] A. SCHWEIZER, "Ob in der Stelle", 99.

[221] A. SCHWEIZER, "Ob in der Stelle", 101.

[222] A. SCHWEIZER, "Ob in der Stelle", 101.

[223] A. SCHWEIZER, "Ob in der Stelle", 107. Likewise, see P.S. CAMERON, *Violence*, 20.29.

[224] A. SCHWEIZER, "Ob in der Stelle", 102. See also *Ibid.*, 114.

[225] P.S. CAMERON, *Violence*, 51–52. See A. SCHWEIZER, "Ob in der Stelle", 101.105.

[226] W. STENGER, "βιάζομαι, βιαστής", *EDNT*, I, 216.

[227] A. SCHWEIZER, "Ob in der Stelle", 108.

[228] P.S. CAMERON, *Violence*, 52.

[229] P.S. CAMERON, *Violence*, 53.

[230] See A. SCHWEIZER, "Ob in der Stelle", 108–113; and P.S. CAMERON, *Violence*, 52–53.

[231] P.S. CAMERON, *Violence*, 53. See A. SCHWEIZER, "Ob in der Stelle", 112.

enburger, Schweizer maintains that, strictly speaking, the latter verse "is not [...] a true parallel"[232]. According to the author, βιάζεται is here to be read as a "middle" (Medium)[233]. Indeed, as he states: "It is not the same word of Christ, which both evangelists recount, but Christ has said something similar on different occasions"[234].

More precisely, as the proximate context in Luke 16,16–18 seems to indicate, the Lucan verse is rather aimed at those who believe they can legitimately break the law for the sake of the kingdom, and is thus meant to emphasize the following truth: "the law remains in force and must be observed [...] in a much stricter sense, for whoever dismisses his wife commits adultery"[235].

Although definitely "epoch-making in several ways"[236], A. Schweizer's arguments present nonetheless a number of weaknesses. P.S. Cameron rightly points out:

His dismissal [in Matt 11,12] of the middle sense of βιάζεται on the grounds of necessary tautology is forced and fallacious [...] in the light of Semitic synonymous parallelism [...] "tautology" in a saying of Jesus is evidence more for its authenticity than anything else [...] The argument that Jesus could not have said "since the days of Judas the Galilean" for fear of provoking the Zealots to further uprising seems particularly weak [...] the linguistic evidence is not so one-sided as Schweizer makes out, or as it has subsequently been held to be. He makes no reference to the interpretations of Hilary, Jerome, Augustine or Clement of Alexandria, each of which is compatible with the meanings he insists on for ἁρπάζειν – a seizing for one's own benefit – and βιάζεσθαι – behaviour which is unnatural or illegal[237].

Moreover, Schweizer's interpretation may have been biased both by his own theological convictions, namely, that the "dignity of Scripture [...] must be asserted in opposition to ecclesiastical tradition"[238], and by the "contemporary revolutionary activities in Germany and France"[239], to which he himself alludes in his article. Finally, although on linguistic, contextual, and historical grounds, according to Schweizer, "there is no reason to abandon the obvious *in malam partem* meaning in favour of a more artificial interpretation"[240], yet, as P.S. Cameron objectively points out:

---

[232] P.S. CAMERON, *Violence*, 53. See M. SCHNECKENBURGER, *Beiträge*, 50–51; and A. SCHWEIZER, "Ob in der Stelle", 118–119.

[233] A. SCHWEIZER, "Ob in der Stelle", 117.

[234] A. SCHWEIZER, "Ob in der Stelle", 119.

[235] A. SCHWEIZER, "Ob in der Stelle", 118.

[236] P.S. CAMERON, *Violence*, 54.

[237] P.S. CAMERON, *Violence*, 54.

[238] O. PFLEIDERER, *The Development*, 128.

[239] P.S. CAMERON, *Violence*, 53. See A. SCHWEIZER, "Ob in der Stelle", 113.

[240] P.S. CAMERON, *Violence*, 53.

The *in bonam partem* sense is not absolutely excluded – the point is that because of the normal meaning of the language an *in bonam partem* interpretation should not be considered before an *in malam partem* interpretation[241].

Indeed, A. Schweizer underlines the importance of the context in determining the positive or negative meaning of these words and, although he considers it insufficient, he still leaves the door open to the possibility of their *in bonam partem* sense[242].

In the decades following his article, other *in malam partem* commentaries shall appear. On the grounds of context, language, and history, quite a few authors shall successively support Schweizer's conclusions, or, in any case, by their own different approaches, advance in similar directions[243]. In particular, as stated by P.S. Cameron:

> Schweizer's Zealotic solution has spawned what is perhaps the only interpretation in the history of the saying which can with a reasonable amount of confidence be dismissed out of hand – that Jesus was himself a Zealot and intended the saying as encouragement to his Zealotic followers[244].

Overall, however, Schweizer's strongest effort is unable to set the scales permanently on the *in malam partem locus*. Contrary to what happens with the Fathers, the pendulum shall never stand in one position again for more than one or two consecutive decades, but shall continue to alternate between the positive and negative hermeneutic orientations under the impulse of various arguments for each position. While some authors shall attempt to make a synthesis, keeping both the positive and negative sides together[245], many others

---

[241] P.S. CAMERON, *Violence*, 52.

[242] See A. SCHWEIZER, "Ob in der Stelle", 98–102.

[243] As P.S. Cameron (*Violence*, 55–56.63) notes, Gfrörer and J. Weiss follow "Schweizer's identification of the βιασταί with the Zealots", whereas Zyro sees in Luke 16,16 no true parallel of Matt 11,12, being, as it is, rather "a denunciation of anti-nomianism". See, e.g., A.F. GFRÖRER, *Geschichte*, II.1, 91–98; F.F. ZYRO, "Erklärung", 409–410; ID., "Neue Auslegung", 663–704; J. WEISS, *Die Predigt*, 196–197; A. VON SCHLATTER, *Johannes*, 66–75; and P.S. CAMERON, *Ibid.*, 66.71–75.178, n. 53.

[244] P.S. CAMERON, *Violence*, 132. Such an interpretation can be rejected simply on the basis of Jesus' assertion to love one's enemies and his typical association with tax-collectors and sinners. Few scholars (e.g., R. Eisler, J. Carmichael, and S.G.F. Brandon) have assiduously held on to this Zealotic trend. See, e.g., M. HENGEL, *Die Zeloten*, 344–348; ID., *Gewalt*, 38–46; S.G.F. BRANDON, *Jesus*, 78.200.300, n. 5; and P.S. CAMERON, *Violence*, 54.116–119.132.190, n. 237. See also M. GOURGUES, "Jésus et la violence", 126–135.143–145; and R.A. HORSLEY, "Ethics and Exegesis", 5.10.

[245] See, e.g., H. OLSHAUSEN, *Biblischer Commentar*, I, 361–362.681–684; ID., *Biblical Commentary*, I, 423–424; II, 73–76; R. STIER, *Die Reden*, I, 470–476; F.J.A. HORT, *Judaistic Christianity*, 26; O. CULLMANN, *The State*, 20–21; and P.S. CAMERON, *Violence*, 59–60.117–118.177, n. 39.

shall react to and reject Schweizer's conclusions, such that the exegetical enquiry of the 19th and 20th cs. shall eventually end with a final deadlock[246].

III. A. von Harnack and the Eventual Polarization of the Discussion

Among the exegetes who, in contrast with A. Schweizer's proposal, find further reasons to retain the traditional interpretation of the Fathers, Adolf von Harnack's study is especially worth mentioning[247]. His understanding closes P.S. Cameron's chronological account of the interpretation of the saying, as the representative example of the opposing modern scholarship, "a consolidation of several centuries of *in bonam partem* interpretation"[248], and as directly offsetting "the equally wide-ranging survey by Alexander Schweizer"[249]. Moreover, in a manner similar to that of our study, and unlike Schweizer, A. von Harnack begins his discussion of the "violence passage"[250] by considering Luke 16,16, and this is also why we highlight it at this point of our discussion.

First of all, according to the German author, and in keeping with J. Weiss' solution, the Lucan version of the saying is "less primitive"[251] than Matthew's, for originally "the good news of the kingdom was not the point"[252]. For Harnack, its Lucan form seems to have "received its colour from the Pauline-Lucan mission"[253]. Accordingly, Luke does not only replace βιάζεται with εὐαγγελίζεται, but also completely "isolates" (isoliert)[254] the saying from its original context[255]. The verse is so "smoothed" (geglättet) by the evangelist's own understanding that, when compared to Matthew's version, Luke's text has for him the appearance of "a [well] hewn stonework" (einem behauenen Quaderstein) beside "a clumsy block" (ein ungefüger Block)[256].

---

[246] See, e.g., C.I. NITZSCH, *System*, 179; W.M.L. DE WETTE, *Kurze Erklärung*, 108–109; C.H. WEISSE, *Die evangelische Geschichte*, II, 70–72; W.G. RINCK, "Über Matth. 11,12", 1020–1021; B. BAUER, *Kritik*, II, 244–268; J.P. LANGE, *Matthäus*, 159–162; F. BLEEK, *Synoptische Erklärung*, I, 451–453; and P.S. CAMERON, *Violence*, 55.57–59.61–62.67.176, n. 21.

[247] See A. VON HARNACK, "Zwei Worte", 947–957; and P.S. CAMERON, *Ibid.*, 77–81.129.

[248] P.S. CAMERON, *Violence*, 79.

[249] P.S. CAMERON, *Violence*, 77.

[250] W. STENGER, "βιάζομαι, βιαστής", *EDNT*, I, 216.

[251] P.S. CAMERON, *Violence*, 77. See J. WEISS, *Die Predigt*, 193–194.

[252] P.S. CAMERON, *Violence*, 77. See A. VON HARNACK, "Zwei Worte", 949.

[253] A. VON HARNACK, "Zwei Worte", 950. See P.S. CAMERON, *Violence*, 77.

[254] A. VON HARNACK, "Zwei Worte", 947.

[255] More precisely, A. von Harnack ("Zwei Worte", 947, n. 1) argues that "Bei Lukas hat der Spruch keinen Kontext [...] alle Versuche, ihn mit v. 15 oder v. 17 zu verbinden, gescheitert", and, likewise (*Ibid.*, 949), the thought of v. 16c "schließt sich inhaltlich nicht gut" with the content of v. 16ab, but "comes like a shot out of a gun" (kommt wie aus der Pistole geschossen).

[256] A. VON HARNACK, "Zwei Worte", 947.

Secondly, as far as βιάζεται is concerned, Harnack argues that, unlike εὐαγγελίζεται, the former verb must be taken here as middle (vs. passive), "since the two sentences [i.e., v. 16b and v. 16c] do not [really] constitute a *parallelismus membrorum*"[257], as some would argue. Luke has found in this saying "nothing unfavourable" (nichts Ungünstiges), has interpreted βιάζεσθαι as "an intransitive active" (intransitives Aktivum), and has paraphrased Matt 11,12c with his own v. 16c[258]. Concerning the actual meaning of the verb, Harnack further affirms:

"[when] connected to εἰς, βιάζεσθαι has [...] everywhere (from Xenophon, Thucydides, Polybius, Plutarch and Philo) the sense of 'penetrating with violence into something'"[259].

However, he maintains that, in formulating his own version of the saying, Luke does not really place any emphasis on it: "βιάζεται is merely preserved from the source and the reader must make of it what he will – it is of seconddary significance"[260].

On the contrary, all the "stress" (Ton)[261] of the Lucan verse is fixed on both εὐαγγελίζεται and πᾶς. More precisely, the πᾶς represents "the actual acme of the sentence" (das eigentliche Akumen des Satzes)[262], whereas the "Gospel-verb", εὐαγγελίζειν, may have been inspired by Matt 11,5 (= Luke 7,22), "in the context of Jesus' speech about John"[263], and used here in a way resembling John 1,17[264].

Finally, among the main intentions justifying the Lucan changes, the author identifies two:

a) Luke primarily wishes to highlight the antithesis between the "old period" (alten Zeit) of "the Law and the Prophets" (ὁ νόμος καὶ οἱ προφῆται)[265] – which, according to Harnack, is "not εὐαγγελία" (keine εὐαγγελία)[266] – and the "new period" (neuen Zeit), "which is essentially marked by the dawning of the kingdom of God"[267] as good news. Right from the start, Harnack grants to Luke

---

[257] A. VON HARNACK, "Zwei Worte", 948.

[258] See A. VON HARNACK, "Zwei Worte", 953.

[259] "hat βιάζεσθαι, mit εἰς [...] überall (bei Xenophon, Thukydides, Polybius, Philo und Plutarch) den Sinn 'gewaltsam in etwas eindringen'" (A. VON HARNACK, "Zwei Worte", 948).

[260] P.S. CAMERON, *Violence*, 77. See A. VON HARNACK, "Zwei Worte", 949.

[261] A. VON HARNACK, "Zwei Worte", 948.

[262] A. VON HARNACK, "Zwei Worte", 949.

[263] A. VON HARNACK, "Zwei Worte", 955, n. 3.

[264] See A. VON HARNACK, "Zwei Worte", 948. See also, "for the Law was given through Moses, grace and truth came about through Jesus Christ" (ὅτι ὁ νόμος διὰ Μωϋσέως ἐδόθη, ἡ χάρις καὶ ἡ ἀλήθεια διὰ Ἰησοῦ Χριστοῦ ἐγήνετο) (John 1,17).

[265] Luke 16,16a.

[266] A. VON HARNACK, "Zwei Worte", 948.

[267] A. VON HARNACK, "Zwei Worte", 950. For A. von Harnack's interpretation of the kingdom of God, see, e.g., B.T. VIVIANO, *The Kingdom*, 113–116; and J. RATZINGER, *Jesus*, I, 51–52.

16,16 the utmost importance precisely insofar as it divides the history of the Jewish religion "into two halves" (in zwei Hälften)[268]. John the Baptist is associated with the first period, marks its "end" (Schluß)[269] and, although he constitutes "its capstone and highest point" (ihr Schlußstein und Höhepunkt)[270], is still to be considered as "excluded" (ausgeschlossen)[271] from the period of the Gospel, which begins only with Jesus Christ, as "the turning point of the times and the end of the law" (die Wende der Zeiten und das Ende des Gesetzes)[272].

b) As evinced by the additions of the pronominal adjective πᾶς and the verb εὐαγγελίζεται, Luke intends to emphasize the good news of the universal call to salvation. Although Luke may have basically reshaped both its original context and its specific features (i.e., ἡ βασιλεία, βιάζεται and βιασταί) also for fear, perhaps, that his readers might not even grasp it[273], Harnack is convinced that:

"he [i.e., Luke] has almost certainly understood the saying [...] in [its] positive sense and compensated the omission [...] through 'εὐαγγελίζεται' and 'πᾶς εἰς αὐτὴν βιάζεται'. Before, there was only prophecy, now, the kingdom has arrived and is proclaimed as good news; before, it was only for the Jews, now, [it is] for the whole world"[274].

In keeping with the "joyful optimism" (freudigen Uptimismus)[275] found in the Acts of the Apostles, A. von Harnack explains:

"The idea of the universality of the Gospel is the main idea; as so often, Luke wants to push it to the forefront: 'Everyone comes now into the kingdom!' [...] The saying in the Lucan version can then be paraphrased thus: 'The law and the prophets' – not a good news and given only to the people of Israel – go until John and have thus fulfilled their task; after John, however, i.e., now, the Gospel of the kingdom of God is proclaimed. It is intended for all people, and they [actually] crowd to enter into it"[276].

---

[268] A. VON HARNACK, "Zwei Worte", 947. As observed by Harnack (*Ibid.*, 955), "Lukas hat den Grundgedanken bewahrt und verstärkt, daß es sich um zwei Perioden handelt".

[269] A. VON HARNACK, "Zwei Worte", 948.

[270] A. VON HARNACK, "Zwei Worte", 955.

[271] A. VON HARNACK, "Zwei Worte", 948. On this point, the author argues against J. Weiss' and T. Zahn's interpretations, according to whom John and his days are rather to be included into the new Gospel times. See *Ibid.*, 950–951; J. WEISS, *Die Predigt*, 192–197; T. ZAHN, *Matthäus*, I, 426–427; and P.S. CAMERON, *Violence*, 74–77.

[272] A. VON HARNACK, "Zwei Worte", 950.

[273] See A. VON HARNACK, "Zwei Worte", 955.

[274] A. VON HARNACK, "Zwei Worte", 955.

[275] A. VON HARNACK, "Zwei Worte", 949.

[276] A. VON HARNACK, "Zwei Worte", 949. Several other authors underline the universal and inclusive character of the kingdom of God in Luke 16,16, as expressed by the subject πᾶς. See, e.g, F. GODET, *Luke*, II, 172; A. PLUMMER, *Luke*, 389; G. SCHRENK, "βιάζομαι, βιαστής", *TDNT*, I, 612; W. GRUNDMANN, *Lukas*, 323; H. PREISKER, "Lukas 16,1–7", 89;

Turning to Matthew 11,12, Harnack identifies it both with an "authentic dominical saying" (echten Herrenworts)[277] – mainly on account of its "harsh brevity and [...] powerful and profound simplicity"[278] – and "a critique of the Baptist movement" (eine Kritik der Täuferbewegung)[279], because, although he is appraised highly, John, but also his followers, are "not [among] the βιασταὶ ἁρπάζοντες τὴν βασιλείαν"[280] and "must submit to be placed beneath the smallest [...] in the kingdom of God"[281].

More precisely, Harnack considers, first of all, Matthew's different and more "extensive context" (umfangreichen Kontextes)[282] and argues that, although the Matthean version of the saying is placed within a discourse of Jesus on John the Baptist, its focus "is not on John at all" (Johannes ist [...] überhaupt nicht die Rede)[283]. On the contrary, as summarized by P.S. Cameron:

v. 12 is principally about the kingdom [...] The idea is really that the kingdom of Heaven not only ἤγγικεν ["has come near"], or ἔφθασεν ["has come upon"] but also βιάζεται ["penetrates by storm"] (cf. Zahn)[284].

Because of its different subject, and in keeping with Zahn's interpretation – as opposed to that of "most exegetes"[285] – Harnack argues that, by reference to Matt 12,28 (= Luke 11,20), and just as in Luke 16,16c, βιάζεται is to be understood, even in this case, "as a middle with an active-intransitive meaning" (als Medium mit aktiv-intransitiver Bedeutung)[286]. The verb "in the present [tense] only seldom has the passive sense"[287]. After all, the thought that the kingdom of God may come with violence is not so surprising, when one considers "that βίαιος is also found as an attribute of [the] 'Spirit'"[288].

Secondly, Harnack affirms that Matthew agrees with Luke not only in keeping the *in bonam partem* and middle sense of the violence-verb, but also

---

C.H. TALBERT, *Reading Luke*, 187–188; L. SABOURIN, *Luke*, 297; and D.J. IRELAND, *Stewardship*, 131–132.

[277] A. VON HARNACK, "Zwei Worte", 956.

[278] A. VON HARNACK, "Zwei Worte", 956, n. 1.

[279] A. VON HARNACK, "Zwei Worte", 957.

[280] A. VON HARNACK, "Zwei Worte", 957.

[281] A. VON HARNACK, "Zwei Worte", 956.

[282] A. VON HARNACK, "Zwei Worte", 950.

[283] A. VON HARNACK, "Zwei Worte", 951.

[284] P.S. CAMERON, *Violence*, 77. See, e.g., Matt 3,2; 4,17; 10,7; 12,28; Luke 10,9.11; 11,20; T. ZAHN, *Matthäus*, I, 428; and A. VON HARNACK, "Zwei Worte", 951.954.

[285] A. VON HARNACK, "Zwei Worte", 952, n. 1.

[286] A. VON HARNACK, "Zwei Worte", 952. See T. ZAHN, *Matthäus*, I, 427–428; A. VON HARNACK, "Zwei Worte", 952, n. 4; and P.S. CAMERON, *Violence*, 76.

[287] P.S. CAMERON, *Violence*, 78. See A. VON HARNACK, "Zwei Worte", 952.

[288] A. VON HARNACK, "Zwei Worte", 954. Along with T. Zahn, the author (*Ibid.*, 954) mentions here, by way of example, "Acts 2,2 πνοὴ βιαία; Isa 11,15; Ps 47,8; JOS., *Bell.* III, 9.3 πνεῦμα βίαιον". See T. ZAHN, *Matthäus*, I, 428, n. 21.

in establishing only two (vs. three) periods in history: namely, "the time up to John (inclusively) and the time after John or the time of the βασιλεία"[289]. By drawing attention (as F.F. Zyro does) to the contrast between these two periods and the implied connection between v. 12 and v. 13 (γάρ), Harnack argues against the *in malam partem* interpretation, observing that, in v. 12, "one expects some fitting characteristic of the second [period as well], the time of the present kingdom"[290], and "if *in malam partem*, the saying fits badly with v. 13"[291].

Thirdly, the author also maintains that, by positively reading both βιάζεται and βιασταί, the ideas expressed in Matt 11,12bc become "simply identical; because ἁρπάζουσιν is, then, already contained in βιάζεται"[292]. In this way, the meaning of the whole sentence is not only simpler, but also richer, for a kingdom that comes with violence requires that those who welcome it be likewise violent themselves[293]. After all, as paraphrased by P.S. Cameron:

The paradoxical use of βιασταί and ἁρπάζειν *in bonam partem* is not nearly so paradoxical as the robbing of the kingdom by evil stormers. In fact the latter is impossible, so the robbing would have to be thought of as conative – but that is difficult to read into ἁρπάζειν[294].

Harnack compares this paradoxical language with other equally shocking images often used by Jesus in his preaching, such as, "the serpent-like wisdom, the unjust steward, the harsh judge, *al.*"[295], and eventually infers: "nothing, nevertheless, prevents the assumption that Jesus has allegorically presented the violent stormers as role models"[296].

---

[289] A. VON HARNACK, "Zwei Worte", 951.

[290] P.S. CAMERON, *Violence*, 78. See F.F. ZYRO, "Erklärung", 402; A. VON HARNACK, "Zwei Worte", 951.953; and P.S. CAMERON, *Violence*, 62.80.178. This argument shall later be followed by other scholars. See, e.g., F. DIBELIUS, "Der Spruch", 285–288.

[291] P.S. CAMERON, *Violence*, 78. See A. VON HARNACK, "Zwei Worte", 953.

[292] A. VON HARNACK, "Zwei Worte", 954, n. 2.

[293] See A. VON HARNACK, "Zwei Worte", 954, n. 2.

[294] P.S. CAMERON, *Violence*, 78. See A. VON HARNACK, "Zwei Worte", 953.

[295] A. VON HARNACK, "Zwei Worte", 952, n. 3. See, e.g., Matt 10,16; Luke 16,8; 18,6; etc. The note on the juxtaposition of the "violence saying" and the parable of "The Shrewd Steward" is already made by Bernard of Clairvaux and C.I. Nitzsch, but can also be traced back to the Fathers. See, e.g., BERNARD OF CLAIRVAUX, *Serm. div.* XCIX (ed. J. LECLERCQ – H. ROCHAIS, VI.1, 365); ID., *Sent.* II.87 (ed. *Ibid.*, VI.2, 42); C.I. NITZSCH, *System*, 179; and P.S. CAMERON, *Violence*, 27.55.80.180, n. 121. As to the paradoxical language, see, e.g., B. RALPH, "The Kingdom", 427; J.-M. LAGRANGE, *Matthieu*, 221; and E. PERCY, *Die Botschaft Jesu*, 197.

[296] A. VON HARNACK, "Zwei Worte", 953. As P.S. Cameron (*Violence*, 35) remarks, other authors shall likely maintain that "Jesus was deliberately […] using violent language to sharpen the image which he wanted to convey". See also *Ibid.*, 55.78–80.92.180, n. 121; and C.S. KEENER, *Matthew*, 340.

Fourthly, by drawing attention to the fact that "ἁρπάζειν means not only 'to rob' but also 'to take hastily'"[297], Harnack points out that the term does not necessarily carry an "unfavourable meaning" (ungünstigen Sinne)[298]. Contrary to all those authors who see, in the βιασταί's action, a violence analogous to that perpetrated by the Zealots against the Romans[299], the βιασταί must actually be "true disciples of Christ"[300], also because "the Zealot party did not begin with John the Baptist"[301]. More precisely, the "violent ones" are those who, like the widow in the parable of the Unjust Judge (see Luke 18,1–8), must resort to the "conquering weapon" (Eroberungswaffe) of their persistent prayers, in order to "take the kingdom of God quickly" (das Reich Gottes hastig ergreifen), since, "in the new period, everything takes place with much violence and in a very short time"[302]. Such an *in bonam partem* interpretation, indeed, finds support, not only in the Fathers' most recurrent paraphrase of the saying or the μετὰ σπουδῆς of Irenaeus of Lyons and John Chrysostom, but also in the understanding of the "oldest interpreter" (älteste Ausleger), Clement of Alexandria[303]. That the latter's evidence is so early is for Harnack particularly significant, because it creates "a presumption in favour of that sense"[304], and shows how, at that time, "as a Greek [speaker], one could understand the saying *in bonam partem*"[305].

Finally, Harnack concludes his discussion by underlining how the Matthean dominical saying sets up decisive evidence "both for the presentness of the kingdom and for the messianic consciousness of Jesus"[306]. In fact, in keeping with both Matt 11,5 and Matt 12,28, the author affirms:

"Our saying (and its context) leaves no doubt on both issues: [...] Jesus refers to himself, not only as a prophet or a 'Messias designatus', but as the Messiah who has already begun his work [...] Back then, it was [about] the right inner preparation for the coming kingdom,

---

[297] A. VON HARNACK, "Zwei Worte", 954, n. 3.

[298] A. VON HARNACK, "Zwei Worte", 952.

[299] See, e.g., J.C.R. ECKERMANN, *Erklärung*, I, 61; A. SCHWEIZER, "Ob in der Stelle", 108–113; A.F. GFRÖRER, *Geschichte*, II.1, 91–98; J. WEISS, *Die Predigt*, 196–197; and J. WELLHAUSEN, *Matthaei*, 53. Cf., also, A. VON HARNACK, "Zwei Worte", 952, n. 3; and P.S. Cameron, *Violence*, 44.52–53.55–56.74–75.

[300] A. VON HARNACK, "Zwei Worte", 953.

[301] P.S. CAMERON, *Violence*, 78. See A. VON HARNACK, "Zwei Worte", 953.

[302] A. VON HARNACK, "Zwei Worte", 954.

[303] See CLEMENT OF ALEXANDRIA, *Quis div.* XXI (ed. G.W. BUTTERWORTH, 312); IRENAEUS OF LYONS, *Haer.* IV, 37.7 (ed. A. ROUSSEAU, II, 939); JOHN CHRYSOSTOM, *Hom. Jo.* VIII (*PG* 59, 301δ); and A. VON HARNACK, "Zwei Worte", 953–954.

[304] P.S. CAMERON, *Violence*, 79.

[305] A. VON HARNACK, "Zwei Worte", 953. Among those scholars who shall later make use of this argument, see M. WERNER, *Die Entstehung*, 70–71; and G.E. LADD, *The Presence*, 162–163.

[306] P.S. CAMERON, *Violence*, 80.

now it is [about] gaining the present kingdom itself [...] But, then again, everything preparatory is now concluded; there, [it was about] the Law and the prophets; here, [it is about] the kingdom of God!"[307].

A. von Harnack eventually paraphrases the Matthean form of the saying in this way:

"'(the least in the kingdom of Heaven is greater than John); this kingdom of Heaven is not only future, however, but it penetrates now, after the days of John, by storm, and only [those] people who are [actually] stormers take it; for all the Prophets and the Law have found their boundary (for their prophetic task) with John (there must, therefore, be something new now); John is nevertheless – if you let this observation apply – the Elijah that must come as a direct precursor of the Messiah'"[308].

As with Schweizer's *in malam partem* interpretation, so with Harnack's article: his *in bonam partem* solution equally "sets the scene for the rest of the 20th century"[309]. The "old interpretations [shall] continue to find followers"[310], and not only the 19th, but even "the 20th century sees in effect a return to the position of the Fathers"[311]. However, in spite of his definite contribution to the late history of the interpretation of the saying, Harnack's discussion presents also a few contradictions, which we would here like to bring to the fore.

Firstly, above and beyond Harnack's arguments in favor of the middle and positive sense of βιάζεται, it is especially his concluding remarks concerning the presentness of the kingdom and Jesus' messianic consciousness that particularly initiate "a new trend of claiming the support of the text"[312]. Yet, as affirmed by P.S. Cameron:

Harnack does not, as he implies he does, deduce from Matt 11,12 the presentness of the kingdom and Jesus' messianic consciousness, but rather [...] convinced already of both, he interprets Matt 11,12 accordingly[313].

---

[307] A. VON HARNACK, "Zwei Worte", 956–957.

[308] A. VON HARNACK, "Zwei Worte", 951–952.

[309] P.S. CAMERON, *Violence*, 80.

[310] P.S. CAMERON, *Violence*, 131.

[311] P.S. CAMERON, *Violence*, 157. See, e.g., M. WERNER, *Die Entstehung*, 70–71; B. RALPH, "The Kingdom", 427; and E. PERCY, *Die Botschaft*, 197.

[312] P.S. CAMERON, *Violence*, 157. See, e.g., A. SCHWEITZER, *The Quest*, 264–266.355.370–374; E.C. DEWICK, *Primitive Christian Eschatology*, 134; J. MOFFATT, *The Theology*, 51–52; R. OTTO, *The Kingdom*, 108–112; E. PERCY, *Die Botschaft Jesu*, 191–202; C.H. DODD, *The Parables*, 48–51; O. BETZ, "The Eschatological Interpretation", 104; E. JÜNGEL, *Paulus*, 190–193; N. PERRIN, *The Kingdom*, 58–64.87.121–127.171–174; ID., *Jesus*, 46; R.H. HIERS, *The Kingdom*, 36–49.56.93–97; and P.S. CAMERON, *Violence*, 74–81.101–102.127–129.189–190.

[313] P.S. CAMERON, *Violence*, 81.

His interpretation, in other words, is heavily biased by earlier convictions of his, previously written on these subjects[314].

Secondly, if the Fathers' *in bonam partem* interpretation of the saying constitutes an important datum in support of its positive meaning, as also noted by Cameron, one wonders why their equal unanimity "in reading βιάζεται as passive does not, apparently, create a similar presumption"[315], at least as far as Matt 11,12b is concerned[316].

Thirdly, if Luke has really understood the saying, as Harnack argues, how come this is so only insofar as its middle, intransitive, positive and history-making meanings are concerned[317]? Commenting on βιάζεται – an admittedly "specific characteristic" (Spezifikum)[318] of the original saying – he writes that "perhaps, he [i.e. Luke] himself was not even entirely sure of understanding it"[319] and, accordingly, must have left it there, unexplained, up to the reader's own imagination[320]. In other words, if the evangelist really understood the "violence passage"[321], as the author claims, why would he then choose to pull it out of its original context, that is, "Jesus' speech on John"[322], and oddly isolate it in a "no context" (keinen Kontext)[323] *locus* of his Gospel? The logical answer Harnack gives is related to Luke's double intention to stress both the antithesis between the old and new historical periods and the universality and missionary effect of the Gospel. However, if this is so, the problem is really why he does not simply use "to go in" (εἰσέρχεται), for instance, instead of βιάζεται. Harnack does ask himself this question, but finds no answer: "one does not understand", he confesses, "why violence or haste is needed to enter the kingdom"[324].

Finally, Harnack also lays emphasis on the fact that "the Law and the Prophets" (John included) have reached their end and "thus fulfilled their task" (damit ihre Aufgabe erfüllt)[325]. However, if this is true, how does he explain

---

[314] See, e.g., A. VON HARNACK, *Das Wesen*, 34.39.83; ID., *What is Christianity?*, 56.66.141; B.T. VIVIANO, *The Kingdom*, 115; J. RATZINGER, *Jesus*, I, 51; and P.S. CAMERON, *Violence*, 80–81.

[315] P.S. CAMERON, *Violence*, 79.

[316] As P.S. Cameron (*Violence*, 21.82) notes, while in Mt 11,12b βιάζεται is "always taken as passive", whenever they consider "the Lucan parallel [...] the Fathers [...] unanimously understood the latter *in bonam partem* with βιάζεται as middle".

[317] Cf. A. VON HARNACK, "Zwei Worte", 953.955.

[318] A. VON HARNACK, "Zwei Worte", 955.

[319] A. VON HARNACK, "Zwei Worte", 955.

[320] See A. VON HARNACK, "Zwei Worte", 949.

[321] W. STENGER, "βιάζομαι, βιαστής", *EDNT*, I, 216.

[322] A. VON HARNACK, "Zwei Worte", 955, n. 3.

[323] A. VON HARNACK, "Zwei Worte", 947, n. 1.

[324] A. VON HARNACK, "Zwei Worte", 949.

[325] A. VON HARNACK, "Zwei Worte", 949.

those other assertions of Jesus attesting the permanent validity of the Law-prophets binomial in the Matthean and Lucan writings[326]? With the advent of the Messiah and his Gospel of the kingdom, the prophetic message of Scriptures may have really been fulfilled, but this should not necessarily amount to a break of the NT with the OT, nor should the weight of the Law, as a condition for righteousness or admission into the heavenly kingdom, be so simply dismissed[327].

Overall, as with Schweizer's *in malam partem* interpretation, Harnack's equally strong thrust in the opposite *in bonam partem* direction shall be unable to settle the exegetical discussion once and for all. In the nearly seventy years separating Schweizer's article (1836) from Harnack's (1907), the situation is such that, if we rely on P.S. Cameron's overall impression, these first modern academic attempts seem to end with "a polarization of the discussion"[328] around the following three central points: a) the positive or negative value of βιάζεται; b) its middle or passive voice; and c) the historically restricted or universally edifying reference of the saying as a whole[329]. This is how P.S. Cameron summarizes the two positions:

According to Schweizer the saying is *in malam partem*, βιάζεται is passive, and the βιασταί are a specific historical group. According to Harnack the saying is *in bonam partem*, βιάζεται is middle, and the βιασταί are the believers, now as then. Each side bases its arguments principally on the linguistic (Greek) evidence and on the context in Matthew, but each side interprets the evidence differently, each formulating methodological principles in support (some, on each side, of questionable validity – for example, Schweizer dismisses what to him is "tautology", and Harnack argues that because βιάζεσθαι in the present tense is rarely passive it should be regarded as middle in Matt 11,12). Each side becomes more and more firmly entrenched, and the position appears to be a stalemate[330].

---

[326] See, e.g., Matt 5,17–19; Luke 16,17.29.31; 24,25.27.44; and Acts 24,14; 26,22; 28,23.31.

[327] See, e.g., Matt 7,12; 19,16–17; 22,40; 23,23; Luke 2,22–24.27.39; 10,25–28; 11,46; 18,18–20; and Acts 7,53; 21,20.24; 22,3.12; 23,3. In one instance, at least, A. von Harnack ("Zwei Worte", 955) cuts the Law from the picture completely, stating: "before, there was only prophecy, now the kingdom" (Früher gab es nur Weissagung, jetzt ist das Reich). A few years after the publication of "Zwei Worte", Harnack shall follow Marcion and propose the abandonment of the OT. See A. VON HARNACK, *Marcion*, 215–223. As regards Matthew's thought on the Law and the kingdom, see, e.g., L. SABOURIN, *Matthew*, 30–32.

[328] P.S. CAMERON, *Violence*, 81.

[329] See P.S. CAMERON, *Violence*, 48.81.

[330] P.S. CAMERON, *Violence*, 81.

D. A Summary of the Major Proposals in Recent Decades

In this fourth and closing stage of our historical analysis, we propose a summary of the great "diversity of solutions and approaches"[331] taken up by modern scholarship as to the interpretation of the "violence passage"[332], mostly in the 20th and 21st centuries. In order to do so, we can consider only some of the major lines of inquiry, typically employed in these past decades, and arrange the section accordingly. The review shall attest the general lack of consensus, which, once again, concomitant with a "secularist reinterpretation of the idea of the kingdom"[333] of God, still characterizes the current discussion over the saying, and shall thus reveal the real need for a fresh solution.

I. The Greek Impasse and the Question of a Conjectural Semitic Original

As we have observed in the previous section, with the rise of modern scholarship, the swing towards the *in malam partem* interpretation slowly progresses and the "desire on the part of commentators to break out of the restraints of the traditional solutions"[334] gradually increases[335]. Yet, by the end of the 19th and the beginning of the 20th century, the result is really an impasse, in which the exegetical research struggles to find a general consensus over the varied proposals. Following A. Schweizer's and A. von Harnack's articles, in fact, any additional academic attempt to break the hermeneutic deadlock around the "violence passage"[336], which is based merely on Greek philological grounds, appears sterile and rather pointless.

If a deeper examination of the linguistic evidence in other Greek sources (for instance, those of M. Dibelius, G. Schrenk, and W. Michaelis) appears to substantiate Schweizer's *in malam partem* interpretation, then again, other studies (specifically, those of B. Ralph, M. Werner and E. Percy) offer equivalent support for Harnack's diametrically opposed proposal[337]. While

---

[331] P.S. CAMERON, *Violence*, 85.

[332] W. STENGER, "βιάζομαι, βιαστής", *EDNT*, I, 216.

[333] J. RATZINGER, *Jesus*, I, 53.

[334] P.S. CAMERON, *Violence*, 67.

[335] Commenting on the 20th c. *in malam partem* interpretation of the saying, P.S. Cameron (*Violence*, 113) argues that it "has itself become what might be characterized as the scholarly consensus in the present century, to the extent that one can speak of a consensus in so disputed a field". However, as he (*Ibid.*, 100–108) himself briefly reviews, the concurrent *in bonam partem* sense is about as much favoured and by almost as many recent authors as is the *in malam partem* one, so that to speak of a consensus on this subject is inappropriate.

[336] W. STENGER, "βιάζομαι, βιαστής", *EDNT*, I, 216.

[337] See, e.g., M. DIBELIUS, *Die urchristliche Überlieferung*, 23–32; B. RALPH, "The Kingdom", 427; G. SCHRENK, "βιάζομαι, βιαστής", *TDNT*, I, 609–614; M. WERNER, *Die Entstehung*, 70–71; W. MICHAELIS, *Der Herr*, 66–70; E. PERCY, *Die Botschaft*, 197;

G.A. Deissmann provides further evidence from a Greek inscription, in favour of the middle reading of βιάζεσθαι, "in an absolute intransitive sense"[338], H. Almquist's and W.E. Moore's respective studies on Plutarch and Josephus separately undergird the same verb's "passive" (*Passivum*)[339] meaning. Ultimately, while arguing for an *in malam partem* sense of ἁρπάζω and διαρπάζω, W.E. Moore admits that these verbs are used in Josephus to refer to a "rightful seizing [...] a legitimate [...] permitted seizing"[340], and he grants that "the matter cannot be decided on purely linguistic grounds"[341].

As a result, throughout these decades, new lines of inquiry gradually develop. As P.S. Cameron remarks, these are not mere "indications of a slightly desperate search for new alternatives"[342], but they also represent hopeful "signs of an imminent breaking up of this polarization"[343]. Thus, while some attempts are made to compare the Greek text of the saying with the ancient versions[344], for instance, other specialists hunt for a solution in a number of daring ventures, including the launch of truly conjectural emendations for the extant texts and the reconstruction of a Semitic original, as this might actually lay concealed behind the Greek wording of the saying.

As to the former trend, mention should be made of an article written by J.H. Michael, in which the author considers the expression "kingdom of Heaven" (βασιλεία τῶν οὐρανῶν), in Matt 11,12b, in the light of Matt 12,29 (cf. the occurrence of ἁρπάζειν in both verses), as a misunderstanding for the supposedly original phrase, "kingdom of Satan" (βασιλεία τοῦ Σατανᾶ). For J.H. Michael, the latter syntagm might have, at its Aramaic level (מלכות דשטנא),

---

W.E. MOORE, "ΒΙΑΖΩ, ΑΡΠΑΖΩ", 519–543; and P.S. CAMERON, *Violence*, 39–40.42. 47.90–93. Additional grounds for the positive understanding of βιάζεσθαι were already offered by W.M.L. de Wette, when he pointed to the textual example of 2Macc 14,41, with "forcing the courtyard's door" (τὴν αὐλαίαν θύραν βιαζομένων). See, e.g., W.M.L. DE WETTE, *Kurze Erklärung*, 132; and P.S. CAMERON, *Violence*, 55.

[338] P.S. CAMERON, *Violence*, 91. See G.A. DEISSMANN, *Neue Bibelstudien*, 86; and Moulton, "βιάζομαι", 109–110.

[339] H. ALMQUIST, *Plutarch*, 38. See P.S. CAMERON, *Violence*, 90–91.

[340] W.E. MOORE, "ΒΙΑΖΩ, ΑΡΠΑΖΩ", 537. See FLAVIUS JOSEPHUS, *A.J.* V.171–173 (ed. B. NIESE, I, 326); *B.J.* I.356 (ed. *Ibid.*, VI, 81); *Ibid.*, II.494 (ed. *Ibid.*, VI, 244); and *Ibid.*, VI.353 (ed. *Ibid.*, VI, 559).

[341] W.E. MOORE, "ΒΙΑΖΩ, ΑΡΠΑΖΩ", 540.

[342] P.S. CAMERON, *Violence*, 83.

[343] P.S. CAMERON, *Violence*, 81.

[344] Thus, A. Merx (*Die vier kanonischen Evangelien*, II.1, 189–191) finds evidence for the *in malam partem* use of the terms and passive sense of βιάζεται. However, as P.S. Cameron (*Violence*, 99–100) notes, "Merx's first argument, that the unanimity of the versions excludes a middle sense of βιάζεται in Matthew and a passive sense in Luke [...] contains its own refutation, since it provides evidence that, at a time when the language was still living, βιάζεσθαι in the present tense could be understood as either passive or middle".

erroneously been confused and replaced with מלכות דשמיא[345]. A. Pallis also
proposes an alternative emendation of the text. Taking βιάζεται as "an error for
βαπτίζεται"[346], he argues that the original verb would have accordingly implied
a certain haste, by all righteous men, "to be baptized in the name of Christ"[347].
These, or analogous emendations, however, shall rightly attract only a few
followers, mainly because of the extreme questionability of the approach, their
lack of any textual evidence, and their basic clash with the principle of *lectio
difficilior*. As explained by P.S. Cameron, "it is scarcely credible that so banal
an idea should have been altered in the direction of such an extreme difficulty"[348].

With regard to the second trend, however, P.S. Cameron notes a more encouraging and growing "awareness of the necessity to enquire into the Semitic
original"[349]. Aside from A. Schweizer's already mentioned suggestion of טרף
("tear, seize")[350], as an equivalent for ἁρπάζειν, the first true contribution in
this direction can be traced back to A. Resch in 1895[351].

By comparing several extra-canonical parallels and looking at some LXX
texts[352], Resch identifies the saying's likely common Hebrew equivalents of
βιάζεται and βιασταί with נפרצה and הפרצים[353], respectively, adducing the following three main reasons: a) the spelling of נפרצה explains both βιάζεται and
βιαστή (*violentum*)[354] since it can either stand for a perfect or a participle; b)
the verb פרץ semantically accounts both for βιάζεται (Matt 11,12b) and
εὐαγγελίζεται (Luke 16,16c), since it can mean not only "to break through"
(Qal), as in Mic 2,13 (see Luke 13,24 = Matt 7,14)[355], but also "to spread out"

---

[345] See J.H. MICHAEL, "A Conjecture", 375–377.

[346] A. PALLIS, *Notes*, 35. See also *Ibid.*, 30.

[347] A. PALLIS, *Notes*, 35.

[348] P.S. CAMERON, *Violence*, 121. See also *Ibid.*, 119–124.

[349] P.S. CAMERON, *Violence*, 81. See also *Ibid.*, 87–89.93–98.156.

[350] BDB, "טרף", 382.

[351] See, e.g., A. SCHWEIZER, "Ob in der Stelle", 98–99; A. RESCH, *Aussercanonische*, II,
439–442; and P.S. CAMERON, *Violence*, 93.

[352] E.g., 1Sam 28,23, 2Sam 13,25.27, Mic 2,13; 2Macc 14,41; JUSTIN MARTYR, *Dial.* LI
(ed. P. BOBICHON, I, 312); IRENAEUS OF LYONS, *Haer.* IV, 37.7 (ed. A. ROUSSEAU, II,
939); CLEMENT OF ALEXANDRIA, *Strom.* IV, II.5.3 (ed. O. STÄHLIN, II, 250); *Ibid.*, V,
III.16.7 (ed. *Ibid.*, II, 336); PSEUDO-MACARIUS, *Lib. cor.* XIII (*PG* 34, 837a); and ID.,
Lib. men. XVIII (*PG* 34, 949c).

[353] Namely, the passive (Niphal) form of פרץ and the (Qal) participle masculine plural
form of the same root.

[354] See, e.g., IRENAEUS OF LYONS, *Haer.* IV, 37.7 (ed. A. ROUSSEAU, II, 939); and PSEUDO-
MACARIUS, *Lib. men.* XVIII (*PG* 34, 949c).

[355] Drawing from Medieval Jewish exegesis, the association between the "violence
passage" (W. STENGER, "βιάζομαι, βιαστής", *EDNT*, I, 216), Mic 2,13, and פרץ, is first made
by J. CALVIN and E. Pocock, but later mentioned also by other scholars. See, e.g., PesR 35.4
(ed. M. FRIEDMANN, 161a); J. CALVIN, *Commentaries*, III, 211; E. POCOCK, *A Commentary*,
21–23; P.P. LEVERTOFF – H.L. GOUDGE, "The Gospel", 154–155; D. FLUSSER, *Jesus in*

(Niphal), as in the Vulgate translation of נפרץ with "manifest" (*manifesta*)[356]; and c) the Hebrew הפרצים can poetically justify the recurrent patristic Greek formula – "the kingdom of Heaven belongs to the violent ones" (βιαστῶν ἐστιν ἡ βασιλεία τῶν οὐρανῶν)[357] – since one may simply dismiss ἁρπάζουσιν αὐτήν as a Matthean expansion "derived" (abgeleitet)[358] from it, and translate Matt 11,12bc as ᵇמלכות השמים נפרצה ᶜומלכות השמים לפרצים.

Resch's conjecture, "that the same root (פרץ) lies behind both halves of the saying"[359], is embraced first by J.T. Marshall, and then by many others as well[360]. In his critical review of Resch's study, however, Marshall also connects, on the one hand, the "breaking through" of the פרצים with "the fence of the Law"[361], thus basically identifying the βιασταί with the law-breakers and sinners of Matt 21,32, and, on the other hand, attributes the translation of βιάζεται with εὐαγγελίζεται to Luke's misreading of "אתפרץ for אתפרס"[362], which as an Aramaic equivalent of פרש can also mean "to spread"[363].

Attempts, moreover, are concurrently made in the hypothetical construction of an original text in the Aramaic language. Thus, behind all of the saying's three Greek terms of violence (i.e., βιάζεται, βιασταί, and ἁρπάζουσιν), A. Meyer, for instance, proposes the single Aramaic root חסן, which not only means "to be strong" (stark sein)[364], but also "to take possession of" (in Besitz nehmen)[365]. According to Meyer, the Lucan βιάζεται perfectly agrees with the meaning of Dan 7,18, which affirms: "the saints of the Most High shall receive [...]

Selbstzeugnissen, 38–40; D. BIVIN – R.B. BLIZZARD Jr., *Understanding the Difficult Words*, 123–125; B.H. YOUNG, *Jesus*, 52–54.62–67; and R.S. NOTLEY, "The Kingdom", 305–307.

[356] 1Sam 3,1 (*Vg.*). See, e.g., M.J. CONRAD, "פרץ", *TDOT*, XII, 104–110.

[357] See, e.g., CLEMENT OF ALEXANDRIA, *Strom.* IV, II.5.3 (ed. O. STÄHLIN, II, 250).

[358] A. RESCH, *Aussercanonische*, II, 441. See *Ibid.*, II, 440–441; and P.S. CAMERON, *Violence*, 93–94.

[359] P.S. CAMERON, *Violence*, 94.

[360] See J.T. MARSHALL, "Aussercanonische", 48–49. See also M. BLACK, *An Aramaic Approach*, 211, n. 2; ID., "The Kingdom", 290, n. 2; O. BETZ, "Jesu", 126–129; ID., "The Eschatological Interpretation", 102–105; B.E. THIERING, "Are the 'Violent Men'", 293–297; G.R. BEASLEY-MURRAY, *Jesus*, 91–96; P.S. CAMERON, *Violence*, 94–95.98–99.141–153; B.H. YOUNG, *Jesus*, 51–55; and R.S. NOTLEY, "The Kingdom", 303–307.

[361] J.T. MARSHALL, "Aussercanonische", 48. In this regard, P.S. Cameron (*Ibid.*, 194, n. 64) refers to J. Levy's dictionary (*NCWTM*, "פרץ", IV, 133) and mentions that the "Rabbinic use of the root פרץ is usually in the context of breaking through the fence around the Law [...] But it is also used in the primary Old Testament sense of the breach created or used by the robber". See also O. BETZ, "The Eschatological Interpretation", 97–98.

[362] J.T. MARSHALL, "Aussercanonische", 48. See P.S. CAMERON, *Violence*, 95.

[363] BDB, "פרש", 831. See also *Ibid.*, "פרס", 828; and *Ibid.*, "פרש", 831.

[364] A. MEYER, *Jesu Muttersprache*, 157.

[365] A. MEYER, *Jesu Muttersprache*, 158. See *Ibid.*, 87–89.157–159; and P.S. CAMERON, *Violence*, 95–96.

and take possession of the kingdom" (ויקבלון[...] קדישי עליונין ויחסנון מלכותא)[366]. Matthew, one can conjecture, may have been in possession of some other textual variant, which read both "חסיניא (powerful, violent ones)"[367], in place of "חסידיא 'the pious ones'"[368], and "חמס> יחמסונה: 'to treat violently, to wrong'"[369], in place of "יחמסונה i.e. 'seize hold of'"[370], and, if this is the case, he may have thus translated his two faulty Semitic readings with the Greek terms, βιασταί and βιάζεται[371]. As P.S. Cameron remarks, A. Meyer eventually recognizes that "the suggested corruption of חסידיא (pious ones) to חסיניא could be avoided by postulating an emphatic infinitive absolute of חסן"[372], and he thus reconstructs the original Aramaic form of the saying in the following way: "מיומין דיוחנן מלכותא דשמיא תתחסן ומחמסן יחמסונה"[373].

Not content with Meyer's proposal, a couple of years later, G. Dalman finds two better Aramaic equivalents for βιάζεται, specifically, the verbs תקף and אנס[374]. In a way similar to חסן, תקף means "in the Peal 'to be strong', and in the Aphel 'to hold fast'"[375], whereas אנס "can mean 'to use force' and 'to rob'"[376]. However, "since תקף has no passive meaning"[377], he ultimately opts for אנס, and proposing it as the only root lying behind βιάζεται, βιασταί, and ἁρπάζουσιν, conjectures the following original Matthean form of the saying: "מלכותא דשמיא מן יומי יוחנן ועד כען מתאנסא ואנוסין אנסוהא"[378]. As to the different Lucan version, Dalman maintains that it may be designated "as peculiarly

---

[366] Dan 7,18. See also, "and the saints took possession of the kingdom" (קדישין ומלכותא החסנו) (Dan 7,22c).

[367] P.S. CAMERON, *Violence*, 95.

[368] A. MEYER, *Jesu Muttersprache*, 89.

[369] P.S. CAMERON, *Violence*, 95.

[370] P.S. CAMERON, *Violence*, 95.

[371] See A. MEYER, *Jesu Muttersprache*, 158.

[372] P.S. CAMERON, *Violence*, 95.

[373] A. MEYER, *Jesu Muttersprache*, 158. Meyer (*Ibid.*, 158) translates it thus: "Seit Johannes Tagen wird das Himmelreich in Besitz genommen; ja, mit fester Hand erfassen sie es [als sicheren Besitz]".

[374] See G. DALMAN, *Die Worte*, 113–116; ID., *The Words*, 139–143; and P.S. CAMERON, *Violence*, 96–98. For Dalman's interpretation of the kingdom of God, see N. PERRIN, *The Kingdom*, 23–28.

[375] G. DALMAN, *The Words*, 140. See ID., *Die Worte*, 114. For an introduction on the Pᵉʳal and Haṗ‘el verbal conjugations and their basic meanings, see Rosenthal, 46–47.

[376] G. DALMAN, *The Words*, 141–142. See ID., *Die Worte*, 115.

[377] P.S. CAMERON, *Violence*, 96. See G. DALMAN, *Die Worte*, 114; and ID., *The Words*, 140.

[378] G. DALMAN, *Die Worte*, 115. The text may be thus translated: "the kingdom of Heaven [is] from the days of John and until now [it] is forced and those who use force rob [or 'use force against'] it". As the author himself (ID., *The Words*, 142) explains, however, "The words ἁρπάζουσιν αὐτήν, corresponding to אנסוהא, are not intended to suggest that the violent rulers seize the theocracy [die Gottesherrschaft], but that they maltreat it in the persons of its representatives". See, also, P.S. CAMERON, *Violence*, 96.

Greek" (als spezifisch griechisch)[379], since "neither the passive εὐαγγελίζεται nor εἰς αὐτὴν βιάζεται can go back to an Aramaic original"[380]. It is Luke himself who has actually reshaped v. 16 into its present form, "so as to accommodate the saying to the context"[381].

Regardless of all these new attempts, the impasse characterizing the interpretation of the "violence passage"[382] persists and, far from reaching a general consensus, the discussion risks becoming even more discordantly intricate. In fact, while "Dalman's אנס is followed by Schrenk [...] and by Black"[383], it is rejected by E. Percy, who opts for Dalman's first option (תקף), mainly because the latter (contrary to the former) can be used in the "reflexive-Passive Stem forms [...] with an intransitive sense"[384]. Other scholars will eventually propose yet more Semitic verbal roots for βιάζεται and/or ἁρπάζουσιν. Among these, we recall the following: חזק, meaning "to grow strong"[385]; כבש, signifying to "subdue, bring into bondage [...] force"[386]; דחק, with the sense of "forcing the end"[387]; גזל, which means to "tear away, seize"[388] and, apparently, also "invariably denotes violent robbery"[389]; חמץ, which, as a possible by-form of חמס, means "to be leavened [...] be sour, hence sharp, violent"[390]; and, last but not least, חבל, with its twofold meaning, to "bind" and "act (ruinously) corruptly [...] wound, injure"[391].

---

[379] G. DALMAN, The Words, 142. See ID., Die Worte, 116.

[380] P.S. CAMERON, Violence, 97. See G. DALMAN, Die Worte, 116; and ID., The Words, 142.

[381] G. DALMAN, The Words, 142. See ID., Die Worte, 116.

[382] W. STENGER, "βιάζομαι, βιαστής", EDNT, I, 216.

[383] P.S. CAMERON, Violence, 98. Note, however, how M. Black concurs, at the same time, with A. Resch, in proposing פרץ, while, as P.S. Cameron (Ibid., 130) notes, G. Schrenk "effectively ignores the implications of the work of Resch, Meyer, Dalman, etc.". See G. SCHRENK, "βιάζομαι, βιαστής", TDNT, I, 612–613; M. BLACK, An Aramaic Approach, 116, n. 1; Ibid., 211, n. 2; ID., "The Kingdom", 290, n. 2; and J. SCHLOSSER, "Le Règne", 524, n. 94.

[384] E. PERCY, Die Botschaft Jesu, 196, n. 7. See also Ibid., 191–202; and B.D. CHILTON, "The Violent Kingdom", 226–229.

[385] BDB, "חזק", 304. As G. Dalman (Die Worte, 114) and others point out, this Hebrew verb is often translated with תקף by the Aramaic versions. See, e.g., TO on Gen 48,2; TO on Num 13,20; TO on Deut 22,25; TJ on Judg 1,28; etc. Among the authors who support חזק, see, e.g., F. DELITZSCH, Die vier Evangelien, 18.137; and R. OTTO, The Kingdom, 110.

[386] BDB, "כבש", 461. Thus, e.g., see C.C. TORREY, Our Translated Gospels, 105.

[387] According to the BDB Lexicon ("דחק", 191), the verb literally means to "thrust, crowd, oppress", but it is used in the context of the messianic redemption to denote a hastening of its coming. See D. DAUBE, The New Testament, 291; and J.D.M. DERRETT, Jesus' Audience, 187–191.

[388] BDB, "גזל", 159.

[389] P.S. CAMERON, Violence, 144. See also Ibid., 143–147.183, n. 68.

[390] BDB, "חמץ", 329–330. See also NCWTM, "חמץ", II, 73–74; and P.S. CAMERON, Violence, 148–151.196, n. 104.

[391] BDB, "חבל", 286–287. See P. DI LUCCIO, "La giustizia", 39, n. 50.

For that reason, one can say that R.S. Notley is right when he remarks that "Suggesting Semitic equivalents for Greek terms is always a precarious task"[392].

It is no surprise then, if, as P.S. Cameron's study shows, the Semitic endeavor eventually leaves "the whole subject more wide open than before"[393]. In his assessment of the entire approach, indeed, the latter author concludes as follows:

The truth of the matter is that the investigation of the Semitic background is necessary precisely because the Greek translations are ambiguous and unsatisfactory and because therefore it is *not* known in advance what the saying means. Indeed the suggestions [...] that one or more words in the second half of Matt 11,12 may be secondary, or that one Semitic root may lie behind both halves, or that the original Aramaic or Hebrew may have had more than one meaning, throw doubt on the possibility of any control from the Greek texts[394].

II. The Question of the Jewish Background

Alongside this first line of enquiry into the saying's conjectural Semitic original, and prompted largely by A. Schweitzer's "eschatological or rather apocalyptic interpretations"[395] of the kingdom of God, there also arises in those years another significant approach to the discussion, which sees the desire for some fresher understanding of the text that may also take into consideration an examination of all its possible Jewish backgrounds.

As we have already mentioned, with the rise of modern scholarship, Schneckenburger already notes that βιάζεται's hostile violence can involve the Jewish belief that the Messianic time "could be, and had been, delayed and prevented by the sins of the people"[396]. Against this first assumption, nearly seventy years later, A. Schweitzer contends that the coming of the Messiah can be accelerated and advanced, specifically by "repentance and moral renewal" (Buße und sittliche Erneuerung)[397], in compliance with that prophetic and rabbinic notion which maintains that Israel would be redeemed by the faithful

---

[392] R.S. NOTLEY, "The Kingdom", 285.

[393] P.S. CAMERON, *Violence*, 93.

[394] P.S. CAMERON, *Violence*, 97.

[395] P.S. CAMERON, *Violence*, 129. See, e.g., A. SCHWEITZER, *The Quest*, 264–266.355.370–374; and P.S. CAMERON, *Violence*, 180, n. 124. For A. Schweitzer's interpretation of the kingdom of God, see, e.g., N. PERRIN, *The Kingdom*, 28–36; V. SUBILIA, *Il Regno*, 149–164; and J. RATZINGER, *Jesus*, I, 52.

[396] P.S. CAMERON, *Violence*, 85. See M. SCHNECKENBURGER, *Beiträge*, 49–51. See also H. SCHOLANDER, "Zu Mt. 11,12", 172–175; G. SCHRENK, "βιάζομαι, βιαστής", *TDNT*, I, 611, n. 13; and P.S. CAMERON, *Violence*, 45.

[397] A. SCHWEITZER, *Das Messianitäts*, 27. See also ID., *The Mystery*, 110–116.125.143–147.260–261; ID., *Reich Gottes*, 137; C. SPICQ, *Agapè*, I, 164–165; ID., *Théologie morale*, I, 214; and P.S. CAMERON, *Violence*, 75–76.

observance of the Law (see bShab 118b)[398]. Even in this case, the opinions that shall follow after these first two apparently opposite positions on the interpretation of the saying are, yet again, quite far from reaching a consensus.

Less than a decade later, W. Brandt argues against A. Schweitzer, on the basis of the proper Jewish understanding of the "expression מלכות שמיא"[399], for the kingdom of God, he claims, cannot be said to suffer violence[400]. However, Brandt's claim is confuted, firstly, by H. Scholander[401], on the grounds of several Talmudic and Midrashic passages (e.g., bKet 111a), and secondly, by P. Billerbeck[402]. The latter scholar, adding even more rabbinic examples, sees the βιασταί along with Joshua ben Levi's interpretation (see WaR 19.118d), as the "hasty of heart" (נמהרי־לב) of Isa 35,4, namely, those who wish "to force" (דחק) and "speed up the advent of the Messianic age"[403]. According to the Rabbis, this can actually be done in at least four different ways: a) through "even one day of penance" (auch nur Einen Tag Buße)[404]; b) through the faithful observance of "only two Sabbaths" (nur zwei Sabbate)[405]; c) through the study of the Torah "for its own sake" (um ihretwillen)[406]; and d) through works of "charity" (Wohltätigkeit)[407]. However, towards the end of his commentary, Billerbeck adds: "Israel will be redeemed (namely, in the days of the Messiah) only if they are all one"[408].

---

[398] See A. SCHWEITZER, *The Mystery*, 114. Among those scholars who shall closely follow Schweitzer's lead on the subject, see, e.g., E.F. SCOTT, "The Kingdom", 462–463; ID., *The Kingdom*, 139–145; F. DIBELIUS, "Der Spruch", 285–288; and M. WERNER, *Die Entstehung*, 70–71. For instance, C.S. Keener (*Matthew*, 340) remarks: "One second-century Jewish tradition praises those who passionately pursue the law by saying that God counts it as if they had ascended to Heaven and taken the law forcibly, which the tradition regards as greater than having taken it peaceably (SifDev 49.2.1). These were the people actively following Jesus, not simply waiting for the kingdom to come their way".

[399] W. BRANDT, "Matthäus", 247–248.

[400] Schweitzer's idea, as to the possibility of forcing God by repentance and fulfilment of the Law, shall likewise be criticized by J. Schniewind (*Matthäus*, 144), who attributes it to a misguided pious Pharisaic hope, and by C. Stratton ("Pressure", 414), who affirms that such a thing would be like "to mock the sovereignty of God". See also W. MICHAELIS, *Der Herr*, 66–70; and W.D. CHAMBERLAIN, "Till the Son of Man", 6.

[401] Contrary to W. Brandt, H. Scholander ("Zu Mt. 11,12", 175) argues that "Der Gedanke, dass das Gottesreich Gewalt erleidet […], ist dann von jüdischen Standpunkt aus völlig verständlich".

[402] See Str-B, I, 598–601; and P.S. CAMERON, *Violence*, 85–87.

[403] Str-B, I, 599.

[404] Str-B, I, 599.

[405] Str-B, I, 600. See also A. SCHWEITZER, *The Mystery*, 114.

[406] Str-B, I, 600.

[407] Str-B, I, 600.

[408] Str-B, I, 600. On the eschatological "unitedness" (יחד) and its Messianic understanding among the members of the Qumran community, see, e.g., O. BETZ, "The Eschatological Interpretation", 90–91.

Most of these assertions, however, are again rejected, a few years later, by W. Michaelis[409], but reconciled by D. Daube[410], who maintains that, for the Rabbis and Jesus' contemporary Jewish milieu, repentance and good deeds go together in forcing the end, and should not be separated[411]. In reality, Daube goes over almost all previous suggestions of a possible Jewish background to the saying and mentions more than a few Jewish sources, some of which refer to "tearing off" (פרק)[412] the yoke of the Law and the kingdom of Heaven[413]; others to the simultaneous "oppression" and "robbing" (אנס)[414] of the poor, heralding the end[415]; some others, consistent with the Fathers' interpretation, speak of the "impudent" (חוצפא)[416] prayer as that which can actually "conquer" (נצח)[417] or "seize hold of" (תפש)[418] God[419]; and still others imply a legitimate kind of violence, in the verbs "to invade" (גוד)[420] and "to urge" (דחק)[421]. However, as P.S. Cameron notes:

> Daube has, of course wittingly, confounded this confusion: in his discussion there appears a plethora of possible roots behind every interpretation. He suggests at least a dozen candidates for βιάζεται, and at least half-a-dozen for ἁρπάζουσιν[422].

Moreover, Daube also repeats most of the previous interpretations. Thus, along with A. Resch, P.P. Levertoff and H.L. Goudge (and against F.C. Burkitt), he supports the idea that the saying might refer to the messianic "breaking out" (פרץ)[423] of the kingdom of God and that, according to some rabbinic interpretations of Mic 2,13, the Messiah and the βιασταί would respectively be a direct descendent of Perez (cf. Gen 38,29) and his followers (פרצים)[424]. In addition to their attention to the double meaning of פרץ, and recalling

---

[409] See W. MICHAELIS, *Der Herr*, 68–70; and P.S. CAMERON, *Violence*, 87.

[410] See D. DAUBE, *The New Testament*, 285–300; and P.S. CAMERON, *Violence*, 87–89.

[411] See, e.g., bBer 64a; bSan 97b; MekhSh on Exod 13,19 (ed. W.D. Nelson, 82); 1QS I.13–15; 1QpHab VII.1–2; and D. DAUBE, *The New Testament*, 289–293.

[412] BDB, "פרק", 830. See, e.g., Gen 27,40.

[413] See, e.g., mAv 3.5; tSot 14.1; A. BÜCHLER, *Sin*, 36–45.52–55.94–96.81–88.117–118.161.465–457; and D. DAUBE, *The New Testament*, 287.

[414] See, e.g., Dan 4,6. Cf. BDB, "אנס", 1081; and *HALOT*, "אנס", II, 1818.

[415] See, e.g., BerR 32.2; and D. DAUBE, *The New Testament*, 288.

[416] BDB, "חצף", 1093. Cf. *HALOT*, "חצף", II, 1879. See, e.g., Dan 2,15–16.23; and 3,22.

[417] BDB, "נצח", 663.

[418] BDB, "תפש", 1074.

[419] See, e.g., bBer 32a; bSan 105a; PesK 161a; and D. DAUBE, *The New Testament*, 290.

[420] BDB, "נוד", 156.

[421] *HALOT*, "דחק", I, 219. See, e.g., bBer 64a; and D. DAUBE, *The New Testament*, 291.

[422] P.S. CAMERON, *Violence*, 99.

[423] BDB, "פרץ", 829.

[424] See, e.g., BerR 38.29; *Ibid.*, 85; bSuk 26a; A. RESCH, *Aussercanonische*, II, 439–442; P.P. LEVERTOFF – H.L. GOUDGE, "The Gospel", 154; F.C. BURKITT, "PHARES", 254–258; D. DAUBE, *The New Testament*, 289; and O. BETZ, "The Eschatological Interpretation", 106–107.

Harnack's observation that the Lucan εὐαγγελίζεται is also found in Matt 11,5, Daube sees the further possibility that the Gospel preaching might have already been connected with the exertion of violence at the level of their common source (*Q*)[425].

Furthermore, adding to Billerbeck's reference to Isa 35,4, he also notes how even its most immediate context (i.e., Isa 35,5–6) is closely related to that of Matt 11,12 (cf. Matt 11,5)[426], and referring to another "tenable explanation"[427] – which claims that Elijah's second coming shall have the specific function of removing and restoring to the nation those families that were respectively restored and removed "by force" (בזרוע)[428] – he additionally suggests that, not only the Matthean, but also the Lucan version of the saying "may proceed from this tradition"[429].

His real conclusion, however, tends to an altogether "different solution"[430]. According to another rabbinic tradition, Solomon is charged in Heaven and reproached for having cancelled the *yod* (י) from the precept, "He shall not multiply [לא ירבה] wives for himself" (Deut 17,17), thus assuming that he could actually have "a multitude [לארבה] of wives for himself" (see 1Kgs 11,1–4)[431]. Daube ultimately maintains that the "violence passage"[432] may allude to this tradition and imply that John the Baptist, in his advent as the second "Elijah who is to come" ('Ηλίας ὁ μέλλων ἔρχεσθαι)[433], "whatever his powers may be, has not abrogated the Law"[434], nor committed adultery (see, e.g., Matt 5,18;

---

[425] See D. DAUBE, *The New Testament*, 293–295. Besides the "double meaning of breaking and spreading, hence Luke's variant '[…] is preached', i.e., spread", P.P. Levertoff and H.L. Goudge ("The Gospel", 154–155) state further that, according to the Talmud (e.g., bBer 34b; bShab 63a; bSan 99a), "All the prophets, and indeed the Law before them […] prophesied for the days of the Messiah". See also R.S. NOTLEY, "The Kingdom", 280.

[426] See Str-B, I, 599; and D. DAUBE, *The New Testament*, 291.

[427] D. DAUBE, *The New Testament*, 297.

[428] D. DAUBE, *The New Testament*, 297. See, e.g., bQid 70a; mEd 8.7; and BDB, "זרוע", 283–284.

[429] D. DAUBE, *The New Testament*, 297. See, e.g., F. WEBER, *Jüdische Theologie*, 352–353; P. VOLZ, *Jüdische Eschatologie*, 192–193; W.C. ALLEN, *Matthew*, 118; J. MOFFATT, *The Theology*, 51–52; J.M.D. DERRETT, *Law*, 84.358–360; P.S. CAMERON, *Violence*, 89–90; and R.S. NOTLEY, "The Kingdom", 289–291.

[430] D. DAUBE, *The New Testament*, 298.

[431] See, e.g., ShemR 6.1–2; ShirR 11.12; WaR 19.2; ySan 2.6; *Ibid.*, 20c; and D. DAUBE, *The New Testament*, 298. See also A.R.C. LEANEY, *Luke*, 224; E. BAMMEL, "Any deyathiqi", 355–358; W.G. KÜMMEL, "'Das Gesetz'", 403; and S.R. LLEWELYN, "The Traditionsgeschichte", 337–338.

[432] W. STENGER, "βιάζομαι, βιαστής", *EDNT*, I, 216.

[433] Matt 11,14.

[434] D. DAUBE, *The New Testament*, 300.

11,14; and Luke 16,16–18), as one might have nonetheless expected "in the New Testament era [...] Hence the importance of making it clear"[435].

Overall, however, and in spite of all this evidence supporting Jewish backgrounds, Daube appends to his conclusion – as one would probably expect at this point – the following final and unhappy remark: "in both Matthew and Luke, the saying [...] with the area surrounding it is a *Trümmerfeld*, a heap of ruins"[436].

Thus, Daube retrieves his very first and foremost compromise:

all interpretations to be found in modern literature, and quite a few not to be found, are reconcilable with a Jewish milieu. In fact, Rabbinic texts do not enable us to arbitrate [...] we cannot clear up the meaning of the saying[437].

Lastly, since, in his judgment, almost all interpretations seem equally plausible, many of the scholars referring to him shall, as a result, have the further possibility of discordantly picking any of them, indifferently, not only from a linguistic Greek angle but, henceforth, even when arguing from the perspective of a Jewish milieu. Along with P.S. Cameron, one could then conclude and wonder:

Has the investigation of the Semitic background achieved anything? J. Weiss said in 1900 that few of the results were at all convincing, and this judgment must still stand [...] Daube's contribution has been to show that there are so many Semitic roots that could conceivably be translated by βιάζεσθαι that more or less any interpretation can plausibly appeal to a Semitic ancestor[438].

III. The Question of the Historical and Narrative Context

Finally, among the most distinctive lines of inquiry, which progressively mark the exegesis of the verse in this last period, one cannot but mention the increasing consideration given to the significance of both the historical and narrative contexts of the saying, as the attempts to unlock its hermeneutic deadlock still persist.

---

[435] D. DAUBE, *The New Testament*, 296. See, e.g., Mal 3,23; Deut 18,15; SifDev 175 (ed. L. FINKELSTEIN, 221); and D. DAUBE, *The New Testament*, 296.298–300. In addition to all of these possible Jewish backgrounds, one could still mention, for example, O. Betz's remarks ("The Eschatological Interpretation", 99–104) on bSan 94a and MekhSh on Exod 15,18 (ed. W.D. Nelson, 156–157), according to which, when robbers and those who rob the robbers come, Israel's redemption shall be near and God's kingship shall be acknowledged in the world. See, e.g., 1QH II.10–16.20–29; VI.25–36; Matt 12,28–29; Matt 21,32–44; P.S. CAMERON, *Violence*, 110–112; and A. GUCCIONE, "Il cielo", 452, n. 19.

[436] D. DAUBE, *The New Testament*, 300.

[437] D. DAUBE, *The New Testament*, 285.

[438] P.S. CAMERON, *Violence*, 130–131. See J. WEISS, *Die Predigt*, 197.

On the subject of the historical context, for example, P.S. Cameron traces a "tendency to 'historicize' the saying"[439] already back to Hilary of Poitiers, Jerome of Stridon and Gregory the Great and, then again, also to P. Melanchthon[440]. The former three Latin Fathers, in fact, supposedly consider this saying as "a response to a historical event"[441] – namely, God's transfer of salvation from Jews to Gentiles, in and through Christ – while the latter Reformed theologian interprets Matt 11,12 "primarily as describing an actual historical reception of the gospel μετὰ σπουδῆς"[442], as opposed to a simple plea to receive it. However, it is predominantly in the past couple of centuries that there progressively arises a perception that the verse's incomprehensibility might also be due to one's own ignorance of the precise "historical context" (geschichtlichen Zusammenhang)[443] in which the sentence may have been uttered, and accordingly the research begins to revolve also around the development of its possible historical origin and transmission[444].

Overall, the leading conviction inspiring these hermeneutic approaches eventually appears to be the following one:

"the sentence cannot be interpreted as a general basic principle ('only violent perpetrators get into the kingdom'), but as an ascertainment of actual historical facts"[445].

The latter belief and its tendentially *in malam partem* solutions often appear to mirror a 20th century secularist and "post-Christian"[446] vision of the kingdom, in which God's good tidings (cf. εὐαγγελίζεται: Luke 16,16b!) are often

---

[439] P.S. CAMERON, *Violence*, 48.

[440] See P.S. CAMERON, *Violence*, 155–156.

[441] P.S. CAMERON, *Violence*, 155. See also *Ibid.*, 11–19.

[442] P.S. CAMERON, *Violence*, 48. See P. MELANCHTHON, *Annotationes*, 839–842. Likewise, P.S. Cameron (*Violence*, 48) continues: "Similarly, Eckermann and Schneckenburger refer [...] to a particular historical phenomenon and not [...] a universally applicable maxim". See, e.g., M. BUCER, *Enarrationes*, 111b–d; J. CALVIN, *Commentarius*, 303–304; ID., *A Harmony*, II, 7–8; J.C.R. ECKERMANN, *Erklärung*, I, 61; M. SCHNECKENBURGER, *Beiträge*, 48–52; and P.S. CAMERON, *Violence*, 35–38.44–45.

[443] J. SCHMID, *Matthäus*, 192. See also A. SCHWEITZER, *Von Reimarus*, 263; M. GOGUEL, *Au seuil*, 68–69; J.M.D. DERRETT, *Law*, 48; P.H. MENOUD, "Le sens", 207–208; E. TROCMÉ, *Jésus*, 47; and P.S. CAMERON, *Violence*, 102.

[444] See, e.g., E. BAMMEL, "Is Luke 16,16–18", 101–106; F.W. DANKER, "Luke 16,16", 241–243; D.R. CATCHPOLE, "On Doing Violence", 50–61; ID., *The Quest*, 45–46.232–241; B.D. CHILTON, "The Violent Kingdom", 203–230; D. KOSCH, *Die Gottesherrschaft*, 19–64; ID., *Die eschatologische Tora*, 427–444; S. LLEWELYN, "The Traditionsgeschichte", 330–349; C.M. TUCKETT, *Q*, 135–137.404–409; C. HEIL, *Lukas*, 119–127.136–140; D. MARGUERAT, "Le règne", 113–127; H.T. FLEDDERMANN, *Q*, 781–792; J. VERHEYDEN, "The Violators", 397–415; and S.J. JOSEPH, "For Heaven", 169–188.

[445] J. SCHMID, *Matthäus*, 192. See, e.g., E. NEUHÄUSLER, *Anspruch*, 84, n. 140; and P. HOFFMANN, *Studien*, 67.71.

[446] J. RATZINGER, *Jesus*, I, 55.

pushed off the exegetical stage and their place gradually taken over by utterly human energy and reasoning[447]. In fact, as the saying is progressively reduced to mere human explanations, entirely consistent with man's world and history, the universally edifying reference of faith and tradition is slowly put aside and often disqualified as disparagingly obsolete or too "ascetic" (ascetischen)[448]. As commented by J. Ratzinger:

It seems like a way of finally enabling the whole world to appropriate Jesus' message, but without requiring missionary evangelization[449].

In other words, the Gospel "violent" saying progressively seems to communicate no longer an extemporal good news, universally valid for and worth proclaiming to all readers, but a concrete hostile situation of NT history, which merely occurs in a given place and time, and is narrowly applicable only to a few intended people.

Beginning from this observation, the historical evidence is progressively examined, and the actual starting point of the saying and potential referents gradually become some of the exegetes' major concerns. Thus, P. Hoffmann argues that the violence of the *Q*-saying might point to the actual situation of persecutions that the early Christians suffer during the Jewish War, as they

---

[447] See, e.g., K. LÖWITH, *Meaning*, 42.208–213; V. SUBILIA, *Il Regno*, 46–49.103–148; J. RATZINGER, *Das Heil*, 63–83; and ID., *Jesus*, I, 52–55.

[448] A. SCHWEIZER, "Ob in der Stelle", 107. See also P.S. CAMERON, *Violence*, 20.29–30.47. On the contrary, the biblical exegesis of the early interpreters, both Jewish and Christians, was closely linked with faith and tradition, also because it presupposed their existence, already in the very authors and literary genres of the sacred texts. See, e.g., G.I. GARGANO, *Il sapore*, 45–54.204–205.

[449] J. RATZINGER, *Jesus*, I, 54. Thus, analyzing the scholars' change of perspectives and research areas as to the topic of violence and the kingdom (e.g., from S.G.F. Brandon and M. Hengel, to J. Jeremias, H. Schürmann and others), following the 1960s and 1970s M. Gourgues ("Jésus et la violence", 126.131–132.135.136) observes a shift from an understanding of Jesus as subject to object of violence and from its positive to a negative interpretation: "durant les années 1960 et surtout vers la fin de la décennie [...] la violence sur laquelle on s'interroge en rapport avec Jésus est une violence d'orientation ou à signification socio-politique [...] on assiste depuis à un changement assez net de perspectives. Alors que la ligne précédente de recherche s'intéressait à Jésus comme sujet ou auteur éventuel de violence, celle qui prédomine maintenant le considère comme objet ou victime de la violence [...] la violence n'est plus située d'abord dans une perspective collective, en tant que moyen de libération socio-politique, mais dans une perspective individuelle, en tant qu'assumée comme expérience personnelle. Ou encore on pourrait dire qu'il ne s'agit plus d'une violence 'positive', c'est-à-dire pointant vers un au-delà positif – comme une libération nationale – mais d'une violence 'négative', absurde, liée à la mort et faisant de celle-ci un échec et un martyre [...] Pensons par exemple au *logion* sur les violents (Matt 11,12 par.)". For M. Gourgues' overview of the interpretation of the latter *logion*, see, esp., *Ibid.*, 141–142.

refuse "to join the revolutionaries"[450], whereas for B.D. Chilton and R. Bultmann, respectively, it would be "best viewed in the context of Temple controversy about John and the law"[451] and the "rivalry between the Christian and the Baptist communities"[452]. P.S. Cameron reads the saying in connection to Luke 13,31–32 and identifies its original Lucan/*Q* context with "a small collection of anti-Herod sayings"[453], deducing as follows: "The saying was probably uttered after the Baptist's death, and perhaps on the occasion of Herod's threat to Jesus"[454].

Similarly, M.W. Bates detects in it a denouncement and a criticism of Herod Antipas, but, as specified by the author, his "proposal goes beyond any previous suggestions in arguing that Jesus [...] is *deliberately speaking in code*"[455]. Thus, according to the author, the saying ultimately expresses the sociopolitical dissatisfaction of an oppressed community by means of veiled remarks and a cryptic language[456].

As regards the possible referents of the term βιασταί, the proposed list of historical characters is definitely quite long and multifarious. We have already mentioned how, for M. Schneckenburger, their violence seems to indicate mainly a Pharisaic opposition to Jesus[457], whereas, for A. Schweizer, they may well represent some Zealotic historically hostile movement[458]. According to F.F. Zyro, their group is marked by a specifically antinomian inclination and would be composed by "those who misunderstand the way in which the law

---

[450] J. VERHEYDEN, "The Violators", 404. See P. HOFFMANN, *Studien*, 71–79.

[451] B.D. CHILTON, "The Violent Kingdom", 223.

[452] R. BULTMANN, *The History*, 164. Cf. A. VON HARNACK, "Zwei Worte", 957.

[453] P.S. CAMERON, *Violence*, 158. See also *Ibid.*, 147–148.152–153.158.

[454] P.S. CAMERON, *Violence*, 158.

[455] M.W. BATES, "Cryptic Codes", 75. Cf., e.g., D.J. WEAVER, "'Suffering Violence'", 10–11.

[456] More precisely, as stated by Bates (*Ibid.*, 76), "Antipas's brutal treatment of John the Baptist created just such a threatening and unstable situation for Jesus – that is, Luke 16,16–18 and Matt 11,12 reflect a *Sitz im Leben* of the historical Jesus in which it was safer and more cleverly pointed to make coded, derisive allusions to Antipas' well-known misconduct than to say such things forthrightly". See, e.g., *Ibid.*, 80–83.88–93. However, as specified by G. Rossé (*Luca*, 637) in regard to v. 18, in paricular: "La forma del *loghion* (stile giuridico) non permette di considerare il detto una parola occasionale di Gesù pronunciata per criticare il comportamento di Erode Antipa che ha ripudiato la propria moglie (la figlia del re nabateo Areta) per sposare una maritata (Erodiade)".

[457] See, e.g., M. SCHNECKENBURGER, *Beiträge*, 49. See also A. HILGENFELD, *Die Evangelien*, 75, n. 2; L. PAUL, *Die Vorstellungen*, 54–56; W.E. MOORE, "ΒΙΑΖΩ, ΑΡΠΑΖΩ", 540–543, P.S. CAMERON, *Violence*, 45.61.108.113; and J. VERHEYDEN, "The Violators", 405–410.

[458] See, e.g., A. SCHWEIZER, "Ob in der Stelle", 108–113. See also A.F. GFRÖRER, *Geschichte*, II.1, 91–98; J. WEISS, *Die Predigt*, 196–197; P. HOFFMANN, *Studien*, 76–79; and P.S. CAMERON, *Violence*, 52–56.108.

has been superseded"[459], while, for M. Dibelius, O. Betz, and others, they would symbolise the devil and his earthly powers, also by analogy with Belial and the Qumran's opponents, the *'ārîṣîm* (עריצים)[460].

Behind the label "violent ones", F.W. Danker discerns the Christians themselves, but as designated by their adversaries[461], and J. Schröter recognizes the opponents of the *Q* community, who essentially reject their Gospel preaching[462]. Finally, on the evidence of the Qumran literature, B.E. Thiering sees in the βιασταί "false teachers of the kind who are referred to in John 10,10–13"[463], thieves who lay their hands on the kingdom as on doctrinal booty, whereas many others distinguish in them some allusion to the actual person of Herod Antipas[464] and either Jesus himself and/or John the Baptist, with or without their disciples[465].

In other words, in the last couple of centuries, the "violence passage"[466] is slowly interpreted with reference to some specific occurrence or historical group, as opposed to its more traditional and long-running understanding of a "timeless moral"[467], but still no consensus has been reached.

---

[459] P.S. CAMERON, *Violence*, 65. See F.F. ZYRO, "Neue Auslegung", 674–675.682–686.694. For a completely opposite opinion, cf., e.g., W.D. CHAMBERLAIN, "Till the Son of Man", 7.

[460] See, e.g., M. DIBELIUS, *Die urchristliche Überlieferung*, 23–25; R. OTTO, *The Kingdom*, 108–111; O. BETZ, "Jesu", 127–129; ID., "The Eschatological Interpretation", 102–105; M. HENGEL, *Die Zeloten*, 345; and P.S. CAMERON, *Violence*, 110–113.131.

[461] See F.W. DANKER, "Luke 16,16", 231–243 (esp. 234–236). Likewise, see G. BRAUMANN, "'Dem Himmelreich'", 107–109; E. NEUHÄUSLER, *Anspruch*, 81–86; R. BANKS, *Jesus*, 220; J. SCHLOSSER, "Le Règne", 522; G. THEIßEN, "Jünger", 200; D. MARGUERAT, "Le règne", 121; and J. VERHEYDEN, "The Violators", 407–409. However, cf. D.J. IRELAND, *Stewardship*, 131, n. 70.

[462] See J. SCHRÖTER, "Erwägungen", 450. See also J. VERHEYDEN, "The Violators", 404, n. 29.

[463] B.E. THIERING, "Are the 'Violent Men'", 297. See *Ibid.*, 293–297; and P.S. CAMERON, *Violence*, 167–169.

[464] See F.E.D. SCHLEIERMACHER, *Über die Schriften*, 206–208; A. VON SCHLATTER, *Matthäus*, 368; ID., *Johannes*, 66–75; W. MICHAELIS, *Der Herr*, 66–70; G. SCHRENK, "βιάζομαι, βιαστής", *TDNT*, I, 612–614; A.R.C. LEANEY, *Luke*, 224; P.S. CAMERON, *Violence*, 152–154.158; and M.W. BATES, "Cryptic Codes", 74–93.

[465] See, e.g., B. WEISS, *Matthäus*, 218–219; C.H. WEISSE, *Die evangelische Geschichte*, II, 70–72; J.P. LANGE, *Matthäus*, 159–162; F.F. ZYRO, "Erklärung", 401–402; S. COX, "Spiritual Forces", 258–259; K.F. NÖSGEN, *Die Evangelien*, 68; A. SCHWEITZER, *Von Reimarus*, 354; A. FRIDRICHSEN, "Neutestamentliche", 470–471; C. STRATTON, "Pressure", 414–420; E. BAMMEL, "Is Luke 16,16–18", 101–106; F.W. DANKER, "Luke 16,16", 240–241; P.W. BARNETT, "Who Were the 'Biastai'", 65–70; J. SCHLOSSER, "Le Règne", 522; W. STENGER, "βιάζομαι, βιαστής", *EDNT*, I, 218–219; G. THEIßEN, "Jünger", 193–194; and C.S. KEENER, *Matthew*, 340.

[466] W. STENGER, "βιάζομαι, βιαστής", *EDNT*, I, 216.

[467] P.S. CAMERON, *Violence*, 155.

In ascertaining the proper understanding of the saying, and linked to such a historical investigation, wide exegetical consideration is progressively given also to its narrative formation and development. New attempts are thus made to critically explain the saying as "a literary development of certain fundamental ideas and suggestions present in Mark"[468] (B. Bauer), "an early stage of John 1,17"[469] (A. von Harnack), or as a genuine account, which may either be wholly consistent with the tradition shown in Justin Martyr (C.H. Weisse)[470], or even partly lengthened with "an anti-Pauline twist"[471] (F.C. Bauer). Nowadays, the majority of researchers considers Matthew's as the most difficult and, therefore, original wording of the βία-saying, whereas they see Luke's as keeping the most primitive order of the clauses[472]. However, even in this case, as G. Theißen notes, "this is not a general consensus"[473].

A similar disagreement applies also to the reconstruction of the original Greek wording of the saying in Q[474]. On the one hand, as P.S. Cameron observes, "the most widely held opinion"[475] holds on to the following form:

[a] The Law and the Prophets up to John;

[b] since then the kingdom of God *biázetai*

[c] and the *biastái* seize it[476].

---

[468] P.S. CAMERON, *Violence*, 57. See B. BAUER, *Kritik*, II, 244–268.

[469] P.S. CAMERON, *Violence*, 180, n. 111. See A. VON HARNACK, "Zwei Worte", 947.

[470] "[a]Ὁ νόμος καὶ οἱ προφῆται μέχρι Ἰωάννου τοῦ βαπτιστοῦ· [b]ἐξ ὅτου ἡ βασιλεία τῶν οὐρανῶν βιάζεται [c]καὶ βιασταὶ ἁρπάζουσιν αὐτήν" (JUSTIN MARTYR, *Dial.* LI.3a). See, e.g., C.H. WEISSE, *Die evangelische Geschichte*, II, 70–72; J.M. ROBINSON – P. HOFFMANN – J.S. KLOPPENBORG, ed., *The Critical Edition*, 465; and P. BOBICHON, ed., *Justin Martyr*, I, 314–315.

[471] P.S. CAMERON, *Violence*, 61. See F.C. BAUER, *Kritische Untersuchungen*, 615–621. See also P.S. CAMERON, *Ibid.*, 57–58.60–61.177, ns. 30–32; and *Ibid.*, 180, n. 111.

[472] See, e.g., J. WEISS, *Die Predigt*, 192–195; G. THEIßEN, "Jünger", 185, n. 5; R.A. EDWARDS, "Matthew's Use", 263–265; J.A. FITZMYER, *Luke*, II, 1115.1118; G. ROSSÉ, *Luca*, 632–633; and S. LLEWELYN, "The Traditionsgeschichte", 333–349.

[473] G. THEIßEN, "Jünger", 184, n. 3. See, e.g., T.W. MANSON, *The Sayings*, 134; S. SCHULZ, *Q*, 261; H.M. MERKLEIN, *Die Gottesherrschaft*, 87; and J. SCHLOSSER, "Le Règne", 512. Among those who argue in favour of an original Matthean order, see, e.g., J. WEISS, *Die Predigt*, 192–197; and P. HOFFMANN, *Studien*, 51–60.

[474] For the whole discussion, see H. SCHÜRMANN, "Das Zeugnis", 169–171; P. HOFFMANN, *Studien*, 51–79; and G. ROSSÉ, *Luca*, 629, n. 41.

[475] P.S. CAMERON, *Violence*, 124.

[476] "[a]Ὁ νόμος καὶ οἱ προφῆται ἕως Ἰωάννου· [b]ἀπὸ τότε ἡ βασιλεία τοῦ θεοῦ βιάζεται [c]καὶ βιασταὶ ἁρπάζουσιν αὐτήν" (*Q* 16,16). See, e.g., S. SCHULZ, *Q*, 262; H.M. MERKLEIN, *Die Gottesherrschaft*, 87; A. POLAG, *Fragmenta*, 74; D. KOSCH, *Die Gottesherrschaft*, 18.79; ID., *Die eschatologische Tora*, 432; J. GNILKA, *Das Matthäusevangelium*, I, 413; D.R. CATCHPOLE, *The Quest*, 234; G. THEIßEN, "Jünger", 185; J.M. ROBINSON – P. HOFFMANN – J.S. KLOPPENBORG, ed., *The Critical Edition*, 464–466;

On the other hand, discordant views are not lacking. B.D. Chilton prefers both the Lucan preposition "until" (μέχρι), in Q 16,16a, and the sentence, "every one biázetai eis it" (πᾶς εἰς αὐτὴν βιάζεται), as Q 16,16c, while D.R. Catchpole eventually changes his mind altogether with regard to his first proposed solution[477]. Likewise, on the subject of the abovementioned Q text, P.S. Cameron mistakenly (?) reports the Matthean expression, kingdom "of Heaven" (τῶν οὐρανῶν), rather than "of God" (τοῦ θεοῦ)[478], and eventually comments:

There are two objections to this reconstruction. First, it does not take into account the words ἕως ἄρτι which, as J. Weiss and M. Dibelius argue, are more likely to have been omitted than added, and second, it implies that the words ἀπὸ δὲ τῶν ἡμερῶν Ἰωάννου, which have a strong Semitic flavor, were added after the saying was translated into Greek[479].

Overall, inasmuch as it entails some "community reconstruction"[480], most of these authors might be said to agree at least in their equal presupposition that the saying must obviously be a later invention. However, not everyone shares this conviction. Many other scholars, as we have already pointed out, consider the verse as rather an expression of Jesus' present perception of the kingdom, his messianic consciousness or theology, and thus maintain that it must necessarily belong to one of his own authentic utterances[481].

Finally, as the question comes to the two different narrative/literary contexts in which the saying is currently found, the exegetical explanations equally disagree, especially as to whether the proximate verses are either "inherited from a source or [...] the result of redactional activity"[482]. On the one hand, the relevance of "both the immediate context and that of the chapter as a whole"[483] is firstly valued by A. Schweizer[484], and then, even more seriously emphasized by F.F. Zyro[485], although the latter understands it in view of his differing antinomian solution[486]. Likewise, by a comparison of the previous chapter's

---

C. HEIL, *Lukas*, 125; D. MARGUERAT, "Le règne", 116; H.T. FLEDDERMANN, *Q*, 783; H. KLEIN, *Das Lukasevangelium*, 546; and J. VERHEYDEN, "The Violators", 399.

[477] See B.D. CHILTON, "The Violent Kingdom", 223; D.R. CATCHPOLE, "On Doing Violence", 57; and ID., *The Quest*, 234.

[478] See P.S. CAMERON, *Violence*, 124.188, n. 192.

[479] P.S. CAMERON, *Violence*, 124. See J. WEISS, *Die Predigt*, 194–195; and M. DIBELIUS, *Die urchristliche Überlieferung*, 24.28–29.

[480] P.S. CAMERON, *Violence*, 126.

[481] See, e.g., P.S. CAMERON, *Violence*, 125–129.

[482] P.S. CAMERON, *Violence*, 134. See also *Ibid.*, 134–141.

[483] P.S. CAMERON, *Violence*, 64.

[484] See A. SCHWEIZER, "Ob in der Stelle", 98–102.

[485] See F.F. ZYRO, "Neue Auslegung", 674–675.

[486] As P.S. Cameron (*Violence*, 63) remarks, F.F. Zyro further distinguishes between "kingdom of God" (βασιλεία τοῦ θεοῦ: Luke 16,16b) and "kingdom of Heaven" (βασιλεία τῶν οὐρανῶν: Matt 11,12b), with "the latter having Christ instead of God at its centre" and being, rather, spiritually invisible and abstract within the hearts of believers. However,

Lucan parable (see Luke 15,11–32) with the Matthean contextual reference to the *metánoia*-preacher (see Matt 3,1–2; and 11,2–15), B. Ralph later underlines repentance as that which "must be violently striven for"[487], and eventually points to the Prodigal Son as the typical βιαστής[488].

Similarly, as to the subject of the Lucan (vs. Matthew's) adjacent verses, not a few of these exegetes contend, on the one hand, that Luke 16,16 receives a considerable amount of light from v. 14, which mentions the Pharisees and their love of money[489]. For most of them, the evangelist has purposely placed Luke 16,15–18 in between vv. 1–13 and vv. 19–31, with v. 14 functioning as a sort of introduction, and it is their conviction that it must accordingly be interpreted in connection with the thematic thread of chapter 16, namely, the right use of riches[490]. Thus, C. Lavergne, for instance, comments: "the [only] way to enter is using some energy and a certain [kind of] violence, which consists in making friends by means of cumbersome riches"[491].

On the other hand, M. Dibelius and others argue that the saying must have originally been foreign to both Gospel narrations[492]. If, in keeping with the results of form, source and redaction criticism, "the Matthean and Lucan

---

on the word of P.S. Cameron (*Ibid.*, 66.73), such a distinction shall eventually be "shown to be untenable", for example, by G. Dalman, whereas quite a number of interpreters (e.g., S. Cox, W. Baldensperger, A. Schweitzer, A. von Harnack, etc.) shall subsequently hold on only to a "spiritualised, indeed etherialised concept of the kingdom". See, e.g., F.F. Zyro, "Neue Auslegung", 663–700; G. Dalman, *Die Worte*, 113–116; and P.S. Cameron, *Ibid.*, 68.73.80–81.

[487] P.S. Cameron, *Violence*, 103.

[488] See B. Ralph, "The Kingdom", 427; and P.S. Cameron, *Violence*, 103. By the same token, while underscoring the importance of the context in Matt 11,12, C. Stratton ("Pressure", 415) expresses his astonishment before the fact that, attracted by this single verse, most commentators have totally forgotten all the rest. On the importance of the Matthean context, see, e.g., G. Strecker, *Der Weg*, 168; A. Kretzer, *Die Herrschaft*, 65–77; and P.S. Cameron, *Violence*, 137.192, n. 24.

[489] See, e.g, C. Stratton, "Pressure", 418.

[490] See, e.g., H.J. Holtzmann, *Die Synoptiker*, 387–388; A. Jülicher, *Die Gleichnisreden*, II, 632–641; E. Klostermann, *Lukasevangelium*, 161; A. Plummer, *Luke*, 379–380; J.-M. Lagrange, *Luc*, 438; F. Hauck, *Lukas*, 206–207; W. Grundmann, *Lukas*, 319; K.H. Rengstorf, *Lukas*, 187; H. Schürmann, "*'Wer daher eines'*", 245–249; E.E. Ellis, *Luke*, 201–202; P. Hoffmann, *Studien*, 54–55; K.E. Bailey, *Poet*, 116–117; J. Ernst, *Lukas*, 468–469; C.H. Talbert, *Reading Luke*, 183–188; E. Lupieri, *Giovanni Battista*, 67–68; W. Wiefel, *Lukas*, 291; D.J. Ireland, *Stewardship*, 128–139; R.A. Piper, "Social Background", 1654–1660; C.-S.A. Cheong, *A Dialogic Reading*, 119; R. Meynet, *Luc*, 650–652; and J. Verheyden, "The Violators", 412–413.

[491] C. Lavergne, *Luc*, 193.

[492] See, e.g., M. Dibelius, *Die urchristliche Überlieferung*, 23; F.W. Danker, "Luke 16,16", 241–243; G. Braumann, "'Dem Himmelreich'", 105–106; and J. Schlosser, "Le Règne", 510.

contexts are independent and secondary"[493], then, the saying must rather be interpreted separately, and "neither context can give any help in exegesis"[494]. According to these other authors, the Lucan vv. 15(16)–18 are too noticeably incomprehensible and logically unrelated to be key in the understanding of either chapter or verse 16[495]. Ultimately, what should really guide the interpretation of the latter verse, for them, is not so much the context[496] as the evangelist's theology, which is, however, "reflected in a different context"[497].

E. Final Remarks and Preliminary Questions

As we have had the occasion to note, unfortunately, even the solutions and arguments proposed in the last decades have ultimately been unable to change the previous stalled situation characterizing the understanding of the "violence passage"[498], from the very rise of modern scholarship and all through the years separating Schweizer's article from Harnack's. This is what P.S. Cameron writes at the culmination of his history of the interpretation of the verse, in 1984:

There were encouraging signs that the new period would provide the methods and the evidence necessary to break out of this deadlock, but these hopes have not been fulfilled[499].

Although at the beginning of this chapter, M.W. Bates' opening remarks had already confirmed for us the survival of such an exegetical *status quo*, even in 2013, our overview of virtually "all" the expositions advanced in the history of

---

[493] P.S. CAMERON, *Violence*, 123.

[494] P.S. CAMERON, *Violence*, 109.

[495] See, e.g., W.G. KÜMMEL, "'Das Gesetz'", 401–404; G. ROSSÉ, *Luca*, 629–630; and F. BOVON, *Luc*, III, 93, n. 81.

[496] Among the authors who recognize little or no connection at all between Luke 16,15(16)–18 and their immediate context, see, e.g., D. SCHULZ, *Über die Parabel*, 120; J.J. VAN OOSTERZEE, *Lukas*, 261–262; C.E. VAN KOETSVELD, *Die Gleichnisse*, 246; A.F. LOISY, *Les Èvangiles*, II, 166; J.M. CREED, *Luke*, 206; R. BULTMANN, *The History*, 23.164–166; W.O.E. OESTERLEY, "The Gospel Parables", 203; E. HIRSCH, *Die Worlagen*, 65–68; J. SCHMID, *Lukas*, 262; T.W. MANSON, *The Sayings*, 133–135; J.A. FITZMYER, "The Story", 25, n. 4; ID., *Luke*, II, 1114; J. DRURY, *Tradition*, 160–161; I.H. MARSHALL, *Luke*, 625; L. SABOURIN, *Luke*, 296–298; and F. BOVON, *Luc*, III, 93, n. 81.

[497] O. BETZ, "The Eschatological Interpretation", 105. See, e.g., H. CONZELMANN, *Die Mitte*, 8.14–15.85–86.95.138–139; W.C. ROBINSON Jr., "The Theological Context", 27, n. 30; A. GEORGE, "Tradition", 105.109–112.120–129; W. WINK, *John*, 20–21.46–49; W.G. KÜMMEL, "'Das Gesetz'", 398–415; J.A. FITZMYER, *Luke*, II, 1114–1116; P.S. CAMERON, *Violence*, 125.188, ns. 197–201; G. ROSSÉ, *Luca*, 634; W. LINKE, "'Gwałt'", 103–107; and F. BOVON, *Luc*, III, 89–90.

[498] W. STENGER, "βιάζομαι, βιαστής", *EDNT*, I, 216.

[499] P.S. CAMERON, *Violence*, 129.

the interpretation of the text has by no means been pointless. The statement that no "satisfactory explanation"[500] has yet been given "in either ancient or modern scholarship"[501] does not prevent one from collecting those clues which have nonetheless been scattered throughout its wide hermeneutic field[502]. In keeping with Augustine of Hippo's suggestion, we are now placed in the right position to catch a glimpse of the larger exegetical picture and thus ask a few preliminary questions as equally valuable starting points for our study[503].

First of all, our survey has revealed to us that the oldest and most long-established understanding of the saying has unanimously been *in bonam partem*. In this regard, as pointed out by G. Häfner, the Fathers' early paraphrase, over and above "such a unanimity in an *in bonam partem* interpretation"[504], is, on the one hand, already a first sign that neither term must necessarily be taken or interpreted *in malam partem*[505]. As he additionally observes, it would actually be unthinkable if the βία-terms carried exclusively negative linguistic connotations[506]. On the other hand, such an ostensibly fair observation is by itself insufficient and must be sustained by further textual and linguistic data, nor is it an adequate indication to determine with certainty either the positive or negative meaning of the words in our text. As a result, the exegetical solution to this issue must clearly be sought somewhere else.

Secondly, this unanimous and long-running positive understanding of the "violence saying" is all the more significant when, in addition to A. von Harnack's remarks on the early Fathers' proximity to and knowledge of the NT Greek language, one considers also the following two further observations: a) the history of interpretation of other popular and seemingly "violent" Gospel passages, such as, the temple incident of John 2,13–25, actually attests the tangible possibility for such texts to be used, otherwise, as a justifying warrant for Christian violence and killing, both by patristic and medieval interpreters[507]; and b) these same authors are definitely aware of the

---

[500] M.W. BATES, "Cryptic Codes", 74.

[501] M.W. BATES, "Cryptic Codes", 74.

[502] As a matter of fact, M.W. Bates admittedly builds his own solution upon the clues of other scholars, who have already long anticipated his own anti-Herod conclusions, at least in part. See, e.g., M.W. BATES, "Cryptic Codes", 87, n. 47.

[503] See AUGUSTINE OF HIPPO, *Enarrat. Ps.* LIV.22 (ed. A. TRAPÈ – P.R. PICCOLOMINI, III.26.2, 114–115).

[504] G. HÄFNER, "Gewalt", 32.

[505] See G. HÄFNER, "Gewalt", 35.

[506] See G. HÄFNER, "Gewalt", 33.

[507] See, e.g., AUGUSTINE OF HIPPO, *C. litt. Petil.* II.10.24 (ed. A. TRAPÈ – P.R. PICCOLO-MINI, I.15.2, 78–79); *Ibid.*, II.80.178 (ed. *Ibid.*, I.15.2, 194–195); ID., *Tract. Ev. Jo.* X.5–6.8 (ed. *Ibid.*, III.24, 238–245); PETER DAMIAN, *Ep.* VII.2 (*PL* 144, 436b); ANSELM OF LUCCA, *Alb. Matt* (*PL* 149, 475d–478c); BRUNO OF SEGNIS, *Comment. Matt* LXXXVI (*PL* 165, 244b–248b); ID., *Comm. Luc.* XLVI (*PL* 165, 440a–c); BERNARD OF CLAIRVAUX, *Laud. mil.*

negative nuances of the βία-terms and are likewise absolutely convinced that "in God [...] there is no violence" (βία [...] οὐ πρόσεστι τῷ θεῷ)[508]. If it is truly possible for both vocabulary and Gospel accounts to carry negative connotations, then one cannot but legitimately wonder why Luke 16,16 has been so consistently interpreted positively.

Finally, the ultimate reasons set forth by the same P.S. Cameron, in order to eventually dismiss an *in bonam partem* interpretation of the saying, are not totally convincing. In fact, the author writes:

> The argument that he [i.e., Jesus] may here have used *prima facie in malam partem* vocabulary with an *in bonam partem* reference (in a hyperbolical fashion in order to arrest the attention of his audience), while not excluded by the Greek vocabulary, is impossible in the light of the associations of ideas which the vocabulary of the reconstructed original would inevitably have sparked off[509].

In other words, the impossibility of such a positive interpretation is founded on a hypothetical reference to an original Semitic textual form, which, although it may sound really accurate and well-reasoned, is nonetheless nothing more than a "virtually certain"[510] conjecture, lacking actual textual support[511]. As he himself acknowledges, the studies conducted as to the possible Semitic background of the saying have actually shown that behind βιάζεσθαι's "several shades of meaning"[512] there exist so many Aramaic or Hebrew roots that almost "any interpretation can plausibly appeal to a Semitic ancestor"[513]. Accordingly,

---

V.9 (ed. J. LECLERCQ – H. ROCHAIS, III, 222); ID., *Ep.* CCCXCIV (ed. *Ibid.*, VIII, 368–369); and A. ALEXIS-BAKER, "Violence", 73–86.

[508] *Diogn.* VII.4 (ed. H.-I. MARROU, 68–69). Clement of Alexandria (*Fr.* XXIX [ed. O. STÄHLIN, III, 217]) clearly states: "God, therefore, is not violent" (οὐ τοίνυν βίαιος ὁ θεός); and elsewhere he (*Quis div.* X [ed. G.W. BUTTERWORTH, 288–289]) specifies: "God, therefore, does not coerce (for violence is hateful to God), but provides to those who seek, and grants to those who ask, and opens to those who knock" (Οὐ γὰρ ἀναγκάζει ὁ θεὸς [βία γὰρ ἐχθρὸν θεῷ], ἀλλὰ τοῖς ζητοῦσι πορίζει, καὶ τοῖς αἰτοῦσι παρέχει, καὶ τοῖς κρούουσιν ἀνοίγει). For similar expressions, seee also IRENAEUS OF LYONS, *Haer.* IV, 37.1 (ed. A. ROUSSEAU, II, 920–921); and JOHN DAMASCENE, *Parall.* (*PG* 95, 1112c.1285a). Finally, alluding to Aristotle, Thomas Aquinas (*C. gent.* I.19 [ed. B.M. DE RUBEIS, 12]) echoes this idea, stating: "in God there can be nothing violent" (*in Deo nihil potest esse violentum*).

[509] P.S. CAMERON, *Violence*, 153. See also *Ibid.*, 144–147.

[510] P.S. CAMERON, *Violence*, 158.

[511] The author himself (*Violence*, 151) seems to admit this when, apropos of another saying used in support of his interpretation (Mark 8,15), he writes: "This of course is only a conjecture and as such is offered only tentatively". Moreover, in the final epitome of his study, he (*Ibid.*, 157) also notes that "Other sayings of Jesus on the subject of entering the kingdom suggest that [...] the verse could still perfectly well be *in bonam partem* [...] and prescriptive", whereas commenting, eventually, on the consequences of his final solution, he (*Ibid.*, 159) judiciously describes it as "an interpretation which itself is at most probable".

[512] P.S. CAMERON, *Violence*, 142.

[513] P.S. CAMERON, *Violence*, 131.

notwithstanding the author's precious contribution as to the saying's hermeneutic history, his final conclusion can justly be considered to rely merely on an ambiguous "degree of probability"[514]. On the contrary, if we wish to find a firm foundation for a solution, we must confidently and *a priori* dismiss any conjectural translation, emendation, or reconstruction of a Semitic "original" as it were mere sand. The exegetical cornerstone of any NT scientific research and the safest way to conduct it should always be the actual Greek text at one's disposal.

For this reason, we presume that the safest clues for understanding Luke 16,16 are most likely to be found in the literary or narrative context in which Luke has actually chosen to place the saying. In fact, as A. Schweizer observes, and as the writing principle of any lexicon also confirms, the context of a word is of primary importance in determining its meaning and establishing whether, in a given account, that word essentially carries either a positive or negative nuance[515]. Besides, as P.S. Cameron notes, "the occurrence of *in malam partem* vocabulary [...] does not make an *in bonam partem* interpretation impossible"[516].

In opposition to what A. Schweizer contends, however, and in agreement with G. Häfner's observation, we further suspect that Luke's context may truly carry enough redactional and compositional signals so as to eventually favour an *in bonam partem* sense of these words[517].

The latter stage of our analysis has shown us how the relevance of both historical and narrative contexts is as contested a point as almost anything else. However, the equally significant number of exegetes who, starting from the extant text (vs. its probably "original" conjecture), actually see the present context as potentially and logically meaningful ought not to be so easily passed over. If Luke is not a blind collector of pre-existing traditions, but rather a skilled evangelist (see Luke 1,1–4), theologically and literarily reshaping his sources so as to address the needs and issues of his intended readers' specific community, as we here presuppose, whether he found the saying originally isolated or already grouped as a coherent unit in his source, then he would not have inserted any of its verses, as pointed out by J.-M. Lagrange, "without

---

[514] P.S. CAMERON, *Violence*, 158.

[515] As K.W. Clark (*The Gentile Bias*, 202) writes, "It may be necessary to remind ourselves occasionally that meaning is not created by a lexicon nor even by the lexicographer". Likewise, M. Silva (*Biblical Words*, 138) remarks: "lexicographers determine meaning by observing word usage, by examining contexts [...] The principle of contextual interpretation is [...] one of the few universally accepted hermeneutical guidelines". See, e.g., A. SCHWEIZER, "Ob in der Stelle", 98–102; M. SILVA, *Biblical Words*, 138–169; and J.B. CORTÉS – F.M. GATTI, "On the Meaning", 257.

[516] P.S. CAMERON, *Violence*, 99.

[517] Cf. A. SCHWEIZER, "Ob in der Stelle", 98–102; and G. HÄFNER, "Gewalt", 24–25.33.47–51.

seriously considering the context"[518]. On the contrary, if he "puts or leaves these verses in their present context", as D.J. Ireland remarks, it must be "for a reason"[519].

Not a few scholars today recognize how Luke wishes to underline a message that is probably historical, but also pastoral and theological, having eternity itself presumably in view[520]. Indeed, if it is true that his words tell a sacred history that is meant to benefit the readers in their personal journey of faith and salvation towards the eternal kingdom of God, then chances are that also Luke 16,16 may be part of this plan, in one way or another.

Moreover, like any other document from antiquity, it is also safe to assume that in an effective act of communication, author and reader must speak the same language and share common expectations as part of their contemporary literary culture, social conventions, and historical setting. An acknowledgement of Luke's and his readers' Judeo-Hellenistic cultured milieu and framework of understanding is thus crucial or, at the very least, necessary to attain an objectively valid understanding of the meaning and message of the Lucan verse[521].

Likewise, to have an effective impact on a given reader and on a predetermined subject, any kind of literature must also be shaped in such a way as to be sensible and persuasive. Source credibility, readability and clearness of language, proper amount and order of information, arrangement and organization of the message, and reader's exposure to repeated variations of a basic theme, are just some of the compositional guides used in both ancient and modern times to bring an audience to a specific course of action[522]. It is then

---

[518] J.-M. LAGRANGE, *Luc*, 438. See also P.S. CAMERON, *Violence*, 141.193, n. 42.

[519] D.J. IRELAND, *Stewardship*, 128.

[520] As pointed out in the prologue (Luke 1,1–4), the aim of Luke-Acts is generally twofold: to set forth the truth of what has happened, in careful and often elaborate detail, and offer the theological significance of the narrated facts. See, esp., "an orderly exposition" (διήγησις: Luke 1,1), as compared to, "gospel" (εὐαγγέλιον: Mark 1,1), and "so that you may know [...] the certainty" (ἵνα ἐπιγνῷς [...] τὴν ἀσφάλειαν: Luke 1,4), in the light of, "know [...] for certain" (ἀσφαλῶς [...] γινωσκέτω: Acts 2,36). For a 1st c. definition of the Lucan term, διήγησις, as a historical narration of "events" (πράγματα), see, e.g., THEON, *Progym.*, IV.8–27 (ed. L. SPENGEL, II, 80). For Luke as a historian and theologian, see, e.g., F.F. BRUCE, *The Acts*, 27–34; I.H. MARSHALL, *Luke. Historian*, esp. 39; and F. BOVON, *Luke the Theologian*, esp., 350–367.497–499.505–513.

[521] Thus, R.F. O'Toole (*The Unity*, 12) points out: "One should not draw a rigid distinction between Judaism and Hellenism. Rather, by the time that Luke wrote, Hellenism and Judaism had merged to a considerable extent [...] The main influence on Luke comes from the Bible which he used, the Septuagint, the Greek translation of the Hebrew Old Testament. This does not deny that Luke was acquainted with the rhetorical norms of Hellenistic literature and that he used them". See also D.E. AUNE, *The New Testament*, 11–16.120–131.

[522] See, e.g., LUCIAN OF SAMOSATA, *Hist. scrib.*, XLIII–LXIII (ed. A.M. HARMON, VI, 58–73); and B. MULLEN – C. JOHNSON, *The Psychology*, 31ff. For instance, S. Principe

also very likely that in composing and arranging the context of the "violence passage"[523], Luke may have made stylistic and literary choices, which are undoubtedly worth studying, but then again, not as ends in themselves. In fact, by nature of their very existence, the function of these features is to guide the reader to the proper understanding of the text and its intended meaning. In other words, as in the setting of design professions, we presume that "form follows function"[524]. Thus, the author's literary concern for the shape of the narrative context of Luke 16,16 is in all likelihood at the service of its envisioned purpose and message, and consequently all exegetical analysis should serve the purpose of its theological interpretation, within a serious consideration of its context.

Unfortunately, not many studies of the saying have been conducted seriously in this sense. In fact, P.S. Cameron himself notes, even if some interpreters continue to a certain extent to build their arguments on the context, "the majority either expressly or tacitly treat the saying as isolated"[525].

Among these, a significant example is J.A. Fitzmyer's study. The author considers Luke 16,16–18, on the one hand, as breaking the unitarian tone of the chapter and as having "almost nothing to do"[526] with the previous partition[527]. On the other hand, he also comments: "It is, consequently, difficult to discern what thread, apart from the theme about the use of material possessions, unites the chapter"[528].

Accordingly, there is a contextual unifying thread against which the saying should first and foremost be assessed, and, as several authors have recognized,

---

("Chi era Luca?", 134) remarks: "Perché la sua testimonianza sia riconosciuta valida, [Luca] deve poter contare sulla validità delle sue fonti".

[523] W. STENGER, "βιάζομαι, βιαστής", *EDNT*, I, 216.

[524] The origin of this motto is at times ascribed to the Jesuit scholar C. Lodoli, but was employed and popularized later, in the 19th c., by L.H. Sullivan, as part of his architectural theories. See, e.g., L.H. SULLIVAN, "The Tall Office Building", 408; J. RYKWERT, "Lodoli", 21–26; E. DI STEFANO, *Ornamento*, esp., 22.24–31; and M.J. NEVEU, "Apologues", 57.

[525] P.S. CAMERON, *Violence*, 132. See also R.J. KARRIS, "Poor and Rich", 121; and D.J. IRELAND, *Stewardship*, 157.

[526] J.A. FITZMYER, *Luke*, II, 1114. See, e.g., D.J. IRELAND, *Stewardship*, 128, n. 53.

[527] See J.A. FITZMYER, *Luke*, II, 1111–1112.

[528] J.A. FITZMYER, *Luke*, II, 1095. According to F. Bovon (*Luc*, III, 66), "A lire l'ensemble du chapitre, le lecteur se rend compte que la thématique des biens matériels est decisive", and yet, he later adds (*Ibid.*, 93, n. 81) what D. Marguerat ("Le règne", 114, n. 3) calls a "remarque désabusé": "Dans mon esprit, les v. 16–18 n'ont guère de rapport entre eux, ni avec leur context". In other words, even those arguing in favour of the disrupting character of vv. (15)16–18 within Luke 16 somehow recognize a certain amalgamating thematic coherence, precisely inasmuch as they actually imply that there is an interrupted train of thought. See, e.g., A.B. BRUCE, *The Parabolic Teaching*, 378; K.H. RENGSTORF, *Lukas*, 195; J. SCHMID, *Lukas*, 262–263; R.C. TANNEHILL, *The Narrative Unity*, I, 185–186; and K.R. SNODGRASS, *Stories*, 405.

that coincides precisely with the proper use of riches[529]. Yet, as our overview of the history of the interpretation of the saying has revealed, the vast majority of modern (vs. Patristic and Medieval) scholars tends rather too easily to either overlook it or give it up altogether.

To his credit, J.A. Fitzmyer does recognize the logical association of vv. 14–15 with v. 13, as well as their transitional value with respect to vv. 19–31, seeing the theme of material goods being already prefigured in the younger son's conduct of chap. 15, then developed in the two parables of chap. 16[530], and, because of the Palestinian marriage's social circumstances, possibly implied also in v. 18[531]. However, while this latter connection – namely, that between the theme of material possessions and v. 18 – is further underlined, already, by other scholars[532], the possible linguistic and semantic links of vv. 16 and 17 with such a contextual theme still require deeper and more thorough investigation. Although some authors (e.g., M. Dibelius) have actually highlighted the possibility of a conflictual relationship between our saying and the Gospel statement "which attributes the kingdom to the poor"[533] (see Matt 5,3; Luke 6,20), a fresher study of the context of these verses in their Lucan Gospel perspective might reveal some kind of compatible link with this theme, even as good news (see, e.g., Matt 11,5; Luke 7,22; and 16,16)[534]. In this sense, J.M.D. Derrett has even gone as far as to remark the following: "the burden of proof lies heavily upon him who asserts that the passages which

---

[529] Thus, G. Rossé (*Luca*, 616) comments: "un argomento domina il c. 16: il problema dell'uso della ricchezza".

[530] See Luke 16,1–8a; and Luke 16,19–31. For the author, the first parable is actually followed by three concrete applications (cf. Luke 16,8b–9.10–12.13) and a clear reprobation of the Pharisees' inward avarice (cf. Luke 16,14–15). See J.A. FITZMYER, *Luke*, II, 1095.1105.1111.1127.

[531] Thus, J.A. Fitzmyer (*Luke*, II, 1119) points out: "Given the Palestinian understanding of the relation of a woman to a man in marriage [...] it [v. 18] indirectly belongs to the topic of a man's possessions". Later (*Ibid.*, II, 1120), he notes how such an understanding implies "the OT ideas of the wife as the chattel of the husband (implicit in such passages as Exod 20,17; 21,3.22; Jer 6,12; Num 30,10–14; Esth 1,20–22; and especially Sir 23,22–27)".

[532] See, e.g., J. ERNST, *Luca*, II, 664; J. RADERMAKERS – P. BOSSUYT, *Lettura pastorale*, 356, n. 190; G. ROSSÉ, *Luca*, 636–638; S. FAUSTI, *Una comunità*, 568–569; S. GRASSO, *Luca*, 435; and B.B. BRUEHLER, "Reweaving the Texture", 64.67.

[533] P.S. CAMERON, *Violence*, 109. M. Dibelius (*Die urchristliche Überlieferung*, 25) rhetorically asks: "Das Evangelium ist die Botschaft vom Reichgottes für die Armen [...] und nun sollte es den Stürmern gehören?".

[534] See, e.g., A. VON HARNACK, "Zwei Worte", 955, n. 3; and D. DAUBE, *The New Testament*, 293–295. As C.H. Talbert ("Between Text and Sermon", 406) observes, the immediate context speaks of the poor hearing good news (see Matt 11,5), an echo of both OT prophecy (see, e.g., Isa 29,19; and 61,1) and "post-biblical Jewish belief. Qumran, 4Q521 (frag. 2, col. 2), associates the poor getting good news [...] with the coming messianic figure".

appear in sequence are not united by a thread of teaching"[535]. While one may
eventually and independently end up agreeing with him, statements as bold as
this require some assessment on our part.

Finally, A. von Harnack's point on Luke's clever reshaping of the original
context may not be limited simply to the Lucan additions of εὐαγγελίζεται and
πᾶς, as the author maintains. A deeper study of the context and its language,
after all, may even show how that could rather include the saying's
"specifically" violent feature, βιάζεται, as well[536]. Perhaps Luke was entirely
sure of understanding its nuances, and it is Harnack rather than Luke who has
eventually left it unexplained[537]. In other words, if our "redactional"
assumption is right that there exists some literary and theological project of
Luke's Gospel – or, as N. Perrin puts it, that "Luke is every bit as much an
author in the case of the Gospel of Luke as he is in the case of the Acts of the
Apostles"[538] – then the properly Lucan narrative *locus* and his better
understanding of the Greek nuances of the terms may actually be related, and
even enlighten each other. Indeed, consistent with A. von Harnack's initial
insight, and far from being either "of secondary significance" (sekundärer
Bedeutung)[539] or "like a shot out of a gun" (wie aus der Pistole geschossen)[540],
Luke's selected context may really and wholly be "a [well] hewn stonework"
(einem behauenen Quaderstein)[541] of literary and theological skill, with neither
βιάζεται, nor any other cut stone whatsoever, having to be rejected. However,
this too must be proven, and that is precisely why we need to move on to the
next chapter.

---

[535] J.M.D. DERRETT, *Law*, 78. Accoding to the author (*Ibid.*, 98), the thread of teaching
that, in Luke 16, goes "from usury to divorce and thence to antisocial and non-God-fearing
conspicuous consumption (the Steward – Mammon – the Law and the Prophets – Divorce – Dives
and Lazarus) has arisen from a pre-existing catena of ideas still traceable in Midrashic texts",
such as, for instance, those commenting on Isa 50,10 (Yalq 473; and DevR 31). See also
Ibid., 49–50.82–85.94–98; P.S. CAMERON, *Violence*, 182, n. 66; and *Ibid.*, 193, n. 41.

[536] See A. VON HARNACK, "Zwei Worte", 955.

[537] Cf. A. VON HARNACK, "Zwei Worte", 949.955.

[538] N. PERRIN, "The Evangelist", 8. In this sense, N. Perrin (*Ibid.*, 9) claims that "Luke
has exercised the freedom [and literary creativity] of an author both in regard to the Gospel
and to the Acts of the Apostles [...] using traditional material but nonetheless [...] for a
definite purpose".

[539] A. VON HARNACK, "Zwei Worte", 949.

[540] A. VON HARNACK, "Zwei Worte", 949.

[541] A. VON HARNACK, "Zwei Worte", 947.

Chapter 3

The Saying in its Context

A. Introduction

In his adroit, well documented and accurate study of the contextual levels and *cruces interpretum* of Luke 16,1–13[1], D.J. Ireland argues that a logical connection between v. 13 and the preceding verses should, at the very least, suggest that Luke, or the tradition he draws on, apparently did not regard it as out of place in such a narrative setting[2]. The same thing could be said concerning v. 16.

The following pages aim to show precisely how Luke 16,16 and the adjacent verses are marked by a unifying literary and thematic coherence. Consistent with such reasoning, then, this information shall encourage us to appreciate that Luke made a deliberate creative choice to assemble this account the way it is, including our verse.

Moreover, "the coherence of the Lucan context"[3] will also throw some light on Luke 16,16 and the apparently unrelated adjacent verses[4]. In fact, if Luke has intentionally shaped its context into a logical and consistent unit, then we have enough reason to believe that he has also provided us with the safest clues for the proper understanding of the saying itself, even as to its positive or negative interpretation.

---

[1] See, e.g., C.L. BLOMBERG, review of D.J. IRELAND, *Stewardship*, 351; W.S. KURZ, review of *Ibid.*, 141; and P.-É. LANGEVIN, review of *Ibid.*, 111.

[2] See D.J. IRELAND, *Stewardship*, 113. In this section, we shall refer to the "author" of the third Gospel and Acts, or "Luke", without differentiating him from the "source tradition" he may be using. The distinction shall be made only later, as the focus of our analysis shall shift from present canonical context to Lucan sources and redaction. For an outline of D.J. Ireland's work, see J.A. TROXLE, Jr., *Doing Justice*, 52–56.

[3] P.S. CAMERON, *Violence*, 138.

[4] See D.J. IRELAND, *Stewardship*, 123.

B. A Look at the Narrative Context:
Some Methodological Premises

As with an arras of fine quality, so it is with an enigmatic text such as ours. One can see either a confusing and rough texture, made up of several stitches, fabrics, and unraveled threads of different colors, hanging disjointedly one from the other and without any apparently logical weft, or one can appreciate an elegant contrapuntal tapestry, richly woven, with interlaced strands of colorful textiles, into a brilliant and articulate design. It all depends on the scientific perspective used to approach it.

In our earlier overview of the major scholarly proposals in recent decades, we have mentioned a conspicuous number of authors who concur in holding the disconnectedness or unrelatedness of vv. 15(16)–18, to both the context and each other[5]. Among these, for instance, claiming that the evangelist placed them together "with scissors and paste" and as well as he could, nevertheless with little success[6], C.E. van Koetsveld goes as far as to remark:

"Luke, perhaps, had nowhere else to accommodate these verses and that is why he wrote them in this place, where his parchment scroll had still some space left"[7].

However, various studies have called such literary statements into question. In our previous section, we have also mentioned a fair number of authors who consider chap. 16 of Luke's Gospel a well thought-out composition, structurally centered around v. 14, and united by a thematic thread of teaching, concerned primarily with the right use of riches[8]. The exegesis of the most recent years reevaluates these conclusions[9]. Thanks to the latest use of the

---

[5] See, e.g., D.J. IRELAND, *Stewardship*, 122. For a list of proponents of this view, see, esp., D.P. SECCOMBE, *Possessions*, 178, n. 200; and Chap. II, p. 81, n. 496.

[6] See, e.g., J.D.M. DERRETT, "Fresh Light", I, 199; and I.H. MARSHALL, *Luke*, 624.

[7] C.E. VAN KOETSVELD, *Die Gleichnisse*, 246. Approximately forty years before him, J.J. van Oosterzee had already mentioned Van Der Palm's similar opinion. According to the author (J.J. VAN OOSTERZEE, *Luke*, 252), the latter "believed that Luke, before beginning on a new page a new parable, in order to make use of the yet vacant space of his almost fully occupied former leaf, noted down some disconnected sayings of the Lord, without any historical connection".

[8] See Chap. II, p. 80, n. 490. See also I.H. MARSHALL, *Luke*, 614.624; A. FEUILLET, "La parabole", 221; D. KOSCH, *Die Gottesherrschaft*, 68, n. 26; J.R. DONAHUE, *The Gospel*, 162; J. NOLLAND, *Luke*, II, 795–796; D. MATHEWSON, "The Parable", 33; and J.B. GREEN, *Luke*, 586–588. Thus, the latter (*Ibid.*, 588, n. 261) remarks: "Donahue [...] speaks for most when he observes of chap. 16 that, '... apart from a concern for material possessions, no thread emerges that gives it thematic unity'".

[9] Among the most recent authors who view Luke 16,1–31 as an organized unit, see, esp., E. LUPIERI, "Mammona iniquitatis", 132; T. BEDNARZ, "Status Disputes", 390–393; and B.B. BRUEHLER, "Reweaving the Texture", 52–53.

contextual, narrative, and rhetorical approaches, these authors have newly shown the existence of quite an articulate narrative structure, which actually keeps the whole chapter together "as a consistent piece of work"[10].

Thus, as H.L. Egelkraut points out, it may indeed be the case that, "At first sight Luke 16,14–18 seems logically incoherent with that which precedes, with that which follows, and within itself"[11]. However, a closer look at its narrative context suggests that such an ostensible "rag-bag collection"[12] or "plop-down of random sayings"[13] – just to mention a couple of notoriously fanciful labels – all in all, is not so logically or thematically disparate as it seems[14]. The context surrounding vv. 14–18 presents various patterns that can help elucidate the meaning and function of Luke 16,16, and among these, the linguistic recurrence of concepts related to wealth and possessions is of primary importance[15]. The present investigation intends to go far beyond that academic trend, which esteems gospel texts as "somewhat unraveled"[16], and, likewise, "gospel writers as merely 'uninvolved collectors' [Sammlern] of tradition"[17].

Indeed, as C.E. van Koetsveld's aforementioned observation indicates, and as D.J. Ireland notes,

An exclusively literary approach [...] cannot account for the arrangement of the material within the [...] section. Why, for instance, is Luke 16 composed of two parables sandwiched around sayings about the law and the kingdom? Why is the material of that chapter juxtaposed to the three parables of chapter 15[18]?

The answers to these questions can be found only if, in addition to the classical literary approach, one employs also the recent tools of rhetorical and narrative

---

[10] J.D.M. DERRETT, "Fresh Light", I, 199. In addition to the previous note, see also G.W. KLINGSPORN, *The Law*, 358.360.371–372; R.C. TANNEHILL, *The Narrative Unity*, I, 130–132.185–186; O. LEHTIPUU, "Characterization", 101–105; and D.B. GOWLER, "'At His Gate'", 249.

[11] H.L. EGELKRAUT, *Jesus' Mission*, 114. See also F. GODET, *Luke*, II, 170; J.M. CREED, *Luke*, 206; and B.J. BYRNE, *The Hospitality of God*, 133–134.

[12] E.E. ELLIS, *Luke*, 202. See also D.J. IRELAND, *Stewardship*, 122.

[13] T. BEDNARZ, "Status Disputes", 377.

[14] See, e.g., B.J. BYRNE, *The Hospitality of God*, 133. One could also recall the way in which D. Daube (*The New Testament*, 300) describes "the saying concerning violence to the kingdom with the area surrounding it [...] a *Trümmerfeld*, a heap of ruins", or mention the following comment, by H. Crouzel (*L'Église*, 26): "on a l'impression d'un fourre-tout, où l'évangéliste loge ce qu'il n'a pas pu mettre ailleurs".

[15] See B.B. BRUEHLER, "Reweaving the Texture", 52.

[16] B.B. BRUEHLER, "Reweaving the Texture", 50.

[17] D.J. IRELAND, *Stewardship*, 148, n. 165.

[18] D.J. IRELAND, *Stewardship*, 148, n. 165.

critical analysis, with the conviction that in order to understand a text correctly one needs to interpret it in its context[19].

This is why, rather than attempting to understand these verses in isolation or in relation to some other hypothetical context[20], we shall try to bring out as many legitimate connections and meaningful relationships as can possibly be found in the Lucan text, between v. 16, the "seemingly disparate dicta"[21] of vv. 14–18, and their present narrative context. By doing so, we also hope to eliminate any need for postulating a different "original" translation, emendation, or reconstruction of a Semitic textual form as the point of departure of our research[22].

C. The Narrative Unit around Luke 16,16: Delimitation and Structure

In his commentary on chap. 16 of Luke's Gospel, R.J. Karris notes:

It seems that the tendency in past scholarship has been to consider the two parables of this chapter in relative isolation from one another and from 16,14–18 or to single out 16,16 as if the rest of the chapter did not exist. I presuppose that chap. 16 forms a unity[23].

In this portion of our study, we intend primarily to found the validity of such a presupposition on firmer evidential bases, thus embarking on what R.J. Karris himself calls, "a relatively unexplored question"[24].

Before any sober analysis of a biblical text may take place, it is first and foremost necessary to establish its proper boundaries and, so doing, define the limits of that space within which meaning is engendered[25]. As rightly phrased

---

[19] See D.J. IRELAND, *Stewardship*, 1. Ignoring the hermeneutic context assigned by the author to a given text can result in dangerous sectarian interpretations. See D. MARGUERAT – A. WÉNIN, *Sapori*, 210.213. For the methodological cooperation in biblical exegesis between the historical-critical and narrative methods, see, e.g., *Ibid.*, 199–200.

[20] See D.J. IRELAND, *Stewardship*, 107.

[21] T. BEDNARZ, "Status Disputes", 400.

[22] In our next chapter, rather than constituting the primary ground for a solution, any reference of ours to the saying's Jewish background shall thus be solely and exclusively a further validation of this section's outcome.

[23] R.J. KARRIS, "Poor and Rich", 121.

[24] R.J. KARRIS, "Poor and Rich", 122. See, e.g., C. STRATTON, "Pressure", 415; J.D.M. DERRETT, "Fresh Light", I, 198; P.S. CAMERON, *Violence*, 132.157; G.W. KLING-SPORN, *The Law*, 360–361.384–387.417; and D.J. IRELAND, *Stewardship*, 123, n. 23.

[25] See D. MARGUERAT – Y. BOURQUIN, *How to Read*, 173. As the two authors (*Ibid.*, 30) point out, "to strip a narrative of its final twist or to ignore what makes it get off the ground is completely to distort it. To cut too early or too late is to disfigure the narrative. To decide the closure of the text is a first interpretative act".

by S. Bazyliński, "the question must be answered as to where the passage starts (*terminus a quo*) and where it ends (*terminus ad quem*)"[26].

In their introductory manual to narrative criticism, D. Marguerat and Y. Bourquin draw attention to the fact that, contrary to modern novelists, biblical authors had no chapters or verses to mark the boundaries inherent in their stories, and the only means which they used to give the readers signs of their intended closures were of a narrative kind[27]. Thus, it may be useful to keep in mind that "the markers (chapters, verses, titles) provided by our Bibles"[28] cannot be considered, uncritically, as trustworthy indications for structuring a biblical text[29].

The same is true as regards modern synopses. The latter cannot be accepted blindly as reliable templates for making a closure, for they too ascribe little impact to the narrative characteristics of the text. In their attempts to be as short and compact as possible, these instruments link the Lucan form of the "violence passage"[30] with either v. 17[31] or vv. 17–18[32], thus ignoring a whole segment of the account, which appears to be concurrently constructed on and defined by a clear set of narrative signals and, despite that, also sensibly associated with its preceding and most proximate surroundings. Since the author has purposely incorporated these narrative indicators into the text to hint at its envisioned internal frontiers, then we wish do justice to the meaning of Luke 16,16 in the present canonical context and we must at least give them proper attention.

---

[26] Bazyliński, 201–202. See D. MARGUERAT – Y. BOURQUIN, *How to Read*, 30–32.

[27] See D. MARGUERAT – Y. BOURQUIN, *How to Read*, 31.

[28] D. MARGUERAT – Y. BOURQUIN, *How to Read*, 32.

[29] As D. Marguerat and Y. Bourquin (*How to Read*, 31) remind us, "When copied on scrolls and codices by the copyists, for more than a thousand years the text was presented in continuous form. For the Hebrew Bible, the first traces of a division into verses go back to the scribes of the Talmudic period (fifth century), but it was not until 1553 that their numbering was adopted. For the New Testament, the numbering of the chapters goes back to the efforts of the Englishman Stephen Langton (1203). The distribution into verses appears for the first time in the edition of the Greek text by the Geneva publisher Robert Estienne in 1551, and from then on was authoritative. But the criteria used for this numbering of the text are practical: they reflect the reading of the theologians and the Greek scholars, and take no account of narrativity".

[30] W. STENGER, "βιάζομαι, βιαστής", *EDNT*, I, 216.

[31] Thus, both A. Poppi (*Nuova Sinossi*, I, 222–225) and K. Aland (*Synopsis*, 197–198) single out vv. 16–17 together under the headings, "*La Legge non passerà*" and "Concerning the Law", respectively, and place v. 18 alone, with the following title: "*Sul divorzio*" or "Concerning Divorce".

[32] See, e.g., J. SCHMID, ed., *Sinossi*, 133; and M.E. BOISMARD – A. LAMOUILLE, *Synopsis*, 248–249.

I. Luke 16,14–31: The Minimum Narrative Segment encompassing v. 16

In keeping with the scientific criteria used to determine the proper narrative perimeter of a text, and the *indicia* scattered in it, the most basic and essential literary segment for perceiving the intended meaning of v. 16 occurs in Luke 16,14–31[33]. In fact, sandwiched between two separate discourses of Jesus to his disciples (cf. Luke 16,1–13; 17,1–10) and characterized by a sufficient number of changes, vv. 14–31 can safely be regarded as a somewhat autonomous narrative unit[34].

Specifically, Luke 16,14 forms the *terminus a quo* of this minimum possible narrative segment encompassing Luke 16,16. Here, we find what D. Kosch calls, a "significant detailed [bedeutend ausführlicher] caesura"[35], as well as a variation in the narrator's identity and position, from *intradiegetic* to *extradiegetic*[36]. Although the Lucan narrator makes no mention of a change of time and place, he nonetheless replaces Jesus' voice (see Luke 16,1b–13) with his own, introducing what appears to be a "new" set of characters and circumstances[37]. Jesus remains the main actor and source of teaching, both before and after v. 14. However, the *extradiegetic* narrator intervenes in the narrative to signal a shift in Jesus' audience, from disciples to Pharisees (see Luke 16,1a.14a). More precisely, he now *tells* his readers that the latter, who loved money (φιλάργυροι), heard all that Jesus had just said to his disciples and, as a result,

---

[33] As D. Marguerat and Y. Bourquin (*How to Read*, 151) point out, these guiding principles are the presence or change of "time, place, characters, theme, model or literary genre". See, e.g., J.-N. ALETTI, *Il racconto*, 226. Thus, we disagree here with G. Giurisato ("Come Luca", 446), for whom the minimum narrative segment to which v. 16 belongs comprises "vv. 1–18". Specifically, he (*Ibid.*, 445–446) argues: "Che il v. 1 e il v. 19 segnino l'inizio di due pericopi sembra evidente in base alla somiglianza degli incipit". Although marking the incipit of two parables, the aforementioned resemblance does not necessarily indicate the beginning of their two corresponding scenes. On a narrative level, these are rather introduced by v. 1a and vv. 14–15a, respectively.

[34] As we shall see, however, vv. 14–31 are also structurally connected with vv. 1–13 and, as such, are to be interpreted accordingly. See, e.g., T. BEDNARZ, "Status Disputes", 390.415; and B.B. BRUEHLER, "Reweaving the Texture", 52–53.

[35] D. KOSCH, *Die Gottesherrschaft*, 69.

[36] All parts of a narrative are generally characterized in terms of an "orderly/detailed exposition" (διήγησις): see, e.g., Judg 7,15; Sir 6,35; 9,15; 22,6; 27,11.13; 38,25; 39,2; 2Macc 2,32; 6,17; and Luke 1,1. Every element which is "within" its limits (actors, actions, plot and spatial-temporal changes) is defined as *intradiegetic*, whereas every other one (narrator/author and reader), which remaining "outside of" it cannot be perceived by the characters, is known as *extradiegetic*. See, e.g., J.-N. ALETTI, *Il racconto*, 226–230; D. MARGUERAT – Y. BOURQUIN, *How to Read*, 39; M. CRIMELLA, *Marta*, 64, n. 19; and *Ibid.*, 347–348.

[37] See, e.g., F.J. MATERA, "Jesus' Journey", 73. A look at the larger context reveals that they are not so "new", after all (cf. Luke 15,2). However, with respect to its immediate narrative context, the change is obvious. Cf. Luke 16,1a.14–15a.

were scoffing at him[38]. Thus, even if only momentarily (see v. 15a), the actions recounted "extradiegetically" by the narrator pass from Jesus' "speaking" (λέγειν)[39] to the Pharisees' "hearing" (ἀκούειν)[40] and "sneering at" (ἐκμυκτη-ρίζειν)[41] him.

In v. 15a, the Lucan narrator's voice ends its short foray into the narrative and Jesus can thus resume his teaching (see v. 15b). Together, as D.J. Ireland remarks, vv. 14–15a function as "the introduction to the rest of the chapter"[42]. As such, they are particularly significant, because, by focusing on the motif of the Pharisees' avariciousness[43], they bring into play the main theme of the entire segment (vv. 14–31) and, as we shall see, of Luke 16 as a whole, namely, the use of material possessions and riches in view of one's future entry into the "house-kingdom" of God[44]. Apart from Luke 12,42, in fact, all of the Lucan uses of terms related to "house management" (e.g., οἰκονόμος, οἰκονομία, οἰκονομεῖν) occur only in chap. 16 of his Gospel, and in connection with words, such as, "rich" (πλούσιος), "mammon" (μαμωνᾶς), "possessions" (ὑπάρχοντα),

---

[38] See F.J. MATERA, "Jesus' Journey", 73. A narrator can either intervene directly in the narration (*telling*), expressing through his own words his omniscient *point of view* (*pdv*) on the characters' inner intentions and attitudes, or give space to the characters' words themselves (*showing*), transferring his own *pdv* on their lips, in the form of a direct discourse. See, e.g., D. MARGUERAT – Y. BOURQUIN, *How to Read*, 69–71; J.L. RESSEGUIE, *Narrative Criticism*, 126–130; and M. CRIMELLA, *Marta*, 65, n. 20.

[39] See Luke 15,3.7.10.11; 16,1 and 9a.

[40] Luke 16,14a. Cf., e.g., Luke 15,1–2.25.

[41] Luke 16,14b. Cf., e.g., Luke 15,2; 19,7; 23,35; and A.A. JUST, Jr., *Luke*, II, 623.

[42] D.J. IRELAND, *Stewardship*, 123. See also J. DUPONT, *Les Béatitudes*, III, 165.167. 173; and J.J. KILGALLEN, "The Purpose", 234.

[43] See, e.g., Luke 11,39–42; 20,47. See also A. PLUMMER, *Luke*, 387–388; J.A. FITZMYER, *Luke*, II, 1113; D.J. IRELAND, *Stewardship*, 124–127; and J.J. KILGALLEN, "The Purpose", 238.

[44] Thus, J. Grant and F.W.S. O'Neill ("The Unjust Steward", 240) observe: "The section Luke 16,1–31 might be headed 'Teaching about Money'". Likewise, according to J.A. Fitzmyer (*Luke*, II, 1095), "the theme [...] in this chapter [...] has to do mainly with the proper attitude toward and use of material possessions". See also J. DUPONT, *Les Béatitudes*, III, 163; D.J. IRELAND, *Stewardship*, 122.124; and D. MARGUERAT, "Le règne", 125, n. 2. Moreover, as W. Lee (*The Conclusion*, 2225–2227) remarks, "In the Bible [...] the house of God is closely related to the kingdom of God [...] God first has a house, and then this house is expanded, enlarged, into a city [...] a city signifies a kingdom. The temple was a symbol of God's house, and the city of Jerusalem was a symbol of God's kingdom. Hence, the temple and the city, the house and the kingdom, are inseparable [...] As the consummation of His work, the house becomes the kingdom [...] Eventually, in the New Jerusalem, this pair becomes a single entity, for the entire kingdom will be God's house". See, e.g., Gen 28,16–17; Exod 15,13b.17–18; 25,8; Num 12,7; 2Sam 7,17; 1Chr 17,14; Pss 87,2; 132,12; 146,10; Jer 8,19; Ezek 36,26–27; Mic 4,6–8; Zeph 3,14–15; Matt 12,25; Mark 3,24–25; Luke 11,17; 1Cor 3,9; Eph 2,19–21; 1Tim 3,15; Heb 3,6; and Rev 21,10–11.22. See also L. SEMBRANO, "Il Regno", 19–140; and F. PANIMOLLE, "Il Regno", 163–224.

"goods" (ἀγαθά), "law" (νόμος) and "kingdom of God" (βασιλεία τοῦ θεοῦ)[45]. It is also very significant, in this sense, that these terms occur seven times within the first parable, and that the only difference between the two forms of the saying recorded in Luke 16,13 and Matt 6,24 consists in Luke's addition of the term, "house-servant" (οἰκέτης)[46]. Thus, J.A. Fitzmyer is right when he argues against E.E. Ellis that the change of audience from disciples (v. 1a) to Pharisees (v. 14a) "does not connote a change of theme"[47]. Time, place, and theme clearly remain the same as in the narration of v. 1[48].

In v. 15b, as we have mentioned, the *extradiegetic* narrator passes the baton of the narrative back to the *intradiegetic* teacher. However, while Jesus' former teaching is an "instruction" to his disciples on the aforementioned primary theme of the chapter (vv. 1–13), the tone of that teaching changes now into an "admonishment" in answer to his critics (vv. 15b–31)[49]. Prompted by their adverse reaction to his instruction (vv. 14–15a), this response includes both a set of sayings (vv. 15b–18) and a parable (vv. 19–31). These two components are slightly separated by the mere coordinating particle, δέ (v. 19a)[50], but kept together by a number of unifying links[51]. As noted by J. Dupont, it is above all the "absence of any [real] introduction at the beginning of the parable"[52], which allows us to attribute such introductory function to vv. 14–15a for the parable as well[53].

---

[45] See, e.g., Luke 16,1–4.8.9.11–14.16–17.19.22.25. See also J. DUPONT, *Les Béatitudes*, III, 163–164; C.H. TALBERT, *Reading Luke*, 183–188; J. NOLLAND, *Luke*, II, 795; and A.A. JUST, Jr., *Luke*, II, 612.

[46] See Luke 16,1.2(2x).3(2x).4.8; and D.J. IRELAND, *Stewardship*, 112, n. 299.

[47] J.A. FITZMYER, *Luke*, II, 1112. Cf. E.E. ELLIS, *Luke*, 202.

[48] See J.A. FITZMYER, *Luke*, II, 1112.

[49] See D.J. IRELAND, *Stewardship*, 122–123.

[50] Thus, referring to J.J.J. van Rensburg's comment on Luke 12,41, G. Giurisato ("Come Luca", 439–440) remarks: "Dal punto di vista sintattico [...] la particella δέ [...] potrebbe segnare l'inizio di una nuova pericope, ma non necessariamente; anzi nel caso nostro ha piuttosto la forza di un οὖν conclusivo, che connette il brano seguente al precedente". The same thing could be said of Luke 16,19. See, e.g., J.J.J. VAN RENSBURG, "A Syntactical Reading", 417.421–422.424; and J. DUPONT, *Les Béatitudes*, III, 165.167.173.

[51] See J. DUPONT, *Les Béatitudes*, III, 167. Among the terms recurring in both subunits, see, e.g., the indefinite adjective, "everyone" (πᾶς: Luke 16,14.16.18.26); the verbs, "being there" (ὑπάρχειν: Luke 16,14.23), "hearing" (ἀκούειν: Luke 16,14.29.31), and "falling" (πίπτειν: Luke 16,17.21); and, esp., the expression, "the Law (Moses) and the prophets" (ὁ νόμος [Μωϋσῆς] καὶ οἱ προφῆται: Luke 16,16.29.31). See also v. 17.

[52] J. DUPONT, *Les Béatitudes*, III, 167.

[53] Thus, J. Dupont (*Les Béatitudes*, III, 167, n. 4) comments: "Pareille absence de transition pourrait étonner chez Luc, si l'on ne tient pas compte que la véritable transition se trouve, dans sa pensée, au v. 14. Mais on peut en trouver un autre exemple en 17,7". In turn, M.-L. Rigato ("'Mosè e i Profeti'", 145) acknowleges "un senso più compiuto dal racconto nella sua globalità considerando Lc 16,16–31 unitariamente".

Finally, in view of the fact that no change of scene or audience takes place until Luke 17,1, we can safely assume that Jesus' response continues all the way up to Luke 16,31[54]. Reclaiming the reins of the narrative, the *extradiegetic* narrator intervenes again in Luke 17,1a, making clear that the previous section has finally reached its end[55]. Here, the recipients of Jesus' teaching revert from Pharisees (see Luke 16,14–15a) to disciples (see Luke 16,1a). Moreover, the *intradiegetic* narrator is no longer Abraham (see Luke 16,29.31), but Jesus (see Luke 17,1b). Thus, Luke 16,31 closes both parable (vv. 19a–31) and chapter (vv. 1–31), and as such constitutes the *terminus ad quem* of our short narrative segment (vv. 14–31). The "inclusion" (*inclusio*) created around the latter verses, by the occurrence of the verb, "to listen" (ἀκούειν), brackets further the whole segment and so confirms its closure[56].

II. Luke 16,1–13: A Closely Associated Narrative Segment

Although Luke 16,14–31 represents the primary narrative segment in which the meaning of Luke 16,16 is produced, it cannot be totally separated from the rest of the chapter as if it were a fully independent unit. On the contrary, as pointed out by some scholars, vv. 14–31 are logically and thematically linked to vv. 1–13 and form with it a well-constructed concentric composition, which, as we shall see better in the next paragraph, finds its midpoint in v. 14[57].

We have already mentioned how, in spite of the several changes in the second narrative segment (vv. 14–31) of chap. 16 (i.e., narrator's identity and position, audience, narrated actions, and teaching tone), space, time and theme continue unaltered from vv. 1–13. As B.B. Bruehler points out, vv. 14–15a are only "one of the two places"[58] in the whole chapter where we hear the narrator speaking directly. His opening words (v. 14a), "were listening to all these things" (ἤκουον δὲ ταῦτα πάντα), in particular, carry the specific function of connecting what follows (vv. 15b–31) to the preceding segment (vv. 1b–13)[59]. Here, the object of the Pharisees' action of "listening" (ἀκούειν) is defined by means of the syntagm, "all these things" (ταῦτα πάντα). Although the latter could very well include *all the things* which Jesus has been teaching since

---

[54] See D.J. IRELAND, *Stewardship*, 125.

[55] See M. CRIMELLA, *Marta*, 418.

[56] The verb occurs four times in Luke 16 (ἀκούειν: vv. 2.14.29.31) and, thus, is also one of its unifying elements. For the literary-rhetorical figure of the *inclusio*, see, e.g., Lausberg, 280–281; and J.L. RESSEGUIE, *Narrative Criticism*, 57–58. For the key value of this particular verb in this narrative section and the author's perspective, see the next two stages of the present study, when it shall be contextualized in connection with the Šᵉmaʿ of Deut 6,4–5 and Luke's own redaction and theology.

[57] See, e.g., D.J. IRELAND, *Stewardship*, 122; and T. BEDNARZ, "Status Disputes", 390–391.

[58] B.B. BRUEHLER, "Reweaving the Texture", 54.

[59] See B.B. BRUEHLER, "Reweaving the Texture", 54.

Luke 14,25, it pertains primarily to the new instructions offered to his disciples in Luke 16,1a–13, which culminate with a saying on the irreconcilableness between the service of God and that of mammon[60]. Unsurprisingly, the Pharisees are characterized not only as "listening" (v. 14a), but also as "money-lovers" (φιλάργυροι)[61].

The other place in which the *extradiegetic* narrator intervenes directly in Luke 16 is v. 1a[62]. His brief remark makes it clear that the previous parabolic account is now ended (see Luke 15,11–32). It also brings the reader's attention to a change of audience: while continuing his teaching to the crowds, including tax collectors, sinners, Pharisees and scribes (see Luke 14,25; and 15,1–2), Jesus turns now to a specific group among them: his disciples[63]. Thus, in v. 1b, the *intradiegetic* narrator is no longer the father within the parable (see Luke 15,31–32), but Jesus himself (see Luke 15,3.11a).

Moreover, the motifs of riches and one's different approach to them create an *inclusio* around the actual message of the whole instruction (vv. 1b–13) and so help identify its main theme[64]. As D.J. Ireland rightly points out, then,

Luke 16,14–31 continues and amplifies the polemic against greed which is the background for Jesus' teaching in vv. 1–13 [...] these verses serve to reinforce Jesus' teaching in vv. 1–13 by warning the disciples of the consequences of trying to serve God and mammon, of being lovers of money, of not using their material possessions for the poor[65].

From a syntactical perspective, the connection between v. 14 and the preceding verses is accentuated further by the imperfect tense of two verbs (ἤκουον and

---

[60] See, esp., J.A. FITZMYER, *Luke*, II, 1071.1112; D.J. IRELAND, *Stewardship*, 123–124; and A.A. JUST, Jr., *Luke*, II, 622.

[61] For instance, J.B. Green (*Luke*, 601) detects "a subtle wordplay" between "making friends by means of mammon" (ποιεῖν φίλους ἐκ τοῦ μαμωνᾶ: v. 9) and, as phrased by B.B. Bruehler ("Reweaving the Texture", 54, n. 22), "being a friend (φίλ-) of money" (φιλαργυρεῖν: v. 14). The link can also be made semantically, between "money-lover" (φιλάργυρος: v. 14), "mammon" (μαμωνᾶς: vv. 9.11.13), and "to love" (ἀγαπᾶν: v. 13).

[62] See B.B. BRUEHLER, "Reweaving the Texture", 54.

[63] Thus, A.A. Just Jr. (*Luke*, II, 612) points out: "Jesus' extended discourse begun at 14,25, with great crowds journeying with him [...] and will terminate at 17,10, after which Luke reports that Jesus is travelling between Samaria and Galilee". See also Luke 14,26–27.33; J.A. FITZMYER, *Luke*, II, 1071; and M. GRILLI, *Matteo*, 352.

[64] See, on the one hand (v. 1b), e.g., "rich" (πλούσιος), "steward" (οἰκονόμος), "to squander" (διασκορπίζειν) and "possessions" (ὑπάρχοντα), and on the other hand (v. 13), "servant" (οἰκέτης), "to serve" (δουλεύειν: 2x), "to hate" (μισεῖν), "to love" (ἀγαπᾶν), "to cling to" (ἀντέχεσθαι), "to despise" (καταφρονεῖν), and "mammon" (μαμωνᾶς). See also J.L. RESSEGUIE, *Narrative Criticism*, 58.

[65] D.J. IRELAND, *Stewardship*, 122. See also J.J. KILGALLEN, "The Purpose", 234.

ἐξεμυκτήριζον)[66], and simultaneously felt, at the textual level, by the manuscript tradition of several readings[67]. By adding a καί to the previous δέ, they establish a relationship between v. 14 and v. 1, and thus emphasize the contrast between the Pharisees and the disciples[68].

Finally, the two narrative segments (vv. 1–13.14–31) are associated also on structural, lexical and semantic levels[69]. Just as in Jesus' admonition to the Pharisees (vv. 14–31), also in his instruction to his disciples (vv. 1–13), parable (vv. 1b–8a) and sayings (vv. 8b–13) resurface concomitant to each other, although in inversed position (see vv. 15b–18.19–31). Linked by internal associations, they likewise occur right after two brief *extradiegetic* introductions (see vv. 1a.14–15a)[70]. Among the lexical and semantic correspondences linking vv. 14–31 and vv. 1–13, the following ones are especially worth noting:

a) the recurrences of the word, "rich" (πλούσιος)[71], and the aforementioned verb, "to listen" (ἀκούειν)[72];

b) the assonances[73] between "law" (νόμος), "steward" (οἰκονόμος), "house" (οἶκος), "servant" (οἰκέτης), "management" (οἰκονομία) and "managing"

---

[66] Thus, A.A. Just Jr. (*Luke*, II, 622) and L.J. Topel ("On the Injustice", 222) comment, respectively: "The imperfect emphasizes the connection to Jesus' teaching" and "expresses continuity with what went before".

[67] A E N P W Δ Θ 1 13 28 565 1582 and $f^{1.13}$.

[68] See, e.g., J.A. FITZMYER, *Luke*, II, 1112; and J. NOLLAND, *Luke*, II, 809. The presence of the conjunction καί, in Luke 16,1, is attested, e.g., in 𝔓[75] ℵ A B D E L N P W Δ Θ Ψ 1 13 28 565 1582 and $f^{1.13}$.

[69] See, esp., A. FEUILLET, "La parabole", 215; B. STANDAERT, "L'art de composer", 342–343; G. GIURISATO, "Come Luca", 462.477; E. LUPIERI, "Mammona iniquitatis", 132; T. BEDNARZ, "Status Disputes", 390–393; and B.B. BRUEHLER, "Reweaving the Texture", 52–53. We shall deal with some of these features again, in our study of both the concentric structure of Luke 16 and the relationship between its two parables.

[70] For the internal associations keeping the first segment (Luke 16,1–13) together, see especially the link created by the recurrence of the substantive, "unrighteousness" (ἀδικία: Luke 16,8a.9), and the adjective, "unrighteous" (ἄδικος: Luke 16,10.11). See also the *assonance* between "house" (οἶκος), "steward" (οἰκονόμος), "management" (οἰκονομία), "managing" (οἰκονομεῖν), and "servant" (οἰκέτης) in Luke 16,1.2.3.4.8.13. For the internal associations keeping the second segment (Luke 16,14–31) together, see the recurrence of the aforementioned verb, "to listen" (ἀκούειν: Luke 16,14.29.31), the indefinite adjective, "all/every" (πᾶς: Luke 16,14.16.18.26), and the substantive, "prophets" (προφῆται: Luke 16,16.29.31). See also the instances of the verbs, "to be [present]" (ὑπάρχειν: Luke 16,14.23), and "to fall" (πίπτειν: Luke 16,17.21).

[71] Luke 16,1.19.21.22.

[72] Luke 16,2.14.29.31.

[73] Commenting on the connective function of assonances, G. Giurisato ("Come Luca", 431, n. 45) specifies: "I termini non hanno solo una funzione semantica, ma anche connettiva: gli stessi termini, anche quando hanno accezioni diverse, colpiscono l'orecchio con la ripetizione degli stessi suoni, collegando così i testi".

(οἰκονομεῖν)[74], and between "entrusting" (πιστεύειν), "trustworthy" (πιστός), and "mammon" (μαμωνᾶς), which in their Aramaic substratum all share the same root, *'āman* (אמן)[75];

c) and last but not least, the common idea of being welcomed or coming into someone else's place[76].

III. Luke 16,14: A Lynchpin for the Whole Narrative Unit

The aforementioned observations encourage us to appreciate a deliberate intention on the part of the author to construct the context of v. 16 into a coherent unit (vv. 1–31), composed of two narrative segments (vv. 1–13.14–31) and centered on v. 14[77]. More precisely, a look at the narrative development of this unit leads us to view these two segments as two scenes (or panels) of one and the same theme-centered narrative diptych. At the center of the diptych, v. 14 functions as the hinge to which the two panels are attached and around which they rotate (see Luke 16,1–13.14.15–31).

On the left and right sides of v. 14, in fact, the hinged narrative panels match each other according to a typical chiastic pattern, made up of an alternation of stories and sayings (A–B/B[1]–A[1])[78]. Two parables, relating to two rich men (A: vv. 1b–8a; and A[1]: vv. 19–31) are sandwiched around two concatenated

---

[74] Luke 16,1.2.3.4.8.13.16.17.27.

[75] Luke 16,9.10.11.12.13. Among the authors who note a connection at the Semitic level of the aforementioned words, see, e.g., G.M. CAMPS – B.M. UBACH, "Un sentido", 75–82; F. HAUCK, "μαμωνᾶς", *TDNT*, IV, 388; G. ROSSÉ, *Luca*, 624, n. 20; F. BOVON, *Luc*, III, 73; A. TOSATO, *Vangelo*, 392, n. 129; and K.R. SNODGRASS, *Stories*, 412. For the etymological explanations of the word "mammon" (μαμωνᾶς), and its connection with the vocabulary of faith and truth, see, e.g., J.A. FITZMYER, *Luke*, II, 1109; M. GRILLI, *L'impotenza*, 18; and ID., *Matteo*, 355–356.360.

[76] See, e.g., Luke 16,2.4.9.22.24.26.27.28.30. See also the assonance between the numbers, "fifty" (πεντήκοντα: v. 6) and "five" (πέντε: v. 28), and the verbs, "bringing (charges)" ([δια-]βάλλειν: vv. 1.20), "call/confort-ing" (προσ/παρα-καλεῖν: vv. 5.25), and "not being able to" (οὐ/μὴ δύνασθαι: vv. 2.13.26).

[77] See, e.g., C.-S.A. CHEONG, *A Dialogic Reading*, 119.

[78] Although differing slightly in the delimitation of the segments, we agree with B.B. Bruehler ("Reweaving the Texture", 53): "The basic repetitive-progressive texture [...] shows us a basic chiastic layout: story (vv. 1–8), sayings (vv. 9–13), sayings (vv. 14–18), and story (vv. 19–31)". Thus, E. Lupieri ("Mammona iniquitatis", 132) explains: "Indeed, the whole of Luke 16 is organized as a 'circular' or chiastic unit, rotating around the ironic reaction of the Pharisees (Luke 16,14), which roughly stands in the middle of the chapter. The 'first wing' of this [...] unit is composed of a parable regarding the administration of unrighteous richness [...] and of a group of apparently loose logia regarding faithfulness and richness [...] After the reaction of the Pharisees, we find the 'second wing', composed of a group of apparently loose logia [...] and of a parable regarding unrighteous richness". See also M. GRILLI, *Matteo*, 349.

sets of sayings (B: vv. 8b–13; and B¹: vv. 15b–18)[79], which are further addressed to two opposite groups of people (disciples and Pharisees: see vv. 1a.14–15a)[80] in what is known as an *exemplum contrarium*[81]. Literary concatenations of sayings-material[82], as well as audience shifts from adversaries to disciples, and vice-versa, are recurring patterns particularly typical of Luke's Travel Narrative (Luke 9,51–19,44)[83].

Within this diptych or chiastic structure, however, v. 14 neither tells a story nor presents sayings. Rather, as B.B. Bruehler points out, it indicates the derision of the Pharisees in such a way as to provide a lynchpin for the unit[84]. In fact, although it is properly part of the second *extradiegetic* introduction of chap. 16 (see vv. 1a.14–15a), the verse stands out also for the different information it supplies as compared to that of v. 1a. Adding to the correspondence between v. 1a, "he was also saying to the disciples" (ἔλεγεν δὲ καὶ πρὸς τοὺς μαθητάς), and v. 15a, "and he said to them" (καὶ εἶπεν αὐτοῖς), it voices further details, which the *extradiegetic* narrator believes necessary for the reader's proper grasp of the narrative that follows.

That v. 14 works as "the pivotal link"[85] between vv. 1–13 and 15–31 is visible also from a syntactic perspective. In fact, the aforementioned use of the imperfect tenses, "were listening to" (ἤκουον) and "were sneering at" (ἐξεμυκτήριζον)[86], does

---

[79] See D.J. IRELAND, *Stewardship*, 148, n. 165. As T. Bednarz ("Status Disputes", 409) points out, "The two parables of the rich persons form an *inclusio* that binds together the concentric composition".

[80] See, e.g., Luke 6,7; 11,53; 12,1; 15,1–2; and 19,39. For the hostile characterization of the Pharisees in Luke, as opposed to that of Jesus' disciples, and as reflecting a conventional typology, a caricature, or a literary device, rather than a historical depiction, see T. BEDNARZ, "Status Disputes", 387, n. 20.

[81] See, e.g., Lausberg, 199–200; and M. CRIMELLA, *Marta*, 419.

[82] See, esp., J.A. FITZMYER, *Luke*, II, 842. According to the author (*Ibid.*, II, 842), "the joining of such disparate material, which is characteristic of the travel account", may actually be a direct consequence of "what Luke meant in his prologue when he protested that he was writing 'systematically' (*kathexēs*, lit. 'in order', 1,3)". See also G. GIURISATO, "Come Luca", 419–420.481.

[83] See A.A. JUST, Jr., *Luke*, II, 613. As noted by J.A. Baird (*Audience Criticism*, 51), "Luke in his travel narrative is extremely obscure regarding his topography, but surprisingly careful in observing changes in audience". See also B.I. REICKE, *Luke*, 38–39; J.L. RESSEGUIE, "Point of View", 43, n. 8; M.R. AUSTIN, "The Hypocritical Son", 310–311; G.W. KLINGSPORN, *The Law*, 137–138.154–155.188–190; L.T JOHNSON, *Luke*, 165; D.J. IRELAND, *Stewardship*, 58.156–157; F.J. MATERA, "Jesus' Journey", 69–73; and K.R. SNODGRASS, *Stories*, 405.

[84] See B.B. BRUEHLER, "Reweaving the Texture", 53. See also J. DUPONT, *Les Béatitudes*, III, 62–63.167; and C.J.A. HICKLING, "A Tract", 257.

[85] D.J. IRELAND, *Stewardship*, 123.

[86] The verb ἐκμυκτηρίζειν lit. means, "to turn up the 'nose' (μυκτήρ)", as a sign of scorn or ridicule toward someone. See, e.g., LXX on Job 22,19; Pss 21,8; 35,16; Prov 15,5; 23,9; Jer 20,7; Luke 23,35; and Thayer, "ἐκμυκτηρίζω", 198.

not only complete and connect what follows with the previous aorist verbs but, insofar as it indicates static background information (second narrative level), it also marks the beginning of a new narrative segment[87]. In other words, paving the way for the upcoming admonishment (vv. 15b–31), these verbs set the stage with key information, which, as remarked by A. Nicacci, "the reader/listener must know in order to understand"[88] what is about to be narrated. Strictly speaking, this also implies that the primary level of the narration in Luke 16,14–31 begins only after this background knowledge has been staged, with the aorist tense of λέγω (εἶπεν: v. 15a)[89]. As the segment reaches its closure, in fact, the first level of narration resumes, and the tenses of the main verbs revert to the aorist tense (see Luke 17,1a.5a.6a).

Finally, the crucial function of v. 14 is palpable also in the "narrational texture"[90] of Luke 16, as well as in its thematic and rhetorical developments. As B.B. Bruehler remarks, parable (vv. 1b–8a) and sayings (vv. 8b–13) together bring about the Pharisees' negative reaction (v. 14), which in turn produces another set of sayings, followed by a related parable[91]. The logical progression of the narrative is perceived also at its thematic level[92]. At the centre of the concentric structure (v. 14), we find a warning against love of money (φιλαργυρία), while at its extremities, the phrase, "a rich man" (ἄνθρωπος πλούσιος), opens the two parables almost like a refrain (see vv. 1b.19a). Indeed, the language of wealth and possessions produces what B.B. Bruehler calls a "repetitive-progressive"[93] pattern, which begins with the

---

[87] See, e.g., Luke 16,1 (ἔλεγεν); Luke 14,25; 15,3.11 (εἶπεν). See also Mark 7,6.9; Luke 5,34.36; 6,3.5; 12,42.54; 13,2.6; John 12,30.33; P. JOÜON, "Imparfaits", 93–96; and A. NICACCI, "Dall'aoristo", 89–94. For the relationship between Imperfect and Aorist, see Smyth, 279; Zerwick, 93; and B.M. FANNING, *Verbal Aspect*, 244.288. Imperfect indicatives generally express background information or circumstances relating to the actions of the main (aorist) verbs. See, e.g., "were grumbling" (διεγόγγιζον: Luke 15,1); A. NICACCI, "Dall'aoristo", 87–99.107; M. CRIMELLA, *Marta*, 61, n. 5; and *Ibid.*, 87.

[88] A. NICACCI, "Dall'aoristo", 97.

[89] Because vv. 14–31 belong to the broader teaching episode (or micro-narrative) of Luke 14,25–17,10, the verb is distinctive of the general dynamics of its first level of narration and actually marks its progression. See, e.g., Luke 14,25b; 15,3.11a; 16,15a; 17,1a.5a.6a; A. NICACCI, "Dall'aoristo", 107; F.J. MATERA, "Jesus' Journey", 72–73; and A.A. JUST, Jr., *Luke*, II, 612.

[90] B.B. BRUEHLER, "Reweaving the Texture", 55.

[91] See B.B. BRUEHLER, "Reweaving the Texture", 53. Thus, the author (*Ibid.*, 53) concludes: "Therefore, one can examine v. 14 as the Pharisees' attempt to discredit Jesus' teaching [i.e., vv. 1–13], and vv. 15–18 (as well as 19–31) as an answer to those implicit challenges".

[92] For instance, R.H. Stein (*Luke*, 421) observes: "The parable of the rich man and Lazarus is connected to the preceding as an example (Luke 16,19–26) both of a man who was a lover of money (16,14) and who foolishly made poor use of his possessions (16,9–13) as well as an example (16,27–31) of the continued validity of the law and the prophets (16,16–18)". See also E.E. ELLIS, *Luke*, 221; and A.A. JUST, Jr., *Luke*, II, 623.

[93] B.B. BRUEHLER, "Reweaving the Texture", 52.

staging of the "rich man", in the first parable (v. 1b); then, develops and, in a section made up of sayings interpreting the parable, becomes "unrighteous mammon" (3x: vv. 9.11.13); shortly after that, it continues and reappears in the negative characterization of the Pharisees, as "money lovers" (v. 14), to end again with the tragic fate of another "rich man" (v. 19), in the second parable.

Accordingly, if the narrative and thematic structure of Luke 16 do rotate around v. 14, then the midpoint of the concentric composition should not only reveal crucial information for the comprehension of the surrounding verses, but also function rhetorically as the lynchpin or pivot of the whole underlying reasoning[94]. As could be expected, a number of exegetes agree that part of the extra-parabolic discourse refers to the first parable, while another foretells the following one[95]. Such a deduction has recently received further confirmation by the study of the "argumentative texture"[96] of the chapter. The rhetorical analysis, in particular, has shown how each single part of the first narrative panel in the chiasm sheds light on its counterpart. The following figure (# 1) portrays the way in which these connections work at the rhetorical level of the narrative structure in Luke 16[97].

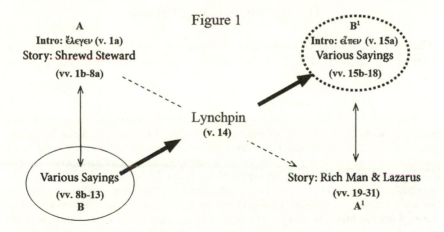

Figure 1

A
Intro: ἔλεγεν (v. 1a)
Story: Shrewd Steward
(vv. 1b-8a)

B¹
Intro: εἶπεν (v. 15a)
Various Sayings
(vv. 15b-18)

Lynchpin
(v. 14)

Various Sayings
(vv. 8b-13)
B

Story: Rich Man & Lazarus
(vv. 19-31)
A¹

As B.B. Bruehler points out, each set of sayings functions as an elaboration of its respective parable (B > A and B¹ > A¹), the first one (B) by way of com-

---

[94] See, e.g., T. BEDNARZ, "Status Disputes", 391.

[95] See, esp., A. FEUILLET, "La parabole", 212. See also F. GODET, *Luke*, II, 159; C.L. BLOMBERG, *Interpreting the Parables*, 116; G. ROSSÉ, *Luca*, 617; R. KRÜGER, "Lucas 16,1–13", 99–100; and A.A. JUST, Jr., *Luke*, II, 612.

[96] B.B. BRUEHLER, "Reweaving the Texture", 53.

[97] The figure is an adaptation of the diagram found in B.B. BRUEHLER, "Reweaving the Texture", 53.

mentary, and the second one (B¹) as a prelude[98]. Because of the concentric construction of Luke 16 and its logical narrative progression, however, the first set of sayings (B) and parable (A) also help interpret the opposite matches (B¹ and A¹, respectively)[99]. As to the central lynchpin of the unit on the subject of the Pharisees' love of wealth (v. 14), its major rhetorical thrust provides the key turning point of the concentric composition, as derision finds its place of exchange and "the target(s) of the innuendo becomes clear"[100].

To conclude, we can say that R.J. Karris' initial presupposition has proved to be valid. A number of textual indicators and thematic links in Luke 16 unify two narrative segments into one coherent unit. At the same time, hermeneutical clues emerge from the context of Luke 16,16, which call for a study of both the parables and the sayings in their role of mutual clarification, and of v. 14, in its crucial function within the thematic thread of the chapter. The following pages shall be devoted specifically to bringing out how each of these elements ultimately enlighten the saying of v. 16.

D. Two Sandwiching Parables

The most evident sign of a deliberate arrangement on the part of Luke, spatially buttressing, so to say, R.J. Karris' aforementioned presupposition, is the strong

---

[98] See B.B. BRUEHLER, "Reweaving the Texture", 53. See also the aforementioned links within each of the two panels, in Chap. III, p. 99, n. 70. As concerns Luke 16,14–31, for instance, C.H. Talbert (*Reading Luke*, 185) observes: "The section [...] is organized into a two-pronged group of sayings (vv. 14–18), followed by a double-edged parable (vv. 19–31). Verses 19–26 of the parable are an exposition of vv. 14–15, while vv. 27–31 serve as an illustration of vv. 16–18 [...] This pattern gives unity to the section". Although there may be some truth as to the inner unifying connections, however, vv. 14–15a contain neither sayings nor parables. The first set of sayings begins rather in v. 15b, as indicated in the figure. For a list of authors who call attention to the relationship between vv. 14–18 and 19–31, see, e.g., J. DUPONT, *Les Béatitudes*, III, 164, n. 1.

[99] François Bovon also observes a certain parallelism between vv. 10–13 and vv. 14–18. However, as B.B. Bruehler ("Reweaving the Texture", 53, n. 21) remarks, "then he differentiates them sharply, vv. 10–13 are related while vv. 15–18 are divergent". F. BOVON, *Luc*, III, 83.

[100] T. BEDNARZ, "Status Disputes", 391. See also *Ibid.*, 390–402. In the concentric composition of chap. 16, the author (*Ibid.*, 391) detects the use of humor by means of a rhetorical device, which "Demetrius calls innuendo", and which "serves to create puzzlement" in the hearer. See DEMETRIUS, *Eloc.*, 282–286 (ed. W.R. ROBERTS, 196–197). Up to v. 14, the Lucan audience is unable to see that the target of Jesus' rhetoric on unrighteous deeds, unfaithfulness, worldly shrewdness, and "loving" slavery to mammon (vv. 1b–13) is the Pharisees (with their upturned noses). The following admonition and story (vv. 15b–31), aimed at them directly, are a call to love God and neighbor by fidelity to the Law, especially as concerns the care of the poor.

nexus existing between the two parables towering above this section[101]. Luke 16, in fact, begins with the parable of the Shrewd Steward and ends with that of the Rich Man and Lazarus[102]. The vast majority of scholars, nowadays, acknowledge the "intimate and surprising connexion"[103] of these two stories as legitimate, and are generally at ease with the fact that these substantial passages, which belong exclusively to Luke, counterbalance one another in a reciprocally clarifying way[104].

For instance, M. Ball observes that, while in the parable of the Good Samaritan (Luke 10,25–37) and, on a larger scale, in the three individual parables of the Lost Sheep, the Lost Coin, and the Lost Son (Luke 15,4–7.8–10.11–32), Luke uses a renowned storyteller's technique known as the "rule of three"[105], "a rule of two" is likewise operative in the parable of the House-builders (Luke 6,47–49) and, on a larger scale, in both complementary pairs of parables on the cost of discipleship (Luke 14,28–30.31–33) and the handling of possessions (Luke 16,1b–8a.19–31)[106]. In particular, as concerns the relationship

---

[101] See, e.g., J. NOLLAND, *Luke*, II, 796; and D.L. BOCK, *Luke*, II, 1322.

[102] See A. FEUILLET, "La parabole", 212.

[103] J.D.M. DERRETT, "Fresh Light", II, 364. Similarly, A. Feuillet ("La parabole", 221–222) writes: "les deux paraboles […] sont intimement liées entre elles". Thus, one could say that a certain "effect of affinity" is here at work. See, e.g., D. MARGUERAT – A. WÉNIN, *Sapori*, 16.172–176.

[104] See, e.g., H. OLSHAUSEN, *Biblischer Commentar*, I, 666–693; ID., *Biblical Commentary*, II, 62–84; J.J. VAN OOSTERZEE, *Luke*, 253; F. GODET, *Luke*, II, 159; A.B. BRUCE, *The Parabolic Teaching*, 378; C.E. VAN KOETSVELD, *Die Gleichnisse*, 247; A. PLUMMER, *Luke*, 390; W. GRUNDMANN, *Lukas*, 325; A. VON SCHLATTER, *Die Evangelien*, 331; J.D.M. DERRETT, "Fresh Light", II, 364.370; F.J. MOORE, "The Parable", 103–105; I.H. MARSHALL, *Luke*, 632; A. FEUILLET, "La parabole", 212.221–222; J.A. FITZMYER, *Luke*, II, 1127; B. STANDAERT, "L'art de composer", 342–343; J. NOLLAND, *Luke*, II, 797; D.J. IRELAND, *Stewardship*, 136–137; R.A. PIPER, "Social Background", 1661; M. BALL, "The Parables", 329–330; R. KRÜGER, "Lucas 16,1–13", 99.108; A.A. JUST, Jr., *Luke*, II, 612.630; G. GIURISATO, "Come Luca", 481, n. 166; B.J. BYRNE, *The Hospitality of God*, 133; C.-S.A. CHEONG, *A Dialogic Reading*, 119–120; J.A. TROXLE, Jr., *Doing Justice*, 220–222; L. SCHOTTROFF, *Le parabole*, 251–273; M. CRIMELLA, *Marta*, 418–419; and J.L. STORY, "Twin Parables", 105.

[105] M. BALL, "The Parables", 329. For the "dramatic triangle", as a specific Lucan development of the σύγκρισις (or *comparatio*), and Luke's rhetoric-narrative use of it in the Gospel, see O. LEHTIPUU, "Characterization", 83–84; M. CRIMELLA, *Marta*, 19–58; and D. MARGUERAT – A. WÉNIN, *Sapori*, 51–57.

[106] See M. BALL, "The Parables", 329–330. In support of the different claim, that Luke 15,1–16,8a form rather a pair of doublets, see, e.g., M.R. AUSTIN, "The Hypocritical Son", 307–315; D. LANDRY – B. MAY, "Honour Restored", 305–308; and A.T. FARNES, "A New Interpretation", 6–10. Although we still recognize some connection between the parables contained in Luke 15 and Luke 16, the latter author (*Ibid.*, 11) goes too far in arguing that, "these certain men [in Luke 15,11; 16,1.19] were in fact the same certain man". See, e.g., *Ibid.*, 12.14–22. His reasoning is illogical and scientifically weak. The two sons' prodigal

between the two parables of Luke 16, his conclusion is that they ought to be compared and contrasted with one another, so that they may eventually interpret each other[107]. D. Marguerat and Y. Bourquin clarify how this is possible on a narrative level: "The interlocking triggers off an echo [...] and this echo produces enhanced meaning"[108].

To unveil the higher meaning produced by the interaction of these "sandwiching" parables and the sayings embedded between them, we shall proceed by indicating, first, only those elements binding the stories together. Secondly, we shall analyze each of the two parables separately, appraising their specific key points and functions. Only after they have been allowed to speak for themselves shall we finally pay attention to the echo they prompt. For the most part, thus, the focus of the following study shall be on the peculiar light the parabolic accounts shed on each other and on v. 16 in particular[109]. However, since the latter receives light also from the first set of sayings (see figure # 1), which in turn is but a clarification of the parable preceding it, our analysis shall be devoted first of all to the story of the rich man and his shrewd steward. Due to the disproportionate difficulty of its interpretation and its foundational value, the study of the first parable (A) shall occupy a considerable number of pages when compared to that of the second parable (A[1]).

I. A Few Shared Features: Introductory Remarks

In support of the intimate connection between the two parables in Luke 16, scholars generally mention a good number of common features[110]. For the most part, these consist of either mere lexical correspondences (e.g., the repetition of sentences, phrases, single terms, verbs and their compounds, synonyms,

---

father and the shrewd steward's rich master should accordingly end up in Hades in the person of the certain rich man of the last parable. The author, however, does not dare argue this.

[107] See M. BALL, "The Parables", 329. A. Feuillet ("La parabole", 217) notes something very similar when he claims that the closing parable, "revêt une signification beaucoup plus profonde quand on y voit la contrepartie de l'intendant astucieux".

[108] D. MARGUERAT – Y. BOURQUIN, *How to Read*, 39.

[109] More precisely, we shall deal first with the two parables (vv. 1b–8a and vv. 19–31) of chap. 16 separately, as integral parts of its two narrative scenes (vv. 1–13 and vv. 14–31). Similar treatment shall then be given to the sayings (vv. 8b–13 and vv. 15b–18) and to their connection with Luke 16,16. However, the study in this section is designed primarily to collect the light scattered throughout the context for the main purpose of demonstrating its coherence. For the actual application of the results of this research, with the detailed exegesis of the text and its related parts, see Section IV.

[110] See, e.g., A. VON SCHLATTER, *Die Evangelien*, 331; A. FEUILLET, "La parabole", 212.221–222; B. STANDAERT, "L'art de composer", 342–343; G. GIURISATO, "Come Luca", 462.477; and T. BEDNARZ, "Status Disputes", 410–411.

antonyms and assonances) or thematic agreements[111]. As we shall see, however, a further degree of resemblance can be detected with regard to their internal structure.

1. Lexical Correspondences

At the lexical level, the recognized correspondences generally include:

a) the very *opening sentence* introducing the two parables, "[now] there was a certain rich man" (ἄνθρωπός [δέ] τις ἦν πλούσιος)[112];

b) entire *expressions*, such as, "so he called (him) and said (to him)" (καὶ αὐτὸς φωνήσας [αὐτὸν] εἶπεν [αὐτῷ])[113], and "into the(-ir) house(-s) of" (εἰς τὸν [τοὺς] οἶκον [οἴκους] τοῦ [αὐτῶν])[114], both of which somehow echo the idea of "someone going from [a place] to" (τις ἀπὸ [...] πορευθῆναι πρός)[115] another;

c) the *verbs*, "hearing" (ἀκούειν)[116], "laying (charges)" ([δια-]βάλλειν)[117], "calling to one's self (or side)" (προσ[παρα-]καλεῖν)[118], "not being able to" (οὐ [μὴ] δύναμαι)[119], as well as, the participle specifying "things (or people) being there" (ὑπάρχ-[ων]οντα)[120];

d) and, finally, the *assonances* occurring between the nouns, "house" (οἶκος), "steward" (οἰκονόμος), and "management" (οἰκονομία), and the verb,

---

[111] See B. STANDAERT, "L'art de composer", 344. Discussing the criteria used to determine when two parabolic texts can be said to be actually parallel, C.L. Blomberg ("When is a parallel", 80) suggests three basic categories of verbal agreement: "(a) [...] words [...] which appear in identical form [...] (b) [...] which are [...] in different lexical or grammatical form, and (c) [...] which are clear synonyms". See also G. GIURISATO, "Come Luca", 426–430.

[112] Luke 16,1b.19a. One can also translate this sentence as follows: "(now) a certain man was rich". However, scholars treat the latter translation as less probable. See, e.g., A. PLUMMER, *Luke*, 391; B.B. SCOTT, "A Master's Praise", 179; R.C. TANNEHILL, *The Narrative Unity*, I, 186; and M. CRIMELLA, *Marta*, 350, n. 29.

[113] Luke 16,2a.24a.

[114] Luke 16,4c.27c.

[115] Luke 16,30b. See, also, "when I am removed from [...] they will receive me" (ὅταν μετασταθῶ ἐκ [...] δέξωνταί με), in Luke 16,4bc; "he was carried off [...] to" (ἀπενεχθῆναι αὐτόν [...] εἰς), in Luke 16,22a; "to go through from here to you [...] may cross over from there to us" (διαβῆναι ἔνθεν πρὸς ὑμᾶς [...] ἐκεῖθεν πρὸς ἡμᾶς διαπερῶσιν), in Luke 16,26bc; "they may come into this place of" (ἔλθωσιν εἰς τὸν τόπον τοῦτον τῆς), in Luke 16,28c; and D.A. DE SILVA, "The Parable", 261–262.

[116] Luke 16,2b.29c.31b.

[117] Luke 16,1c.20b.

[118] Luke 16,5a.25d. See also the similar use of the verb φωνέω, in Luke 16,2a.24a.

[119] Luke 16,2d.26b.

[120] Luke 16,1c.23b.

"managing" (οἰκονομεῖν)[121], as well as that between the numbers "fifty" (πεντήκοντα)[122] and "five" (πέντε)[123].

2. Thematic Correspondences

In addition to these features, both stories appear to be intertwined also on the thematic level[124]. Besides the aforementioned shared idea of movement from one place to another, some interpreters argue that a careful analysis cannot possibly fail to recognize the mutual presence of two "themes", that is, money and eschatology[125]. Thus, even if the parables are separated from each other by various verses, F. Godet points out: "The idea common to both is that of the relation between the use made of earthly goods and man's future beyond the tomb"[126].

Indeed, not a few scholars emphasize the thematic concern of the two parables with wealth, and the contrasting angle of their approach to the subject of its use[127]. We prefer to consider this motif later, while dealing with the main point of each parable and the thematic thread of Luke 16. For the moment, we wish to draw attention to the less assiduously examined motif of eschatology.

According to some authors, a number of eschatological nuances characterizes both accounts, either explicitly or implicitly.

For instance, before unfolding itself directly into its characters' final destiny, the plot of the second story speaks plainly of "good" (ἀγαθός) and, "evil" (κακός)[128], as well as of the possibility "to convert" (μετανοεῖν)[129] during one's earthly life. Its eschatological tones, then, go without saying: both the rich man and poor Lazarus "die" (ἀποθνήσκειν)[130] and are sentenced to a fate of either "torment" (βάσανος)[131] or consolation[132], with all dialogues (see Luke 16,24–

---

[121] See Luke 16,1b.2cd.3ac.4bc.8a.27c.

[122] Luke 16,6c.

[123] Luke 16,28a.

[124] See, e.g., J.-N. ALETTI, *L'arte*, 17–18; and G. GIURISATO, "Come Luca", 431.

[125] See, esp. J.A. TROXLE, Jr., *Doing Justice*, 222. See also S.E PORTER, "The Parable", 134–137; J.J. KILGALLEN, "Luke 15 and 16", 376; and D.L. BOCK, *Luke*, II, 1322.

[126] F. GODET, *Luke*, II, 159.

[127] See, e.g., A. PLUMMER, *Luke*, 379–380; J.A. FITZMYER, "The Story", 24–25; C.H. TALBERT, *Reading Luke*, 183–188; B. STANDAERT, "L'art de composer", 342–343; D.J. IRELAND, *Stewardship*, 7–12.48.159.217; and A. BOLIN, *Du bon usage*, 33.

[128] Luke 16,25b.

[129] Luke 16,30b. See also the verb, "to persuade" (πείθειν), in Luke 16,31c.

[130] Luke 16,22 (2x).

[131] Luke 16,23b.28c. See also the verb, "to torment" (ὀδυνεῖν), in Luke 16,24c.25c; and the mention of the "flame" (φλόξ), in Luke 16,24c.

[132] See, e.g., the verb "to console" (παρακαλεῖν), in Luke 16,25c; and, likewise, the mention of "water" (ὕδωρ), in Luke 16,24b.

31) being staged in some "place" (τόπος)[133] of the afterlife, between "Abraham's bosom" (κόλπος ʼΑβραάμ)[134] and "Hades" (ᾅδης)[135].

Albeit implicitly, the first story contains similar shades of meaning. As D.J. Ireland argues, and as other scholars likewise point out, the parable of the Shrewd Steward has a real eschatological dimension[136], which is especially detectable in its crisis motif and summons to action[137]. Indeed, commentators have repeatedly interpreted both the steward's call to give account of his management and his impending dismissal (see vv. 2.4b) allegorically, as referring to man's final judgment and death[138]. The motif is present likewise in the parable of the Rich Man and Lazarus, as a way of recapitulation. Without realizing it, even the five brothers of the rich man are confronted with this crisis and sooner or later will have to face it[139]. As has rightly been noted, mention of them embodies Luke's intention to bring the message of the story back to the living:

> the readers [...] should understand more fully their responsibilities to those less fortunate and act accordingly, lest they be like the rich man, his five brothers, and the Lucan Pharisees[140].

Moreover, a few interpreters observe some eschatological implications in Luke 16,8a, specifically in the verb, "to praise" (ἐπαινεῖν), the adverb, "shrewdly" (φρονίμως), and the epithet, "of unrighteousness" (τῆς ἀδικίας). For instance, referring to H. Preisker's article, K.E. Bailey grounds his argument

---

[133] Luke 16,28c. See also Luke 16,23c.

[134] Luke 16,22b.

[135] Luke 16,23a. See, e.g., M.R. AUSTIN, "The Hypocritical Son", 314–315. The spatial notion of the afterlife here may have a significant impact on the interpretation of the kingdom of God, in Luke 16,16.

[136] See, esp., D.J. IRELAND, *Stewardship*, 2. See also D.R. FLETCHER, "The Riddle", 19; A. FEUILLET, "La parabole", 222; and D.A. DE SILVA, "The Parable", 259–260.

[137] See, esp., D.J. IRELAND, *Stewardship*, 82. See also J. JEREMIAS, *The Parables*, 46–48.182; J.A. FITZMYER, "The Story", 32, n. 21; R.H. HIERS, "Friends", 32.36; T. HOYT, Jr., "The Poor", 160–161; L.J. TOPEL, "On the Injustice", 219.226–227; K.E. BAILEY, *Poet*, 105–107; D.P. SECCOMBE, *Possessions*, 172; M. KRÄMER, *Das Rätsel*, 67–68.238; D.J. IRELAND, *Stewardship*, 12–22; D.A. DE SILVA, "The Parable", 260–263.266; and D. LANDRY – B. MAY, "Honour Restored", 292, n. 22.

[138] See, e.g., A. BOLIN, *Du bon usage*, 9.11–14.16. In turn, J.S. Kloppenborg ("The Dishonoured Master", 479, n. 15) notes: "The phrase *apodidonai ton logon* (v. 2) occurs elsewhere as a metaphor for God's judgment (Matt 12,36; cf. 25,19; Rom 14,12; 1Pet 4,5) [...] always in contexts which make clear its eschatological sense". Unfortunately, however, he (*Ibid.*, 479, n. 15) immediately states: "Nothing in the context of Luke 16,1–8a suggests an eschatological sense". Cf., e.g., Heb 13,17; D.A. DE SILVA, "The Parable", 259; D. MATHEWSON, "The Parable", 36, n. 42; and M.D. GREENE, "The Parable", 86, n. 19.

[139] See, e.g., J.A. FITZMYER, *Luke*, II, 1128–1129.

[140] D.B. GOWLER, "'At His Gate'", 257. See also R.A. PIPER, "Social Background", 1661.

on the usage of the noun, "praise" (ἔπαινος), to claim that even the occurrence of the corresponding verb in the story (v. 8a) constitutes outward evidence of the eschatological concern of the parable[141]. Likewise, more than one interpreter recognizes an implicit eschatological nuance in the adverb, "shrewdly" (φρονίμως)[142]. Although it is a biblical *hapax legomenon*, eight of the nine Gospel uses of the related adjective (φρόνιμος) are definitely eschatological in nature[143]. The only exception seems to be the occurrence in Matt 10,16b, wherein Jesus sends the twelve out on their mission, exhorting them to be as "shrewd" (φρόνιμοι) as serpents and as innocent as doves[144].

Finally, as to the eschatological tone of the epithet, "of unrighteousness" (τῆς ἀδικίας), on a grammatical level, the phrase, "the steward of unrighteousness" (ὁ οἰκονόμος τῆς ἀδικίας), essentially corresponds to the other phrase, "the unrighteous steward" (ὁ οἰκονόμος ἄδικος)[145]. However, on a semantic level, the expression seems to have a slightly deeper nuance and may already imply within itself the same eschatological dualism as that stated in v. 8b, between this world and age and the next[146]. In spite of the grammatical equivalence with the adjective, for instance, H. Kosmala cites Qumran evidence to support his view that the expression was often used to signify someone who was totally caught up in the mentality of this world[147]. Moreover,

---

[141] See K.E. BAILEY, *Poet*, 107. See also H. PREISKER, "ἔπαινος", *TDNT*, II, 587; D.J. IRELAND, *Stewardship*, 67; and A.A. JUST, Jr., *Luke*, II, 616.

[142] See, e.g., J. JEREMIAS, *The Parables*, 46; H. PREISKER, "Lukas 16,1–7", 85–92; K.E. BAILEY, *Poet*, 106; J.A. FITZMYER, "The Story", 32, n. 21; ID., *Luke*, II, 1102; and D.J. IRELAND, *Stewardship*, 82–83.

[143] See Matt 7,24; 24,45 (= Luke 12,42); 25,2.4.8.9; and Luke 16,8. See also D.J. IRELAND, *Stewardship*, 83.

[144] As far as the eschatological use of the term in Luke's Gospel is concerned, however, what really matters are primarily its Lucan instances. Moreover, D.J. Ireland (*Stewardship*, 83, n. 140) observes: "Whether or not the adjective has an eschatological nuance in this verse [...] the verse is often cited as a parallel to the quality being commended in our parable". See, e.g., Matt 10,16b; and Luke 16,8a. See also H. OLSHAUSEN, *Biblical Commentary*, II, 68–69; A. VON HARNACK, "Zwei Worte", 952, n. 3; T. ZAHN, *Lukas*, 574; J.M. CREED, *Luke*, 202; B.A. HOOLEY – A.J. MASON, "Some Thoughts", 53–54; and D.R. FLETCHER, "The Riddle", 17–18.

[145] As M. Zerwick (Zerwick, 14) specifies, this is one of the best known examples of the "attributive" or "Hebrew" genitive, which "owing to Semitic influence [...] the Greeks used not [as] a genitive but an adjective". See also BDF, 91–92, §165.

[146] See, esp., D.J. IRELAND, *Stewardship*, 71. See also J. KÖGEL, "Zum Gleichnis", 590.597; M. KRÄMER, *Das Rätsel*, 149; I.H. MARSHALL, *Luke*, 620; K.E. BAILEY, *Poet*, 106; D.J. IRELAND, *Stewardship*, 70–72; and A.A. JUST, Jr., *Luke*, II, 616.

[147] See H. KOSMALA, "The Parable", 114–115. As D.J. Ireland (*Stewardship*, 99) points out, however, H. Kosmala goes too far when he maintains that, like the world itself, so all its "wealth and material possessions are [...] inherently evil". Although they can be acquired through "unrighteousness" (ἀδικία), and used in a way that is antagonistic to God (cf. vv. 9.11.13; and 1Tim 6,9–10), they too are part of God's good creation (cf. Gen 1,4.10.12.18.21.25.31) and, if

as pointed out by E.E. Ellis, in Luke's Gospel the substantive, "unrighteous-ness" (ἀδικία), occurs only in three parabolic passages (see Luke 13,27; 16,8–9; and 18,6), two of which, at least, relate clearly to eschatological contexts[148]. If this is the case, vv. 8b–13 may be simply expanding on one of the ruling principles that worldly people usually work for (i.e., wealth), and the expression, "unrighteous mammon" (μαμωνᾶς τῆς ἀδικίας)[149], be just a standard idiom for all money, "much as one might today use the expression 'filthy lucre'"[150].

3. Structural Correspondences

In addition to the lexical and thematic features mentioned thus far, there exist also a couple of correlated observations of a structural nature, which associate the two parables. The latter concern mostly the characters of the stories and interplay of their focalizations.

On their earthly podium, both accounts are equally staged around two protagonists or main participants: on the one hand, a *certain rich man* (or master) and his shrewd steward, and on the other hand, another *certain rich man* and poor Lazarus[151]. Likewise, both narratives introduce an additional

---

used shrewdly, can gain both heavenly friends and an eternal abode (cf. vv. 4.9; and 1Tim 6,17–19). The problem with them is whenever they begin to take the place of God. See, e.g., Luke 16,13; and M. GRILLI, *Matteo*, 360–361.

[148] See E.E. ELLIS, *Luke*, 199.

[149] Luke 16,9a.

[150] C.L. BLOMBERG, *Interpreting the Parables*, 246. Similarly, commenting on the polysemic value of the phrase, "the steward of unrighteousness" (ὁ οἰκονόμος τῆς ἀδικίας), R. Krüger ("Lucas 16,1–13", 104) mentions the possibility that it indicate an "'administrador de los bienes injustos o de lo que en sí es injusto', a saber, la riqueza, el Mamón. Es decir, administrador de bienes injustos".

[151] See D.J. IRELAND, *Stewardship*, 50; and J. DURKIN, "A Cultural Reading", 11. Strictly speaking, as pointed out by M. Crimella (*Marta*, 380–381), a third key character does come into play in the dramatic triangle of the second parable. Portrayed as, "un ministro o un plenipotenziario di Dio", Abraham functions as the "determinante (o sovrano dell'azione) [...] il ricco e Lazzaro hanno il ruolo di rispondenti". However, Abraham appears only after the first two characters have died and, as noted by D.L. Bock ("The Parable, 64), the development of the afterlife is "unusual", characterizing as it does only the plot of the second story. It aims at showing that, even then, nothing really happens. As specified by F. Schnider and W. Stenger ("Die offene Tür, 277), all the expectation of a contact between the two characters fails and "der Reiche beharrt in Beziehungslosigkeit zu dem Armen". Thus, when one considers the second parable as a whole, M. Crimella (*Marta*, 57, n. 110) is right: the first story follows "una logica differente: al determinante (l'uomo ricco) risponde un solo rispondente principale (l'amministratore) che, a sua volta, ha una relazione con un altro rispondente subordinato (i debitori)". However, when one considers solely the first earthly scene of the second parable, the parallel between the two main characters in both stories holds true. As generally acknowledged by the latter (*Ibid.*, 30), in fact, even "se le storie

collective character, namely, the first rich man's *debtors* and the second rich man's *brothers*. These secondary figures can be classified as "flat" characters, in that they are constructed by means of a single trait (i.e., their being debtors and brothers, respectively)[152]. Although both R.W. Funk and M. Crimella treat the debtors of the first story as "subordinate respondents", nothing prevents us from considering both debtors and brothers also as "simple" or "walk-on" agents, to the degree that they play only a passive or quasi-passive (background) function in the denouement of their respective plots[153].

Moreover, in both accounts, the narration proceeds similarly from one character to the other, causing a dramatic change of view or perspective in the development of the story. In fact, the protagonists are staged according to a chiastic pattern: *rich man # 1* (vv. 1b–2), *steward* (vv. 3–4), *steward* (vv. 5–7), *rich man # 1* (v. 8a), and, likewise, *rich man # 2* (v. 19), *Lazarus* (vv. 20–21), *Lazarus* (v. 22a), *rich man # 2* (v. 22b)[154]. This alternating presentation of the main characters, however, goes hand in hand with another narrative technique, known as, "change of focalizer". As D. Marguerat and Y. Bourquin clarify, the latter consists precisely in the alternation of the subjects of focalization, so that the presentation of the narrative also adopts the view of the characters, alternately[155]. As concerns our two parables, in particular, the authors remark:

This procedure is obvious in the parable of the rich man and the poor Lazarus (Luke 16,19–31): the first scene (vv. 19–21) is depicted from the perspective of Lazarus and his impotent distress; there is a reversal in the second scene (vv. 22–31), in which Lazarus is dumb while the narrator introduces the reader to the despair of the rich man. The dramatization of the

---

raccontate sono differenti la costruzione del racconto ha interessanti parallelismi e singolari comunanze". See, e.g., R.W. FUNK, "Structure", 51–56; D. MARGUERAT – Y. BOURQUIN, *How to Read*, 18–20; O. LEHTIPUU, "Characterization", 97–100; M. CRIMELLA, *Marta*, 20–30.367–368.424–427; and A. BOLIN, *Du bon usage*, 52.

[152] See, e.g., D. MARGUERAT – Y. BOURQUIN, *How to Read*, 173; and O. LEHTIPUU, "Characterization", 77–79. For the distinction between *round* and *flat* characters, see, esp., D. MARGUERAT – Y. BOURQUIN, *How to Read*, 60–61; and J.L. RESSEGUIE, *Narrative Criticism*, 123–124.

[153] See, e.g., D. MARGUERAT – Y. BOURQUIN, *How to Read*, 60; *Ibid.*, 178; and M. CRIMELLA, *Marta*, 403. As admitted by R.W. Funk ("Structure", 52–53), "subordinate figures may be stage pawns [...] in no case [they] play more than ancillary roles". See also *Ibid.*, 55.69; and M. CRIMELLA, *Marta*, 57, n. 110.

[154] More precisely, as M. Crimella (*Marta*, 379) points out, the portrayal of the two characters in the second story "procede per mezzo dell'artificio retorico della reduplicatio [...] cioè [...] attraverso un doppio chiasmo, alternando il ricco e il povero". See also Lausberg, 277–279; F. SCHNIDER – W. STENGER, "Die offene Tür", 278; J. KREMER, "Der arme Lazarus", 574–575; and O. LEHTIPUU, "Characterization", 90–91.94.

[155] See D. MARGUERAT – Y. BOURQUIN, *How to Read*, 74. The sequence of focalizations is one of those narrative techniques in which Luke notably excels and can be used also as a structural marker to link various scenes thematically, so that they illumine each other. See, e.g., D. MARGUERAT – A. WÉNIN, *Sapori*, 155–163.

parable is fed by this change of focalizer, which brings the reader, successively, under the skin of the two protagonists[156].

In this parable, specifically, the disproportionate *number of verses* dedicated to the second scene (precisely, 10 vv. as compared to 3, in the first scene), the fact that the poor man *never speaks* a word in the whole story, and the most noteworthy "singularity of the parable"[157] itself, namely, that a character in the fictitious story carries *a name*, have all a specific effect on both Jesus' immediate addressees and Luke's Gospel readers: "they are asked to identify with the dynamics that concern the rich man and his brothers[158]. Indeed, it is the anonymous rich man who is "the main person"[159] in the story. On a narrative level, in fact, the mention of the character's name forces one to re-cognize one's difference from him and keep distance, whereas anonymity facilitates wider identification[160]. As a result, the *intradiegetic* storyteller intends primarily to convey a fearful and disquieting admonishment against the rich and, only secondarily, an encouragement for the poor[161]. Even though the characterization of the rich man must sound quite rough to Jesus' hearers – that of Lazarus is definitely more attractive – they are nonetheless invited to enter the narrated world by wearing the rich man's shoes and no other's, and this is so precisely because the intended primary audience of the parable is the money-loving assemblage of the Pharisees (see Luke 15,1–3; 16,1a.14–15a)[162].

---

[156] D. MARGUERAT – Y. BOURQUIN, *How to Read*, 74. See also O. LEHTIPUU, "Characterization", 91–93; M. CRIMELLA, *Marta*, 377–378; and D. MARGUERAT – A. WÉNIN, *Sapori*, 147. At the pragmatic level (i.e., at the level of the effects of the text upon the reader), Luke may here be employing this technique to question his reader concerning the identity of the true disciple in relation to his use of wealth. See, e.g., *Ibid.*, 162–163.

[157] M. CRIMELLA, *Marta*, 427. As pointed out by A. Plummer (*Luke*, 391), "Nowhere else does Christ give a name to any character in a parable". M. Crimella (*Ibid.*, 358) notes further that the nominalization of the character is supplied by means of "a well-known Lucan formula, "ὀνόματι + nominativo". See, e.g., Luke 1,5; 5,27; 10,38; 16,20; 23,50; 24,18; Acts 5,1; 8,9; 9,10–12.33.36; 10,1; 11,28; 12,13; 16,1.14; 17,34; 18,2.7.24; 19,24; 20,9; 21,10; 27,1; and 28,7. See also BDF, 71, §128.3; D.L. BOCK, "The Parable", 64–65; and O. LEHTIPUU, "Characterization", 89.93.

[158] M. CRIMELLA, *Marta*, 427. See also *Ibid.*, 349–365.378–382.386–387.391–395.415–417.421–427.

[159] H. KVALBEIN, "Jesus", 84.

[160] See, e.g., M. CRIMELLA, *Marta*, 367; and J.L. RESSEGUIE, *Narrative Criticism*, 67.129–130.

[161] See, e.g, O. LEHTIPUU, "Characterization", 101–104; and T. BEDNARZ, "Status Disputes", 414.

[162] As O. Lehtipuu ("Characterization", 102) writes, "The story is told mainly from the rich man's point of view […] because the Pharisees are the primary audience. In this way, the Pharisees are led to identify themselves with the rich man and experience what their life is going to be like if they do not repent, if they do not share their goods with others". See also M. CRIMELLA, *Marta*, 348. Thus, we strongly disagree with those who maintain that the author's intended impact of this parable on the audience is simply that of sympathizing with

Although less obvious and in a slightly different fashion, the same procedure (*change of focalizer*) is employed in the parable of the Shrewd Steward (Luke 16,1b–8a). Here, the plot begins (vv. 1b–2) and ends (v. 8a) with the rich man's judgment (or perspective), but centers on the shrewd steward's thoughts and actions (vv. 3–4.5–7)[163]. Thus, also in this case, the staging of the protagonists conforms to an alternating pattern (rich man, shrewd steward, rich man), and this brings the reader again beneath their different focalizations.

By listening to the charges made against his steward (vv. 1b–2), the rich master seems at first to endorse the accusers' perspective and dismiss the steward[164]. However, the story ends with the master praising him (v. 8a)[165]. Authors explain this utter change of mind differently. A minority of scholars distinguishes here a quite logical and even expected development, mostly on account of the character's social status and the fact that his initially discredited honor is ultimately restored[166]. Conversely, the majority opinion understands it as a rather unexpected and paradoxical statement[167].

We shall have occasion again to evaluate the two trends in our study of the parable itself, mostly favoring the latter. However, what is particularly worth noting here is that, regardless of its more or less illogical development, it is still the rich master's focalization that is brought to the fore in v. 8a. What is more, the change of focalization is made easier by the use of a paradox. In fact, the purpose of the latter rhetorical figure is that of grabbing the reader's

---

the poor Lazarus and of rejecting the rich man. See, e.g., H.-G. GRADL, "Von den Kosten", 310. The intended identification of the Pharisees with the rich man is supported further by the association of Lazarus with the younger son (cf. Luke 15,16 and 16,21) and that of the rich man with the elder son (cf. Luke 15,31 and 16,25): both rich man and elder son are an image of the Pharisees' own attitude, respectively, towards money and sinners. See, e.g., M.-L. RIGATO, "'Mosè ed i Profeti'", 163, n. 41; *Ibid.*, 168, n. 56; and M. CRIMELLA, *Marta*, 327–329.420–421.423–424.

[163] See, e.g., G. GIURISATO, "Come Luca", 446.

[164] As B.B. Scott ("A Master's Praise", 182) points out, "The rich man's [initial] response aligns him with the accusers, living up to the reader's expectations".

[165] For instance, C. Paliard (*Lire l'écriture*, 26) notes: "le texte dise [...] que l'homme riche qui avait condamné celui qui était accusé d'avoir dilapidé ses biens, est devenu le maître qui fait l'éloge de son trompeur, à cause de son habileté".

[166] See, e.g., K.E. BAILEY, *Poet*, 101–102; J.S. KLOPPENBORG, "The Dishonoured Master", 492; B.J. MALINA – R.L. ROHRBAUGH, *Social-Science*, 375; and D. LANDRY – B. MAY, "Honour Restored", 294–305.309.

[167] Thus, J.D. Crossan ("The Parable", 465) remarks: "the quite immoral story of the Unjust Steward [...] stands as a deliberately shocking story". See also R.W. FUNK, "Structure", 66; R.H. STEIN, *An Introduction*, 40; D.P. SECCOMBE, *Possessions*, 162; J. GILLMAN, *Possessions*, 81; D.J. IRELAND, *Stewardship*, 22.81–82; and H.J.B. COMBRINK, "A Social-Scientific Perspective", 293–294. In fact, as D. Marguerat (*Sapori*, 170–171) observes, "Luca coltiva il piacere di costruire personaggi paradossali [...] Luca ama i paradossi [...] Il burlesco o il paradosso rappresentano per il narratore la svolta narrativa della sorpresa della grazia".

attention and eliciting surprise, by "showing a linking of facts which goes against common sense"[168]. If the logic of the plot calls for the steward's condemnation (vs. commendation), the final surprise has then an unsettling and enduring effect on the reader[169]. He is left in a situation where he needs to make sense of a story which ultimately defies his "implicit world" and its view of justice[170]. Specifically, the rich man's final commendation obliges Jesus' listeners, as well as Luke's readers, to engage in retrospection and to re-evaluate the characterization of the parable[171]. By doing so, however, the object of their thoughts once more becomes the master's seemingly illogical and sudden view[172].

Yet, this does not necessarily mean that he is the main character and focalizer of the parable[173]. The "shock factor"[174] of the paradox, in fact, guides the narrative structure of the account only in the background[175]. The construction of the plot centres rather on the shrewd steward's attitude and actions (vv. 3–7). He is the leading and polarizing figure of the parable, who devises and implements a strategy, and so solves his problem[176]. He is also the only one to be portrayed as a round, earthly character, with an interior monologue[177]. While the rich master in the story remains in the dark[178], Luke's reader and Jesus' audience are informed of the way in which the steward confronts his unexpected crisis, as well as his true values, emotions and motivations[179]. This "private" revelation effectively introduces the hearers and

---

[168] D. MARGUERAT – Y. BOURQUIN, *How to Read*, 176. More precisely, we have here an instance of what H. Lausberg (Lausberg, 36) calls, "παράδοξον σχῆμα", namely, a kind of paradox, "which shocks the audience's sense of justice (or to generalize in extra-juridical terms: their sense of value and truth)".

[169] See, e.g., H.J.B. COMBRINK, "A Social-Scientific Perspective", 293–294.304.

[170] See, e.g., B.B. SCOTT, "A Master's Praise", 185, n. 42; *Ibid.*, 187; H.J.B. COMBRINK, "A Social-Scientific Perspective", 303; and J.A. TROXLE, Jr., *Doing Justice*, 230–231.

[171] See, e.g., B.B. SCOTT, "A Master's Praise", 187.

[172] See, e.g., B.B. SCOTT, "A Master's Praise", 182.

[173] M. Barth ("Dishonest Steward", 72) goes too far when he concludes: "The real hero of this story is, therefore, the lord, not the steward". Cf., e.g., D.J. IRELAND, "A History", 302, n. 42; and G. GIURISATO, "Come Luca", 446, n. 90.

[174] D.J. IRELAND, *Stewardship*, 81.

[175] See, e.g., D. MARGUERAT – Y. BOURQUIN, *How to Read*, 110.

[176] See, e.g., D.J. IRELAND, *Stewardship*, 112, n. 299; D. MATHEWSON, "The Parable", 32; and G. GIURISATO, "Come Luca", 446–447.

[177] See, e.g., D.R. FLETCHER, "The Riddle", 28; P. SELLEW, "Interior Monologue", 245; and A. BOLIN, *Du bon usage*, 52.

[178] See, e.g., P. SELLEW, "Interior Monologue", 247; D. MATHEWSON, "The Parable", 39, n. 56; and D. LANDRY – B. MAY, "Honour Restored", 305.

[179] See, e.g., J.L. RESSEGUIE, "Point of View", 43; and P. SELLEW, "Interior Monologue", 247. In reality, the rich man is aware of the steward's own dilemma, but only insofar as he is its cause. As a result of his own actions (vs. monologue), again, he will come to know the steward's strategy. Thus, the master's final commendation can concern only the steward's

readers into the steward's inner world, creating empathy and leading them to associate themselves with his take on the situation[180].

His perspective, then, is very significant and must not be overlooked. In fact, the steward's inner soliloquy is also a device used "to get to the point of the story"[181]. The Pharisees and crowds may still be present, listening to Jesus, at least implicitly (see Luke 15,1–3; and 16,1a.14–15a), but, this time, it is the disciples who constitute the explicit audience (see Luke 16,1a)[182]. They are asked to identify with the steward, but so is the reader. Specifically, the parable asks both, disciples and readers, to ponder a very practical and, at the same time, eschatological question: what are we "to do" (ποιεῖν)[183] with the "possessions" (ὑπάρχομντα: v. 1c) we have been entrusted to manage before the settlement of accounts comes?

II. The First Parable (vv. 1b–8a)

A few generic features immediately link v. 16 with the interpretation of the parable that opens its harmonious chapter.

Firstly, in quite a similar way to commentaries on the aforementioned verse, scholars keep striving with the difficulty of arriving at a satisfactory explanation of the true teaching of this story as well[184]. Indeed, it is often noted that the parable of the *Shrewd Steward*[185] is one of the most difficult parabolic

---

concrete business, not his moral values, thoughts, or even selfish motivations, which remain otherwise wholly unknown to him.

[180] As specified by B.B. Scott (183–184), "Drawing the reader into the steward's subjectivity makes identification possible". See, e.g., R. ALTER, *The Art*, 84–86; D.A. DE SILVA, "The Parable", 260; D. MARGUERAT – Y. BOURQUIN, *How to Read*, 58–59.65–70.75.132.162–163.174; and A. BOLIN, *Du bon usage*, 48. See also J.S. KLOPPENBORG, "The Dishonoured Master", 491; and D. LANDRY – B. MAY, "Honour Restored", 300. Finally, as J.A. Metzger (*Consumption*, 115) notes, "neither the subject of the verb δέξωνται nor the referent of the possessive genitive αὐτῶν (v. 4) is revealed […] refusing to disclose the identity of the steward's potential hosts […] heightens suspense and draws readers yet further into the story".

[181] O. LEHTIPUU, "Characterization", 81. See also J. DURKIN, "A Cultural Reading", 12; and J.A. TROXLE, Jr., *Doing Justice*, 232–233.

[182] See, esp., J. DURKIN, "A Cultural Reading", 9.11. See also Luke 14,25; 15,1–3; 16,14–15a; and A.A. JUST, Jr., *Luke*, II, 612.614.

[183] In Luke's Gospel, the verb, "to do" (ποιεῖν), is often linked to the relationship between masters and slaves (see, e.g., Luke 7,8c; 12,43.47–48; 16,3–4.8; and 17,9–10). Only the Lucan Jesus, that is, the Lord (see, e.g., Luke 2,11; 6,5.46; and 18,41) and yet a servant (see, e.g., Luke 12,37; 17,7–8; and 22,26–27), asks his Father to forgive his executioners, because "they do not know *what they do* [τί ποιοῦσιν]" (Luke 23,34b).

[184] See, e.g., W.O.E. OESTERLEY, "The Gospel Parables", 15; B.A. HOOLEY – A.J. MASON, "Some Thoughts", 49; and A.T. FARNES, "A New Interpretation", 1, n. 3.

[185] The parable has been dubbed with different appellations throughout the history of its interpretation. See, e.g., A.T. FARNES, "A New Interpretation", 1. We shall call it here by

sections of the Gospels and has long been classified accordingly, just like v. 16, as a *crux interpretum*[186].

Secondly, the list of interpretations concerning the steward's identity is curiously reminiscent of the one already seen with regard to the *biastái* (Matt 11,12c). As A. Plummer remarks:

the variety of the interpretations is very great. A catalogue of even the chief suggestions would serve no useful purpose: it is sufficient to state that the steward has been supposed to mean the Jewish hierarchy, the tax-collectors, Pilate, Judas, Satan, penitents, St. Paul, Christ [...] The literature on the subject is voluminous and unrepaying[187].

Finally, just as with v. 16, part of the difficulty is that scholars often tend to approach the account in isolation. In keeping with the contextual take on this chapter, we agree with those authors who argue for the insufficiency of an exclusively literary approach for the proper understanding of the parable: an awareness of both Gospel setting and religious, social, or economical aspects is fundamental[188].

Contrary to our treatment of v. 16, however, we shall avoid here a full discussion of the history of the interpretation of the parable, to the extent that it lies beyond the scope of the present study[189]. Accordingly, we shall concentrate on three of its most basic issues: a) the identity of "the master/Lord" (ὁ κύριος), in v. 8a; b) the proper ending and structure of the

that which we think encapsulates the main point of the story, pointing directly to the shrewdness of the steward.

[186] See, e.g., A. JÜLICHER, *Die Gleichnisreden*, II, 495; P. GÄCHTER, "The Parable", 121; D.R. FLETCHER, "The Riddle", 15; M.A. BEAVIS, "Ancient Slavery", 38; D.J. IRELAND, "A History", 293; ID., *Stewardship*, 1; H.J.B. COMBRINK, "A Social-Scientific Perspective", 289; J.A. TROXLE, Jr., *Doing Justice*, 1, n. 3; J. DURKIN, "A Cultural Reading", 7; and A. BOLIN, *Du bon usage*, 4. To the extent that many commentators actually stumble on its interpretation, J.J. van Oosterzee (*Lukas*, 236.240) calls it, not only a "*crux interpretum*", but even a "λίθος προσκόμματος".

[187] A. PLUMMER, *Luke*, 380–381. See also F. GODET, *Luke*, II, 167–168; and L.J. TOPEL, "On the Injustice", 216. In addition to A. Plummer's list, we wish to mention the interpretation of Cyril of Alexandria (*Comm. Luc.* XVI.1 [*PG* 72, 812cd]), whereby the "steward" (οἰκονόμος) is linked etymologically to "domestic goods" (οἰκεῖα), as opposed to "house" (οἶκος). Thus, the steward represents all rich Christians who have the duty of distributing their God-given goods to the poor generously. See, e.g., P. MONAT, "L'exégèse", 93, n. 16; and A. BOLIN, *Du bon usage*, 8.

[188] See, e.g., J.A. FITZMYER, "The Story", 23; J.S. KLOPPENBORG, "The Dishonoured Master", 487; S.E. PORTER, "The Parable", 134; D. MATHEWSON, "The Parable", 30.33; H.J.B. COMBRINK, "A Social-Scientific Perspective", 294; and R. KRÜGER, "Lucas 16,1–13", 101.

[189] The history of its interpretation is available in several studies. See, e.g., M. KRÄMER, *Das Rätsel*, 15–28; D.J. IRELAND, "A History", 293–318; ID., *Stewardship*, 5–47; P. MONAT, "L'exégèse", 89–123; D. LANDRY – B. MAY, "Honour Restored", 288–294; B.C. DENNERT, "A Survey", 145–152; and A. BOLIN, *Du bon usage*, 7–28.

story; and c) the very meaning of the final approval of the shrewd steward's actions[190]. These three questions are closely related not only with each other, but also with v. 8[191]. Indeed, the latter can be considered as the true "crux" and "key" of the interpretation of the parable and, as such, shall be the starting point of our reflection[192].

1. The Identity of "the Master/Lord" (ὁ κύριος) in v. 8a

Without entering into much detail as to its discussion, we concur with the large number of scholars who consider the first character, in v. 8a, to be the same as the "master" (κύριος) of vv. 3 and 5, that is, the previous "certain rich man" (ἄνθρωπός τις πλούσιος) of v. 1[193]. As J.A. Fitzmyer argues, this is the most reasonable and expected reading of the segment[194]. As opposed to v. 9, where the unprecedented occurrence of "I" (ἐγώ) can refer only to Jesus, no indication of a variation of subject occurs in v. 8a[195]. Therefore, in referring to the same character, it is only natural that the narrator's voice uses the same appellative as that of his last mention of him (see v. 5a), that is, "master" (κύριος).

Surely, as a result of this reading, one is faced with the difficulty of explaining the meaning of the master's change of mind, which is the true "root problem"[196] of the interpretation of the parable. However, the latter fits well with the chiastic structure, pattern of reversal, alternation of *focalizers*, and

---

[190] Thus, I.H. Marshall (*Luke*, 614) speaks similarly of "three closely linked problems". See also J.D.M. DERRETT, "Fresh Light", I, 198–199; G. ROSSÉ, *Luca*, 618; D.L. BOCK, *Luke*, II, 1340; and R. KRÜGER, "Lucas 16,1–13", 103, n. 4.

[191] See, e.g., B.A. HOOLEY – A.J. MASON, "Some Thoughts", 51.

[192] Thus, I.J. Du Plessis ("Philanthropy", 6) comments: "The decisive point for understanding this story is found in verse 8a". See also M. KRÄMER, *Das Rätsel*, 139; D.J. IRELAND, "A History", 294; H.J.B. COMBRINK, "A Social-Scientific Perspective", 294; and M. GRILLI, *Matteo*, 353.

[193] See, e.g., J.-M. LAGRANGE, *Luc*, 433; D.R. FLETCHER, "The Riddle", 16–17; J.A. FITZMYER, "The Story", 27–28; K.E. BAILEY, *Poet*, 104; I.H. MARSHALL, *Luke*, 619–620; R.H. STEIN, *An Introduction*, 107; B.B. SCOTT, "A Master's Praise", 175; D.J. IRELAND, *Stewardship*, 64–65; J.S. KLOPPENBORG, "The Dishonoured Master", 476–477; H.J.B. COMBRINK, "A Social-Scientific Perspective", 293; G. GIURISATO, "Come Luca", 447; D. LANDRY – B. MAY, "Honour Restored", 294; C.M. HAYS, *Luke's Wealth Ethics*, 142–143; J.K. GOODRICH, "Voluntary Debt Remission", 547, n. 2; and T. BEDNARZ, "Status Disputes", 395. For a brief summary of the main arguments in support of this view, see, e.g., R.S. SCHELLENBERG, "Which Master?", 265.

[194] See J.A. FITZMYER, "The Story", 27–28.

[195] See, e.g., J.A. FITZMYER, "The Story", 28; and J.S. KLOPPENBORG, "The Dishonoured Master", 476.

[196] L. MORRIS, *Luke*, 245. See also D.J. IRELAND, *Stewardship*, 65; É. FUCHS, "L'Évangile", 195; J.S. KLOPPENBORG, "The Dishonoured Master", 476–477; and H.J.B. COMBRINK, "A Social-Scientific Perspective", 291.

paradox, and should thus be retained[197]. On the contrary, to understand the κύριος of v. 8a as pointing to Jesus is not only at odds with its "narrative probability", but it implies reading back into v. 8a, by reflection, the same subject as in vv. 8b–9[198]. Lastly, if one eradicates the difficulty, by denying that the master could commend his steward, then one assumes precisely that which needs to be demonstrated and, as B.B. Scott points out, thus "eliminates the unexpected from the art of the story telling"[199].

2. The Proper Ending of the Story

As far as the proper boundaries of the parable are concerned, its *terminus a quo* is generally uncontested. The expression, "a certain man" (ἄνθρωπός τις), in v. 1b, is often used elsewhere by Luke as a parabolic incipit[200]. The entire scholarly debate focuses rather on its *terminus ad quem*, which is variously fixed either in v. 7, 8a, 8b, or 9[201].

Our stance on the issue follows that of a majority of scholars who maintain that the first parable comes to an end in the middle of v. 8, with the key words, "because he had done shrewdly" (ὅτι φρονίμως ἐποίησεν)[202], and who consider vv. 8b–13 to be its appended commentary or application unit[203].

---

[197] See, e.g., D.O. VIA, Jr., "Parable", 124; R.W. FUNK, "Structure", 60; and D. MARGUERAT – Y. BOURQUIN, *How to Read*, 40–42.74.110–111.

[198] See, e.g., J.A. FITZMYER, "The Story", 28; and J.S. KLOPPENBORG, "The Dishonoured Master", 477.

[199] B.B. SCOTT, "A Master's Praise", 175, n. 8. See also *Ibid.*, 174–177. In fact, as we have already suggested and J.S. Kloppenborg ("The Dishonoured Master", 492–493) specifies further, "The genius of the parable consists in bringing about narrative closure, but only at the expense of fracturing the cultural codes and expectations of the listener".

[200] See, e.g., Luke 10,30; 12,16; 14,16; 15,11; 16,1.19; 19,12; the longer reading in Luke 20,9 (A W Θ *f*[13] 1241 2542 syᵖ); and D.A. DE SILVA, "The Parable", 256.

[201] See, e.g., D.A. DE SILVA, "The Parable", 256; and H.J.B. COMBRINK, "A Social-Scientific Perspective", 290.

[202] In favour of the parable ending in v. 8a, see, e.g., F. GODET, *Luke*, II, 164; W.O.E. OESTERLEY, "The Gospel Parables", 197.290–292; D.O. VIA, Jr., *The Parables*, 156–157; ID., "Parable", 124; M. KRÄMER, *Das Rätsel*, 174–182; L.J. TOPEL, "On the Injustice", 218; É. FUCHS, "L'Évangile", 4–5; I.H. MARSHALL, *Luke*, 620; B.B. SCOTT, "A Master's Praise", 174–177; J.S. KLOPPENBORG, "The Dishonoured Master", 477; J. NOLLAND, *Luke*, II, 796.801; P. SELLEW, "Interior Monologue", 247; D.A. DE SILVA, "The Parable", 257; D.L. BOCK, *Luke*, II, 1332; H.J.B. COMBRINK, "A Social-Scientific Perspective", 292; M.D. GREENE, "The Parable", 84; D. LANDRY – B. MAY, "Honour Restored", 288.303; J.A. TROXLE, Jr., *Doing Justice*, 11; J. DURKIN, "A Cultural Reading", 8; and F. UDOH, "The Tale", 314.

[203] See, e.g., D. MATHEWSON, "The Parable", 33.35; D.L. BOCK, *Luke*, II, 1324–1326; H.J.B. COMBRINK, "A Social-Scientific Perspective", 290–292; J.A. TROXLE, Jr., *Doing Justice*, 7.202–208; J.A. METZGER, *Consumption*, 123, n. 59; and M. GRILLI, *Matteo*, 350–351.

As we have already suggested and are soon to explain better, the phrase, "doing shrewdly" (φρονίμως ποιεῖν), in v. 8a, encapsulates very well the main point of the parable (see ποιεῖν: vv. 3.4), which is then logically explained and applied by Jesus to his primary audience (the disciples) in the immediately following sayings[204].

Once again, J.A. Fitzmyer offers one of the most convincing reasons for this hermeneutic choice:

Without v. 8a the parable has no real ending. From the beginning, the reaction of the master to the manager's conduct is expected; it is finally given in v. 8a[205].

Since narratives generally involve closures, and this is indeed given here, there is no reason one should do without it, whether its content is according to one's expectations or not[206]. In fact, if the story has a surprising finale, it may be simply because Luke wants it to end that way, leaving the reader in a situation of uneasiness[207].

Moreover, the simultaneous mention of the two main characters of the story, both times in the *telling* mode, creates an "inclusion" (*inclusio*) around vv. 1b–8a[208]. On the one hand, at the very beginning of the story, Luke 16,1bc introduces both characters, as "a certain rich man" (ἄνθρωπός τις ἦν πλούσιος) and as a "steward" (οἰκονόμος) indicted "as squanderer" (ὡς διασκορπίζων), respectively. On the other hand, just as the story reaches its closure, the narrator's voice again refers to them in Luke 16,8a, calling the former, "master" (κύριος), just as it was the steward's custom (see vv. 3.5b)[209], and the latter, "unrighteous" (τῆς ἀδικίας). This last narrative trait seems to be a negative development of the initial detail used in the characterization of the steward, in Luke 16,1c[210]. As we shall see better later, the two features are most likely related to each other.

---

[204] See, e.g., "shrewder" (φρονιμώτεροι: v. 8b) and "do" (ποιήσατε: v. 9b); as well as, "Now he was also saying to the disciples" (Ἔλεγεν δὲ καὶ πρὸς τοὺς μαθητάς: v. 1a) and "And I say to you" (Καὶ ἐγὼ ὑμῖν λέγω: v. 9a).

[205] J.A. FITZMYER, "The Story", 27. See also *Ibid.*, 26–30; and ID., *Luke*, II, 1096–1097.1101; and M. GRILLI, *Matteo*, 351.

[206] See, e.g., B.B. SCOTT, "A Master's Praise", 175.

[207] See, e.g., B.B. SCOTT, "A Master's Praise", 179.184–185.

[208] As A. Bolin (*Du bon usage*, 47) notes, "Au niveau du récit proprement dit, seuls les v. 1 et 8a sont présentés en mode telling avec une série de verbes au passé". See also J.A. METZGER, *Consumption*, 113, n. 16.

[209] See the steward's own appellative, "my master" (ὁ κύριός μου), in vv. 3.5b, and the narrator's, "his master" (τοῦ κυρίου ἑαυτοῦ), in v. 5a.

[210] Although in a different narrative context, the initial trait, "squanderer" (διασκορπίζων), has also a clear literary antecedent, in Luke 15,13.

Furthermore, as we have already mentioned, most interpreters treat the following sayings (vv. 8b–13) as comments on the parable[211]. In fact, among the few recognizably Lucan expressions of the section, the formula, "I tell you" (ἐγὼ ὑμῖν λέγω), in v. 9a, is a clear sign indicative of a commentary, since it is often used elsewhere in Luke's Gospel to introduce Jesus' own applications of the main points of other parables[212]. Moreover, this formula follows naturally the discussion introduced in v. 8b, by the conjunction, "for/since" (ὅτι)[213]. Both the evident explanatory character of this conjunction and the logical link between vv. 8b and 9a suggest that the utterance is not that of the master in the parable, but Jesus' own comment on it[214]. Indeed, the latter verses function as the introduction of the whole application unit (vv. 8b–13)[215].

Finally, a few more explanations support the thesis. At the grammatical level, the use of indirect (v. 8b) and direct (v. 9) speech allows us to treat both verses as Jesus' own utterances[216]. Likewise, at the level of form and content,

---

[211] See, e.g., H.J.B. COMBRINK, "A Social-Scientific Perspective", 291. For instance, based on some of K. Paffenroth's statistics, J.A. Troxle Jr. (*Doing Justice*, 205) supports the majority scholarly opinion by suggesting that, "the parable and the applications [...] have different styles and probably derive from different sources". See also G. ROSSÉ, *Luca*, 623–629; and K. PAFFENROTH, *The Story*, 74–85.92–93.

[212] See, e.g., Luke 11,8.9; 14,24; 15,7.10; 18,8.14; 19,26; B.B. SCOTT, "A Master's Praise", 175–176; and D.J. IRELAND, *Stewardship*, 86. The verb, "to fail" (ἐκλειπεῖν), in v. 9b, and the noun, "domestic slave" (οἰκέτης), in v. 13a (cf. Matt 6,24), are also Lucan. He is the only evangelist to make use of them. See, e.g., Luke 12,33 (ἀνέκλειπτον); 22,32; 23,45; Acts 10,7; and G. ROSSÉ, *Luca*, 625.628, ns. 23.37.

[213] See, e.g., F. UDOH, "The Tale", 327, n. 91; and M. GRILLI, *Matteo*, 350.354.

[214] Thus, as K.R. Snodgrass (*Stories*, 412) remarks, the parable "extends through v. 8a, and vv. 8b–9 are Jesus' explanation of the parable". The link between vv. 8b and 9a is corroborated further by the occurrences of the expressions, "the sons of this age" (οἱ υἱοὶ τοῦ αἰῶνος τούτου: Luke 16,8b), and "unrighteous mammon" (μαμωνᾶς τῆς ἀδικίας: Luke 16,9a), inasmuch as they denote "worldly" people and wealth, respectively. See, e.g., Luke 20,34; John 8,35; CD XX.34; J.M. CREED, *Luke*, 203; H. KOSMALA, "The Parable", 114–115; E.E. ELLIS, *Luke*, 199; I.H. MARSHALL, *Luke*, 620–621; J.A. FITZMYER, *Luke*, II, 1107–1108; and D.J. IRELAND, *Stewardship*, 84–85.

[215] The juxtaposition of vv. 8b–9 to v. 8a, by means of a couple of catchwords, makes it possible for the former to be a commentary on the parable. See, e.g., "unrighteous steward" (ὁ οἰκονόμος τῆς ἀδικίας) and "shrewdly" (φρονίμως), in v. 8a; "shrewder" (φρονιμώτεροι), in v. 8b; and "unrighteous mammon" (μαμωνᾶς τῆς ἀδικίας), in v. 9. See also D.J. IRELAND, *Stewardship*, 68–72; H.J.B. COMBRINK, "A Social-Scientific Perspective", 292; G. ROSSÉ, *Luca*, 624, n. 20; C.L. BLOMBERG, *Interpreting the Parables*, 246; and K.R. SNODGRASS, *Stories*, 402.

[216] As D.J. Ireland (*Stewardship*, 64) points out, "in vv. 8–9 we have a mixture of indirect and direct speech. If v. 8b is indirect speech and v. 9 direct, Jesus could still be the speaker in both and the master the one who praises the steward in v. 8a". See also J. SCHMID, *Lukas*, 259; J. DUPONT, "L'exemple", 69; I.H. MARSHALL, *Luke*, 619; and A. BOLIN, *Du bon usage*, 47–48.

the wisdom and parenetic language employed in vv. 8b–9 confirms their function as a commentary and/or application of the parable[217]. Finally, the vocabulary of these verses shows signs of Palestinian origins[218], thus indicating that the thought expressed in them may go back even to Jesus himself.

Based on all the aforementioned reasons, we can recapitulate with J. Durkin thus:

> The second half of v. 8 [...] is seemingly incongruent; the rich man who speaks of practical matters in vv. 1–2 would probably not break into a sermon on the "sons of this world" and the "sons of light". Thus, it is safe to say that the break between parable and sermon comes in the middle of v. 8[219].

3. The Narrative Plot and Structure of the Story

Having established the boundaries of the parable, we can now turn to the examination of its narrative plot and structure. Generally, whether one considers the plot from the rich man's point of view (see Table I) or from that of his steward (see Table II), the story complies with the threefold pattern: *crisis – response – denouement*[220].

a) The Plot from the Rich Man's Perspective

From the rich man's point of view, the parable opens with a decisive verdict[221]. The character is first introduced as being rich and as having a steward (v. 1b), and immediately after, he is unexpectedly informed of the latter's prodigal handling of his possessions (v. 1c). This news opens before him a situation of

---

[217] As H.J.B. Combrink ("A Social-Scientific Perspective", 292) argues, "verse 8b is not part of the parable because its inclusion would introduce *topoi* like οἱ υἱοὶ τοῦ αἰῶνος τούτου and οἱ υἱοὶ τοῦ φωτός which are not inherently part of the narrative structure of the parable, and thus signal the beginning of the commentary on the parable". See also J.A. FITZMYER, "The Story", 28; T. SNOY, "Approche littéraire", 48; L.J. TOPEL, "On the Injustice", 219; B.B. SCOTT, "A Master's Praise", 176; and A. BOLIN, *Du bon usage*, 48.

[218] Thus, I.H. Marshall (*Luke*, 621) notes: "The verse [8b] makes use of a dualism similar to that found at Qumran". See, e.g., 1QS I.9; II.16; III.13.24.25; 1QM I.3.9.11.13; etc. See also John 12,36; Eph 5,8; 1Thess 5,5; 1En CVIII.11; J.A. FITZMYER, *Luke*, II, 1108; C.L. BLOMBERG, *Interpreting the Parables*, 246; and R. KRÜGER, "Lucas 16,1–13", 110–111.

[219] J. DURKIN, "A Cultural Reading", 8. In a similar vein, D.J. Ireland (*Stewardship*, 84) remarks: "The eschatological dualism here between 'the sons of this age' and 'the sons of light' is out of place in the mouth of one who is himself a son of this age and for whom the distinction would have little meaning".

[220] See, e.g., D.O. VIA, Jr., "Parable", 123–124.129; R.W. FUNK, "Structure", 61; and E. FUCHS, *L'éthique chrétienne*, 67.

[221] See, e.g., B.B. SCOTT, "A Master's Praise", 178.

crisis: to avoid loss of money and prestige, he must do something[222]. Second (v. 2), he promptly *responds* to this situation, calling the steward to himself and asking him to turn in the account of his administration, so that he may dismiss him, because he is no longer capable of managing his possessions. At this point, the master's response sets up the steward's own crisis, and the "baton" of the narrative is handed on to the steward. As we have seen, however, the story reaches its closure only in v. 8a[223]. Here, the master takes back the strands of the plot and, although unexpectedly, gives his last verdict[224]. In this way, the narrative tension is resolved and the plot finds its *denouement*.

Table I: The Narrative Plot from the (A) Master's Perspective		
Scene I: Introduction & Crisis	A "certain man" (ἄνθρωπός τις) is first introduced as being rich (ἦν πλούσιος) and as having a steward (ὃς εἶχεν οἰκονόμον). Then, the latter (οὗτος) is suddenly "reported to him" (διεβλήθη αὐτῷ) "as squandering" (ὡς διασκορπίζων) "his possessions" (τὰ ὑπάρχοντα αὐτοῦ).	v. 1bc
Scene II: Response	The rich man summons (φωνήσας) his steward (αὐτόν), questions him on account of what he hears about his being wasteful (τί τοῦτο ἀκούω περὶ σου), and asks him to turn in (ἀπόδος) the accounting (τὸν λόγον) of his "stewardship" (οἰκονομίας), since he is no longer capable of managing (οὐ δύνῃ ἔτι οἰκονομεῖν)[225].	v. 2

---

[222] See, e.g., H.J.B. COMBRINK, "A Social-Scientific Perspective", 301. As the author (*Ibid.*, 303) explains, according to the ancient Mediterranean culture, his steward's wasteful management (see διασκορπίζων: v. 1c) implied most likely a "threat to the honour of a rich landowner" as well. See also I.H. MARSHALL, *Luke*, 617; J.S. KLOPPENBORG, "The Dishonoured Master", 487–492; D. LANDRY – B. MAY, "Honour Restored", 298–301; J.A. TROXLE, Jr., *Doing Justice*, 10, n. 33; J.A. METZGER, *Consumption*, 112–113; and F. UDOH, "The Tale", 331–334.

[223] See, e.g., B.B. SCOTT, "A Master's Praise", 178.

[224] Thus, E. Fuchs (*L'éthique chrétienne*, 67) observes: "la maître change radicalement d'attitude; loin de condamner l'intendant pour son escroquerie, il le loue pour son intelligence".

[225] Several mss. (e.g., A E G H K L Δ Π Ψ 33 etc.) have the future verbal form, "you shall be able" (δυνήσῃ). The present tense (δύνῃ) is nonetheless better attested (e.g., 𝔓[75] ℵ B D P W Θ 1 346 788 1582 and *f*[1.13]). Moreover, as J.A. Metzger (*Consumption*, 112) points out, "The phrase οὐ δύνῃ ἔτι οἰκονομεῖν is ambiguous and may be rendered 'for you are no longer capable of stewarding' or 'for you can no longer serve as steward'. The first translation would constitute a matter-of-fact commentary on the steward's lack of proficiency in administrative matters, but the second would imply immediate termination". We consider the first meaning to be the most appropriate in this context. The master is making a remark based on something, which he has just heard. The present tense forms of the verbs, "to be capable" (δύνασθαι) and "to manage" (οἰκονομεῖν), point back to the previous analogous forms in the present tense, namely, "squandering" (διασκορπίζων), "possessions" (ὑπάρχοντα), and "I hear" (ἀκούω).

Scene III: Dénouement & Conclusion	The "master" (κύριός) praises (ἐπῄνεσεν) his "unrighteous steward" (οἰκονόμον τῆς ἀδικίας), "because he had done shrewdly" (ὅτι φρονίμως ἐποίησεν).	v. 8a

b) The Plot from the Shrewd Steward's Perspective

Analogously, the steward is first introduced as belonging to a certain rich man (v. 1b) and, immediately after, described as squandering his possessions (v. 1c). Because of his alleged wasteful management, he is then called up and questioned by his master (v. 2), who asks him to submit the accounting of his stewardship. This event places the steward in a situation of *crisis*, which obliges him to act. His *response* unfolds into a two-stage process of reflection and action (vv. 3–7). After describing the steward's soliloquy (vv. 3–4), the narrator shows us how he then carries out his unstated decision (vv. 5–7), calling two of his master's representative debtors to himself and reducing the amounts of the debts they owe his master[226]. The inner dialogue discloses some information only to Jesus' audience and Luke's reader: they are told of the steward's goal (specifically, to be welcomed into the houses of his master's debtors); of the options he takes into account (i.e., digging and begging); and of his reasons for discarding them (i.e., his lack of strength and sense of shame: οὐκ ἰσχύω and αἰσχύνομαι)[227]. From this revelation, they can sense also how the matter is rather urgent (see ταχέως: v. 6) and the solution carried out by the steward consistent with his own job as a financial administrator[228]. Finally (v. 8a), owing to the shrewdness of these specifically economic actions, the steward is surprisingly commended (vs. condemned) by the rich man. Once again, therefore, the narrative tension is resolved and the plot finds its *denouement*[229].

---

[226] A dual pattern marks the whole process: in v. 3, we hear of two possible routes of action being discarded, i.e., "to dig" (σκάπτειν) and "to beg" (αἰσχύνομαι); and again, in vv. 5–7, only two examples are offered in representation of the whole selected action. See, e.g., G. ROSSÉ, *Luca*, 621–622; and J.A. METZGER, *Consumption*, 117, n. 34.

[227] See, e.g., J.A. METZGER, *Consumption*, 114; and A. BOLIN, *Du bon usage*, 50.

[228] Several terms, in vv. 4–7, carry legal or financial nuances: see, e.g., "steward" (οἰκονόμος): 1x (v. 3); "stewardship" (οἰκονομία): 2x (vv. 3.4); "to discharge from a position" (μεθιστάναι): 1x (v. 4); "to take the promissory note" (δέχεσθαι τὰ γράμματα): 2x (vv. 6.7; however, cf., also, vv. 4.9, where the verb means "to receive/welcome"); "to call in for official inquiry" (προσκαλεῖν): 1x (v. 5); "debtor" (χρεοφειλέτης): 1x (v. 5); "to owe something to someone financially" (ὀφειλεῖν): 2x (vv. 5.7); and "to set down" or "to draw up" (γράφειν): 2x (vv. 6.7). See, also, A. BOLIN, *Du bon usage*, 51–52.

[229] The master's paradoxical praise, thus, represents the true turning point of the story from both men's perspectives. See, e.g., D. MARGUERAT – A. WÉNIN, *Sapori*, 171.

Table II: The Narrative Plot from the (B) Steward's Perspective		
Scene I: Introduction & Crisis (vv. 1b–2)	The "steward" (οἰκονόμος) is first introduced as belonging to a "certain rich man" (ἄνθρωπός τις πλούσιος) and then described, "as squandering" (ὡς διασκορπίζων) "his possessions" (τὰ ὑπάρχοντα αὐτοῦ). Being called (φωνήσας) by his master, he is then questioned as to that which the master hears about him (τί τοῦτο ἀκούω περὶ σου), and asked to turn in (ἀπόδος) the accounting (τὸν λόγον) of his "stewardship" (οἰκονομίας).	
	Deliberation (vv. 3–4)	*Application (vv. 5–7)*
Scene II: Response (vv. 3–7)	Because his master (ὁ κύριός μου) is "taking the stewardship" (ἀφαιρεῖται τὴν οἰκονομίαν) away from him (μεταστάθω ἐκ τῆς οἰκονομίας), the "steward" (οἰκο-νόμος) wonders and realizes (ἔγνων) what to do (τί ποιήσω: 2x): so as to be received (ἵνα [...] δέξωνταί με) "into the homes" (εἰς τοὺς οἴκους) of his master's debtors, he discards two options, i.e., "digging" (σκάπτειν) and "begging" (ἐπαιτεῖν).	Acting on his undisclosed solution, the steward calls in (προσκαλεσάμενος) "each one of his master's debtors" (ἕνα ἕκαστον τῶν χρεοφειλετῶν τοῦ κυρίου ἑαυτοῦ) and reduces the debts which, by way of example, two of them owe to his master (τῷ κυρίῳ μου), by 50 and 20 percent, respectively[230].
Scene III: Dénouement & Conclusion (v. 8a)	The "unrighteous steward" (οἰκονόμον τῆς ἀδικίας) is praised (ἐπήνεσεν) by his "master" (κύριός), for acting shrewdly (ὅτι φρονίμως ἐποίησεν).	

c) The Overall Chiastic Structure of the Story

As far as the overall structure of the story is concerned, framed within the mention of the two main characters in the *telling* mode of exposition (vv. 1b.8a), the parable begins and ends with the master's judgment, as "a carefully formed mini-drama [...] elegantly constructed"[231].

Specifically, when one considers it from the point of view of the aforementioned alternation of the main actors on the stage, the parable is composed of three major sections: *master* (A: vv. 1–2), *steward* (B: vv. 3–7), and *master* (A[1]: v. 8a)[232]. However, based on the distinction between the steward's inner dialogue with *himself* and his actual dealings with the master's *debtors*, the central part (B: vv. 3–7) can then be split into two further subunits (B: vv. 3–4; and

---

[230] See, e.g., J.A. METZGER, *Consumption*, 118–119.

[231] J.D. CROSSAN, "Servant Parables", 32. See also G. GIURISATO, "Come Luca", 446; and A. BOLIN, *Du bon usage*, 47.50.

[232] See, e.g., M. GOURGUES, *Les Paraboles*, 168; and A. BOLIN, *Du bon usage*, 52.

B[1]: vv. 5–7). The final construction is made up accordingly of four narrative scenes arranged in a chiastic (or ring) shape (see Table III: A – B – B[1] – A[1])[233].

Table III: The Overall Chiastic Structure of the Story		
(A) Master & Steward (vv. 1b–2)	a) The master (M) has a steward (S) (εἶχεν οἰκονόμον): v. 1b; b) M is informed about S (διεβλήθη αὐτῷ): v. 1c.	b[1]) M hears about S (ἀκούω περὶ σου): v. 2a; a[1]) M decides to dismiss S (οὐ δύνῃ ἔτι οἰκονομεῖν): v. 2b.
(B) Steward & Self (vv. 3–4)	a) S says to himself: "What shall I do?" (τί ποιήσω;): v. 3a; b) S discloses the problem (ὅτι [...] τὴν οἰκονομίαν): v. 3b; c) S discards two options (οὐκ ἰσχύω [...] αἰσχύνομαι): v. 3c.	a[1]) S realizes what he shall do (ἔγνων τί ποιήσω): v. 4a; b[1]) S refers to the problem (ὅταν [...] τῆς οἰκονομίας): v. 4b; c[1]) S decides on his goal (ἵνα [...] δέξωνταί με εἰς τοὺς οἴκους): v. 4c.
(B[1]) Steward & Debtors (vv. 5–7)	a) S speaks to the first debtor (ἔλεγεν τῷ πρώτῳ): v. 5a; b) S asks him: "How much do you owe?" (πόσον ὀφείλεις;): v. 5b; c) the first debtor answers: "A hundred" (ὁ δὲ εἶπεν· ἑκατόν): v. 6a; d) S says to the first debtor: "Take your promissory note[234]	a[1]) S speaks to the other debtor (ἑτέρῳ εἶπεν): v. 7a; b[1]) S asks him: "How much do you owe?" (πόσον ὀφείλεις;): v. 7b; c[1]) the second debtor answers: "A hundred" (ὁ δὲ εἶπεν· ἑκατόν): v. 7c; d[1]) S says to the second debtor: "Take our promissory note and

---

[233] While J.D. Crossan recognizes in the parable only three scenes (vv. 1–2.3–4.5–7), he also notes (*Ibid.*, 33) that, "in setting up both the problem and the avenue of solution", the chiastic structure of the first scene is particularly important. Generally, his subdivision is quite close to ours, but, as D.A. De Silva ("The Parable", 256) remarks, "Crossan's scheme is missing its last scene, the return to the steward/master relationship for closure" (v. 8a). One explanation for the omission is that, in fitting the story of the Shrewd Steward into the thematic unity of the *Servant* parables ("Group B"), J.D. Crossan is too intent to compare such a story with that of the Unmerciful Servant (Matt 18,23–35). In the latter, he identifies a three-scenic structure (vv. 23–27.28–30.31–34) that leaves its conclusion (v. 35) out of the picture. He does the same thing with our parable. However, if v. 8a is returned to the story, then the author's scheme is enhanced. Not only does the story reach its closure, but the aforementioned comment on the chiastic structure of vv. 1–2 can then be extended to include the overall construction of the parable itself (see A – B – B[1] – A[1]). See, e.g., J.D. CROSSAN, "Servant Parables", 17.28.32; D.O. VIA, Jr., "Parable", 124; B.B. SCOTT, "A Master's Praise", 177–179; D.J. IRELAND, *Stewardship*, 19; and M. GRILLI, *Matteo*, 350.

[234] Both in v. 6b and v. 7d, as J.A. Metzger (*Consumption*, 116, n. 32) notes, "some manuscripts (notably A K P W *Byz*) preserve the singular τὸ γράμμα. The plural (τὰ γράμματα) is the better attested reading". See, e.g., 𝔓[75] ℵ B D L N Ψ 579 and *f*[1].

	and [...] set down" (δέξαι σου τὰ γράμματα καὶ [...] γράψον): v. 6b.	set down" (δέξαι σου τὰ γράμματα καὶ γράψον): v. 7d.
(A¹) Master & Steward (v. 8a)	M (κύριός) surprisingly praises (ἐπήνεσεν) S (τὸν οἰκονόμον), because of his "shrewd doing" (ὅτι φρονίμως ἐποίησεν).	

Within this structure, three things emerge in particular: a) every scene contains an internal diptych, with the exception of the last one[235]; b) the chiastic pattern of the first scene (vv. 1b–2) ushers in and reflects that of the whole story (vv. 1b–8a); and c) the only single panel (v. 8a) occurring at the end of the story brings it to a closure and unveils its intrinsic message.

In fact, within the *central* part of the structure (B–B¹), and in connection with its *main* character (S), a key role in the parable must be attributed to the verb "to do" (ποιεῖν: vv. 3.4.8a; see also v. 9a). Not only does it encapsulate the steward's management actions and solution, but it also reveals in some way all its dynamics in connection with the two aforementioned motifs of money and eschatology[236]. The steward's question (v. 3a), "What shall I do?" (τί ποιήσω;), and the sudden realization of the answer immediately following it (v. 4a), "I know what I shall do" (ἔγνων τί ποιήσω)[237], express a somewhat intense tension towards the future, which nonetheless demands an immediate and urgent (see ταχέως: v. 6) managerial activity[238]. Likewise, in the verses following the parable (see v. 9), the present-future dimension of the steward's earthly life is taken and interpreted eschatologically, as an application to the disciples' afterlife[239]. However, as we have already mentioned, eschatology

---

[235] See, e.g., J.D. CROSSAN, "Servant Parables", 32; G. GIURISATO, "Come Luca", 446–447; and J. DURKIN, "A Cultural Reading", 11–13.

[236] See, e.g., M. GOURGUES, *Les Paraboles*, 167; and A. BOLIN, *Du bon usage*, 41.51–52. For instance, M. Gourgues (*Ibid.*, 168) points out: "l'action [...] [est] d'abord rendue impérieuse (v. 2), puis cherchée (v. 3), trouvée (v. 4), exécutée (vv. 5–7), et finalement reconnue comme habile (v. 8a)".

[237] The verb, "to know" (γινώσκειν), is here used dramatically, in the aorist tense, to indicate the state of mind just reached and the grasping of the solution (lit. "I have come to know"). See, e.g., J.A. METZGER, *Consumption*, 115, n. 23. The "dramatic aorist" (*aoristus tragicus*) is often used in Greek classical poems and dialogues to give to a statement greater intensity than that given by the present tense. See, e.g., Brugmann, 160; Burton, 22; Zerwick, 84–85; and Wallace, 564–565.

[238] See, e.g., F. BOVON, *Luc*, III, 69; and A. BOLIN, *Du bon usage*, 45–46. See also the significance given to the steward's realization (v. 4), by K.E. BAILEY, *Poet*, 95; F. BOVON, *Luc*, III, 68–74; R. MEYNET, *Luc*, 478; and A. BOLIN, *Du bon usage*, 41.45.50.

[239] See, e.g., T. SNOY, "Approche littéraire", 55; and A. BOLIN, *Du bon usage*, 46.

mingles here with right, or even better, "shrewd" (v. 8a) management of "properties" (see v. 1c). The same commentary verses apply the verb "to do" to one's relationship with "worldly wealth" (see μαμωνᾶς: vv. 9.11.13; esp., v. 9a).

Thus, the opening scene (vv. 1b–2), with its chiastic structure, sets the stage for the story and its message. The notions of possessions and management (see πλούσιος, εἶχεν, οἰκονόμον, and ὑπάρχοντα: v.1bc), as well as those of time and its upcoming expiration (see v. 2) are introduced. Then, as the story advances slowly in detail, they develop and become expectation and need to ponder, judge (see vv. 3–4), take action (see vv. 5–7). Finally, in the last verse and scene of the parable (v. 8a), the steward is praised because of his acting or dealing (lit. "doing") shrewdly (ὅτι φρονίμως ἐποίησεν)[240]. The expression encloses the message of the parable as in a nutshell and launches it towards its audience.

Indeed, the final commendation and its justification (v. 8a) leave both disciples (see v. 1a) and readers "in an uncomfortable position"[241]. The steward's "shrewd doing" obliges them to reconsider his actions (vv. 5–7) and make sense of them[242]. In this endeavor, however, Luke's Gospel comes to the aid of the reader, who can recall how the same question has been asked and answered before (see τί ποιήσ-ω/ωμεν;: Luke 3,10.12.14a; 10,25; 12,17; and 16,3), both by John the Baptist (see Luke 3,11.13.14b) and Jesus (see ποιήσατε: 12,33; and 16,9)[243], and often in the context of possessions and their eschatological use[244]. The outcome of this recollection, for him, is more than just a hint of suspicion.

---

[240] See, e.g., J.S. KLOPPENBORG, "The Dishonoured Master", 479. What the verb "to do" (ποιεῖν) and the adverb "shrewdly" (φρονίμως) entail in this story specifically shall be dealt with later, as we shall discuss the main point of the parable.

[241] B.B. SCOTT, "A Master's Praise", 185.

[242] See, e.g., B.B. SCOTT, "A Master's Praise", 185, n. 42.

[243] See, e.g., L.T. JOHNSON, ed., *Luke,* 245; and R. KRÜGER, "Lucas 16,1–13", 108.

[244] Generally, Luke includes the question, "What shall I do?" (τί ποιήσω;), in the context of parables whose characters' interior dilemma concerns their attitude towards possessions (see, e.g., Luke 12,17; 16,3; and 20,13), whereas, in the rest of his Gospel, the answer to this same question frequently involves generosity in dealing with one's neighbor (see, e.g., Luke 3,10–14; 10,25.27.29.33–35; and 18,18.22). As G. Rossé (*Luca,* 130) comments, for the Lucan Baptist, "il frutto concreto della conversione è la comunione dei beni", a theme which is "apparentato al problema della ricchezza caro a Luca". John's message could be compared here to that of the angelic watcher, in king Nebuchadnezzar's dream (see Dan 4,7.10–11.14.17–24; and Luke 1,17; 3,2–4.9.11–14). As in John's exhortation, Daniel's final advice to the pagan king is to break away from sin, "by [doing] righteousness" (Dan 4,24: cf. MT בצדקה; LXX ἐν ἐλεημοσύναις) and by showing mercy to the poor, since those who trust in the abundance of their riches are like senseless beasts that are destroyed (see Dan 4,13.20.22.26–30; and Ps 49,2.6.12.20). As regards Jesus, Origen of Alexandria (*Comm. Luc.* XXIII.3 [ed. H. CROUZEL – F. FOURNIER – P. PÉRICHON, 314–315]) comments, that he too wants his disciples not to wear two robes (see Luke 3,11; 9,3; and 16,13): "just as we must not serve two masters, so neither [we must] have two tunics, nor be wrapped by a twofold vestment"

4. The Meaning of the Master's Praise: A Hermeneutical Crux

The meaning of the master's final approbation of his steward's actions (v. 8a) is for most commentators the major hermeneutic crux of the entire parable[245]. The issue is whether or how one can ever praise any dishonest conduct[246].

Interpreters have attempted to either evade or resolve the problem primarily in three different ways. Following J. Jeremias' lead, a number of exegetes tried to avoid the question entirely by considering the "master" (κύριος) of v. 8a to be Jesus himself, the "Lord" (Κύριος)[247]. However, as we have already pointed out, this is not the case. Besides, even if one interpreted the praise in v. 8a as uttered by Jesus, the difficulty to understand how the steward might still be used as a model for Jesus' disciples would remain unresolved[248]. Others then decided to treat the final praise voiced by the master as rhetorical irony, and the parable as a negative example to avoid[249]. Yet, linguistic considerations as to the use of the verb in the NT seem to rule irony out of this verse as a spurious explanation of the problem[250]. Finally, starting in the early 1960s and 1970s, a third major group of scholars (see, esp., J.D.M. Derrett and J.A. Fitzmyer) strove to solve the problem by choosing to exonerate the steward's actions (vv. 5–7) of all wrongdoing directly, mainly on the basis of all kinds of socio-

---

(*quomodo non debemus duobus dominis servire, sic nec duas habere tunicas, nec duplici veste circumdari*). Finally, as to the context of almsgiving, the verb "to do" (ποιεῖν) is used also in the expression, "what your right hand does" (τί ποιεῖ ἡ δεξιά σου), in Matt 6,3.

[245] See, e.g., D.J. IRELAND, *Stewardship*, 65–82, esp. 74.

[246] See, e.g., G. ROSSÉ, *Luca*, 618.

[247] For a list of authors following this trend, see, e.g., J.A. FITZMYER, *Luke*, II, 1101; J.S. KLOPPENBORG, "The Dishonoured Master", 476, n. 4; and J.K. GOODRICH, "Voluntary Debt Remission", 550, n. 12. See also R. KRÜGER, "Lucas 16,1–13", 107.

[248] See, e.g., C. FOCANT, "Tromper", 547; D.J. IRELAND, *Stewardship*, 66; and J.K. GOODRICH, "Voluntary Debt Remission", 550.

[249] See, e.g., D.R. FLETCHER, "The Riddle", 15–30; S.E. PORTER, "The Parable", 127–153; D.J. IRELAND, *Stewardship*, 27–33.77–78; and J.K. GOODRICH, "Voluntary Debt Remission", 551. For instance, D.R. Fletcher ("The Riddle", 29) appeals to the "irony of Jesus' play on the story" (see v. 9) as the only way to answer the riddle of the parable, and writes: "'Make friends for yourselves', he seems to taunt; 'imitate the example of the steward; use the unrighteous mammon; surround yourselves with the type of insincere, self-interested friendship it can buy; how far will this carry you when the end comes and you are finally dismissed?'".

[250] Thus, D.L. Bock (*Luke*, II, 1332) remarks: "Irony or sarcasm in this verse is excluded by the use of ἐπαινέω (*epaineō*, to praise), which is uniformly positive in the NT". See, e.g., Rom 15,11; and 1Cor 11,2.17.22. See also F.E. WILLIAMS, "Is Almsgiving", 293–297; and J.K. GOODRICH, "Voluntary Debt Remission", 551. Indeed, as D.J. Ireland (*Stewardship*, 78) comments, "irony seems to have suggested itself because of the difficulty of explaining the praise in v. 8 or Jesus' exhortation in v. 9. Difficulty alone, however, is no proof of irony".

economic assumptions[251]. Although on first consideration their interpretation seems quite fair and sensible, it does present a few weak points which are worth noting.

The basic claim of these scholars is that the steward does nothing but reduce *selflessly*, from his master's debtors, only those amounts that constitute his own profits or commissions, whether they are actually an illicit usurious component (J.D.M. Derrett) or his interest rate for the loans (J.A. Fitzmyer). Indeed, according to these authors, the steward's own "doing" (ποιεῖν) does earn his master's favor *genuinely*, so that the latter's praise is actually legitimate and wholly predictable[252]. Moreover, while the positive notion of "shrewdness" (see φρονίμως: v. 8a) is predicated of the steward's final actions, the epithet, "unrighteous" (τῆς ἀδικίας: v. 8a), with which the parable explicitly closes his negative characterization, is only a mere reference to his former way of life and wasteful management (see vv. 1–2) and has nothing to do with his most recent managerial arrangements (see vv. 5–7)[253]. In other words, the steward undergoes a true conversion, now giving up what belongs to him, as opposed to lavishing that which is his master's, as he used to do before. Thus, in praising the steward the master ratifies the latter *stealthy* but righteous actions. Since these eventually increase his own reputation for piety and generosity, he actually endorses them and makes them appear as if they were his own idea from the very beginning[254].

Some later interpreters have vindicated the steward by adding to this latter notion. Inferring from social-scientific cultural evidence, they generally take the honor-shame paradigm of the ancient Mediterranean world and apply it to this parable[255]. Since, in such a culture, honor was presumed to be worth more than a person's wealth, land, or properties, their claim is that the master logically

---

[251] See, e.g., J.D.M. DERRETT, "Fresh Light", I, 198–219; J.A. FITZMYER, "The Story", 23–42; H. MOXNES, *Economy*, 140–141; J.S. KLOPPENBORG, "The Dishonoured Master", 479–486; D.J. IRELAND, *Stewardship*, 35–46.79–81; R. KRÜGER, "Lucas 16,1–13", 104–106; J.A. TROXLE, Jr., *Doing Justice*, 22–23; and J.A. METZGER, *Consumption*, 121–123. For recent efforts to defend the steward against all unlawful activity, see, e.g., J.A. TROXLE, Jr., *Doing Justice*, 9, n. 32; and *Ibid.*, 22–30.57–59. Although the origin of this hermeneutic trend is generally attributed to J.D.M. Derrett, R. Krüger is right to trace it further back to P. Gächter's article, in 1950. See P. GÄCHTER, "The Parable", 121–131; and R. KRÜGER, "Lucas 16,1–13", 104.

[252] See, e.g., D. LANDRY – B. MAY, "Honour Restored", 303. For a list of authors in support of this interpretation, see, esp., J.K. GOODRICH, "Voluntary Debt Remission", 548, n. 4.

[253] See, e.g., J.D.M. DERRETT, "Fresh Light", I, 204; J.A. FITZMYER, "The Story", 32–33; and D.J. IRELAND, *Stewardship*, 69, n. 93. This standpoint is officially approved of, for instance, also by the *NJB*, p. 1717, n. *b*.

[254] See, e.g., J.D.M. DERRETT, "Fresh Light", I, 210.216–217.

[255] See, e.g., H.J.B. COMBRINK, "A Social-Scientific Perspective", 303; D. LANDRY – B. MAY, "Honour Restored", 301; S.E. WRIGHT, "Parables", 225–227; J.G. LYGRE, "Of What Charges?", 23–27; J.A. TROXLE, Jr., *Doing Justice*, 62–73; J. DURKIN, "A Cultural Reading", 9–15; J.K. GOODRICH, "Voluntary Debt Remission", 549, n. 7; and L. MARULLI, "'And How Much'", 201.

praises his steward's faultless actions, for they are "wise" enough to convert the latter kind of good (i.e., money belonging to the steward) into the former (i.e., honor and good reputation), with no financial loss for the master and, even more, to the latter's advantage[256]. Moreover, by enhancing the master's prestige, the steward reinstates his own name and loyalty. He is now a good and trustworthy manager, gaining approval among his master's debtors, and can thus hope again for future employment[257]. In other words, the master praises the steward because his shrewd strategy ultimately yields advantageous results for all the individuals involved: it reduces the debtors' debts, enhances the master's reputation and, at the cost of the steward's own profit, allows him to vindicate his own name, for the sake of another job opportunity[258].

Indeed, as we have already suggested, this kind of interpretation does sound reasonably good at first glance. It explains the master's praise logically, as something that is even expected, and makes it easier to understand why the steward is proposed as an example to imitate. However, the suppositions on which it rests have never been widely accepted among scholars, primarily because of flaws in their arguments[259]. For instance, one of the reasons the theory is not wholly convincing is that it entails a fairly difficult and unspoken number of assumptions in relation to the nature of the steward's economic transactions[260]. Besides, the large amounts reduced by the steward do not seem to conform to the interest rates typically imposed for contemporary loan practices[261]. Even if they did, the steward questions the debtors on how much they owe *his master* (see vv. 5.7), which clearly implies that he is actually

---

[256] See, e.g., D. LANDRY – B. MAY, "Honour Restored", 304; and J. DURKIN, "A Cultural Reading", 10.

[257] See, e.g., J.D.M. DERRETT, "Fresh Light", I, 204.216; J.R. DONAHUE, *The Gospel*, 164; J.S. KLOPPENBORG, "The Dishonoured Master", 491, n. 58; D. LANDRY – B. MAY, "Honour Restored", 300; J.L. STORY, "Twin Parables", 108–109; and J.K. GOODRICH, "Voluntary Debt Remission", 550.564–565.

[258] See, e.g., J.K. GOODRICH, "Voluntary Debt Remission", 565.

[259] See, e.g., D. LANDRY – B. MAY, "Honour Restored", 289. For a summary of the various problems found so far with such an interpretation, see, e.g., *Ibid.*, 289–290; J.A. METZGER, *Consumption*, 118–121; and L. MARULLI, "'And How Much'", 204–207.213–214.

[260] See, e.g., J.D.M. DERRETT, "Fresh Light", I, 201–216; J.A. FITZMYER, "The Story", 33–37; B.B. SCOTT, "A Master's Praise", 177; J.S. KLOPPENBORG, "The Dishonoured Master", 479–480; and J.K. GOODRICH, "Voluntary Debt Remission", 553–563. Thus, J.S. Kloppenborg ("The Dishonoured Master", 486) argues: "the narrative would have had to include much clearer indications [...] a Palestinian audience would not suppose that either usury or the manager's commission was the focal point of the story".

[261] See, e.g., J.S. KLOPPENBORG, "The Dishonoured Master", 482–483; B.J. MALINA – R.L. ROHRBAUGH, *Social-Science*, 374; D. LANDRY – B. MAY, "Honour Restored", 290; and B.L. IHSSEN, *They Who Give*, 89.

reducing his master's earnings rather than his own[262]. In other words, he is being "generous", as it were, but only with his master's wealth. His actions are indeed injurious; nevertheless his own pocket remains untouched and the narrator has all the reasons in the world to call him unjust (τῆς ἀδικίας: v. 8a)[263]. Finally, the study of Luke's use of the interior monologue technique suggests that the steward's motivations are in all likelihood anything but altruistic[264].

As a result, then, the most reasonable interpretation of the parable is that according to which the steward's actions affect detrimentally only the master. In fact, vindicating the steward's unlawful behavior, as if his debt-reduction caused damage to his own riches, is not only inappropriate but also unnecessary. It is not appropriate insofar as it fails to do justice to the steward's final qualification as "unrighteous" (τῆς ἀδικίας), in v. 8a[265], as well as to the object of his initial accusations, which clearly relate to the loss of "possessions" (τὰ ὑπάρχοντα: v. 1) rather than simply honor[266]. The issue of endangered honor may still have an incidental bearing on the parable, but it is not what is primarily at stake[267]. Indeed, the "justification" of the steward's actions is not even needed.

---

[262] See, e.g., R.H. STEIN, *An Introduction*, 109; B.B. SCOTT, "A Master's Praise", 177; J.S. KLOPPENBORG, "The Dishonoured Master", 481; and D. LANDRY – B. MAY, "Honour Restored", 289. Thus, J. Durkin ("A Cultural Reading", 15) clarifies: "if these two [debtors] had negotiated an agreement including a commission for the steward, the question would have been more likely phrased 'how much do you owe me?'".

[263] See, e.g., J.S. KLOPPENBORG, "The Dishonoured Master", 486.

[264] For instance, P. Sellew ("Interior Monologue", 242) observes: "None of the personalities whose thoughts are described [in Luke's Gospel] is particularly commendable [...] The self-satisfied, amoral, or even immoral individuals who star in these portrayals [...] are looking out for their own interests [...] but [...] seem able to use their craftiness or amoral reasoning to escape punishment". See, e.g., Luke 12,17–19.45; 15,17–19; 16,3–4; 18,4–5; and *Ibid.*, 244–249. See also M.R. AUSTIN, "The Hypocritical Son", 312; D.A. DE SILVA, "The Parable", 260; J.-N. ALETTI, *Il racconto*, 189–197; J.A. TROXLE, Jr., *Doing Justice*, 231–235; and M. CRIMELLA, *Marta*, 258–272.

[265] As D.J. Ireland (*Stewardship*, 69) comments, "As much as inefficiency and dishonesty may have been typical of the steward's management of his master's goods before his dismissal, his *adikia* is still not established clearly enough in vv. 1–2 to justify this characterization in v. 8a [...] If, however, something in vv. 3–7 reveals a quality of dishonesty in the steward, which is central to the parable, the description becomes necessary [...] it is 'reasonable' that *tes adikias* would be omitted in v. 8a if it did not refer to the actions in vv. 5–7". See also M. GRILLI, *Matteo*, 348.

[266] See, e.g., J.K. GOODRICH, "Voluntary Debt Remission", 549.

[267] The idea of honor-shame, just like that of strength (see οὐκ ἰσχύω [...] αἰσχύνομαι: v. 3c), is certainly present in the parable, but not to the point of being the main stated concern of the text. Thus, M.D. Greene ("The Parable", 84) argues: "if honor-shame is the real issue, why do the appended interpretations in verses 8b–13 not understand the parable this way?". See also D. MATHEWSON, "The Parable", 32.

First of all, he is not really looking for a new job[268]. If a new employment were truly the goal of his actions, then the narrator would have explicitly stated so or, at least, given some hints, just as in the case of the previous parable on the prodigal son[269]. His aim is rather that of finding a welcoming place for his future, an abode where he can dwell, which strictly speaking is not even his, just as the possessions he deals with. The solution or strategy, which he is able to come up with, is simply a means to this end. Cutting down the amounts owed to his master by his debtors prompts their benevolence and hospitality, and he can now hope to be received into their homes with gratitude (see Luke 16,4–5.9)[270].

Second, the honor-shame paradigm offers sufficient reasons to explain the master's praise, even when the steward's actions are not vindicated as lawful[271]. As the master supposedly gets back the accounting of his steward's management, and upon his realization of the benefits conferred by the latter on his own debtors, he is likely to face a dilemma[272]. Should he annul the steward's unrighteous actions and get his money back, yet causing disappointment or anger among his debtors and a bad reputation for himself as ungenerous, or should he rather keep silent and endorse them, so that his generous and noble name may ultimately profit from the whole business[273]? Precisely because money is, according to these studies, less valuable than honor, he is most likely to choose the latter over the former, and still praise his steward because of his shrewd checkmate[274]. Thus, even if at the price of his master's money, the steward still provides insurance for his own future, decreases the leaseholders' debts, and heightens his master's honor[275].

Finally, in addition to the aforementioned three leading theories, a few interpreters have proposed other minor explanations of the meaning of the master's praise, which are nevertheless somewhat "farfetched"[276]. For instance, a couple of authors have claimed that Luke 16,8a was originally an interrogation

---

[268] Thus, F. Udoh ("The Tale", 333) points out: "the manager [...] does not undertake a job search for new 'employment', as scholars usually assume. He prepares to flee, and in such a way that he subsequently will not be reduced to begging (vv. 3–4)".

[269] See Luke 15,14–15.17–19. Moreover, as J.A. Metzger (*Consumption*, 116, n. 31) argues, because of their state, "it is highly unlikely that the debtors with whom he speaks would be able to fund the position of a fulltime steward".

[270] See, e.g., M. CRIMELLA, *Marta*, 263–269; and J.K. GOODRICH, "Voluntary Debt Remission", 550, n. 9.

[271] See, e.g., J.S. KLOPPENBORG, "The Dishonoured Master", 486–493; and H.J.B. COMBRINK, "A Social-Scientific Perspective", 293–304.

[272] See, e.g., K.E. BAILEY, *Poet*, 101–102; D. LANDRY – B. MAY, "Honour Restored", 302, n. 60; and L. MARULLI, "'And How Much'", 216.

[273] See, e.g., J.A. TROXLE, Jr., *Doing Justice*, 12.

[274] See, e.g., D. LANDRY – B. MAY, "Honour Restored", 302, n. 60.

[275] See, e.g., J.G. LYGRE, "Of What Charges?", 27.

[276] J.A. FITZMYER, *Luke*, II, 1101.

(vs. affirmation), or that the verb, "to praise" (ἐπαινεῖν), and the adverb, "shrewdly" (φρονίμως), represent *senso bono* mistranslations of their original *senso malo* Aramaic terms, "to bless/curse" (בֶרֶךּ), and "wise/sly" (עֲרִים), respectively[277]. However, as S.E. Porter rightly comments, "resorting to mistranslation of a non-existent document or body of material seems an implausible, to say nothing of unverifiable, solution"[278].

Besides, while we have no extant textual proof that the Gospels were originally written in Aramaic, as they stand in the actual Greek text, one cannot properly translate these propositions by questions[279]. Finally, a *senso malo* hardly fits the context[280], and even if it did, in the LXX the verb בֶרֶךּ is neither translated with ἐπαινεῖν nor used to express the meaning of cursing, when directed to a man[281].

5. The Point of the Parable: Wise Use of Money with Eternity in View

All in all, as we have already mentioned, the efforts to bypass the difficulty and exonerate the "Unjust Steward" have had no great appeal among scholars[282]. They generally fail to recognize the intended distinguishing trait of the parable, and by removing the unforeseen from the art of the story-telling actually rob it of its surprise factor[283].

Consequently, we concur with the vast majority of interpreters who, at least until the middle of the 20th c., have rather understood the steward's actions as being fraudulent and unrighteous (just as v. 8a seems to indicate), and his shrewdness (see φρονίμως: v. 8a) as relating to the prudent use of material possessions to the advantage of his own future benefits[284]. According to this

---

[277] See, e.g., C.C. TORREY, *The Four Gospels*, 157, n. 311; P.G. BRETSCHER, "The Parable", 756–762; G. PAUL, "The Unjust Steward", 192; G. SCHWARZ, "...lobte den betrügerischen Verwalter?", 94–95; I.J. DU PLESSIS, "Philanthropy", 9–10; D.M. PARROTT, "The Dishonest Steward", 513–514; and D.J. IRELAND, *Stewardship*, 33–35.66.77–79.

[278] S.E. PORTER, "The Parable", 128–129. The results of our previous review, as regards the application of a similar approach to the violence passage, totally confirms this statement.

[279] See, e.g., J.B. PHILLIPS, *The Gospels*, 243.

[280] Thus, I.J. Du Plessis ("Philanthropy", 10) notes: "verses 8b and 9 do not really make sense if verse 8a is translated *senso malo*; [...] a *senso malo* translation would not be in correlation with the logical course of the story and the remaining pronouncements in verses 10–13".

[281] See, e.g., C. FOCANT, "Tromper", 549–550; and G. ROSSÉ, *Luca*, 619, n. 4.

[282] See, e.g., D.R. FLETCHER, "The Riddle", 23.

[283] See, e.g., B.B. SCOTT, "A Master's Praise", 175, n. 8; J.S. KLOPPENBORG, "The Dishonoured Master", 492; and D.J. IRELAND, *Stewardship*, 81.

[284] Thus, in his survey of the history of the interpretation of the parable, J.A. Troxle Jr. (*Doing Justice*, 22) observes: "The most common interpretation even up to 1960 was that the steward was dishonest and that the main point of the parable is an exhortation to be wise in the use of material possessions". As D.J. Ireland (*Stewardship*, 8, n. 8) specifies, such an understanding corresponds precisely to that of more than one third of "the 140 or so interpreters"

"conventional" vision, then, the parable promotes a concrete form of charity to the poor, such as, almsgiving, inasmuch as this can help one keep one's eye turned towards one's eschatological "end" (ἔσχατον)[285].

In addition to the aforementioned considerations, the resolution that such a view is to be preferred rests also on the following reasons.

Indeed, if the steward does act unjustly, from start to finish, and if the parable does teach what Christians are to do with their possessions and money with a view to getting an eternal abode in heaven, then one may wonder how this is possible, since the steward is not using his own money but that of his master[286]. The problem, however, ceases to exist as soon as one realizes a few things.

First, such a teaching is essentially conveyed through the *qal waḥômer* (or *a fortiori*) biblical method of reasoning (see v. 8b)[287]. The *a fortiori* argument would here go like this: if the unjust steward was shrewd in his worldly and temporal sphere of existence, how much more should a Christian be shrewd in the spiritual and eternal sphere[288]! Strictly speaking, then, the steward is not a true model or example to imitate[289]. He is truly unrighteous and selfish, for he

---

consulted by him in his survey. See also C.M. HAYS, *Luke's Wealth Ethics*, 144. For a list of the authors who argue in support of this interpretation, see, e.g., D.J. IRELAND, "A History", 295–309; ID., *Stewardship*, 7–35; P. MONAT, "L'exégèse", 89–123; D. LANDRY – B. MAY, "Honour Restored", 289–293; B.C. DENNERT, "A Survey", 145–150; and A. BOLIN, *Du bon usage*, 7–24.

[285] See, e.g., J.A. FITZMYER, "The Story", 32.37; D.J. IRELAND, *Stewardship*, 7–14; and J.A. TROXLE, Jr., *Doing Justice*, 9.30–32.39–41.74–76.81. As J. Lightfoot (*A Commentary*, III, 159–160) notes, in fact, the expression, "unrighteous mammon" (μαμωνᾶς τῆς ἀδικίας) can be also read, "in opposition to *mammon* צדיקה *of righteousness*, i.e., *of mercy*, or *almsgiving*". Jesus' exhortation to make friends for oneself out of the "mammon of unrighteousness" becomes then an encouragement to make use "of those riches which you have not yet laid out in צדיקה *righteousness*, or *almsgiving*". Thus, C.H. Pickar ("The Unjust Steward", 252) points out: "Alms given to the poor will be a means of attaining heaven". For a list of the authors in favour of this view, see, esp., D.J. IRELAND, *Stewardship*, 11, n. 26; and J.A. TROXLE, Jr., *Doing Justice*, 31, n. 55.

[286] See, e.g., D.J. IRELAND, *Stewardship*, 10.

[287] See, e.g., Luke 11,13; 12,6–7.24.28; 13,15–16; 17,10; 18,6–8. See also F.E. WILLIAMS, "Is Almsgiving", 294–295; J.A. FITZMYER, *Luke*, II, 957.978–979.1011.1177. 1147.1180; D.J. IRELAND, *Stewardship*, 10; R.H. STEIN, *Luke*, 444–445; A.A. JUST, Jr., *Luke*, II, 673–674; and Bazyliński, 181–182. As J. Durkin ("A Cultural Reading", 17) notes, "This is a type of parable [that] is characterized by [the] 'how much more ...?' logic". See also S. PRINCIPE, "Chi era Luca?", 140–141.

[288] See, e.g., D.J. IRELAND, *Stewardship*, 10; and J.A. TROXLE, Jr., *Doing Justice*, 12. T.W. Manson (*The Sayings*, 292–293) phrases it analogously: "If a bad man will take infinite trouble [...] for his own selfish interests, the good man will surely take some trouble [...] in a better way and for better ends [...] by disposing of worldly wealth in the proper way, one will have a treasure in heaven".

[289] See, e.g., D.J. IRELAND, *Stewardship*, 66.

mishandles his master's property for his own benefit[290]. However, he is still praised because of his *shrewd doings* (ὅτι φρονίμως ἐποίησεν: v. 8a)[291]. But praising an unrighteous steward because he acted shrewdly is quite different from praising a shrewd steward because he acted unrighteously[292]. Thanks to the *a fortiori* reasoning, therefore, the shrewdness of an unrighteous steward can still be used to encourage almsgiving as the wisest investment possible for the advantage of one's own future[293]. After all, is that not what the Greek root of the term is all about? Although the meaning of the adverb (φρονίμως) is generally explained in different ways, and often described as, "savoir-faire", "astuteness", "cleverness", "shrewdness", "prudence", or "wisdom", in its biblical use it describes often someone who, considering the shortness of time and the options at hand (cf. vv. 3–4), chooses the best course of action foresightedly, so as to provide wisely for his or her hereafter[294].

Secondly, the use which the steward makes of his master's property can still be compared with that which is at stake whenever one gives alms. Indeed, the fact that the steward is "playing", as it were, with someone else's wealth helps explain his "unrighteous" management in terms of the Judeo-Christian notion of almsgiving and its underlying belief that nothing of what we possess here on earth is really ours, in the strict sense of the word[295]. According to this

---

[290] See, e.g., D.J. IRELAND, *Stewardship*, 73.

[291] See, e.g., J.A. TROXLE, Jr., *Doing Justice*, 11–12. As B.B. Scott ("A Master's Praise", 184, n. 41) points out, "*pistos* and *phronimos* are normal adjectives describing a steward's expected activity (Luke 12,42), loyalty and shrewdness in his master's behalf". See, e.g., Luke 12,42–43; 16,8a.10–12; and 1Cor 4,2. See also D. LANDRY – B. MAY, "Honour Restored", 304–305; R.S. SCHELLENBERG, "Which Master?", 274. 278; and F. UDOH, "The Tale", 328–331. However, instead of a "faithful and shrewd steward" (ὁ πιστὸς οἰκονόμος ὁ φρόνιμος: Luke 12,42) of "someone else's property" (ἐν τῷ ἀλλοτρίῳ: Luke 16,12), the main character of this parable is "shrewd" (φρόνιμος: Luke 16,8ab) but "unrighteous" (τῆς ἀδικίας: Luke 16,8a), that is, unfaithful or disloyal. For a list of authors maintaining this distinction, see, e.g., D.J. IRELAND, *Stewardship*, 73, n. 106.

[292] See, e.g., T.W. MANSON, *The Sayings*, 290–293; and D.J. IRELAND, *Stewardship*, 9.74.

[293] See, e.g., F. GODET, *Luke*, II, 166–167. F.E. Williams ("Is Almsgiving", 295) sums up the argument thus: "If even worldlings are shrewd enough to recognize the value of handing out their master's money, should not the servants of God realize the value of almsgiving? Unfortunately, they do not act as though they did – the children of this world are wiser, in their way, than the children of light [...] This is indeed an exhortation to imitate the steward, but not in his dishonesty; the auditors are being urged to be like the steward in the point at which he is rightly imitable, namely, in the distribution of their master's property".

[294] See, e.g., Gen 41,33–39; Josh 9,4; Ps 90[89],12; Prov 8,12; 12,16; 13,16; 14,8.15.24; 22,3; 27,12; Sir 40,20; Hos 13,13; Matt 7,24–25; 24,44–46; 25,1–13; and Luke 12,42–43. See also D.R. FLETCHER, "The Riddle", 23–24; D.J. IRELAND, *Stewardship*, 72, n. 111; and R. KRÜGER, "Lucas 16,1–13", 107. According to Merriam[11] ("shrewd", 1154), a shrewd person is one particularly "marked by clever discerning awareness [...] practical, hard-headed cleverness and judgment".

[295] For instance, F.E. Williams ("Is Almsgiving", 294) observes: "The parable of the Unjust Steward [...] would counsel the believer to give away as much money as possible

notion, almsgiving is considered as a sort of financial generosity, which can nonetheless grant the person who practices it also some supernatural eschatological reward[296]. Thus, W. Barclay notes:

The Rabbis had a saying, "The rich help the poor in this world, but the poor help the rich in the world to come" [...] It was a Jewish belief that charity given to poor people would stand to a man's credit in the world to come. A man's true wealth would consist not in what he kept, but in what he gave away[297].

Consequently, if by giving to the poor, someone is able to trade one's ephemeral wealth with that which is truly eternal, then this kind of "managerial activity" can also be branded "unrighteous", primarily because of the "selfish" incentive which may often inspire it[298]. Jesus makes a similar point in his commentary on the parable (see vv. 10–11), as he distinguishes between that which is worth "very little" (ἐλάχιστον) and that which is worth "much" (πολύ), and between "worldly" (ἄδικος) "wealth" (μαμωνᾶς) and "true" (ἀληθινός) wealth[299]. Additionally, in the parable closing chap. 16, we have a perfect *"exemplum contrarium"*[300]: the poor Lazarus will not be able to help the anonymous rich man in the world to come, since the rich man did not help the poor Lazarus in this world (see Luke 16,19–31).

Finally, although the issue of the master's honor is "on the periphery"[301] of the story and vv. 8b–13 pass over it in silence, the following reasoning may also apply. Just as the steward's "management" (οἰκονομεῖν) of his master's goods, when it is shrewdly "done" (see ποιεῖν: vv. 3.4.8) in the latter's name,

---

here, in order to obtain eternal shelter in the world to come. Underlying its symbolism is the idea, familiar to Jewish piety, that a man in practicing almsgiving distributes, not his own property, but property which is already God's". Scripture testifies to this idea: all that we own belongs to God, whether materially or spiritually. See, e.g., Exod 9,29; Deut 10,14; 1Chr 29,16; Ps 24,1; Luke 20,25b; John 3,27; Rom 12,6; 1Cor 3,22–23; 4,7–8; and 10,26. See also D.J. IRELAND, *Stewardship*, 12–13.

[296] See, e.g., Tob 4,5–11; Prov 10,2; 19,17; Sir 29,9–13; Matt 6,20; 13,44; 19,21; Luke 12,33; 18,11; 1Tim 6,18–19; PsSol 9,5; and 2Bar 14.12. See also mAv 3.7; K.R. SNODGRASS, *Stories*, 421; and N. EUBANK, "Storing up Treasure", 79–84.

[297] W. BARCLAY, *Luke*, 209.

[298] As F.E. Williams ("Is Almsgiving", 293) clarifies, "If the parable is intended to encourage almsgiving, its appeal is to a motive which may be called 'eschatological self-interest'; that is, the hearer is urged to do without certain worldly advantages, in the expectation of obtaining reward in an eschatological future".

[299] J. Duncan and J.D.M. Derrett (*Law*, 81, n. 1) note a "play upon words: *māmon shel 'emet* is the opposite of *m. dishᵉḵār*". See also M. GRILLI, *L'impotenza*, 18; and ID., *Matteo*, 351.357.

[300] M. CRIMELLA, *Marta*, 419. See, e.g., Lausberg, 199–200.

[301] M.D. GREENE, "The Parable", 84. Thus, J.A. Troxle Jr. (*Doing Justice*, 11) remarks: "Any additional benefit to the debtors or to his master [...] was merely coincidental or, at best, a subordinate concern".

reduces his possessions but enhances his honor, so do believers' alms ultimately give glory to God, whenever they are given prodigally to the poor and in the name of God (see ποιεῖν: v. 9; and Luke 12,33). Giving to the poor those possessions which God has entrusted to us during our earthly life, but which ultimately belong to Him, is certainly one of those good deeds that glorify not only the givers themselves, but also their heavenly Father[302].

Of course, some authors criticize this approach, as a sort of carefully pre-meditated life insurance, which is ostensibly foreign to Jesus' teaching[303]. For instance, I.J. Du Plessis states:

Self-interest […] seems inappropriate within the general tenor of the whole pericope of Luke 16,1–13 […] In verses 10–12 the readers are warned that someone who is dishonest with earthly goods will also be dishonest with spiritual goods […] This sharply contrasts with any interpretation of verse 9 as a recommendation to use earthly goods in a selfish way to earn some kind of eternal reward[304].

However, the premises of such an argument suppose that the terms, "dishonest" (ἄδικος: vv. 10–11) and "dishonesty" (ἀδικία: v. 8a), have nothing to do with "prodigal" (ἄσωτος: cf. Luke 15,13) and "squandering" (διασκορπίζων: v. 1c; cf. Luke 15,13). If, however, these characteristics are connected, then someone who is selfishly wasteful for earthly purposes can still be used, in an *a fortiori* argument, as an encouragement to be selfishly "wasteful", as it were, for heavenly intents.

As far as the characterization of the steward in the parable is concerned, it is perfectly possible that his dishonesty or unrighteousness refers both to the prior wasting of goods for which he is first summoned by his master (v. 1c) and to his later dealings with the latter's debtors (vv. 5–7)[305]. Indeed, a few authors

---

[302] See, e.g., Exod 25,2; 35,21; Deut 15,10; 1Chr 29,9.17; Tob 2,14; 4,7–11.16.19; 12,8–9; 14,2.8–11; Sir 16,14; 17,22; 40,17; Matt 5,16; 6,2.4.29.33; Luke 12,27–33.42–48; Acts 10,4. 31; Rom 2,10; 12,8; 2Cor 8,12; 9,7; Phil 4,18–20; 1Pe 2,12; and 4,10–11.

[303] See, e.g., D.R. FLETCHER, "The Riddle", 25; J.S. KLOPPENBORG, "The Dishonoured Master", 478; I.J. DU PLESSIS, "Philanthropy", 14; and D. LANDRY – B. MAY, "Honour Restored", 292–293. A. Bolin (*Du bon usage*, 18) notes that the latter group of interpreters is represented mainly by Protestant scholars, who "évitent de voir dans le v. 9 une question de mérite". See also D.J. IRELAND, *Stewardship*, 11.102–105.

[304] I.J. DU PLESSIS, "Philanthropy", 15.

[305] The argument put forward, among others, by J. Durkin ("A Cultural Reading", 15), namely, that since "the steward is characterized as dishonest only in verse 8 […] his dishonesty lies not in the wasting of goods for which he is dismissed [vv. 1–2] but [only] in his actions in verses 5–7", is weak. For instance, in the parable of the persistent widow (Luke 18,2–6), the judge is qualified as "unrighteous" (τῆς ἀδικίας) only right after he has acted righteously. In Luke 13,27, by contrast, if one accepts J. Durkin's argument, then the house master's final judgment, "doers of unrighteousness" (ἐργάται ἀδικίας), is bound to refer to the knockers' previous actions of eating and drinking in their householder's presence. That, however, is not the case. Indeed, J. Durkin himself acknowledges (*Ibid.*, 11)

do recognize a certain relationship between the two[306]. According to their view, the steward's "unrighteousness" does not only concern his dishonest bargain with his master's debtors, but it appears to embrace also his entire personality and career[307]. Let us see why.

On a narrative level, the initial occurrence of the verb (v. 1c), "to squander" (διασκορπίζειν), reminds the reader of the one just mentioned in the previous chapter (see Luke 15,13)[308]. Most likely before the same audience (see Luke 14,25; 15,1–3; and 16,1a.14–15a), Jesus portrays the younger son of the preceding parable as one who "squandered his [father's] substances with wasteful living" (διασκόρπισεν τὴν οὐσίαν αὐτοῦ ζῶν ἀσώτως)[309]. A few verses later, the older brother heightens this negative portrayal and accuses him of "devouring [...] the means of subsistence with harlots" (καταφαγών [...] τὸν βίον μετὰ πορνῶν)[310]. To the reader, this sounds more like an accusation than a fact, since, although the latter immoral lifestyle may be implied in the former wasteful living, the narrator never states so expressly. Analogously, in Luke 16,1c, on hearing that the steward is charged (see διεβλήθη) with squandering, whether falsely or not, the reader's mind is unconsciously led to associate him again with the prodigal son[311]. In fact, we are never told whether the charges made against the steward are actually founded, just as one may not positively assume that the elder brother's words are really slandering and

---

that the master's final qualification of his steward as "unrighteous" (τῆς ἀδικίας), in Luke 16,8a, could also mean "that the steward is a habitual schemer", and that (*Ibid.*, 13) vv. 1.8a "form the bookends" of the parable. See, e.g., J.D.M. DERRETT, "Fresh Light", I, 204, n. 1; J.A. FITZMYER, "The Story", 33; D. LANDRY – B. MAY, "Honour Restored", 289.304; and J.K. GOODRICH, "Voluntary Debt Remission", 563.

[306] See, e.g., B.B. SCOTT, "A Master's Praise", 177. For instance, commenting on the steward's actions in vv. 5–7, A. Plummer (*Luke*, 382) writes: "there is no hint that this fraud was a new departure". In turn, D.J. Ireland (*Stewardship*, 70, n. 97) observes: "The actions of vv. 5–7 are not unrelated to the accusations of v. 1".

[307] See, e.g., A. PLUMMER, *Luke*, 382; and D.J. IRELAND, *Stewardship*, 70, n. 97.

[308] See, e.g., A.A. JUST, Jr., *Luke*, II, 611; D. LANDRY – B. MAY, "Honour Restored", 297–298; J.A. METZGER, *Consumption*, 110–111; and J.K. GOODRICH, "Voluntary Debt Remission", 563–564. For instance, B.L. Ihssen (*They Who Give*, 89) suggests that, "Luke 16,1–13 [...] forms half of a duet of parables about squandering of money", and then (*Ibid.*, 89, n. 161) notes: "The parable of the Prodigal Son is the second in this set". In turn, A. Guccione ("Il cielo", 491) associates the younger son of the latter parable directly with the saying in Luke 16,16: "Con quale violenza, nella parabola menzionata, il fratello minore, dissoluto, si impadronisce dei beni del padre".

[309] See, e.g., Luke 12,19.29.45; 16,19; and M. CRIMELLA, *Marta*, 270–272.420.

[310] Luke 15,30. See also Luke 20,47a.

[311] This link shall then be strengthened even further, by the inner dialogue of both characters (see Luke 15,17–19; and Luke 16,3–4). Thus, F. Godet (*Luke*, II, 162) points out: "The words: *he said within himself* [16,3], have some relation to those of 15,17: *when he came to himself*".

false[312]. What these purposely ambiguous charges do point at with certainty is rather the steward's association with the younger son's desire to live with no constraints and in egotistic pleasure[313].

However, whereas the prodigal son's action of squandering his substance is viewed as a whole (see διασκόρπισεν: Luke 15,13), the present tense of the participle, "one squandering" (διασκορπίζων), in Luke 16,1b, indicates rather the continuation of the action[314]. Thus, J.A. Metzger writes:

We may infer that the steward had been in the habit of living wastefully for some time; this was not, at least according to his accusers, a one-time occurrence[315].

---

[312] Based on the association of the verb, διαβάλλειν (cf. διεβλήθη: Luke 16,1c), with the clearly adverse noun, διάβολος (see, e.g., Luke 4,3.6.13; and 8,12), some authors agree to evaluate the former negatively. For instance, D.A. De Silva ("The Parable", 258) writes: "The verb is a hapax here in the gospels, but is linguistically related to *diabolos*, the 'accuser', or more often 'false accuser', as in 2Tim 3,11, or Tit 2,3. With the noun having such overtones, one might well ask whether or not the verb *diaballein* has more to do with slander than faithful testimony". See also B.B. SCOTT, "A Master's Praise", 180–181; M.A. BEAVIS, "Ancient Slavery", 48; and D. LANDRY – B. MAY, "Honour Restored", 297. However, the verb has by itself no exclusively negative meaning. As specified by the BDAG Lexicon ("διαβάλλω", 226), it neutrally means, "to [...] *bring charges, inform* either justly or falsely". See, e.g., I.H. MARSHALL, *Luke*, 617; S.E PORTER, "The Parable", 140; R. KRÜGER, "Lucas 16,1–13", 103; J.G. LYGRE, "Of What Charges?", 23–24; J.A. TROXLE, Jr., *Doing Justice*, 90–94.245–249; and J. DURKIN, "A Cultural Reading", 12.

[313] See, e.g., J.-N. ALETTI, *Il racconto*, 190; J. DURKIN, "A Cultural Reading", 11; and J.A. METZGER, *Consumption*, 115. Aristotle (*EN* IV.1,4–5 [R.W. BROWNE, ed., 86]), for instance, describes prodigal squanderers (ἀσώτοι: see Luke 15,13) as "people [...] who [...] profuse in their expenditure for purposes of intemperance", and have the "single vice [...] of wasting [...] fortune". See, e.g., G. WILKINSON, ed., *Aristotelis*, 132; and M. CRIMELLA, *Marta*, 248–249. At the pragmatic level, such an ambiguous characterization has the effect of causing a certain indecision in the reader concerning the steward's own righteousness: if he is really as selfish and squandering as the younger son in the previous parable, then is he a model for the disciple's management of earthly riches? See, e.g., D. MARGUERAT – A. WÉNIN, *Sapori*, 181. As C.L. Blomberg (*Interpreting the Parables*, 93) specifies, v. 8a shall clarify how it is "the steward's cleverness (not his injustice!) [that] models a character trait needed for discipleship". Both younger son and shrewd steward illustrate how what is needed to gain access to God's kingdom is not one's moral righteousness, but one's personal shrewdness. See, e.g., Matt 22,10; Luke 5,32; 6,35; and 11,13. A similar association occurs also in the second parable of Luke 16: both the squandering son and the poor Lazarus "long to be fed" (cf. ἐπιθύμ-ει[ῶν] χορτασθῆναι: Luke 15,16a and 16,21a) and do associate with impure animals (i.e., pigs and dogs). See, e.g., M.-L. RIGATO, "'Mosè ed i Profeti'", 163, n. 41; and *Ibid.*, 167–168.

[314] When compared with the present and imperfect tenses, which, as D.B. Wallace (Wallace, 555) suggests, "portray the action as an ongoing process [...] it may be helpful to think of the aorist as taking a snapshot of the action". See, e.g., K.L. MCKAY, "Aspect", 203–204.225; and B.M. FANNING, *Verbal Aspect*, 97–98.

[315] J.A. METZGER, *Consumption*, 111. See also *Ibid.*, 115–116; and A. BOLIN, *Du bon usage*, 52–53.

Indeed, if the steward's worldly wastefulness (see διασκορπίζων: v. 1b) and prodigality (see ἀσώτως: Luke 15,13) are a well-established habit of his character, then, in all likelihood, this characterization with which the parable begins in v. 1 is going to have some logical repercussions also on the self-oriented motivations guiding the later management of his master's resources (vv. 5–7) and, accordingly, also on his final characterization, as "dishonest" or "unrighteous" (τῆς ἀδικίας: v. 8a)[316].

Of course, much depends on the point of view from which one looks at the concepts of dishonesty and squandering. However, just as the parable presents two different perspectives and focalizations (the master's and the steward's), so does its commentary, which clearly distinguishes children of light from children of the world and the former's love of God from the latter's love of worldly wealth (see vv. 8b–13). While the children of light consider the steward's earthly management of properties as selfishly unrighteous and wasteful (see, e.g., Luke 12,15–21), so the children of this world view the Christians' eschatologically self-interested investment by almsgiving as an unfair act ("the poor should work harder for themselves!") and a "waste" of money.

Moreover, in light of v. 8b, the shrewdness the master praises clearly sets the steward (see φρονίμως: v. 8a), as well as his master's debtors (i.e., his subordinate respondents), on one side, as children of this world and age (see οἱ υἱοὶ τοῦ αἰῶνος τούτου φρονιμώτεροι [...] εἰς τὴν γενεὰν τὴν ἑαυτῶν: v. 8b)[317], while it singles out the swindled rich master on the side of the children of light (see ὑπὲρ τοὺς υἱοὺς τοῦ φωτὸς: v. 8b)[318]. Eventually, in light of the final distinction (v. 13), one can associate the rich master directly with God. Like God, the master is above both steward and debtors. Like the master, in the final judgment, God will praise those who will have gained a heavenly abode through almsgiving, that is, by their shrewd management of his property[319].

---

[316] Thus, F. Udoh ("The Tale", 334) comments: "the parabolic manager persists in his disloyalty, and it is precisely as 'the unrighteous/unfaithful manager' (τὸν οἰκονόμον τῆς ἀδικίας) that he is praised (v. 8a). He acted 'prudently' (φρονίμως ἐποίησεν) in the pursuit of his own interests".

[317] See, e.g., R.W. FUNK, "Structure", 55–56; M. CRIMELLA, *Marta*, 57, n. 110; and M. GRILLI, *Matteo*, 354. On the debtors' implicit shrewdness and their active participation in the steward's dubious practice of debt-reduction, see, e.g., J.A. METZGER, *Consumption*, 117–118.

[318] We disagree here with those who, as D.J. Ireland (*Stewardship*, 74) writes, consider the master "himself as a man of the world [...] [who] recognizes and admires shrewdness when he sees it, and cannot help but commend his steward for it". See, e.g., G. MURRAY, "Steward", 308; and K.E. BAILEY, *Poet*, 103, n. 68.

[319] Thus, C.L. Blomberg (*Interpreting the Parables*, 93) sums up: "the master's praise reflects God's commendation of his followers, the steward's cleverness (not his injustice!) models a character trait needed for discipleship, and the debtors' future welcome of the steward mirrors the heavenly reception awaiting God's people". See, e.g., H. PREISKER, "ἔπαινος", *TDNT*, II, 587; and L.T. JOHNSON, *The Literary Function*, 156–158.

Thus, to conclude, by means of *a fortiori* reasoning, the parable encourages both Jesus' disciples (see ὑμῖν λέγω: v. 9a) and all children of light (i.e., Christians) to be shrewder than the children of the world and to give alms to the poor, insofar as the latter practice allows one to deal with worldly wealth generously, for the unrighteous or selfish sake of a heavenly (vs. earthly) abode, treasure, or reward[320]. When this prodigal self-interested management shall eventually become a habit, it shall cause the giver's left hand to ignore what his right hand is doing (see Matt 6,1–4), which is precisely what I.J. Du Plessis himself calls, Jesus' "true spirit of charity"[321]. All in all, therefore, W.O.E. Oesterley is right when he writes:

The expression in verse 1, "[...] that he was wasting his goods" [...] implies, as Luke 15,13 shows, that the steward had spent money extravagantly on self-indulgence; instead of serving his lord he had served himself[322].

Afterwards, when the steward decides to act (vv. 4–7), he does it in keeping with his worldly, unrighteous, selfish, and wasteful habit, thus causing damage to his master's property all over again; however, by this time, his doings are also well-thought out and ingenious inasmuch as they are foresightful[323].

Eventually, all parties end up profiting from his self-interested (unrighteous) shrewd (eschatological) strategy: the master suffers the loss of some of his property, but gains honor and glory in exchange; the debtors accept to collaborate actively in the fraud as the steward's accomplices, thus having their debts reduced and their hearts filled with gratitude; and the steward has again defrauded his master, but with very good chances to find a place and be welcomed among his master's debtors, who shall likely be ready to return his act of kindness with joy. However, in light of the commentary (vv. 8b–13) which follows the parable (vv. 1b–8a), the main point of the story can be summed up with F. Godet's words, as follows:

all we have is God's [...] if we give it away, it is with *His* goods (*that which is another's*, v. 12) that we are generous in so acting. Beneficence from this point of view appears as a sort of holy unfaithfulness. By means of it we prudently make for ourselves, like the steward, personal friends, while we use wealth which, strictly speaking, is that of our Master. But differently from the steward, we do so *holily* because we know that we are not acting [...] contrary to the will of the divine Owner, but that, on the other hand, we are entering into His purposes of love, and that He

---

[320] See, e.g., Luke 6,30.38; 12,33; 16,9; and 18,18.22. For instance, C. Pellegrino (*Maria di Nazaret*, 300–301) notes a "prospettiva escatologica" in the Lucan use of the expression, "the children of this age" (οἱ υἱοὶ τοῦ αἰῶνος τούτου), both in Luke 16,8b and Luke 20,34.

[321] I.J. Du Plessis, "Philanthropy", 15. See also D.R. Fletcher, "The Riddle", 25.

[322] W.O.E. Oesterley, "The Gospel Parables", 196.

[323] See, e.g., W.O.E. Oesterley, "The Gospel Parables", 197. Thus, the author (*Ibid.*, 198) remarks: "The steward first defrauds his lord by wasting his goods; consistently with this he deliberately and for his own ultimate benefit directs the debtors to deduct a portion from the debts owing to his lord".

rejoices to see us thus using the goods which He has committed to us with that intention. This unfaithfulness is faithfulness (v. 12)[324].

III. The Second Parable (vv. 19–31)

The parable of the Rich Man and Lazarus (Luke 16,19–31) has been branded at times as the "parable in reverse", that is, a negative illustration paralleling the positive one of the earlier story (Luke 16,1b–8a)[325]. The feature of *commendation* in the first parable plainly contrasts that of *condemnation* in the second one[326].

Both parables, in fact, deal with the relationship between the use of earthly riches and futurities[327]. However, the two pictures portrayed in them are designed to complement each other: by showing the negative consequences of what it means not to follow the call of vv. 9–13, the fate of the rich man in the second story functions now as a deterrent, discouraging the audience from engaging in the love of mammon[328].

---

[324] F. GODET, *Luke*, II, 163–164. Then, linking it with the parable of the Prodigal Son, the author (*Ibid.*, 169–170) further adds: "Like a rich father, who should trust his son with a domain of little value, that he might be trained later in life to manage the whole of his inheritance, thus putting his character to the proof, so God exposes external seeming goods of no value to the thousand abuses of our unskillful administration here below, that from the use which we make of them there may one day be determined for each of us whether we shall be put in possession, or whether we shall be deprived of our true eternal heritage". Other authors prefer to speak of a "holy prudence" or a "most ingenious fraud". For instance, D.J. Ireland (*Stewardship*, 11) comments: "Taken with the subsequent sayings (vv. 9–13), the parable seems to be intended to commend prudence of a specific kind, that is, prudence in the use of wealth. As the dishonest steward displayed prudence in earthly, temporal things for his own earthly future, so the disciples of Christ are to demonstrate an analogous prudence with earthly things for spiritual, eternal goals". See also *Ibid.*, 8–10.107–108.

[325] See, e.g., J.D.M. DERRETT, "Fresh Light", II, 370; D.J. IRELAND, *Stewardship*, 136; and C.-S.A. CHEONG, *A Dialogic Reading*, 119. As already mentioned, M. Crimella (*Marta*, 419) speaks of an "*exemplum contrarium*". See also Lausberg, 199–200.

[326] See, e.g., D.J. IRELAND, *Stewardship*, 136; and C.-S.A. CHEONG, *A Dialogic Reading*, 120. Among the authors who point out the contrast between the two parables, see, e.g., J.J. VAN OOSTERZEE, *Luke*, 253; C.E. VAN KOETSVELD, *Die Gleichnisse*, 247; A. PLUMMER, *Luke*, 390; W. GRUNDMANN, *Lukas*, 325; I.H. MARSHALL, *Luke*, 632; B. STANDAERT, "L'art de composer", 343; D.J. IRELAND, *Stewardship*, 136–137; R.A. PIPER, "Social Background", 1661; and M. CRIMELLA, *Marta*, 418–419.

[327] For a list of some of the authors supporting this view, see, e.g., D.J. IRELAND, *Stewardship*, 136, n. 105.

[328] See, e.g., F. GODET, *Luke*, II, 159; D.J. IRELAND, *Stewardship*, 137–138; and M. GRILLI, *Matteo*, 351.

Since the delimitation and interpretation of this account, unlike those of the first parable, pose no serious question to scholars, we shall deal with them here rather expeditiously[329].

1. The Delimitation of the Story

On the one hand, the parable of the Rich Man and Lazarus begins clumsily, with no real break or introduction (see the only coordinating particle, δέ: v. 19a)[330]. As we have already mentioned, this is so simply because it follows directly from the discourse begun in v. 14[331]. In fact, just as in v. 1b, so in v. 19a, the expression, "a certain man" (ἄνθρωπός τις), is by itself a sufficient narrative marker signaling the incipit of a new story[332]. Besides, here the narration changes *genre*. From a juridical saying on marriage and divorce (v. 18), the reader is almost catapulted into the stage of a new fictitious account (v. 19), with a new set of characters and situations, and so the previous set of dicta (vv. 15b–18) yields place to a direful parable concerning a rich man's neglect to care for the poor and his fearsome end (vv. 19–31)[333].

On the other hand, the literary *genre* changes for a second time in Luke 17,1a, immediately after Abraham's strong and final response (see v. 31) to the rich man's last and desperate request (see v. 30)[334]. As the audience switches back from Pharisees (see vv. 14–15a) to disciples (see v. 1a), and the narrator's identity and position, from *intradiegetic* (see v. 31a) back to *extradiegetic* (see vv. 1a.14–15a), the primary narrator signals the end of the previous account, introducing the reader to a new concatenation of sayings-material (see Luke 17,1–10)[335]. Here is how Y.-G. Kwon describes the latter new narrative segment:

---

[329] See, esp., G. GIURISATO, "Come Luca", 467. For a list of studies concerning the delimitation and composition of the parable, see *Ibid.*, 467, n. 138.

[330] See, e.g., J.A. FITZMYER, *Luke*, II, 1125.

[331] See, e.g., J. DUPONT, *Les Béatitudes*, III, 167. Thus, G. Rossé (*Luca*, 638) points out: "La parabola del ricco epulone e del povero Lazzaro è già stata annunciata da Luca nel v. 14".

[332] See, e.g., Chap. III, p. 119, n. 200.

[333] See, e.g., G. ROSSÉ, *Luca*, 636; and T. BEDNARZ, "Status Disputes", 392–393. Here as elsewhere, the characters of the story can represent "exemplary concretizations" of the preceding *logia* (vv. 15b–18), to the extent that they offer either a model or a counter-model of what is stated just before. See, e.g., Luke 7,36–50; and D. MARGUERAT – A. WÉNIN, *Sapori*, 172–176.

[334] As T. Bednarz ("Status Disputes", 413–414) notes, vv. 30–31 are linked together by an assonance: "the rich person's clause: ἀλλ'ἐάν τις ἀπὸ νεκρῶν πορευθῇ ('rather if someone went to them from the dead') [is] reflected by the harsh-sounding Abrahamic riposte, οὐδ'ἐάν τις ἐκ νεκρῶν ἀναστῇ ('not even, if someone might rise from the dead')".

[335] See, e.g., M. CRIMELLA, *Marta*, 418.

a very interesting, indeed highly significant, collection of sayings of Jesus where the nature of Christian life, characterized by unconditional forgiveness (vv. 3–4), is explained in terms of eschatology (vv. 1–2), faith (vv. 5–6), and the disciples' relationship with the Lord (vv. 7–10)[336].

2. The Structure of the Story

An issue which perhaps deserves a little more attention is the inner layout and construction of the parable. In spite of some attempts to depart from the general view, the vast majority of commentators recognize in the structure of the one story two main sections[337]. These are then analyzed and segmented differently, according to the authors' distinct approaches and emphases.

Some separate the earthly scene of the rich man and Lazarus (vv. 19–22) from that of the conversation beyond the tomb between the rich man and Abraham (vv. 23–31)[338]. Others follow more formal (vs. thematic) criteria, making a distinction between a narrative account in the third person (vv. 19–23) and the dialogic format characterizing the rest of the account (vv. 24–31)[339]. Yet others focus on the reversal of fortunes of the first two characters after death and the impossibility of coming back to life (vv. 19–26), with its subsequent summon to repentance on earth (vv. 27–31)[340]. Whatever sub-division is adopted, there can be no doubt as to both its unity and its concern with the proper use of wealth, as well as the importance of listening to the testimony of the Law and the Prophets, in view of the life to come[341].

Taking into account the observations noted by D. Marguerat and Y. Bourquin as regards the change of focalizer, and based on the structural analysis of F. Schnider and W. Stenger, we adhere to the narrative coherence of

---

[336] Y.-G. KWON, "Forgiveness", 613.

[337] See, e.g., G. GIURISATO, "Come Luca", 467. For a list of the authors who divide the parable into two sub-units, see R.F. HOCK, "Lazarus", 449, n. 5. Among those who deviate from this course, see, e.g., W. VOGELS, "Having", 26–47; G. GIURISATO, "Come Luca", 468, n. 143; R. MEYNET, *Luc*, 653; and M. CRIMELLA, *Marta*, 346, n. 19. For instance, from a semiotic perspective, W. Vogels identifies in the death of the characters (v. 22) the turning point of the story, and in the binomial "having-longing" its actual denouement (vv. 19–21.23–31). According to his rhetorical-Semitic approach, instead, R. Meynet subdivides the parable into five sections (A: vv. 19–23; B: v. 24a; C: vv. 25–26; B¹: vv. 27–28; and A¹: vv. 29–31), concentrically.

[338] See, e.g., F. GODET, *Luke*, II, 176–184; E. PAX, "Der Reiche", 257; and A.A. JUST, Jr., *Luke*, II, 632–637.

[339] See, e.g., R.F. HOCK, "Lazarus", 454; G. GIURISATO, "Come Luca", 468–469; D.L. BOCK, *Luke*, II, 1363–1364; H.-G. GRADL, "Von den Kosten", 309.313; and M. CRIMELLA, *Marta*, 346–347.

[340] See, e.g., J. DUPONT, *Les Béatitudes*, III, 173.178; A. FEUILLET, "La parabole", 216; J.A. FITZMYER, *Luke*, II, 1128; J. NOLLAND, *Luke*, II, 826; A.A. JUST, Jr., *Luke*, II, 632; G. GIURISATO, "Come Luca", 469, n. 145; and M. CRIMELLA, *Marta*, 346, n. 19.

[341] See, e.g., A.A. JUST, Jr., *Luke*, II, 632.

vv. 19–21, as distinct from vv. 22–31[342]. In contrast to the one centered on the reversal theme, this subdivision respects the internal unity of the whole conversation and the direct speech of the two speakers (the rich man and Abraham)[343]. It grants death the role of introducing one of the main novelties characterizing this parable[344]. And lastly, it has the further advantage of taking into account the narrative hints signaling a break between v. 21 and v. 22, namely, the change of time (life-death) and place (earth-afterlife), the introductory formula, "now it happened that" (ἐγένετο δέ + infinitive, with accusative subject)[345], and the appearance of a new character (Abraham). Besides, v. 22 proves fairly adequate to establish a connection between the two scenes of the parable (see Table IV)[346].

Table IV: The Structure of the Whole Story			
Scene I: Antithetical Presentation in Life (vv. 19–21)			
A Great Gap on Earth from the Poor Man's Helpless Point of View	"Now a certain [δέ τις] **rich man** was clothed in purple cloth and fine linen, living gaily every day in splendor" (v. 19).	vs.	"Now a certain [δέ τις] **poor man** named Lazarus was laid at his gate, covered with *sores* [εἰλκωμένος], longing to be fed [...] from the **rich man**'s table, even the dogs [...] licked his *sores* [ἕλκη]" (vv. 20–21).
Scene II: Antithetical Presentation in Death (vv. 22–31)			
A Great Gap in the Afterworld from the Rich Man's Helpless Point of View	"Now *it happened that the* **poor man** died [ἐγένετο δὲ ἀποθανεῖν] and [καί] was carried away by the angels to Abraham's bosom [κόλπον]" (v. 22ab).	vs.	"Now the **rich man** also died [ἀπέθανεν δὲ] and [καί] was buried [...] in his bosom [κόλποις] [...] send Lazarus [...] send him [...] from the dead [...] Abraham [...] from the dead" (vv. 22c–31).

The first scene (vv. 19–21) begins and ends with the presentation of the two characters' earthly *life* and their remarkable gap as "rich" (v. 19) and "poor"

---

[342] See F. SCHNIDER – W. STENGER, "Die offene Tür", 275–276; D. MARGUERAT – Y. BOURQUIN, *How to Read*, 74; and D. MARGUERAT – A. WÉNIN, *Sapori*, 147.

[343] See, e.g., R.F. HOCK, "Lazarus", 454; and G. GIURISATO, "Come Luca", 468–469, ns. 143.145.

[344] As D.L. Bock ("The Parable, 64) specifies, this "is one of the few parables to discuss the world to come and afterlife in some detail beyond a mere reference to future judgment". For an overview of the discussion on the possible dependence of this parable upon Egyptian, Jewish or Hellenistic sources and their visions of the underworld, see, e.g., T.W. MANSON, *The Sayings*, 297–298; J.A. FITZMYER, *Luke*, II, 1125–1129; R.F. HOCK, "Lazarus", 448–455; O. LEHTIPUU, *The Afterlife*, 25–29.45–54; D.B. GOWLER, "'At His Gate'", 258–260; K.R. SNODGRASS, *Stories*, 419–423; and M. CRIMELLA, *Marta*, 341–347.

[345] See, e.g., L.J. TOPEL, "On the Injustice", 222, n. 34; J.A. FITZMYER, *Luke*, I, 118–119; and D.L. BOCK, *Luke*, I, 478.

[346] See, e.g., A. PLUMMER, *Luke*, 392.

(vv. 20–21), the second, instead, opens and closes with the motif of *death*, showing how that same gap carries on ominously[347].

The unity of the first scene is established particularly at the literary level, between v. 19 and vv. 20–21. Thus, the repetition of the expression, "now a certain" (δέ τις), unites v. 19 with v. 20. Moreover, the correspondences between, "*of* his" (αὐτοῦ) and "covered with *sores/ulcers*" (εἰλκωμένος), on the one hand, and "*of* the rich [man]" (πλουσίου) and "*sores/ulcers*" (τὰ ἕλκη), on the other, tie vv. 20 and 21 together. Finally, the latter verses are also connected with v. 19 by means of both the same subjects (see, e.g., the *inclusio* around the term πλουσίος, in vv. 19a.21a), and the phrases, "at his gate" (πρὸς τὸν πυλῶνα αὐτοῦ), and "from the rich man's table" (ἀπὸ τῆς τραπέζης τοῦ πλουσίου).

The second scene includes vv. 22–31. Sandwiched in between a double occurrence of terms relating to the notion of death, the unity of its verses is literarily marked by the parallel construction between the two requests, "Father Abraham, have mercy on me, and send Lazarus so that" (πάτερ᾽ Ἀβραάμ, ἐλέησόν με καὶ πέμψον Λάζαρον ἵνα), in v. 24, and "Then, I beg you, father, so that you send Lazarus to" (Ἐρωτῶ οὖν σε, πάτερ, ἵνα πέμψῃς αὐτόν [...] ὅπως), in vv. 27–28; as well as, by the repetition of the words, "Abraham" (Ἀβραάμ), in vv. 22.23.24.25.29.30, "father" (πατήρ), in vv. 24.27(2x).30, and "torment" (βάσανος), in vv. 23.28[348].

The scene begins by echoing the same opposition between poor (v. 22ab) and rich (v. 22bc), as in vv. 19–21[349]. However, while the first scene puts side by side the two characters' circumstances in *life*, the following verses contrast them in their *death* and what follows after it[350]. Moreover, as we have already mentioned, the main subject of focalization is no longer Lazarus. Because of the sympathy gained among the readers as a result of his relatively more developed

---

[347] See, e.g., ἀποθανεῖν (v. 22a); ἀπέθανεν (v. 22c); and νεκρῶν (2x: vv. 30.31). See also F. SCHNIDER – W. STENGER, "Die offene Tür", 275; V. TANGHE, "Abraham", 566–567; and G. GIURISATO, "Come Luca", 469. As to vv. 19–21, K.M. Hatcher ("In Gold", 278) observes how they mainly illustrate "the stark contrast between the living conditions of haves and have-nots". See, e.g., the two antitheses, "covered with purple cloth vs. sores" (ἐνεδιδύσκετο πορφύραν vs. εἰλκωμένος), on the one hand, and "living gaily vs. longing to be fed" (εὐφραινόμενος vs. ἐπιθυμῶν χορτασθῆναι), on the other. The merriment of an unwise rich man is for the reader an eloquent *déjà vu* (see εὐφραινεῖν: Luke 12,19c and 16,19c) pointing to idolatry (cf. Acts 7,41). Moreover, just as in the prophet Nathan's story (cf. 2Sam 12,1), the contrast between the two characters is emphasized here also by their geographic proximity. See D. MARGUERAT – A. WÉNIN, *Sapori*, 231–233.

[348] See, e.g., the aforementioned footnote (# 347); and F. SCHNIDER – W. STENGER, "Die offene Tür", 275–276.

[349] See, esp., the parallelism between poor man's "dying" (ἀποθανεῖν), in v. 22a, and the clause "the rich man also died" (ἀπέθανεν δὲ καὶ ὁ πλούσιος), in v. 22c. See also F. SCHNIDER – W. STENGER, "Die offene Tür", 275; G. GIURISATO, "Come Luca", 469; and D. MARGUERAT – Y. BOURQUIN, *How to Read*, 74.

[350] See, e.g., K.M. HATCHER, "In Gold", 279.

and empathetic characterization, he is the main focalizer in vv. 19–21. Now, however, the narrative of the story borrows the perspective of the rich man in Hades[351]. After his death, in his new situation of "torment" (cf. vv. 23.28), he raises his eyes and sees Abraham and Lazarus at his side[352]. The plot moves then onto the latter's conversation with Abraham (vv. 24–31) and finally mentions the collective character of the five brothers (v. 28), which allows the focalization to revert to the listener's earthly life and possibility to convert[353]. In other words, at the parable's and chapter's closure, the dramatic effect resumes and, as K.M. Hatcher points out,

> The unspoken question that hangs in the air draws the audience into the story. Will the brothers renounce their idolatry before it is too late and adopt a proper attitude toward their wealth? Will the listeners, the "money-loving" Pharisees? Will the modern-day readers?[354]

Ironically, the word of admonishment that is denied to the rich man's brothers on earth is actually given by the parable to all those who do listen, whether Pharisees (see Luke 16,14), disciples (see Luke 16,1a; and 17,1a), or Gospel readers.

3. The Main Point and Function of the Story

In his commentary on the Gospel of Luke, J.A. Fitzmyer refers to the parable of the Rich Man and Lazarus (vv. 19–31) as one providing a suitable conclusion to the chapter[355]:

> It further illustrates the teaching of the Lucan Jesus about the prudent use of material possessions and gives new meaning to the "dwellings that are everlasting" (v. 9)[356].

---

[351] See, e.g., D. MARGUERAT – Y. BOURQUIN, *How to Read*, 74.

[352] The link between v. 22 and v. 23 is validated by the same subject (see the rich man, in vv. 22c–23), syntactic structure (see the previous infinitives for Lazarus, in v. 22a, and the 3rd pers. sing. indicatives for the Rich Man, in vv. 22b–23), and by the phrase "in the bosom of" (εἰς τὸ-[ιϛ]ν κόλπο-[ιϛ]ν), in vv. 22a–23. See, e.g., F. SCHNIDER – W. STENGER, "Die offene Tür", 275; and G. GIURISATO, "Come Luca", 472.

[353] As J. Dupont (*Les Béatitudes*, III, 178) remarks, "Nous avons évidemment affaire à un procédé littéraire permettant de revenir aux vivants et à leur conduite". See also G. GIURISATO, "Come Luca", 471–473.

[354] K.M. HATCHER, "In Gold", 281. See also A. FEUILLET, "La parabole", 216.

[355] See J.A. FITZMYER, *Luke*, II, 1125. See also D.J. IRELAND, *Stewardship*, 134; and A.A. JUST, Jr., *Luke*, II, 632.

[356] J.A. FITZMYER, *Luke*, II, 1127. Analogously, A. Plummer (*Luke*, 390) notes: "It continues the lesson respecting the right employment of earthly possessions". The parable recounts how Lazarus finds shelter ultimately in the "bosom" (κόλπος) of Abraham (cf. vv. 22–23). As K.M. Hatcher ("In Gold", 279) observes, this term denotes the "enclosure within which are stored up the good things that await the righteous", and is thus a reminder both of earthly houses and eternal tents. See, e.g., Luke 16,4.9.27.

Indeed, the parable does not simply repeat the teaching of the first story (vv. 1b–8a). As we have already pointed out, there exists a narrative progression in Luke 16, and therefore this second account does bring in its own distinctive features (e.g., the name of a fictitious character and the detailed discussion of the afterlife)[357]. However, when viewed in the context of the chapter as a whole, its connections to the preceding verses are unmistakeable.

More precisely, the parable provides a clear visual example of some of the earlier teachings, especially as contained in vv. 1–13 and 14–18, and sheds further light on the concepts of the Law and the kingdom of God advanced in v. 16[358]. Indeed, the final destiny of this second, "certain rich man" (ἄνθρωπός τις πλούσιος), drives home the *key point* that what is witnessed by the Law, particularly as far as the treatment of the poor and the eschatological rewards connected to it are concerned, is still valid (cf. vv. 16–17.29.31)[359]. In other words, in the story of the Rich Man and Lazarus, the use of possessions already introduced by the first parable is portrayed now as the *litmus test* for admission into the eternal abodes (see vv. 4.9.22)[360].

Thus, if, as explained by vv. 8b–13, the first parable (vv. 1b–8a) illustrates the call for disciples (see v. 1a) to use their possessions as shrewdly as the steward, i.e., with eternity in view, showing the good that can ensue from it, the second parable portrays the consequences of neglecting to do that, and is thus a warning for those who, like the money-loving Pharisees (see v. 14), fail to listen to the direction provided by Moses and the prophets in such matters[361].

---

[357] See, e.g., D.L. BOCK, "The Parable, 63–64; K.R. SNODGRASS, *Stories*, 419; and Chap. III, p. 111, n. 151. After the opening expression of v. 19a, "now, there was a certain rich man" (ἄνθρωπός δέ τις ἦν πλούσιος), few mss. (see esp. 𝔓[75] sah 36 and 37) add the phrase, "by the name of Neues" (ὀνόματι Νευης), "Nineveh" (Νινευης), "Phineas" (Φίνεες), "Dives" (*dives*), or "Amenophis" (*Amonofis*). However, as J.A. Fitzmyer (*Luke*, II, 1130) points out, "In the majority of the Greek mss. the rich man is nameless". Also, on internal grounds, these minor variants can be explained as *lectiones facilior*. Thus, B.M. Metzger (Metzger², 140) remarks: "It was probably *horror vacui* that prompted more than one copyist to provide a name for the anonymous Rich Man". See *Ibid.*, 140–141; J.A. FITZMYER, *Luke*, II, 1130; and M. CRIMELLA, *Marta*, 351–353.

[358] See, e.g., A. PLUMMER, *Luke*, 390; and E.E. ELLIS, *Luke*, 202. It is a characteristic trait of Luke's own narrative art to stage his characters in such a way as to crystallize a specific motif of the plot, either by way of anticipation or confirmation. See D. MARGUERAT – A. WÉNIN, *Sapori*, 182.

[359] See, e.g., C.H. TALBERT, *Reading Luke*, 158. As the author (*Ibid.*, 158–159) remarks, "the evangelist wants to accent the point about the continuing validity of the law and its teaching on the use of wealth on behalf of the poor". See also A.A. JUST, Jr., *Luke*, II, 636–637.

[360] See, e.g., K.M. HATCHER, "In Gold", 277.

[361] Within its larger narrative episode (14,25–17,10), the call to discipleship is expressed mostly in terms of renunciation and at times in contrast with the Pharisees' point of view and their greedy concern with possessions. See, e.g., Luke 14,1.18–19.26.33; 15,1–2.4.8.11–

The dialectic force is thus clear: confronted with two opposite attitudes, the reader is encouraged to consider the options at hand and make a choice for either God or mammon (v. 13)[362]. Ultimately, T. Bednarz points out:

> The parable of the rich person and Lazarus functions as a sort of rhetorical reservoir in which Luke cleverly brings together and graphically depicts the themes expressed earlier [...] In particular, the motif of the hoarding of wealth in verse 1 [...] [that] regarding the [...] acquisition of wealth (vv. 9–10) [...] The status of a beggar (vv. 3.20), the various eternal places (vv. 9.22.23.28), the reference to small matters (vv. 10.17.21.24), and the refusal to dismiss that which has been deemed insignificant (vv. 17.22) are just a few of the striking commonalities linking the [...] composition together[363].

E. Two Embedded Concatenations of Sayings

In spite of a number of discordant voices, we thus agree with the vast majority of scholars in that the main thematic thread of chap. 16 consists in the right use of riches in view of one's future entry into the "house-kingdom" of God[364]. However, we do not consider vv. 16–18 an exception to, or an interruption of, such a thread, as several of them do.

As we have already mentioned in the first section of our study, J.A. Fitzmyer is representative of many other scholars with regard to this issue[365]. Indeed, he does recognize the logical association of vv. 14–15 with v. 13, as well as their transitional value with respect to vv. 19–31. He also views the theme of material

---

12.25–30; and 16,14–31. See also A. PLUMMER, *Luke*, 390; J.L. RESSEGUIE, "Point of View", 46–47; and C.H. TALBERT, *Reading Luke*, 159.

[362] Thus, B. Standaert ("L'art de composer", 343–344; and *Ibid.*, 344, n. 18) notes: "en confrontant son lecteur à des positions polaires, l'évangéliste le place devant des options contraires entre lesquelles il est progressivement acculé à choisir [...] Le 'Pharisien' lucanien et les 'riches' en général relèvent du même pôle que Luc place en contraste à celui du disciple. Au lecteur à prendre l'option qui s'impose".

[363] T. BEDNARZ, "Status Disputes", 409–410. Similarly, for J.D.M. Derrett ("Fresh Light", II, 371), the parable "summarizes pictorially the message of the earlier portions, supplies the answer to questions which they have raised, and adds, with an intriguing touch of irony, the reference to current notions of individual retribution after death".

[364] See, e.g., H.J. HOLTZMANN, *Die Synoptiker*, 387–388; A. JÜLICHER, *Die Gleichnisreden*, II, 632–641; E. KLOSTERMANN, *Lukasevangelium*, 161; A. PLUMMER, *Luke*, 379–380; J.-M. LAGRANGE, *Luc*, 438; C. LAVERGNE, *Luc*, 193; F. HAUCK, *Lukas*, 206–207; W. GRUNDMANN, *Lukas*, 319; K.H. RENGSTORF, *Lukas*, 187; H. SCHÜRMANN, "'*Wer daher eines*'", 245–249; E.E. ELLIS, *Luke*, 201–202; P. HOFFMANN, *Studien*, 54–55; K.E. BAILEY, *Poet*, 116–117; J. ERNST, *Lukas*, 468–469; C.H. TALBERT, *Reading Luke*, 183–188; E. LUPIERI, *Giovanni Battista*, 67–68; W. WIEFEL, *Lukas*, 291; D.J. IRELAND, *Stewardship*, 128–139; R.A. PIPER, "Social Background", 1654–1660; C.-S.A. CHEONG, *A Dialogic Reading*, 119; R. MEYNET, *Luc*, 650–652; and J. VERHEYDEN, "The Violators", 412–413.

[365] See Chap. II, pp. 86–87.

goods as prefigured first in chap. 15 (see vv. 4.8.13.19), then developed in the two parables of chap. 16 (see vv. 1b–8a.19–31), and possibly implied also in v. 18. However, when dealing with Luke 16,16–18, the author considers the verses as breaking the unitary tone of the chapter[366].

The study of the narrative and thematic unity of Luke 16 (see figure # 1) has directed our attention to the suggestion that vv. 16–18 are linked to the contextual theme of the chapter. In the remaining pages, we intend to explore better how this connection does actually take shape and effect.

I. A Thematic Thread of Thought

Among the concomitant themes, which scholars generally bring up when discussing chap. 16 of Luke's Gospel, there emerge, for instance, eschatology, discipleship, conflict, reversals, righteousness, validity of the Law, universality of salvation, and the proper attitude toward or use of wealth[367]. Without taking anything away from these, we still believe that the theme which stands out the most in this chapter is that of the right use of riches in view of one's future entry into the "house-kingdom" of God[368]. In addition to what we have observed thus far, a few more explanations need our attention.

Firstly, the repetition of the very opening words in the two parables of Luke 16 is a clear narrative signal, strongly suggesting an intention on the part of Luke to impart here a lesson on which attitude one should have towards

---

[366] See, e.g., J. SCHMID, *Sinossi*, 213; J.A. FITZMYER, *Luke*, II, 1095.1105.1111–1112.1114.1119–1120.1127; D.J. IRELAND, *Stewardship*, 128, n. 53; and F. BOVON, *Luc*, III, 93, n. 81.

[367] Thus, G. Schrenk ("βιάζομαι, βιαστής", *TDNT*, I, 612) identifies the main theme of Luke 16 with "the righteousness of the Pharisees and the validity of the Law". C.J.A. Hickling ("A Tract", 255) and D.B. Gowler (*Host*, 261) underline, respectively, the "criticism of the Pharisees" and their "warning [for them] to repent". A.J. Hultgren (*Jesus*, 191) and J. Tyson ("Conflict", 318) focus rather on the themes of "discipleship" and "conflict", while G.W. Klingsporn (*The Law*, 361) stresses those of "the law and Jesus' conflict with his opponents". Finally, J. Nolland (*Luke*, II, 795) speaks of "human responsibility, focused sharply on the use of, and attitude toward, wealth". For the themes of conflict with Pharisees and that of the inclusiveness of the kingdom in Jesus' preaching, see also F.W. DANKER [1958], "Luke 16,16", 231–243; and G.W. KLINGSPORN, *The Law*, 362–365.383–384.

[368] As noted by J.M.D. Derrett (*Law*, 50), "The main theme appears to have an embroidery of minor themes, but the whole seems to fit together as a consistent piece of work". For a list of authors who are in favour of such a view, see, e.g., Chap. III, p. 150, n. 364. In spite of the semantic polyvalence of the term and the different academic approaches to the discussion, we here hold on to the distinction of a "theme" from a "motif" and identify the latter, with a smaller or more recurrent (e.g., a *Leitmotif*) semantic unit, whereas we conceive the former as consisting of a network of motifs and arising generally as a consequence of their interaction. See, e.g., C. SEGRE, *Avviamento*, 102.331–359, esp. 348–349; and R. LUPERINI, *La fine*, 45–48.

possessions and what kind of shrewd use of riches God calls all to make[369]. In the first parable, being characterized as "rich" is a redundant feature[370]. The man is said to have both debtors and a steward looking after his property, and so the note on his riches is rather indicative of a specific design, which places the entire unit within a thematic and chiastic frame (see figure # 1)[371].

Secondly, at the narrative level, the phrase brings the reader's mind back to the only other "certain rich man" (ἄνθρωπός τις πλούσιος)[372] to be mentioned in the Gospel as a character of a fictitious story (Luke 12,16–21)[373]. Also in this case, the underlying theme of one's relationship with material possessions dominates a whole narrative segment, connecting the parable of the Rich Fool with its adjacent verses (Luke 12,13–15.22–37)[374].

A few striking similarities exist between these two chapters. In both Luke 16,1b–8a and Luke 12,16–21, the main question is the same: "What shall I do?" (τί ποιήσω;)[375]. Moreover, the rich man in these three stories shares similar traits: he is generally characterized as one who trades with "grain" (σῖτος)[376], or has got a large quantity of "goods" (ἀγαθά)[377], and, at least in two out of three cases, he chooses to use them so as "to enjoy himself"

---

[369] See, e.g., A.A. TRITES – W.J. LARKIN, *Luke*, 227.

[370] See, e.g., B.B. SCOTT, "A Master's Praise", 179.

[371] Thus, A.A. Just, Jr. (*Luke*, II, 557.612.630), comments: "Luke typically casts significant passages in chiastic frames [...] Luke 16,1–31 opens with one story unique to Luke (the steward of unrighteousness) and closes with another (the rich man and Lazarus). In each story the disciple's attitude toward possessions is an important theme [...] these two stories frame Luke 16". This suggestion is substantiated further by the frequency of the word, "rich" (πλούσιος), in Luke 16,1.19.21.22, and by the possible – although for A. Plummer (*Luke*, 391) "less probable" – nuanced translation of the opening sentence (Luke 16,1b), "a certain man was rich who had a steward" (ἄνθρωπός τις ἦν πλούσιος ὃς εἶχεν οἰκονόμον). See also J.S. KLOPPENBORG, "The Dishonoured Master", 487; J. GILLMAN, *Possessions*, 81; D.A. DE SILVA, "The Parable", 257; H.J.B. COMBRINK, "A Social-Scientific Perspective", 300; and J. DURKIN, "A Cultural Reading", 11.

[372] See Luke 12,16b.

[373] See, e.g., G.W. KLINGSPORN, *The Law*, 366–371; H.D.M. SPENCE – J.S. EXELL, ed., *Luke*, II, 60; and B.B. BRUEHLER, "Reweaving the Texture", 52.

[374] Thus, G. Giurisato ("Come Luca", 435–436) argues: "trattano tutti lo stesso tema [...] di fondo: il rapporto dell'uomo con le cose terrene". Also, J.-N. Aletti (*Il racconto*, 187) remarks: "Quando Luca inizia una parabola con le parole 'un uomo ricco', vuol dire che il tema sul quale egli invita a riflettere è proprio quello".

[375] Luke 12,17b and 16,3b. Moreover, in both instances the answer is similar: "this is what I shall do" (τοῦτο ποιήσω), in Luke 12,18a; and "I know what I shall do" (ἔγνων τί ποιήσω): Luke 16,4a. See also J. DUPONT, *Les Béatitudes*, III, 119; C.L. BLOMBERG, "Midrash", 241; R.C. TANNEHILL, *The Narrative Unity*, I, 247; and B. SHELLARD, *New Light*, 120.

[376] Luke 12,18c and 16,7b.

[377] Luke 12,18c.19b and 16,25b. See, e.g., O. LEHTIPUU, "Characterization", 97.

(εὐφραίνειν)[378]. Besides, when it does not narrate the destiny of the rich man directly, the parabolic course of action is followed by some remark concerning either the world to come or the rich man's impending death[379]. Finally, the central question as to the wise use of "possessions" (ὑπάρχοντα)[380] is eventually resolved by Jesus' authoritative answer: "make for yourselves" (ποιήσατε ἑαυτοῖς)[381] an "unfailing" (ἀνέκλειπτος)[382] treasure in Heaven, through "almsgiving" (ἐλεημοσύνη)[383]. Indeed, an idolatrous use of possessions can become a genuine impediment for the salvation of the Christian[384].

Thus, chaps. 12 and 16 appear somehow connected in Luke's Gospel, not only from a literary and thematic perspective but, as noted by J.A. Fitzmyer, also at the level of their contextual narrative structure:

A similar combination of two parables separated by independent sayings is found in Luke 12,13–37 (the parable of the Rich Fool, 12,13–21; logia, 12,22–34; the parable on watchfulness, 12,35–37)[385].

These connections, along with those in chap. 18 (see, esp., Luke 12,33–34; 16,9.15.18.19–25 and 18,20.22–25)[386], strengthen the impression that, as in

---

[378] Luke 12,19c and 16,19c. As observed by B. Shellard (*New Light*, 120), "It is perhaps noteworthy that whereas the Parable of the Rich Fool was addressed to the multitude (12,13), that of the Dishonest Steward is aimed at the disciples, as 16,1 makes clear". See also C.L. BLOMBERG, "Midrash", 241.

[379] See Luke 12,20.25 and 16,8a–9.22–31. See also D.J. IRELAND, *Stewardship*, 69–72.82–83.99–105.136.138–139.159.204–205; and B. SHELLARD, *New Light*, 120.

[380] See Luke 12,33a and Luke 16,1c.

[381] Luke 12,33b and 16,9b. See, e.g., R. KRÜGER, "Lucas 16,1–13", 108.

[382] Luke 12,33c. See also the verb, "to fail" (ἐκλειπεῖν), in Luke 16,9b.

[383] Luke 12,33a. The English expression, "giving alms", is rendered in Greek literally with the verb "doing" (ποιεῖν ἐλεημοσύνην). See, e.g., Tob 1,3.16; 4,7–8.11.16; 12,8–9; 14,2.8.10–11; Sir 7,10; 16,14; 35,2; Matt 6,2–3; Acts 9,36; 10,2; and 24,17.

[384] See, e.g., Luke 12,15–22.29–34; 16,1–31; and 17,1–2. See also A.A. JUST, Jr., *Luke*, II, 617–618.

[385] J.A. FITZMYER, "The Story", 25.

[386] See, e.g., "rich" (πλούσιος): Luke 12,16; 16,1.19.21.22; 18,23.25; "poor" (πτωχός): Luke 16,20.22; 18,22; "eternal" (αἰώνιος): Luke 16,9; 18,18.30; "life" (ζωή): Luke 12,15; 16,25; 18,18.30; "kingdom" (βασιλεία): Luke 12,31–32; 16,16; 18,24–25.29; "heaven" (οὐρανός): Luke 12,33.56; 16,17; 18,22; "it is easier" (εὐκοπώτερον ἐστιν): Luke 16,17; 18,25; "to have" (ἔχειν): Luke 12,17.19; 16,1.28; 18,22.24; and "to commit adultery" (μοιχεύειν): Luke 16,18; 18,20. See also J. DUPONT, *Les Béatitudes*, III, 157; I.H. MARSHALL, *Luke*, 683; and J.A. FITZMYER, *Luke*, II, 1177. Some authors draw special attention to the expression, "it is easier" (εὐκοπώτερον ἐστιν: Luke 16,17; and 18,25). See E. HIRSCH, *Die Worlagen*, 65–68; P.S. CAMERON, *Violence*, 138; and F. BOVON, *Luc*, III, 92. It is worth noting here that, in the NT, the latter occurs only in connection with forgiveness of sins and entrance into the kingdom of God. See, e.g., Matt 9,5; 19,24; Mark 2,9; 10,25; Luke 5,23; and 18,25. On the association of almsgiving with the forgiveness of sins and the concept of a heavenly treasure in Second Temple Judaism, see, esp., J.D. WOODINGTON, "Charity and Deliverance", 639–646.

Luke 12, so in Luke 16, the primary thematic train of the chapter is that of the disciple's use of and approach to material possessions, wealth and money although considered in the latter in relation to one's future entry into the "house-kingdom" of God[387].

Thirdly, as it usually happens with thematic threads, also in this noticeable recurrent theme of Luke's two-volume work, we find proleptic elements scattered within the narrative episode to which Luke 16 belongs (Luke 14,25–17,10)[388]. In the preparatory scenes preceding the aforementioned chapter (Luke 14,25–35; 15,1–10; and 15,11–32), this thread takes the form of a secondary motif, along with that of "law" and "conflict"[389]. Then, in Luke 16, it gradually evolves into a real theme, but within the larger enclosing concern for teachings on and conditions of discipleship (see Luke 14,25–35; and 17,1–10)[390].

---

[387] See, e.g., R.H. HIERS, "Friends", 33; L.J. TOPEL, "On the Injustice", 221, n. 26; J.A. FITZMYER, *Luke*, I, 247; C.L. BLOMBERG, "Midrash", 241; R.C. TANNEHILL, *The Narrative Unity*, I, 129–132.186–187.246–248; I.J. DU PLESSIS, "Reading Luke", 226; D.J. IRELAND, *Stewardship*, 157–159.174–180.204–205; A.A. JUST, Jr., *Luke*, II, 613; G. GIURISATO, "Come Luca", 419–484; S.E. WRIGHT, "Parables", 217–239; B. SHELLARD, *New Light*, 120; J.L. STORY, "Twin Parables", 105; R.D. SCHUMACHER, "Saving Like a Fool", 269–276; and A.P. SHEROUSE, "The One Percent", 285–293.

[388] In addition to the changes of place, characters, and situation, the whole episode is marked by the mention of Jesus' travelling, both in Luke 14,25 (συμπορεύομαι) and in 17,11 (πορεύομαι), as well as by the Septuagintal expression, "and it happened that" (καὶ ἐγένετο, or וַיְהִי... ן), accompanied by the temporal clause, "as/when/while" (ἐν τῷ, or בְּ) + inf., in Luke 17,11. The latter are every so often used together by Luke to indicate a new narrative incipit. See, e.g., Luke 5,12; 7,11; 8,1; 9,18; 11,1; and 14,1. See also L.J. TOPEL, "On the Injustice", 221–223; G. SELLIN, "Komposition", 101–113; J.A. FITZMYER, *Luke*, I, 118–119; D. KOSCH, *Die Gottesherrschaft*, 68–73; D.L. BOCK, *Luke*, I, 478; and R.C. TANNEHILL, *Luke*, 103.

[389] See, e.g., B. SHELLARD, *New Light*, 120. In the same way, for instance, S.E. Wright ("Parables", 233) speaks of it as "an often unnoticed sub-theme", present already in the parables of the Lost Sheep, the Lost Coin, and the Lost Son (Luke 15,1–32), while B.B. Bruehler ("Reweaving the Texture", 52) recognizes it as a "piece of repetitive-progressive texture" that gradually emerges, eventually, in Luke 16.

[390] See, e.g., D. KOSCH, *Die Gottesherrschaft*, 70–71; I.J. DU PLESSIS, "Philanthropy", 3–5; D.J. IRELAND, *Stewardship*, 158; A.A. JUST, Jr., *Luke*, II, 579; E. LUPIERI, "Mammona iniquitatis", 133, n. 6; Y.-G. KWON, "Forgiveness", 613–642; B.B. BRUEHLER, "Reweaving the Texture", 52; and M. GRILLI, *Matteo*, 349. In the third Gospel as a whole, the theme of the use of wealth twines together often with that of the eschatological reversal of fortunes. In both of its real and fictitious characters, Mary's (Luke 1,53) and her Son's (Luke 6,24) words prove true: some of these "rich" (πλούσιος) individuals are sent away emptyhanded (see Luke 12,16; and 18,23), having already received their rewarding consolation while being on earth (see Luke 14,12; and 16,19). Others, however, by dealing with wealth shrewdly, find salvation (see Luke 16,8; and 19,2). For the unique position of Zacchaeus, as combining the poles of reversal in himself, see C.M. HAYS, *Luke's Wealth Ethics*, 176.

Finally, as visible in figure # 1, both the concentric structure of the chapter as a whole and the parables' related content, their framing position as well as their connections with the corresponding sayings, all draw attention to this theme[391]. It is thus perfectly possible for Luke 16,1–31 to come together under a common topic or concern. The theme of the use of wealth is very dear to Luke[392]. Similarly, that of uniting related material to form one same episode is a recurrent characteristic pattern of the Travel Narrative[393]. Indeed, advocates of topical, chiastic, and parable-source hypotheses, note how the subdivision and structure of the latter larger narrative section of Luke's Gospel does include pericopes which are essentially composed of true collections of related teachings[394].

II. The Role of the Sayings in the Overall Pattern

If the space where the meaning of Luke 16,16 is produced is represented by vv. 1–13 and vv. 14–31 together, not only the parables but also the sayings must play a key role in the overall pattern of the narrative unit[395]. When we let the two scenes reverberate upon each other, the emphasis of the overarching structure lies on both the two embedded sets of sayings and on v. 14, as Jesus' and Luke's reliable words, respectively. The Lucan use of two different levels of narration, with their two narrators' respective voices, suggests that, whatever the subject at issue in it is, it must indeed be a matter of extraordinary importance, and as such, it deserves our attention.

---

[391] Thus, B. Standaert ("L'art de composer", 344) points out: "Luc rassemble ses matériaux en tenant compte des genres. Une parabole en appelle une autre, une controverse se trouve en parallèle avec un autre point litigieux [...] en antithèse avec un bout de discours eschatologique. Il est par exemple notoire qu'il y a, dans chaque paragraphe, des paraboles, placées chaque fois de façon symétrique par rapport au centre". As to Luke 16, he specifies (*Ibid.*, 342): "la structure concentrique se dégage aisément". See also G. GIURISATO, "Come Luca", 427–428.

[392] As noted by C.L. Blomberg (*Interpreting the Parables*, 116), the theme of the "use and abuse of riches [...] is one of the most prominent in both Luke and Acts". See, e.g., the following exclusively Lucan verses: Luke 3,10–14; 8,1–3; 10,35–37; 12,15–21; 14,33; 16,1–8a.19–26; 19,1–10; Acts 2,44–45; 4,34–5,11; 8,18–20; 9,36; 10,2.4.31; 20,35; as well as, Luke's following modifications of his sources' related material: Luke 5,11 (cf. Matt 4,20.22; Mark 1,18.20); 6,30.34–35 (cf. Matt 5,42.44–47); 11,41 (cf. Matt 23,26); 12,33 (cf. Matt 6,19); and 18,22 (cf. Matt 19,21; Mark 10,21). See also J.A. FITZMYER, *Luke*, I, 247–251.269; and *Ibid.*, II, 969–975.981–983.1045.1059–1067.1094–1136.1204.1227–1228.

[393] See, e.g., B. STANDAERT, "L'art de composer", 344.

[394] See, e.g., J.-M. LAGRANGE, *Luc*, xxxiii–xlii; I.H. MARSHALL, *Luke. Historian*, 152; C.H. TALBERT, "Lucan Patterns", 55; J.A. FITZMYER, *Luke*, I, 825–826; C. BLOMBERG, "Midrash", 220.236.244–245; and H.K. FARRELL, "The Structure", 54.

[395] See, e.g., B.J. BYRNE, *The Hospitality of God*, 133.

So far, we have already indicated how, because of the co-axial construction of Luke 16 and its logical narrative progression, each single part of the first narrative panel sheds light on its corresponding counterpart, and we have also mentioned how the former set of sayings should help interpret the latter opposite match (see figure # 1). Moreover, we have already allowed the two sandwiching parables to echo their higher meaning; however, we have not yet done so with the sayings. The time has come now for us to display the illuminating effect which each of the sayings in the first set has on its respective complement.

A study, in particular, confirms our results. In her recent effort to understand the rhetorical thrust of Luke 16,14–18, the assistant professor of New Testament Studies at the Loyola University of New Orleans, T. Bednarz, observes a precise rhetorical aim, on the part of Luke, to shape the chapter the way it is[396]. Having recognized in Luke 16 a "cleverly constructed concentric composition"[397], consisting, as we have already seen, of two framing parables about rich men (vv. 1–8a and 19–31) placed around two framed sets of four dicta each (vv. 8b–13 and 15–18) and a midpoint (v. 14), the author affirms that, just as the second parable hearkens back to the first one, so does each of the latter four sayings with regard to the previous four:

The first set of dicta (vv. 8b–13) forms a concentric pattern with the second set of dicta (vv. 15–18) so that the first set of dicta serves to clarify the second set [...] the first dictum connects the shrewd ones with the unjust Pharisees (vv. 8b and 15[b]). The second dictum links those who befriend wealth by unjust means with those who enter the kingdom of God by unjust means (vv. 9 and 16). The third dictum associates those who do not demonstrate loyalty in small matters with those who do not demonstrate loyalty in the small matters of the law (vv. 10–12 and 17). Finally, the fourth dictum relates those who are disloyal to God with those who commit adultery (vv. 13 and 18)[398].

---

[396] See, e.g., T. BEDNARZ, "Status Disputes", 377–378.

[397] T. BEDNARZ, "Status Disputes", 390. For a bibliographic note on the author, see, e.g., http://cas.loyno.edu/religious-studies/bios/terri-bednarz-rsm [accessed on-line: 07. 11.2016].

[398] T. BEDNARZ, "Status Disputes", 390–391. In turn, W.O.E. Oesterley ("The Gospel Parables", 195–196.199–201) speaks of a striking logical consistency in vv. 9–13, while M. Grilli (*Matteo*, 351) points out: "*Le istanze che ne conseguono (vv. 9–13) contengono tre sequenze* che, in realtà, racchiudono tre temi diversi, raccolti, però, tutti attorno a un asse centrale: *mamôna* (vv. 9.11.13). In questo modo, l'uso del *denaro* funge da perno catalizzatore dei diversi detti, costringendo il lettore a focalizzare la sua attenzione sul tema". As we shall see in Chap. V of our study, the same thing can be affirmed also as far as the second set of sayings (vv. 15b–18).

The following figure (see figure # 2) summarizes these patterns by illustrating how each of the elements in the first narrative segment illumines the corresponding one in the second narrative segment[399].

Figure 2

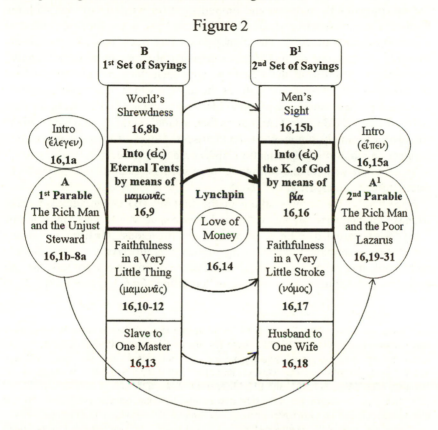

Thus, within the first set of sayings (B), the first saying compares the wisdom of the children of this age with that of the children of light (cf. v. 8b). As implied in the earlier parable, this comparison primarily sets the former's worldly outlook – specifically, as concerns unrighteous management and shrewdness in selfish business solutions – against that of the Christian faithful. The latter implies a sense of faith and foresight that extend beyond this world, and which concretely materialize into a provident care for one's eternal destiny through generous acts of mercy or almsgiving. Rather than begging (see v. 3c),

---

[399] The figure is an adaptation of that found in T. BEDNARZ, "Status Disputes", 392. Within it, our emphasis is laid upon the correspondence between the two sets of sayings, and the illuminating thrust of v. 9 onto Luke 16,16, in particular.

thus, a son of light gives alms to the poor so as to have a treasure in heaven and a welcome into eternity (see vv. 3–4.5–7.8a.9)[400].

Within the second set of sayings (B[1]), likewise, the corresponding first dictum compares the outward and limited sight (or wisdom) of men with the limitless and introspective vision of God (cf. v. 15b), in the specific context of a warning against greed[401]. The money-lover Pharisees, just like the earthly stewards or children of this age, esteem earthly mammon very "highly" (see ὑψηλόν). Besides, in their dealings with men, they run also the risk of becoming "proud", that is, as "high" as the idols in which they "trust", for their being rich is often considered a sign of blessing from God and a reward for their righteousness[402]. However, Jesus retorts that, in God's sight, "that which is high" (τὸ ὑψηλόν), namely, "money" or the Pharisees' "love" of it (see φιλαργύριον), is rather an idolatrous "abomination" (βδέλυγμα) of the heart[403].

In a similar way for the following three sayings, each dictum in vv. 9–13 relates to its counterpart in vv. 16–18.

Specifically, the second saying in the first set (B) encourages "to make friends" (cf. ποιήσατε φίλους: v. 9b; and φιλάργυροι: v. 14) who can welcome "into" (εἰς) eternal dwellings, by means of "fugacious" (ἐκλίπῃ: v. 9c) and unrighteous mammon (μαμωνᾶς τῆς ἀδικίας: v. 9b). As we have already mentioned, this exhortation implies concretely selling one's possessions and giving alms to the poor, so as to have an "unfailing" (ἀνέκλειπτον: Luke 12,33)

---

[400] See, e.g., Luke 6,20; 12,17b.33–34; 16,3b.9b and 18,22. Whereas some authors object that tents cannot be eternal, W.O.E. Oesterley answers by citing Ps 60[LXX],5a: "I will dwell in your tent for ever" (παροικήσω ἐν τῷ σκηνώματί σου εἰς τοὺς αἰῶνας). See W.O.E. OESTERLEY, "The Gospel Parables", 200–201. See also W. MICHAELIS, "σκηνή", *TDNT*, VII, 377–381; and I.H. MARSHALL, *Luke*, 621–622.

[401] See, esp., the recurrence of the reflexive genitive pronoun, ἑαυτῶν: vv. 8b and 15b. See also 1Sam 16,7; D.J. IRELAND, *Stewardship*, 122; and J.J. KILGALLEN, "The Purpose", 234.

[402] See, e.g., mAv 4.9. See also Ps[LXX] 115[113],4–8[12–16]; and Jer 2,5. Lovers tend to resemble the object of their love. See, e.g., C.M. HAYS, *Luke's Wealth Ethics*, 148–150. In fact, the term, "high" (ὑψηλός), can also mean "proud", while "mammon" means most likely, "that in which one puts one's trust", deriving as it does from the Semitic root, √אמן. See, e.g., BDAG, "ὑψηλός", 1044; J.A. FITZMYER, *Luke*, II, 1109; and M. GRILLI, *Matteo*, 360–361.

[403] See, e.g., 2Kgs 17,32–41; 23,13; Prov 16,5; Luke 11,39–42; and 15,29. The phrase, "abomination before" (βδέλυγμα ἐνώπιον: Luke 16,15c), in particular, occurs elsewhere in the Scriptures only in Prov 11,1, which deals with the so called, "scales of deception", i.e., dishonest or false balances: again, a reference to monetary dealings. Generally, the Law condemns all dishonest business transactions as an "abomination" (βδέλυγμα). See, e.g., Lev 19,35–36; Deut 25,13–16; Prov 20,10.23; and Mic 6,10–12. See also G. ROSSÉ, *Luca*, 631, n. 49; and F. BOVON, *Luc*, III, 89. Thus, D.J. Ireland (*Stewardship*, 127) points out: "In the present context, 'that which is highly esteemed among men [*to en anthrōpois hypsēlon*]' may have specific reference or application to mammon or the love of it. In God's eyes this human value is 'detestable', it is an 'abomination [*bdelygma*]'. This word recalls OT language, particularly with regard to idol worship (e.g., 1Kgs 11,5.7)".

treasure in Heaven[404]. Correspondingly, the second saying of the second set (B¹) speaks of all those who come up "into" (εἰς)[405] the kingdom of God, via βία (see v. 16).

The third saying in the first set (B) deals with faithfulness and unrighteousness in "very little" (ἐλάχιστον) and in "much" (πολύ) as to wealth and property (see vv. 10–12). In fact, the verses form "an integrated unit"[406] composed of three juxtapositions, one affirmative (v. 10) and two interrogative (vv. 11–12), and centered primarily around the idea of a "faith-filled" (see πιστός: vv. 10[2x].11.12; ἀληθινός and πιστεύω: v. 11) use of "unrighteous mammon" (ἄδικος μαμωνᾶς: v. 11)[407]. The corresponding saying in the second set (B¹) concerns also faithfulness and unrighteousness in the "small matters" (κεραία) of the "law" (νόμος), but within the context of the latter's "un-failing" validity (see v. 17)[408].

---

[404] See also Chap. III, pp. 134–135, ns. 284–285.

[405] Among the correspondences semantically linking vv. 1–13 with vv. 14–31, we have already mentioned the common idea of going into someone else's place. From a literary and structural perspective, this correspondence is reflected also in the use of the preposition εἰς. The latter occurs 3x in the first segment (vv. 4.8b.9) and 4x in the second (vv. 16.22.27.28). However, only two of the former three occurrences (vv. 4.9) deal with a place (in v. 8b it is a group of people) and, as such, match well with twice their number, in the latter four. In v. 9 and v. 16, particularly, εἰς occurs within a saying (vs. a parable, as in vv. 4.22.27.28) and only in vv. 4.9 and vv. 16.22 the place is clearly described in a positive light (cf. its questionable or negative character in vv. 27.28). Finally, when added to the occurrences of the other preposition used to express direction, "to/towards" (πρός) places or people (vv. 1.20[2x].26.30), a total number of 4 instances in the first segment (vv. 1.4.8b.9) agrees with double their amount, in the second (vv. 16.20[2x].22.26.27.28.30).

[406] J. NOLLAND, *Luke*, II, 806.

[407] For the connection of these syntagmas, at their Semitic level, see, e.g., Chap. III, p. 100, n. 75. Commenting on vv. 10–12, J.A. Fitzmyer (*Luke*, II, 1107) remarks: "Three points are made: the contrast of faithfulness in little things of life and in big things (the smallest amount and much) [...] a contrast of handling ordinary possessions and really valuable goods; and a contrast of responsibility in handling what belongs to another and what may become one's own. The three contrasts thus sum up the role of fidelity in Christian life". As J. Nolland (*Luke*, II, 806) points out, the contrasting effect resulting from a comparison of the first members in the juxtapositions (see ἐν ἐλαχίστῳ: v. 10[2x]; ἐν τῷ ἀδίκῳ μαμωνᾷ: v. 11; and ἐν τῷ ἀλλοτρίῳ: v. 12) shows that, "it is money to which Luke wants to apply the category of 'the least thing'" belonging to another.

[408] The expression, μία κεραία (Luke 16,17), lit. means, "one horn" (from κέρας). It is commonly translated as, "one stroke of a letter", and refers to the little hook or hornlike projection placed upon the extremities of the Hebrew letters (*serif*). It is used here, as well as in Matt 5,18, in the sense of the smallest part or most insignificant detail of the Law. See, e.g., Thayer, "κεραία", 344; and I.H. MARSHALL, *Luke*, 630. Besides the ideas of "faithfulness" and "littleness", the sayings are associated also by their use of the superlative and comparative (cf. ἐλαχίστῳ: v. 10; and εὐκοπώτερον: v. 17), respectively.

Lastly, the fourth and final saying of the first set (B) urges Jesus' disciples to be personal and faithful domestic-slaves in God's household (see v. 13), called to love and cling to God, and simultaneously hate and despise "wealth" (μαμωνᾶς). Moreover, just as the opening verses of the first segment of the narrative unit have a chiastic structure (see Table III), so does its closing verse (see vv. 1b–2.13):

A (v. 13a): no one can (simultaneously) be a personal domestic slave to two lords;
B (v. 13b): for, either he will hate the "One" (εἷς) and love the "other" (ἕτερος);
B¹ (v. 13c): or he will cling to "one" (εἷς) and despise the "other" (ἕτερος) [One];
A¹ (v. 13d): you cannot simultaneously be a slave to God and mammon[409].

By dissuading from dismissing one's wife and marrying another, the corresponding fourth saying in the second set (B¹) encourages likewise to be a loving and faithful husband to only one woman (see v. 18)[410]. Although the saying might seem out of place here[411], at first glance, it fits within the thematic thread of the chapter on the use of possessions, primarily because of the OT Jewish understanding of marriage, which viewed a wife as a chattel or merchandise, "owned" or acquired by the "husband/owner" (בַּעַל) by means of a sort of financial "contract" (כְּתוּבָה), in which her "purchase-price" (מֹהַר) was readily apparent[412]. According to the Mishnah, in fact, a wife was one of the

---

[409] See, e.g., A.A. JUST, Jr., *Luke*, II, 620. From a literary and structural perspective, the terms "one" (εἷς) and "other" (ἕτερος), in the first segment (Luke 16,1–13), find a counterpart in the second (Luke 16,14–31): see εἷς: vv. 5.13[2x].17; and ἕτερος: vv. 7.13[2x].18.

[410] See, esp., the recurrence of the indefinite adjective, ἕτερος, in vv. 13[2x] and 18. The message of this saying can be considered as the negative (or reverse) side of that in v. 13: if v. 13 is a positive exhortation to be a loving and loyal servant to God alone, v. 18 is a negative warning not to be an unloving and disloyal husband to one's only wife. As we have seen, v. 14 is the hinge which allows the second narrative panel to rotate and, consequently, produce a mirroring effect. If we were to translate the message of v. 18 into the complementary female perspective, it would be a positive exhortation to be a loving and loyal wife to only one husband (see figure # 2) and, inasmuch as the disciples (see v. 1a) mystically embody the Church, also act as a faithful and devoted bride to the One Lord, Jesus Christ. See, e.g., 1Cor 8,6; Eph 4,1–6; and 5,31–32.

[411] See, e.g., G.W. KLINGSPORN, *The Law*, 414–425.

[412] See, e.g., Jastrow, I, "כְּתוּבָה", 680; *Ibid.*, I, "כְּתוּבְתָּה", 680; BDB, "מֹהַר", 555; and *HALOT*, I, "בַּעַל", 142. See also Gen 34,12; Exod 22,15–16; Deut 22,29; etc. As the latter lexicon (*Ibid.*, I, "מהר", 553–554) specifies, the Hebrew root √מהר can mean, "to acquire as one's wife", but also "to hasten [...] be violent". See also J. ERNST, *Luca*, II, 664; J. RADERMAKERS – P. BOSSUYT, *Lettura pastorale*, 356, n. 190; J.A. FITZMYER, *Luke*, II, 1119–1120; G. ROSSÉ, *Luca*, 636–638; S. FAUSTI, *Una comunità*, 568–569; S. GRASSO, *Luca*, 435; and B.B. BRUEHLER, "Reweaving the Texture", 64.67. Rightly, C. Pellegrino (*Maria di Nazaret*, 289, n. 171) notes the male perspective with which Luke "vieta che un uomo che ripudia una donna ne sposi un'altra o che un uomo sposi una ripudiata (a differenza

goods that a Jew could obtain simply by paying money or its equivalent. Thus, F. Udoh remarks:

> *mQid.* 1,1–4 opens with a discussion of four categories of property that can, and the means by which they can, be "acquired": the woman (wife), a Hebrew slave, the Canaanite slave, and cattle. The Canaanite slave falls into the subcategory of "property for which there is security", that is, immovable property, which "can be acquired by money or by writ or by usucaption (that is, by long uninterrupted possession for a specified length of time)" (*mQid* 1,5). See *mBB* 3,1; 4,7; 9,7; *mGit* 2,3; *mBQ* 4,5; also, *mKet* 2,7; 8,5; *mBQ* 8,1.3–5; 9,2; *mYev* 7,1–3[413].

III. An Encouraging Analogous Case

The echo triggered by vv. 13 and 18 (see figure # 2), and the convergence of the two sets of sayings on the concept of the love of money (v. 14), prompts us to consider also the case of the Matthean parallel to Luke 16,13, namely, Matt 6,24. Here, the same saying, "You cannot serve God and mammon" (οὐ δύνασθε θεῷ δουλεύειν καὶ μαμωνᾷ), is placed in the narrative context of other sayings of Jesus, which concern primarily wealth and the proper way to approach it (cf. Matt 16,19–34)[414]. However, the relationship of these sayings

---

dell'ottica anche femminile di Mc 10,11–12)". See, esp., Mark 11,12; but, also, Matt 5,32; and 19,9. As suggested by G. Rossé (*Ibid.*, 637), this exclusive standpoint may be intended here as a reproach of the materialistic, male-oriented Halakhic interpretation of the marriage law endorsed by the Pharisees (see v. 15a), and the "usanza nella quale il divorzio è un diritto che spetta essenzialmente all'uomo (e non alla donna)". Accordingly, it would also echo the stress on the woman's legal and social protection, already intended by Deut 24,2, and further fostered by both מֹהַר and כְּתוּבָּה. Already in the 4th c., Gregory of Nazianzus (*Or.* XXXVII.5–7 [*PG* 36, 287b–292a]) gives voice to a similar concern, although in the context of a commentary on Matt 19,3–5. In her commentary on Luke 16,18, finally, M.-L. Rigato ("'Mosè ed i Profeti'", 158, n. 33) speaks of an "'apertura evangelica' […] per indicare la lettura della Torah nell'ottica di Gesù". See also *Ibid.*, 176–177.

[413] F. UDOH, "The Tale", 316, n. 28. See, e.g., P. BLACKMAN, ed., *Mishnayoth*, III, 451–452; and B. COHEN, *Jewish and Roman Law*, 289–291.

[414] See, e.g., W.D. DAVIES – D.C. ALLISON, Jr., *Matthew*, I, 625; and S.J. HULTGREN, "The Apostolic Church", 206. See also the contrast between the terms, "light" (φῶς) and "darkness" (σκότος), in Matt 6,23, and the expressions, "the children of light" (οἱ υἱοὶ τοῦ φωτός) and "the children of this age" (οἱ υἱοὶ τοῦ αἰῶνος τούτου), in Luke 16,8b. See, e.g., C.R. MOSS, "Blurred Vision", 769. In other words, the love of money takes away the discernment of faith. See also Dan 4,13.20.22.26–30; Pss 49(48),2.6.12.20; 115(113),4–8(12–16); 135(134),15–18; Sir 20,29; and 1Tim 6,9–10. Thus, Cyprian of Carthage (*Or. Dom.* XX [PL 4, 533b]) remarks: "The Lord teaches us that riches [*divitias*] are not only to be despised [*contemnendas*] but that they are also dangerous [*periculosas*], because in them is the root of every seductive evil and it produces the blindness of the mind [*cæcitatem mentis*] which becomes exposed to every error".

with such a thread of thought is not clear as far as a couple of verses are concerned, just as with Luke 16,16–18[415].

Specifically, the Matthean version of the *dictum* on God and mammon (v. 24) occurs in between Jesus' warning not to lay up treasures on earth but have one's "heart" (καρδία) turned heavenward (vv. 19–21), the saying about the eye as being the lamp of the body (vv. 22–23), and the teaching not to be anxious about food and clothing (vv. 25–34). While the thematic connection to material possessions is easily understood in vv. 19–21 and 25–34, this is not so as concerns vv. 22–23[416]. In a way analogous to βιάζεται (Matt 11,12 and Luke 16,16), the term ἁπλοῦς occurs only 2x in the NT (Matt 6,22 and Luke 11,34), and its ambiguity is generally interpreted either in connection with the "two masters saying" (v. 24), that is, in terms of a "single-minded" love and loyalty to God, or with that of the "treasure in Heaven" (vv. 19–21), as signifying a liberal or "generous" heart, as opposed to a "greedy" one[417].

Now, in biblical tradition, an "evil eye" (עַיִן רַע) is often a metaphor for envy, stinginess or greed, while a "good eye" (עַיִן־טוֹב) is used often to refer to generosity or almsgiving[418]. While Luke juxtaposes the saying on the ὀφθαλμός ἁπλοῦς and ὀφθαλμός πονηρός (Luke 11,34–36) with a call to purity through almsgiving (Luke 11,37–41), Matthew places it directly in the context of the love of money (Matt 6,24)[419]. Being himself most likely a tax collector and a Jew (see Matt 9,9; and 13,52), the latter is undeniably cognizant of the monetary nuance of such a figure of speech and thus makes use of it in a plain manner (cf. Matt 20,15)[420].

---

[415] For instance, G. Rossé (*Luca*, 630) wonders: "se l'argomento del capitolo riguarda l'uso della ricchezza, cosa stanno a fare al centro della composizione i vv. 16–18 sulla Legge?".

[416] For a survey of the various scholarly approaches and theories used to explain this saying, see, e.g., C.B. BRIDGES – R.E. WHEELER, "The Evil Eye", 69–79; and C.R. MOSS, "Blurred Vision", 762–771.

[417] See, e.g., BDAG, "ἁπλοῦς", 104; W.D. DAVIES – D.C. ALLISON, Jr., *Matthew*, I, 638–639; and C.R. MOSS, "Blurred Vision", 760–762. For a list of authors favouring either one of the two views, see C.B. BRIDGES – R.E. WHEELER, "The Evil Eye", 71, ns. 6–7.

[418] See, e.g., Deut 15,9; Tob 4,7; Prov 22,9; 23,6; 28,22; Sir 14,8–10; 31,13; 35,7.9; Rom 12,8; 2Cor 8,2; 9,11.13; Gal 3,1; and Jas 1,5. See also H.J. CADBURY, "The Single Eye", 69–74; S. EASTMAN, "The Evil Eye", 76–77; and S.J. HULTGREN, "The Apostolic Church", 206–207. For similar references to "greed" and "evil eye" in the pseudepigraphic work of The Testaments of the Twelve Patriarchs and rabbinic traditions, see J.H. ELLIOTT, "The Evil Eye", 68–78. For instance, the latter (*Ibid.*, 78) notes: "A midrash on the book of Numbers (*Sifre Num.* 110) makes clear the conceptual association of Evil Eye and mammon and their common fate: 'The wealthy person whose eye is evil and his mammon go out of this world'".

[419] See, e.g., S.J. HULTGREN, "The Apostolic Church", 206–207.

[420] See, e.g., W.D. DAVIES – D.C. ALLISON, Jr., *Matthew*, I, 635. For a discussion on Matthew's traditional Judeo-Christian identity and authorship, see, e.g., *Ibid.*, I, 7–146. It may be interesting to note here also the threefold (exclusively Matthean) NT occurrence of the term, "friend" (ἑταῖρος), which is used negatively to describe the workers of the vineyard, complaining

Thus, the idea behind the two occurrences of ἁπλοῦς is probably the same in both the Matthean and Lucan contexts: a person with an "evil eye" is one who, being full of "evil" love for mammon or "greed" (see πονηρία), can even so be purged on the inside through almsgiving (ἐλεημοσύνη)[421]. However, Matthew seems to have grasped and clearly emphasized a semantic trait of the expression while others (Luke included) have not. Could the same reasoning apply to Luke 16,16 as opposed to Matt 11,12? In other words, could Luke have been aware of a monetary nuance of the verb βιάζεσθαι, which he has then wanted to emphasize by means of a specific context?

F. Concluding Remarks and Questions

Thus, although at first sight, Luke 16,14–18 may seem disjointed with the surrounding verses and entirely unravelled, after careful analysis of this point of the narrative, the aforementioned remarkable features strongly discount that view.

As we have seen, the contextual unit in which the "violence passage"[422] actually occurs, in its present canonical form, appears to be logically associated to that context by a good number of literary techniques, rhetorical devices, and textual indicators (e.g., introductory statements, catchwords, transitional expressions, changes in audience and writing styles, and repetitions of key phrases, refrains, or motifs, often counterpoising one another), which are all distinctive features of conscious artistry and narrative intentionality on the part of Luke[423].

Finally, from recent studies, it is clear that Luke 16,1–31 follows a concentric arrangement, which is literarily, narratively, rhetorically, and thematically structured around a mid-turning point on the subject of money (v. 14), and that Luke 16,15b–18 plays a key role in the overall pattern of the narrative unit with respect to Luke 16,8b–13[424].

---

because they expect more money (Matt 20,13), the man without the wedding garment in the wedding feast of the kingdom of Heaven (Matt 22,12), and Judas Iscariot, who betrays Jesus for thirty pieces of silver (Matt 26,50; cf., also, 26,15–16; John 12,4–6; and 13,26–29). Could the notion of greed be implicit in this other term as well? See, e.g., K.H. RENGSTORF, "ἑταῖρος", *TDNT*, II, 699–701; and J. NALPATHILCHIRA, *"Everything is Ready"*, 210–212.

[421] See, e.g., Tob 4,7.9–11.17; 12,9; Matt 6,2–4.22–23; Luke 11,33–36.39.41 (vs. Matt 23,25); 12,33; Mark 7,17–23; Acts 15,9; 1Cor 5,7–8; and 1Tim 6,10. See also S.J. HULTGREN, "The Apostolic Church", 207.

[422] W. STENGER, "βιάζομαι, βιαστής", *EDNT*, I, 216.

[423] See, e.g., A. FEUILLET, "La parabole", 212–223; B. STANDAERT, "L'art de composer", 342–343; I.J. DU PLESSIS, "Reading Luke", 221–223; and G. GIURISATO, "Come Luca", 444–475.477.

[424] See, e.g., C. STRATTON, "Pressure", 418; and K.R. SNODGRASS, *Stories*, 405. See also F. GODET, *Luke*, II, 184; R. MORGENTHALER, *Die lukanische Geschichtsschreibung*, I, 142; F.J. MOORE, "The Parable", 105; J. DUPONT, *Les Béatitudes*, III, 62–63.167; C.J.A. HICKLING,

The correspondence between the sayings in v. 9 and v. 16, in particular, suggests that the latter verse also must somehow deal with the concepts of possessions and use of wealth. However, the matter requires a thorough study of the "violent" language of the verse, which is why we must now move on to the next chapter.

"A Tract", 256–257; A. FEUILLET, "La parabole", 212.221–222; B. STANDAERT, "L'art de composer", 342–343; A.A. JUST, Jr., *Luke*, II, 557.612. 630; R. MEYNET, *Luc*, 650–652; J.L. STORY, "Twin Parables", 105; E. LUPIERI, "Mammona iniquitatis", 132; T. BEDNARZ, "Status Disputes", 377–415; and B.B. BRUEHLER, "Reweaving the Texture", 53. Thus, M. Grilli (*Matteo*, 351) remarks: "L'ultima sequenza (v. 13) contiene una massima che si trova anche in Matt 6,24 e probabilmente proviene da una fonte comune a Matteo e Luca. È però interessante come il nostro autore, l'abbia fortemente valorizzata, ponendola come vertice di tutta l'unità letteraria che comprende i vv. 1–13".

Chapter 4

The Linguistic Spectrum of the "βία-based" Lexemes

A. Introduction

The preceding study of the contextual coherence of Luke 16 leads to the suggestion that v. 16 was consciously selected by the author of the third Gospel to form part of a unified and creative whole with the rest of the chapter.

Literary, lexical, syntactical, narrative, rhetorical, structural, semantic, and thematic considerations all seem to converge in pointing out the connection of this verse with the main thematic thread of the unit, namely, the temporal use of wealth and material possessions for the sake of a future abode in the "house-kingdom" of God. The two parables framing the chapter (vv. 1b–8a.19–31), the two concatenated sets of sayings sandwiched in between them (vv. 8b–13.15b–18), and the idea of the Pharisees' love of money (φιλαργυρία), strategically placed at the midpoint of the concentric arrangement (v. 14), are all significant elements of conscious artistry on the part of Luke, pointing in this direction. Most of all, however, it is the resonance prompted by the second and third sayings in each of the two sets (see figure # 2) that shows clearly how both βία (v. 16) and νόμος (v. 17) are somehow linked to and illumined by the term μαμωνᾶς (vv. 9.10–12).

As a result of the hermeneutical thrust produced by these and other textual indicators, we wonder whether Luke may have indeed been aware of a semantic nuance belonging to the "βία-based" verb, which, connecting v. 16 to v. 17, has then been somehow overlooked or forgotten by the exegetes. By means of a diachronic reappraisal of the "several shades of meaning"[1] of βιάζεσθαι (v. 16), its cognates, and their actual connections with the notions of "law" (νόμος: v. 17), "wealth" (μαμωνᾶς: vv. 9.10–12) and "that which belongs to another" (τὸ ἀλλότριον: v. 12), this third stage of our study aims precisely at showing the possibility of such a deduction.

To do this, after some brief etymological considerations, we shall set out the widest semantic field of the "βία-terms", by looking at both literary and papyrological sources, pagan and religious writings, as well as at the various philosophical, mythological, poetical, medical, juridical and economical contexts of the Greek world. The correlations, differences and developments,

---

[1] P.S. CAMERON, *Violence*, 142.

in these different types of literature, will allow the literal meaning of the terms to surface, together with their additional applied senses or metaphorical significations. Following this initial inquiry, we shall establish how this wide-ranging sematic field is actually narrowed in the 2nd Temple Jewish and early Christian literature by taking into consideration the LXX translation and other Greek-speaking Jewish or Christian related sources. Finally, we shall explore how the terms are appropriated and generally used in the apocryphal and canonical New Testament writings and, particularly, by Luke himself, within the body of his Hellenistic, Jewish, and very early Christian sources.

The linguistic and semantic data explored shall warrant a new look at the teachings on violence, kingdom, and riches surrounding the "violence passage"[2]. Particularly, when understood in the light of the *Shared Aggadic Targumic Traditions* (Satt)[3] on Deut 6,5, the concept of "strength", which characterizes the most basic meaning of the verb βιάζεσθαι, shall plausibly account for many of the strategic "signals for comprehension"[4] found in the narrative context of the Lucan verse. In other words, the evidence offered by the lexical tendencies and semantic patterns emerging from the Hellenistic, Jewish, and Christian background shall lead us to see the *Šᵉmaʿ Yiśrāʾēl* of Deut 6,4–5 as that hypothetical "broad reference"[5] suitable for the contextual and semantic whole of Luke 16,16.

B. The Widest Semantic Field of the "βία-terms" in Ancient Greek

From a linguistic perspective, the verb βιάζεσθαι is a phenomenon difficult to define. Literary and psychological studies of its various significations generally come together in ascertaining a certain element of ambivalence, an intrinsic tension between good and evil[6].

Overall, the analysis of ancient Greek literary sources shows how the verb is commonly associated with the notion of "injustice" (ἀδικία) and, as such, often linked to an act of transgression of the "law" (νόμος) or a condition of

---

[2] W. STENGER, "βιάζομαι, βιαστής", *EDNT*, I, 216.

[3] See A. SHINAN, *The Embroidered Targum*, 23–34; and P. DI LUCCIO, *The Quelle*, 31–41.211–214.274–275.

[4] D. MARGUERAT – Y. BOURQUIN, *How to Read*, 145.

[5] P.S. CAMERON, *Violence*, 133.

[6] For the ambivalent aspect of βία in ancient Greek poetry, see, e.g., G. NAGY, *The Best of the Achaeans*, 319–323.326–333.345–347. F. D'Agostino (*BIA*, 25) speaks of a certain "ambiguità intrinseca di βία". See also *Ibid*, 35. For the ambiguity of the term "violence", in general, and its range of meanings, see E.A. STANKO, ed., *The Meanings of Violence*, 1–16.

"lawlessness" (ἀνομία)[7]. The transgressive or evil nuance of the verb can involve also a "violation" of other kinds of boundaries, from those characterizing a physical space or property (e.g., house, land, city, etc.), to those relating to more social or emotional values, such as human dignity, life, rights, and freedom (e.g., abuse, theft, murder, suicide, etc.)[8]. However, the verb occurs also in conjunction with the opposite concepts of "virtue" (ἀρετή), "justice" (δίκη), and acts of "righteousness" (δικαιοσύνη), in a logic that involves the life-giving gift of love[9]. In this sense, it may also carry either the overtones of duty and obligation, urgency and zeal, firmness and "obstinate determination"[10] in accomplishing a mission, or simply imply the "affectionate pressure of friendship"[11].

A similar ambiguity also marks the definition of human violence from a psychological perspective. Its essence seems to embrace simultaneously the instincts of death and life, as well as the powers of hatred and love, so much so that J. Bergeret, a French physician, psychoanalyst, and professor at the University of Lyon, states: "violence is neither good nor bad, in itself"[12]. Field specialists understand the phenomenon of human violence primarily as an innate expression of the existence of man, often associated with hostile connotations and feelings (e.g., aggression, destruction, cruelty, humiliation,

---

[7] See, e.g., X. LÉON-DUFOUR, "Violence", *VTB*, 1360–1361; and F. D'AGOSTINO, *BIA*, 17.20.25.

[8] For instance, D. Daube ("The Linguistics", 402) observes how, from a linguistic perspective, the substantives βιαιοθάνατος and βιαιοθανασία tend to be "associated with savage suicide", typically in "the Christian era". See also *Ibid.*, 408–409; and F. D'AGOSTINO, *BIA*, 85–92.

[9] Consider, e.g., the semantic relationship between the Greek term, δικαιοσύνη, and its Hebrew equivalent (צדקה), as an act of charity or "almsgiving" (ἐλεημοσύνη), or think of the military valor (ἀρετή) of those men who were ready to give their lives out of love for a given ideal or value. See, e.g., Deut 6,25; 24,13; Dan 4,24; F. D'AGOSTINO, *BIA*, 17.20; Adrados, "βία", IV, 710; and A. JELLAMO, *Il cammino*, 21.25. Thus, M.S. Porrello ("Omicidio", 142) remarks: "La società descritta da Omero era costituita dagli eroi. Gli eroi erano uomini forti, coraggiosi, rispettati [...] che sapevano lottare [...] fino al sacrificio della stessa vita [...] che si distinguevano per le proprie eccelse virtù. Ma la virtù di questi uomini era essenzialmente virtù guerriera: coraggio, forza fisica, senso dell'onore. Dell'onore faceva parte anche la violenza".

[10] C. SPICQ, "βιάζομαι", *TLNT*, I, 291.

[11] P.H. MENOUD, "Le sens", 210. See also Adrados, "βιάζω", IV, 710–711.

[12] J. BERGERET, "Adolescence", 418. See, e.g., ID., *La violence fondamentale*, 171–214; ID., *La violence et la vie*; M. VAUCHER, "Un couple infernal", 13–16; ID., "Vie, violence", 13–33; and J.-D. CAUSSE, "La violence", 67.71–77. Thus, F. D'Agostino (*BIA*, 119–120) speaks of "la violenza insita nell'amore [...] come il naturale effetto di una legittima pulsione sessuale, che può, a seconda dei casi, trovare onesto sfogo (nella coniugalità, nell'intimità degli amanti o comunque nella corrispondenza dei sentimenti) o un brutale e illegittimo dispiegarsi: è il caso dello stupro o delle nozze forzate".

hatred, and transgression)[13], but also linked to a functional impulse for self-preservation, which is deeply rooted in the mental and emotional texture of our nature and generally directed against a sense of anguish for the loss of something or someone[14]. Accordingly, the aforementioned authority in the field observes:

Contemporary psychology tends to consider that natural violence is nothing more than an instinct of defense and survival; the other [person] exists only as a diffuse threat to the existence of the subject [...] Such violence serves essentially to protect and reassure in relation to a very primitive fear of annihilation stemming from the threatening image that the subject has constructed of the other[15].

---

[13] For instance, the American Psychological Association (http://www.apa.org/topics/violence/) defines "violence" as "an extreme form of aggression, such as assault, rape or murder". Also, for E.K. Englander (*Understanding Violence*, 2), "violence is aggressive behaviour with the intent to cause harm (physical or psychological)", whereas according to the World Health Organization (E.G. KRUG – *al.*, ed., *World Report*, 5), the term designates "the intentional use of physical force or power". For a comprehensive and recent psychological review of the phenomenon of violence on a global scale, see A. BUTCHART – C. MIKTON, ed., *Global Status Report*, 1–274. For the relationship between violence and aggression, instead, see, e.g., T.G. MOELLER, *Youth*, 2–3.

[14] See J.-D. CAUSSE, "La violence", 67–71. Similar considerations concern the related term, "aggression", in connection with the positive notions of creativity, assertiveness, and adaptation, and its irreplaceable function for the survival of human nature. See, e.g., Bonino, "aggressività", 30–34.

[15] J. BERGERET, "Adolescence", 419. In an article on the primary prevention of drug addiction, the author (ID., "Toxicomanies", 192) specifies: "La violence constitue donc une sorte d'instinct de vie, un besoin de survivre, envers et contre tout, présent chez tous les êtres humains, comme chez tous les êtres vivants en général. Il ne s'agit pas de confondre la violence avec l'agressivité, ni avec la haine, encore moins avec ce qu'on désigne parfois sous les termes d''instinct de mort'. La violence humaine naturelle n'a aucunement pour but de faire souffrir l'autre, de lui nuire et encore moins de chercher à le tuer. Elle vise seulement à protéger l'existence du sujet, a tous les registres. Si la violence dégénère parfois en comportements nocifs pour l'autre ceci provient seulement de la façon dont l'autre est vécu comme obstacle à l'existence du sujet et non des sentiments a priori hostiles à l'autre [...] La violence n'est donc ni bonne ni mauvaise à l'origine; elle existe comme garante de la vie [...] Si le sujet ne parvient pas à intégrer cette violence naturelle au sein du courant amoureux, libidinal, si bien décrit par Freud, si les obstacles à une telle évolution logique et heureuse sont trop importants dans l'enfance ou l'adolescence, alors cette violence va dégénérer en haine, en agressivité, en exactions les plus diverses, tournées vers les autres ou retournées contre soi-même [...] Le destin heureux, au contraire, de la violence naturelle, celui auquel une prévention primaire bien conduite doit contribuer, consiste, dès l'enfance, puis au moment de l'adolescence, non pas à une répression, à un déni ou à un refoulement de la violence constitutionnelle, mais à une opération progressive d'intégration positive de cette violence, mise au service des pulsions amoureuses pour donner naissance à un courant de tendresse et de créativité signant la réussite du long processus psychogénétique con-

Thus, a question spontaneously comes to mind: was it always like that? Did the Greek verb for violence initially imply both a force of death and a power of life[16]? As we are about to see in the following pages, the Greek "βία-based" lexemes in their infancy were quite distant from taking on such an ambivalent meaning. The etymological history of these terms shows how, at their linguistic dawn, they embraced an entirely different kind of semantic liaison. Because of its relevance to the comprehension of our verse, our study of the widest semantic field of the Greek terms shall begin precisely from the following etymological implications.

I. BÍA and BÍOΣ: An Etymological Liaison

In spite of the limits involved in such a quest, studies of the Indo-European language and Vedic Sanskrit, specifically, show that, in its etymological beginnings, that described by the verb βιάζεσθαι was properly speaking a phenomenon related only to the power of life[17].

According to modern researchers, the very sound of the prepositive syllable "bi-" would set in motion the entire semantic dynamics of the nominal-root (βία) of the Greek verb for violence (βιάζεσθαι) and direct it towards the meaning of "life" (βίος)[18]. Originally, such an explosive sound emerged in order to replace that of the pre-existing nominal or verbal prefix "vi-" (cf. *vis*), with its fricative voiced consonant (v), to express the *energy* required by an action of continuous detachment or separation[19]. Moreover, while the semantic value of the final vowel sound "-a" (βία) indicates the fulfilment or effect of the action[20], the original meaning attributed to the very first consonant "b" was

---

duisant à la maturité". For a more thorough discussion of the subject, see ID., *La violence fondamentale*, 171–214; ID., *La violence et la vie*; and ID., *Sigmund Freud*, 199–226.

[16] See J.-D. CAUSSE, "La violence", 71.

[17] For the definition of the concept of "etymology" and its history, see V. PISANI, *L'etimologia*, 11–80. As to the relationship between Sanskrit and the classical Greek and Latin languages, as well as the linguistic Indo-European unity, see ID., *Le lingue indo-europee*, 13–27.32–34.92–117. Finally, on the etymological and philosophical link between life and violence, see, esp., D. KISHIK, "Life", 143–149; and ID., *Power*, 92–98.

[18] For instance, A.J. van Windekens ("βινέω", 43) states: "Je crois que βι- signifie tout simplement 'vivre'".

[19] See Rendich, "b", 355; and *Ibid.*, "vi", 512. For some general hints on the semantic value of vocalic and consonantal sounds, see also *Ibid.*, 10–21.37–38.78–80. The idea of separation may here recall the aforementioned psychological trait of the "fear" (*bhayá*) of loss. See, e.g., Monier, "*bhayá*", 747. J. Bergeret ("Adolescence", 418) acknowledges how, "etymologically speaking, violence is a vital force, a life instinct, or, more particularly, a survival instinct, and [...] how important it is to recognize this meaning as a [...] positive starting point for all the meanings that are derived from it".

[20] See Rendich, 28.80.

that of *a vital and luminous "force"* (*váyas*)[21], exemplified by the Greek and Sanskrit terms for "life" (βίος) and "light" (*bhás*), respectively[22].

Such an initial concept of a "force" or "energy" (βία), standing in direct connection with the power of "life" (βίος), matches the one expressed also by the Latin word, *vis* (cf. *vita*), from which the other term for "violence" (*violentia*) and its cognates derive as from a diminutive form[23]. Although *vis* may have been originally equivalent to ἴς (for Fίς or γίς), namely, the ancient Greek nominal-root for the word "strength" (ἰσχύς), the latter was then supplanted by the most common term, βία[24]. Indeed, these terms may have shared similar etymological roots (cf. Greek: βίος/βία; Latin: *vita*/*vis*; Sanskrit: *jīvá*/*j*[*i*]*yá*; and Indo-European: **guiuos*/**guiie*)[25]. This is further evinced by the fact that, in composition, the substantive βία is sometimes joined with some prepositions (cf., e.g., ὑπέρ and ἀντί) to form adjectives and adverbs ending in -βιος, which imply the notion of an overwhelming or hostile strength, as opposed to "life" (βίος)[26].

Thus, contrary to what one would initially expect, both the Greek and Latin terms for "violence" (βία, and *vis*/*violentia*) appear to have been etymologically linked to the natural thrust of life. Moreover, as F. D'Agostino observes, as such, they were originally devoid of any moral connotation[27]. What they

---

[21] From the Sanskrit *váyas* there came the Lat. *vis*. See Monier, "*váyas*", 920; and V. PISANI, *Glottologia*, 184.

[22] See, e.g., Monier, "*bhás*", 755–756; and Rendich, "b", 355. See also Monier, "*jyá*", 426–427; and *Ibid.*, "*jyut*", 427.

[23] See, e.g., *CCLEE*, "*violentia*", 1635; *Ibid.*, "*vis*", 1638; Bailly, "*vis*", 442; *Ibid.*, "*vīvo*", 444; Meillet, "*uīs*", 740; and Windekens, "βινέω", 43.

[24] See, e.g., Bailly, "*vis*", 442; Boisacq, "ἴς", 382; Chantraine, "ἴς", 469; and G. NAGY, *The Best of the Achaeans*, 89.229–230.321. However, cf. Boisacq, "ἰσχύς", 386.

[25] See, e.g., Buck, "Strong", 295–298; X. LÉON-DUFOUR, "Violence", *VTB*, 1360; D. KISHIK, "Life", 143; and J.-D. CAUSSE, "La violence", 72. Etymologically, βία and the Greek term for "bow" or "bow-string" (βιός) derive from the Sanskrit word, *j*(*i*)*yá*, meaning "oppression" or "dominion", yet both βιός and βίος appear to have originated from *jīvá*, meaning "life". See, e.g., Monier, "*jīvá*", 422; *Ibid.*, "*jyá*", 426–427; Boisacq, "βία", 119; *Ibid.*, "βιός", 120; *Ibid.*, "βίος", 120; V. PISANI, *Manuale*, 82; ID., *Glottologia*, 15.48.69.122.184; Chantraine, "βία", 175; *Ibid.*, "ἴς", 469; Windekens, "βινέω", 43; T. RÖMER, "Des meurtres", 35–36; and R.S.P. BEEKES – M. DE VAAN, *Comparative Indo-European Linguistics*, 38. By sharing the same Greek spelling, βίος and βιός are also phonetically and phonologically lumped together with βία. See, e.g., C. BRIXHE, *Phonétique*, 85–86. Playing on their semantic and phonetic nuances, for instance, an ancient Greek fragment (*Fr.* 22B 48 [ed. H. DIELS – W. KRANZ, I, 161]) reads: "life, thus, is the name of the bow, but death is its deed" (τῶι οὖν τόξοι ὄνομα βίος, ἔργον δὲ θάνατος). See F. D'AGOSTINO, *BIA*, 104, n. 18. For the root morphemes *guei* ("to live") and *gueiə* ("to overpower"), used in the Indo-European reconstructed terms mentioned above, see N. BIRD, *The Distribution*, 37.

[26] See, e.g., ὑπέρβιος, ἀντίβιος, ἐναντίβιος; as compared to ἔκβιος, ἔμβιος, ἐπίβιος. See also Chantraine, "βία", 174.

[27] See F. D'AGOSTINO, *BIA*, 17.33.

underlined was simply the meaning of a force "in action"[28], in the sense of a vital power inherent in nature and concerning, for instance, the wind, the storm and its lightings, but also those passions and instincts that were intrinsically part of human existence[29]. This explains why, for instance, the very loss of βία implied also an impoverishment of bodily force, which could sometimes even cause death[30].

However, as pointed out by H.-J. Ritz, in contrast to the other Greek term for "life" (ζωή), βίος signifies not only "life" itself, but also "livelihood", that is, those very possessions and riches by means of which human life is sustained[31]. Likewise, the Sanskrit verb linked with βίος (*jīv*) can mean not only "to live" or "be alive", but also "to remain" in such a state, and therefore, as M. Monier-Williams proposes, "to support life [...] seek a livelihood, wish to live by"[32] and have appropriate means of subsistence.

Thus, at this point we ask ourselves a second question: What about βία? Could analogous considerations affect the Greek βία-root verb for "violence" as well? Considering the etymological connections of these words, it is quite plausible that the latter term concerns not only the natural instinct for self-preservation but, somehow, also the worldly affairs of human existence. In fact, as M. Monier-Williams writes, the Sanskrit verb (*jyā*) underlying βιάζεσθαι means not only "to overpower" or "oppress", but also "to deprive any one (acc.) of property"[33]. Indeed, from its very beginning, among the nuances expressed by the verb βιάζεσθαι, one of them may have referred directly to wealth, possessions or, more generally, "that which belongs to another" (τὸ ἀλλότριον). However, if this is the case, then a further question must be asked and answered: what evidence do we have in support of such a hypothesis? The following analysis of the uses of the "βία-terms" in Greek literature and papyri shall address the issue directly and provide us with a suitable response.

II. The Ancient Greek Usage: Ambiguity and "Strength"

In the preface to his lexical investigation of the term βία in ancient Greek thought, F. D'Agostino makes this general remark:

---

[28] Meillet, "*uīs*", 740.

[29] Thus, see, e.g., the etymological and semantic relationship between *vis, vir, virilia, viriosus, virtus*. See also Boisacq, "ἴς", 382; Meillet, "*uīs*", 740; and G. NAGY, *The Best of the Achaeans*, 321.

[30] See, e.g., HOMER, *Ody.* IV.668 (ed. A.T. MURRAY, I, 154–155); *Ibid.*, XXII.219 (ed. *Ibid*, II, 352–353); and Adrados, "βία", IV, 710.

[31] See H.-J. RITZ, "βίος, βιωτικός", *EDNT*, I, 219. See also Thayer, "βίος", 102; and Adrados, "βίος", IV, 714–715.

[32] Monier, "*jīv*", 422.

[33] Monier, "*jyā*", 426.

"the term runs through all the stages of the Greek literary culture, from Homer to the 4th c. philosophers, from the Greek-Roman authors up to the Byzantines"[34].

Despite its extent, the body of literature is not definitive when it comes to defining the lexeme[35]. On the basis of the large number of Greek texts studied in his survey, the author attempts to reconstruct a unified image of βία, as a neutral activity, which can become either a legitimate and civilized virtue (ἀρετή) or a brute and ruthless force (ὕβρις), based on whether it is guided by δίκη and νόμος or set against them[36]. Nevertheless, his survey ultimately shows two things: first, that the understanding of the lexeme undergoes a clear "pendulum movement"[37] between the poles of condemnation and commendation; and, second, that the term is used in various contexts to express the general idea of "strength" (ἰσχύς)[38].

In the following pages, we shall look at the contexts in which βία and its cognates occur and see how their different "shades of meaning"[39] can ultimately be grouped under the notion of "strength", as their widest semantic boundary or common denominator. In this process, moreover, two considerations shall guide our study. Since the idea of "strength" (ἰσχύς) is rendered by other Greek terms as well (e.g., ἀλκή, δύναμις, κράτος, μένος, ῥώμη and σθένος), βία should be able to carry some distinctive nuances, which, each time and in different contexts, allow one to choose this term instead of another[40]. However, precisely because of the aforementioned ambivalent connotations of the lexeme, no text as such, regardless of its clarity, shall be used to give a univocal semantic key, as if that were the exclusive meaning of βία to the detriment of all others[41].

---

[34] F. D'AGOSTINO, *BIA*, viii. Running to about 130 pages, F. D'Agostino's study is arguably the best such survey in recent times and, as such, shall be used here as the main guiding reference for this first subsection on literary sources.

[35] See, e.g., PSEUDO-PLATO, *Def.*, 415e–416a (ed. J. BURNET, V, 539–540); and F. D'AGOSTINO, *BIA*, 21. The latter (*Ibid.*, 21) also wonders whether the lack of a satisfactory definition of the term in ancient Greek literature may be due to the common knowledge of its meaning, "quasi che il concetto fosse ritenuto troppo evidente per richiedere un esplicita delucidazione".

[36] See F. D'AGOSTINO, *BIA*, 101–102. See also the occurrences of οἱ δικαιοῦντες ἑαουτούς, in Luke 16,15; ὁ νόμος, in Luke 16,16a; and τοῦ νόμου, in Luke 16,17.

[37] F. D'AGOSTINO, *BIA*, x. See, e.g., G. NAGY, *The Best of the Achaeans*, 317–323.

[38] The terms βία and ἰσχύς are used equivalently by philosophers, historians, and poets, to express the use of strength, either negatively, as an unjust and savage force, or positively, as the wise power of the gods. See, e.g., EURIPIDES, *Med.*, 536–538 (ed. L. MÉRIDIER – *al.*, I, 143); THUCYDIDES, *Hist.* IV.62.3–4 (ed. C.F. SMITH, II, 316–317); ANONYMUS IAMBLICHUS, *Fr.* 89.3.1 (ed. H. DIELS – W. KRANZ, II, 401); PLUTARCH, *Is.* 351d (ed. M. GARCÍA VALDÉS, 56–57); and F. D'AGOSTINO, *BIA*, 17–19.

[39] P.S. CAMERON, *Violence*, 142.

[40] See, e.g. Buck, "Strong", 295–298; É. BENVENISTE, *Le vocabulaire*, II, 72; and F. D'AGOSTINO, *BIA*, 17.

[41] See F. D'AGOSTINO, *BIA*, 19.

Finally, as a result of these reflections, the papyrological investigation following our first analysis of the ancient literary sources shall highlight merely one legal nuance of "violence", on which Luke may have consciously drawn when placing v. 16 in chap. 16, without for that reason turning that nuance into its only possible meaning. Specifically, the evidence obtained through the papyri shall open before us an original hermeneutic "pattern"[42] for a "satisfactory explanation"[43] of the saying, in keeping with its context, language, and theology. The notion of "acquisition by *usucapio* or *ḥazaqah*"[44] (חזקה) may in fact be the key to understanding the way in which violence can be used so as to take possession of an eternal abode in the "immovable" property of the kingdom of God.

1. The Greek Literary Source Material: Several Shades of Meaning

As we have already mentioned, this section shall examine the evidence to be found in the literary sources of the ancient Greek world and, regardless of the various contexts in which they occur, try to establish especially whether and how the "βία-based" lexemes are used to convey the general idea of "strength" (ἰσχύς) in connection with the possession, use, or dispossession of wealth and properties, both positively and negatively.

a) A Philosophically "Naturalistic" (vs. "Moral") Phenomenon

One of the first considerations which F. D'Agostino makes in his survey pertains to the contrast emerging in Greek philosophy between the longing for the lost "simple life" (ἁπλοῦς βίος) of the golden age and the "violence" (βία) proper to a more worldly and materialistic kind of existence[45]. Such a contrast reminds us indirectly of the aforementioned semantic liaison between βία and βίος. The watershed separating these concepts is not as crystal clear as it sounds; however, they intersect and mingle with each other at a specific point of convergence, namely, in their rapport with either "justice" (δίκη) and "law" (νόμος) or, conversely, "injustice" (ἀδικία) and "lawlessness" (ἀνομία).

Generally, although some ancient Greek thinkers do try to define βία, their definitions either do not fit moral categories at all, or are unable to tell whether the phenomenon of violence really belongs ultimately to one or the other side of "the pendulum movement"[46].

---

[42] P.S. CAMERON, *Violence*, 161.

[43] M.W. BATES, "Cryptic Codes", 74.

[44] S. LLEWELYN, "The Introduction", 156.

[45] See, e.g., DEMOCRITUS, *Fr.* 68B 5.3 (ed. H. DIELS – W. KRANZ, II, 138); and F. D'AGOSTINO, *BIA*, 6–8. Cf., also, the occurrence of the adjective ἁπλοῦς, in Matt 6,22–23; BDAG, "ἁπλοῦς", 104; and Chap. III, pp. 161–163.

[46] F. D'AGOSTINO, *BIA*, xi–xii.

For instance, in the pseudo platonic collection of definitions, βία occurs only indirectly, when dealing with the definitions of "anger" (θυμός) and "self-indulgence" (ἀκρασία), namely, a "violent impulse" (ὁρμὴ βίαιος) and a "forcible state" (ἕξις βιαστική), respectively, "without" (ἄνευ) and "contrary to right reason" (παρὰ τὸν ὀρθὸν λογισμόν)[47]. Here, however, the focus is more on the power of these instincts than on their moral character. The only direct definition the author makes of a clearly negative "evil leading to dishonor" (ἀδικία πρὸς ἀτιμίαν φέρουσα)[48] regards rather ὕβρις, that is, "wanton violence or insolence"[49], not βία. Contrary to what happens in the aforementioned definitions, these two concepts are not explained in terms of each other[50].

In Classical Greek usage, the linguistic concept of βία is originally distinct from that of ὕβρις[51]. Although the two terms are often associated dyadically, they are never totally assimilated to one another[52]. The former is generally neutral or ambiguous, and sometimes associated with "justice" (δίκη)[53] or the heroic "virtue" (ἀρετή) of courageous warriors[54], whereas the latter is always negative, and often linked to "injustice" (ἀδικία) and "ignominy" (ἀτιμία).

For instance, while Aristotle understands ὕβρις as a source of "injustice" (ἀδικία) and "hatred" (μῖσος), he describes βία unemotionally, as a means to an end[55]. Similarly, the Pseudo-Aristotle links "injustice" (ἀδικία) with ὕβρις, as

---

[47] See, e.g., PSEUDO-PLATO, *Def.*, 415e (ed. J. BURNET, V, 539); *Ibid.*, 416a (ed. *Ibid.*, V, 540); and F. D'AGOSTINO, *BIA*, 21.

[48] PSEUDO-PLATO, *Def.*, 415e (ed. J. BURNET, V, 540). See F. D'AGOSTINO, *BIA*, 21.

[49] LSJ, "ὕβρις", II, 1841. See, e.g., C. DEL GRANDE, *Hybris*, 1; and F. D'AGOSTINO, *BIA*, 25, n. 16.

[50] See F. D'AGOSTINO, *BIA*, 21–22.

[51] Thus, commenting on the definition of "violence" in antiquity, J. Hahn ("Violence", BNP, XV, 439) specifies: "Violence embraces a range of meanings covered by the Latin expressions *imperium, potestas, potentia, vis,* and *violentia*; in Greek literature, the term ὕβρις (*hýbris*) comes closest to expressing the modern concept of the use of illegitimate force".

[52] See, e.g., HOMER, *Ody.* XV.329 (ed. A.T. MURRAY, II, 98–99); *Ibid.*, XVII.565 (ed. *Ibid.*, 192–193); THEOGNIS, *El.*, I.835–836 (ed. J. CARRIÈRE, 104); and F. D'AGOSTINO, *BIA*, 26, ns. 19–20.

[53] See, e.g., SOLON, *Fr.* 32.2 (ed. M.L. WEST, II, 159); *Ibid.*, 36.16 (ed. *Ibid.*, II, 161); PLATO, *Leg.*, IV.718b (ed. J. BURNET, V, 133); R. HIRZEL, *Themis*, 129–137; and F. D'AGOSTINO, *BIA*, 20, n. 83. The latter (*Ibid.*, 10, n. 42) also notes: "è del tutto simile all'opposizione tra βία e δίκη quella, tipicamente romana, tra *vis* e *jus*".

[54] Thus, M.S. Porrello ("Omicidio", 142) remarks: "La violenza è forza, e, come il coraggio, parte della ἀρετή". See, e.g., HOMER, *Ily.*, IX.496–498 (ed. A.T. MURRAY – W.F. WYATT, I, 430–431); and *Ibid.*, XXIII.578 (ed. *Ibid.*, II, 534–535). In turn, F. D'Agostino (*BIA*, 20) observes: "Aristotele […] proclama che la βία implica sempre una qualche ἀρετή". See ARISTOTLE, *Pol.*, I.2, 1255a.16–17 (ed. O. IMMISCH, 10); F. D'AGOSTINO, *BIA*, 20, n. 86; and *Ibid.*, 96–97.

[55] Thus, F. D'Agostino (*BIA*, 32) writes: "La βία è invece descritta con freddezza, in modo del tutto adiaforo, come uno strumento". See, e.g., ARISTOTLE, *Pol.*, V.3, 1304b.8–18 (ed. O. IMMISCH, 169); *Ibid.*, V.5, 1305b.18–22 (ed. *Ibid.*, 172); *Ibid.*, V.8, 1311a.27–33 (ed. *Ibid.*, 189);

an evil in itself, whereas he deals with βία from a merely economical (vs. moral) perspective, or as F. D'Agostino specifies, in a morally "cold and objectively utilitarian spirit"[56]: a slave is not to suffer βία simply because he must be nourished to increase his master's profit. More precisely, the Greeks conceive βία as "strength" per se, beyond any ethical or social qualification[57]. That is why one can be exhorted poetically "to drink to violence" (πρὸς βίαν πίνειν)[58] cheerfully, for instance, "when the news is good"[59], or argue through a "violent" (βίαιον) rhetorical technique, also known as *violenta argumentatio*, which occurs whenever a statement of the opponent is taken and converted to the speaker's purposes[60].

However, as far as ὕβρις is concerned, there is no ambiguity whatsoever: the concept is always understood negatively[61]. As A. Jellamo points out:

"*Hybris* is the excess, the exaggeration of those who demand more, the arrogance of those who violate their limits. For the Greek spirit, [it is] the worst of evils, the greater guilt. *Hybris* is the claim to transcend the human condition, the presumption to consider ourselves as gods; but it is also the pretension to invade the other's 'part': *hybris* is unjust violence, predominance, dominion, oppression. At the time of Heraclitus, these meanings were already patrimony of the Greek culture"[62].

Thus, even when one considers Xenophon's negative equivalence of the βία-root lexemes with the concept of "lawlessness" (ἀνομία), his definition remains quite ambiguous, not only because of the indistinctness of his moral system

---

Ibid., V.8, 1313a.8–10 (ed. *Ibid.*, 195); ID., *Ath.*, 38 (ed. M. CHAMBERS, 33–34); and F. D'AGOSTINO, *BIA*, 32–34.

[56] F. D'AGOSTINO, *BIA*, 33. See PSEUDO-ARISTOTLE, *Oec.*, I.5, 1344a.35–1344b.3 (ed. F. SUSEMIHL, 6).

[57] See F. D'AGOSTINO, *BIA*, 17. Thus, the latter (*Ibid.*, 33) specifies: "la βία non possiede in sé nessun connotato, né nel bene, né nel male".

[58] See, e.g., ALCAEUS, *Fr.* 332 (ed. G. LIBERMAN, II, 144); SOPHOCLES, *Fr.* 735 (ed. A.C. PEARSON, III, 3–4); and ARISTOPHANES, *Ach.* 73 (ed. B.B. ROGERS, I, 12–13). D. Page (*Sappho*, 238) and D.A. Campbell (ed., *Greek Lyric*, I, 372–373) translate the expression in the Alcean verse differently, namely, as "drink with might and main" and "drink with all their strength", respectively. However, the reading selected by these authors follows the edition of E. Lobel and D. Page (*Poetarum*, 266), which reads πὲρ βίαν rather than the πρὸς βίαν πίνειν. See also B. MARZULLO, *Studi*, 97–98.

[59] C.M. BOWRA, *Greek Lyric Poetry*, 157.

[60] See, e.g., HERMOGENES, *Eur.* III.3 (ed. H. RABE, 138–140); Ernesti, "βίαιον", 57–58; R. HIRZEL, *Themis*, 131, n. 1; J. MARTIN, *Antike rhetorik*, 129–131; F. D'AGOSTINO, *BIA*, 17; M. PATILLON, *La théorie du discours*, 53; G. LIBERMAN, *Alcée*, II, 144, n. 272; G.A. KENNEDY, *Greek Rhetoric*, 89; and ID., *Invention*, 82–85.

[61] See F. D'AGOSTINO, *BIA*, 25–26, ns. 16–18.

[62] A. JELLAMO, "Alle radici", 250. See, e.g., HERACLITUS, *Fr.* 22B 43 (ed. H. DIELS – W. KRANZ, I, 160); PLATO, *Leg.*, III.691c (ed. J. BURNET, V, 100); *Ibid.*, X.906a (ed. *Ibid*, V, 358); ARISTOTLE, *Rhet.* II.2.1378b (ed. W.D. ROSS, 71–72); and G. NAGY, *The Best of the Achaeans*, 319.

and education, but also on account of the equivocal dialectic context in which it occurs[63]. As F. D'Agostino suggests, the text itself makes it impossible to establish whether the concept of βία carries here a positive or negative nuance, and this may actually reflect the intrinsically ambiguous reality of the term itself[64].

Indeed βία does take on ambivalent meanings. Starting in the 6th c. BCE, the term occurs as set directly against "justice" (δίκη or δικαιοσύνη) and "gentleness" (πραότης), or connected with "illicit seizure" (ἁρπαγή), "greediness" (πλεονεξία), "fraud" (ἀπάτη), "transgression" (παρανομία), "ignorance" (ἀμαθία), "anger" (θυμός), "enmity" (ἔχθρα), "incontinence" (ἀκράτεια), "cruelty" (ὠμότης), "incivility" (βαρβαρότης), "wanton violence" (ὕβρις), "lack of mercy" (οὔτ'ἐλεῶν), and "injustice" (ἀδικία)[65]. However, contrary to sometimes too hasty modern identifications with the latter concept[66], Greek philosophers are quite far from condemning violence per se. As F. D'Agostino points out, βία is not on their list of faults or vices[67]. Quite the opposite, being linked to the concepts of "war" (πόλεμος) and "strife" (ἔρις), the term is often valued by the Greeks as an honorable military skill, often connected with life and beauty, even at a later date[68]. The truth, then, is that just as there can be a good and a bad ἔρις, so there can exist a good and a bad βία[69].

---

[63] See, e.g., XENOPHON, *Mem.*, I,2.39–46 (ed. M. BANDINI – L.-A. DORION, I.1, 19–21); *Ibid.*, II,1.30–31 (ed. K. HUDE, 56–57); F. D'AGOSTINO, *BIA*, 22–25; M. BANDINI – L.-A. DORION, ed., *Xénophon*, I.1, 83–87, ns. 82–87; *Ibid.*, 105–106, ns. 134–135; and H. LU, *Xenophon's Theory*, 123–152.

[64] See F. D'AGOSTINO, *BIA*, 25. Perhaps, it is in this light that one should read also the ostensibly negative statement in which Xenophon (*Mem.* I,2.12 [ed. M. BANDINI – L.-A. DORION, I.1, 11–12]) writes: "Critias was the most thievish, violent [βιαιότατος], and bloodthirsty man of all [those who were included] in the oligarchy".

[65] See, e.g., AESOP, *Fab.*, 195 (ed. É. CHAMBRY, 84–85); CLEOBULUS, *Fr.* 10A 5.11 (ed. H. DIELS – W. KRANZ, I, 63); SOPHOCLES, *Aia.*, 1334–1335 (ed. A. DAIN – P. MAZON, II, 56); GORGIAS, *Fr.* 82B, 11a.1–2.35–36 (ed. H. DIELS – W. KRANZ, II, 295.303); ISOCRATES, *Pac.*, VIII.45 (ed. G. MATHIEU – É. BRÉMOND, III, 4); ID., *Phili.*, V.16 (ed. *Ibid.*, IV, 23); XENOPHON, *Mem.* I,2.10–12 (ed. M. BANDINI – L.-A. DORION, I.1, 11–12); DEMOSTHENES, *Phil.*, XI.7 (ed. M. CROISET, II, 156–157); ID., *Mid.*, XXI.101 (ed. O. NAVARRE – *al.*, II, 52); PLUTARCH, *Ser.*, XXVI.565d (ed. P.H. DE LACY – *al.*, VII, 282–283); DIO CHRYSOSTOM, *Or.*, LXXV.1–4 (ed. J.W. COHOON – *al.*, V, 240–245); and F. D'AGOSTINO, *BIA*, 37–39.43–44.

[66] See, e.g., F. CHATELET, "Remarques", 34; and F. D'AGOSTINO, *BIA*, 19.

[67] See F. D'AGOSTINO, *BIA*, 14.

[68] See, e.g., HERACLITUS, *Fr.* 22B 8 (ed. H. DIELS – W. KRANZ, I, 152); *Ibid.*, 22B 80 (ed. *Ibid.*, I, 169); *Ibid.*, 53B (ed. G.S. KIRK, 245–249); PLATO, *Resp.* III.399a.6–7 (ed. J. BURNET, IV, 399a); PROCLUS, *Athen.*, v. 24 (ed. R.M. VAN DER BERG, 298); and F. D'AGOSTINO, *BIA*, 9–13. For instance, Aristotle (*Rhet.* I.5.1361b [ed. W.D. ROSS, 22]) has no problems associating it with the athletic "beauty" (κάλλος) of the youth. See also F. D'AGOSTINO, *BIA*, 20, n. 85.

[69] See, e.g., E. WOLF, *Griechisches Rechtsdenken*, I, 136; J.-P. VERNANT, *Myth and Thought*, 240; Chantraine, "ἔρις", 372; and F. D'AGOSTINO, *BIA*, 13, n. 59.

This semantic ambivalence of the term is quite visible, for instance, in Plato's writings. As F. D'Agostino observes, Plato is the first thinker known to have asked himself radically the question of the "reason" for the existence of violence (i.e., *why does it exist?*); however, he never answers the question directly. His explanation concerns rather the problem of its genesis (i.e., *whence does it come?*). By resorting to Greek mythology, in fact, he ultimately finds the "origin" (ἀρχή) of the existence of βία in the gods' withdrawal from the world[70].

Generally, Plato uses βία to describe the amoral power of natural agents, but then mentions it again within the legal and ethical context of retribution[71]. Indeed, βιάζεσθαι does occur in connection with the definitions of negative concepts, such as, "the perfectly unjust man" (ὁ τελέως ἄδικος), "wanton violence" (ὕβρις), "injustice" (ἀδικία), "lawlessness" (ἀνομία), and even "suicide" (ἑαυτὸν βιάζεσθαι)[72], but it can also be linked more neutrally with the legal and economic concepts of "law" (νόμος), "supreme justice" (τὸ δικαιότατον), "poverty" (πενία), "theft" (κλέπος), and "riches" (πλοῦτος)[73]. For example, Plato writes: "love of riches (ἐπιθυμία [...] τῶν χρημάτων) is one of the greatest causes of murder cases involving violence (τὰ [...] βίαια [...] περὶ φόνους)"[74].

In this regard, and in connection with Luke 16,12 (ἐν τῷ ἀλλοτρίῳ), it is interesting to note how, by looking at the nature of "violent acts" (βίαια) themselves, Plato establishes a general principle, whereby he associates βία directly with "that which belongs to another" (τὸ ἀλλότριον):

---

[70] See, e.g., PLATO, *Symp.*, III.195c.4–196c.3 (ed. J. BURNET, II, 182–183); *Ibid.*, III.199c.3–204b.9 (ed. *Ibid.*, II, 187–195); and F. D'AGOSTINO, *BIA*, x–xi.15–16.97–100. 107–117.121–124. For an understanding of mythology as providing an answer to the question of the origin of things, see, e.g., C.G. JUNG – K. KERÉNYI, ed., *Essays on a Science*, 7–18. According to F. D'Agostino (*Ibid.*, 110), "La filosofia della violenza diviene così in Platone una mito-logia della violenza".

[71] See, e.g., PLATO, *Leg.*, IX.872e.5–6 (ed. J. BURNET, V, 315); *Ibid.*, IX.874b.8–e.1 (ed. *Ibid.*, V, 317); *Ibid.*, XI.919a.3 (ed. *Ibid.*, V, 373); and F. D'AGOSTINO, *BIA*, 51–55.

[72] The expression, "to do violence to oneself" (ἑαυτὸν βιάζεσθαι), occurs twice in *Phae.*, 61c.9–d.5, and is used often to indicate suicide. Plato (*Leg.*, IX.873c.4 [ed. *Ibid.*, V, 316]) defines the person who commits suicide as one who withdraws himself from his destiny "with violence" (βίᾳ). See, e.g., D. DAUBE, "The Linguistics", 400.402; and F. D'AGOSTINO, *BIA*, 85–88.

[73] See PLATO, *Phae.*, 61c.9–d.5 (ed. J. BURNET, I, 84–85); ID., *Polit.*, 291e.1–2 (ed. *Ibid.*, I, 495); *Ibid.*, 292c.5–9 (ed. *Ibid.*, I, 496); ID., *Resp.* II.361a.5–b.5 (ed. *Ibid.*, IV, 361a); *Ibid.*, III.413b.1–10 (ed. *Ibid.*, IV, 413b); ID., *Leg.*, X.890a.4–5 (ed. *Ibid.*, V, 334); and F. D'AGOSTINO, *BIA*, 38.80–81.

[74] PLATO, *Leg.*, IX.869e.3–870c.5 (ed. J. BURNET, V, 311–312).

this one principle about forcible acts (τοιόνδε τι νόμμον βιαίων πέρι) must be stated above all: no-one (is) to carry off or lead away anything belonging to others, nor (is he) to use anything belonging to his neighbour, unless he persuade its owner[75].

The *"pendular movement* of Greek thought"[76] between condemnation and commendation becomes particularly manifest when one considers Plato's use of βία in the context of "law" (νόμος) and "justice" (δίκη)[77]. On the one hand, Plato esteems "persuasion" (πειθώ) and "violence" (βία) as noble methods for wise legislators and pedagogues, and yet, on the other hand, he sees βία also as a harmful weapon in the hands of the oppressor, a negative trait of the tyrant against his people[78], for whoever is superior, whether good or bad, has the right to rule "with violence and justice" (βίᾳ καὶ δίκη)[79]. In this sense, even the "law" (νόμος) itself, which is a good per se, can be considered a tyrant, insofar as it performs acts of violence, mainly against man and nature[80].

---

[75] S.R. LLEWELYN, "Forcible Acquisition", 148. "Μετα δὲ τὰς αἰκίας περὶ παντὸς ἓν εἰρήσθω τοιόνδε τι νόμμον βιαίων πέρι· Τῶν ἀλλοτρίων μηδένα μηδὲν φέρειν μηδὲ ἄγειν, μηδ᾽ αὖ χρῆσθαι μηδενὶ τῶν τοῦ πέλας, ἐὰν μὴ πείσῃ τὸν κεκτημένον" (PLATO, *Leg.*, X.884a.1–4 [ed. J. BURNET, V, 327]). Thus, N.R.E. Fisher (*Hybris*, 483) comments: "At the start of book X, Plato moves to enunciate a general regulation on 'violent acts' (*biaia*), namely that no one should take away what belongs to another without consent". Similarly, in a speech allegedly uttered by Demosthenes (*Macar.*, I.1.4–5 [ed. J.H. VINCE – N.W. DEWITT – A.T. MURRAY, V, 60–61]), we read of "lawless and violent men" (παρανομοῦντες καὶ βιαζόμενοι) trying to have what does not belong to them (cf. ὥστ᾽ ἐκ παντὸς τρόπου τὰ μὴ προσήκονθ᾽ ἑαυτοῖς ἔχειν). See also ID., *Lacr.*, 26 (ed. *Ibid.*, IV, 294– 295); ISAEUS, *Pyr.*, 62 (ed. P. ROUSSEL, 66–67); ID., *Apoll.*, 40 (ed. *Ibid.*, 139); ID., *Ciron.*, 2 (ed. *Ibid.*, 145); and S.R. LLEWELYN, "Forcible Acquisition", 149. According to the latter (*Ibid.*, 147), "a nexus between Plato's legal principle concerning acts of force [...] and the examples of 'violence directed against property' in the papyri can be observed". We shall come back to this nexus later, when dealing with the papyrological occurrences of the term.

[76] F. D'AGOSTINO, *BIA*, x.

[77] As we have already mentioned, these two concepts occur also in chap. 16 of Luke's Gospel. See Luke 16,15.16a.17.

[78] See PLATO, *Resp.* XVIII.569b.3–4 (ed. J. BURNET, IV, 569a). For similar considerations, see also SOLON, *Fr.* 32.2 (ed. M.L. WEST, II, 159); *Ibid.*, 34.8 (ed. *Ibid.*, II, 160); PSEUDO-PLATO, *Thea.*, 126a.7–8 (ed. J. BURNET, III, 125d); ARISTOTLE, *Pol.*, V.8, 1313a.9–10 (ed. O. IMMISCH, 195); and F. D'AGOSTINO, *BIA*, 38–39.

[79] PLATO, *Leg.*, IV.718b.3 (ed. J. BURNET, V, 133). See, e.g., *Ibid.*, III.690c.1–3 (ed. *Ibid.*, V, 98); *Ibid.*, IV.711c.3–8 (ed. *Ibid.*, V, 124); *Ibid.*, IV.722b.4–c.4 (ed. *Ibid.*, V, 138); ID., *Resp.* II.365d.2–7 (ed. *Ibid.*, IV, 365a); *Ibid.*, VIII.548b.4–10 (ed. *Ibid.*, IV, 547d). See also ARISTOTLE, *Met.*, III.5, 1009a.18 (ed. W. JAEGER, 75); and F. D'AGOSTINO, *BIA*, 58.60.80–81. For the understanding of βία as a characteristic trait of every kingdom, as opposed to tyranny, see E. WOLF, *Griechsches Rechtsdenken*, I, 215–216.

[80] See PLATO, *Prot.*, 337d.1–3 (ed. J. BURNET, III, 336d–337d); ID., *Gorg.*, 484b.4–8 (ed. *Ibid.*, III, 483d); and F. D'AGOSTINO, *BIA*, 79–82. In turn, laws can also suffer violence. For instance, Plato (*Cri.*, 51c.1–3 [ed. J. BURNET, I, 73]) has Socrates affirm that violating

Overall, these considerations lead us towards a deeper realization that, strictly speaking, behind the ambiguously positive or negative view of "violence" (βία) there lies a reasonably "practical" (vs. "moral") process of argumentation. Even when βία is linked with the notions of "life" (βίος) and "death" (θάνατος), they intersect the concepts of "justice" (δίκη) or "injustice" (ἀδικία) essentially as far as the established order of things is concerned.

The ancient idea of "violent death" (βιαιοθανασία) as such, for instance, is described merely "from a *naturalistic* point of view"[81], as an unnatural or artificial "violation" of the set order of life in the cosmos. The popular belief, that the souls of the people who die by such a death (βιαιοθάνατοι) would keep roaming the earth in anger, haunting their murderers, is rather enlightening, in this regard[82]. Behind these beliefs, F. D'Agostino discerns the conviction that natural "life" (βίος), as such, should not be touched, and that any human intervention upon "nature" (φύσις) is considered an "unjust" (ἄδικος) act of "violence" (βία), mainly because nature itself has its own objectively inherent "justice" (δίκη)[83].

This kind of philosophical reasoning is especially evident in Aristotle's writings. The Greek thinker explains how a distinctive element of βία is precisely that of intruding upon the natural course of nature and upsetting its order from the outside: all "that [which is performed] with violence", he writes, "is [directed] against nature" (ἔστι τὸ βίᾳ παρὰ φύσιν)[84].

According to Aristotle's thought, each being or element in nature moves towards its own prefixed "place" (τόπος), "of necessity" (ἀνάγκη): fire goes upwards; earth travels downwards; etc. Whenever an "external cause" (ἐκτός ἡ

---

a "law" (νόμος) would be as "doing violence" (βιάζεσθαι) to one's father and mother. See also F. D'AGOSTINO, *BIA*, 82–83; and J.-D. CAUSSE, "La violence", 76.

[81] F. D'AGOSTINO, *BIA*, 41.

[82] See, e.g., HERODOTUS, *Hist.*, I.159.3–4 (ed. PH.-E. LEGRAND, I, 165); GORGIAS, *Fr.* 82B, 11a.3–5 (ed. H. DIELS – W. KRANZ, II, 295); THUCYDIDES, *Hist.* VII.82.2–3 (ed. C.F. SMITH, IV, 168–169); PLATO, *Leg.*, IX.865d–e (ed. J. BURNET, V, 306); ID., *Resp.* VIII.566b (ed. *Ibid.*, IV, 565e); ARISTOTLE, *Met.*, VI.3.2, 1027b (ed. W. JAEGER, 126); ID., *Respir.*, XVII–XVIII.478b–479b (ed. H. TREDENNICK – *al.*, VIII, 470–475); and F. D'AGOSTINO, *BIA*, 40–43.

[83] See F. D'AGOSTINO, *BIA*, 44. Thus, as we have already mentioned, for Plato (*Leg.*, IX.873c.4 [ed. J. BURNET, V, 316]) the suicidal is one who uses "violence" (see βίᾳ) to walk away from his own destiny. See Chap. IV, p. 177, n. 72.

[84] ARISTOTLE, *Phys.*, VI.230a.29–30 (ed. W.D. ROSS, 230b). See also ID., *Coel.*, II.14, 297b.22–23 (ed. C. PRANTL, 66); *Ibid.*, III.2, 300a.23 (ed. *Ibid.*, 71); and F. D'AGOSTINO, *BIA*, 44–47. For instance, Aristotle (*Pol.*, I.2, 1253b.18–23 [ed. O. IMMISCH, 6]) affirms that, since "lording it over" (δεσπόζειν) a slave is "against nature" (παρὰ φύσιν), then it is "violent" (βίαιον). However, since βία can be associated also with "virtue" (ἀρετή), he never rejects slavery in itself totally. See, e.g., *Ibid.*, I.2, 1255a.9–19 (ed. *Ibid.*, 10); F. D'AGO-STINO, *BIA*, 93, n. 62; and *Ibid.*, 95, n. 68. For a discussion of violence and slavery in ancient Greek thought, see *Ibid.*, 92–97.

αἰτία), as opposed to an "internal" (ἐντός) one, *forces* something to deviate from its natural direction or destination, one does "violence" (βία) to it[85]. As a result, one can "violate" (βιάσασθαι) a "stone" (λίθον), by throwing it in the air; "fire" (πῦρ), by pushing it down to earth; a "horse" (ἵππον), by forcing it to veer from its galloping route; or even a man, by forcing him "to do" (ποιεῖν) something either "against nature" (παρὰ φύσιν) or "against his resolves" (παρ'ἃ βούλεται)[86]. Once this kind of violence is over, the element returns to its natural place, regaining its lost equilibrium, order and state of rest[87].

To conclude, then, the philosophical explanation of the phenomenon of βία is given primarily in terms of "physicalist" (vs. "moral") concepts, that is, linked to the notions of motion and rest in the cosmic order. Its cause stands outside of nature, and specifically, in the capacity of the divine or human will to upset such an established order and balance of things[88]. This reasoning ultimately explains why God himself cannot suffer βία: since God is the perfectly eternal and unmovable mover, no change can affect him from the outside[89]. This also explains why the life dedicated to trade is qualified by him as being violent (see ὁ δὲ χρηματιστὴς βίαιός τίς ἐστιν)[90]: since such a life (lit. "the life of money-making") is primarily oriented towards the pursuit of "wealth" (πλοῦτος), which is only a means to an end rather than a true end in itself; it is thus against the aforementioned understanding of nature and balance.

b) A Traditional Epic Theme and its Mythological Domains

As one moves from the philosophical Greek world to that of ancient poetry, epic and mythology, linguistic studies yield analogous results. "Violence" (βία), as G. Nagy observes, is "a traditional epic theme"[91], generally characterized by

---

[85] See, e.g., ARISTOTLE, *Nic.*, III.1.3, 1110a.1–4 (ed. J. BURNET, 111–112); *Ibid.*, III.1.10, 1110b.2–8 (ed. *Ibid.*, 115–116); *Ibid.*, III.1.12, 1110b.16–18 (ed. *Ibid.*, 116–117); *Ibid.*, V.8.3, 1135a.26–34 (ed. *Ibid.*, 235–236); and F. D'AGOSTINO, *BIA*, 50, n. 71.

[86] See ARISTOTLE, *Magn.*, I.14–15, 1188b.1–18 (ed. F. SUSEMIHL, 22). See also the oc-currences of the verb ποιεῖν, in Luke 16,3.4.8.9.

[87] See ARISTOTLE, *Coel.*, II.300a.23–27 (ed. C. PRANTL, 71).

[88] See ARISTOTLE, *Magn.*, I.15, 1188b.12–14 (ed. F. SUSEMIHL, 22); ID., *Phys.*, VIII.215a.1–4 (ed. W.D. ROSS, 215a); and F. D'AGOSTINO, *BIA*, 45–46. As the latter (*Ibid.*, 46, n. 56) notes, the physical dimension of βία, as an effect of the "hastiness" and "swiftness" (ταχυτής) of motion, had already been observed by both Anaxagoras and Antiphon. See, e.g., ANAXAGORAS, *Fr.* 59B 9.3–4 (ed. H. DIELS – W. KRANZ, II, 36); and ANTIPHON, *Fr.* 87B 29.8–9 (ed. *Ibid.*, II, 344).

[89] See, e.g., ARISTOTLE, *Met.*, V.4, 1015b.14–15 (ed. W. JAEGER, 94); and F. D'AGO-STINO, *BIA*, 47–50.

[90] See, e.g., ARISTOTLE, *Nic.*, I.5, 1096a.5–7 (ed. J. BURNET, 22–23); H. RACKHAM, ed., *Aristotle*, XIX, 16–17; and F. D'AGOSTINO, *BIA*, 48, n. 64.

[91] G. NAGY, *The Best of the Achaeans*, 318.

a certain ambivalence of positive and negative meanings, used in combination with "cosmic and heroic aspects"[92].

On the positive side, and in a way similar to the aforementioned philosophical consideration of "war" (πόλεμος), the Greek epic tradition also esteems "strife" (ἔρις) and "violence" (βία) as "virtues" (ἀρεταί)[93]. Athletes and mythological figures, warriors and heroes, all need both "violence" (βία) and "might" (κράτος) in order to win in battle[94]. Titans, Centimanes, and Zeus himself, all fight each other with their own βία, and when the sky and thunder god eventually triumphs over everyone else, he grants his βία to his own son, Heracles, and to those heroes with whom he is pleased[95].

All in all, as F. D'Agostino observes, βία "is defined as favourable, εὐμενής, because it belongs to Zeus"[96]. For instance, Aeschylus classifies the "grace" (χάρις) of the gods as βίαιος[97]. Pindar considers "extreme violence" (τὸ βιαιότατον) justifiable by the supreme νόμος governing both gods and men, while Sophocles thinks that the gods may use βία positively, in order to prevent evil deeds[98]. Not only is βία considered as a positive dimension of reality, but, as F. D'Agostino points out, it is elevated even to the rank of a divinity "worthy of veneration"[99]. In fact, coinciding with the Roman deity *Vis*, Βία represents

---

[92] G. NAGY, *The Best of the Achaeans*, 323. See also *Ibid.*, 321.

[93] See, e.g., HESIOD, *Erga*, vv. 11–26 (ed. F. SOLMSEN – *al.*, 49–50); and HOMER, *Ily.*, IV.439–445 (ed. A.T. MURRAY – W.F. WYATT, I, 196–197). For the epic meaning of βία as "valor", in Homer's Iliad, see, e.g., Thurber, "βίη", 34.

[94] See, e.g., HESIOD, *Th.*, 385–401.437 (ed. F. SOLMSEN – *al.*, 21–23); E. WHITE – H. GERARD, ed., *Hesiod*, 106–111; G. NAGY, *The Best of the Achaeans*, 90.317–323.326–333.345–347; F. D'AGOSTINO, *BIA*, 35–36; and *Ibid.*, 63, n. 58.

[95] See, e.g., HESIOD, *Th.*, 670–678 (ed. F. SOLMSEN – *al.*, 33); *Ibid.*, 687–693 (ed. *Ibid.*, 34); and F. D'AGOSTINO, *BIA*, 63. For Heracles' virtuous violence, see H.H.O. CHALK, "*APETH* and *BIA*", 7–18.

[96] F. D'AGOSTINO, *BIA*, 20. See also AESCHYLUS, *Sup.*, 1068 (ed. H.W. SMITH, I, 104–105). The fact that, at times, βία is seen from a negative perspective, often as an equivalent of ὕβρις or πειθώ, may also be due to the latter two's mythological opposition to the gods and, specifically, to Zeus and Δίκη, one of his daughters. See, e.g., HOMER, *Ily.*, XVI.387–388 (ed. A.T. MURRAY – W.F. WYATT, II, 190–191); HESIOD, *Th.*, 901–906 (ed. F. SOLMSEN – *al.*, 43–44); ID., *Op.*, 248–262.274–277 (ed. *Ibid.*, 59–60.61); AESCHYLUS, *Sept.*, 663.742–749 (ed. P. MAZON, I, 133.136); ID., *Choeph.*, 947–952 (ed. *Ibid.*, II, 116–117); ID., *Ag.*, 381–385 (ed. *Ibid.*, II, 24); PAUSANIAS, *Graec.*, II.1.5–6 (ed. W.H.S. JONES, I, 250–251); PINDAR, *Ol.*, XIII.1–10 (ed. W.H. RACE, I, 188–189); PLATO, *Resp.* II.365d.6–7 (ed. J. BURNET, IV, 365d); PLUTARCH, *Ser.*, XXV.564e (ed. P.H. DE LACY – *al.*, VII, 278–281); and F. D'AGOSTINO, *BIA*, 35–36.60–61.

[97] See, e.g., AESCHYLUS, *Ag.*, 182–183 (ed. P. MAZON, II, 16); F. D'AGOSTINO, *BIA*, 20, n. 84; and *Ibid.*, 67, n. 2.

[98] See, e.g., PINDAR, *Fr.*, 169a.1–19 (ed. B. SNELL – H. MAEHLER, IV, 133–134); SOPHOCLES, *Ph.*, 601–602 (ed. A. DAIN – P. MAZON, III, 32); and F. D'AGOSTINO, *BIA*, 67–78.

[99] F. D'AGOSTINO, *BIA*, 55. See also *Ibid.*, 55–66.

in the Greek mythology the personification of bodily force or raw energy, a concept which parallels, perhaps, that of the Egyptian *Ba* or *Ka*[100].

More precisely, in the ancient literary Greek world, Βία is a winged Olympian Daemon (a demigod or supernatural spirit), daughter of the Titan Pallas and the Oceanid water Nymph Styx[101], and sister of Νίκη (i.e., the goddess of victory), Κράτος and Ζῆλος (i.e., the personifications of power and zeal/jealousy, respectively)[102]. Literary sources show us Βία primarily as a guard and personal attendant at Zeus' side, together with her siblings, and never leaving his throne. For instance, we are told how she supports the latter's overthrowing of Κρόνος for the control of Olympus and all the gods of ancient Greece during the Titan War; how she defends the aforementioned mount from Τυφωεύς (i.e., the god of monsters), and also how she brings Prometheus to be chained to a rock, at the Caucasus mountains[103]. In a story recorded by Herodotus and Plutarch, Βία appears suddenly also in connection with "money" (ἀργύριον): when the Athenian statesman, Themistocles, tries to exact tributes from the Andrians, he claims to be escorted by two goddesses, namely, Πειθώ and Βία[104].

---

[100] In Ancient Egypt, *Ba* (or *Ka*) is a manifestation of the constitutive principle or energy existing in every living being, whether human or divine. For a description of this notion, see, e.g., Corteggiani, "*Ba*", 69–71; and *Ibid.*, "*Ka*", 252–254. See also GORGIAS, *Fr.* 82B, 11.6 (ed. H. DIELS – W. KRANZ, II, 289–290); E. SIMON, "Bia et Kratos", LIMC, III.1, 114–115; Turner, "*Ba*", 86; ID., "*Bia (A)*", 101; ID., "*Ka*", 254; and R. BLOCH, "Bia", BNP, II, 621. The Roman equivalent goddess of Βία is *Vis*, which, as K.N. Daly (*Greek and Roman Mythology*, 27) points out, however, is most likely "a name that appears to be a mere translation".

[101] Styx ruled over one of the Underworld Rivers marking the boundary between the land of the living and the world of the dead. See, e.g., Turner, "*Styx*", 441. See also the eschatological theme and crisis motif of Luke 16.

[102] See, e.g., HESIOD, *Th.*, 374–403 (ed. F. SOLMSEN – *al.*, 21–22); AESCHYLUS, *Prom.*, 12–13 (ed. P. MAZON, I, 161); PLATO, *Prot.*, 321d (ed. J. BURNET, III, 321d); PSEUDO-APOLLODORUS, *Bibl.*, I.2.4–5 (ed. P. SCARPI, 10–11); MOSCHION, *Fr.* 6.16 (ed. A. NAUCK – B. SNELL, 814); W. SMITH, ed., *Dictionary*, I, 486; F. D'AGOSTINO, *BIA*, 62, n. 53; A. JELLAMO, *Il cammino*, 12–13; and A.J. ATSMA, "BIA", Abstract Personifications.

[103] See J.-P. VERNANT, *Myth and Thought*, 17.196.240; and R. HARD, *The Routledge Handbook*, 49.95.695. In the prologue to his tragic play, *Prometheus Bound*, Aeschylus stages Κράτος and Βία, side by side with Hephaestus, while the latter tries to arouse pity in his assistants at the unbearable sight of the Titan's torture. Here, Κράτος speaks with Hephaestus and shows no pity whatsoever for Prometheus, but Βία remains silent. See, e.g., AESCHYLUS, *Prom.*, 36–87 (ed. P. MAZON, I, 162–164); F. D'AGOSTINO, *BIA*, ix.64–65; and D.L. MUNTEANU, *Tragic Pathos*, 173–175. As F. D'Agostino observes, this silence appears to "shout" the very ambivalence of violence, as a reflection of the ambivalence of Prometheus' action, that is, both an illegitimate theft and a legitimate gift. See F. D'AGOSTINO, *BIA*, 65.

[104] See, e.g., HERODOTUS, *Hist.*, VIII.111 (ed. PH.-E. LEGRAND, VIII, 110–111); PLUTARCH, *Them.*, XXI.30–31 (ed. C. SINTENIS, I, 239); J. LANGHORNE – W. LANGHORNE, ed., *Plutarch's Lives*, I, 376; H.A. HOLDEN, ed., *Plutarch's Life*, 32–33.135–136; and F. D'AGOSTINO, *BIA*, 57. According to Gorgias, both πειθώ and βία are irresistible forces. See, e.g., GORGIAS, *Fr.* 82B, 11.1–21 (ed. H. DIELS – W. KRANZ, II, 288–294); and F. D'AGOSTINO, *BIA*, 58.

In other words, both the rhetorical art of "persuasion" (πειθώ) and "violence" (βία) can be used to achieve the same goal, namely, the appropriation of material resources belonging to someone else[105].

Recent archeological discoveries confirm these literary sources, not only as to the existence of a cult of Βία and of sanctuaries dedicated to it, but also as regards the deity's association with the notion of wealth[106]. For instance, in the curse tablet found in a tomb at Kenchreai, near Corinth, the goddess is actually asked to get involved in punishing a thief "and even to correct the injustice by returning the stolen property"[107].

On the negative side, and beyond the confines of an idealized world, βία is thought to occur among humans in opposition to "justice" (δίκη), mainly because of hunger, and being tied to the life of the wild beasts is sometimes assimilated to ὕβρις[108]. However, in this case also, violence is connected with wealth and property. In fact, "war" (πόλεμος) is opposed to "peace" (εἰρήνη), which is in turn associated with "riches" (πλοῦτος)[109]. Moreover, Homer speaks of men working "violent deeds" (ἔργα βίαια), either when they are "lawless" (ἀθεμίστιοι), that is, whenever they drive out "justice" (δίκη), give crooked judgments and thus stir the gods' anger, or when they "waste possessions" (κτήματα κείροντας) and devour the houses of people who might not come back home[110]. In a way analogous to that described in Plato's aforementioned legal principle, thus, the epic poet connects "violent acts" (βίαια) with someone else's property[111].

Furthermore, the literary association of βία with the notion of wealth and property goes back all the way to the end of the 8th c. BCE, or the beginning

---

[105] In his commentary to this story, M. Foley ("*Peitho*", 175) tries to reconcile the paradoxical relationship between the two divine personifications by referring to Aristotle's description of βία, as "a mode of external compulsion". See ARISTOTLE, *Nic.*, III.1–5, 1110b–1114a (ed. J. BURNET, 114–136). However, his arguments evolve eventually into very intricate speculations that require more effort than they are worth, at least as far as we are concerned in this study. For the ambiguity of the association between πειθώ and βία, see F. D'AGOSTINO, *BIA*, 55–62.

[106] See, e.g., PAUSANIAS, *Graec.*, II.4.6 (ed. W.H.S. JONES, I, 268–271); *CIG*, III, 190–191, I.43790.1–2; F. D'AGOSTINO, *BIA*, 56, n. 26; and C.A. FARAONE – J.L. RIFE, "A Greek Curse", 141–157.

[107] C.A. FARAONE – J.L. RIFE, "A Greek Curse", 151.

[108] See, e.g., HESIOD, *Erga*, vv. 213.274–280 (ed. F. SOLMSEN – *al.*, 58.61); CRITIAS, *Fr.* 88B 25.15–16 (ed. H. DIELS – W. KRANZ, II, 387–389); ATHENAEUS, *Deipn.* I.12d–e (ed. C.B. GULICK, I, 54–55); F. D'AGOSTINO, *BIA*, 8; *Ibid.*, 35, n. 3; and M. FOLEY, "*Peitho*", 174.

[109] See, e.g., HOMER, *Ody.* XXIV.486 (ed. A.T. MURRAY, II, 438); and F. D'AGO-STINO, *BIA*, 11.

[110] See HOMER, *Ily.*, XVI.387–388 (ed. A.T. MURRAY – W.F. WYATT, II, 190–191); ID., *Ody.* II.235–238 (ed. A.T. MURRAY, I, 52–53); *Ibid.*, XVIII.138–142 (ed. *Ibid.*, II, 206–207); and F. D'AGOSTINO, *BIA*, 36–37.

[111] See PLATO, *Leg.*, X.884a.1–4 (ed. J. BURNET, V, 327); and Chap. IV, pp. 177–178.

of the 7th, and can be said to reflect that ambivalence proper of βία, between justice and injustice, about which we have already spoken.

On the one hand, for instance, Hesiod refers to those who acquire "riches" (χρήματα) unjustly in terms of βία, and admonishes: "if someone takes great riches violently and with force [...] the gods [will] quickly blot him out"[112].

Later, in the 5th c. BCE, Euripides writes about the gods' hatred for the "violence" (βία) used to hold on to "what belongs to others" (τἀλλότρια)[113]. For the great tragic dramatist, such "unjust wealth" (ὁ πλοῦτος ἄδικος) must "be given up" (ἐατέος), rather than clung to (see μὴ σχεῖν)[114].

On the other hand, an anonymous sophistic treatise, written sometime after the Peloponnesian War (4th c. BCE), mentions the enigmatic oxymoron of Cleobulina, an ancient and well-known poetess of Rhodes, who back in the 6th c. BCE identifies stealing and swindling "violently" (βιαίως) with a "just" (δίκαιον) kind of violence:

"it is just [δίκαιον] to tell lies and to deceive [...] to steal the belongings of one's friends and to use force [καὶ βιῆσθαι] against those one loves most, is just [δίκαιον] [...] it is right [δίκαιον], isn't it, to steal these things [...] and to take it away by force [ἀφελέσθαι βίαι]? [...] And it is right [δίκαιον] to plunder a temple [...] I want also to present the testimony of older poetry, of Cleobulina, for instance: 'I saw a man stealing and deceiving by force [βιαίως], and to do this by force [καὶ τὸ βίαι ῥέξαι] was an action most just [τοῦτο δικαιότατον]'"[115].

---

[112] R.K. BALOT, *A Genealogy*, 152. "εἰ γάρ τις καὶ χερσὶ βίη μέγαν ὄλβον ἕληται [...] ῥεῖα δέ μιν μαυροῦσι θεοί" (HESIOD, *Op.*, 320–326 [ed. F. SOLMSEN – *al.*, 63]).

[113] Specifically, Euripides (*Hel.*, 903–908 [ed. A.M. DALE, 37]) has Helen state: μισεῖ γὰρ ὁ θεὸς τὴν βίαν, τὰ κτητὰ δὲ κτᾶσθαι κελεύει πάντας οὐκ ἐς ἁρπαγάς. Ἐατέος δ' ὁ πλοῦτος ἄδικός τις ὤν. Κοινὸς γάρ ἐστιν οὐρανὸς πᾶσιν βροτοῖς καὶ γαῖ', ἐν ᾗ χρὴ δώματ' ἀναπληρουμένους τἀλλότρια μὴ σχεῖν μηδ' ἀφαιρεῖσθαι βίᾳ. A.S. Way (ed., *Euripides*, I, 545–547) translates these verses thus: "For God abhorreth violence, bidding all not by the spoiler's rapine get them gain. Away with wealth – the wealth amassed by wrong! For common to all mortals is heaven's air, and earth, whereby men ought to enrich their homes, nor keep nor wrest by violence others' goods".

[114] The passage is regarded sometimes as an interpolation. See, e.g., A.S. WAY, ed., *Euripides*, I, 547, n.1; L. MÉRIDIER – *al.*, ed., *Euripide*, V, 87, n. 1; A.M. DALE, ed., *Euripides*, 126–127, ns. 903–904; and F. D'AGOSTINO, *BIA*, 37. As far as we are concerned, its vocabulary sounds very close to that used in Luke 16,16 and its proximate context. As we have seen, the shrewd steward of the first parable manages that which belongs to his master, and the reader is encouraged to give up that which belongs to God in almsgiving! See, e.g., οἴκους (Luke 16,4b); μαμωνᾶ τῆς ἀδικίας (Luke 16,9); ἄδικος (Luke 16,10[2x]); ἐν τῷ ἀδίκῳ μαμωνᾷ (Luke 16,11); ἐν τῷ ἀλλοτρίῳ (Luke 16,12a); μισήσει (Luke 16,13b); θεός (Luke 16,13d); βιάζεται (Luke 16,16c); ἀποθανεῖν (Luke 16,22a); ἀπέθανεν (Luke 16,22b); and οἶκον (Luke 16,27). See also οὐρανῶν (Matt 11,12b); and ἁρπάζουσιν (Matt 11,12c).

[115] R.K. SPRAGUE, "Dissoi Logoi", 160–161. See ANONYMOUS, *Dialex.*, XC, 3.3–4.7.11 (ed. H. DIELS – W. KRANZ, II, 410–411); CLEOBULUS, *Fr.*, 10.3a.5 (ed. *Ibid.*, I, 63); GORGIAS, *Fr.* 82B 11a.5 (ed. *Ibid.*, II, 295); and CRITIAS, *Fr.* 88B 25.10 (ed. *Ibid.*, II, 387).

Contemporary to Cleobulina, Theognis of Megara mentions βία also in the context of the seizure of wealth and gain: "they plunder the wealth", he writes, "by force" (χρήματα δ᾽ ἁρπάζουσι βίη)[116]. During approximately the same period, Pindar describes Heracles as walking the "path of violence" (βίας ὁδόν) while performing his "virtuous" theft[117]. Finally, much later, Plutarch will use often the verb βιάζεσθαι together with ἁρπάζειν and, as we have seen in the aforementioned story of Themistocles, in the context of the force of language and the craving for wealth[118]. For instance, after comparing the way "idle talkers" (οἱ ἀδόλεσχοι) long for listeners with such a "disease of the soul" (νόσημα τῆς ψυχῆς) as "love of money" (φιλαργυρία)[119], he observes how talkative people "do violence [by] speaking" (βιάσωνται λαλεῖν)[120]. However, he is also well aware of how "a lot of silver and gold" (χρυσῶν καὶ ἀργυρῶν πλῆθος) can be used to make friends for oneself (cf. φίλον οὐδένα σεαυτῷ πεποίηκας), which recalls for us directly the analogous expression occurring in Luke 16,9[121].

c) Minor Uses and Contexts

The Greek terms for "violence" are used in other circumstances and contexts as well, from love to cult, from medicine to history. These occurrences are less pertinent to our contextual understanding of Luke 16,16. As a result, we shall only glimpse them briefly here, whereas we shall analyze the juridical and

---

Although some authors struggle to find the solution to this enigma, whether in a "dagger", in "strife", or "war", we are here interested in the fact that the riddle itself may be exploiting a nuance of the term βία relating directly to wealth and property. See J.M. EDMONDS, ed., *Elegy*, I, 165, n. 2; and F. D'AGOSTINO, *BIA*, 39, n. 33.

[116] R.K. BALOT, *A Genealogy*, 150. See THEOGNIS, *El.*, I.677 (ed. J. CARRIÈRE, 96); and R.K. BALOT, *A Genealogy*, 148–150.

[117] See, e.g., PINDAR, *Fr.*, 169a.1–19 (ed. B. SNELL – H. MAEHLER, IV, 133–134); and F. D'AGOSTINO, *BIA*, 67–78. The Pindaric citation is mentioned, among others, also by Herodotus, in relation to the violent deeds of the Persian king, Cambyses, and the intrinsic force of the events themselves, and by Plato, in relation to Heracles' theft and the guiding violence of law and justice. See, e.g., HERODOTUS, *Hist.*, III.38.20–21 (ed. PH.-E. LEGRAND, III, 66); PLATO, *Gorg.*, 484a.2–484c.3 (ed. J. BURNET, III, 483d–484c); and ID., *Leg.*, X.890a.4–5 (ed. *Ibid*, V, 334).

[117] F. D'AGOSTINO, *BIA*, 55. See also *Ibid.*, 55–66.

[118] See, e.g., PLUTARCH, *Apoph. Rom.*, II.203c.3 (ed. P.H. DE LACY – *al.*, III, 206–207); ID., *Ser.*, XX.562d (ed. *Ibid.*, VII, 264–265); ID., *Amat.*, XI.755c (ed. *Ibid.*, IX, 342–343); and H. ALMQUIST, *Plutarch*, 38. Plutarch traces the root of βία back to the primordial nature of man and his farthest titanic origins. See PLUTARCH, *Carn.*, I.996c (ed. P.H. DE LACY – *al.*, XII, 558–561). See also DIO CHRYSOSTOM, *Or.*, XXX.10 (ed. J.W. COHOON – *al.*, II, 408–409); and F. D'AGOSTINO, *BIA*, 111–112.

[119] PLUTARCH, *Garr.*, II.502e (ed. P.H. DE LACY – *al.*, VI, 398–399). See Luke 16,14.

[120] PLUTARCH, *Garr.*, II.503b (ed. P.H. DE LACY – *al.*, VI, 402–403).

[121] See PLUTARCH, *Apoph. Reg.*, IV.175e (ed. P.H. DE LACY – *al.*, III, 30–31); and H. ALMQUIST, *Plutarch*, 68.

economical usage of the βία-terms with more interest later, when dealing with the papyrological data.

Within the Greek literary vocabulary, βία is sometimes predicated also of "[passionate] love" (ἔρως), often in conjunction with the notion of "abduction" (ἀρπαγή)[122]. In the ambit of erotic typologies and love theories, the term can be used either positively, to win a girl's heart, or negatively, to force her into a marriage or even rape[123]. Finally, in an account narrated by Strabo, "violence" (βία) occurs also in connection with the young Cretans' traditional pederastic initiation to adulthood[124]. According to such a tradition, if during the ritual "kidnapping" (ἀρπαγή) – which was usually preceded by an agreement between the abductor and the young man's family – the aristocratic adult male used any βία against the boy, the latter was legally free to break off the relationship with the former and could rightfully ask for retribution.

The verb βιάζεσθαι is then used also in the ritual context to express the violation of a regulation or the trespassing of a place. For instance, in the epigraphic rules (ca. 400 BCE) for the cult of Men Tyrannos (i.e., the moon god), in a sanctuary founded by Xanthus the Lycian, the latter bans all sacrifices offered in his absence or without his permission. In l. 8 of this inscription (ἐὰν δέ τις βιάσεται ἀπρόσδεκτος ἡ θυσία παρὰ τοῦ θεοῦ)[125], the verb indicates primarily a transgression of such an injunction but, as suggested by G.A. Deissmann, it may also refer intransitively to someone who "comes forward violently or enters by force"[126] into the sanctuary.

Furthermore, within the medical language of the ancient Greek physicists, as observed by C. Spicq, the verb βιάζεσθαι is also "frequently used with respect

---

[122] See, esp., F. D'AGOSTINO, *BIA*, 119–120. Rather than associating it with βία, other authors poetically set ἔρως against ὕβρις. For instance, Paulus Silentiarius (*Anth.*, V.255 [ed. H. STADTMÜLLER, I, 195]) writes: "wanton violence is the dissolution of passionate love" (ὕβρις ἔρωτας ἔλυσε). See F. D'AGOSTINO, *BIA*, 125, n. 34.

[123] See, e.g., HERODOTUS, *Hist.*, IX.108.2–5 (ed. PH.-E. LEGRAND, IX, 100); EURIPIDES, *Ion*, 10–11 (ed. L. MÉRIDIER – al., III, 183); ID., *Andr.*, 390–391 (ed. *Ibid.*, II, 127); ID., *Anth.*, IX.57 (ed. H. STADTMÜLLER, III, 40); LYSIAS, *Erat.*, I.32–33 (ed. L. GERNET – M. BIZOS, I, 36–37); PLUTARCH, *Amat.*, V.751d.8 (ed. R. FLACELIÈRE, 50–51); *Ibid.*, XXII.768b.4–6 (ed. *Ibid.*, 112–113); ID., *Apoph. Lac.*, II.202b.3–4 (ed. P.H. DE LACY – al., III, 200–201); and F. D'AGOSTINO, *BIA*, 59–60.120. As the latter (*Ibid.*, 120) specifies, "ratto e violenza carnale coincidevano infatti nel termine onnicomprensivo di βία; la βιασθεῖα era per definizione la donna rapita e violentata".

[124] See STRABO, *Geo.*, X.4.21, 483c (ed. G. AUJAC – F. LASERRE, VII, 102–104); and F. D'AGOSTINO, *BIA*, 59–60.

[125] See *Pap. Syll.* 1042.8 (ed. G. DITTENBERGER, III, 196). Thus, K. Dowden (*European Paganism*, 33) translates the line: "and if anyone forces their way the sacrifice is unaccepted by the god".

[126] G.A. DEISSMANN – A. GRIEVE, *Bible Studies*, 258. However, cf. C. SPICQ, "βιάζομαι", *TLNT*, I, 291.

to surgery"[127]. This usage recalls that of the aforementioned philosophical naturalistic phenomenon, inasmuch as the terminology of "violence" (βία) is meant also in this case to describe essentially an external, abnormal, or artificial intervention, which, as such, goes against "nature" (φύσις) and "justice" (δίκη)[128]. Thus, a donkey is said to "do violence" (βιάζεται) to a mare, when it mounts it and copulates with it "unnaturally" to produce a mule, or a plant is "violated" (βιασαμένος) when it is forced to blossom prematurely, for its fruits are not allowed to ripen as nature wishes[129].

Finally, in the world of ancient history, Greek writers use βία mostly to qualify the force or power of natural agents (such as, winds, seas, etc.)[130], to describe the human violence present especially in the midst of "war" (πόλεμος)[131], and in the context of legal rights and tribunals, where those who can "do violence" (βιάζεσθαι) do not require "to be judged" (δικάζεσθαι)[132]. Sometimes, however, the βία-lexemes are used also in other historical circumstances, to indicate someone's entry into someone else's place, or one's seizure of that which belongs to another.

For instance, Thucydides mentions βία in connection both with forcing one's way into a place and with "greedy gain" (πλεονεξία) or "unjust wealth" (ὁ πλοῦτος

---

[127] C. SPICQ, "βιάζομαι", *TLNT*, I, 288. For a list of Greek medical sources referring to βιάζεσθαι, βίαιος and βία, see W.K. HOBART, *The Medical Language*, 179–180.

[128] See, e.g., GORGIAS, *Fr.* 82B, 11a.1–2 (ed. H. DIELS – W. KRANZ, II, 295); HIPPOCRATES, *Fract.*, II.30.5–6 (ed. J.E. PETREQUIN, II, 196–197); F. HEINIMANN, *Nomos*, 42.97.131.135.151; and F. D'AGOSTINO, *BIA*, 41–42.

[129] See, e.g., DEMOCRITUS, *Fr.* 68B, 150–151 (ed. H. DIELS – W. KRANZ, II, 124–125); EPICTETUS, *Diatr.*, IV.8.36–40 (ed. W.A. OLDFATHER, II, 388–391); and F. D'AGOSTINO, *BIA*, 42.

[130] See, e.g., THUCYDIDES, *Hist.* II.52.3 (ed. C.F. SMITH, I, 350–351); *Ibid.*, III.89.24 (ed. *Ibid.*, II, 158–159); POLYBIUS, *Hist.*, I.47.4 (ed. P. PÉDECH – *al.*, I, 83); *Ibid.*, IV.41.4 (ed. *Ibid.*, IV, 80); *Ibid.*, V.48.6 (ed. *Ibid.*, V, 99); and F. D'AGOSTINO, *BIA*, 48, n. 64.

[131] For instance, Herodotus recounts how king Darius, in his desire to punish the satrap Oroetes for his wrongdoing, thought it best not to resort to "violence and numbers" (βίη τε καὶ ὁμίλῳ), by sending an "army" (στρατόν) openly against him, but to use cunning or "cleverness" (σοφίη) instead. Similarly, in Thucydides, when Cleon, "the most violent citizen" (βιαιότατος τῶν πολιτῶν), argues in favour of the Mytilenaeans' death, his claims are countered by Diodotus with a persuasive reasoning: the Mytilenaeans should be spared so that they can be their allies in war. See HERODOTUS, *Hist.*, III.127 (ed. PH.-E. LEGRAND, III, 162–163); THUCYDIDES, *Hist.* III.36.6 (ed. C.F. SMITH, II, 56–57); and *Ibid.*, III.47.5 (ed. *Ibid.*, II, 84–85). Thucydides (*Hist.* III.82.2 [ed. *Ibid.*, II, 142]), in particular, defines "war" (πόλεμος) as a true "teacher of violence" (βίαιος διδάσκαλος). For a study of this concept in ancient Greece, see, e.g., J.-P. VERNANT, *Mythe et société*, 31–56. For an unfavourable view of war, after the Peloponnesian War, see D. FOURGOUS, "L'invention", 1155. However, the historical realization expressed by Aristotle, in *Pol.* VII.14, 1333a–b (ed. O. IMMISCH, 258–261), seems to contradict this opinion. See F. D'AGOSTINO, *BIA*, 9–11.38.

[132] See, e.g., THUCYDIDES, *Hist.* I.77.2 (ed. C.F. SMITH, I, 130–131); and *Ibid.*, III.82.2 (ed. *Ibid.*, II, 142). See also οἱ δικαιοῦντες ἑαυτούς, in Luke 16,15; and πᾶς [...] βιάζεται, in Luke 16,16c.

ἄδικος)[133]. As R.K. Balot notes, the Greek historian has "the Corinthians call the Corcyraeans 'violent and grasping'"[134] (βίαιοι καὶ πλεονέκται), meaning that they are characterized by an excessive desire for money[135]. In like manner, Polybius speaks of the appetite for "that which belongs to others" (τὰ ἀλλότρια) as a deterioration, from democracy "to a government of violence and force" (εἰς βίαν και χειροκρατίαν)[136], and mentions βία in the context of a forced passage[137]. Finally, Diodorus of Sicily speaks later of the "superiority of the man who does violence" (τὴν ὑπεροχὴν τοῦ βιαζομένου)[138] in terms of the power or authority to do as one pleases, and uses the term βία also to mean the forcible seizure or conquest of a city[139].

2. The Greek Papyrological Source Material: A Significant Nuance

As we move from literary to both learned and popular Greek papyrological usage, the extant source material at our disposal discloses a few significant details that are worth underlining.

The preceding analysis of literary documents has indeed revealed a mixed usage of βία and its cognates primarily in the ambiguous or morally unspecified terms of "strength" and in relation to wealth and possessions as well. However, the following selection of papyrological examples shall shed a significant amount of light on the existence of a specific legal nuance of the βία-lexemes, which can help explain the occurrence of βιάζεται in Luke 16,16 as a lawful and ethically acceptable seizure of the kingdom of God. Specifically, whenever the βία-terms occur in reference to an immoveable property (e.g., house, land, etc.), which, as S.R. Llewelyn phrases it, is being "acquired without the consent of its lawful owner or possessor"[140] because of an interrupted use of it for a set period of time, law and justice concur in vindicating such an acquisition from all negative connotations.

Most of the instances cited in the following pages are thus "petitions against either dispossession or disturbance of possession"[141], in which the plaintiffs use the substantive βία and its verbal (βιάζεσθαι) or adverbial (βιαίως) cognates

---

[133] See, e.g., THUCYDIDES, *Hist.* VII.83.5 (ed. C.F. SMITH, IV, 170–171). See also the expression, μαμωνᾶς τῆς ἀδικίας, in Luke 16,9.

[134] R.K. BALOT, *A Genealogy*, 270. See THUCYDIDES, *Hist.* I.40.1 (ed. C.F. SMITH, I, 70–73).

[135] See R.K. BALOT, *A Genealogy*, 233–239.269–270.303–305.

[136] POLYBIUS, *Hist.*, VI.9.7–9 (ed. P. PÉDECH – *al.*, VI, 79).

[137] See, e.g., POLYBIUS, *Hist.*, V.4.9 (ed. P. PÉDECH – *al.*, V, 45).

[138] DIODORUS OF SICILY, *Histor.*, XVI.27.1 (ed. I. BEKKER – *al.*, IV, 43). See also F. D'AGO-STINO, *BIA*, 37.

[139] See, e.g., DIODORUS OF SICILY, *Histor.*, II.19.7 (ed. I. BEKKER – *al.*, I, 201); and *Ibid.*, XVII.68.2 (ed. *Ibid.*, IV, 239).

[140] S.R. LLEWELYN, "Forcible Acquisition", 147.

[141] S.R. LLEWELYN, "Forcible Acquisition", 134. See W. DAHLMANN, Ἡ βία, 18–22.

to describe "the alleged force used by the accused"[142] directly against their property, and for that reason, also against their person, although only indirectly[143]. For the sake of convenience, the following list shall be numbered in chronological order.

a) Violence as a "Force" Used Against Someone Else's Property

Among the numerous extant papyri discovered in the last one or two centuries, some illustrate a specific use of βιάζεσθαι and βία, which is comparable with both the proximate context of Luke 16,16 and its specific linguistic expression, βιάζεται εἰς[144]. We shall limit ourselves to reporting here only some more significant examples of such a use, noting from time to time some of the lexical equivalents, as they occur[145].

1. In a letter of Ptolemy Philadelphus to Antiochus (middle of 3rd c. BCE), Ptolemy mentions the rumors that soldiers are "using some excessive violence" (πλείω τινὰ βίαν γίνεσθαι), because they are not receiving an accommodation "from the administrators" (παρὰ τῶν οἰκονόμων)[146]. Their violence consists in "breaking into the houses" (εἰς τὰς οἰκίας εἰσπηδεῖν) and "settling [in them] by force" (βίαι ἐνοικεῖν)[147].

2. In a petition (222 BCE) addressed by Polemaios, a Macedonian commander of the cavalry units of Pythangelos, to king Ptolemy III Euergetes, the plaintiff accuses Polemon and Aristomachos of sowing in his allotment, without asking his authorization, and for refusing to pay him rent for the use

---

[142] S.R. LLEWELYN, "Forcible Acquisition", 140.

[143] Thus, W. Dahlmann (H βία, 26) points out: "At no time does the word [βία] here have the meaning of force in the sense of a physical prevailing over another but it is used in the sense of an illegal dispossession which ignores the will of the possessor". See also S.R. LLEWELYN, "Forcible Acquisition", 147. The latter (Ibid., 132) remarks further: "Violence was not necessarily an action against a person in any direct sense. In fact, a delict of violence might be committed against an owner by a person who makes use of his property without consent".

[144] Most of the uses of βιάζεσθαι and βία cited in this section relate to either verbs or nouns expressing the notions of entrance, building, dwelling, etc. See, esp., the following phrases: βεβιασμένους [...] κατεσπαρκέναι; βιαζόμενον [...] οἴεσθαι κατοικοδομεῖν; βιάζεται [...] οἰκοδομεῖν; εἰς τὰς οἰκίας εἰσπηδεῖν [...] βίαι ἐνοικεῖν; εἰσβιάζεσθαι εἰς τοὺς προκειμένους τόπους; ἐνοικοῦσιν βιαίως; οἰκίας [...] εἰσβεβιασμένων; βιαιότερον ἐμβατεῦσας; and the few analogous concepts, in Luke 16.

[145] For other uses of these lexemes in the papyri, however, see, esp., Moulton, "βιάζομαι", 109–110; and C. SPICQ, "βιάζομαι", TLNT, I, 288, ns. 6–7.

[146] See Pap. Hal. 1, II.207.166–170 (ed. A.S. HUNT – C.C. EDGAR – D.L. PAGE, II, 54–55); and S.R. LLEWELYN, "Forcible Acquisition", 134–135. Cf., also, Luke 16,1–4.8.13.

[147] See A.S. HUNT – C.C. EDGAR – D.L. PAGE, ed., Select Papyri, II, 54–55.

of his own land[148]. The wrong suffered by Polemaios, namely, "their sowing" (αὐτοὺς κατεσπαρκέναι) in his plot of land and, consequently, their illegal possession and use of it, is referred to as "having acted with violence" (βεβιασμένους)[149].

3. In a petition (222–204 BCE) addressed to king Ptolemy IV Philopator, the plaintiff, a woman named Hediste, alleges to have been wronged by a doctor named Demetrios[150]. The wrong is such that, as S.R. Llewelyn remarks, Hediste "sees herself as treated violently by virtue of actions of the accused in regard to property owned by her"[151]. Specifically, the woman writes:

"For though I own a portion of vacant land [...] the aforementioned, entering on this place, did me violence by carrying brick(s) and digging foundation(s) so as to build"[152].

4. A petition (182–181 BCE) addressed to the strategos Daimachos by a farmer from Diospolis Magna, named Petearoeris, makes reference to Pempsais' improper appropriation of a plot of land belonging to Petearoeris' wife: Pempsais is described here as "acting with violence" (βιαζόμενος)[153].

5. Similarly, in another formal request (175 BCE) to the strategos Ptolemaios, three brothers complain of an intrusion on their territory and mention an earlier petition concerning someone's "violent" (βιαζόμενον) attempt to build upon the vacant land they had inherited from their father[154].

---

[148] See *Pap. Magd.* 1 (ed. P. JOUGUET – *al.*, II, 57–64); and S.R. LLEWELYN, "Forcible Acquisition", 141–143.

[149] See *Pap. Magd.* 1.17–18 (ed. P. JOUGUET – *al.*, II, 58); and S.R. LLEWELYN, "Forcible Acquisition", 143.

[150] See *Pap. Magd.* 27 (ed. P. JOUGUET – *al.*, II, 151–153); and S.R. LLEWELYN, "Forcible Acquisition", 143–144.

[151] S.R. LLEWELYN, "Forcible Acquisition", 144.

[152] S.R. LLEWELYN, "Forcible Acquisition", 143–144. "Ὑπάρχοντος γάρ μοι μέρος τι ψίλου [...] ὁ προγεγραμμένος, ἐπιπορευόμενος ἐπὶ τὸν τόπον, βιάζεται με πλίνθον προσάγων καὶ θεμέλιον σκάπτων ὥστε οἰκοδομεῖν" (*Pap. Magd.* 27.2–4 [ed. O. GUÉRAUD, II, 171]). The edition by P. Jouguet and others (*Papyrus grecs*, II, 151) reads "having come" (ἐρχόμενος) rather than "having entered upon" (ἐπιπορευόμενος). The meaning, however, remains unaffected. As S.R. Llewelyn ("Forcible Acquisition", 147) notes, here "the indicative verb shows that the object of the use of force was perceived to be a person, i.e. βιάζεται με. The so-called 'violence directed against immovables' is actually violence against persons through the use of their property without consent". Such an idea may help explain why the Church Fathers speak of a violence directed both against God and his kingdom.

[153] See P. COLLART – P. JOUGUET, "Un papyrus ptolémaïque", 23–40; S.R. LLEWELYN, "Forcible Acquisition", 145–147; and A. JÖRDENS, "Griechische Briefe", 411–412. The latter (*Ibid.*, 412) translates the expression, παρὰ τὸ κ[αθ]ῆκον βιαζόμενον (l. 15), as follows: "gegen alles H[erk]ommen mit Gewalt an".

[154] "ἐπεδώκα[μ]έν σοι ὑπόμνημα [...] ὑπὲρ τοῦ βιαζόμενον αὐτὸν οἴεσθαι κατοι[κο-δομεῖν τὸν καταλελειμμένον ὑπ[ὸ τοῦ] πατ[ρὸς ἡμῶν ἐπὶ οἰκήσει" (*Pap. Tebt.* 779.4–7 [ed. B.P. GRENFELL – *al.*, III, 212–213]). S.R. Llewelyn ("Forcible Acquisition", 145) translates it thus: "We

6. A couple of years later (171 BCE), in another petition addressed to the same person by Herieus, a cultivator of Crown land, the petitioner claims to have suffered violence (cf. βιασαμένη με) because of some encroachments on a piece of land inherited from his father, first by a woman and then, upon her death, also by her alleged heirs[155].

7. In a petition (ca. 160–159 BCE) to king Ptolemy VI Philometor and his wife, Cleopatra, Ptolemaios claims that some neighbors have "done violence" (πεποίηται βίας) by taking advantage of his inability to attend to his own business in order "to force their way into" (εἰσβιάζεσθαι εἰς) the courtyard and site of his house, appropriating the latter ones to their own uses, and erecting extra buildings of their own[156].

8. A decree of Ptolemy VIII Euergetes (140–139 BCE), which "takes the shape of a letter to all the civil officials of the country, from the strategoi downwards"[157], refers to some violence being exerted on the priests of a temple dedicated to Arsinoë (or Berenice), through the embezzlement of their revenues: occupation and "compulsory cultivation of agricultural land"[158] belonging to the temple (see ἱερὰ γῆ) is taking place without any knowledge

---

presented to you a petition [...] concerning his thinking forcibly to [build upon] the vacant land which was left by [our father for] (our) residence".

[155] The text reads thus: "My father having died when I was still young, Thareus, a woman of Thebes, doing violence to me [...] in defiance of all right built a tower ten cubits high on the unoccupied plot which came to me from my father. But the ordinance declares, 'If any person builds upon the land of another, let him be deprived of the building'. And whereas Thareus has since died and a certain Petesouchus and his sister Kamous lay claim to her property, I request you to [...] compel them to leave the plot" (ἐπεὶ τοῦ πατρός μου μεταλλάξαντος τὸν βίον ἔτι νεωτέρου μου ὄντος Θαρεῦς τις Θηβαία βιασαμένη με [...] ᾠκοδόμησαν ἐν τῶι ἐμῶι πατρικῶι ψιλῶι τόπωι πυργίον (δεκά)π(ηχυ) παρὰ τὸ καθῆκον, τὸ δὲ διάγραμμα διαγορεύει ἐάν τις ἐν ἀλλοτρίωι χωρίωι οἰκοδομήσηι, στερέσθω τοῦ οἰκοδομήματος. Ἀξιῶ σ', ἐπεὶ ἡ μὲν Θαρεῦς τετελεύτηκεν Πετεσοῦχος δέ τις καὶ ἡ τούτου ἀδελφὴ Καμοῦς ἀντιποιοῦνται τῶν ταύτης, προσκαλεσάμενον αὐτοὺς [...] συναναγκάσαι ἐκχωρεῖν ἐκ τοῦ τόπου) (*Pap. Tebt.* 780.3–22 [ed. B.P. GRENFELL – *al.*, III, 214–215]). In this case also, the violence used against a person's property is felt as being directed against the person.

[156] "διαστείλῃ ταυτοῖς μηκέτι εἰσβιάζεσθαι εἰς τοὺς προκειμένους τόπους παραδοῦναι δὲ τοῖς παρ' ἐμοῦ περὶ δὲ ἧς πεποίηται βίας διαλαβεῖν μισοπονήρως" (*Pap. Lond.* 45.29–32 [ed. F.G. KENYON – H.I. BELL, I, 36]). S.R. Llewelyn ("Forcible Acquisition", 135) translates the text as follows: "that he might give orders to them no longer to force their way into the aforementioned places, but give (them) back to my representatives, and concerning the force which they used that he decide justly". See also Moulton, "βιάζομαι", 109–110; R. TAUBENSCHLAG, *The Law*, 443, n. 70; ποιεῖν, in Luke 16,3.4.8.9; and εἰς [...] βιάζεται, in Luke 16,16c.

[157] B.P. GRENFELL – *al.*, ed, *The Tebtunis Papyri*, I, 59.

[158] S.R. LLEWELYN, "Forcible Acquisition", 141, n. 30.

or consent having been previously formalized by some contract or agreement (see τινὰς δὲ καὶ βιαζομέν[ου]ς ἄνευ συναλλάξεων)[159].

9. A petition from the priests of Soknopaios to Apollonios (132 BCE), strategos and superintendent of the revenues, mentions "violence" (see βίας) in the context of a suit against the chief priest Petesouchos: the offense implicates here the latter's fraudulent exaction or extortion (see παραλογισάμενος) upon the priests' farmers and his "doing violence to them" (βιασάμενος αὐτούς), by getting possession of 225 artabae of wheat (see μετενήνοχεν πυροῦ ἀρτάβας)[160].

10. A petition (ca. 127 BCE) written by the cavalryman Apollonios, to Ptolemy VIII Euergetes and his wife, Cleopatra, refers to five "keepers of mummies" (χοαχύται) assuming possession of Apollonios' property and "dwelling [in it] violently" (ἐνοικοῦσιν βιαίως)[161].

11. In the legal proceedings of Hermias (119–117 BCE), the latter accuses another group of χοαχύται of "making use of violence" (βίαι χρώμενοι), since they are laying claim to a house of his, unlawfully (see ἀντιποιούμενοι ἀδίκως)[162]. Hermias petitions the officials that those people may withdraw from his property and that a judicial decision be given for their having forced their way into it (see ἐκ τῆς οἰκίας ἐκχωρεῖν, περὶ δὲ αὐτῶν εἰσβεβιασμένων [...] διαλαβεῖν)[163]. However, his appeal for legal defence against the alleged forcible seizure of his house eventually fails, not only because of his lack of documents (ἀποδείξεις) providing proof of his forefathers' earlier ownership, but also on account of the length of time in which the χοαχύται had used the house un-

---

[159] See *Pap. Tebt.* 6.2.20–32 (ed. B.P. GRENFELL – *al.*, I, 60–61); B.P. GRENFELL – *al.*, *The Tebtunis Papyri*, I, 58–65; and S.R. LLEWELYN, "Forcible Acquisition", 141, n. 30. See also the LXX on Isa 58,6, with its mention of "violent contracts" (βίαια συναλλάγματα).

[160] See *Pap. Amh.* 35, VII.274.12–42 (ed. A.S. HUNT – C.C. EDGAR – D.L. PAGE, II, 248–251). This is another instance of a violence directed only indirectly to a person, through the direct appropriation of his or her property. See also Luke 16,6–7.

[161] See *Pap. Taur.* 3.6–24 (ed. U. WILCKEN, II, 114); *Pap. Par.* 14.22 (ed. *Ibid.*, II, 115); and S.R. LLEWELYN, "Forcible Acquisition", 135–136. U. Wilcken (ed., *Urkunden*, 38–39) explains how a χοαχύτης was someone entitled to officiate the "cultic liturgies" (λειτυργίαι) in the Egyptian funeral and burial system, with invocations, libations and offerings. See also S.R. LLEWELYN, "Forcible Acquisition", 136, n. 23; and the *assonance* between "house" (οἶκος), "steward" (οἰκονόμος), "management" (οἰκονομία), "managing" (οἰκονομεῖν), and "servant" (οἰκέτης), in Luke 16,1.2.3.4.8.13.

[162] See *Pap. Taur.* 2.26–28 (ed. U. WILCKEN, II, 48); *Ibid.* 1.1.29–1.2.31 (ed. *Ibid.*, II, 62); *Pap. Par.* 15.1.18 (ed. *Ibid.*, II, 52); S.R. LLEWELYN, "Forcible Acquisition", 136–138; and ID., "The Introduction", 157–159. See also ποιεῖν, in Luke 16,3.4.8.9; and ἀδικία, in Luke 16,8.9.10.11.

[163] See *Pap. Par.* 15.2.31–32 (ed. U. WILCKEN, II, 53); *Pap. Taur.* 1.4.33–34 (ed. *Ibid.*, II, 64); and S.R. LLEWELYN, "Forcible Acquisition", 138–139. See also εἰς [...] βιάζεται, in Luke 16,16c.

disputedly[164]. As pointed out by S.R. Llewelyn, the advocate of the accused party here "appeals to the legal principle of *usucapio* to justify their claims"[165], and eventually wins the case because the plaintiff "had failed to dispute possession over a period far in excess of the maximum period of three years"[166]. Thus, rather than restoring the property to Hermias, the final judgment authorizes the χοαχύται to remain in possession of the house (see κρατεῖν καθὼς καὶ ἀπὸ τῆς ἀρχῆς διακατεῖχον) and proscribes the former's forceful entrance into it (see μὴ εἰσβιάζεσθαι)[167].

12. In a royal edict of king Ptolemy Euergetes II (118 BCE) concerning the proclamation of a list of indulgences (e.g., the possibility of returning home, resuming former occupations, recovering properties, enjoying tax-releases and remission of penalties, etc.), the people are prohibited from "taking away with violence anything of what has been dedicated to the gods" (παραιρεῖσθαι μηθὲν τῶν ἀνιερωμένων τοῖς θεοῖς μετὰ βίας), whether villages, lands, or other sacred revenues, such as, taxes[168].

13. In another document (ca. 116–111 BCE), the petitioners (two sisters, Apollonia and Aphrodisia) request that a certain man, named Ariston, may give back to them the "ground of tilled vineyard" (see ἀπὸ ἐδάφους ἀμπελῶνος αὐρουρῶν), which they had lawfully inherited from their father, and in which Ariston "had entered with much violence" (βιαιότερον ἐμβατεῦσας), thus "doing violence" (πεποίηται βίας) by turning it to his own use[169].

14. In a notification (ca. 112 BCE) sent to Poseidonios, the epistates of Tebtunis, the verb βιάζεσθαι is used in the context of robbery, to indicate someone's forcing his way and entering into someone else's house, by night (see ἐβιάσαντό τινες εἰς τὴν ὑπάρχουσάν μοι οἰκίαν καὶ [...] εἰσῆλθον εἰς τὴν προστάδα)[170].

---

[164] See *Pap. Par.* 15.3.67–68 (ed. U. WILCKEN, II, 54); *Pap. Taur.* 1.7.2–13 (ed. *Ibid.*, II, 66); *Ibid.* 1.9.5–29 (ed. *Ibid.*, II, 67–68); and S.R. LLEWELYN, "Forcible Acquisition", 137.

[165] S.R. LLEWELYN, "Forcible Acquisition", 154. See, e.g., *Pap. Par.* 15.3.57–62 (ed. U. WILCKEN, II, 54); and *Pap. Taur.* 1.7.22–27 (ed. *Ibid.*, II, 66); and S.R. LLEWELYN, "Forcible Acquisition", 154–155.

[166] S.R. LLEWELYN, "Forcible Acquisition", 155. See also the use of the following temporal expressions: "since [...] until now" (ἀπό [...] μέχρι τοῦ νῦν), in *Pap. Taur.* 1.6.1 (ed. U. WILCKEN, II, 65); "until [...] since then" (μέχρι [...] ἀπὸ τότε), in Luke 16,16a–b; and "from the days [...] up to now [...] up to" (ἀπὸ δὲ τῶν ἡμερῶν [...] ἕως ἄρτι [...] ἕως), in Matt 11,12a.13.

[167] See *Pap. Taur.* 1.10.1–5 (ed. U. WILCKEN, II, 68); and S.R. LLEWELYN, "Forcible Acquisition", 139. See also εἰς [...] βιάζεται, in Luke 16,16c.

[168] See *Pap. Tebt.* 5, II.210.57–61 (ed. A.S. HUNT – C.C. EDGAR – D.L. PAGE, II, 62–63).

[169] See *Pap. Lond.* 401.11–31 (ed. F.G. KENYON – H.I. BELL, II, 14); R. TAUBEN-SCHLAG, *The Law*, 443, n. 70; and S.R. LLEWELYN, "Forcible Acquisition", 139. See also ποιεῖν, in Luke 16,3.4.8.9; and εἰς [...] βιάζεται, in Luke 16,16c.

[170] See *Pap. Tebt.* 804.9–15 (ed. B.P. GRENFELL – *al.*, III.1, 258). See also ὑπάρχειν, in Luke 16,1.14.23; οἶκος, in Luke 16,4.27; and εἰς [...] βιάζεται, in Luke 16,16c.

15. A petition (1st c. BCE) to the strategos, Andromachos, mentions two women's attempt "to alienate" (ἐξηλλοτριωκέναι) a vacant land, which a certain Castor had legally inherited upon his mother's death, stating that they are actually "making use of their own force and self-will" (ἑαυτὰς βίαι καὶ αὐθαδίᾳ συνχρησαμένας)[171].

16. In a petition (14 BCE) to Nearchos, the rightful owner claims that his neighbor "has violently taken" (πρὸς βίας προσείληπται) his plot of land, forcing (see ἀποβεβίασται) a quarter of its produce away from him[172].

17. As we move to the 1st c. CE, an edict of Germanicus Caesar (19 CE) mentions how "lodging tents are being seized by force" (ἐπὶ σκηνώσεις καταλαμβάνεσθαι ξενίας πρὸς βίαν), while proscribing the violent appropriation of beasts of burden (see ὑποζύγια [...] πρὸς βίαν περιαιρεῖσθαι)[173].

18. In a letter of Sarapion (22 CE) to his brother, Dorion, the former makes use of the verb βιάζεσθαι to draw attention to the pressure used by some friends to have him enter Apollonios' household, that is, the chief usher at the prefect's court, which would eventually give him an advantage at the upcoming judicial inquiry (see ἐγὼ δὲ βιάζομαι ὑπὸ φίλω[ν] γενέσθαι οἰκιακὸς τοῦ ἀρχιστάτορος Ἀπολλωνίου)[174].

19. A petition of Apollonios (ca. 1st c. CE) to the Egyptian prefect describes Harsiesis as a "violent" (βίαιος) man, merely because of his seizure of a part of the house belonging to Apollonios (see ὑπάρχοντί μοι μέρει οἰκίας [...] ἐπικρατῆσαι)[175].

---

[171] S.R. LLEWELYN, "Forcible Acquisition", 139. See *Pap.* 1187.18–24 (BGU, IV.11, 325).

[172] See *Pap.* 1060.13–22 (BGU, IV.3, 93–94); and S.R. LLEWELYN, "Forcible Acquisition", 140.

[173] See *Pap.*, II.211.1–30 (ed. A.S. HUNT – C.C. EDGAR – D.L. PAGE, II, 76–77). See also σκηνάς, in Luke 16,9b.

[174] See *Pap. Oxy.* 294.16–19 (ed. B.P. GRENFELL – *al.*, II, 294–295). I.L.E. Ramelli ("Luke 16,16", 752) cites only this papyrological example in favor of her claim that, in Luke 16,16, βιάζεται is being used in the passive voice: "The meaning is identical to that of Luke 16,16", she argues, "and the date is close as well". Notwithstanding the roughly "close" date between the papyrus and the Gospel text, strictly speaking, in order to be really "identical" the Lucan verse would require the occurrence of the preposition ὑπό. Besides, a number of papyri could be equally cited in support either of an active or intransitive meaning as well. What the letter indicates with enough clarity, however, is rather the relationship of the verb βιάζεσθαι with the notion of becoming, literally, a member of a household, which implies metaphorically the idea of joining or entering into someone's house. See also φίλους, in Luke 16,9a; φιλάργυροι, in Luke 16,14; and the assonance around the root οἰκ-, in Luke 16,1.2.3.4.8.13.

[175] See *Pap. Oxy.* 3468.10–25 (ed. B.P. GRENFELL – *al.*, XLIX, 127–128); and S.R. LLEWELYN, "Forcible Acquisition", 130. See also the expression, τὰ ὑπάρχοντα αὐτοῦ, in Luke 16,1c.

20. In a letter (end of the 1st c. CE) by the strategos Paniscos, we read about βία in the context of the lightening of the burden of some tax-farmers who are "carried off by force" (τοὺς πρὸς βίαν ἀγομένους)[176].

21. In an agreement (131 CE), dealing with the partition of a deceased soldier's possessions between his wife and two fellow-soldiers to whom he owed money, the verb βιάζεσθαι is used to indicate a violation of the bequeathed inheritance (see ἐπίτροπος βιάσηται τὸ ληγᾶτον)[177].

22. An edict, enacted by Marcus Petronius Mamertinus (133–137 CE), refers to the improper claim that some soldiers are laying to the use of boats, animals and men, for without any warrant they are "dragging them away by violence" (πρὸς βίαν ἀποσπῶντας), chiefly out of "greed and injustice" (ἐπὶ πλεονεξίᾳ καὶ ἀδικίᾳ)[178].

23. A petition (164 CE or 196 CE) by a woman named Tamystha, presents the case of some relatives who, being coheirs with her of some other shares of her deceased father's house and palm-grove, are "violently laying claim" (βιαίως ἀντιλαμβάνονται) also to her portion[179].

24. In another petition (187–188 CE) addressed to the strategos of the Heracleid division, Ptolemaios, the plaintiffs (a court official of grains and his associate) complain that the inhabitants of the neighboring village of Theogenous "are violently laying claim to" (βιαίως ἀντελάβοντο) their land on the border of the lake[180].

25. About a century later, in relating the minutes of some legal proceedings before an epistrategos, a papyrus (280–281 CE) refers the request of an advocate to stop an "act of violence" (τὴν βίαν), which entails the coveting and seizing of animals belonging to some orphans, by a man named Syrion (see ἐποφθαλμιάσας τοῖς θρέμμασιν [...] ἥρπασεν), and their restoration to their legitimate owners[181].

As S.R. Llewelyn observes, most of the examples listed above illustrate a specific nuance of βία and its cognates, which recalls Plato's aforementioned general legal principle on "violent acts" (βίαια)[182]. Basically, these papyrological

---

[176] See *Pap. Oxy.* 44, XIV.420.12–16 (ed. A.S. HUNT – C.C. EDGAR – D.L. PAGE, II, 570–573).

[177] See *Pap. Wisc.* 14.14 (ed. P.J. SIJPESTEIJN, I, 54–55); and C. SPICQ, "βιάζομαι", *TLNT*, I, 291, n. 16.

[178] See *Pap.*, II.221.5–9 (ed. A.S. HUNT – C.C. EDGAR – D.L. PAGE, II, 110–111). See also φιλάργυροι, in Luke 16,14; and ἀδικία, in Luke 16,8.9.10.11.

[179] See *Pap.*, VII.284.9–10 (ed. A.S. HUNT – C.C. EDGAR – D.L. PAGE, II, 272–273); and S.R. LLEWELYN, "Forcible Acquisition", 140.

[180] See *Pap. Lond.* 924.10–14 (ed. F.G. KENYON – H.I. BELL, III, 134–135); and S.R. LLEWELYN, "Forcible Acquisition", 140.

[181] See *Pap.* VI.262.6–16 (ed. A.S. HUNT – C.C. EDGAR – D.L. PAGE, II, 208–211).

[182] See PLATO, *Leg.*, X.884a.1–4 (ed. J. BURNET, V, 327); and S.R. LLEWELYN, "Forcible Acquisition", 147.

occurrences indicate that the usage of someone's property without its owner's consent is generally understood as an act of "violence" or "force" being directed primarily against the property, and secondarily against its owner[183]. Whether the alleged wrongful acts occur because of confusion over some inheritance, or the assumption that the latter has been forfeited because of the owner's flight or failure to act in accordance with his obligation, or whether it is an actual abuse committed by someone against it in the absence of its lawful proprietor, the person accused has infringed the latter's right to control and manage his/her property by a non-consensual use of it[184]. The fact that such a use ignores the owner's will is sufficient for it to be defined as a "violent act" (βία)[185].

Since this property-owner *violation* is a legal concept that may be crucial for the understanding of the use of βιάζεσθαι in Luke 16,16, we shall pass now to a succinct examination of those lawsuits used in ancient Greece to institute legal proceedings against dispossession or disturbance of tenure, and which are directed against acts of violence.

b) Property-Owner Violation and Lawsuits Against "Violent Acts"

In Athenian law, the concept of βία is often used within the notion of a "lawsuit against acts of force"[186] (δίκη βιαίων), that is to say, a prosecution conducted against private "violent actions" (βίαια) that are directly linked with the *violation*, seizure, or use of property without its owner's knowledge or consent. For instance, S.R. Llewelyn notes:

This suit was brought against the person who sought to satisfy his claim through self-help (by seizure of movable property) before a legal decision. Such an act was not robbery but the individual was said to have acted with βία[187].

A similar delict could also be performed against immovable property. In this case, H. Lipsius maintains that it could be prosecuted also by a δίκη ἐξούλης, which nonetheless, just like a δίκη βιαίων, arose from disturbance of possession, applied to the seizure of moveable property (even slaves)[188], and imposed the penalty that the property be returned to the plaintiff together with a com-

---

[183] See S.R. LLEWELYN, "Forcible Acquisition", 133.152.

[184] See S.R. LLEWELYN, "Forcible Acquisition", 147.

[185] See PLATO, *Leg.*, X.884a.4 (ed. J. BURNET, V, 327); W. DAHLMANN, ῾Η βία, 26; and S.R. LLEWELYN, "Forcible Acquisition", 148.

[186] S.R. LLEWELYN, "Forcible Acquisition", 147.

[187] S.R. LLEWELYN, "Forcible Acquisition", 133, n. 8.

[188] Thus, A.Z. Bryen (*Violence*, 55) specifies: "Slaves were counted as property, and what we might call 'violence' against property and financial interests was in Roman Egypt called *bia* (which can translate to 'damage' or 'harm', but which always indicates harm not to full people but to inanimate objects, financial interests, and slaves)". See also ID., "Visibility", 192, n. 29.

pensation for any incurred losses[189]. The real or potential presence of violence (βία) was also a peculiar characteristic of the legal procedures for the theft of public and private property (see, e.g., the aforementioned papyrological examples, # 14.16–17.22 and 25), which generally involved a delict of seizure (ἁρπαγή or λωποδυσία) against the will of the owner[190]. Overall, nonetheless, S.R. Llewelyn points out:

> Whether a case of disputed possession was prosecuted by δίκη βιαίων, δίκη ἐξούλης or a third type of suit (e.g., δίκη κλοπῆς, δίκη οὐσίας, διαδικασία etc.), it is interesting to note the use of the terms βία and βιάζομαι in connection with property[191].

Moreover, whenever a delict entailing βία took place, intentionality was always of central importance[192], but to different kinds of deliberately violent intentions corresponded different kinds of legal lawsuits.

In this case also, ὕβρις was quite distinct from βία: in spite of their recurrent "dyadic relationship"[193] in classical Greek, whether in the literary source material studied above or in legal terminology, no intrinsic assimilation occurred between the two concepts[194]. As attested by a number of legal papyri, ὕβρις was considered to be a delict against an individual, which included bodily injuries, verbal insults and contemptuous conduct[195]. Specifically, A.Z. Bryen points out:

> In Roman Egypt, *hybris* has a narrower sense than it did in fifth-century Athens. *Hybris* can refer to violent or offensive conduct against a person's body (a beating or cudgeling, for instance), or against a person's reputation (insults, threats, or public abuse, Loidoria)[196].

---

[189] See H. LIPSIUS, *Das attische Recht*, II, 426; and S.R. LLEWELYN, "Forcible Acquisition", 148–149. As the latter (*Ibid.*, 148, n. 37) underlines, H. Lipsius himself eventually "concludes: 'The distinction between the jurisdictions of both (the δίκη ἐξούλης and the δίκη βιαίων) is at least for us not discernible; we must therefore be satisfied also here again to acknowledge the already repeatedly verified fact that Attic law was fond of offering different ways to prosecute the same offence'".

[190] See, e.g., PLATO, *Resp.* IX.574a.1–b.5 (ed. J. BURNET, IV, 573d); ID., *Leg.*, XI.933e.6 (ed. *Ibid.*, V, 392); *Ibid.*, XI.934c.2–4 (ed. *Ibid.*, V, 393); *Ibid.*, XII.941b.2–8 (ed. *Ibid.*, V, 398); *Ibid.*, XII.942a.1–4 (ed. *Ibid.*, V, 399); DEMOSTHENES, *Mid.*, XXI.44–45 (ed. O. NAVARRE – al., II, 33); D. COHEN, *Theft*, 16.60–68.83.92; and S.R. LLEWELYN, "Forcible Acquisition", 149–152.

[191] S.R. LLEWELYN, "Forcible Acquisition", 149.

[192] Thus, R. Taubenschlag (*The Law*, 444) observes: "Unintentional violence is inconceivable".

[193] F. D'AGOSTINO, *BIA*, 26.

[194] See, e.g., PINDAR, *Ol.*, XIII.10 (ed. W.H. RACE, I, 188–189); R.E. DOYLE, "ΌΛΒΟΣ", 293–303; F. D'AGOSTINO, *BIA*, 27–32; and A.Z. BRYEN, "Visibility", 189. Thus, F. D'Agostino (*Ibid.*, 27) points out: "Un rapporto così intrinseco tra ὕβρις e βία è di fatto assente nell'universo concettuale greco".

[195] See, e.g., R. TAUBENSCHLAG, *The Law*, 435–442.

[196] A.Z. BRYEN, *Violence*, 55. See also N.R.E. FISHER, *Hybris*, 36–85.122 (esp., 45).

Βία, however, could be directed also "against immovables disregarding the person"[197]. From Ptolemaic to Roman law, and all the way down to the Byzantine period, violence with respect to immovable property (e.g., the unlawful seizure or use of someone else's land) was considered as βία[198]. More precisely, as A.Z. Bryen remarks, the latter referred "to what we would understand as violence against property, forced appropriation of goods"[199]. In a number of the papyrological examples cited above, βία and its cognates are used to indicate one's entering someone else's property in order to take possession of it, in the absence of its owner, as opposed to theft or simple disturbance of domestic peace, which was rather an act of ὕβρις[200]. As S.R. Llewelyn points out, one can see how "the issue was generally not one of 'aggravated' theft"[201], but one entailing often the specific notion of *usucapio*[202].

Finally, while the specific intentional element of the perpetrator of "violent acts" (βίαια), namely, seizing or using a property belonging to another person without the latter's knowledge or consent, was prosecuted by a δίκη βιαίων, a subject acting deliberately against another person or his/her rights with an act of ὕβρις was brought to justice by a γραφὴ ὕβρεως[203]. But, in the former case not much weight was given to the moral character of the action[204]. Accordingly, βία was not as bad as ὕβρις: whereas the former was not really punishable in

---

[197] R. TAUBENSCHLAG, *The Law*, 443. See S.R. LLEWELYN, "Forcible Acquisition", 132.

[198] See, e.g., *Pap.* 1060.13–22 (BGU, IV.3, 93–94); *Pap. Lond.* 358.5–6 (ed. F.G. KENYON – H.I. BELL, II, 172); *Ibid.* 924.11–12 (ed. *Ibid.*, III, 134–135); *Pap. Tebt.* 278.26–27 (ed. B.P. GRENFELL – *al.*, II, 34); *Pap. Thead.* 15.4–7 (ed. P. JOUGUET, 98–99); *Ibid.* 23.4–11 (ed. *Ibid.*, 134–135); *Ibid.* 24.5–14 (ed. *Ibid.*, 136–137). See also R. TAUBENSCHLAG, *The Law*, 446–448; and S.R. LLEWELYN, "Forcible Acquisition", 131.

[199] A.Z. BRYEN, "Visibility", 189. See also *Ibid.*, 189, n. 21; and ID., *Violence*, 55.

[200] See R. TAUBENSCHLAG, *The Law*, 444, n. 73.

[201] S.R. LLEWELYN, "Forcible Acquisition", 147.

[202] See, e.g., the examples # 10.16.24 and, esp., # 11. Thus, S.R. Llewelyn ("Forcible Acquisition", 147) observes: "The legal proceedings of Hermias against the choachytai are central to the discussion of usucapio in Hellenistic law". See also ID., "The Introduction", 156–159. For a discussion of usucapio, see our following paragraph.

[203] See, e.g., R. TAUBENSCHLAG, *The Law*, 442–447; W. DAHLMANN, ʾΗ βία, 18–22. 38–41; and S.R. LLEWELYN, "Forcible Acquisition", 130–149.

[204] For instance, F. D'AGOSTINO (*BIA*, 28) comments: "L'elemento soggettivo del reato (se di reato si può in questo caso effettivamente parlare) non veniva assolutamente ad emergere. Ben diverso il caso della γραφὴ ὕβρεως, un azione che colpiva soggetti che avessero agito con una specifica intenzionalità [...] contro l'altro nel disconoscimento dell'altro, delle sue spettanze, delle leggi e del rispetto che ad esse è dovuto".

itself (only when it offended the person directly, as in the case of rape)[205], the latter was always to be punished because of its subtler and evil will[206].

c) "Violent Acts" and Acquisition by Usucapio or Ḥazaqah

In a number of the aforementioned papyri, the legal concept of the δίκη βιαίων associates βία with a direct "violation" or "forcible seizure of" property, i.e., a "violent act" directed primarily against possessions, and only secondarily, against their owners[207]. Not only βία and its cognates, but also ἁρπαγή and its related lexemes (cf. Matt 11,12) occur frequently in such a juridical context with reference to forcible acquisition[208].

Moreover, the petitions and lawsuits referred to in the papyri sometimes involve a principle known as "usucaption" (*usucapio*), which corresponds generally to what we would nowadays more commonly call "squatting" (lawyers tend to speak also of "squatter's rights", "adverse possession", "preemption", or "acquisitive prescription")[209].

For instance, a clear example of this is visible in the legal proceedings of Hermias (see example # 11, above), dating back to the 2nd c. BCE. Here is how S.R. Llewelyn expounds the instance:

---

[205] See, e.g., PLATO, *Resp.*, V.464e (ed. S.R. SLINGS, 196); F. D'AGOSTINO, *BIA*, 32; and S.R. LLEWELYN, "Forcible Acquisition", 147–148. According to the latter (*Ibid.*, 148), "Α δίκη βιαίων differs from a δίκη βίας": while the former implies generally a forcible entrance into someone else's estate or house and the seizure of something belonging to another, the latter may indicate also rape.

[206] See, e.g., LYSIAS, *Simon.*, III.6–8 (ed. L. GERNET – M. BIZOS, I, 69); ID, *Erat.*, I.2 (ed. *Ibid.*, I, 30); DEMOSTHENES, *Mid.*, XXI.46–47 (ed. O. NAVARRE – *al.*, II, 34–35); and F. D'AGOSTINO, *BIA*, 27–32. Thus, the latter (*Ibid.*, 29, n. 30) specifies: "nel linguaggio giudiziario greco ὕβρις denota di per sé un *malum* (se non sempre un delitto), mentre βία richiede ulteriori qualificazioni, per assumere il connotato di un atto illecito; ad es. [...] che sia βία ἀδίκως, cioè 'illegalmente violenta'". See, e.g., DEMOSTHENES, *Arist.*, XXIII.60 (ed. O. NAVARRE – *al.*, II, 125).

[207] As S.R. Llewelyn ("Forcible Acquisition", 147) specifies: "βία and its cognates were used in a context where possession of property had been acquired without the consent of its lawful owner or possessor".

[208] See, e.g., *Pap. Oxy.* 3240.11–12 (ed. B.P. GRENFELL – *al.*, XLV, 98); and S.R. LLEWELYN, *Ibid.*, 154, n. 65.

[209] Thus, S.R. Llewelyn ("The Introduction", 156) observes: "An analysis of Ptolemaic law shows that the use of force/violence (βία) characterised possession without an owner's consent and that the term and its cognates were used by an owner protesting acquisition by usucaption. Indeed, the frequency of reference to 'force/violence' in petitions complaining of the use of property without the owner's consent supports the conclusion that force/violence constituted the delict". See, e.g., Anderson, "pre-emption", 800; *Ibid*, "squatter", 963; and *WEAL*, "adverse possession" [accessed on-line: 05.07.2016], http://legal-dictionary.thefreedictionary.com/Squatters+rights.

The plaintiff in the case alleges in his petitions that the defendants were in possession of his property (house) by a forcible action and he seeks its return. From his perspective possession is illegal in that it was without his consent. The *choachytai* defend their claim on the property and their advocate, as one of the arguments on behalf of his clients, appeals to the legal principle of *usucapio* to justify their claim[210].

As the Latin etymology of the term implies, usucaption means, literally, "holding by use" (*usus-capere*). Specifically, it is "a method of acquiring ownership by civil law"[211] through the uninterrupted use of a property, without the explicit knowledge or consent of its lawful owner, for a specified length of time. As is clear from Hermias' legal proceedings, such a "violent" use of someone else's possession, in Ptolemaic law, "created ownership"[212], invalidating any appeal against the "possessor's adduced legal ground of possession"[213].

For the most part, the conditions required for *usucapio* in the Ptolemaic legal system were not so different from those of Roman and Jewish laws[214]. According to "the earliest Roman code of laws, known as the XII Tables"[215] (451–449 BCE), the usucaption of moveable and immoveable properties required undisputed possession for at least one and two years, respectively, for it to be recognized as such[216]. In Jewish Law, however, the occupier was entitled to retain an immoveable property against the claims of the previous legal owner if he could prove his undisturbed possession for at least three consecutive years[217]. This same legal concept granting title to property was

---

[210] S.R. LLEWELYN, "Forcible Acquisition", 154. Thus, the author (*Ibid.*, 137, n. 24) notes that the plaintiff's possession of the house was actually undisputed for a long time: "In the hearing of year 51 the defendants' advocate states that they and their parents had undisturbed possession for 35 years (*UPZ* II 161 col. 3 *l.* 57). In the hearing of year 54 two figures are given: 37 years of undisturbed possession of the property within the *choachytai*'s families (*UPZ* II col. 162 *l.* 21) and 88 years since the plaintiff or his father had lived in Diospolis (*UPZ* II 162 col. 5 *l.* 32)". See also ID., "The Introduction", 157–159.

[211] E.H. WARMINGTON, ed., *Remains of Old Latin*, III, 460, n. 3.

[212] S. LLEWELYN, "The Introduction", 160.

[213] S. LLEWELYN, "The Introduction", 159.

[214] Thus, S. Llewelyn ("The Introduction", 164) specifies: "Details may have differed between the three legal systems (e.g. prescribed periods and the effect of distance on acquisition), but there remained substantial agreement in the basic conditions of it".

[215] B. COHEN, *Jewish and Roman Law*, 15. See, e.g., S. LLEWELYN, "The Introduction", 160.

[216] See *Tabu.* VI.3 (ed. E.H. WARMINGTON, III, 460–461); and B. COHEN, *Jewish and Roman Law*, 19. Moreover, as S. Llewelyn ("The Introduction", 160, n. 13) notes, in Roman Law, *usucapio* was one of those privileges which "only applied to Roman citizens and to property susceptible to Quiritian ownership [...] e.g., Italic land including *coloniae* located outside Italy which possessed *ius Italicum*. Peregrines and provincial lands [...] were not covered by it".

[217] See, e.g., mBB 3.1–6; mPea 3.6; mQid 1.3; 1.5; P. BLACKMAN, ed., *Mishnayoth*, IV, 179–180, ns. 1–2; and B. COHEN, *Jewish and Roman Law*, 19. In Jewish Law, as S. Llewelyn

known as *ḥazaqah* (חזקה). The latter was a general technical term used to denote possession in the Tannaitic legal system (10–220 CE)[218], but in its Mishnaic understanding, as B. Cohen remarks, it actually meant "entering into or taking possession of land by some physical act"[219]. As regards the nature of such an act, this could entail, for instance, the occupancy and use of an agricultural plot of land, such as a vineyard, the gathering and enjoyment of the harvest, or its enclosing with a fence[220]. Even in this case, slaves were regarded as a kind of property, which could be acquired legally by usucaption[221].

An important element of this principle was that the claim to ownership of an estate was vested in a period of one's undisturbed possession of it[222]. The period, as we have seen, could vary from one to three years, depending on the kind of jurisdiction at hand, and also on the plaintiff's alleged "presence in or absence from the situation of the disputed property"[223]. As J. Neusner observes, in the context of the Jewish Law, the assumption underlying the acquisition by *ḥazaqah* was that the owner would contest possession within that specific period of time:

Anything which is valuable and is allowed to remain in the hands of a person for a period of three years is assumed to belong to that person. If there were a valid claim against the squatter, any other party would have made it within the specified time[224].

A biblical example of *usucapio* is that narrated, for instance, in Gen 21,22–34[225]. The account stresses the fact that, although Abraham has been previously invited by king Abimelech to "dwell" (see Gen 20,15: ישב and κατοικεῖν) in a land, in the Negeb of Judah, which happens to be in Gerar's domain and thus under the king's political control, he is now simply "sojourning" (see vv. 23.34: גּוּר and παροικεῖν) in it, and will do so "for many days" (v. 34: יָמִים רַבִּים; and

---

("The Introduction", 162) observes, "The effect of geographical/political distance on *ḥazaqah* was a matter of dispute". See *Ibid.*, 162–163.

[218] See B. COHEN, *Jewish and Roman Law*, 291, n. 45.

[219] B. COHEN, *Jewish and Roman Law*, 291. See, esp., mBB 3.3; and S. LLEWELYN, "The Introduction", 161–164.

[220] See B. COHEN, *Jewish and Roman Law*, 291, n. 47; and S. LLEWELYN, "The Introduction", 162.

[221] See, e.g., mQid 1.5; P. BLACKMAN, ed., *Mishnayoth*, III, 451–452; B. COHEN, *Jewish and Roman Law*, 289–291; and F. UDOH, "The Tale", 316, n. 28.

[222] See S.R. LLEWELYN, "The Introduction", 154–167.

[223] S.R. LLEWELYN, "Forcible Acquisition", 155. See also R. TAUBENSCHLAG, "Periods and Terms", 174.

[224] J. NEUSNER, *The Talmud*, XXX, 58. See S.R. LLEWELYN, "The Introduction", 162.

[225] See, esp., the *NIV.ASB*, 36–37; but, also, K. GRAY, *Elements of Land Law*, 282–311; and A.M. KITZ, "Undivided Inheritance", 601–618.

ἡμέρας πολλάς)[226]. This means that he is only a temporary resident, with no original ownership rights to it[227]. In addition, however, the episode relates that, before the actual "purchase" of the field (see vv. 27–31), Abraham claims ownership of a portion of it, as a result of the fact that he had been "using" that plot by digging a well into it (see v. 25)[228]. More precisely, Abraham here defends his right to access the well, complaining that Abimelech's servants are trying to take the well away from him, probably by means of the same legal principle that he used in the first place, namely, *usucapio*.

Literally, the servants are said to have "seized" (וַיִּגְזְלוּ) or "taken away" (LXX: ἀφείλαντο)[229] the well from Abraham "with force"[230]. The TO on Gen 21,25 interprets the text by using the Aramaic expression אנסו, which can be translated thus: "took forcible possession of (seized)"[231] it. The verb אנס, in fact, means primarily, "to force, rape [...] compel"[232] or "to do violence"[233], but is used often in a way that resembles the aforementioned juridical use of βιάζεσθαι. Thus, S.R. Llewelyn points out:

> The Aramaic אנס (*'anas*) and its Hebrew cognates confirm not only that it was used in a legal context but also that it had a semantic range similar to that of βιάζομαι in Greek. For example, at Esth 1,8 the term has the meaning "force", "compel"; at Dan 4,6 "oppress", "distress"; at Tg. Isa 21,2 the term translates the Hebrew בגד which can mean "to cheat or to act treacherously in matters of property". At Tg. Isa 5,7 the term translates the Hebrew מִשְׁפָּח – the context implies a meaning opposite to "justice". However, at *m.Kil* 7.6 ha'anas is used to refer to the usurper who takes possession of property which is not his. Again, a ruling of the Qumran community states (*CD* 16.13): "Let no man vow to the altar anything unlawfully acquired (אנוס)". The term was also used to denote the agents of the Roman *Annona* who confiscated land. Jastrow [...] defines the 'annas as "one who is in possession

---

[226] Thus, J.G. Janzen (*Abraham*, 76) remarks: "It is as though, not taking the offer of 20,15 at face value, Abraham has dug the well on the sly and kept quiet about it like a poacher on someone else's land". See also J.C.L. GIBSON, *Genesis*, II, 106.

[227] See, e.g., BDB, "גּוּר", 157; and Thayer, "παροικέω", 489.

[228] The LXX on Gen 21,25 reads plural, "wells of water" (φρεάτων τοῦ ὕδατος). See G.W. WENHAM, *Genesis*, II, 89, n. 25b. The latter (*Ibid.*, 94) observes: "The return of Abimelek and Phicol to the land of the Philistines [see v. 32] implies not only that Abraham had a legal claim to a well but that he had *de facto* possession of the region near it (cf. 12,6)". The treaty, in fact, settles the issue of the violation of Abraham's right to the well by ratifying it. As the author (*Ibid.*, 94) continues, "By granting Abraham rights to a well, Abimelek had made it possible for Abraham to live there permanently and had acknowledged his legal right [...] the promises of land and descendants at last seem on their way to fulfillment".

[229] See also the *Vg.*: *abstulerant.*

[230] On the meaning of the verb גזל, G.W. Wenham (*Genesis*, II, 92) suggests, "'seize', 'steal with force', 'the forceful tearing away of an object from its owner' by a stronger person usually illegally, cf. [Gen] 31,31; Lev 19,13; Job 20,19; Mic 2,2".

[231] Jastrow, "אֲנַס", I, 86. For the Aramaic text of Gen 21,25 see Sperber, I, 30.

[232] M. SOKOLOFF, *DJPA*, "אנס", 66.

[233] Jastrow, "אֲנַס", I, 86.

of property bought from one who obtained it by force or confiscation, owner of reclaimable property"[234].

On the basis of such considerations, S.R. Llewelyn suggests that a juridical interpretation of the violence saying in terms of the legal principle of *usucapio* is possible even at the level of its "Semitic *Vorlage* and that linguistic inter-ference may have influenced its translation into Greek"[235]. The scholar humbly expresses regret at having been unable to find a use of '*anas* with reference to *hazaqah*; however, at least two occurrences can be cited in support of this hypothesis in the rabbinic literature (bBB 45a and tBQ 55a).

Moreover, as far as the Greek text of the *logion* goes, it may be noted how comparable temporal expressions (i.e., ἀπό ... μέχρι/ἕως) occur in both the aforementioned papyrological examples of *usucapio* and the "violence passage"[236]. In other words, the characteristic temporal dimension of the saying, together with the eschatological and economical perspective of chap. 16 of Luke's Gospel, may indicate that, behind its idea of violence for or against (see εἰς αὐτὴν βιάζεται) the kingdom of God, what could be really at stake is its "acquisition by force or more particularly by *usucapio*"[237].

This seems perfectly possible for the two following reasons. First, as S.R. Llewelyn points out,

That the kingdom of Heaven/God could metaphorically be conceived as a property subject to possession is shown in a number of other *logia* of the Jesus-tradition. For example, certain persons could be said to hold keys to it (Matt 16,19; 23,13; par. Luke 11,52) and the kingdom

---

[234] S.R. LLEWELYN, "Forcible Acquisition", 161–162. See also Jastrow, "אנס", I, 86; and M. GIL, "Land Ownership", 40–45.

[235] S.R. LLEWELYN, "Forcible Acquisition", 162. Thus, the scholar argues: "there is an Aramaic rendering of the *logion* which reflects the legal concepts and associations in Greek". As we have already seen (see Chap. II, pp. 67–68), G. Dalman, G. Schrenk, and M. Black do translate βιάζεσθαι with the verbal root אנס in their conjectural Semitic texts. See G. DALMAN, *Die Worte*, 115; G. SCHRENK, "βιάζομαι, βιαστής", *TDNT*, I, 612–613; M. BLACK, *An Aramaic Approach*, 116, n. 1; *Ibid.*, 211, n. 2; and ID., "The Kingdom", 290, n. 2.

[236] W. STENGER, "βιάζομαι, βιαστής", *EDNT*, I, 216. See, esp., S.R. LLEWELYN, "Forcible Acquisition", 154–156.162; and the expressions: "from the former times until now" (ἀπὸ τῶν ἔμπροσθεν χρόνων μέχρι τοῦ νῦν), in *Pap. Taur.* 1.6.1 (ed. U. WILCKEN, II, 65); "until John; since then" (μέχρι Ἰωάννου· ἀπὸ τότε), in Luke 16,16a–b; and "from the days of John the Baptist up to now [...] up to" (ἀπὸ δὲ τῶν ἡμερῶν Ἰωάννου τοῦ βαπτιστοῦ ἕως ἄρτι [...] ἕως), in Matt 11,12a.13.

[237] S.R. LLEWELYN, "Forcible Acquisition", 156. See also ID., "The Introduction", 166. Thus, the author ("Forcible Acquisition", 162) concludes: "At Matt 11,12 βιάζεται (passive) describes an action to acquire possession of the kingdom by force, i.e., without God's consent. The para-tactic extension of the verse (καὶ βιασταὶ ἁρπάζουσιν αὐτήν) further confirms the interpretation as does also the temporal expression, ἀπὸ δὲ τῶν ἡμερῶν Ἰωάννου τοῦ βαπτιστοῦ ἕως ἄρτι. The *logion* manifests the fundamental legal association between the use of force and the act itself. The original *logion* would have read thus (or similar): *From the days of John the Baptist until now the kingdom of Heaven is acquired by force and violent men plunder it*".

is said to belong to the poor, to those persecuted for righteousness and to children (Matt 5,3.10; 19,14)[238].

Second, the element of "economic belief" is very well known in the ancient world. To "believe" and to be a "creditor" (by making loans) are two concepts that are linguistically linked in several languages (e.g., Latin, Akkadian, etc.)[239]. Almsgiving was the best means of delivering goods to God: the hand of the poor was like a conduit (an ATM!) used for transferring funds from earth to Heaven[240].

Thus, when we apply this reasoning to our passage and its context, the saying in Luke 16,16 could be interpreted in the following way: by placing money into God's kingdom, by way of a physical act, such as, almsgiving, even without seeking God's own explicit consent, one could claim the right of ownership of some portion of the "divine estate" by the principle of *usucapio*. In other words, "all" (πᾶς) would have a chance to deposit their belongings into God's own lawful property, "using" such a "parcel" for an undisturbed period of time. At the hour of death, all will have to give account of their earthly management of those goods which belong to God and be judged accordingly, as either worthy or unworthy of an eternal abode[241].

C. The Narrower Semantic Field of the "βία-terms" in Second Temple Period

Thus far, our initial inquiry into the widest semantic field of the "βία-lexemes" has shown how the Greek terminology is used in both the literary and papyrological

---

[238] S.R. LLEWELYN, "Forcible Acquisition", 154, n. 66. Generally, in the NT, the kingdom of God is described mainly as a royal palace, having not only a key, but also a way leading to it, a door, rooms or dwellings where one can store one's treasure and banquet halls where one may recline and drink at table for a meal. See, e.g., Matt 6,20–24; 7,13–14; 8,11; 12,25; 16,19; 19,21; 25,1.10; 26,29; Mark 3,24–25; 10,21; 14,25; Luke 11,17; 12,33; 13,18.20.23–29; 14,15; 18,22; 22,16.18.29–30; John 10,1.6–7.9–10; 14,2; Acts 14,27; 1Cor 16,9; 2Cor 2,12; 5,1–2; Col 4,3; and Rev 3,7–8.20. Moreover, it entails the local sense of right and left (see Matt 20,21.23; Mark 16,19; Acts 7,55–56; and Heb 8,1) or outside and inside (see Matt 8,12; and Luke 13,28). See also S. AALEN, "'Reign' and 'House'", 220.228–240 (esp. 231); K. KOCH, "Offenbaren", 158–165; P.S. CAMERON, *Violence*, 146.153; and D.C. ALLISON, Jr., *Constructing Jesus*, 171–179.

[239] See G.A. ANDERSON, "Faith and Finance", 29–31. For the themes of poverty, riches and almsgiving in the intertestamental period (5th c. BCE – 1st c. CE), as evinced by apocryphal, pseudepigraphic, and Dead Sea Scrolls literature, see, e.g., C.L. BLOMBERG, *Neither Poverty Nor Riches*, 91–101.

[240] See G.A. ANDERSON, "Faith and Finance", 30; and N. EUBANK, "Storing up Treasure", 77–92.

[241] See, e.g., the crisis motif and the eschatological theme of the two parables sandwiching chap. 16 of Luke's Gospel, as well as the echo prompted by them upon our saying.

source material, in a variety of contexts, and with a plurality of both positive and negative meanings. Moreover, the examination of the philosophical, mythological and legal implications deriving from the usage of these terms, as well as their actual connections with the notions of wealth and property, has also launched us in a new hermeneutic direction, which attaches the idea of violence to law, justice, time, and the acquisition of immovable properties belonging to someone else.

In this second stage of our analysis we shall attempt to determine how such a wide-ranging sematic field is actually narrowed in the Greco-Jewish literature of the Second Temple Period (STP). To do this, we will take into consideration specifically the way in which the verb βιάζεσθαι and its substantival (βία), adjectival (βίαιος) and adverbial (βιαίως) cognates are used in Aquila, Symmachus, Theodotion, the LXX, and other Greek-speaking Jewish sources as well, such as, pseudepigraphic literature, Philo's and Josephus' writings. At its different stages, we shall take into account the MT, the Targumim, as well as the Syriac and Latin translations, and thus consider a complex of terms and ideas associated with βία-terminology, as they appear also in Hebrew, Aramaic, and Latin.

The study will reveal how, in this case also, the most common and distinctive meaning characterizing the plurality of ambiguous nuances of the βία-terms can be summarized by the concept of "strength", and how this occurs sometimes in connection with the notions of love and wealth, in ways that recall the context of Luke 16,16[242].

A rather peculiar and significant connection between the ideas of "strength" (ἰσχύς) and "mammon" (ממון) will emerge particularly from the Satt on Deut 6,5 and its related rabbinical writings. This background material will provide us with a "broad reference"[243] that can help us find a solution to the basic problem of how to combine *force* with *love* and the *kingdom of God*, in Luke 16,16[244].

I. The Greek Jewish Literature: Ambiguity and "Strength"

In a recent article, W. Linke observes that, in those LXX texts which do have a Hebrew counterpart, the same Greek verb is used to translate as many as seven Hebrew verbs (i.e., הרס, חזק, כבש, עצר, פצר, פרץ, and תפש)[245]. From this comparison, and after a discussion of the different meanings behind the LXX's and other translations' uses of the verb βιάζεσθαι, the biblical scholar eventually concludes that the Greek verb has a wider semantic field than its

---

[242] See, esp., 4Macc 2,8; Luke 16,14.16–17; and G. GIURISATO, "Come Luca", 462–466.

[243] P.S. CAMERON, *Violence*, 133.

[244] See I.H. MARSHALL, "The Hope", 230, n. 47.

[245] See W. LINKE, "'Gwałt'", 93.

Hebrew equivalents[246], and that their only common denominator is "the use of force, coercion or pressure"[247]. The study of the ancient Greek OT translations, apocryphal and Hellenistic Jewish writings, which is presented below, confirms his result.

1. The Jewish OT Greek Versions, LXX and Apocrypha

The analysis of the uses of the βία-based terms in OT studies shows mainly how their extant occurrences carry various meanings, which can ultimately be grouped under the general idea of "strength" and can sometimes be related to the concepts of wealth and possessions.

a) The Use of the βία-verb, its Prefixed Forms and Translations

Commenting on the Greek versions of the Hebrew OT texts, by Aquila, Symmachus, and Theodotion, W. Linke observes:

"Outside of the Septuagint, ancient translations of the Bible do not form an independent basis for a better understanding of the verb βιάζομαι. Translators used the verb not as a reference to any specific Hebrew term, but to the idea of the use of violence or coercion. This is consistent with the practice of translation and understanding of the meaning of the word in the Septuagint"[248].

Specifically, in his OT translation, Aquila resorts to the use of the verb βιάζεσθαι 4x (Ps 68[69],5; Isa 10,2; Ezek 18,16; and 22,29), to that of the substantive βία 3x (Ps 61[62],11; Isa 61,8; and Ezek 18,16), and to that of the adjective βίαιος other 3x (Gen 10,8; and Jer 37[30],12.15)[249].

Of these ten occurrences, seven are used in conjunction with the Hebrew verb, גָּזַל or the corresponding noun, גֵּזֶל, meaning to "tear away, seize"[250] (see LXX: ἁρπάζειν) and "robbery"[251] (see LXX: ἅρπαγμα or ἁρπαγή), respectively[252], whereas three of them refer either to "a strong, valiant man" (see גִּבּר: Gen 10,8; see also LXX: γίγας) or to an "incurable wound" (see אָנוּשׁ: Jer 37[30],12.15)[253]. As W. Linke notes, in Ps 68(69),5, "it is the Hebrew verb

---

[246] According to the author the phenomenon may be actually due to the fact that the LXX often replaces the wealth of Hebrew terms with a considerably more technical and poorer Greek terminology. See W. LINKE, "'Gwałt'", 94; and ID., "Anioł", 75–94.

[247] W. LINKE, "'Gwałt'", 100.

[248] W. LINKE, "'Gwałt'", 102–103. For a discussion of the some of the occurrences of the verb in these translations, see *Ibid.*, 101–103. For a review of the main features characterizing Aquila's translation, see *Ibid.* 101, n. 36.

[249] See J. REIDER – N. TURNER, *An Index*, 42.

[250] BDB, "גָּזַל", 159.

[251] BDB, "גֵּזֶל", 160.

[252] See Pss 61[62],11; 68[69],5; Isa 10,2; 61,8; Ezek 18,16[2x]; and 22,29.

[253] See BDB, "גִּבּוֹר", 150; *Ibid.*, "אָנַשׁ", 60; and J. REIDER – N. TURNER, *An Index*, 42. Thus, Aquila never uses the βία-terminology to translate חָמָס. In Ps 61[62],11, moreover, the

צמת to be translated"[254], meaning either to "force to silence"[255] or to "annihilate"[256], while in Ezek 18,16 and 22,29 βιάζεσθαι stands for הבל (i.e., "to hold by a pledge")[257] and עשׁק (i.e., "to oppress [...] practice extortion")[258], in that order. Finally, it may be noted how Aquila uses the term ἰσχύς to translate Hebrew terms meaning both "strength" and "wealth", such as, חַיִל (see Jer 15,13; and 26[46],22) and אוֹן (see Hos 12,4), but also the noun חֶזְקָה (see Jonah 3,8; and Dan 11,2)[259]. The latter means, "strength, force, violence"[260], but with a different vocalization can also refer to the aforementioned technical term for *usucapio* (חֲזָקָה)[261].

As concerns Symmachus and Theodotion, we can observe briefly how they use the verb βιάζεσθαι to translate or amend any of the following Hebrew verbs, indistinctly: אפק (i.e., "to force, compel oneself", in the hithpael: see, e.g., 1Sam 13,12)[262], נכר (i.e., to acknowledge or "be acquainted with", in the hiphil: see, e.g., Job 24,17)[263], סאן (i.e., to "tread, tramp": see, e.g., Isa 9,4)[264], צוה (i.e., to "charge, command": see, e.g., Isa 38,1)[265] עצר (i.e., to "detain": see, e.g., Judg 13,15)[266], and פרץ (i.e., "to urge someone on, to force someone": see, e.g., 2Kgs 5,23)[267]. In particular, as W. Linke remarks, Theodotion uses βιάζεσθαι "there where it appears in the LXX, although less frequently (cf. Judg 13,15; and 2Kgs 5,23)"[268]. As far as we are concerned, within this

---

invitation is not to lust after or set one's "heart" (לֵב or καρδία) on "wealth" (חַיִל or πλοῦτος). See Luke 16,1.14–15.19.21–22; and *Ibid.*, 278.

[254] W. LINKE, "'Gwałt'", 101. See F. FIELD, *Origenis Hexaplorum*, II, 205.

[255] W. LINKE, "'Gwałt'", 101.

[256] BDB, "צָמַת", 856.

[257] BDB, "הָבַל", 286. See F. FIELD, *Origenis Hexaplorum*, II, 814.

[258] BDB, "עָשַׁק", 798. See F. FIELD, *Origenis Hexaplorum*, II, 829; and W. LINKE, "'Gwałt'", 101.

[259] See, e.g., F. FIELD, *Origenis Hexaplorum*, II, 613.708.929.959.986; BDB, "אוֹן", 20; *Ibid.*, "חַיִל", 298; and J. REIDER – N. TURNER, *An Index*, 120.

[260] BDB, "חֶזְקָה", 306.

[261] See, e.g., BDB, "חֶזְקָה", 305; and *Ibid.*, "חֲזָקָה", 306

[262] BDB, "אָפֵק", 67. The LXX on 1Sam 13,12 translates אֶתְאַפַּק as ἐνεκρατευσάμην, thus pointing to the power of self-control and mastery over one's passions. Cf. F. FIELD, *Origenis Hexaplorum*, I, 507, n. 21; Thayer, "ἐγκρατεύομαι", 167; and W. LINKE, "'Gwałt'", 101–102.

[263] BDB, "נָכַר", 647. See F. FIELD, *Origenis Hexaplorum*, II, 45–46; L.J. LIEBREICH, "Notes", 400–401; and W. LINKE, "'Gwałt'", 102.

[264] BDB, "סָאַן", 684. See F. FIELD, *Origenis Hexaplorum*, II, 448; and W. LINKE, "'Gwałt'", 102.

[265] BDB, "צָוָה", 845. See F. FIELD, *Origenis Hexaplorum*, II, 505. Inadvertently, W. Linke ("'Gwałt'", 102) refers here his reader to Isa "38,14", in place of 38,1.

[266] BDB, "עָצַר", 783. See F. FIELD, *Origenis Hexaplorum*, I, 445, n. 34; and W. LINKE, "'Gwałt'", 102.

[267] *HALOT*, II, "פּרץ", 972. See F. FIELD, *Origenis Hexaplorum*, I, 661–662; and W. LINKE, "'Gwałt'", 102.

[268] W. LINKE, "'Gwałt'", 102.

large variety of meanings the latter instance (2Kgs 5,23) is particularly worth mentioning, mainly insofar as the concept of violence occurs here in close relation with that of money[269].

Finally, in the LXX, the verb βιάζεσθαι occurs 17x in its plain form[270], and 16x in its prefixed forms: παραβιάζεσθαι (7x)[271], ἐκβιάζεσθαι (5x)[272], καταβιάζεσθαι (2x)[273], διαβιάζεσθαι (1x)[274], and ἀποβιάζεσθαι (1x)[275]. Moreover, its nominal-root (βία), with the adjectival (βίαιος) and adverbial (βιαίως) cognates, occur 30x[276], 12x[277], and 3x[278], respectively. What follows is an analysis of the aforementioned βία-root verb in both canonical and apocryphal Greek OT writings. As we shall see, in this case also, the meanings of these occurrences vary considerably, and embrace negative, neutral, as well as positive nuances.

Thus, on the *negative* side of the spectrum, βιάζεσθαι can indicate a hostile physical violence, such as, homosexual assault (see, e.g., Gen 19,9)[279] or rape (see, e.g., Deut 22,25.28; Esth 7,8; and Sus 1,19)[280]; a presumptuous and obstinate

---

[269] In fact, in 2Kgs 5,23, Naaman "urges" or "forces" Gehazi, namely, Elisha's servant, to take two talents of silver. This verse shall be noted again later, when dealing with the LXX's occurrences of the βία-lexemes.

[270] See Gen 33,11; Exod 19,24; Deut 22,25.28; Judg (A) 13,15.16; 19,7 (= B); 2Sam 13,25.27; Esth 7,8; 2Macc 14,41; 4Macc 2,8; 8,24; 11,25; Sir 4,26; and 31,21. These and the following statistics are based on all "βία-based" lexemes as they occur in Rahlfs' edition of the Septuagint, which includes also those writings that do not form part of the accepted Canon of Scripture. See, e.g., E. HATCH – H.A. REDPATH, *A Concordance*, I, 218; and R.H. CHARLES, ed., *The Apocrypha*, I, vii–xi.

[271] See Gen 19,9; Deut 1,43; 1Sam 28,23; 2Kgs 2,17; 5,16; Amos 6,10; and Jonah 1,13.

[272] See Judg (B) 14,15; Ps 37(38),13; Prov 16,26; Wis 14,19; and Sus 1,19.

[273] See Gen 19,3; and Exod 12,33.

[274] See Num 14,44.

[275] See Prov 22,22.

[276] See Exod 1,13.14; 14,25; Neh 5,14.15.18; 1Macc 6,63; 3Macc 2,28; 3,15; 4,7; 4Macc 11,26; 17,2.9; Od 4,6; Wis 4,4; 5,11; 7,20; 17,5.17; 19,13; Sir 20,4; PsSol 17,5; Hab 3,6; Isa 17,13; 28,2; 30,30; 52,4; 63,1; Ezek 44,18; and Dan 11,17.

[277] See Exod 14,21; 3Macc 4,5; 4Macc 2,15; 5,16; 7,10; Ps 47(48),8; Job 34,6; Wis 13,2; 19,7; Isa 11,15; 58,6; and 59,19.

[278] See Esth 3,13g; Isa 30,30; and Jer 18,14.

[279] See, e.g., G.J. GORDON, *World Biblical Commentary*, II, 56; and J. MONTGOMERY BOICE, *Genesis*, 618.

[280] In Deut 22,25.28 the violence is compared with the murder of one's neighbor (see Deut 22,26) and paralleled to the "hatred" (see Deut 22,13.16) against a woman, her "humiliation" (see Deut 22,24.29) or "defamation" (see Deut 22,14.19). In Sus 1,19, as E.C. Bissell (ed., *The Apocrypha*, 457) notes, the verb ἐξεβιάζοντο "means, first, to drive out; then, to wrest from, which is nearly the sense here. They used violence against her, for the purpose of obtaining her acquiescence in their vile designs". Similarly, in Esth 7,8, it occurs in the context of an alleged subjugation (שבכ) of a woman, and is thus explained by the Aramaic translations with the intention of laying down with her (בכש). See, e.g., L.B. PATON, *Esther*, 263; *HALOT*, I, "בכש", 460; *Ibid.*, II, "שכב", 1486–1488.1993; and

rebellion against God's command (see, e.g., Num 14,44; and Deut 1,43)[281] or a direct transgression of the law (see, e.g., 4Macc 8,24)[282]; an enticing utterance of empty idolatrous words (see, e.g., Ps 37[38],13)[283] or the skilful activity of an artist, who strives to enhance the beauty of his abominable representation (see, e.g., Wis 14,29)[284].

However, the verb can also express a strenuous (*neutral*) effort to stand and struggle against the current of a river (see, e.g., Sir 4,26)[285], for instance, or to row

---

B. GROSSFELD, *The Two Targums*, 77–78.178. For the Aramaic text of the latter, see Sperber, IV, 198. However, it is worth noting how, although βιάζεσθαι does occur in the context of a rape, the OT text prefers sometimes to use other verbs to express it (e.g., ταπεινόω and ענה; or κραταιόω and חזק). This is the case, for instance, in 2Sam 13,12.14: the verb is used here to indicate Absalon's urging (ἐβιάσατο αὐτόν) of king David, Amnon, and all of David's other sons, to come and join his feast.

[281] See, e.g., G.B. GRAY, *Numbers*, 166–167; J. SCHARBERT, "זור", *TDOT*, IV, 47–48; E.H. MERRILL, *Deuteronomy*, 85, n. 58; and I. DRAZIN, ed., *Targum Onkelos to Numbers*, 167, n. 75.

[282] From the proximate context (see 4Macc 8,25), the verb βιάζεσθαι in 4Macc 8,24 appears to be associated with one's violation or transgression (breaking) of the "law" (νόμος). Thus, according to *Codex Sinaiticus* (S) and the Syriac version. The *Codex Alexandrinus* reads "temple" (ναός) instead. See, e.g., R.L. BENSLY, ed., *The Fourth Book*, xvii; Swete, III, 743; and Rahlfs, I, 1169. Only if the Maccabean martyrs were to disobey the law, they would think or say, "Let us not do violence to necessity" (μὴ βιαζώμεθα τὴν ἀνάγκην), in the sense of not striving against the "pressure" (ἀνάγκη) set in motion by the instruments of torture and the fear of death (see 4Macc 8,25) caused by the tyrant. However, ready obedience to the law is "more forcible" (βιαιοτέραν) than any necessity (see 4Macc 5,16b).

[283] Based on the parallelism of the verse (see οἱ ζητοῦντες τὴν ψυχήν μου [מְבַקְשֵׁי נַפְשִׁי] in parallel with οἱ ζητοῦντες τὰ κακά μοι [וְדֹרְשֵׁי רָעָתִי]; and ἐξεβιάσαντο [וַיִּנָקְשׁוּ] in parallel with ἐλάλησαν ματαιότητας [דִּבְּרוּ הַוּוֹת]), the "violence" (see *Vg.*: *"facere vim"*) in Ps 37[38],13 is compared with one's enemies' speaking empty words. As Thayer ("ματαιότης", 393) remarks, ματαιότης is often "the Septuagint for הֶבֶל [...] also for שָׁוְא [...] *what is devoid of truth and appropriateness*". These "violent" words may concern either a prompt to idolatrous worship, since as *HALOT* ("הבל", I, 237) specifies, הֶבֶל or הֲבָלִים indicates "idols, things that do not really exist" (see, e.g., Deut 12,29–13,19), or some loot of properties (see, e.g., √ נקש, in Ps 109,11; הַוּוֹת, in Prov 10,3). The Hebrew (נקש) and Aramaic (עבד פחין) expressions here refer to the image of someone laying snares against another. See, e.g., C.A. BRIGGS – E.G. BRIGGS, *Psalms*, I, 342–343.

[284] See, e.g., J.D.G. DUNN – J.W. ROGERSON, ed., *Eerdmans Commentary*, 773; and D. WINSTON, *The Wisdom*, 269.

[285] See, e.g., P.W. SKEHAN – A.A. DI LELLA, *The Wisdom*, 177. For the Hebrew text of Sir 4,26, see P. BOCCACCIO – G. BERARDI, ed., *Ecclesiasticus*, 2. See also *HALOT*, I, "עמד", 841.

hard against the power of the sea storm and back to dry land (see, e.g., Jonah 1,13)[286], or even to carry bones out of a house (see, e.g., Amos 6,10)[287].

Finally, the verb is also used to convey the *positive* power of the natural appetite for food, as it impels or motivates a person to endure the toil of daily work (see, e.g., Prov 16,26)[288], as well as the pressure exerted to get people to change their mind and do something (see, e.g., 2Kgs 2,17). This latter kind of "persuasive" violence, in particular, can be *either negative*, as when someone is forced to eat against dietary laws and moderation (see 4Macc 11,25; and Sir 31,21), *or positive*, as when the pressure upon someone to eat occurs in the context of a generous reception and entertainment of guests (see, e.g., 2Sam 13,12.14) and an invitation to stay overnight (see, e.g., Judg [A] 13,15.16; and 19,7).

The "violence" implied in these latter instances can be expressed also through prefixed forms of the verb βιάζεσθαι, and sometimes strengthened by the presence of the Hebrew adverb, מְאֹד[289].

Overall, one must agree with W. Linke[290], in noting that the LXX uses the verb βιάζεσθαι and its prefixed forms to translate no less than the following seven Hebrew verbs: הרס (1x: Exod 19,24), כבש (1x: Esth 7,8), תפש (1x: Deut 22,28), חזק (2x: Deut 22,25; and Exod 12,33), עצר (2x: Judg 13,15–16), but primarily פצר (6x: Gen 19,3.9; 33,11; Judg 19,7; 2Kgs 2,17 and 5,16), or

---

[286] See, esp., J.A. BEWER, *Jonah*, 38–40; E.B. ZVI, *Signs of Jonah*, 74; and A. NICACCI – M. PAZZINI – R. TADIELLO, *Il libro di Giona*, 14.63–64. As to the Hebrew text, see, e.g., BDB, "חתר", 369; *HALOT*, I, "חתר", 365; D. STUART, *Hosea-Jonah*, 463; R.F. PERSON, Jr., *In Conversation with Jonah*, 147–148; T.M. BOLIN, *Freedom Beyond Forgiveness*, 85–86; W.D. TUCKER, Jr, *Jonah*, 40; and J.M. SASSON, *Jonah*, 130.

[287] See, e.g., *HALOT*, I, "סרף", 770; J. DE WAARD, "Translation Techniques", 344; and G.F. ZEOLLA, ed., *Analytical-Literal Translation*, 142. Closer to the LXX translation (παραβιῶνται), perhaps, there exists a Jewish medieval interpretation according to which the much disputed meaning of the Hebrew hapax (וּמְסָרְפוֹ) can also refer to "one who is inflamed with zeal for him". See I.D. MARKON, ed., *Commentarius*, 37; Barthélemy, III, 670; and S.M. PAUL – F.M. CROSS, *Amos*, 215, n. 21.

[288] See, e.g., H.T. CRAWFORD, *Proverbs*, 331.334; R.E. MURPHY, *Proverbs*, 118, n. 26a; J.W. MILLER, *Proverbs*, 80; and G. TAUBERSCHMIDT, *Secondary Parallelism*, 99.197–198.228.

[289] See, esp., παραβιάζεσθαι (1Sam 28,23) and καταβιάζεσθαι (Gen 19,3; and Exod 12,33). In Gen 19,3, the reading with καταβιάζεσθαι (i.e., κατεβιάζετο αὐτούς) is supported by the *Codex Cottonianus Geneseos* (D) and *Codex Bodleianus Geneseos* (E), as opposed to the *Codex Alexandrinus* (παρεβιάζετο αὐτούς), and is preferred by Rahlfs. See, e.g., Swete, I, 28; and Rahlfs, I, 25. Ironically, in Gen 19,3, the Hebrew text uses the same verb (פצר), together with the addition of מאד, as in Gen 19,9, thus proleptically contrasting Lot's positive urging of the angels to enter, with the sodomite men's hostile pressure upon Lot. See G.J. GORDON, *World Biblical Commentary*, II, 54. Similarly, in Exod 12,33, the Hebrew Text uses the verb, "to be(come) strong" (חזק), which as W.H.C. Propp (*Exodus 1–18*, 411) comments, "also has the nuance 'urge' (cf. 2Sam 24,4; 2Kgs 4,8; perhaps Jer 20,7). Previously, *ḥzq* described the 'strengthening' of Pharaoh's heart. Now, ironically, his people are 'strong' to release Israel". See, e.g., Exod 4,21; 7,13.22; 8,15; 9,12.35; 10,20.27; 11,10; and 14,4.8.17.

[290] See W. LINKE, "'Gwałt'", 93–100.

פרץ (3x: 1Sam 28,23; and 2Sam 13,25.27), which is either a by-form or a meta-thesis of the former[291]. In the Aramaic translations of the same texts (i.e., TO, TJI, TJII, and CN), these verbs are often rendered by other verbs (e.g., דחף, דחק, זרז, פייס and esp. תקף), which generally express the ideas of pressure, persuasion, haste and strength, sometimes also in connection with money (see, e.g., פסק)[292].

Moreover, it should be observed that in some of these Greek OT occurrences, the βία-root verbal lexemes relate also (more or less directly) to the idea of breaking through some physical boundaries, so as to enter a place belonging to someone else (see, e.g., Exod 19,24; and 2Macc 14,41), the use of wealth (see, e.g., Gen 33,11; 2Kgs 5,16.23; and 4Macc 2,8), and the possession or dis-possession of properties (see, e.g., Judg [B] 14,15; and Prov 22,22).

For instance, in Exod 19,24, Moses goes up to the top of the Lord's mountain and enters the Lord's presence (see Exod 19,20–25), but both priests and people are charged solemnly "not to force their way and go up towards the Lord" (μὴ βιαζέσθωσαν ἀναβῆναι πρὸς τὸν θεόν: Exod 19,24), which, as the context itself clarifies, implies not to approach the Lord past those barriers (boundaries, lines) that had been set out for them (see μήποτε ἐγγίσωσιν πρὸς τὸν θεόν: Exod 19,21), lest the Lord "break out against them"[293]. Likewise, in 2Macc 14,41, the verb of violence is placed in the context of breaking through the outer door of the courtyard (see τὴν αὐλαίαν θύραν βιαζομένων)[294], and since locked doors have the function of protecting some property from

---

[291] See, e.g., *HALOT*, II, "פצר", 954; *Ibid.*, II, "פרץ", 971–972; Thayer, "παραβιάζομαι", 479; BDAG, "παραβιάζομαι", 759; W.F. SMELIK, *The Targum of Judges*, 609; E. VAN STAALDUINE-SULMAN, *The Targum*, 464; F.M. CROSS – al., *Qumran*, 149; and D.T. TSUMURA, *The First Book of Samuel*, 629. For the use of βιάζεσθαι as a translation of פרץ, see also 2Kgs 5,23, both in the Theodotian version and the Lucian recension of the text. See also W. LINKE, "'Gwałt'", 99. In addition to the aforementioned Hebrew verbs, one must also mention the LXX rendering of זיד, חתר and שרף (or סרף) with παραβιάζεσθαι (3x: Deut 1,43; Amos 6,10; and Jonah 1,13), of נזל with ἀποβιάζεσθαι (1x: Prov 22,22), and of עפל with διαβιάζεσθαι (1x: Num 14,44).

[292] See also M. SOKOLOFF, *DJPA*, "דחף", 143; *Ibid.*, "דחק", 143; *Ibid.*, "זרז", 181; *Ibid.*, "פייס", 430; *Ibid.*, "פסק", 441; and *Ibid.*, "תקף", 590.

[293] See Exod 19,12.23; *HALOT*, I, "נבל", 173; and BDAG, "ἀφορίζω", 158. See also the pun in Exod 19,22.24 (פן־יפרץ בהם). The *Vg.* reads "*ne transeant terminos*", thus underlining the nuance. Other variants read "*transeat*" (A) and "*transcendant*" (G). The former Floren-tine *Codex Amiatinus* limits the same "violent" action only to the people (cf. sing.), to the exclusion of the priests; the latter *Pentateuchus Turonensis* keeps the plural form (thus, including the priests), but prefers to translate with the verb "to climb over". See, e.g., *CCLEE*, "*transcendo*", 1557; and the critical apparatus in Weber, 104.

[294] See, e.g., the Syriac translation of the Peshiṭta: ܟܕ ܗܘܐ ܕܢܦܬܚ ܬܪܥܐ (i.e., "was [about] to open the gate") (2Macc 14,41), from √ܦܬܚ (ptaḥ), which as J.P. Smith (ed., *A Compendious Syriac Dictionary*, "ܦܬܚ", 470) writes, means: "to open, unlock, unbar [...] remove [...] to be taken by storm". See also W.M. THACKSTON, *Introduction*, 216.

unwanted intruders, the intended meaning is that of trespassing into someone else's property.

With respect to the use of the verb in connection with money and properties, the following examples should suffice.

In Gen 33,11, βιάζεσθαι is used to express the insistence with which Jacob "urges" (ἐβιάσατο αὐτόν) his brother, Esau, to accept a "gift" of his (lit. "blessing": εὐλογία and ברכה). The idea of "violence" (βία) is placed here in the context of whatever properties Jacob has got (people, sheep and cattle: more than 550 animals)[295], and thus the intention behind this insistence is that of "buying" Esau off with it, so as to be kindly accepted by him (see Gen 32,21)[296].

In Judg (B) 14,15, the Philistines invite Samson's wife to seduce/deceive him so that he may reveal to her the solution to the riddle. They also threaten to burn her, together with her father's house, since they start to fear that she may have actually invited them there to force/impoverish (ἐκβιάσαι) them[297].

Similarly, in Prov 22,22a, the violence expressed by the verb is directed towards money or possessions, insofar as it exhorts to do no violence to the poor beggar (see μὴ ἀποβιάζου πένητα πτωχὸς γάρ ἐστιν; and *Vg.*: *non facias violentiam*) in the sense of not robbing (lit. stealing away [ἀπό-] from) him[298].

---

[295] See, e.g., Gen 32,10–11.14.15–24; and 33,9–10.

[296] It may be noted how Jacob's famous fight with ("violence to"?) God is placed in this same context (see Gen 32,25–33). An analogous kind of "pressure", namely, that of forcing someone to accept some monetary "gift" (see "two silver talents" [διτάλαντον ἀργυρίου]: 2Kgs 5,23), is visible also in 2Kgs 5,16 (καὶ παρεβιάσατο αὐτὸν λαβεῖν), and in 2Kgs 5,23. Although in the latter verse the LXX skips the translation of the verb of violence, this is nonetheless witnessed by the correction of the Alexandrian Codex (A¹), by Origen's and Lucian's recensions (cf. καὶ ἐβιάσατο αὐτόν), as well as by the aforementioned Theodotian translation or that of the other OT versions (see *Vg.*: *coegit eum*; TJ: ואתקיף ביה; and the *Peshiṭta*: ܐܠܨܗ). See, e.g., the critical apparati in Swete, I, 752; and Rahlfs, I, 704. For the Aramaic and Syriac texts, see Sperber, I, 283; and IPS, II.4, 97–98. As T.R. Hobbs (*2 Kings*, 66) remarks, "Naaman's urging and Elisha's refusal to accept any gift echoes the encounter between Jacob and his alienated brother (Gen 33:11). Esau, however, finally accepts the gift".

[297] Judg (B) 14,15 reads: ἢ ἐκβιάσαι ἡμᾶς κεκλήκατε;, while the MT has הלירשנו, i.e., Qal or Piel inf. cnstr. of ירש, with pronominal 1st pers. com. plur. suffix, meaning "to take possession of, dispossess, be heir to someone, oust someone from his possessions" (*HALOT*, I, "ירש", 441). Moreover, the A codex, in place of ἐκβιάσαι has: ἢ πτωχεῦσαι ἐκαλέσατε ἡμᾶς; (Judg [A] 14,15). The verb πτωχεύω means "to be or become poor", and is probably a translation of the conjectural reading, "הלהורישנו" (*BHS*, 428, n. 15c), or "הֲלְהָרִשֵׁנִי", i.e., the hifil inf. cnstr. of רוש. See *Ibid.*, I, "ירש", 441; and II, "רוש", 1209. Finally, the TJ on Judg 14,15 reads: הלמסכינותנא קריתון לנא הלכא. W.F. Smelik (*The Targum of Judges*, 573) translates the text as follows: "Have you invited us here to impoverish us?", from √ מסכן, namely, "to make poor, impoverish" (*HALOT*, "מְסְכֵּן", I, 605). Similarly, the *Vg.* has: *ut spoliaretis* (i.e., "so that you [plur.] may rob [us]?"). See *CCLEE*, "spolio", 1450. For the Aramaic text, see Sperber, I, 77.

[298] In fact, the verb of violence is used here by the LXX to translate the MT, "do not rob the poor" (אַל־תְּגְזָל־דָּל). Thus, according to the BDB ("גזל", 159), the verb means, to "seize,

As concerns the latter verse, a couple of points are also worth mentioning here, as a result of their resemblance with the Lucan saying and its context. In the parallelism of Prov 22,22, the poor is likened to the "weak" lying "at the gates" (ἐν πύλαις)[299], and the verb ἀποβιάζεσθαι is compared with the verb ἀτιμάζειν, which implies a deprivation of honor or shame[300]. In the following verse (Prov 22,23), then, by repeating the same verb (see וְקָבַע אֶת־קֹבְעֵיהֶם נָפֶשׁ)[301], the HT suggests that, in keeping with the law of retaliation, the Lord shall do to the robbers what they themselves have done to the poor, namely, rob them of their lives (ψυχή)[302].

Finally, a text which deserves special attention is 4Macc 2,8. This apocryphal text is very close to Luke 16,16, its immediate context, and their association with the ideas of monetary love and laws[303].

The verse is part of a section (4Macc 2,6–14) which aims at demonstrating how, by following the commandments, "reason masters the 'emotions that hinder

---

rob [...] take violent possession of [...] plunder". See, e.g., R.N. WHYBRAY, *Wealth and Poverty*, 93–94.98.114–115. While the Hebrew text uses 2x the same word for poor (דל), the LXX differentiates between πένης and πτωχός. As the BDAG ("πένης", 795) suggests, the former pertains "to being obliged to work for a living, but not being reduced to begging, for the latter πτωχός, q.v., is ordinarily used".

[299] See Luke 16,20. Lit., ἀστενής means, "the one who is without strength or power".

[300] As the BDAG ("ἀτιμάζω", 148) specifies, the verb means "to deprive someone of honor or respect, to dishonor/shame, an especially grievous offense in the strongly honor-shame oriented Semitic and Gr-Rom. societies". See ἀισχύνομαι, in Luke 16,3.

[301] The *BHS* (p. 1304) suggests emending the text into וְעָקַב אֶת־עֹקְבֵיהֶם, with the verb "to betray" (עקב). However, we agree here with *HALOT* (II, "קבע", 1062) in affirming that for Prov 22,23, the MT should be kept as it is and "קבע Arm. for קבע [...] to seize, take, grab [...] should be accepted".

[302] Thus, according to the original hand of *Codex Sinaiticus*, whereas the *Codex Alexandrinus* and the later correctors of *Codex Sinaiticus* have "justice" (δίκην), in place of "soul" (ψυχήν). See, e.g., the critical apparati in Swete, II, 459; and Rahlfs, II, 220. Although in v. 22, the actual term for the "thing" being "taken" or "stolen" (see גזל: Prov 22,22; and קבע: Prov 22,23) "away from" (ἀπό) the poor is not explicitly mentioned, its parallelism with v. 23 would make of βίος an excellent candidate (see ἀποβιάζομαι: Prov 22,22; and ψυχήν: Prov 22,23).

[303] Thus, C.L. Brenton (*The Septuagint*, 229) translates 4Macc 2,8: "A man, therefore, who regulates his course by the law [τῷ νόμῳ], even if he be a lover of money [φιλάργυρός], straightway puts force upon his own disposition [βιάζεται τὸν αὐτοῦ τρόπον]; lending to the needy without interest, and cancelling the debt of the incoming Sabbath". See, esp., the recurrences of the lexemes, "money-lovers" (φιλάργυροι), "violates" (βιάζεται), and "law" (νόμος), in Luke 16,14.16.17. Thus, G. Giurisato ("Come Luca", 462) notes "sorprendenti punti di contatto" between these two verses, not only at their lexical level, but also as regards their common invitation to conform oneself to God's "economic" laws, triumph over one's love of or servitude to money, and master the temptation of laying with someone else's wife (see Gen 39,7–20; Exod 20,17; and 4Macc 2,2–9). See also *Ibid.*, 462–466.

one from justice'"[304]. "Justice" (δικαιοσύνη) is one of the four forms of wisdom – the other three being "insight" (φρόνησις), "manliness" (ἀνδρεία), and "temperance" (σωφροσύνη) – through which pious reasoning bears sway over the passions (see 4Macc 1,14.18). Thus, having dealt with the vices that go against temperance, namely, gluttony (4Macc 1,31–35) and lust (4Macc 2,1–5)[305], in 4Macc 2,6–9 the author moves on to deal with that which hinders justice, specifically, "greed and love of money"[306].

The guiding principle leading one to act justly is always the Torah. Thus, D.A. deSilva remarks:

> While love of money might make one set financial gain above social relationships and dealing with fellow Jews according to God's standards, the Torah commands that money be lent to the poor within the community without interest (Exod 22,25; Deut 23,19–20) and that all debts be cancelled in the seventh year [...] The prohibitions against gleaning the field and gathering up the last of the grapes (Exod 23,10–11; Lev 19,9–10), which provide a sort of welfare for the poor who come to glean (Ru 2,2–3), also cause one to choose justice over greed[307].

Specifically, the aforementioned laws on interest-free almsgiving[308], debt-cancelling[309] and gleaning[310], guide the "lover of money" (φιλάργυρος: 4Macc 2,8) towards justice: by following them, such a person does violence or "puts force upon his own disposition"[311] (βιάζεται τὸν αὐτοῦ τρόπον)[312], and is thus "ruled

---

[304] D.A. deSilva, *4 Maccabees*, 60. Thus, deSilva (id., "The Human Ideal", 62–63) notes: "The author gives extended consideration to how particular commandments within that Law assist reason to tame and master particular unruly passions (1,31–2,19) as evidence for his claims about the human potential for virtue and the value of the Torah in the pursuit of virtue. The ability of pious Jews to follow particular statutes of the Torah provides the proof that reason can master the passions by the power of self-control (1,31–35; 2,1–6), but the Torah also provides the discipline – the exercise regimen – that trains and empowers a person's reason to overcome his or her inclinations and desires (2,7–9a, perhaps also vv. 9b–14). Doing conscientiously what the Torah stipulates makes one work against one's own greed or stinginess or against one's feelings of dislike or enmity". Similarly, see Luke 16,16–17.29.31.

[305] See, e.g., S.D. Moore – J.C. Anderson, "Taking it Like a Man", 258.

[306] D.A. deSilva, *4 Maccabees*, 61.

[307] D.A. deSilva, *4 Maccabees*, 61. See also D. Sweet, "'Noble Sweat'", 18. For a study of the concept and function of the Law/Torah in 4Macc, see, e.g., P.L. Reddit, "The Concept", 249–270.

[308] See, e.g., Exod (LXX) 22,24(25); Lev 25,35–37; Deut 15,7–11; and 23,20(19)–21(20). See also S. Stein, "The Laws", 161–170; and E. Neufeld, "The Prohibition", 355–412.

[309] See, e.g., Lev 25,8–17; and Deut 15,1–3.9; 31,10.

[310] See, e.g., Exod (LXX) 23,10–11; Lev 19,9–10; 23,22; and Deut 24,19(21)–21(23).

[311] C.L. Brenton, *The Septuagint*, 229. A. Pietersma and B.G. Wright (ed., *A New English Translation*, 531) translate differently: "one overpowers one's own bent".

[312] According to the BDAG ("τρόπος", 1017), the term τρόπος means "the way in which a person behaves or lives, ways, customs, kind of life [...] conduct, character". Thus, in his

by the law through reasoning" (ὑπὸ τοῦ νόμου κρατεῖται διὰ τὸν λογισμόν)[313]. In other words, if his reasoning is "regulated by the law" (τῷ νόμῳ πολιτευόμενος)[314], the "lover of money" (φιλάργυρος: 4Macc 2,8) is in the position of "mastering" (ὁ λογισμὸς κρατῶν)[315] his love (i.e., φιλαργυρία), one of the most violent passions (or affections) of the soul (see 4Macc 1,26; 2,15)[316]. Although devout reasoning cannot by itself eradicate the passion completely, it enables one at least not to be enslaved to it (see 4Macc 3,2–5) and so master it[317].

Finally, the following two verses (see 4Macc 2,10–12) illustrate how reason can also rule over the passions of conjugal, parental or friendly love, and eventually overcome even the hatred of one's enemy (see 4Macc 2,13–14)[318]: the one who lives by the law will not destroy the enemy's crops, even in times of war (see, e.g., Deut 20,19–20), but shall rescue and preserve the latter's property (see, e.g., Exod 23,4–5; and Deut 22,1–4)[319].

To recapitulate, then, devout reasoning, namely, a reason that is informed and guided by the wisdom contained in the laws of the Torah (see 4Macc 1,15–17), is able "to control even the most violent/strongest passions" (βιαιοτέρωον δὲ παθῶν κρατεῖν)[320]. One of these is that same "love of money" (φιλαργυρίας) which leads the Pharisees to scoff at Jesus (Luke 16,14), after having listened to his words on the use of riches and the incompatibility between love of God and love of mammon (Luke 16,1–13), and which inspires Jesus himself to

---

commentary on 4Macc 2,8, G. Scarpat (*Quarto Libro*, 137) observes in the verb of violence a certain power of persuasion: "il λογισμός ha la forza (βιάζεται) di convincere a prestare χωρὶς τόκων e a cancellare il debito all'inizio del settenato". For the Greek text and his Italian translation, see *Ibid.*, 130–131.

[313] 4Macc 2,9.

[314] 4Macc 2,8.

[315] 4Macc 2,9.

[316] For the significant textual differences in 4Macc 2,15, see the critical apparati in Swete, III, 732; and Rahlfs, I, 1160. The former specifies how the Alexandrian (A) reading, φιλαρχίας, reappears in later corrections (S^c.b) of the original version (S*) of *Codex Sinaiticus*, dating to the 7th c. See Swete, I, xxi. Thus, D.A. deSilva ("The Sinaiticus", 60) notes: "In S, the reader encounters φιλαργυρίας ('love of money') in a list of the 'more violent passions' where Rahlfs has elected to read φιλαρχίας ('love of offices': 2,15). The reader of S encounters the more mundane economic interests among the list of vicious and debasing traits, something that might have convicted a broader segment of the readership than would have been the case for readers of those ancient manuscripts (preferred by Rahlfs) naming the 'love of offices', which suggests the ambitious social climbing [...] a preoccupation limited to the elite".

[317] See, e.g., the expression, "without love of money" (ἀφιλάργυρος ὁ τρόπος), in Heb 13,5. See also 1Tim 3,3; and Luke 16,13.

[318] See, e.g., P.L. REDDIT, "The Concept", 252. See also our figure # 2; and Luke 16,13.18.

[319] See D.A. DESILVA, *4 Maccabees*, 61–62.

[320] 4Macc 2,15. See also 4Macc 2,16–20; Luke 16,16.17.29.31; and D.A. DESILVA, *4 Maccabees*, 62–63.

address them and utter the very saying in Luke 16,16 (Luke 16,15–31). If read in this light, the fact that Jesus points to the law and the prophets (see Luke 16,16–18.29.31) in the context of the proper use of wealth would suggest an attempt on his part to appeal to the Pharisees' own devout reasoning, so as to help them master this strong passion of theirs.

b) The Use of the substantive βία, its Cognates and Translations

Overall, in the aforementioned Greek speaking religious Jewish literature[321], the substantive βία occurs 30x.

Of these, it appears 17x in the context of some kind of oppressive, burdensome, and even physically violent doing of *man*, such as, the rigorous slavery and hard labor of Israel in Egypt (2x: Exod 1,13.14); their deportation and oppression by the Assyrians (1x: Isa 52,4); the heavy extortion or levy for food allowance by the Persian governors (3x: Neh 5,14.15.18)[322]; the warlike campaigns and diplomatic operations of Antiochus III (1x: Dan 11,17)[323] and the treacherous overtaking of the city of Jerusalem by the young king, Antiochus V, under the control of Lysias (1x: 1Macc 6,63); the hostile measures taken by the tyrant Ptolemy IV for any antagonist to his decrees, such as: death sentence (1x: 3Macc 2,28), repression by spear (1x: 3Macc 3,15), harassment and deportation (1x: 3Macc 4,7), as well as physical tortures by fire and other instruments (3x: 4Macc 11,26; and 17,2.9); the justice-making of an abusive or wicked judge (1x: Sir 20,4)[324]; the act of stealing by proud and sinful Gentiles (1x: PsSol 17,5)[325]; and finally, also the girding of one's loins in a way contrary to the law, by the Levitical priests (1x: Ezek 44,18)[326].

---

[321] Namely, the LXX and other related documents of second Temple period as contained in Rahlfs' edition.

[322] Although these texts present several problems of translation, βία has something to do here both with "bread" (לחם) and the former acts of extortion made by those who held the office of "governor" (פחה) before Nehemiah, which may be understood as a "pit used as a grave […] metaphorically for ruin" (*HALOT*, II, "פחת", 924), "calamity" (BDB, "פחת", 809). See L.W. BATTEN, *Ezra and Nehemiah*, 248; H.G.M. WILLIAMSON, *Ezra, Nehemiah*, 233–234.241–245; *BHS*, 1438; and Rahlfs, I, 931.

[323] See, e.g., J.A. MONTGOMERY, *Daniel*, 432–435.441–442.

[324] See P.W. SKEHAN – A.A. DI LELLA, *The Wisdom of Ben Sira*, 300.381–383; I. BALLA, *Ben Sira*, 152–154.264–265; and S. BUSSINO, *The Greek Additions*, 403–404.

[325] See R.B. WRIGHT, ed., *The Psalms of Solomon*, 178–179.

[326] The LXX text with βία may here be a scribal error for βιζα, namely, a transcription of the HT (בזיע). See, e.g., W. ZIMMERLI, *Ezekiel 2*, 449, n. 18b. However, later halakhic commentaries (e.g., Rashi's) mention girding one's loins "with the sword", as opposed to the Levitical peaceful function. See, e.g., G.A. COOKE, *Ezekiel*, 484; and S.H. LEVEY, ed., *The Targum of Ezekiel*, 120, n. 15.

Additionally, βία occurs 9x in the context of some kind of force or powerful element of *nature*, such as, the wind (2x: Wis 4,4; and 7,20)[327] or the whoosh of air caused by the rush of wings (1x: Wis 5,11); the regular recurring motion of flowing waters (1x: Wis 17,17) or the rumbling of heavy downpours and hailstones (3x: Isa 17,13; 28,2; and 30,30)[328]; and the bright flames of fire (1x: Wis 17,5) or thunderbolts (1x: Wis 19,13).

Finally, it occurs 4x in connection with some kind of powerful action of *God* (or a divine agent). For instance, it is used when God causes the Egyptian charioteers to drive their chariots with difficulty, heaviness, or hardship (1x: Exod 14,25); when marching confidently, in royal attire, as a blood-stained warrior coming to save (1x: Isa 63,1); and as He dissolves or shatters mountains and hills (2x: Od 4,6; and Hab 3,6). With regard to the original Hebrew text, the substantive (βία) is used to translate or paraphrase lexemes, such as, פֶּרֶךְ (Exod 1,13.14)[329], אֶפֶס (Isa 52,4)[330], פַּחַת (Neh 5,14.15.18)[331], תֹּקֶף (Dan 11,17)[332],

---

[327] See D. WINSTON, *The Wisdom*, 175.

[328] See, e.g., R.L. TROXEL, *LXX-Isaiah*, 260–261.

[329] According to the BDB ("פֶּרֶךְ", 827), the term means, "harshness, severity", but as specified by *HALOT* (II, "פרך", 968), can also mean, "violence, slavery". Elsewhere, the LXX translates it with μόχθος (see., e.g., Lev 25,43.46), which for Thayer ("μόχθος", 419) can denote, "hard and difficult labor, toil [...] distress".

[330] According to the BDB ("אֶפֶס", 67), the term means, "end, extremity [...] extreme limits [...] used esp. hyperbolically [...] בְּאֶפֶס for nought". See also *HALOT*, I, "אפס", 79. Elsewhere, the LXX translates the expression, בְּאֶפֶס, differently: e.g., ἐν κενῇ ἐλπίδι (i.e., "in vain/empty hope": Job 7,6) and ἐν πολλοῖς (i.e., "with much": Prov 26,20).

[331] According to the *HALOT* (II, "פחת", 924), the term means, a "pit used as a grave [...] metaphorically for ruin". See also "fig. of calamity" (BDB, "פחת", 809). Although the MT reads, "charcoal" (פֶּחָם), and the scholarly "general agreement" (H.G.M. WILLIAMSON, *Ezra, Nehemiah*, 242) follows the critical apparatus of the *BHS* (p. 1438), which suggests "governor" (פֶּחָה), L.W. Batten (*Ezra and Nehemiah*, 248) notes: "βία represents a different Heb. word in almost every place it is used. It is therefore difficult to ascertain what the Gk. translators had before them. It is certain, however, that they had neither לחם nor הפחה. In v. 18, we have ἄρτους τῆς βίας, so βία represents some word which was read in place of פחה in all three places". Thus, פַּחַת seems to be a good selection, not only on account of the graphic similarity with פֶּחָה, but also because it coincides with its attested construct form. See, e.g., 2Kgs 18,24; Isa 36,9; and Hag 2,21.

[332] According to the BDB ("תֹּקֶף", 1076), the Hebrew term means, "power, strength, energy". See *HALOT*, II, "תקף", 1786–1787. Elsewhere, the LXX translates it also with ἰσχύς, which as Thayer ("ἰσχύς", 309) specifies means, "ability, force, strength, might". See, e.g., Esth 10,2; and Theodotion's version of Dan (Θ) 11,17, in Rahlfs, II, 930.

יֶזַע (Ezek 44,18)[333], כַּבִּיר (Isa 17,13; and 28,2)[334], and כְּבֵדָת (Exod 14,25)[335]. Hence, it may be noted here that, in spite of the too often misused association between them, βία is never utilized by the LXX to translate the Hebrew term, חָמָס, which "in the OT is used almost always in connection with sinful violence"[336].

In a similar way, the occurrences of βίαιος in Rahlfs' edition of the LXX and other related documents of the STP show analogous results.

The adjective occurs altogether 12x. Out of these, it is used 7x to qualify the power of some *natural* element: for instance, the scorching East wind, drying up and dividing the Red Sea before the Israelites (2x: Exod 14,21; and Isa 11,15) or shattering the ships of Tarshish (1x: Ps 47[48],8); the rushing water of seas and rivers (3x: Wis 13,2; 19,7; and Isa 59,19); as well as, the human passions controlled or directed by devout reasoning (1x: 4Macc 2,15). Additionally, 4x it describes some kind of oppressive and burdensome doing of *man*, physically (e.g., the swift and cruel deportation of Jewish elders, women, and children to the outskirts of Alexandria by Ptolemy IV: 3Macc 4,5)[337], metaphorically (e.g., the human bargains as bonds of wickedness or fetters of slavery: Isa 58,6)[338], and ironically (e.g., the ready obedience to the divine law by Eleazar: 4Macc 5,16; and 7,10). Finally, it occurs 1x as an expression of *divine* activity, when God inflicts the painful arrow of his wrath on Job (1x: Job 34,6)[339].

---

[333] According to the *HALOT* (I, "יֶזַע", 405), the term means, "clothes that cause sweat Ezek 44,18". See also BDB, "יֶזַע", 402. The TJ on Ezek 44,18 connects the verse with the girding of the "hearts" (לבהון), as opposed to their "loins" (הרציהון). See, e.g., G.A. COOKE, *Ezekiel*, 484; S.H. LEVEY, ed., *The Targum of Ezekiel*, 120, n. 15; and Sperber, I, 373–374.

[334] According to the *HALOT* (I, "כביר", 458), the term means, "strong, mighty [...] great things, much". See also BDB, "כַּבִּיר", 460. Elsewhere, the LXX translates it with other adjectives, such as, βαρύς (see, e.g., Job 15,10), ἀναρίθμητος (see, e.g., Job 31,25), ἔντιμος (see, e.g., Isa 16,14), and δυνατός (see, e.g., Job 36,5), i.e., "able, powerful, mighty, strong [...] mighty in wealth and influence" (Thayer, "δυνατός", 160).

[335] According to the BDB ("כְּבֵדָת", 459) and *HALOT* (I, "כבדת", 456–457), the term means, respectively, "heaviness [...] (difficulty)" and "hardship".

[336] R.L. HARRIS, "חָמָס", *TWOT*, I, 297. Thus, in his study of the term, the author (*Ibid.*, 297) continues: "It [i.e., חָמָס] does not refer to the violence of *natural* [emphasis added] catastrophes or to the violence as pictured in a police chase on modern television. It is often a name for extreme wickedness". See also BDB, "חָמָס", 329; and W.E. MOORE, "ΒΙΑΖΩ, ΑΡΠΑΖΩ", 537, n. 1.

[337] See, e.g., J.H. CHARLESWORTH, ed., *The Old Testament*, II, 509.

[338] See, e.g., BDB, "אגדה", 8; BDAG, "στραγγαλία", 947; and B. HROBON, *Ethical Dimension of Cult*, 178–180.195–205.

[339] See, e.g., F. DELITZSCH, *Job*, II, 247–248.

With regard to its Hebrew equivalents, βίαιος is used by the LXX to translate either specific attributes, such as, עַז (Exod 14,21)[340] and צַר (Isa 59,19)[341], or substantives, such as, עֹצֶם (Isa 11,15)[342], רֶשַׁע (Isa 58,6)[343], and אֱנוֹשׁ (Job 34,6)[344].

Finally, the same thing can be said also as concerns βιαίως. This occurs 3x: once to describe a violent *human* action, namely, the death sentence of all Jews by Ahasuerus at Hamman's instigation (Esth 3[B],13[7])[345]; a second time to qualify the *natural* force of the wind impelling a watercourse (Jer 18,14)[346]; and a third time to refer to *God*, as he launches his flaming thunderbolts (Isa 30,30).

---

[340] According to the BDB ("עַז", 738), the term means, "strong, mighty, fierce". See also "עַז נֶפֶשׁ greedy Isa 56,11, Sir 40,30" (*HALOT*, I, "עַז", 804). For the Hebrew text of Ben Sira, see, e.g., P.C. BEENTJES, *The Book of Ben Sira*, 71.114.161. Elsewhere, the LXX translates it with adjectives denoting either the idea of power and strength (e.g., ἰσχυρός: Judg 14,14.18; Prov 21,14; and Isa 43,16; κραταιός: Ps 59[58],4; and Cant 8,6; δυνατός: Ps 18[17],18; σφοδρός: Neh 9,11; and σκληρός: Isa 19,4), or that of arrogance and boldness (e.g., αὐθάδης: Gen 49,3.7; and ἀναιδής: Deut 28,50; Isa 56,11; and Dan 8,23).

[341] According to the BDB ("צַר", 865), the term means, "narrow, tight [...] כִּנָהָר צָר Isa 59,19 like a contracted (and hence swift, powerful) river". See also *HALOT*, II, "צוּר", 1015. Elsewhere, the LXX translates it with adjectives, such as, στενός (Num 22,26) and ἐχθρός (Job 6,23; 36,16; and 38,23); substantives, such as, λιθός (Job 41,7) and θλῖψις (Isa 30,20); or verbs, such as, θλίβω (Ps 78[77],42; and Lam 1,5.7.10).

[342] According to the BDB ("עֹצֶם", 782), the term means, "might, bones". In reality, the MT has עַיִם, which is a "hapax legomenon, with uncertain meaning" (*HALOT*, I, "עַיִם", 817). Among the few conjectural emendations of the text, בְּעֹצֶם רוּחוֹ seems to be the most plausible one, supported as it is also by the LXX (πνεύματι βιαίῳ) and the *Vg.* (*in fortitudine spiritus sui*). See, e.g., the critical apparatus, in the *BHS*, 693. See also BDB, "עַיִם", 744; *HALOT*, I, "עַיִם", 817; and *Ibid.*, I, "עֹצֶם", 869. Elsewhere, the LXX translates its root-related terms either with adjectives, such as, δυνατός (Gen 26,16), κραταιός (Dan[Θ] 8,24), and ἰσχυρός (Dan 11,23), or verbs, such as, ἰσχύω (Exod 1,20; Jer 5,6; and Dan[Θ] 8,8), κατισχύω (Exod 1,7; and Dan 8,8), κραταιόω (Pss 38[37],20; 69[68],5; 105[104],24; and 139[138],17), στερεόω (Dan 8,24) and πληθύνω (Ps 40[39],6.13; Jer[LXX] 15,8; and 30[37],14).

[343] According to the BDB ("רֶשַׁע", 957), the term means, "wickedness, as violence and crime against civil law". See also "אוֹ(וֹ)צְרוֹת רֶשַׁע unrighteous treasures (or treasures of wickedness) Mic 6,10; Prov 10,2, חַרְצֻבּוֹת רֶשַׁע unrighteous fetters (or fetters of wickedness) Isa 58,6, לֶחֶם רֶשַׁע the bread of wickedness Prov 4,17" (*HALOT*, II, "רֶשַׁע", 1296). Elsewhere, the LXX translates it with substantives or adjectives contrary to law and piety, such as, πλημμέλεια (1Sam 24,14), ἀνομία (Pss 5,5; and 45[44],8), ἀσέβεια (Prov 4,17; Qoh 8,8; and Hos 10,13), ἀσεβής (Job 34,8; and Qoh 7,25), ἁμαρτωλός (Ps 84[83],11), κακός (Prov 16,12), and ἄνομος (Ezek 7,11; and Mic 6,10).

[344] According to the *HALOT* (I, "אֱנוֹשׁ", 70), the term means, "incurable [...] disastrous". See also BDB, "אֱנֹשׁ", 60. Elsewhere, the LXX translates it either with the substantive, ἄνθρωπος (Jer 17,9.16), or the adjective, ἀλγηρός (Jer 37,12), i.e., "causing pain" (Muraoka, "ἀλγηρός", 24).

[345] See, e.g., D.J.A. CLINES, *The Esther Scroll*, 69–70; and C.V. DOROTHY, *The Books of Esther*, 81–102.

[346] For the difficulties in the translation of this verse, see, e.g., W.L. HOLLADAY, *Jeremiah 1*, I, 523–524; and W. MCKANE, *Jeremiah*, I, 429–432 (esp. 431).

Where the LXX does not differ from the MT (Esth 3[B],13[7] and Isa 30,30)[347], the former Greek version uses the adverb, βιαίως, to translate the Hebrew adjective, זֵד (Jer 18,14)[348].

2. The Hellenistic Jewish Writings

As one moves from OT ancient versions, LXX and Apocrypha, to other Jewish writings in Greek, the semantic and linguistic study leads to analogous results, independently of whether the analyzed sources are religious or pagan. Due to their importance in NT studies, we shall limit here our research only to the pseudepigraphic literature and the works of Philo of Alexandria and Flavius Josephus[349].

a) The Pseudepigrapha of the OT

In his extensive research on the relationship between the Pseudepigraphic literature and the New Testament, James H. Charlesworth challenges Biblical scholars at the end of the 2nd millennium to consider the Pseudepigrapha as requisite reading and as a source of valuable insights for understanding and reconstructing both the historical and literary contexts of Early Judaism, Christian Origins, and specifically the writings of the New Testament[350]. Before moving to Flavius Josephus' and Philo's works, therefore, we shall explore the meanings of the βία-terms as they occur in the vast panorama of

---

[347] These two occurrences have no direct equivalents in the MT. While in Isa 30,30, the adverb (βιαίως) is annexed to the Hebrew text in order to underline the power of God's anger, which is compared to the flame of a consuming fire, between vv. 13 and 14 of chap. 3 of the book of Esther, it occurs within a considerable addition which retells the contents of king Ahasuerus' decree in detail.

[348] According to the BDB ("זוּר", 266), the term means, "press[ed] down and out". See also *Ibid.*, "זֵד", 279; *Ibid.*, "צָר", 865; *HALOT*, I, "זֵד", 263; *Ibid.*, I, "זָידוֹן", 268; *Ibid.*, I, "זֵד", 279; *Ibid.*, I, "זוּר", 283; *Ibid.*, II, "צָרַר", 1015; and W. MCKANE, *Jeremiah*, I, 431. Elsewhere, the LXX translates it with the substantive, μίσθωμα (Ezek 16,32), or the adjectives, ἀσεβής (Isa 25,2), ἀλλογενής (Isa 61,5; Jer[LXX] 51[28],51; and Obad 1,11), and ὑβριστής (Jer[LXX] 51[28],2). Most of the times, however, the term is rendered in Greek with ἀλλότριος (see, e.g., 2Kgs 19,24; Pss 54[53],5; 109[108],11; Prov 5,10; Isa 1,7[2x]; Jer 2,25; 5,19; 30,8; Ezek 11,9; 28,10; 30,12; etc.).

[349] For an overview on these writings in the historical and literary contexts of the STP, see, e.g., M.E. STONE, ed., *Jewish Writings*, esp., 1–27.89–156–282.325–442.

[350] Thus, in the preface to the new edition of his book, J.H. Charlesworth (*The OTPE & the NT*, vii) writes: "Texts reveal their author's meaning (or range of meanings) when we understand their original contexts […] To perceive what Jesus may have meant, according to Paul or the authors of the gospels, requires studying what he reputedly said and did within his context; that is, within the world of Early Judaism". See also *Ibid.*, xviii.1–26; ID., "In the Crucible", 20–43; and J.A. SANDERS, "Introduction", 13–19.

these early Jewish texts and fragments, and see what nuances these words may have had in Luke's own literary world[351].

Upon a general look at the early Jewish and Christian Greek writings produced at the turn of the Common Era, our findings show how the aforementioned negative, neutral, and positive understandings of the βία-related terminology continue to coexist in relative harmony[352].

The substantive, βία, for instance, is used in the *Testament of Solomon* to designate the positive power of coercion or necessity obliging Beelzebul, the prince of demons, to become subject to Solomon (see καὶ ἀναστὰς [...] μετὰ βίας καὶ ἦλθε πρός με)[353]. However, the author of this work also uses it in a more neutral sense, to relate the strength and haste used by Solomon's servant to tie up tightly a leather flask (see σπουδαίως μετὰ βίας δῆσον τὸν ἀσκόν)[354]. Similarly, in the *Pseudo-Hecateus*, the substantive indicates simply the "violence of the winds" (ἀνέμων βίαν), in the context of the One Creator God (see εἷς ἐστι[ν] θεός) and over against the idols[355].

The substantive is used more or less neutrally also in the *History of the Rechabites* and the *Testament of Joseph*. In spite of the negative contexts in which it occurs, it is meant primarily to convey, respectively, the *force* of the devil's desperate cry of weeping and lament (see κλαυθμῷ μεγάλῳ καὶ βιαίῳ)[356], and the strength used by "the Egyptian woman" (ἡ Αἰγύπτια) to take hold of Joseph's garments and drag him to lie with her[357].

---

[351] For a discussion of how Luke's writings may reflect traditions contained in the pseudepigraphic literature of the Judaism of his day, see, e.g., C.A. EVANS, "Luke", 175–179.190–194.199–201; ID., "The Pseudepigrapha", 139–150; D.P. MOESSNER, "Suffering", 215–227; and G.S. OEGEMA, "The Pseudepigrapha", 151–165.

[352] By way of simplification, we will use "the Pseudepigrapha of the OT", to refer specifically to that body of non-canonical bible-related Greek documents composed approximately during the period 200 BCE to 200 CE, which are neither contained in Rahlfs' edition of the Septuagint nor classified as rabbinic literature. See, e.g., R.H. CHARLES, ed., *The Apocrypha*, II, iv–xi; J.H. CHARLESWORTH, ed., *The Old Testament*, I, xxi–xxxiv; and T.C. VRIEZEN – A.S. VAN DER WOUDE, *Ancient Israelite*, 564–658.

[353] See TSol, III.4–5 (ed. C.C. MCCOWN, 17). See also J.H. CHARLESWORTH, ed., *The Old Testament*, I, 964; A. COSENTINO, "The Testament of Solomon", 1–45; ID., ed., *Testamento di Salomone*; and H.F.D. SPARKS, ed., *The Apocryphal Old Testament*, 733.

[354] See TSol, XXII.11 (ed. C.C. MCCOWN, 67). See also A. COSENTINO, "The Testament of Solomon", 42; J.H. CHARLESWORTH, ed., *The Old Testament*, I, 984; *Ibid.*, 984, n. c; and H.F.D. SPARKS, ed., *The Apocryphal Old Testament*, 749.

[355] See, e.g., PsHec, IV.2; CLEMENT OF ALEXANDRIA, *Strom.* V, XIV.113.1–2 (ed. O. STÄHLIN, II, 402–403); and J.H. CHARLESWORTH, ed., *The Old Testament*, II, 912.

[356] See HistRech, XXI.5–6 (ed. M.R. JAMES, 108); and J.H. CHARLESWORTH, ed., *The History*, 86.100. For a discussion of this work and its origin, see, e.g., R. NIKOLSKY, "The *History*", 185–207; and C.H. KNIGHTS, "The Rechabites Revisited", 307–320.

[357] See TJos VIII.2–3 (ed. M. DE JONGE – *al.*, 153); and J.H. CHARLESWORTH, ed., *The Old Testament*, I, 821.

Finally, the term occurs also in its clear negative connotation. For instance, in the *Letter of Aristeas*, the term is used in the context of a digression on the Law in Judaism, to denote that "strength" (ἰσχύς) or "power" (δύναμις) of oppression, injustice and "robbery" (see ἀφαιρεῖσθαι), which men of "wisdom" (see συνετοῖς) must avoid (see μηδὲν ἐπιτελεῖν βίᾳ), as a lesson drawn from the laws of abstention from the meat of impure birds of prey[358]. In the *Apocalypse of Moses*, moreover, the word, βιασμός, designates a physical pain to the eyes, as the result of a plague[359].

As far as the verb is concerned, βιάζεσθαι and its compound forms occur again in the context of sexual intercourse, in both the *Testament of Reuben* and the *Testament of Solomon*. However, whereas the former uses the simple form of the verb to refer plainly to a woman's deceptive and harmful impact over a man, to lead him to fornication[360], the latter resorts to the use of παραβιάζεσθαι to connote only the power of persuasion used by some Jebusite priests upon a woman, with whom Solomon had fallen in love, to convince her not to go to bed with him unless he gave in to their idolatrous worship[361].

The negative connotation of the verb comes back again, for instance, in the context of a series of woes and doom against Thebes and its idolatry: on the lips of an ecstatic Sybilline prophetess it refers plainly to the "violence" of a devouring fire, which will turn the earth to smoke (see βιαζομένη [...] γαῖα), teaching its inhabitants how hard it is to put "God's law" (θεοῦ νόμος) to the test[362]. Moreover, in the *Book of Enoch* and the *Book of Jubilees*, it expresses, respectively, the power of oppression, murder and persecution of the sinners over the righteous[363],

---

[358] See Aris, I.146–148 (ed. P. WENDLAND, 41–42). Cf. H.ST.J. THACKERAY, ed., *The Letter of Aristeas*, 31; and J.H. CHARLESWORTH, ed., *The Old Testament*, II, 22. The text conveys clearly a parallel between the concept of "violence" (βία) with that of "strength" (ἰσχύς). See, esp., the contiguous expressions, "by violence" (βίᾳ) and "by [...] their own strength" (τῇ [...] ἰσχύι). For an overview of the letter and its focus on piety and the law, see, e.g., D. DE CROM, "The *Letter of Aristeas*", 141–160. For a discussion on its date (between 3rd and 1st cs. BCE), see, e.g., B.G. WRIGHT, "The Letter of Aristeas", 303–325; and U. RAPPAPORT, "*Defining* the Letter", 285–303.

[359] See ApMos, VIII.2 (ed. C. VON TISCHENDORF, 4); and J.H. CHARLESWORTH, ed., *The Old Testament*, II, 273.

[360] See TReu V.4 (ed. M. DE JONGE – *al.*, 10); and J.H. CHARLESWORTH, ed., *The Old Testament*, I, 784.

[361] See TSol, XXVI.4 (ed. C.C. MCCOWN, 73). See also J.H. CHARLESWORTH, ed., *The Old Testament*, I, 986; and H.F.D. SPARKS, ed., *The Apocryphal Old Testament*, 751.

[362] See Sib, VII.126–131 (ed. J. GEFFCKEN, 139). See also M.S. TERRY, ed., *The Sibylline Oracles*, 155.

[363] See 1En XCVI.14–15 (ed. M. BLACK, 36); *Ibid.*, XCVII.3 (ed. *Ibid.*, 37); and J.H. CHARLESWORTH, ed., *The Old Testament*, I, 77. M. Black (*The Book of Enoch*, 315) notes that in its Ethiopic Version (*ḥēda*) the Greek verb βιάζεσθαι corresponds less to the Hebrew, "to do violence to, to wrong" (חמס), than to the verb, "to rob" (גזל). See also *Ibid.*, 97–98.315–317.381.

and Judah's incitement to his father Jacob to strike Esau down violently, with bow and arrow (see βιασθεὶς Ἰακὼβ ὑπὸ τοῦ Ἰούδα)³⁶⁴.

The positive character of the verb of violence appears, nevertheless, in the *Sybilline Oracles*, in a way which closely recalls the vocabulary used in Luke 16,16. The Sybil resorts to it with reference to her "heart" (ἦτορ) and its inner urge to "announce" the oracle to "all" men, according to the will of God (see βιάζεται ἔνδοθεν αὐδήν ἀγγέλλειν πᾶσιν)³⁶⁵. Likewise, in the *Book of Joseph and Aseneth*, βιάζεσθαι is used to convey Aseneth's earnest invitation to Joseph (see ἐβιάσατο αὐτόν), to enter her house and have his feet washed by her, as a sign of hospitality and service³⁶⁶.

Lastly, the monetary or property-related nuance of the verb surfaces discreetly in at least one instance, in the *Sybilline Oracles*. Here, βιάζεσθαι occurs as one of the Sibyls describes the ruin of Rome in keeping with its name, as a punishment for its idolatry:

"And three times three hundred and forty-eight years you will make complete when, an ill-fated violating lot [δύσμορος μοῖρα βιαζομένη] will come upon you and fulfil your name"³⁶⁷.

As to the βία-related adjective, our research brings out analogous results. Thus, in the *Sybilline Oracles*, βίαιος occurs in the positive context of an exhortation to honor the Messiah, and with reference to the laws and ordinances: a Sibyl urges the Daughter of Zion to rejoice, because her King comes to lift the heavy yoke from her neck and break her "established godless [...] and violent bonds" (θεσμοὺς ἀθέους [...] δεσμούς τε βιαίους)³⁶⁸. On its neutral level, the adjective is used also in the *Book of Jubilees*, to convey the strength of "a mighty wind"

---

³⁶⁴ See Jub, XXXVIII.1 (ed. J.C. VANDERKAM, I, 206–207.292). See also R.H. CHARLES, ed., *The Book of Jubilees*, 219; J.H. CHARLESWORTH, ed., *The Old Testament*, II, 127; and J.C. VANDERKAM, ed., *The Book of Jubilees*, II, 250, n. 1. For a survey of recent studies on the *Book of Jubilees*, see, e.g., ID., "Recent Scholarship", 405–431.

³⁶⁵ See Sib, III.5–7 (ed. J. GEFFCKEN, 46); and εὐαγγελίζεται, πᾶς, and βιάζεται, in Luke 16,16. See also H.N. BATE, ed., *The Sibylline Oracles*, 45.

³⁶⁶ See JosAs, XX.3 (ed. P. BATIFFOL, 70); and J.H. CHARLESWORTH, ed., *The Old Testament*, II, 234. For an article on Christian ethics in the chaps. 22–29 of this pseudepigraphic work, see R. NIR, "'It is not Right'", 1–29.

³⁶⁷ See Sib, VIII.148–150 (ed. J. GEFFCKEN, 149). As M.S. Terry (ed., *The Sibylline Oracles*, 168, n. 195) notes, "The number 948 is the numerical value of the Greek letters in the name Rome (ρ = 100, ω = 800, μ = 40, η = 8, = Ρώμη). Nine hundred and forty-eight years after the founding of Rome extends to about 196 of our era, and the reign of Septimius Severus". The verb is clearly related to the term, "portion, lot, share" (μοῖρα), which is in turn used often with reference to the distribution of a land, country, or booty. See, e.g., BDAG, "μοῖρα", 656.

³⁶⁸ See Sib, VIII.324–328 (ed. J. GEFFCKEN, 163). See also M.S. TERRY, ed., *The Sibylline Oracles*, 177.

(ἄνεμος βίαιος), blowing against the tower of Babel and overthrowing it[369]. Finally, the negative connotation appears in one of the Sibyl's prophecies: while the divine voice describes the mythical gigantic race of Gen 6,4 as "wantonly violent" (ὑβριστήρ), Moses calls openly his people "violent sinners" (ἁμάρτωλοί τε βίαιοι), and he does so after they have heard him speak a first time and reacted by "turning up their nose" (ἐμυκτήριζον), just like the Pharisees in Luke 16,14[370].

Finally, in the *Sybilline Oracles*, the adverb, βιαίως, occurs on Noah's lips to discourage the people from fighting with each other violently[371], and in the sentences of the *Pseudo-Phocylides* it is used to refer to the discipline of children: "Do not apply your hand violently to tender children" (νηπιάχοις ἀταλοῖς μὴ ἄψῃ χεῖρα βιαίως)[372].

b) *Philo of Alexandria*

Native of Alexandria in Egypt, "a man held in esteem in every respect [...] and not unskilled in philosophy" (ἀνὴρ τὰ πάντα ἔνδοξος [...] καὶ φιλοσοφίας οὐκ ἄπειρος)[373], Philo is certainly acquainted with the βία-root lexemes, considering that they occur regularly in his writings (see, esp., *Spec.*, *Mos.* and *Aet.*)[374].

As far as the verb βιάζεσθαι is concerned, this is used, sometimes, whether in conjunction with εἰς or not, to indicate forced entry into some place (such as, the human body, a country fit for habitation, etc.)[375]. Other times, it

---

[369] See Jub, X.26 (ed. J.C. VANDERKAM, I, 64–65). This additional remark to the story narrated in Genesis corresponds to an ancient tradition. See, e.g., Gen 11,8; Sib, III.98–103 (ed. J. GEFFCKEN, 53); and FLAVIUS JOSEPHUS, *A.J.*, I.118 (ed. H.ST.J. THACKERAY – *al.*, IV, 56–57). See also R.H. CHARLES, ed., *The Book of Jubilees*, 84, n. 26; J.H. CHARLES-WORTH, ed., *The Old Testament*, II, 77; J.C. VANDERKAM, ed., *The Book of Jubilees*, I, xi–xii.267; and *Ibid.*, II, 63.

[370] See Sib, I.171–176 (ed. J. GEFFCKEN, 14); and ἐξεμυκτήριζον, in Luke 16,14. See also M.S. TERRY, ed., *The Sibylline Oracles*, 23. The same expression, "violent sinners" (ἁμάρτωλοί τε βίαιοι), occurs as a Sybil describes the ruinous idolatry and greed of Rome. See Sib, VIII.185 (ed. J. GEFFCKEN, 151). See also M.S. TERRY, ed., *The Sibylline Oracles*, 170.

[371] See Sib, I.154 (ed. A. RZACH, 15). See also M.S. TERRY, ed., *The Sibylline Oracles*, 22; and J. GEFFCKEN, ed., *Die Oracula Sibyllina*, 13.

[372] See PsPho, I.150 (ed. P.W. VAN DER HORST, 98–99); J.H. CHARLESWORTH, ed., *The Old Testament*, II, 579; and W.T. WILSON, *The Sentences*, 220. For a commentary on this verse, see, e.g., *Ibid.*, 174–175.

[373] FLAVIUS JOSEPHUS, *A.J.*, XVIII.259 (ed. H.ST.J. THACKERAY – *al.*, IX, 154–155).

[374] Specifically, according to the statistical data generated by the BibleWorks computer program for Windows, the verb (βιάζεσθαι) occurs 90x; the substantive (βία) occurs 61x; the adjective (βίαιος) occurs 39x; and the adverb (βιαίως) occurs 9x. To these, one should also add the occurrences of βιαστικός (4x), ἀντιβιάζεσθαι (7x), ἐκβιάζεσθαι (4x), παραβιάζεσθαι (2x), εἰσβιάζεσθαι (2x), ἀποβιάζεσθαι (1x), and καταβιάζεσθαι (1x).

[375] See, e.g., PHILO, *Mos.*, I.19.108 (ed. R. ARNALDEZ – *al.*, XXII, 74–75); *Ibid.*, I.39.215 (ed. *Ibid.*, XXII, 130–131); A. VON HARNACK, "Zwei Worte", 948; Moulton, "βιάζομαι", 109–

indicates the kind of violence applied by a person against one's natural inclinations[376] or the pressure used by a tyrant to motivate an unlawful behaviour[377]. It can occasionally be preceded or followed by an infinitive verb, "in the sense of 'to do a thing violently'"[378], as when it refers, for instance, to the "upsetting" (ἀνατρέψαι βιάζονται)[379] of the soul's faculties. A "pleasure-loving mind" (φιλήδονος νοῦς), in fact, can lure people by offering them wealth or "properties" (ὑπάρχοντα), and thus "draw them violently into a prison of exceeding bitterness" (ἀντισπᾷ βιαζόμενος δεσμωτηρίῳ πάνυ πικρῷ παραδοῦναι)[380]. For the Hellenistic Jewish philosopher, wealth and possessions are not evil in themselves, but only insofar as they become the object of one's unrestrained cravings[381].

Philo makes use also of some prefixed βία-verbs. Thus, the unique occurrence of καταβιάζεσθαι indicates the pressure exerted over the soul by "folly" (ἀφροσύνη), as this "compels" (ἀναγκάζει) it to commit all kinds of sins[382]; that of ἀποβιάζεσθαι designates the drive of the eyes, which compel one to see what he or she does not wish to see[383]; and ἀντιβιάζεσθαι can express that exercised by the "antagonist weight of mortality" (ἀντίπαλον θνητὸν ἄχθος)[384] or by the transient goods of this earth[385]. While those who are able to "use violence against" (ἀντιβιάσασθαι) such a downward force of attraction, by their "superior

---

110; and C. Spicq, "βιάζομαι", *TLNT*, I, 288, n. 7. See also the occurrences of εἰσβιάζεσθαι, in Philo, *Decal.* XXVIII.144 (ed. F.H. Colson – *al.*, VII, 78–79); and Id., *Spec.* I.40.325 (ed. *Ibid.*, VII, 288–289).

[376] See, e.g., Philo, *Deus* XXII.100–101 (ed. F.H. Colson – *al.*, III, 58–61).

[377] See, e.g., Philo, *Somn.* II.18.124 (ed. F.H. Colson – *al.*, V, 498–499).

[378] F.H. Colson – *al.*, ed., *Philo*, III, 446, n. *b.*

[379] Philo, *Somn.* II.21.145 (ed. F.H. Colson – *al.*, V, 508–509). See, e.g., Id., *Ebr.* XXXV.143 (ed. *Ibid.*, III, 392–393); and Id., *Sobr.* II.6 (ed. *Ibid.*, III, 442–445). It is Philo's opinion (*Mut.* XLI.239 [ed. *Ibid.*, V, 264–267]) that a person's thoughts have the power to pour on, like a rushing torrent, "and upset its whole being with their violence" (καὶ πᾶσαν αὐτὴν βιαίως ἀνατρέποντα).

[380] See Philo, *Mut.* XXXII.172–173 (ed. F.H. Colson – *al.*, V, 228–231). Accordingly, in Luke 16, Jesus could very well be warning, as it were, the "money-loving mind" (φιλάργυρος νοῦς) of the Pharisees of such an impending possible danger! Indeed, as T.E. Schmidt ("Hostility", 88) points out, "love of money" (φιλαργυρία) is "a standard phrase used by Philo in condemning greed".

[381] See, e.g., T.E. Phillips, "Revisiting Philo", 114–121.

[382] See Philo, *Somn.* II.30.198 (ed. F.H. Colson – *al.*, V, 532–533).

[383] See Philo, *Spec.* III.31.177 (ed. F.H. Colson – *al.*, VII, 586–587).

[384] Philo, *Mut.* XXXIV.185 (ed. F.H. Colson – *al.*, V, 236–237).

[385] See Philo, *Deus* XXXII.148–151 (ed. F.H. Colson – *al.*, III, 84–87); and Id., *Somn.* II.2.12–13 (ed. *Ibid.*, V, 448–449). In one instance, at least, Philo uses this verb in a way akin to Aristotle's, when he speaks of the stationary place of the natural elements and the order and balance of things. See Aristotle, *Magn.*, I.14–15, 1188b.1–18 (ed. F. Susemihl, 22); and Philo, *Aet.* VII.32–33 (ed. F.H. Colson – *al.*, IX, 206–209).

power" (κραταιοτέρα δυνάμει), are called "blessed" (μακάριοι)[386], they who drop down and are overcome by it are worthy of disgrace and "laughter" (γέλως)[387].

Moreover, in one instance, the author interprets the OT occurrence of παρα-βιάζεσθαι, in Deut 1,43, as referring to those people who make useless and fictitious efforts against their natural inclinations so as to gain wisdom or virtue, but are not sincere in their worship of God[388]. Sooner or later their *hypocritical violence* will be made manifest, "for [such a] violence is of short duration" (τὸ γὰρ βίαιον ὀλιγοχρόνιον)[389]. As Philo explains in the following lines, it lasts for a brief time because of the etymology of the term, βίαιον (i.e., "a violent action"), which is here thought to derive from the adverbial use of another adjective, meaning "a little" (βαιόν).

Last but not least, in addition to conveying the experience of constraint and the impulse of the passions (e.g., hatred, anger, etc.)[390], the verb ἐκβιά-ζεσθαι is used to express the compulsion felt when taking an oath, and it is thus paralleled with the obligation to make good one's word by the use of "all the strength and means" (παντὶ σθένει καὶ μεχανῇ πάσῃ) in one's power[391]. The phrase is particularly significant: the violence expressed by the verb is compared with the human exertion of *all one's strength*, as well as the use of *all the means at one's disposal*[392].

As to the substantive (βία) and its adjectival cognates (βίαιος and βιαστικός), they denote primarily the force of *natural elements* (e.g., hail, winds, rainstorms, etc.), *animals*, *enemies*, but also the power of *temperance* or self-control, as well as the impulses of the human *passions*[393].

---

[386] PHILO, *Spec.* IV.21.115 (ed. F.H. COLSON – al., VIII, 78–79).

[387] PHILO, *Praem.* I.5 (ed. F.H. COLSON – al., VIII, 314–315). See also *Ibid.*, XVI.94 (ed. *Ibid.*, VIII, 370–371).

[388] See PHILO, *Deus* XXII.99–103 (ed. F.H. COLSON – al., III, 58–63).

[389] PHILO, *Deus* XXII.103 (ed. F.H. COLSON – al., III, 62–63). See also ID., *Aet.* VI.30 (ed. *Ibid.*, IX, 204–205).

[390] See, e.g., PHILO, *Spec.* II.4.16 (ed. F.H. COLSON – al., VII, 314–315).

[391] PHILO, *Spec.* II.3.9 (ed. F.H. COLSON – al., VII, 310–311). See also *Ibid.* II.1.2 (ed. *Ibid.*, VII, 306–307); and ID., *Decal.* XVII.85 (ed. *Ibid.*, VII, 48–49).

[392] This concept shall come back, again, when dealing with the Jewish interpretation of Deut 6,5.

[393] See, e.g., PHILO, *Mos.*, I.6.25 (ed. R. ARNALDEZ – al., XXII, 38–39); *Ibid.*, I.8.41 (ed. *Ibid.*, XXII, 46–47); *Ibid.*, I.9.49 (ed. *Ibid.*, XXII, 50–51); *Ibid.*, I.20.115 (ed. *Ibid.*, XXII, 78–79); *Ibid.*, I.20.118 (ed. *Ibid.*, XXII, 80–81); *Ibid.*, I.21.120 (ed. *Ibid.*, XXII, 82–83); *Ibid.*, I.21.123 (ed. *Ibid.*, XXII, 84–85); *Ibid.*, I.23.131 (ed. *Ibid.*, XXII, 88–89); *Ibid.*, I.32.176 (ed. *Ibid.*, XXII, 110–111); *Ibid.*, I.38.211 (ed. *Ibid.*, XXII, 128–129); and *Ibid.*, II.27.139 (ed. *Ibid.*, XXII, 252–253). See also ID., *Somn.* II.13.92 (ed. F.H. COLSON – al., V, 484–485); and ID., *Spec.* II.31.191 (ed. *Ibid.*, VII, 426–427). For a complete list of occurrences of the aforementioned lexemes in Philo's works, see P. BORGEN – K. FUGLSETH – R. SKARSTEN, *The Philo Index*, 59.

For instance, in his account of the world's creation given by Moses, Philo mentions the "violence of the winds" (βία πνευμάτων)[394] or that of the fish, which allows the latter creatures to "push their way up" (βία τὴν φορὰν ἀνωθοῦντα)[395] into stormy waters. The wind becomes actually a metaphor for the very activity of God, whose power can hinder human deeds[396]. Elsewhere, βία refers also to the "rush and violence" (φορᾶς καὶ βίας)[397] of the "tides" (ἀμπωτίζοντα)[398], which can cause even death at times, or it is "the winter-flowing river of life" (χειμάρρουν ποταμὸν τοῦ βίου), which, with its worldly affairs, dashes upon us "with utmost violence" (βιαιοτάτην)[399].

Accordingly, "the entire life of a statesman" (πᾶς ὁ τοῦ πολιτευομένου βίος) can be seized, as it were, by spiritual "diseases" (νόσους), which "violently" (βιαίως) strive "to overthrow and cast it down" (ἀνατρέψαι καὶ καταβαλεῖν)[400]. The soul is compared to a vessel, tossed around by the violence of the passions[401]. These are like mighty winds blowing against the human soul, so as to make it side with either the mind or the body[402]. Thus, in his allegorical interpretation of Genesis, Philo talks about the "violence of the impulse" (βία τῆς ὁρμῆς)[403] of the passions and offers us an example of it. The wife of Joseph's master, burning with the fire of lawless lust, employs βία, that is, "the force of passion" (τοῦ πάθους ἰσχύν)[404], to draw Joseph to her bed. However, Joseph resists and replies: "Why are you doing violence [to me]?" (τί βιάζῃ;)[405]. Later, when recounting her version of the facts, Joseph is said to

---

[394] PHILO, *Opif.* XXVI.80 (ed. F.H. COLSON – *al.*, I, 64–65). See also *Ibid.*, XIX.58 (ed. *Ibid.*, I, 44–45); *Ibid.*, XXXVIII.113 (ed. *Ibid.*, I, 90–91); and ID., *Abr.* XXXI.160 (ed. *Ibid.*, VI, 80–81). Philo (*Aet.* XXVI.139 [ed. *Ibid.*, IX, 280–283]) believes such kind of violence to be responsible even for the formation of Sicily, which being originally part of the mainland, "was [then] forced to become an island" (νῆσος ἐβιάσθη γενέσθαι)!

[395] PHILO, *Opif.* XX.63 (ed. F.H. COLSON – *al.*, I, 48–49).

[396] See, e.g., PHILO, *Virt.* VIII.49 (ed. F.H. COLSON – *al.*, VIII, 192–193); and W.T. WILSON, ed., *Philo*, 151.

[397] PHILO, *Abr.* VIII.44 (ed. F.H. COLSON – *al.*, VI, 26–27).

[398] See, e.g., PHILO, *Deus* XXXVII.177 (ed. F.H. COLSON – *al.*, III, 96–97); and ID., *Mut.* XXXV.186 (ed. *Ibid.*, V, 236–237).

[399] See PHILO, *Fug.* IX.49 (ed. F.H. COLSON – *al.*, V, 36–37); and ID., *Prob.* X.63 (ed. *Ibid.*, IX, 46–49). Here, the concept of "violence" (βία) is somehow linked to that of "life" (βίος).

[400] See PHILO, *Somn.* I.38.222 (ed. F.H. COLSON – *al.*, V, 414–415).

[401] See, e.g., PHILO, *Abr.* XVI.76 (ed. F.H. COLSON – *al.*, III, 146–147); and *Ibid.*, XIX.89 (ed. *Ibid.*, III, 152–153).

[402] See PHILO, *Somn.* II.12.81 (ed. F.H. COLSON – *al.*, V, 478–479).

[403] PHILO, *Leg.* I.23.73 (ed. F.H. COLSON – *al.*, I, 194–195). See also *Ibid.*, III.25.80 (ed. *Ibid.*, I, 352–353).

[404] PHILO, *Ios.* IX.41 (ed. F.H. COLSON – *al.*, VI, 162–163). See also *Ibid.*, X.52–53 (ed. *Ibid.*, VI, 168–169).

[405] PHILO, *Ios.* IX.42 (ed. F.H. COLSON – *al.*, VI, 162–163).

have attempted "to violate" (βιάζεσθαι)[406] her, sexually[407]. The constraining "charm" (φίλθρον) of love, "affection" (εὔνοια), or "pleasure" (ἡδονή), is qualified as being "the most forcible" (βιαστικώτατον) of all[408].

Finally, Philo deals directly with the acts of violence that go against the 6th and 7th commandments, in book III of his treatise on special laws[409]. Generally, whether they apply to adultery or murder, if the violence of these acts occurs in connection with ὕβρις, it frequently assumes the negative traits of an injustice, as in the example of the gaolers' cruelty, or of the adulterer's outrageous conduct, which is stained either by seduction or rape[410]. In book IV, he further classifies the person that carries away "that which belongs to another [τὰ ἑτέρου] with violence and publicly [βίᾳ καὶ φανερῶς]", as a "common enemy" (κοινὸς πολέμιος)[411], who, as such, must be legally prosecuted. However, as C.J. Cornthwaite remarks, Philo is also well acquainted with the notion of violence as a requisite for virtue[412]. In order for a person to act according to the dictates of the Torah, and in a way contrary to one's natural inclinations (see 4Macc 2,8), βία becomes somehow for him like a "necessity" (ἀνάγκη)[413] and, as such, can also occur in conjunction with the eagerness needed to discharge one's obligations (see σπουδάζειν)[414].

---

[406] PHILO, *Ios.* X.51 (ed. F.H. COLSON – *al.*, VI, 168–169).

[407] For Philo's use of βία and βιάζεσθαι in the sense of a sexual assault or violation, see, esp., PHILO, *Spec.* III.13.76–77 (ed. F.H. COLSON – *al.*, VII, 520–523); and ID., *Hypoth.* VII.1 (ed. *Ibid.*, IX, 422–423).

[408] PHILO, *Abr.* XXXV.194–195 (ed. F.H. COLSON – *al.*, VI, 94–97). See also ID., *Spec.* I.2.9 (ed. *Ibid.*, VII, 104–105); and *Ibid.* III.6.35 (ed. *Ibid.*, VII, 496–497).

[409] See, e.g., F.H. COLSON – *al.*, ed., *Philo*, VII, 471–607.

[410] See, e.g., PHILO, *Ios.* XV.80–84 (ed. F.H. COLSON – *al.*, VI, 180–183); ID., *Praem.* IX.52 (ed. *Ibid.*, VIII, 342–343); and ID., *Spec.* III.12–13.72–78 (ed. *Ibid.*, VII, 518–523). See also *Ibid.*, I.37.204 (ed. *Ibid.*, VII, 214–217); *Ibid.*, III.11.64 (ed. *Ibid.*, VII, 514–515); and *Ibid.*, III.14.79–80 (ed. *Ibid.*, VII, 522–525). Although the concepts of βία and ὕβρις are often associated, their meaning is not identical. The former, for instance, can convey the constraint over a soul by an emotion, such as, a woman's love for her husband (see φιλανδρία), whereas the latter points specifically to the outrage of rape or sexual assault. See, e.g., *Ibid.*, III.30.168 (ed. *Ibid.*, VII, 580–581); and *Ibid.*, III.31.173 (ed. *Ibid.*, VII, 582–585).

[411] PHILO, *Spec.* IV.1 (ed. F.H. COLSON – *al.*, VIII, 6–7).

[412] See, e.g., PHILO, *Ebr.* XXXV.143 (ed. F.H. COLSON – *al.*, III, 392–393); and C.J. CORNTHWAITE, *Torah*, 101.

[413] PHILO, *Decal.* XVII.85 (ed. F.H. COLSON – *al.*, VII, 48–49). See also ID, *Spec.* IV.21.115 (ed. *Ibid.*, VIII, 78–79); and ID, *Virt.* XXIV.122 (ed. *Ibid.*, VIII, 236–237).

[414] See, e.g., PHILO, *Ios.* XXXV.209 (ed. F.H. COLSON – *al.*, VI, 240–241); and K. BERTHELOT, "Zeal", 113–129.

c) Flavius Josephus

In a way akin to Philo of Alexandria, "Josephus, son of Matthias" ('Ιώσηπος Ματθίου παῖς)[415], is quite conversant in βία-terminology and resorts to it regularly in his writings. In his study of Josephus' usage of βιάζεσθαι and its cognates, W.E. Moore notes "some 120 occurrences of the verb"[416], and although he fails to provide a precise number as to the occurrences of the corresponding noun (βία), adjective (βίαιος), and adverb (βιαίως), he does nonetheless state that their "usage [...] corresponds to that of the verb"[417].

According to Moore's analysis, Josephus often uses the verb βιάζεσθαι in the military context, to signify, for instance, the force of arms used in war (e.g., fire, flurries of blows and flying arrows)[418], but he also resorts to it in other circumstances, to indicate, for instance, "a forced expression" (βιασάμενος τὸν λόγον)[419]. The verb can point as well to "physical violence, or the threat or fear of it"[420], as in the case of punitive tortures (e.g., crucifixion)[421], or to sexual kinds of violent behaviour (e.g., rape)[422], but then again, it is used regularly in the context of "nature" (φύσις), to denote either the intrinsic force of its elements

---

[415] FLAVIUS JOSEPHUS, B.J., I.1.3 (ed. H.ST.J. THACKERAY – al., II, 2–3).

[416] W.E. MOORE, "ΒΙΑΖΩ, ΑΡΠΑΖΩ", 519.

[417] W.E. MOORE, "ΒΙΑΖΩ, ΑΡΠΑΖΩ", 523. More precisely, the BibleWorks computer program for Windows lists a total of 138 hits of the verb (βιάζεσθαι), for a number of 54 forms, in 136 verses (63x in A.J., 61x in B.J., 7x in V., and 7x in Ap.). To these, one should also add the further 11 following occurrences: 5 of ἐκβιάζεσθαι (4x in A.J., and 1x in B.J.), 2 of εἰσβιάζεσθαι (B.J., I.498; and Ibid., VI.74), 1 of ἀποβιάζεσθαι (B.J., III.270), 1 of διαβιάζεσθαι (A.J., XIX.173), 1 of παραβιάζεσθαι (Ap., II.233), and 1 of ὑπερβιάζεσθαι (A.J., IX.212). See also the following occurrences: the substantive (βία) occurs 91x (49x in A.J., 40x in B.J., and 2x in V.); the adjective (βίαιος) occurs 24x (17x in A.J., 6x in B.J., and 1x in Ap.); and the adverb (βιαίως) occurs 4x (3x in A.J., and 1x in Ap.). On the basis of these results, we must disagree with W.E. Moore (Ibid., 521), when he states: "the great majority of these occur in the War".

[418] See, e.g., FLAVIUS JOSEPHUS, B.J., III.7.257 (ed. H.ST.J. THACKERAY – al., II, 650–651); Ibid., V.6.286 (ed. Ibid., III, 288–289); ID., V., XXII.108 (ed. Ibid., I, 42–43); and W.E. MOORE, "ΒΙΑΖΩ, ΑΡΠΑΖΩ", 521, n. 1. See also a similar use of the substantive (βία), in ID., B.J., III.7.244 (ed. Ibid., II, 646–647).

[419] FLAVIUS JOSEPHUS, Ap., II.165 (ed. H.ST.J. THACKERAY – al., I, 358–359). See, e.g., W.E. MOORE, "ΒΙΑΖΩ, ΑΡΠΑΖΩ", 532, n. 1.

[420] W.E. MOORE, "ΒΙΑΖΩ, ΑΡΠΑΖΩ", 521.

[421] See, e.g., FLAVIUS JOSEPHUS, A.J., XVI.47 (ed. H.ST.J. THACKERAY – al., VIII, 226–227); Ibid., XVI.391 (ed. Ibid., VIII, 364–365); ID., B.J., I.24.496 (ed. Ibid., II, 234–235); Ibid., VII.6.201 (ed. Ibid., III, 562–563); and W.E. MOORE, "ΒΙΑΖΩ, ΑΡΠΑΖΩ", 521, n. 2.

[422] See, e.g., FLAVIUS JOSEPHUS, A.J., II.46 (ed. H.ST.J. THACKERAY – al., IV, 188–189); Ibid., II.58 (ed. Ibid., IV, 192–193); Ibid., VII.168–170 (ed. Ibid., V, 450–453); and W.E. MOORE, "ΒΙΑΖΩ, ΑΡΠΑΖΩ", 522, ns. 1–4.

(e.g., wind, water, etc.), or that which goes against "the natural or normal tendency of things" (e.g., agricultural production)[423].

Finally, it may be noted also how the Romano-Jewish historian employs the verb for violence in a way similar to Philo, to indicate "the pressure, or stress, of necessity"[424] (ἀνάγκη), or some forced entry into a place (e.g., Jerusalem, Hebron, or the temple)[425], often in connection with greed and the acquisition of treasures[426].

As to the use of the prefixed βία-verbs, one notes how Josephus makes use of ἐκβιάζεσθαι in conjunction with ἀνάγκη or ὕβρις, to express, for instance, the necessity of an army to fight boldly[427], the pressure felt by God when imposing a just punishment on the people on account of their "outrageous" (ἐξύβριζον) crimes[428], or the power exercised by passionate love (see ὑπ' ἔρωτος πρὸς τοῦτο [...] ἐκβιάζωνται) over a young free man wishing to marry a female slave or a prostitute, regardless of all legal prohibitions and the latter's "outrageous use of the body" (ὕβριν τοῦ σώματος)[429].

The context of sexual desire and immoral "mingling" recurs in the author's use of εἰσβιάζεσθαι, although here the verb refers mostly to Salome's supposed

---

[423] W.E. MOORE, "ΒΙΑΖΩ, ΑΡΠΑΖΩ", 522. See, e.g., FLAVIUS JOSEPHUS, A.J., IV.226 (ed. H.ST.J. THACKERAY – al., IV, 584–585); Ibid., V.17 (ed. Ibid., V, 8–11); ID., B.J., I.17.330 (ed. Ibid., II, 154–155); Ibid., III.10.518 (ed. Ibid., II, 720–721); Ibid., IV.8.477 (ed. Ibid., III, 140–141); W.E. MOORE, "ΒΙΑΖΩ, ΑΡΠΑΖΩ", 522–523; and S.R. LLEWELYN, "Forcible Acquisition", 161.

[424] W.E. MOORE, "ΒΙΑΖΩ, ΑΡΠΑΖΩ", 523. See, e.g., FLAVIUS JOSEPHUS, A.J., II.114 (ed. H.ST.J. THACKERAY – al., IV, 216–217); Ibid., III.5 (ed. Ibid., IV, 322–323); and W.E. MOORE, "ΒΙΑΖΩ, ΑΡΠΑΖΩ", 523, n. 1.

[425] See, e.g., FLAVIUS JOSEPHUS, A.J., XVII.253 (ed. B. NIESE, IV, 117–118); ID., B.J., II.262 (ed. Ibid., VI, 204); Ibid., II.328 (ed. Ibid., VI, 216); Ibid., III.491 (ed. Ibid., VI, 339); Ibid., IV.292 (ed. Ibid., VI, 385); Ibid., V.59 (ed. Ibid., VI, 442); Ibid., V.112 (ed. Ibid., VI, 449); Ibid., VI.74 (ed. Ibid., VI, 522); Ibid., VI.248 (ed. Ibid., VI, 545); C. SPICQ, "βιάζομαι", TLNT, I, 288, n. 7; and W.E. MOORE, "ΒΙΑΖΩ, ΑΡΠΑΖΩ", 520. For a similar use of the substantive (i.e., βία + εἰς), see, e.g., FLAVIUS JOSEPHUS, A.J., XVIII.37 (ed. B. NIESE, IV, 147); and ID., B.J., IV.203 (ed. Ibid., VI, 373).

[426] See, e.g., "for he also did violence to take over the citadels, and zealously began to search for the royal treasures with violence, being eager for gain and greedy in his desire" (τάς τε γὰρ ἄκρας ἐβιάζετο παραλαμβάνειν καὶ τῶν βασιλικῶν χρημάτων ἐπ' ἐρεύνῃ προθύμως ὥρμητο βίᾳ διὰ κέρδη καὶ πλεονεξιῶν ἐπιθυμίας) (FLAVIUS JOSEPHUS, A.J., XVII.253 [ed. B. NIESE, IV, 117–118]). See also Ibid., XVI.45–47 (ed. Ibid., IV, 11); ID., B.J., II.41–50 (ed. Ibid., VI, 162–163); Ibid., IV.312–314 (ed. Ibid., VI, 388); and Ibid., VII.261 (ed. Ibid., VI, 604). For a similar use of the substantive, see, e.g., FLAVIUS JOSEPHUS, A.J., I.61 (ed. Ibid., I, 15); ID., B.J., II.264–265 (ed. Ibid., VI, 204–205); Ibid., II.562–564 (ed. Ibid., VI, 256); Ibid., II.595–597 (ed. Ibid., VI, 262); and W.E. MOORE, "ΒΙΑΖΩ, ΑΡΠΑΖΩ", 527–529.

[427] See FLAVIUS JOSEPHUS, A.J., XV.150–151 (ed. H.ST.J. THACKERAY – al., VIII, 72–73).

[428] See FLAVIUS JOSEPHUS, A.J., I.100 (ed. H.ST.J. THACKERAY – al., IV, 48–49).

[429] See FLAVIUS JOSEPHUS, A.J., IV.244–245 (ed. H.ST.J. THACKERAY – al., IV, 592–593).

and forced nocturnal *entry into* Alexander's chamber, without the latter's consent (see μιγῆναί ποτε αὐτῷ μὴ θέλοντι νύκτωρ εἰσβιασαμένην)[430]. As W.E. Moore notes, the middle voice of the verb is habitually used by Josephus with the accusative, with or without the preposition εἰς, "in the sense of 'forcing a way for oneself'"[431], as also the other occurrence of εἰσβιάζεσθαι indicates[432].

Elsewhere, the Hellenistic writer uses ἀποβιάζεσθαι to convey the forced withdrawal of the Roman troops from the battlefield, and their subsequent replenishment[433]. Lastly, Josephus borrows the Thucydidean phrase, "the evil pressing exceedingly heavily upon them" (ὑπερβιαζομένου τοῦ κακοῦ)[434], to excuse the sailors for casting Jonah into the sea (see Jonah 1,12–16), and makes use of the strengthened compound forms for βιάζεσθαι (διαβιάζεσθαι and παραβιάζεσθαι) in the context of the Jewish law, either negatively, as in the instance of Julius Caesar's intention to overcome the wise democratic "legal system" (τὸν κόσμον τῶν νόμων)[435] of his people, or positively, to praise their heroic endurance and fidelity to it[436].

As far as the substantive, βία, and its adjectival and adverbial cognates are concerned, they are sometimes associated with the concepts of "greed" (πλεονεχία) and "riches" (χρήματα)[437], and often likened to those of "strength" (ἰσχύς) and "power" (δύναμις), as when Josephus mentions Adam's prediction on the destruction of the world, for instance, "at one time by the force [κατ' ἰσχύν] of fire and at another by the violence and abundance [κατὰ βίαν καὶ πλῆθος] of water"[438], or when he recounts king Darius' question on what

---

[430] See FLAVIUS JOSEPHUS, *B.J.*, I.25.498 (ed. H.ST.J. THACKERAY – *al.*, II, 234–235).

[431] W.E. MOORE, "ΒΙΑΖΩ, ΑΡΠΑΖΩ", 520.

[432] See FLAVIUS JOSEPHUS, *B.J.*, VI.1.74 (ed. H.ST.J. THACKERAY – *al.*, III, 396–397).

[433] See FLAVIUS JOSEPHUS, *B.J.*, III.7.270 (ed. H.ST.J. THACKERAY – *al.*, II, 654–655).

[434] FLAVIUS JOSEPHUS, *A.J.*, IX.212 (ed. H.ST.J. THACKERAY – *al.*, VI, 112–113). See THUCYDIDES, *Hist.* II.52.3 (ed. C.F. SMITH, I, 350–351); and H.ST.J. THACKERAY – *al.*, ed., *Josephus*, VI, 113, n. *b*.

[435] FLAVIUS JOSEPHUS, *A.J.*, XIX.173 (ed. H.ST.J. THACKERAY – *al.*, IX, 294–295).

[436] See FLAVIUS JOSEPHUS, *Ap.*, II.233 (ed. H.ST.J. THACKERAY – *al.*, I, 386–387).

[437] See, e.g., FLAVIUS JOSEPHUS, *A.J.*, I.54 (ed. H.ST.J. THACKERAY – *al.*, IV, 24–27); *Ibid.*, I.61 (ed. *Ibid.*, IV, 28–29); *Ibid.*, XVII.253 (ed. B. NIESE, IV, 117–118); *Ibid.*, XVIII.291 (ed. H.ST.J. THACKERAY – *al.*, IX, 170–171); and ID., *B.J.*, I.16.317 (ed. *Ibid.*, II, 148–149).

[438] FLAVIUS JOSEPHUS, *A.J.*, I.70 (ed. H.ST.J. THACKERAY – *al.*, IV, 32–33). The association of βία with the notions of abundance and strength will be underlined later, in the context of the Satt on Deut 6,5. See, e.g., *Ibid.*, VI.69 (ed. *Ibid.*, V, 200–201); *Ibid.*, VII.310 (ed. *Ibid.*, V, 526–527); *Ibid.*, XI.43 (ed. *Ibid.*, VI, 334–335); *Ibid.*, XVI.401 (ed. *Ibid.*, VIII, 162–163); *Ibid.*, XVIII.291 (ed. *Ibid.*, IX, 170–171); ID., *B.J.*, IV.1.77 (ed. *Ibid.*, III, 24–25); *Ibid.*, V.12.491 (ed. *Ibid.*, III, 352–353); and *Ibid.*, VI.8.399 (ed. *Ibid.*, III, 490–491). For a similar linkage between the corresponding verbs, see, e.g., ID., *A.J.*, VII.124 (ed. *Ibid.*, V, 426–427); and ID., *B.J.*, IV.1.23 (ed. *Ibid.*, III, 10–11). For the connection between ἰσχύς, δύναμις, πολύς, and βία, see, esp., ID., *A.J.*, XI.43 (ed. *Ibid.*, VI, 334–335); and, also, *Ibid.*, XIV.28 (ed. *Ibid.*, VII, 462–463). Finally, for a discussion of the extra-biblical traditions on

should be considered to be the "strongest" (ἰσχυροτάτος) or "most violent" (βιαιότατος) of all things, whether wine, kings, women, or truth[439].

Finally, just like its corresponding verb, so also the substantive refers frequently to the power of natural elements (e.g., water, fire, wind, etc.)[440], and can indicate the force needed to "cross" and enter a territory (see βίᾳ περαιῦσθαι)[441]. Whenever it occurs concomitantly with ὕβρις or ὑβρίζειν, it conveys usually some negative sexual lustful connotation (e.g., sodomy, rape, etc.)[442], whereas alongside πειθώ or πειθεῖν, it points to the use of physical violence as opposed to simple persuasion[443]. It is quite often used in conjunction with both "plunder" (ἁρπαγή or ἁρπάζειν) and "wealth" (χρῆμα)[444], and can also carry with it the overtones of "haste" (σπουδή)[445] and "necessity" (ἀνάγκη)[446].

Adam's prediction, in pseudepigraphic and rabbinic sources, see S. MANSON, ed., *Flavius Josephus*, III, 24, ns. 165–166.

[439] See FLAVIUS JOSEPHUS, *A.J.*, XI.36–56 (ed. H.ST.J. THACKERAY – *al.*, VI, 330–341); and W.E. MOORE, "ΒΙΑΖΩ, ΑΡΠΑΖΩ", 524–525.

[440] See, e.g., FLAVIUS JOSEPHUS, *A.J.*, I.78 (ed. H.ST.J. THACKERAY – *al.*, IV, 36–37); *Ibid.*, II.349 (ed. *Ibid.*, IV, 316–317); *Ibid.*, III.110 (ed. *Ibid.*, IV, 368–369); *Ibid.*, IV.51 (ed. *Ibid.*, IV, 500–501); *Ibid.*, IV.55 (ed. *Ibid.*, IV, 502–503); *Ibid.*, IX.210 (ed. *Ibid.*, VI, 110–111); ID., *B.J.*, III.9.424 (ed. *Ibid.*, II, 694–695); *Ibid.*, IV.1.77 (ed. *Ibid.*, III, 24–25); *Ibid.*, IV.4.286 (ed. *Ibid.*, III, 84–85); and *Ibid.*, VII.3.55 (ed. *Ibid.*, III, 520–521).

[441] See FLAVIUS JOSEPHUS, *A.J.*, IV.77 (ed. H.ST.J. THACKERAY – *al.*, IV, 512–513). See also *Ibid.*, XVIII.37 (ed. B. NIESE, IV, 147); and ID., *B.J.*, IV.203 (ed. *Ibid.*, VI, 373). For the seizure of a territory by force, see, e.g., ID., *A.J.*, XVI.42–43 (ed. *Ibid.*, VII, 468–471).

[442] See, e.g., FLAVIUS JOSEPHUS, *A.J.*, I.200 (ed. H.ST.J. THACKERAY – *al.*, IV, 98–99); *Ibid.*, V.143–146 (ed. *Ibid.*, V, 66–69); *Ibid.*, V.339 (ed. *Ibid.*, V, 150–151); *Ibid.*, VII.170–172 (ed. *Ibid.*, V, 450–453); and W.E. MOORE, "ΒΙΑΖΩ, ΑΡΠΑΖΩ", 539–540.

[443] See, e.g., FLAVIUS JOSEPHUS, *V.*, XXXVII.185 (ed. H.ST.J. THACKERAY – *al.*, I, 68–71); ID., *B.J.*, II.1.8 (ed. *Ibid.*, II, 324–327); *Ibid.*, II.20.562 (ed. *Ibid.*, II, 538–539); ID., *A.J.*, IV.17 (ed. *Ibid.*, IV, 484–485); and W.E. MOORE, "ΒΙΑΖΩ, ΑΡΠΑΖΩ", 534–535.

[444] See, esp., FLAVIUS JOSEPHUS, *A.J.*, I.61 (ed. H.ST.J. THACKERAY – *al.*, IV, 28–29); ID., *B.J.*, II.13.264–265 (ed. *Ibid.*, II, 426–427); *Ibid.*, II.20.562–564 (ed. *Ibid.*, II, 538–539); *Ibid.*, II.21.595–597 (ed. *Ibid.*, II, 550–553); *Ibid.*, VII.8.261 (ed. *Ibid.*, III, 578–579); and W.E. MOORE, "ΒΙΑΖΩ, ΑΡΠΑΖΩ", 528–530. As the latter notes (*Ibid.*, 537), the verb ἁρπάζειν is used also to qualify "rightful seizing". See, e.g., FLAVIUS JOSEPHUS, *B.J.*, I.18.356 (ed. *Ibid.*, II, 166–167); *Ibid.*, VI.6.353 (ed. *Ibid.*, III, 478–479); and ID., *A.J.*, V.171–173 (ed. *Ibid.*, V, 78–79).

[445] Thus, W.E. Moore ("ΒΙΑΖΩ, ΑΡΠΑΖΩ", 524) speaks of "the suddenness of βία". See, e.g., FLAVIUS JOSEPHUS, *A.J.*, II.53 (ed. H.ST.J. THACKERAY – *al.*, IV, 190–191); *Ibid.*, VII.141 (ed. *Ibid.*, V, 436–437); *Ibid.*, XVI.101 (ed. *Ibid.*, IX, 40–41); and ID., *B.J.*, III.7.218 (ed. *Ibid.*, II, 638–639).

[446] See, e.g., FLAVIUS JOSEPHUS, *A.J.*, II.114 (ed. H.ST.J. THACKERAY – *al.*, IV, 216–217); *Ibid.*, IX.99 (ed. *Ibid.*, VI, 52–55); *Ibid.*, XII.281 (ed. *Ibid.*, VII, 144–145); and W.E. MOORE, "ΒΙΑΖΩ, ΑΡΠΑΖΩ", 530–534.

II. The Shared Aggadic Targumic Traditions on Deut 6,5: "Strength" and "Mammon"

Thus, summarizing the latter results, one can see how, in both religious and pagan Greek Jewish writings of the STP, the wide-ranging semantic field of the literary and papyrological source material is slightly narrowed to an analogous variety of positive, neutral and negative meanings, to denote sometimes the power of the natural elements and the human passions, but also the violation of physical boundaries, one's entry into someone else's property by means of "force", the use of wealth and gifts, the dispossession of properties, occasionally in connection with notions that seem to recall the context of Luke 16,16 (e.g., love of wealth, poverty and shame). All in all, however, whether it is a military, physical, sexual, or monetary kind of violence, βία has to do always with the general concept of "strength".

Although such an outcome may sound, at first, rather banal, it is nonetheless quite significant, with respect to Luke 16, to see that, at the time when the Gospels were composed, the Hellenistic idea of "force" or "strength" mingled together with the Jewish notion of "abundance", "wealth" and "properties". Hints of such a relationship are already discernible in the synonymous parallelism of some OT Psalms[447], or also in some of Philo's and Josephus' aforementioned uses of the βία-lexemes[448]. However, clearer indications of such an association are to be found especially in the context of the interpretation given to Israel's profession of "faith" (אמונה)[449], on the basis of its Hebrew and Aramaic texts.

In other words, the foregoing complex of words or concepts, frequently associated with βία-terminology, appears also in some non-Greek Jewish religious texts that comment on the meaning and ritual recitation of Deut 6,5. The body of evidence found by recent studies supports the view that, at the time when the Gospels were written, the ritual recitation of the latter Hebrew text was known to Jews and Christians alike. It is very likely that, during approximately the same period, the interpretative Aramaic traditions (Satt) accompanying and commenting on such a text, circulated freely, not only

---

[447] See, esp., Pss 49[48],7ab; 52[51],9bc; and 62[61],11bc.

[448] See, esp., PHILO, *Mut.* XXXII.172–173 (ed. F.H. COLSON – *al.*, V, 228–231); ID., *Spec.* II.3.9 (ed. *Ibid.*, VII, 310–311); and FLAVIUS JOSEPHUS, *A.J.*, I.70 (ed. H.ST.J. THACKERAY – *al.*, IV, 32–33). An analogous association between "strength" and "abundance" is visible also in the transferred meaning of the Latin term, *vis*, which as E.A. Andrews (*CCLEE*, "*vis*", 1638) points out, is used to translate not only the concept of "*violence*, βία", but also that of "*Quantity, number, abundance*".

[449] This term is sometimes found also in association with "money" (כסף), "wealth" (πλοῦτος), or "treasures" (θησαυροί), and in opposition to "malice of deceit" (בעולא דנשתר). See, e.g., MT on 2Kgs 12,16 and 22,7; LXX on Ps 36,3 (cf. MT on Ps 37,3); TgProv on Prov 28,20; and LXX on Isa 33,6.

among Jews but also among early Christians, whether in Synagogues or in other buildings dedicated to the study of the Torah and to community prayer[450]. Although the vast majority of these texts date after the 1st c. CE, because of the significance of the oral transmission of faith in Jewish thought and practice, the centrality of the Deuteronomic text itself in the life of this people, and the typically conservative tendency of liturgical (prayer) passages, it is quite possible that the hermeneutic traditions contained in them go back to an earlier time, at least, at the oral level.

The relevance of this material for understanding the semantic range of the Lucan βία-lexeme of v. 16, and the analogous connections of these texts with the concepts of law, love, strength, life, and kingdom of God, prompt us to make a brief analysis of these sources and their significance.

1. The Ritual Recitation of the Šᵉma' in 1ˢᵗ c. Palestine

According to several authors, and on the basis of testimonies, such as, the Nash Papyrus, a few *tefillin* found at Qumran, the NT, Flavius Josephus, Justin Martyr, and the Mishnah, Israel's profession of faith (the text of which was based on Deut 6,4–9; 11,13–21; and Num 15,37–41) was already recited in 1ˢᵗ c. Palestine at the beginning of the morning liturgical service of the Temple and in the Synagogue[451]. It was generally preceded by the recitation of the "Ten Commandments" (see Exod 20,1–17; and Deut 5,4–21) or "Words of life"[452]. Scholars seem to agree that, at Jesus' time, there probably existed independent

---

[450] See, e.g., E.P. SANDERS, "Common Judaism", 1–15; K.H. TAN, "The Shema", 181–206; and P. DI LUCCIO, *The Quelle*, 36–37. Thus, F.H. Chase (*The Lord's Prayer*, 8) points out: "The lessons from the Law and the Prophets must have had an honored place in the Christian as in the Jewish Synagogues, and 'the exhortation' would often be based upon some prophetic saying or some ancient type". See also Luke 4,18–21; Acts 13,15; and Chap. IV, p. 166, n. 3.

[451] See, e.g., 1QPhyl; and 4QPhyl 1–2.7.10.12.15; Mark 10,18–19; 12,29–30; Matt 19,17–19; 22,37.39; Luke 10,27; 18,18–20; FLAVIUS JOSEPHUS, *A.J.*, IV.212–213 (ed. H.ST.J. THACKERAY – *al.*, IV, 576–579); JUSTIN MARTYR, *Dial.*, XCIII.2.3 (*PG* 6, 697b); ID., 1 *Apol.*, XVI,6 (*PG* 6, 353a); mBer 1,3; and mTam 4,3–5,1. See also J. MANN, "Changes", 288; E. CORTÉS, *Los Discursos*, 338; E.P. SANDERS, *Judaism*, 196; M. MCNAMARA, *Targum*, 190–192; F. MANNS, *La Preghiera*, 140–143; F.G. VOLTAGGIO, *La oración*, 373; and D. FORTUNA, *Il Figlio dell'ascolto*, 205–224.

[452] As M. Rooker (*The Ten Commandments*, 3) elucidates, "The Ten Commandments are literally the 'Ten Words' (*ăseret haddᵉbārîm*) in Hebrew. The use of the term *dābār*, 'word', in this phrase distinguishes these laws from the rest of the commandments (*miṣwâ*), statutes (*hōq*), and regulations (*mišpāṭ*) in the Old Testament". See, e.g., the Lucan expression, "living words" (λόγια ζῶντα), in Acts 7,38. Listening to these words is equal to articulating the biblical masculine form of the written law (*haddᵉbārîm*) with the Talmudic feminine one of the oral law (*haddibrôt*), and thus enter into the dialectics of life, love and fecundity. See M.-A. OUAKNIN, *Le Dieci Parole*, 31–38.

versions of the love commandment, which were recited daily, and no fixed form of this liturgical passage had yet taken over[453].

2. The Interpretations of the Text in the Jewish World

When one looks at the targumic paraphrases of Deut 6,5, as well as the rabbinic commentaries concerning it, the variety of interpretations illumines further the semantic range of the concept of "strength" (ἰσχύς) generally associated with the βία-based Greek terminology, linking it directly with the Aramaic term for "wealth" (מָמוֹן; μαμωνᾶς)[454].

Thus, one reads in the Targums: "And you shall love *the teaching of the Law of* [emphasis added] the Lord with all your heart, and with all your soul, and with all your *money* [emphasis added]"[455]; or, "And you shall love the Lord your God with all your heart, and with all your soul, and with all your *properties* [emphasis added]"[456]; or, else, "that you may love the Lord your God with *the two dispositions of* [emphasis added] your heart, and *even if it takes* [emphasis added] your soul and *the service of* [emphasis added] all your *money* [emphasis added]"[457]. The italics serve to emphasize here the significant differences with respect to the MT on Deut 6,5, which reads: "And you shall love the Lord your God with all your heart, and with all your soul, and with all your *strength* [מְאֹד]"[458].

The Tg. Pseudo-Jonathan in particular expands the MT of Deut 6,5 on a few subjects, which would come back again in rabbinic commentaries. Let us look then at these hermeneutic developments.

---

[453] See, e.g., F. NOËL, *The Travel Narrative*, 378. For instance, the author (*Ibid.*, 378–379) remarks: "The fact that also the human capacities are varied in the Septuagint texts of the love command makes this hypothesis still more likely [...] the variation in the Septuagint explains the diversity of the wording of the love command in the Synoptic Gospels". See, e.g., the LXX on Deut 6,5; Josh 22,5*b*; 2Kgs 23,25; 2Chr 35,19*b*; 2Macc 1,3–4; 4Macc 13,13; Sir 6,26; 7,27–30; and Mark 12,30.33*a*.

[454] See Luke 16,9.11.13. For a brief summary on the rabbinic exposition of Deut 6,5, see B. GERHARDSSON, *The Testing*, 71–76.

[455] "ותרחמין ית אולפן אורייתה דייי בכל לבבכון ובכל נפשיכון ובכל ממוניכון" (CN on Deut 6,5). See A. DÍEZ MACHO, ed., *Neophyti 1*, V, 70; and M. MCNAMARA, *Targum Neophyti 1*, 49–50.

[456] "ותרחם ית יוי אלהך בכל ליבך ובכל נפשך ובכל נכסך" (TO on Deut 6,5). See B. GROSS-FELD, ed., *The Targum Onqelos*, 33–34; and Sperber, I, 302.

[457] "ותרחמון ית ייי אלקכון בתרי יצרי ליבכון ואפילו נסיב ית נפשכון ובכל ממונכון" (TJI on Deut 6,5). See H. NÖLDEKE, *Targum Jonathan*, 313; and E.G. CLARKE, ed., *Targum Pseudo-Jonathan: Deuteronomy*, 25. See also sy[p] on Deut 6,5; 1QS I,11–13; and P. DI LUCCIO, *The Quelle*, 274–275.

[458] "ואהבת את יהוה אלהיך בכל לבבך ובכל־נפשך ובכל מאדך" (MT on Deut 6,5). See *BHS*, 297.

First of all, concerning the love of God with all one's heart, it mentions a heart that loves with both its two "inclinations" or "dispositions" (יצרי)[459]. This idea rests probably on the notion that, when the Lord God created man, he created him "with two inclinations"[460], i.e., "the inclination to do good and the inclination to do evil" (SifDev 32,59), and later, after our progenitors' fall, gave Cain and his seed the power to control his evil inclination and to be either righteous, by doing God's will, or sin, by disobeying it[461]. As B. Gerhardsson remarks, the rabbis would speak of the "doubter" or "unbeliever" as someone having "two hearts" (שני לבבות) or a "divided heart" (לב חלוק), whereas they would refer to the "righteous" man, as one having "a clean, whole and undivided, 'perfect' heart (לבב שלם or תם לבב, בר לבב)"[462], who both "seeks" (דרש) and "loves" (אהב) God "with his whole heart" (בכל־לבבו)[463]. This kind of love would mainly imply, for them, blessing God in both good and bad times (see Ps 34[33],2), and thus, in a certain sense, loving God gratefully, even when things do not go the way one would expect (see SifDev 32,59; and mBer 9,5)[464].

The Pseudo-Jonathan continues its interpretation of Deut 6,5 and, as F. Manns comments, affirms:

"'love the Lord your God [...] *even if it takes your soul* [emphasis added]', implying that one must love God by being ready even to give up one's own very *life* [emphasis added]"[465].

In the Scriptures, in fact, the Hebrew word for "soul", *nepeš* (נפש; see also ψυχή in Greek) designates that "principle of life" which, according to the OT, is located in the blood, and turns the person's or animal's "flesh" (בשר or σάρξ) that possesses it into a living being[466]. A propos of this, the rabbis, both in the

---

[459] See Jastrow, "יֵצֶר", I, 590. The targumic tradition on the two inclinations of the heart is sometimes related to the presence of a single or double *bêt* (ב), in the Hebrew word for "heart" (לֵב or לֵבָב), and of the single or double *yôd* (י), in the Hebrew verb used to describe man's *artistic* "fashioning" (יָצַר) by God. See, e.g., MT: וַיִּיצֶר, in Gen 2,7; יֵצֶר, in Gen 6,5; and יוֹצֵר, in Jer 18,2–4. See also Str-B, IV, 466–483.

[460] See "ובְרא יי אלקים ית אדם בתרין יצרין" (TJI on Gen 2,7).

[461] See "ובידך מסרית רשותיה דיצרא בישא [...] ואנת תהי שליט ביה בין למיזכי בין למיחטי" (TJI on Gen 4,7). Curiously, the Hebr./Aram. term יֵצֶר (i.e., "inclination") per se is sometimes rendered by the LXX with the word διάνοια, that is, the same term which the Synoptic Gospels unanimously add when referring to Deut 6,5 (see, e.g., Gen 6,5; 8,21; 1Chr 29,18; Matt 22,37; Mark 12,30; and Luke 10,27b). For the Jewish concept of the two inclinations of the heart and the *Šᵉmaʿ*, see, e.g., B. GERHARDSSON, *The Testing*, 48–50; and E.E. URBACH, *The Sages*, I, 471–483.

[462] B. GERHARDSSON, *The Testing*, 48.

[463] The Palestinian targumic exegesis on Deut 6,4 mentions thus the undivided or "perfect heart" (בליבא שלמה) of the twelve sons of Jacob (see CN and TJII on Deut 6,4).

[464] See, e.g., D. FORTUNA, *Il Figlio dell'ascolto*, 214.

[465] F. MANNS, *La Preghiera*, 140. See B. GERHARDSSON, *The Testing*, 75–77. See also the aforementioned etymological link of "violence" with "life".

[466] See, e.g., Gen 9,4; Lev 17,11; Deut 12,23; and BDAG, "ψυχή", 1098.

Mishnah (e.g., mBer 9,5) and the Talmud (e.g., bBer 61b; yBer 9,7; and Sot 5.7), mention the instance of Rabbi Akiba's joy for being finally able to fulfil the love commandment of the *Š^ema'*, by loving God with all his soul, through his very martyrdom[467].

As far as the interpretation of the Hebrew term *m^e'ōd* (מאֹד) is concerned, what immediately catches the attention is the almost unanimous Jewish under-standing of the word, as meaning "money" (Aram. מָמוֹן), "wealth" (Aram. הוֹן), "properties" (Aram. נִכְסִין), or "possessions" (Aram. קִנְיָן), as compared to the rather general sense of "strength" (ἰσχύς) or "might" (δύναμις), rather visible in the Greek and Latin ancient translations of the MT[468]. A similar association between riches and strength is already visible, for instance, in the synonymous parallelism of some OT Psalms (see, e.g., Pss 49[48],7ab; 52[51],9bc; and 62[61],11bc), and other Hellenistic Jewish writings (e.g., Philo and Josephus)[469]. However, the extant Aramaic traditions common to all the Targums (Satt), specifically, those on Deut 6,5, make it utterly clear[470].

Bible dictionaries point out how the term *m^e'ōd* occurs 300x in the OT and almost always as an adverb, deriving its sense possibly from the Assyrian word for "abundance" (*mu'du*), and thus meaning "very", "exceedingly", or "greatly"[471].

---

[467] See J.W. VAN HENTEN – F. AVEMARIE, ed., *Martyrdom*, 151–153.

[468] For this interpretative tradition (i.e., *m^e'ōd* = *māmôn*, or *hôn*, *niḵsîn* and *qinyān*), see sy^p, TJI, CN and TO on Deut 6,5; SifDev 55; TJ on Jer 17,1; Cant 4,9; 8,9; and Prov 3,3; 1QS 1,11; mSan 74a; SifDev 32,59; mBer 54a, 61b; Pes 25a; and bYom 82a. See also Jastrow, "הוֹן", I, 339; *Ibid.*, "מָמוֹן", II, 794; *Ibid.*, "נכסין", II, 911; *Ibid.*, "קִנְיָן", II, 1393; M. MCNAMARA, *Targum*, 99–100; and P. DI LUCCIO, *The Quelle*, 206. Conversely, cf. the LXX: δύναμις (Deut 6,5); and ἰσχύς (2 Kgs 23,25); and the *Vg.*: *fortitudine* (Deut 6,5); and *virtute* (2 Kgs 23,25). For Thayer ("δυνατός", 160), a δυνατός is a person who is "able, powerful [...] strong [...] mighty in wealth and influence". See also E. KUTSCH, "הון", *TDOT*, III, 364–368 (esp. 367).

[469] Synonymous parallelism can be defined as that symmetrical poetic disposition in which, as S. Bazyliński (*A Guide*, 164) points out, "the second member of a unit repeats with other words the thought of the first member". For instance, in Ps 49[48],7ab, the first term in the parallelism, "strength" (MT: חיל; LXX: δύναμις), is paralleled with "the abundance of riches" (MT: רב עשרם; LXX: πλῆθος τοῦ πλούτου), and translated by the TgPs with "properties" (נכסין). Likewise, in Sir 5,1–2.8 (see μὴ ἔπεχε ἐπὶ τοῖς χρήμασίν σου [חילך אל תשען על] in parallel with μὴ ἐξακολούθει τῇ ψυχῇ καὶ τῇ ἰσχύι σου [כוחך אל תשען על] and μὴ ἔπεχε ἐπὶ χρήμασιν ἀδίκοις [אל תבטח על נכסי שקר]), "wealth" is first paired with both "soul" and "strength", and then spelled out in greater detail in terms of "unrighteous wealth", by way of *inclusio*. See also Sir 8,1–2; PHILO, *Mut.* XXXII.172–173 (ed. F.H. COLSON – *al.*, V, 228–231); ID., *Spec.* II.3.9 (ed. *Ibid.*, VII, 310–311); FLAVIUS JOSEPHUS, *A.J.*, I.70 (ed. H.ST.J. THACKERAY – *al.*, IV, 32–33); J.T. WILLIS, "The Juxtaposition", 471.477; J. ZIEGLER, ed., *Sapientia Iesu*, 147.149; G. RAVASI, *Il libro dei Salmi*, II, 76, n. 14; P.C. BEENTJES, *The Book of Ben Sira*, 26; and F. UEBERSCHAER, *Weisheit aus der Begegnung*, 171–172.

[470] A. Shinan refers to these traditions with the expression, "shared aggadic targumic traditions" (המסורת הכלל תרגומית). See Chap. IV, p. 166, n. 3.

[471] See W.C. KAISER, "מאֹד", *TWOT*, I, 487; *HALOT*, "מאֹד", 4719; and BDB, "מאֹד", 547.

For that reason, מְאֹד may be compared also with כַּבִּיר, which, as we have seen, in a couple of instances, at least, is actually rendered by the Greek substantive βία (Isa 17,13; and 28,2), whereas in Gen 19,3.9 it is used in conjunction with פָּצַר and translated by the LXX with the verb παραβιάζεσθαι[472]. Curiously enough, Deut 6,5 and 2Kgs 23,25 are the only two OT exceptions in which the term מְאֹד is used as a substantive (lit. meaning "muchness") and both of them do refer to the *Š^ema'*[473].

The rabbis, too, in expanding further on this hermeneutical reading of "strength" (מְאֹד) as "money" (מָמוֹן)[474], would sometimes associate the latter with "life" (נֶפֶשׁ), thus echoing what we have already mentioned a propos of βίος. For instance, in San 74*a* we read:

If it says "with all your soul" why should it also say "with all your might", and if it says "with all your might" why should it also say "with all your soul"? Should there be a man who values his *life* [emphasis added] more than his *money* [emphasis added], for him it says: "with all your *might* [emphasis added]"[475].

Finally, the sincere recitation of the *Š^ema' Yiśrā'ēl* was regarded generally as a binding legal oath and referred to as *taking up on one's shoulders the yoke of the kingdom of God*[476]. Thus, J. Ratzinger explains:

the one who prays it accepts God's lordship, which, consequently, through the act of praying, enters the world [...] helps to bear it on his shoulders, and through his prayer, God's lordship shapes his way of life, his day-to-day existence, making it a locus of God's presence in the world[477].

---

[472] According to the *HALOT* (I, "כביר", 458), the Hebrew term means, "strong, mighty [...] neuter, great things, much". See also BDB, "כַּבִּיר", 460.

[473] For instance, as regards 2Kgs 23,25, J.A. Montgomery (*Kings*, 536) observes: "Josiah's piety is expressed in terms of the Shema [...] with its tripartite analysis of human nature". See also T.R. HOBBS, *2 Kings*, 338.

[474] For instance, according to the translation of B. Grossfeld (ed., *The Targum Onqelos*, 34, n. 2), mBer 9,5 reads: "'With all your might' (Deut 6:5) means with all your money". In turn, S. Lieberman (ed., *Midrash Devarim Rabba*, 70) reports the following story, about Yossi ben Simmai: "when a fire took place in his garden on a Sabbath and the quaestor from Zippori came down to extinguish it [...] he did not let him, saying: "How can I fulfil [the command]: 'With all your money?' [היאך אני מקיים בצל ממונך]". See also SifDev 32,59; Ber 54*a*; *Ibid.*, 61*b*; Pes 25*a*; Yom 82*a*; P. BLACKMAN, ed., *Mishnayoth*, I, 71–73; J. NEUSNER, ed., *Sifre*, I, 86–90; and D. FORTUNA, *Il Figlio dell' ascolto*, 205–219. Thus, the latter author (*Ibid.*, 242) eventually remarks: "Il termine *mammona* [...] corrisponde al modo in cui, al tempo di Gesù, era interpretato il termine ebraico מְאֹד di Deut 6,5".

[475] B. GROSSFELD, ed., *The Targum Onqelos*, 34, n. 2. See also D. FORTUNA, *Il Figlio dell'ascolto*, 215, ns. 62.64.

[476] See, e.g., mBer 2,2; bBer 61b; J. NEUSNER, *The Theology of the Halakhah*, 326ff; A. BERLIN – M.Z. BRETTLER, ed., *The Jewish Study Bible*, 380; P. DI LUCCIO, *The Quelle*, 192, n. 50; D. FORTUNA, *Il Figlio dell'ascolto*, 211–212; and *Ibid.*, 215, n. 61.

[477] J. RATZINGER, *Jesus*, I, 57.

Accordingly, when understood in the light of the Satt on Deut 6,5 and its relationship between the concepts of "strength" (characterizing the most basic meaning of the verb βιάζεσθαι) and that of wealth or "mammon", many of the strategic "signals for comprehension"[478] released by the narrative context of Luke 16,16 become more recognizable: the framing occurrences of the verb "to listen" (ἀκούειν) around vv. 14 and 31; the eschatological use of μαμωνᾶς, suggested by both parables and sayings; the very notion of faith presupposed by almsgiving, as a φρονίμως ποιεῖν (v. 8a; cf. vv. 3.4.8b.9a)[479]; the relationship between βασιλεία (v. 16), βιάζεται (v. 16), μαμωνᾶς (vv. 9.11.13), νόμος (vv. 16.17; cf. vv. 29.31), and other key words, such as, εἰς (vv. 5.13[2x].17), θεός (vv. 13.15[2x].16), ἀγαπήσει (v. 13), and καρδία (v. 15); the association of the expression ὁ νόμος καὶ οἱ προφῆται (v. 16a) with Deut 6,5 and Lev 19,18[480]; the idea of love underlying the wordplay between ποιήσατε φίλους (v. 9), φιλάργυροι (v. 14), ἀγαπήσει (v. 13) and μαμωνᾶς (vv. 9.11.13); and the assonance, at their Aramaic level, between πιστός (v. 10[2x]), πιστοί (vv. 11.12), πιστεύσει (v. 11), μαμωνᾶς (vv. 9.11.13), and the Semitic verb for faith, 'āman (אמן). Last but not least, such an understanding answers also the question how the resonance prompted by the second and third sayings in each set (see figure # 2) joins concretely βία (v. 16) and νόμος (v. 17) with the term μαμωνᾶς (vv. 9.10–12).

D. The Appropriation and Use of the "βία-terms" in Early Christian Literature

As one turns to the early Christian literature (ECL), both canonical and non-canonical writings reaffirm what has emerged so far, namely, the idea of "force", as the most prevalent common meaning in the nuances of our terms, and their ambiguous or neutral use.

In canonical writings, in particular, what immediately draws the attention is the distinctive rate of "βία-root" lexemes occurring in Luke-Acts. This exceptional number of occurrences reflects how Luke was influenced by the Semitic literature he knew, especially the LXX and other Jewish sources, but not exclusively. His 1st c. CE literary and educational background, reflected

---

[478] D. MARGUERAT – Y. BOURQUIN, How to Read, 145.

[479] See also the expression, "giving [lit. 'doing'] alms" (ποιεῖν ἐλεημοσύνην): Tob 1,3.16; 4,7–8.11.16; 12,8–9; 14,2.8.10–11; Sir 7,10; 16,14; 35,2; Matt 6,2–3; Acts 9,36; 10,2; and 24,17.

[480] See, e.g., Deut 6,5; Lev 19,18; 2Kgs 23,25; Tob 4,15–16; Matt 5,17–18; 7,12; 11,13; 22,37–40; Mark 12,30–31; Luke 6,30–31; 10,26–27; 16,16–17.29.31; Did. I.2 (ed. W. RORDORF – A. TUILIER, 142–143); G. RESCH, Das Aposteldecret, 132–141; M.-L. RIGATO, "'Mosè ed i Profeti'", 165–166.175; and P. DI LUCCIO, The Quelle, 115, n. 48. The NT notion that "the whole law" (πάντα τὸν νόμον) is summarized by the Šᵉma' is already expressed in a nutshell, in 2Kgs 23,25. See also Rom 13,9; Gal 5,14; and Jas 2,8.

also in his knowledge of the Hellenistic Greek language and style[481], may account for a better awareness on his part even of the other meanings and uses that these words had in the non-religious literature. Within the wide semantic field of these terms, it is quite possible that Luke would have understood also those legal and economical nuances observed in the papyri. Indeed, the fact that the evangelist places the teaching contained in v. 16 within a section of his Travel Narrative (specifically, chap. 16 of his Gospel), in which the primary (vs. exclusive) thematic concern is the use of money or property, argues in favor of such a hypothesis.

I. The NT Apocryphal Literature

The NT Apocrypha may be of less relevance than the writings of Philo or Josephus. However, even if only briefly and by way of conclusion, it may be helpful to take a look at how the early Christians understood and used the βία-based lexemes in the non-canonical literature of the first four centuries of the Common Era, and whether one can discern any insights into the earliest stages of the Gospel tradition or, as T.A. Wayment would say, any "developing Christian attitudes [...] towards the texts"[482]. According to some scholars, some of these writings are ostensibly contemporary to those of the NT Canon and might potentially draw from the same sources, at least in part[483].

Generally, our analysis of these sources confirms the results seen thus far. Negative and positive readings of the βία-terms continue to occur, one alongside the other, yet with the former slowly outnumbering the latter.

Contrary to the Latin text of the Pseudo-Matthean Gospel (cf. *violentiam fecisses*)[484], for instance, the earlier Greek text of the Proto-Gospel of James avoids altogether the use of the βία-terminology and, even when the context may require it, prefers to use other verbs (see, e.g., μιαινεῖν and ταπεινεῖν) to

---

[481] Jerome (*Vir. ill.* VII [*PL* 23, 649b]) describes Luke explicitly as being "not unskilled in the Greek language" (τοῦ Ἑλληνικοῦ οὐκ ἄπειρος). For some bibliographic notes on Luke's elevated Greek style, see, e.g., P. WALTERS, *The Assumed Authorial Unity*, 90–92, ns. 1–8.

[482] T.A. WAYMENT, *The Text*, 2.

[483] See, e.g., E. HENNECKE – W. SCHNEEMELCHER, ed., *NT Apocrypha*, I, 61. For a recent introduction on the scholarship and studies of the NT Apocrypha, see P. HELDT, "New Testament Apocrypha", 652–675. For a collection of some of their earliest mss., see, e.g., T.A. WAYMENT, *The Text*, 9–409. For a discussion on the dates of the NT papyri, see H. KOESTER, "Apocryphal and Canonical Gospels", 107–110. Luke's own use of the term may have then been influenced by some oral or written collection of Jesus' sayings, traceable also in the so called apocryphal traditions. For a discussion of the relationship between *Q* and *Ev. Thom.*, see, e.g., *Ibid.*, 112–119.

[484] *Ps.-Mt.*, XII.1 (ed. B.D. EHRMAN – Z. PLEŠE, 94–95). See also *Ev. Phil.*, LXI; and A. DE SANTOS OTERO, *Los Evangelios Apócrifos*, 399.

express the same immoral alleged violation of the Virgin Mary[485]. In the Gospel of Nicodemus, the lexeme indicates the positive "power" (δύναμις), which a word of the risen Lord has to "forcefully" (βίᾳ) drag Lazarus out of the entrails of Hades[486]. The majority of the other texts, however, do use the substantive and its adjectival or adverbial cognates negatively, to predicate, for instance, the "violent" (βίαιος) trait of one of the two "bandits" (λῃσταί) crucified with Jesus[487], the "ill-treatment" (βία) accorded to prisoners[488], the vicious character of Jesus' death, together with those of Caiaphas and Annas (see, esp., the combination of the concepts of *violence* and *life* in the phrase, Καϊάφαν δυστήνως καὶ βιαιῶς τὸν βίον ἀπορρῆξαι, in l. 41)[489], and the sexual union with a woman by the Gnostic elect[490]. Finally, in the Gospel of Thomas, βιάζεσθαι is used also neutrally of Christ, to narrate the effort of the child Jesus, as he "forces his way through" the crowds (see καὶ βιασάμενος διῆλθεν τὸν ὄχλον)[491].

Last but not least, the verb occurs also in the Gospel of the Nazarenes, in the form of a marginal note on Matt 11,12, which indicates an alternative reading of this "synoptic-like"[492] material: here, βιάζεσθαι is replaced altogether by διαρπάζεσθαι[493]. The direct reference to the Matthean verse is particularly significant, insofar as it attests the possibility for the authors of these writings to have drawn from traditions known also by the evangelists of the NT Canon[494].

II. The NT Canon and Luke's Exclusive Use of the "βία-terms"

Whenever the NT authors wish to convey the notion of "violence", they usually use Greek adjectives, such as, βαρύς, ἰσχυρός, ὑβριστής, πλήκτης, or their cog-

---

[485] See, e.g., *Prot. Iac.*, XIII.1–2 (ed. B.D. EHRMAN – Z. PLEŠE, 54–55); *Ibid.*, XV.2–3 (ed. *Ibid.*, 56–57); and J.K. ELLIOTT, *A Synopsis*, 50–51. As B.D. Ehrman and Z. Pleše (ed., *The Apocryphal Gospels*, 73) remark, the Gospel of Pseudo-Matthew "is a Latin reworking of the (Greek) Protoevangelium Jacobi, based probably on one or more Latin editions of that work that have long since been lost".

[486] See, e.g., *Ev. Nic.* I.B, XX.3 (ed. B.D. EHRMAN – Z. PLEŠE, 480–481); and C. VON TISCHENDORF, ed., *Evangelia Apocrypha*, 174.

[487] See *Narr. Ios.*, I.2 (ed. B.D. EHRMAN – Z. PLEŠE, 572–573); and C. VON TISCHENDORF, ed., *Evangelia Apocrypha*, 201.

[488] See *Narr. Ios.*, IV.1 (ed. B.D. EHRMAN – Z. PLEŠE, 580–581); and C. VON TISCHENDORF, ed., *Evangelia Apocrypha*, 208.

[489] See, e.g., *Ep. Tib. Pil.*, l. 5 (ed. B.D. EHRMAN – Z. PLEŠE, 532–533); *Ibid.*, l. 41 (ed. *Ibid.*, 534–535); and *Ibid.*, l. 51 (ed. *Ibid.*, 534–535).

[490] See, e.g., *Ev. Phil.*, CIV; and A. DE SANTOS OTERO, *Los Evangelios Apócrifos*, 406.

[491] See, e.g., *Ev. Thom.*, X.2 (ed. B.D. EHRMAN – Z. PLEŠE, 16–17); and J.K. ELLIOTT, *A Synopsis*, 155.

[492] B.D. EHRMAN AND Z. PLEŠE, ed., *The Apocryphal Gospels*, 202.

[493] See, e.g., *Ev. Naz.*, X.5 (ed. B.D. EHRMAN – Z. PLEŠE, 208–209); D. DAUBE, *The New Testament*, 288; and S.R. LLEWELYN, "Forcible Acquisition", 161, n. 89.

[494] See, e.g., A.F.J. KLIJN, *Jewish-Christian Gospel Traditions*, 36.

nates[495]. Above and beyond the occurrence of βιάζεται in the "violence passage"[496] (Matt 11,12; Luke 16,16), Luke is the only NT author who makes use of the "βία-based" terms to describe the intrinsic force of an act of persuasion, a situation of mob pressure, or an element of nature[497]. Thus, if any of the NT authors is entitled to know better the nuances of the verb βιάζεσθαι and its cognates it is certainly Luke.

Overall, in the Greek New Testament, the verb βιάζεσθαι occurs 2x, that is, in Matt 11,12 and Luke 16,16. It suffices here to say that G. Schrenk is probably right in suggesting that the two verses require to be treated separately, because of the different linguistic structures and contexts in which the verb occurs[498].

To these occurrences, one must add also those of the verb, παραβιάζεσθαι (2x), in Luke 24,29 and Acts 16,15. In both cases, Luke uses the verb in the context of hospitality and the power of persuasion, generally following closely its LXX usage[499]. By their entreaties, the two Emmaus disciples press/invite (παρεβιάσαντο) the anonymous pilgrim (Jesus) to stay with them, as an expression of their insistence and hearty welcome (Luke 24,29)[500]. Likewise, Lydia

---

[495] See, e.g., Matt 22,6; Rom 1,30; 2Cor 10,10; 12,10; 1Thess 2,2; 1Tim 1,13; 3,3; and Titus 1,7.

[496] W. STENGER, "βιάζομαι, βιαστής", *EDNT*, I, 216.

[497] See παραβιάζεσθαι: Luke 24,29; Acts 16,15; βία: Acts 5,26; 21,35; 27,41; and βίαιος: Acts 2,2. The NT writer does use other terms as well (e.g., μέγας, ἰσχύω, ὑβρίζω, and βαρύς), especially whenever he has to express the kind of negative violence present in a persecution or mistreatment, the beating by an evil spirit, the rapacity of wolves, and the loss or damage of a shipwreck. See, e.g., Luke 18,32; Acts 8,1; 14,5; 19,16; and 20,29. It is also significant that the clearly hostile actions of extorting money or properties by force and threat of violence and putting pressure on someone for personal gain are not conveyed by Luke with any βία-related verb, but by means of διασείω and συκοφαντέω, respectively (see Luke 3,14; and Luke 19,8). See also BDAG, "διασείω", 236; and *Ibid.*, "συκοφαντέω", 955. Finally, Luke uses the word βίος more than the other Synoptic writers. While the lexeme is totally absent in Matthew's Gospel, it is used only 1x by Mark (12,44) and 5x by Luke (8,14.43; 15,12.30; and 21,4), often in the context of riches (see all of the above, with the exception of Luke 8,43).

[498] See G. SCHRENK, "βιάζομαι, βιαστής", *TDNT*, I, 609.

[499] See, e.g., Gen 19,3; Judg(A) 13,15.16; 19,7(= B); 1Sam 28,23; 2Kgs 2,17; 5,16; and Sus(LXX) 1,19. In the MT of Judg 13,15.16, the idea of a hospitable and persuasive pressure is expressed by the verb √ עצר (see v. 15: נַעְצְרָה־נָּא אוֹתָךְ; and v. 16: אִם־תַּעְצְרֵנִי), which as G.F. Moore (*Judges*, ICC, 321–322) notes, "generally implies forcible restraint, and here elegantly expresses the urgency of the invitation to stay". The LXX (A Codex) translates it with the verb βιάζομαι (see v. 15: βιασώμεθα δή σε; and v. 16: ἐὰν βιάσῃ με). The B Codex, however, prefers the verb κατέχω (see v. 15: κατάσχωμεν ὧδέ σε; and v. 16: ἐὰν κατάσχῃς με), which, as Thayer ("κατέχω", 339–340) specifies, means to "retain [...] from going away", but also "to get possession of". In Luke's Gospel, the latter verb is used 2x to speak of Jesus and of God's word (see Luke 4,42; 8,15).

[500] The Latin translation makes the persuasive nuance clearer: *et coegerunt illum* (*Vg.*). See *CCLEE*, "*cogo*", 300. The Syriac versions, however, translate the Greek verb differently, namely, the *Peshiṭta* (P) uses √ܐܠܨ (see "and they urged him strongly": ܘܐܠܨܘܗܝ); whereas both the *Synaiticus* (S) and *Curetonian* (C) mss. of the *Vetus Syra* have √ܥܨܐ (see "and they

persuades (see παρεβιάσατο) Paul and Luke to stay/lodge in her house (Acts 16,15)[501].

As far as the substantive βία is concerned, it likewise occurs only 3x and always in the *Opus Lucanus* (Acts 5,26; 21,35; and 27,41). Of these, 2x it is contextualized as a human activity and 1x as an element of nature. Specifically, in the context of hardship, difficulty and persecution, the apostles are captured in the temple courts and arrested (lit. "brought" before the Sanhedrin), but "without force/violence" (see ἦγεν αὐτοὺς οὐ μετὰ βίας; and ἄγω: Acts 5,19.21.27)[502], since the high priest and the Sadducees (see Acts 5,17–18.21) are afraid of the people's reaction (see Luke 20,19). Likewise, in Acts 21,35, Paul is being arrested and "brought" (ἄγω: Acts 21,34) into the barracks or headquarters of the Roman troops in Jerusalem. However, this time the violence is not that of the soldiers, but it refers to the "turmoil" (θόρυβος: Acts 21,34) of the crowd. Ironically, thus, Paul is being protected by what appears to be true mob violence (lit. "because of the violence of the crowd": διὰ τὴν βίαν τοῦ ὄχλου). In Acts 27,41, however, βία is used in the context of Paul's shipwreck (see Acts 27,15.17) to describe the powerful force of an element of nature, namely, the stormy waves of the sea (see, e.g., Wis 13,2; 17,17; 19,7; and Acts 27,18.20)[503]. Although Paul is still being led to Rome in chains (see, e.g., Acts 26,31–27,2.42–43; 28,17), this time the violence implies no hostile action of man: the "stern [of the ship where Paul is kept prisoner] is being destroyed by the violence/force of the sea waves" (ἡ δὲ πρύμνα ἐλύετο ὑπὸ τῆς βίας τῶν κυμάτων)[504].

A similar use is made by Luke, as regards the only NT occurrence of the adjective βίαιος, in Acts 2,2, in the context of the descent of the Holy Spirit on the day of Pentecost (see Acts 2,1–4). Here, the lexeme is used again to describe the powerful force of an element of *nature*, namely, that "of a gust of

---

begun to": ܐܘܣܝܦ). See also J.P. SMITH, ed., *A Compendious Syriac Dictionary*, "ܐܠ", 18; *Ibid.*, "ܐܠܐ", 595–596; W.M. THACKSTON, *Introduction*, 221; and G.L. CARREGA, *La Vetus Syra*, 202–203.

[501] See the *Vg.*: *et coegit nos*; and the *Peshiṭta*: "and she constrained/urged us much" (ܐܠܨܬܢ). See also J.P. SMITH, ed., *A Compendious Syriac Dictionary*, "ܗܓܡ", 360; and W.M. THACKSTON, *Introduction*, 211.

[502] See, also, the MT of Isa 52,4 (בְּאֶפֶס עֲשָׁקוֹ), wherein Assyria oppresses God's people for no reason, i.e., "without cause [...] Isa 52,4" (*HALOT*, I, "אפס", 79). The LXX (A. PIETERSMA – B.G. WRIGHT, ed., *A New English Translation*, 865) translates it thus: "they were led by force" βίᾳ ἤχθησαν). For the critical text of Acts 5,26 and its minor variants, see NA[28], 394.

[503] See "be violently beaten by a storm Acts 27,18" (BDAG, "σφοδρῶς", 980) and "of the pressure of a violent tempest [...] Acts 27,20" (Thayer, "ἐπίκειμαι", 239). See also Exod 14,21 and Neh 9,11: the LXX translates the same Heb. term, עז (i.e., "strong, mighty, wind Exod 14,21" [BDB, "עז", 738]), with either βίαιος or σφοδρός (i.e., "pert. to being excessive, vehement [...] violent" [BDAG, "σφοδρός", 980]), to describe the force/violence of the wind and the sea, respectively.

[504] For the textual commentary of the verse, see Metzger[2], 500; and R.L. OMANSON, *A Textual Guide*, 288–289.

wind"[505] (φερομένης πμοῆς βιαίας) or "breath of life"[506], rushing and roaring (see ἦχος: Luke 21,25 and Acts 2,2) all over the house where the apostles were gathered[507].

Overall, then, as the *Analytical Lexicon of the Greek New Testament* points out, βιάζεσθαι and its cognates occur in the NT Canon "always with a component of force"[508]. Specifically, as far as Luke 16,16 is concerned, the most probable meaning of the verb would be, *"to enter forcibly into something"*[509]. As we have already seen, literary and religious Greek documents use the verb in conjunction with the preposition εἰς and the accusative to mean precisely that. Thus, G. Schrenk states:

in Greek βιάζεται εἰς does not mean "to exert force against" but "forcefully to press into"; "to fight against" would be βιάζεσθαι with the accusative, and if a preposition were used it would be πρός or ἐπί[510].

The same can be said concerning the use of this expression in the papyri. For instance, S.R. Llewelyn notes:

When the verb βιάζομαι had as its object a person, it meant "to pressure" or "to compel" [...] When used absolutely or applied to an impersonal object, as in the case of Luke 16,16, βιάζομαι like εἰσβιάζομαι (cf. Luke 16,16 εἰς αὐτὴν βιάζεται) could mean "enter by force"[511].

The problem remains that of establishing which kind of "force" or violence is at stake in the context of the Lucan saying, which allows "everyone" (πᾶς) to

---

[505] Thayer, "φέρω", 650.

[506] Thayer, "πνοή", 524.

[507] See, e.g., Exod 14,21; Wis 4,4; 5,11; 7,20; Isa 11,15; Jer 18,14; and Ps 47[48],8. Just as in Wis 7,20 (πνευμάτων βίας), so in Acts 2,2 (πμοῆς βιαίας), the authors may be playing with the polisemic value of their expressions. See, e.g., D. WINSTON, *The Wisdom*, 175. The forceful nuance of the Greek adjective is underlined by the *Vg.*, which reads: "a vehement spirit" (*spiritus vehementis*). See *CCLEE*, "*vehemens*", 1609. The Syriac *Peshiṭta* (P) translates: "a powerful wind" (ܪܘܚܐ ܬܩܝܦܬܐ). See J.P. SMITH, ed., *A Compendious Syriac Dictionary*, "ܐ", 408; and W.M. THACKSTON, *Introduction*, 213.

[508] Friberg, "βιάζω", 91. In the "violence passage", the use of force inherent within the occurrence of the Greek verb, is brought out by the *Vg.*'s understanding: *et omnis in illud vim facit* (Luke 16,16); and, *vim patitur et violenti rapiunt illud* (Matt 11,12).

[509] BDAG, "βιάζω", 175.

[510] G. SCHRENK, "βιάζομαι, βιαστής", *TDNT*, I, 612. In reality, according to the author (*Theologisches*, I, 611), the Greek expression βιάζεται εἰς literally means "to penetrate violently" (*"gewaltsam eindringen in"*) or "forcibly find one's way into", rather than "forcefully to press into", as if it were merely a synonymous expression of παραβιάζομαι or ἀναγκάζω. Indeed, Luke might have found βιάζομαι in his source, but then he may have also chosen to place it in the context of chap. 16 precisely because of its slightly different nuance. See, e.g., Luke 14,23; 24,29; Acts 16,15; P.-H. MENOUD, "Le sens", 210–212; and P.S. CAMERON, *Violence*, 134–135.142.

[511] S.R. LLEWELYN, "Forcible Acquisition", 132, n. 2. See also Moulton, "βιάζομαι", 109–110; R. TAUBENSCHLAG, *The Law*, 442–447; and S.R. LLEWELYN, "Forcible Acquisition", 130–152.

"penetrate" or "find one's way into" (βιάζεται εἰς) the kingdom of God, most likely "through attempts to *occupy* (an area) *by force* (a territory, APPIAN, *Bell. Civ.* 3,24 §91)"[512].

E. Concluding Remarks and Remaining Questions

In the opening remarks of his article on the meaning of βιάζεσθαι in ordinary Greek, G. Schrenk has stated:

Like βία and its Sanskrit cognates, βιάζομαι always denotes a forced as distinct from a voluntary act [...] Whether the reference is to compulsion by higher powers (nature or fate), or whether man compels himself or natural forces, there is always the effective achievement of an act of force, or an attempt as such. In the rich use in relation to military action, maltreatment, compulsion of various kinds and even religious constraint, we can see clearly this basic sense of the exercise of hostile force[513].

Based on the linguistic and semantic analysis conducted in this section of ours, we can agree with Schrenk's assertion only in part. Indeed, the βία-root lexemes do refer generally to "an act of force, or an attempt as such". However, their "basic sense" is not necessarily "hostile", nor does the verb βιάζομαι "always" stand for "a forced as distinct from a voluntary" action[514].

Specifically, our analysis has shown how one cannot really speak of an "un-equivocal" (eindeutigen)[515] negative use of the terms. Quite the reverse, their usage is so persistently marked by an intrinsic semantic ambivalence between good and evil that the context in which they occur becomes key to their proper understanding, time and again[516].

---

[512] BDAG, "βιάζω", 175.

[513] G. Schrenk, "βιάζομαι, βιαστής", *TDNT*, I, 609.

[514] It suffices to recall here the observation made by R. Taubenschlag (*The Law*, 444): "Unintentional violence is inconceivable". Unfortunately, compared with several other articles in the *Theological Dictionary of the New Testament*, G. Schrenk's review on the nuances of the verb in the secular Greek usage is too short to be judged "conclusive" (only 14 lines!) and, as such, cannot be taken simply for granted, as do, for instance, S. Schulz or J. Schlosser. See S. SCHULZ, *Q*, 265; and J. SCHLOSSER, "Le Règne", 517–518. It would seem rather that the author may have overlooked the ambivalence of the data quite hurriedly and in favor of his biased negative outlook. Similar observations have already been made by other scholars. See, e.g., G. HÄFNER, "Gewalt", 24.31–32.

[515] U. LUZ, *Das Evangelium*, II, 178. Cf. G. HÄFNER, "Gewalt", 24.

[516] Thus, C. Stratton ("Pressure", 414–415) rightly observes: "*Biazō* comes from *bia* which carries the simple meaning of strength. It does not bear in the root a necessary inference of physical violence [...] *Biazō* fully denotes an action done with gusto, with effort, and with strength [...] It is surprising that expositors have not heeded the context of this verse more than they have. In many cases the attraction of this single sentence has been so strong that the context has been forgotten".

Moreover, literary and papyrological evidence confirms our etymological considerations and provides solid ground in support of our initial hypothesis. Within its rich and
wide semantic field, the βία terminology does carry a specific nuance in relation to βίος
and in keeping with the meaning of the Sanskrit verb *jyā*: βιάζεσθαι can be used to refer
directly to wealth, possessions or "that which belongs to another" (τὸ ἀλλότριον).

In line with the context of the Lucan saying, Luke may indeed have drawn on
his knowledge of the Greek verb's economic "shades of meaning"[517] to refer to
a not necessarily hostile "potential use of force"[518], which, consistent with the
legal notion of "acquisition by *usucapio* or *ḥazaqah*"[519] (חזקה), is then needed
to take possession of the "immovable" (spatial) property of God's kingdom[520].
The term βία, in this sense, would imply the "seizing" (cf. Matt 11,12c) of such
a divine space, "without the consent of God"[521] (its true lawful owner) and by
means of almsgiving[522]. The *biastái*, in turn, may simply be "all" (πᾶς)[523] those
who stand or "come up" (στῆναι)[524] in God's kingdom, loving him with all their
strength or mammon (see the Satt on Deut 6,5), by way or means of *bía*[525].

However, a few questions still remain unanswered: which sources did Luke
use in his formulation of the saying? What redactional changes did he make?
What was the rhetorical logic guiding his composition and which theological
message did he wish to convey, and to whom? What concrete implications or
"good news" on the kingdom of God (see ἡ βασιλέια τοῦ θεοῦ εὐαγγελίζεται)
does our interpretation of the verse have both for Luke's particular community
and for the believers of all times (see πᾶς)? These questions prompt us to go
back to the text and move on to our next and final chapter.

---

[517] P.S. CAMERON, *Violence*, 142.

[518] S.R. LLEWELYN, "Forcible Acquisition", 152. Indeed, Luke must be aware of a positive
meaning of βία as well, because he uses the latter as an attribute of the Holy Spirit. See πνοῆς
βιαίας (Acts 2,2) and πνεύματος ἁγίου (Acts 2,4). Thus, F. Hadjadj (*Et les violents*, 188–189)
rightly remarks: "Aussi est-il périlleux de réserver le terme de la violence au mal, comme il devient
de plus en plus d'usage de le faire, suivant en cela la spécieuse morale à la mode [...] Il est dit
en effet: 'Il vint du ciel un bruit comme celui d'un souffle violent'". See also *Ibid.*, 188–195.

[519] S.R. LLEWELYN, "The Introduction", 156.

[520] See, e.g., D.C. ALLISON, Jr., *Constructing Jesus*, 171–179; and D. FORTUNA, *Il Figlio
dell'ascolto*, 102, n. 13.

[521] S.R. LLEWELYN, "The Traditionsgeschichte", 348.

[522] See, esp., F. D'AGOSTINO, *BIA*, 1–126; C. SPICQ, "βιάζομαι", *TLNT*, I, 288; S.R. LLEWELYN,
"Forcible Acquisition", 130–162; ID., "The Introduction", 154–167; A. TOSATO, *Vangelo*, 307–457;
G.A. ANDERSON, "Faith", 29–34; and N. EUBANK, "Storing up Treasure", 77–92.

[523] Luke 16,16. Thus, not only the Hebrew people who had access to the revelation contained
in the law and the prophets, but also the Gentiles. These were also considered to be "violent"
(*'annās*) in Rabbinic Literature. See, e.g., bBB 45a; Jastrow, "אנס", I, 86; and S.R. LLEWELYN,
"Forcible Acquisition", 161–162. See also PsSol 17,5.

[524] See BDAG, "ἵστημι", 482–483.

[525] See, e.g., Matt 5,3; 6,31–33; 13,44; 19,16.21–24.29; Mark 10,17.21–25; Luke 6,20;
10,25; and 18,18.22–25.29–30.

Chapter 5

Exegesis and Theology of Luke 16,16 in Context

A. Introduction

"Kingdom of God" and "Violence", "Love" and "Strength" ... the question, which we set out to answer at the beginning of our quest, has finally reached its fourth and concluding stage and we are about to give as objective a "satisfactory explanation"[1] as possible, grounded as it is upon the long-established positive reception of the saying (Chap. II), the coherent narrative arrangement of its context (Chap. III), and the literary acquaintance with the βία-related verb (Chap. IV).

Going back to the text of Luke 16,16, this final stage of our study aims at showing our understanding of the intended meaning and message of the verse, which, building on the results reached thus far, takes into account the rhetorical thrust of its adjacent "peculiarly placed dicta"[2] (Luke 16,15b.17–18), the theological lens used by the evangelist in editing and adapting his source material, and the meaningful interlocking of sayings and parables, along with their echo of one another[3]. Specifically, we shall present first a brief review of the results of prior scholarship on the redactional critical questions of author, audience, sources, and form, and see what redactional changes the evangelist has probably made in relation to the latter. We shall then proceed with the exegesis and theology of the saying, within both its remote and proximate contexts, underscoring the rhetorical logic and message that step by step guides the whole composition. Finally, we shall conclude by exposing the universal import of the never-ending force of its good news.

B. Tradition and Redaction of the Text

To come to a proper appreciation of Luke's redactional artistry, the βία-related passage and its immediate context need first of all to be put in perspective with the identity of their author and reader, sources and form. Locating briefly the Lucan author in the literary world and age of his audience, reflecting on the

---

[1] M.W. BATES, "Cryptic Codes", 74.
[2] T. BEDNARZ, "Status Disputes", 377.
[3] See D. MARGUERAT – Y. BOURQUIN, *How to Read*, 39; and Chap. III, pp. 104–106.

shape he has given to his source material, and paying attention to the differences between them will allow us to see the stylistic and literary signals
of his redactional composition as vehicles ordered to the communication of a
coherent theological message.

I. Author and Audience

Although scholars address the issue of how the phenomenon is to be interpreted
differently, it is a matter of fact that, every now and then, the narrator of Luke-
Acts uses the first person singular or plural personal pronoun to refer to himself
(with or without others) and, in a couple of instances (Acts 16,15; cf. 27,41),
to describe even some βία-related personal experiences[4]. Are these instances
fictitious or real references to the author's presence at the scenes? Or else, are
they vestiges of a previous source (or sources)? Could they be regarded rather
as narrative techniques, either left or placed intentionally by Luke to bring his
audience into the story, enhance the credibility of the accounts, or point to his
own identity as a good historian, or that of his own community[5]?

Unfortunately, no consensus has yet been reached in contemporary
scholarship around the exact meaning and function of these self-disclosing
occurrences, and as researchers continue to discuss their different possible
explanations, the identity of either the (individual or collective) person hiding
behind them, or that of the real addressee(s) of these writings above and beyond
the name of Theophilus, remain a matter of debate.

---

[4] Specifically, the narrator's first-person singular pronoun occurs twice, once explicitly,
in the prologue to Luke (cf. Luke 1,3a: "it seemed good to me [κἀμοί] too"), and another time
implicitly, in that to the Acts of the Apostles (cf. Acts 1,1a: "the first account I composed
[ἐποιησάμην]"). As for the first-person plural pronoun, it occurs twice in the prologue to the
Gospel (cf. Luke 1,1: "the things accomplished among us [ἐν ἡμῖν]"; and Luke 1,2: "just as
they handed them down to us [ἡμῖν]"), and a few more times in the so-called "we-passages"
of the book of Acts (see Acts 16,10–17; 20,5–15; 21,1–18 and 27,1–28,16; see, also, Acts 11,28,
in [D] Codex Bezae Cantabrigensis). In Acts 16,15, in particular, Luke reports what
happened to him while being the object of a βία-related verb: "and she pressed us hard
[παρεβιάσατο ἡμᾶς]". See also Luke 24,29; and Acts 27,41. If one takes the "we-sections" as
Luke's direct participations in the narrated events, then this is a further sign of his familiarity
with the βία-terminology. For a discussion of the "we-sections", see, e.g., W.S. KURZ,
"Narrative Approaches", 208–212; ID., *Reading Luke-Acts*, 111–124; J.A. FITZMYER,
The Acts, 98–103; C.K. BARRETT, *The Acts*, II, xxv–xxx; and R.I. PERVO, *Acts*, 392–396.

[5] Thus, W.S. Kurz ("Narrative Approaches", 208–209) observes: "Our implied author,
traditionally called Luke, is plotting a narrative around events of which most are already
known to the implied readers, since they concern deeds that were accomplished 'among us'.
Who are the 'us'? The easiest reading of 'us' would include both the implied author and
readers within the same set, not to exclude from 'us' Theophilus and other implied readers.
If the 'us' includes the implied readers, the events to be narrated are in the public domain
shared by Luke and Theophilus". See *Ibid.*, 208–212.215–220.

Generally speaking, the long-standing traditional view on the matter associates the author of Luke-Acts closely with "Luke" (Λουκᾶς), namely, a Gentile Syrian of Antioch converted to Christianity, physician by profession, and companion or disciple of Paul[6]. A few scholars cite evidence also in support of his Jewish (vs. ethnic) origin[7]. Granting that what may be validly affirmed on the basis of internal evidence is merely that the author of the two-volume work prefers to remain anonymous, just as the other three evangelists do, the substantial evidence of the tradition makes "Luke" a very likely candidate for Lucan authorship[8]. Because of the Septuagint style and language of his writings, one may also assume that Luke belonged most likely to a higher class of society, which allowed him to acquire a literary education and an acquaintance with both Greek rhetoric and Jewish exegesis, and so develop a remarkable taste and talent for writing[9].

As regards the addressee(s) of Luke-Acts, the important questions to be asked are who Theophilus is and whom he represents as Luke's implied reader[10]. Judging from the fine Greek of the prologue to the first volume (Luke 1,1–4) and the

---

[6] See, e.g., Col 4,14; 2Tim 4,11; and Phlm 24. See also F.H. HESSE, *Das Muratori'sche Fragment*, 67–82; G. KUHN, *Das muratorische Fragment*, 10.38–44; H.M. GWATKIN, *Selections*, 76–77; H. LIETZMANN, *Das muratorische Fragment*, 4–5.14; H.J. CADBURY, "The Tradition", 209–264; J.M. CREED, *Luke*, xiii–xxi.23–24; K. ALAND, ed., *Synopsis Quattuor Evangeliorum*, 531–481; J.A. FITZMYER, *Luke*, I, 35–53; ID., *The Acts*, 49–51; J. WENHAM, "The Identification", 3–44; C.K. BARRETT, *The Acts*, I, 30–48; and *Ibid.*, II, xliv–liii.

[7] For instance, in her re-reading of the earliest sources, M.-L. Rigato claims that Luke was most likely a Jew, probably a Pharisee and a *nomikós* (i.e., an expert in the Torah and the Midrash technique), bilingual (with a knowledge of both Greek and Hebrew), and possibly of Levite descent. See M.-L. RIGATO, "Luca originario Giudeo", 391–422. See also EUSEBIUS OF CAESAREA, *Hist. Eccl.* III, 4.6 (ed. K. LAKE, I, 196–197); IRENAEUS OF LYONS, *Haer.* III, 11.8 (*PG* 7.1, 887b); G. ROSSÉ, *Luca*, 8, n. 3; and S. PRINCIPE, "Chi era Luca?", 131–146.

[8] Thus, J.A. Fitzmyer (*Luke*, I, 35) remarks: "The Third Gospel is anonymous, as are the other three canonical Gospels. Nowhere in it does its author reveal his identity, and it cannot be deduced from the extant text [...] Acts is equally anonymous; nothing in its text-tradition reveals the identity of the author". The ancient subscription found in P[75] (ευαγγελιον κατα λουκαν), for instance, attributing the authorship of the third Gospel to "Luke", is a late 2nd to early 3rd c. scribal addition, separating the latter from the Gospel of John. See, e.g., V. MARTIN – R. KASSER, ed., *Papyrus Bodmer*, I, 61. Despite this, as G.B. Caird (*Luke*, 17) argues, one must also admit that "an ancient scholar [...] would have had no means of putting a name to the author if there had not been a valid tradition connecting the books with the name Luke". Besides, as noted by W.S. Kurz (*Reading Luke-Acts*, 123), "The anonymity can also convey that the implied readers knew the author's identity, as would Theophilus to whom the work is addressed".

[9] See, e.g., J.A. FITZMYER, *Luke*, I, 35.107–127; ID., *The Acts*, 114–118; and F. BOVON, *Luc*, I, 27.

[10] For instance, R.F. O'Toole ("Theophilus", *ABD*, VI, 512) remarks: "There is a dialogic setting between Luke and Theophilus; thus, even more important than the insoluble question of his personal identity is the question of whom Theophilus represents. This question is closely related to Luke's purpose". See also W.S. KURZ, "Narrative Approaches", 208–212.

high quality of its sentence structure, I.H. Marshall observes: "It claims a place for the Gospel as a work of literature, worthy of an educated audience"[11].

Thus, Theophilus (Θεόφιλος), that is to say, the person to whom Luke dedicates his work (see Luke 1,3; and Acts 1,1), may be an actual historical character, learned and, perhaps, even rich enough to make his work known to a threefold kind of public: educated Gentiles, Greek speaking Jews and, above all, Christian believers, perhaps worried by false rumors about the continuity between ancient Judaism and Christianity, or simply needing further instruction[12]. The fact that the name of this otherwise unknown personality, "was used by both Gentiles and Jews"[13], leaves the question as to his ethnic identity open[14]. However, J.A. Fitzmyer rightly notes:

Because Luke dedicates the two volumes to Theophilus, it means that his opus is not a private writing; Theophilus stands for the Christian readers of Luke's own day and thereafter[15].

Above and beyond the critical opinion concerning the historicity of the person lying behind such a dedication, "the name readily yields to a symbolic interpretation"[16] as well, which, as shown by the Church Fathers, could also be pointing to the implied reader as a "lover of God" (φίλος and Θεός) as opposed to a "lover of money" (φίλος and ἀργύρον)[17]. Indeed, the audience of Luke's

---

[11] I.H. MARSHALL, *Luke*, 38. See also BDF, 242, §464; J.A. FITZMYER, *Luke*, I, 287–302; J. NOLLAND, *Luke*, I, 4; and R.F. O'TOOLE, "Theophilus", *ABD*, VI, 511–512.

[12] See, e.g., Luke 1,4; 2,22–24.27.39; 5,39; 10,26; 16,16–17; 24,44; Acts 7,53; 15,5–6; 16,3; 21,20–26; 22,3.12.30; 24,5–6.13–21; 25,8.26; and 28,23. See also Luke's own use of the adjective, "most noble" or "excellent" (κράτιστε), in Luke 1,3; Acts 23,26; 24,3; 26,25; J.A. FITZMYER, *Luke*, I, 300; and F. BOVON, *Luc*, I, 28.41.

[13] J.A. FITZMYER, *Luke*, I, 299. See, e.g., R.F. O'TOOLE, "Theophilus", *ABD*, VI, 511–512; and L.H. FELDMAN, *Jew and Gentile*, 58.

[14] For a discussion of the traditions around Theophilus' identity, see, e.g., J.A. FITZMYER, *Luke*, I, 299; and R.F. O'TOOLE, "Theophilus", *ABD*, VI, 511–512.

[15] J.A. FITZMYER, *Luke*, I, 300. Thus, the author (*Ibid.*, I, 59) concludes: "There may have been some Jews and Jewish Christians among them – as the quotation of Isaiah at the end of Acts suggests. But the audience envisaged by Luke [...] is one that is predominantly Gentile Christian, and Theophilus is one of them". See, e.g., Isa 6,9–10; and Acts 28,26. See also W.S. KURZ, *Reading Luke-Acts*, 12–16; and R.F. O'TOOLE, "Theophilus", *ABD*, VI, 512. For different opinions, as to the identity of Luke's ideal reader, cf., e.g., J. NOLLAND, *Luke*, I, xxxii–xxxiii; M.A. POWELL, *What Are They Saying*, 57; and D. WENHAM – al., ed., *Exploring the New Testament*, I, 294.

[16] R.I. PERVO, *Acts*, 35. Thus, the author (*Ibid.*, 35) point out: "The characterization of Theophilus in Luke 1,1–4 functions also to define the implied reader. In the latter sense, at least, few commentators on Acts have improved upon Bede: 'Theophilus means "lover of God" or "loved by God". All lovers of God may therefore believe that [Acts] was written to them, because Luke the Physician wrote so that they might find health for the soul here'". See BEDE THE VENERABLE, *Exp. Act.* I (ed. M.L.W. LAISTNER, 6).

[17] For instance, W.S. Kurz ("Narrative Approaches", 211) points out: "The implied author obviously is aiming to communicate with his implied reader [...] whether Theophilus is a real

writings may have been primarily and predominantly a Christian community of non-Jewish origin for whose faith journey money-mammon represented a danger[18]. Finally, the two-volume work manifests also the author's double care of admonishing the many disciples coming from the Gentiles not to forget the Jewish roots of their faith, and reassuring those few others coming from Judaism that the Law was still valued and valid[19].

II. Sources and Form

As any other ancient historian, and as he himself implies in his prologue (see, esp., Luke 1,1–2), Luke must have availed himself of some written sources to write his own accurate narrative account of the facts (διήγησις)[20]. Among the documents alluded to, scholars recognize generally three: a written collection of Jesus' sayings (*Q*), which Luke shared with Matthew, but which has not come to us; the Gospel of Mark (*M*), which he also shared with Matthew; and some other source material peculiar to him (*L*), whether written or oral, with parallels neither in Matthew nor Mark[21].

---

person or a symbolic 'lover of God' [...] Theophilus is a fiction like any addressee of a letter: he is the implied reader created by the text itself". In the light of Luke 16,13–14, the meaning of the name, Theophilus (Θεόφιλος), clashes strikingly with the presentation of the Pharisees, as "money-lovers" (φιλάργυροι), and may define such a creation further. For additional observations on Luke's implied author and reader, see also ID., *Reading Luke-Acts*, 9–16.

[18] See, e.g., Luke 3,14; 7,5; 8,3; 9,3; 11,41; 12,13–34; 14,33; 16,1–13.14–31; 19,8.15.23; 22,5; Acts 3,3.6; 4,32.34–37; 5,1–11; 8,9–24; 9,36; 10,2.4.31; 19,19; 20,33; and 24,17. See also F. BOVON, *Luke the Theologian*, 444. The reappearance in Acts of motifs found in the Gospel regarding the theme of the use of money (e.g., generosity, almsgiving, greed, selfishness, etc.), confirms not only the view that Luke-Acts form a single literary composition, but also that the proper use of riches must have been an issue Luke felt the need to address. For the reasons in favor of a predominantly non-Palestinian origin of Luke's intended readers, see, e.g., J.A. FITZMYER, *Luke*, I, 57–59.

[19] See, e.g., J.S. JERVELL, *Luke and the People*, 41–74; and M.-L. RIGATO, "'Mosè ed i Profeti'", 176–177. Thus, J.A. Fitzmyer (*Luke*, I, 58–59) remarks: "it seems to me that he has made a convincing case for the idea that the Gentiles have gained a share in what had been given to Israel, i.e. the salvation of God sent first to reconstituted Israel (Acts 15,16–18; cf. 3,23) is by God's own design sent further to the Gentiles without the law, especially when part of Israel rejects the invitation (Acts 13,46). Thus, Luke explains the relationship of the Gentile Christians for whom he is writing to Israel of old [...] They are not, indeed, the new people of God, but belong to the reconstituted people of God [...] his treatment of Paul actually constitutes an excellent portrayal of the 'continuity between Judaism and Christianity'". Cf., also, Rom 11,16–29.

[20] For instance, J.A. Fitzmyer (*Luke*, I, 63) points out: "The prologue thus hints at a complex literary history behind it". See also J. NOLLAND, *Luke*, I, 6–8; and F. BOVON, *Luc*, I, 25.36–37.

[21] Cf., e.g., I.H. MARSHALL, *Luke*, 30–31; J.A. FITZMYER, *Luke*, I, 63–106; and F. BOVON, *Luc*, I, 25–27.

When we look at the broader narrative context of Luke 16,16, the entire sequence (Luke 14,25–17,10) to which the saying belongs is for the most part (ca. 79%) composed of material which Luke may have derived from *L* (66 verses out of 84, altogether)[22]. The same thing can be affirmed, even more so, concerning the narrower concentric unit of Luke 16: here, out of thirty-one verses, twenty-seven (i.e., ca. 87% of the chapter) have no counterpart in any other Gospel, three (vv. 13.16–17) have parallels only in Matthew (cf. Matt 6,24; 11,12–13 and 5,18), and just one (v. 18) is shared with both the other Synoptics (cf. Mark 10,11–12; Matt 5,31–32; and 19,9)[23]. From the form-critical point of view, moreover, all four of the verses shared by Luke with Matthew and/or Mark (vv. 13.16–18) can be classified as "dominical sayings"[24].

This means also that, out of the eight sayings occurring in the entire chapter, only four are supposedly derived from sources which Luke shared with other evangelists. Based on our analysis of the concentric patterns between the two sets of sayings in Luke 16, it is likely that Luke may have inserted these sayings into his own material and/or creation because of their common relation to the theme of possessions and wealth and his theological interest in their proper use in view of one's entry into the kingdom of God[25].

Unfortunately, despite the progress made by recent studies in the reconstruction of the *Q* and *L* source material, their "postulated entity"[26] (over against *M*) cautions us to be aware of the limitations of coming to any conclusion as to their use

---

[22] Specifically, in Luke 14,25–17,10, the *L* material could include: Luke 14,25.28–33; 15,1–3.8–16,12.14–15.19–31; and 17,7–10. The remainder of the narrative sequence (ca. 13% and 8%, respectively) contains material derived possibly from *Q* (11 verses, altogether: Luke 14,26–27 [cf. Matt 10,37–38]; 15,4–7 [cf. Matt 18,12–14]; 16,13 [cf. Matt 6,24]; 16,16–17 [cf. Matt 11,12–13; and 5,18]; and 17,3b–4 [cf. Matt 18,15]) and *M* (7 verses, in total: Luke 14,34–35 [cf. Mark 9,49–50; and Matt 5,13]; 16,18 [cf. Mark 10,11–12; and Matt 19,9]; 17,1–3a [cf. Mark 9,42; and Matt 18,6–7] and 17,5–6 [cf. Mark 9,28–29; Matt 17,19–21; and 21,21]). See, e.g., K. ALAND, ed., *Synopsis*, 193–201; and J.M. ROBINSON – P. HOFFMANN – J.S. KLOPPENBORG, ed., *The Critical Edition*, vii–viii.447–493.

[23] For instance, A. Dettwiler ("The Source Q", 46) speaks of "a Mark-Q overlap for Luke 16,18". In turn, J.A. Fitzmyer (*Luke*, II, 1095) ponders: "Since most of the material of chap. 16 is exclusive to Luke (vv. 1–12.14–15.19–31), one wonders why he inserted here the sayings on the law and divorce, which have counterparts in the Synoptic tradition".

[24] See, e.g., R. BULTMANN, *The History*, 132.138.164–166. Within the broad category of "dominical sayings", the author treats the logia in v. 16 and vv. 17–18 under the headings, "Legal Sayings and Church Rules" and "'I'-Sayings", respectively. For discordant voices, as to the dominical form of *Q* 16,16 and the *Q* origin of vv. 13.16–18, respectively, cf., e.g., D.A. CARSON, "Do the Prophets", 193, n. 2; and F.C. GRANT, "Where Form Criticism", 18.

[25] See, esp., the illuminating thrust of vv. 9.10–12.13 (cf. μαμωνᾶς) onto vv. 16.17.18, respectively, as shown in Chap. III, p. 157, fig. 2.

[26] J.A. FITZMYER, *Luke*, I, 75.

and redaction on the part of Luke[27]. Therefore, in keeping with the general approach and style of our study, we shall here go over only a summary of the results of prior scholarship on the issue, and inevitably regard any possible deduction as only a reasonable speculation[28].

III. Redaction of Luke 16,16

As things stand in the present text, Luke has grouped together the sayings in Luke 16,16–18, whereas Matthew has them distributed in three different locations, two within the Gospel narrative of the Sermon on the Mount (see Matt 5,18.32), and one in a section dealing with the figures and roles of Jesus and John the Baptist in relation to the kingdom of Heaven (see Matt 11,12–13)[29]. In spite of a few interpreters' reservations, the vast majority of modern critics agree in assigning some or all of these sayings to *Q*, "an ethnically Judean text [...] of first-century Judaism"[30]. Their lack of consensus, however, concerns whether they were originally separate or already linked together in their source[31].

---

[27] For instance, nothing precludes the material peculiar to Luke from being his own creation. See, e.g., I.H. MARSHALL, *Luke*, 30–31. For an overview of the most recent research and innovative studies on the coherence of *Q* and its hypothetical stages of composition, see, e.g., P. DI LUCCIO, *The Quelle*, 27–31. For the Jewish, almost Pharisaic legal characteristics of the source(s) peculiar to Luke, see, e.g., A.M. PERRY, "A Judeo-Christian Source", 181–194 (esp. 192).

[28] Thus far, we have dealt primarily with traceable extant material (e.g., the historical reception, narrative context, and linguistic spectrum of the saying), with the hope of coming to a conclusion as objectively grounded as possible. A detailed analysis of the source-critical issue of the text would thus go beyond the scope of our study and its approach. However, such a line of research could still be suitable material for a further promising article or monograph.

[29] See, e.g., D. MARGUERAT, "Le règne", 114; A. DETTWILER, "The Source Q", 50; and Chap. I, pp. 4–8.

[30] S.J. JOSEPH, "For Heaven", 171. See also P. DI LUCCIO, *The Quelle*, 29–30. Among the authors who indicate some uncertainty concerning the *Q* origin of the three sayings, see, e.g., B.H. STREETER, *The Four Gospels*, 286–287; F.C. GRANT, *The Gospels*, 60; and F.W. DANKER, "Luke 16,16", 242. As to the majority opinion and in favour of their *Q* origin, see, e.g., B.S. EASTON, *Luke*, 249; V. TAYLOR, *Behind the Third Gospel*, 157; ID., "The Order of Q", 27–31; B.H. BRANSCOMB, *Jesus and the Law*, 198.205–207.213–218; W. MANSON, *Luke*, 187; D. DAUBE, *The New Testament*, 292–300; H. SCHÜRMANN, "'Wer daher eines'", 238–250; G.B. CAIRD, *Luke*, 189; R. BANKS, *Jesus*, 213.247; R.A. EDWARDS, *A Theology of Q*, 137–138; J.P. MEIER, *Law and History*, 57–60.85–86.103–104.140–141; I.H. MARSHALL, *Luke*, 626–631; R.A. GUELICH, *The Sermon*, 137.165–166.244.270; and G.W. KLINGSPORN, *The Law*, 354, n. 11.

[31] In support of *Q* 16,16–18, as being an original sequence kept unaltered by Luke, see, e.g., W. MANSON, *Luke*, 187; D. DAUBE, *The New Testament*, 294; H. SCHÜRMANN, "'Wer daher eines'", 238–250; G.B. CAIRD, *Luke*, 189; J. SCHLOSSER, "Le Règne", 509–510; D. KOSCH, *Die Gottesherrschaft*, 63; J. VERHEYDEN, "The Violators", 402, n. 21; and P. FOSTER,

Moreover, on the basis of the majority opinion, it is highly probable that Matthew may have taken *Q* 16,16 and placed it in a context focused on John the Baptist, mostly because of the occurrence of the latter's name in the opening phrase of the saying (cf. v. 16a)[32]. Scholars agree that Luke tends to follow the sequence of *Q* sayings generally more closely than Matthew[33]. It is then more reasonable to believe that the primitive unity of *Q* 7,24–28 may have been preserved intact by Luke and expanded by Matthew (cf. Luke 7,24–28; and Matt 11,7–11.12–13), rather than the contrary[34]. Indeed, consistent with his habit of grouping thematically, Matthew has most likely placed the three sayings into two different suitable contexts, whereas in keeping with his technique of "grouped integration"[35] Luke has probably preferred to preserve the original sequence of his source[36]. Consequently, as A. Dettwiler points out, the odds are that "Luke 16,16–18 forms a traditional block which would seem to go back to Q"[37].

"Matthew's Use", 184. Among the authors who argue that the three sayings were originally separate in *Q* and were later joined together in Luke's Gospel, see, e.g., W.L. KNOX, *The Sources*, II, 99; F.W. DANKER, "Luke 16,16", 242; P. HOFFMANN, *Studien*, 53–56; H. HÜBNER, *Das Gesetz*, 15–31; and R.A. GUELICH, *The Sermon*, 199. Finally, some maintain that only *Q* 16,16–17 formed an original unity, but have doubts about v. 16. See, e.g., I.H. MARSHALL, *Luke*, 626–627; and C. HEIL, *Lukas*, 129.136.139. For further discussion on the whole issue, see, e.g., J. VERHEYDEN, "The Violators", 402, n. 21; and A. DETTWILER, "The Source Q", 47–60.

[32] See, e.g., G. HÄFNER, "Gewalt", 48–51; J. VERHEYDEN, "The Violators", 401–402; and D.R. BURKETT, *Rethinking the Gospel Sources*, II, 207–208. Thus, A. Dettwiler ("The Source Q", 50) concludes: "Matthew 11,11–12, in arrangement, slots well into this context [...] Matthew took the sentence Q 16,16 – the only fragment of Q on the Baptist outside of Q 3 and Q 7 – and put it in a position in Q 7 which seemed to him appropriate, both formally (cf. the key words 'John the Baptist' and 'kingdom' in Q 7,28 and Q 16,16) and topically". See also D.A. CARSON, "Do the Prophets", 190.

[33] See, e.g., J.S. KLOPPENBORG, *Q, the Earliest Gospel*, x.

[34] See J. SCHLOSSER, "Le Règne", 510. See also J.S. KLOPPENBORG, *Q, the Earliest Gospel*, 129–130.

[35] D. MARGUERAT, "Le règne", 117.

[36] Thus, A. Dettwiler ("The Source Q", 50) concludes: "The positioning of Matt 5,18 and 5,32 is most likely redactional [...] Matthew 11,12–13 results from an editorial and coherent effort on the part of Matthew, and forms a kind of explanatory addition, following on from the middle block on John the Baptist (Q 7,24–28//Matt 7,7–11)". See also J. SCHLOSSER, "Le Règne", 509–510; J.S. KLOPPENBORG, "*Nomos*", 44; and D. MARGUERAT, "Le règne", 116. Finally, as J. Verheyden ("The Violators", 400) points out, "J.S. Kloppenborg rightly observes, 'if Luke had seen 16,16 in its present Matthean location (in a cluster of sayings about John the Baptist), it is hard to imagine why he would have moved it to its current location'".

[37] A. DETTWILER, "The Source Q", 49. Thus, the author (*Ibid.*, 49) continues: "The fact that Luke 16,16–18 appears at first sight to lack internal consistency is not itself a counter-argument: rather it supports the antiquity of this sequence, all the more because Luke 16, vv. 16–17 are linked by the key word νόμος ('law'), and because Luke 16,18 clearly con-

If that is the case, then the question that arises spontaneously is why Luke has inserted *Q* 16,16–18 in a chapter whose main theme is the proper use of riches with eternity in view. Despite the efforts to reconstruct the source, the original context of these verses in *Q* is ultimately unknown to us[38]. It could be that Luke was influenced by some other hint pointing in that direction, which he derived from the context of his source (e.g., the previous saying on loving either God or mammon, in *Q* 16,13)[39]. However, based on his understanding of the terms, it is more likely that the evangelist saw a certain thematic link occurring already within this block of sayings, which he then expressed by inserting it in a chapter for the most part composed of material peculiar to him with respect to that same theme[40].

As regards v. 16, in particular, it is thus possible that Luke may have inherited a tradition of the teaching of Jesus (very likely already in Greek), in which this saying with βιάζεσθαι is found, and that this tradition came to Matthew as well (see Matt 11,12–13)[41]. As we have seen in Chapter IV, within the semantic field of the βία-related terminology, there are various possibilities. Consistent with the way it was used in Jewish and Hellenistic sources, Luke may have understood the βία-verb in the light of its specifically

---

stitutes an application of v. 17". For the unity of *Q* 16,16–18, based on common theme and catchword association, see also S.J. JOSEPH, "For Heaven", 169–188 (esp. 175).

[38] See, e.g., D. MARGUERAT, "Le règne", 117; J. VERHEYDEN, "The Violators", 400; A. DETTWILER, "The Source Q", 51; and S.J. JOSEPH, "For Heaven", 171, n. 17.

[39] According to the hypothetical reconstruction of the *Q* text, *Q* 16,16 occurs immediately after *Q* 16,13. Moreover, the allegedly traditional block *Q* 16,16–18 is in turn followed by *Q* 17,1–2. The latter contains a "woe" (οὐαί) against the person placing "stumbling blocks" (σκάνδαλα: *Q* 17,1; cf., also, σκανδαλίζειν: *Q* 7,23 and 17,2) before the little ones, which may recall the first "woe" (οὐαί) of the Lucan Gospel against the rich, in Luke 6,24 (see πλὴν οὐαι: Luke 6,24; and 17,1). See, e.g., J.M. ROBINSON – P. HOFFMANN – J.S. KLOPPENBORG, ed., *The Critical Edition*, 125.462–477; and J. VERHEYDEN, "The Violators", 401–402. Thus, the latter (*Ibid.*, 413, n. 59) notes: "When 16,16–18 is read together with 16,13 (and 14–15) one also might be able to give an explanation for the somewhat strange choice of the example in v. 18. In 16,13[–14] the Pharisees are accused of φιλαργυρία; 16,18 gives the impression that they are implicitly associated with adulterers. The combination of both is not unknown in ancient philosophical texts". See also R.A. PIPER, "Social Background", 1659, n. 80.

[40] For instance, as A. Dettwiler ("The Source Q", 49) points out, "the majority of sentences in Q are, *de facto*, grouped in thematic blocks".

[41] Thus, J. Schlosser ("Le Règne", 510) remarks: "Les ressemblances étroites, dans le vocabulaire et dans le contenu, entre Matt 11,12–13 et Luc 16,16 supposent que les deux évangélistes utilisent une même tradition". In turn, A. Dettwiler ("The Source Q", 52) explains: "The two versions go back to a common form (spoken or written), as is shown by the following points of convergence: the link between the person of John the Baptist and the kingdom; the expression, 'the Law and the prophets' (in the reverse order in Matthew, 'the prophets and the Law'); the rare verb βιάζεται in the passive sense in Matthew ('subject to violence'), but in the active and intransitive sense in Luke ('forces a way in'); a temporal format using prepositions and adverbs of time (Matthew: ἀπό, ἕως ἄρτι, ἕως; Luke: μέχρι, ἀπό, τότε)".

legal and property-related nuance, and so made that understanding clear by placing this teaching within a particular section (Luke 16) of the Travel Narrative in which the primary (vs. exclusive) thematic concern is precisely the use of money or property[42]. With that interpretation of the βία-related term, then, things begin to fall into place, and we can come to a better understanding of the coherence of Luke 16 as well.

Although a reconstruction of "an original version on the basis of Matthew and Luke proves very complex"[43], for the sake of clarity and completeness, the following Table summarizes the results of the large majority of modern scholarship with reference to the wording of the allegedly original saying in *Q* 16,16, along with our own translation[44].

Table V: Luke 16,16 vs. Matt 11,12(–13) and the Reconstuction of Q 16,16	
Luke 16,16	Matt 11,12(–13)
(a) Ὁ νόμος καὶ οἱ προφῆται μέχρι Ἰωάννου· (b) ἀπὸ τότε ἡ βασιλεία τοῦ θεοῦ εὐαγγελίζεται (c) καὶ πᾶς εἰς αὐτὴν βιάζεται.	(a) ἀπὸ δὲ τῶν ἡμερῶν Ἰωάννου τοῦ βαπτιστοῦ ἕως ἄρτι (b) ἡ βασιλεία τῶν οὐρανῶν βιάζεται (c) καὶ βιασταὶ ἁρπάζουσιν αὐτήν (13 πάντες γὰρ οἱ προφῆται καὶ ὁ νόμος ἕως Ἰωάννου ἐπροφήτευσαν).
Q 16,16	
(a) Ὁ νόμος καὶ οἱ προφῆται ἕως Ἰωάννου· (b) ἀπὸ τότε ἡ βασιλεία τοῦ θεοῦ βιάζεται (c) καὶ βιασταὶ ἁρπάζουσιν αὐτήν.	(a) The Law and the prophets up to John; (b) since then the kingdom of God is violated, (c) and the violators take possession of it.

---

[42] Thus, A. Dettwiler ("The Source Q", 48) points out: "According to Luke 16,29–31, the only possibility of escaping condemnation after death is to listen to 'Moses and the prophets', that is to say, scripture. The conclusion of Luke 16 stresses that the right ['just'] relationship with money is a demand testified by 'Moses and the prophets', or, in other words, 'the Law and the prophets' (Luke 16,16). Luke 16,16–18 therefore prepares the ground for Luke 16,19–31, by affirming the validity of the Law as an 'ethical code' for the proper use of material possessions, for the Christian era too".

[43] A. DETTWILER, "The Source Q", 51. Thus, the author (*Ibid.*, 52) continues: "As Helmut M. Merklein has rightly remarked, the major problem in any attempt at reconstruction resides in the fact that each of the two versions can be seen as a revision of the other". See H.M. MERKLEIN, *Die Gottesherrschaft*, 84.

[44] For the Greek texts in Table V, see, esp., J.M. ROBINSON – P. HOFFMANN – J.S. KLOPPENBORG, ed., *The Critical Edition*, 464–466; A. DETTWILER, "The Source Q", 51.53; Chap. I, pp. 2–6; and Chap. II, pp. 78–79. For bibliography and reconstruction, see, e.g., B.D. CHILTON, "The Violent Kingdom", 203–230; J. VERHEYDEN, "The Violators", 399–402; and S.J. JOSEPH, "For Heaven", 171, n. 17.

As a rule, scholars base this reconstructed text for the saying in Q 16,16 primarily on the following assumptions:

a) "is preached [as good news]" (εὐαγγελίζεται) and "everyone" (πᾶς) are Lucan, whereas the expression, "the kingdom of Heaven" (ἡ βασιλεία τῶν οὐρανῶν) is Matthean[45];

b) the inversion of the usual order of the expression, "the Law and the prophets" (ὁ νόμος καὶ οἱ προφῆται: Luke 16,16a), into "all the prophets and the Law" (πάντες οἱ προφῆται καὶ ὁ νόμος: Matt 11,13) is a Matthean redactional touch, since such an order is unknown to both LXX and NT[46];

c) in line with his general tendency, Luke has remained faithful to his source and preserved the order of its elements[47];

d) the Matthean form of the saying, in Matt 11,12, is generally preferred as a *lectio difficilior*[48].

---

[45] The occurrences of these syntagmas in the Synoptics are as follows: "to preach a good news" (εὐαγγελίζειν) occurs 1x in Matthew (Matt 11,5) and 25x in Luke (10x in Luke and 15x in Acts); "everyone" (πᾶς) occurs 120x in Matthew, 306x in Luke (145x in Luke and 161x in Acts) and 64x in Mark; "Heaven" (οὐρανός) occurs 72x in Matthew, 58x in Luke (34x in Luke and 24x in Acts) and 17x in Mark; the expression "the kingdom of Heaven" (ἡ βασιλεία τῶν οὐρανῶν) occurs 31x in Matthew and never in Mark or Luke; while the expression "the kingdom of God" (ἡ βασιλεία τοῦ θεοῦ) occurs 5x in Matthew, 37x in Luke (31x in Luke and 6x in Acts) and 14x in Mark. As far as the temporal expressions are concerned, the statistics do not provide sufficient grounds for definitive judgments: "until" (μέχρι) occurs 2x in Matthew (Matt 11,23 and 28,15) and 3x in Luke (Luke 16,16, Acts 10,30 and 20,7); "up to" (ἕως) occurs 43x in Matthew, 49x in Luke (27x in Luke and 22x in Acts) and 14x in Mark; "since then" (ἀπὸ τότε) occurs 3x in Matthew (Matt 4,17, 16,21 and 26,16) and 1x in Luke (Luke 16,16). See, e.g., J. SCHLOSSER, "Le Règne", 512, n. 17; *Ibid.*, 513–515; and A. DETTWILER, "The Source Q", 52.

[46] See, e.g., J.P. MEIER, *Law and History*, 86; and D.R. BURKETT, *Rethinking the Gospel Sources*, II, 208. Moreover, A. Dettwiler ("The Source Q", 52) suggests: "structurally Matt 11,12 links closely with Matt 11,11: twice in succession there is exactly the same designation, ᾿Ιωάννου τοῦ βαπτιστοῦ ('John the Baptist') and Matthew's preferred expression, 'the kingdom of Heaven'. Then again, Matt 11,13 prepares for Matt 11,14: 'the scriptures', and in particular, 'the prophets' – Mal 3,23 – had announced the eschatological return of Elijah. Furthermore, the insistence on the prophetic dimension of the scriptures (Matt 11,13 with the surprising inclusion of 'the prophets' before 'the Law') corresponds so well with the aims of the first evangelist that it is difficult to avoid attributing this feature to his editing".

[47] For instance, J. Schlosser ("Le Règne", 512) notes: "L'ordre des éléments en Matt 11,12–13 est la conséquence d'un remaniement et [...] sur ce point, Luc est resté fidèle à la source". In turn, A. Dettwiler ("The Source Q", 52) specifies: "Luke [...] probably kept the original order of the two central affirmations (Luke 16,16a–b // Matt 11,12–13) [...] Furthermore, it is obvious that the phrase, Luke 16,16b, ἡ βασιλεία τοῦ θεοῦ εὐαγγελίζεται, 'the good news of the kingdom of God is proclaimed', belongs to the Lucan editing".

[48] Thus, A. Dettwiler ("The Source Q", 52) remarks: "The version in Matt 11,12 is more archaic, very difficult to understand, and that is why the great majority of scholars consider it as original".

Starting off from this reconstruction, we can finally draw a few conclusions relating to Luke's redactional work and interpretation of his earlier source.

If, along with the majority opinion, we understand the verb βιάζεται in *Q* 16,16b as passive, and take the conjunction, καί, in *Q* 16,16c, epexegetically, then the last part of the sentence (i.e., "the violators take possession of it") can explain the previous one (i.e., "the kingdom of God is violated"), specifying that the kind of βία at stake here is the "seizing" of the divine space (see ἁρπάζουσιν αὐτήν)[49]. With such an understanding in mind, Luke may have simply wished to abbreviate the original saying, by incorporating the idea of the forcible acquisition of the kingdom of God (i.e., βιασταὶ ἁρπάζουσιν αὐτήν: *Q* 16,16c) into that of the "lawful" and active entry into it (i.e., εἰς αὐτὴν βιάζεται: Luke 16,16c) by dint of the notions of *usucapio* (see the use of the temporal expressions, "until", "up to", and "since then"), the love commandment (see the NT use of the expression, "the Law and the prophets"), and the "economic belief" of fund transfer through almsgiving (see the understanding of "strength" as "mammon", in the Satt on Deut 6,5)[50].

Then, in harmony with his Gospel theology and approach, and in view of his predominantly Gentile Christian audience, Luke may have complemented the ethnically Jewish taste of his source with the addition of πᾶς (Luke 16,16c) and εὐαγγελίζεται (Luke 16,16b), to underline the universal and positive aspect of such an entry, and address the issue of the danger that an improper use of riches must have constituted for his intended readers, as a hindrance to the right response of the heart before the gift of the kingdom of God and its good news[51].

---

[49] See, e.g., BDF, 228–229, §442(9); J. SCHLOSSER, "Le Règne", 525; and D.R. BURKETT, *Rethinking the Gospel Sources*, II, 209.

[50] In this sense, Luke 16,16 may be a further and more implicit instance of a deliberate Lucan interpretation of a *Q* saying, in line with the Jewish teaching on the value of almsgiving. See, e.g., "give alms from that which is within" (τὰ ἐνόντα δότε ἐλεημοσύνην: Luke 11,41a), as opposed to, "cleanse […] the inside" (καθάρισον […] τὸ ἐντός: Matt 23,26); or even, "give alms […] make for yourselves […] an unfailing treasure in Heaven" (δότε ἐλεημοσύνην […] ποιήσατε ἑαυτοῖς […] θησαυρὸν ἀνέκλειπτον ἐν τοῖς οὐρανοῖς: Luke 12,33), as opposed to, "do not store up for yourselves treasures upon earth […] but […] in Heaven" (μὴ θησαυρίζετε ὑμῖν θησαυροὺς ἐπὶ τῆς γῆς […] δὲ […] ἐν οὐρανῷ: Matt 6,19–20). See also M. BLACK, *An Aramaic Approach*, 2; J.S. JERVELL, *Luke and the People*, 150; I.H. MARSHALL, *Luke*, 496; and G.W. KLINGSPORN, *The Law*, 324–328.

[51] For instance, P. Di Luccio (*The Quelle*, 29–30) remarks: "the contents of the source of sayings would have been Jewish in origin, and addressed – at least some of it, or at some point – to Israel. While Jewish in character, however, Q would have been composed in a Greek-speaking milieu […] many critics today maintain that the Palestine of the first century CE was the cultural, social and religious context within which the source of sayings was formed. The early community of Jesus' followers of Jerusalem, or a Galilee community, could have been responsible for its formation and final composition". For the Judean ethnicity of *Q*, see also *Ibid.*, 29–30, ns. 30–38; and S.J. JOSEPH, "For Heaven", 171, n. 13. In turn, J. Schlosser ("Le Règne", 521) deduces: "Luc 16,16b doit être compris, dans l'intelligence lucanienne du passage, *in bonam partem*". Thus, as J. Verheyden ("The Violators", 412)

These deductions, as reasonable as they may sound, remain ultimately hypothetical in nature. Indeed, if it were possible to know with certainty the text itself of *Q* 16,16, whether Luke found some or all of the sayings in Luke 16,16–18 already linked in *Q*, or whether he was rather responsible for joining originally separate sayings, then such a knowledge would provide us with some strong insights as to the meaning of these sayings in Luke's redaction. However, because of the absence of any hard evidence of *Q* or document verification for it, no firm conclusion can be reached on the matter and, therefore, our primary concern shall be here the analysis of the meaning and function of these verses as they stand now in the text, from the standpoint of the final form of the Lucan narrative, beyond or outside the source historical question[52].

C. Exegesis and Theology of the Saying in Its Remote Context

The probability of such redactional choices adds value to the actual narrative strategies analyzed previously in our study (Chap. III). Proceeding from wider to narrower context, the following investigation shall take into account, first of all, and without much detail, the meaningfulness of the narrative sequence (Luke 14,25–17,10) in which Luke 16,16 occurs, to see how the issue of the disciples' proper use of riches unfolds, scene after scene. The rhetorical development and progression of the teaching conveyed in it and the orderly arrangement of its scenes shall come to light as vehicles ordered towards the communication of a coherent good news.

I. Luke 14,25–17,10: A Narrative Sequence Within the Travel Section

Before turning to an examination of each sentence within the second set of sayings (Luke 16,15b–18), it will be helpful to consider the remote context of Luke 16,16

---

rightly concludes, "Luke may have changed some of the wording of Q in the second half of v. 16, but he has not really changed the meaning of the verse".

[52] For a similar approach, see, e.g., G.W. KLINGSPORN, *The Law*, 356–357. Above and beyond the hypothetical nature of *Q* itself, Matthew and Luke might have also used different recensions of this common source. Thus, despite the considerable increase in the number of publications and studies on this postulated source of sayings, the early warning of I.H. Marshall (*Luke*, 31) still holds true: "we must be cautious in drawing conclusions about Luke's redactional activity from his use of Q material". For a general overview of the Two Source Hypothesis and the formation of *Q*, see, e.g., H.K. MCARTHUR, "The Origin", 119–120; P. DI LUCCIO, *The Quelle*, 23–31; and C.M. TUCKETT, "The Current State", 9–50. For a treatment of the problem of the *Q* theory itself and its critique, as a working literary supposition in contrast with a historical fact, see, esp., M.D. GOULDER, "Is Q a Juggernaut?", 667–681; and M. GOODACRE, "A Monopoly", 583–622.

and see how the arrangement of its narrative sequence (Luke 14,25–17,10), with its various scenes and motifs (esp., the use of riches), illumines the verse in one way or another.

Luke presents Jesus' public ministry in three distinct stages: in Galilee (Luke 4,14–9,50), on the way to Jerusalem (Luke 9,51–19,44), and in Jerusalem itself (Luke 19,45–21,38)[53]. However, whereas the Matthean Jesus utters the βία-related saying as he travels throughout the whole region of Galilee, preaching the good news of the kingdom in its towns, villages, and synagogues, the Lucan Jesus voices it while journeying south towards Jerusalem, presumably outside the Galilean territory[54].

The very placement of Luke 16,16 within the wider setting of the Travel Narrative (Luke 9,51–19,44) potentially has impact on our understanding of its meaning, insofar as the physical journey may imply also the idea of a Christian *hălākāh*, that is, a metaphorical walk among the divine commandments, which translates itself into a teaching on the moral living of God's people based on the primary premise of the love commandment[55]. Those who, while still in Galilee (Luke 4,14–9,50), "left everything" (Luke 5,11) to follow Jesus (i.e., the disciples) are now invited to go after him all the way to Jerusalem (Luke 9,51–19,44)[56]. The journey offers them the opportunity to *walk* (*hālak*) with their master and learn further what discipleship entails. In fact, among the primary concerns guiding Luke's composition of this Gospel section, special emphasis is given to the training of the disciples, regarding the interpretation of the law, for instance, the openness of the mission to the Gentiles, the experience of re-

---

[53] This subdivision is based on our considered judgment that the proper ending of the Travel Narrative is to be found in Luke 19,44. See Chap. I, p. 6, n. 34.

[54] For the geographical indications of the locations and movements of Jesus prior to the occurrence of the saying in both Gospel narratives, see, e.g., Matt 9,1.10.14.23.26–27.31–32.35; 11,1.12–13; Luke 9,51–52.56–57; 10,38; 11,1.37.53; 12,1.13; 13,1–2.10.22.31–33; 14,1.25; 15,1; and 16,1.14–16.

[55] See, e.g., *HALOT*, "הלך", I, 246; P.J. BERNADICOU, "The Spirituality", 455–466 (esp. 466); P. SIGAL, *The Halakhah*, 54–58, esp. 57; and M. GRILLI, *L'impotenza*, 10–12. 41–43.108. "Walking" or "journeying" (πορεύομαι) in God's statutes, ordinances, precepts, commandments, or words, is "the way of the righteous" (ὁδός δικαίων: Ps 1,6) and is equivalent to one's "moral living" (*hălākāh*; see OSArb. *Alāku*: "to behave"), for "the commandment of the law is […] the way of life" (ἐντολὴ νόμου [...] ὁδὸς ζωῆς: Prov 6,23). See, e.g., Pss 1,1–5; 15(14),2; Prov 4,18–19; 10,17; Sir 17,11; Isa 33,15; Ezek 18,9; and Hos 14,9(10). See also Luke 1,6; 8,14; Acts 9,31; and 14,16.

[56] As compared to leaving their nets, boats, and fathers (cf. Matt 4,18–22 and Mark 1,16–20), the disciples are pictured in Luke as those who, "leaving everything" (ἀφέντες πάντα: Luke 5:11), are totally detached from material possessions. See also Luke 5,28; 14,33; and 18,22 (see, esp., Luke's addition of "all" [πάντα], as opposed to Mark 10,21).

jection and opposition, but also the right relationship with money and one's proper use of possessions[57].

The narrative sequence (Luke 14,25–17,10) to which Luke 16,16 belongs offers a particular instance of how such an instruction unfolds, one scene after another. The sequence is well demarcated by two travel notes (see συμπορεύομαι: Luke 14,25; and πορεύομαι: Luke 17,11), which are each in turn preceded and followed by the occurrences of two healing accounts (see Luke 14,1–6 and 17,12–19), the expression, "the kingdom of God" (see Luke 14,15 and 17,20; see also Luke 16,16b), and varied teachings on discipleship (see Luke 14,25–35 and 17,1–10).

Specifically, in both Luke 14,25 and 17,11, place, characters, time, and situation change. After "healing" (ἴασαι: Luke 14,4) a man suffering from dropsy, on the Sabbath day (see Luke 14,1–6), and talking about "first" (πρωτοκλισίαι: Luke 14,8) and "last places" (ἔσχατοι τόποι: Luke 14,9–10; see also Luke 14,22), Jesus leaves the "house" (οἶκος: Luke 14,1) of one of the leaders of the Pharisees and resumes his journey towards Jerusalem, accompanied by large crowds (see Luke 14,25)[58].

The next mention of the continuation of such a journey occurs in Luke 17,11, with its construction marking a new narrative incipit[59]. Here, Luke indicates how, in their journey towards Jerusalem, Jesus and his disciples reach a new geographical boundary, namely, the borderlands of Samaria and Galilee[60]. After

---

[57] Throughout this narrative section of the journey to Jerusalem (Luke 9,51–19,44), the Lucan disciples are instructed to perform varied deeds, such as, proclaim the kingdom of God (e.g., Luke 9,60 and 10,9.11), expect rejection, persecutions and sufferings (e.g., Luke 9,52–53; 10,3.10–11 and 12,11), pray (e.g., Luke 11,2–13 and 18,1–14), forgive (e.g., Luke 11,4 and 17,3–4), be found ready for their master's return (e.g., Luke 12,35–40 and 17,7–10), put God first (e.g., Luke 9,59–62; 10,25–28 and 12,31), hear and do God's word (e.g., Luke 10,25–42 and 11,28; cf., also, Luke 6,47–49 and 8,21), carry the cross (e.g., Luke 14,27; cf., also, 9,23 and 23,26), etc. As we have just noted, however, when the Lucan Jesus calls and thus "creates" his first disciples, they are said to "leave everything" behind, to follow him (see Luke 5,11.28). Then, prior to the journey, Luke's Jesus addresses them directly as "poor" (Luke 6,20). What this characterization hints to shall be elucidated primarily and progressively in the Travel Narrative, mostly in terms of the requirement to be both detached from their possessions and shrewd in their use of money. See, e.g., Luke 9,57–62; 10,4; 11,41; 12,13–34; 14,28.33; 16,1–31; 18,22.28 and 19,8.15.23.

[58] Several motifs, occurring also later in Luke 16 (e.g., shame, honor, reversal of fortunes, poor, recompense, buying, getting married, and strong urge or call to enter [see καὶ ἀνάγκασον εἰσελθεῖν: Luke 14,23] into the heavenly banquet of God's kingdom) are introduced here, in this smaller unit (Luke 14,7–24), as a preparatory stage for the following narrative sequence (Luke 14,25–17,10).

[59] See Chap. III, p. 154, n. 388.

[60] Although suggesting a movement East to West (vs. North to South, towards Jerusalem), the mention of Samaria serves to prepare for the following account (see Luke 17,12–19), where Jesus sets a Samaritan "foreigner" (ἀλλογενής: Luke 17,18) as an example to his followers,

"entering" (εἰσερχομένου αὐτοῦ εἰς: Luke 17,12; see also εἰς: Luke 16,16c) a certain village and "healing" (ἴασαι: Luke 17,15) ten lepers, the expression, "the kingdom of God", reappears: the Pharisees ask Jesus about its coming and Jesus replies by pointing to the fact that it is already within their reach, accessible in and through his preaching and his person (see Luke 17,20–22)[61].

In between these two travel notes, the whole narrative sequence consists of six scenes (Luke 14,25–35; 15,1–10; 15,11–32; 16,1–13; 16,14–31; and 17,1–10), in which Luke presents primarily a few teachings on the full meaning and implications of discipleship[62]. At the structural level, and by way of *inclusio*, both the first (Luke 14,25–35) and last (Luke 17,1–10) scenes comprise ten verses conveying several aspects of discipleship, mostly by means of images (e.g., tower, battle, salt, millstone, mustard seed, and mulberry tree)[63]. In between them, two diptychs (Luke 15,1–10.11–32 and Luke 16,1–13.14–31), focusing on two separate themes (joyous welcoming of repentant sinners and right use of riches in view of one's entry into the kingdom of God), are addressed to the same mixed audience (see Luke 15,1–3.11a; and 16,1a.14–15a), mostly by means of parables (see Luke 15,4–6.8–9.11b–32; and 16,1b–8a.19–31)[64].

As one advances from one scene to the next, the wider initial public made up of the "large crowds" (ὄχλοι πολλοί: Luke 14,25) travelling with Jesus is progressively identified as a composite group, counting among its members three kinds of people: tax-collectors and sinners (see Luke 15,1.2), Pharisees and scribes (see Luke 15,2 and 16,14), disciples and apostles (see Luke 16,1 and 17,1.5)[65]. Another development throughout these scenes has to do with the proper attitude toward possessions and their use. Right from the start of the

---

most of whom are presumably Israelites. "Everyone" (πᾶς), even the "outsiders", are gaining access to God's kingdom (see Luke 16,16c)!

[61] See, e.g., H.J. CADBURY, "The Kingdom of God", 172–173; J.A. FITZMYER, *Luke*, II, 1160–1162; and D.L. BOCK, *Luke*, II, 1414–1419.

[62] For a discussion of Luke's understanding of discipleship, see, e.g., F.J. MATERA, *Passion Narratives*, 202–205.

[63] The two scenes are associated also by the occurrence of the same formula, "which one of you" (τίς ἐξ ὑμῶν), in Luke 14,28 and 17,7. See also Luke 15,4.

[64] Thus, I.H. Marshall (*Luke*, 597) comments: "There can be no doubt that chap. 15 forms one self-contained and artistically constructed unit with a single theme". J.A. Fitzmyer (*Luke*, II, 1072–1073), likewise, remarks: "That chap. 15 is an artistic unit in the Lucan Gospel must be admitted [...] The pair of parables (vv. 4–6 and 8–9) has a counterpart [...] in the pair of sayings on the conditions of discipleship in 14,28–32 [...] and [...] is clearly marked by the introductory 'or' (v. 8), resembling that of 14,31". For the change of theme, from chap. 15 to chap. 16, see, e.g., *Ibid.*, II, 1095. Behind these two separate themes and diptychs, the notion of almsgiving may well function as a broadly unifying factor, insofar as it can be used to gain forgiveness of sins and entry to the "house-kingdom" of God. See, e.g., Chap. III, p. 153, n. 386; Chap. V, p. 288; and Chap. VI, p. 312.

[65] For the distinction between the labels, "disciple" and "apostle", in Luke-Acts, see, e.g., F.J. MATERA, *Passion Narratives*, 200–201; and R.D. WITHERUP, *101 Questions*, 32–33.

narrative sequence, this subject matter is set out by the Lucan Jesus as one of the requirements of true discipleship (see Luke 14,33). It continues then to appear in some of the motifs occurring in the scenes preceding Luke 16 (Luke 14,25–35; 15,1–10 and 15,11–32), but it is only in this last chapter that it develops gradually into a unifying theme[66].

Specifically, in the first scene (Luke 14,25–35), Luke presents a few sayings on discipleship, some of which are unique to him[67]. Over and above the requirements of loving God more than family or self, and carrying one's own cross, Luke adds the need for a true follower of Jesus to "first sit down and estimate the amount of the expense" (πρῶτον καθίσας ψηφίζει τὴν δαπάνην: Luke 14,28), so as to avoid embarrassment and public shame (see Luke 14,29–30 and 16,3.6–7)[68]. Then, however, the Lucan Jesus explains: "In the same way, therefore, everyone [πᾶς] of you who does not detach himself [ἀποτάσσεται] from all his possessions cannot be my disciple" (Luke 14,33)[69].

Following the closing remark of this first scene, on the call "to listen" (ἀκούειν) and heed carefully (see Luke 14,35 and 16,14.29.31), Luke combines a pair of scenes (Luke 15,1–10 and 15,11–32) in which Jesus touches on motifs that are related to money in various ways[70]. Three parables are told in the presence of two categories of people, that is, "tax-collectors" (τελῶναι) and sinners, and Pharisees and scribes (see Luke 15,1–3.7)[71].

---

[66] See, e.g., J.A. FITZMYER, *Luke*, II, 1095; S.E. WRIGHT, "Parables", 233; B. SHELLARD, *New Light*, 120; and B.B. BRUEHLER, "Reweaving the Texture", 52. For the distinction between theme and motif, see Chap. III, p. 151, n. 368. Among the other Lucan motifs emerging from Luke 15, M. Grilli (*Matteo*, 341), for instance, identifies especially that of the "condivisione della gioia". For the progressive appearance of the theme of riches in Luke's Gospel, see, e.g., Luke 4,18; 6,20.24; 9,3; 10,4; 12,15–34; 14,33; 16,1–31; 18,18–27; 19,1–10; 21,1–4. See also M. GRILLI, *Matteo*, 345–346.

[67] Apart from Luke 14,26–27 (cf. Matt 10,37–38) and 14,34–35 (cf. Mark 9,49–50 and Matt 5,13), the verses of this subunit are distinctively Lucan material.

[68] Both, "to compute, reckon, or calculate" (ψηφίζειν means, lit., "to count with pebbles"), and, "expense, or cost" (δαπάνη), belong to the economic terminology. See, e.g., Ezra 6,4.8; Luke 14,31; and Acts 19,19. See also Thayer, "δαπάνη", 125; and *Ibid.*, "ψηφίζω", 676.

[69] See, e.g., G. DELLING, "τάσσω", *TDNT*, VIII, 33–34. In Luke, the verse is followed immediately by the saying about salt (see Luke 14,34–35), an image synthesizing the whole teaching on the cost of discipleship: to give flavour to other foods, a pinch of salt needs to dissolve entirely and give all its "property" away! In Matthew, this saying follows rather the Gospel of the Beatitudes (see Matt 5,13), to express more generally the identity of every adult Christian disciple.

[70] A few authors observe rightly how "money" plays a significant role in Luke 15, especially in the parable of the prodigal son, where the economic situation marks the times of the narrative. See, e.g., F. BOVON, *L'œuvre de Luc*, 39. Another motif that slowly emerges in Luke 15 is also that of the "house". See, e.g., *Ibid.*, 45.

[71] It is worth underlining the presence of the tax-collectors, who as Thayer ("τελώνης", 620) points out, "were, as a class, detested not only by the Jews but by other nations also,

In all of these stories, the main characters are said to "possess" (ἔχειν: Luke 15,4.8.11), "lose" (ἀπολλύειν: Luke 15,4.6.8.9.24.32) and "find" (εὑρίσκειν: Luke 15,4–6.8–9.24.32) something or someone, whether it is one of a hundred sheep, ten silver coins, or two sons (see Luke 15,4.8.11)[72]. Economic images succeed one another gradually and in an ever clearer way, from that of "small cattle" (πρόβατα, lit., "sheep": Luke 15,4.6), to those of "coins" (δραχμά: Luke 15,8–9), "property" (οὐσία: Luke 15,12–13) and "livelihood" (βίος: Luke 15,12.30). In the third parable, in particular, the loss of the younger son is associated with the "squandering" (διασκορπίζειν) of property and thus tied directly with that of the Shrewd Steward, in the next scene (see Luke 15,13 and 16,1c). Moreover, the boy's departure from home as well as his return to his father are motivated primarily by economic criteria, job performance, and the benefits which he can derive from them (see Luke 15,12.17.19b)[73]. In other words, though the boy's characterization revolves predominantly around the use of money and the desire for it, that of his father rotates around his generous habit of "giving" (δοῦναι: Luke 15,12.22.29; see also 15,23.27.31)[74].

Then, in Luke 16, the motif evolves gradually into a real theme, although as we have already mentioned the larger enclosing concern of the sequence remains always that of discipleship (see Luke 14,25–35; and 17,1–10)[75]. Finally, in the closing scene of the narrative sequence, Luke depicts Jesus teaching his disciples about the nature and implications of discipleship with respect to neighbor (see Luke 17,1–4) and God (see Luke 17,5–10) and in terms of accountability (see Luke 17,1–2), forgiveness (see Luke 17,3–4), faith (see Luke 17,5–6) and service (see Luke 17,7–10)[76]. Thus, while the sequence resumes its larger emphasis on the theme of discipleship (see Luke 14,25–35), that on the right

---

both on account of their employment and of the harshness, greed, and deception, with which they prosecuted it". Etymologically, the name τελώνης may derive from τέλος ("end") and ὦνος ("price, sum paid"), thus indicating a person whose purpose in life is the accumulation of wealth. In Luke 16, Jesus will set his warning against greed before these same groups of people (see Luke 15,1–3.11; 16,1.14–15a). A similar antagonism between these characters occurs in Luke 5,27–32 and 19,1–10. See, e.g., J.-N. ALETTI, *Il racconto*, 210–214; and M. CRIMELLA, *Marta*, 324–329.

[72] See, e.g., M. CRIMELLA, *Marta*, 327.

[73] See, e.g., J.-N. ALETTI, *Il racconto*, 187–197; and M. CRIMELLA, *Marta*, 265–269.

[74] Thus, J.-N. Aletti (*Il racconto*, 205) observes: "Il suo essere padre consiste nel condividere tutto con i propri figli, nel non custodire nulla gelosamente […] vivere di questa liberalità". See also L.T. JOHNSON, *The Literary Function*, 159–161.

[75] See, e.g., Chap. III, pp. 151–155.

[76] For instance, concerning Luke 17,1–10, J.A. Fitzmyer (*Luke*, II, 1136) comments: "The only link that they [i.e., the sayings] seem to have is a bearing on various aspects of discipleship". See also *Ibid.*, II, 1136–1148; and Y.-G. KWON, "Forgiveness", 613.

use of riches in view of one's entry into the kingdom of God (see Luke 16,1–31) is attenuated substantially, though perhaps not shelved entirely[77].

D. Exegesis and Theology of the Saying in Its Proximate Context

In the third chapter of our study, we dealt extensively with the peculiar light that the two parabolic accounts (vv. 1b–8a and vv. 19–31) and sets of sayings (vv. 8b–13 and vv. 15b–18) in Luke 16 shed on each other and on v. 16. To avoid unnecessary repetition, and thus facilitate the final comprehension of the saying, this final section shall be primarily an application of those new lights. Specifically, the following pages shall include the explanation and function of Luke 16,16, as the main point of reference, within a close reading of its most adjacent verses (vv. 15b–18), that is to say, the most basic and proximate literary context in which its meaning is produced. The application to this verse of the hermeneutic answers from our present study shall allow us to go beyond its preliminary neutral translation. To assess the functions and repercussions of Luke's strategic choices upon his intended readers, some of the questions we shall ask will concern the pragmatic effects or changes the author wants to bring about in the readers' minds and the kind of persuasive language he uses for that purpose in these verses.

I. Luke 16,15b–18: A 2nd Set of Sayings Within a Concentric Unit

As already mentioned, when it comes to the exegesis and theology of Luke 16,15b–18, many early interpreters argue in favour of their independent nature, mostly

---

[77] In fact, a couple of hints to it can still be detected by the attentive reader. For instance, the severe tone of the interjection, "but woe to" (πλὴν οὐαὶ τῷ: Luke 17,1), is used two more times by the Lucan Jesus: once against the rich, who have already received their consolation (Luke 6,24; see also Luke 6,20; and 16,1.19.25), and another time against Judas Iscariot (Luke 22,22). It is worth underlining here that Luke portrays Judas, not as hanging himself (cf. Matt 27,5), but as "purchasing" (κτάομαι) a piece of land "with a wage of unrighteousness" (ἐκ μισθοῦ τῆς ἀδικίας: Acts 1,18; see also Acts 1,19 and Matt 27,7; as well as, Luke 10,7 and 1Tim 5,18), "to go to his own place" (πορευθῆναι εἰς τὸν τόπον τὸν ἴδιον: Acts 1,25). The literary connection between such a characterization and Luke 16 (see, esp., vv. 8–9.11.22 and 28) is all the more accentuated when one considers also that greed is the primary motive for Judas' betrayal in both Matt 26,15 (vs. Mark 14,10–11) and John 12,6 (see, also, Luke 22,3 and John 6,70–71; 13,2.27). Finally, a further hint to the theme of riches and the kingdom of God can be seen in the occurrence of the verb, "to stumble or cause to stumble" (σκανδαλίζειν: Luke 17,2), which is mentioned only one other time in Luke-Acts, in the context of John the Baptist and Jesus, and immediately after the sentence, "the poor [πτωχοί] have the Good News preached [εὐαγγελίζονται] to them" (see Luke 7,22–23 and Matt 11,4–6.11–12; see also Luke 16,16.20.22).

because of their seeming lack of connection with the Lucan context and with each other, and as a result, Luke 16,16 is often singled out and analyzed in isolation from the rest of the narrative[78]. However, we have also seen that, with the advent of rhetorical and narrative criticism, more recent scholarship has challenged the previous general skepticism about their internal and con-textual coherence and led gradually to the view that these verses possess both an inner logical progression of thought and a meaningful connection with the surrounding context[79]. Indeed, rather than representing independent dominical sayings tied together artificially, they do play a logical role in the redactional structure and unity of Luke 16[80]. In that case, we must ask ourselves what message Luke intends to convey through them. To determine the meaning and implications of Luke 16,16, an exegetical and theological analysis of the individual sayings contained in these verses is imperative[81].

---

[78] See, e.g., B.H. STREETER, *The Four Gospels*, 286–287; M. GOGUEL, *Au seuil*, 62; J.M. CREED, *Luke*, 206; H.L. EGELKRAUT, *Jesus' Mission*, 114, n. 3; R.J. KARRIS, "Poor and Rich", 121–122; and Chap. III, pp. 90–92. A widely-known instance of such an approach is H. Conzelmann's study of the verse as the key to Luke's so-called three-stage schema of salvation history. See, e.g., H. CONZELMANN, *The Theology*, 16.20–21.25–26.101.112–123.160–161.185. For a criticism of the latter's interpretation, see W.G. KÜMMEL, "'Das Gesetz'", 398–415; and G.W. KLINGSPORN, *The Law*, 360–361.

[79] For instance, G.W. Klingsporn argues that the common link between Luke 16,14–18 and its wider context in Luke 14–16 is to be found in the relationship between the theme of the validity of the law and that of Jesus' conflict with his opponents. See, e.g., G.W. KLINGSPORN, *The Law*, 361–365.371–372.383. Although we recognize the value of his arguments in favor of the existence of these themes, in our view the main contextual link uniting the sayings with their surroundings is provided rather by the primary theme of riches, property, and their proper use in view of one's entry into the kingdom of God, as it occurs in Luke 16. The author himself (*Ibid.*, 366) acknowledges this approach as being "more traditional", but eventually discards it because of his own difficulty in recognizing "how vv. 16–18 fit into the unity of the chapter [...] with the theme of the right use of possessions". See, e.g., *Ibid.*, 366–372.383–384.

[80] See, e.g., G.W. KLINGSPORN, *The Law*, 358.372.

[81] The Greek text of these verses shall follow that of the NA[28] critical edition. Moreover, since these verses present no significant textual problems, we shall only note the variants we consider relevant or interesting to our study, without however altering the critical texts. The biblical Committee of the GNT[4] (Metzger[2], 140–141) does not comment on them. For a list of all the insignificant variants, see, e.g., the critical apparati in Merk[9], 265; Tischendorf, I, 624; NA[27], 214; NA[28], 253; the CNTTS database, on Luke 16,15–18; and M. KLINGHARDT, *Das älteste Evangelium*, II, 868.1254.

1. Verse 15b:

"You are those who keep justifying yourselves in men's sight, but God knows your hearts, [he knows] that what among men is high [-ly exalted] is an abomination in God's sight"[82].

Following immediately after the second extradiegetic introduction of the chapter (see vv. 1a.14–15a), these simultaneously admonitory and wise words constitute the beginning of the second set of sayings (vv. 15b–18) in Luke 16[83]. Through them, Jesus addresses directly the money-loving Pharisees. Analogously to v. 8b, this utterance expresses primarily a comparison between two perspectives, one human (see ὑμεῖς) and one divine (see ὁ δὲ θεός): while men stop at outward appearances (see ἐνώπιον τῶν ἀνθρώπων), God (see ἐνώπιον τοῦ θεοῦ) is able to look straight to the human heart (see, e.g., 1Sam 16,7)[84]. "God judges otherwise than human beings"[85]: as a result, that which among men is esteemed to be "of high quality, noble, sublime"[86] (ὑψηλός), can be, before God, "something that causes revulsion or extreme disgust, a 'loathsome, detestable thing'"[87] (βδέλυγμα).

---

[82] "ὑμεῖς ἐστε οἱ δικαιοῦντες ἑαυτοὺς ἐνώπιον τῶν ἀνθρώπων, ὁ δὲ θεὸς γινώσκει τὰς καρδίας ὑμῶν· ὅτι τὸ ἐν ἀνθρώποις ὑψηλὸν βδέλυγμα ἐνώπιον τοῦ θεοῦ" (Luke 16,15b). Two textual variants worth mentioning are the replacements of the substantive, "God" (θεοῦ), with, "Lord" (κυρίου), within the final expression, "in the sight of" (ἐνώπιον τοῦ), in (B) Codex Vaticanus, and that of the adjective, "high" (ὑψηλόν), with, "strong" (ἰσχυρόν), in the minuscule ms. 579. Both remind us of the text of Deut 6,5 (cf. Luke 10,27). Consistent with its Satt, the latter may also be read as a further allusion to mammon.

[83] Thus, G. Rossé (*Luca*, 630) remarks: "Gesù [...] combina una sorta di profezia di minaccia (v. 15a) con un detto a carattere sapienziale (v. 15b)". See also J.A. FITZMYER, *Luke*, II, 1112.

[84] For the relationship of v. 15b with v. 8b, see, esp., Chap. III, p. 157, fig. 2. Behind the saying contained in v. 15b there might be an allusion to God's words to Samuel. See, e.g., the occurrences of the syntagmas, "man" (ἄνθρωπος), "God" (θεός), "that" (ὅτι), and "heart" (καρδίας), in both 1Sam 16,7 and Luke 16,15b. See also the expressions, "the height of stature/size" (see MT on 1Sam 16,7: גבה קומה; and LXX: τὴν ἕξιν μεγέθους), and "that which is high" (τὸ [...] ὑψηλὸν: Luke 16,15b); as well as, "for man looks at the eyes/[sur-]face but God looks at the heart" (see MT on 1Sam 16,7: כי האדם יראה לעינים ויהוה יראה ללבב; and LXX: ὅτι ἄνθρωπος ὄψεται εἰς πρόσωπον ὁ δὲ θεὸς ὄψεται εἰς καρδίαν: 1Sam 16,7), and "but God knows the hearts" (ὁ δὲ θεὸς γινώσκει τὰς καρδίας: Luke 16,15b). In Hebrew the same word (עין) is used to indicate both "eye" and "source, spring". Accordingly, to see what "springs" out of the human heart, man needs to look into the eyes, whereas God can see directly into it (see, e.g., Matt 6,22–23 and Luke 11,34–36). The TJ on 1Sam 16,7 reads: "for the children of men see into the eyes, but before God the thoughts of the heart are uncovered" (ארי בני אנשא חזן בעיניהון וקדם יוי גלין מחשבת לבא). See, e.g., E. VAN STAALDUINE-SULMAN, *The Targum*, 338–339. The latter expression sounds much like the words of Mary: "He has scattered the proud in the thoughts of their hearts [διανοίᾳ καρδίας αὐτῶν]" (Luke 1,51).

[85] J.A. FITZMYER, *Luke*, II, 1112.

[86] BDAG, "ὑψηλός", 1044.

[87] BDAG, "βδέλυγμα", 172.

What this abominable "thing" (see τό [...] ὑψηλόν) refers to exactly is suggested by the context. Through his extradiegetic intervention into the narrative, the omniscient narrator has just revealed to his readers that which lies hidden in the Pharisees' hearts, which God alone sees directly: their "love of money" (see φιλάργυροι: v. 14)[88]. Jesus could have humanly stopped at their outward appearance, seeing the way they had turned up their nose to deride him (see ἐξεμυκτήριζον αὐτόν: v. 14). However, he chooses to go deeper (see, e.g., Luke 11,39) and, continuing the train of thought of v. 13, aims forthrightly at the love of their hearts, equating it to an idolatrous "abomination" (βδέλυγμα)[89]. The OT use of this term is succinctly summed up by L.T. Johnson:

The contrast between what is "exalted" (ὑψηλός) and "low" is typical of Luke, but in this case, the language is stronger: the "abomination" (βδέλυγμα) occurs in Gen 43,32, Exod 8,26, Lev 5,2, 7,21, 11,10–42, Deut 17,1, as something utterly reprehensible or "unclean" in thing or act. In Deuteronomy, it is mainly associated, however, with idolatry (see Deut 7,25; 12,31; 18,12; 27,15; 29,17; 32,16), and that association is continued in Isaiah (2,8.20; 17,8; 41,24; 44,19). In Dan 9,27, 11,31 and 12,11, the "abomination of desolation" is the supreme representation of idolatry (cf., also, Mark 13,14 and Matt 24,15). The word choice by Luke, in short, corresponds to the portrayal of Mammon in *L* as an idol competing for human allegiance against God, which portrayal the Pharisees mock. In light of the sayings which follow, it is instructive to note that the term βδέλυγμα is also used to designate sham outward worship (Isa 1,13 and 66,3), immoral financial dealings (Deut 25,16), and the remarrying of a divorced wife (Deut 24,4)[90]!

---

[88] Although differently, the Pharisees' avarice (Luke 16,14) shall come back in the characterizations of Judas (Acts 1,18–19), Symon the magician (Acts 8,9–24), and the Ephesian traders (Acts 19,23–27). See, e.g., F. BOVON, *L'œuvre de Luc*, 233–235.

[89] Thus, C.H. Talbert (*Reading Luke*, 156) remarks: "The Pharisees scoff at Jesus' statement, 'You cannot serve God and mammon' (v. 13). Given their assumptions, this was predictable. For them tragedy is a sign of God's displeasure; success (e.g., financial prosperity) is evidence of one's righteousness and of God's pleasure. It is no wonder they scoffed at Jesus' 'either God or money' stance [...] Money for them was a sign, a sure sign, of God's favor and of their place in the kingdom. Their position had roots in their scriptures (e.g., Deut 28,12–13 where wealth and plenty are a sign of God's blessings). Jesus' response to their scoffing was to contrast their outer-public appearance with their inner-private reality (cf. 11,39–41; 18,9–14)". In turn, J.A. Fitzmyer (*Luke*, II, 1112) comments: "Coming immediately after Jesus' saying about serving God or mammon in the present Lucan context, they [i.e., Jesus' words] offer a commentary on v. 13, especially the last part of it: Coveting mammon is the real abomination in God's sight". See also G. ROSSÉ, *Luca*, 631.

[90] L.T. JOHNSON, ed., *Luke*, 250. See, e.g., Luke 16,15b–18; D.J. IRELAND, *Stewardship*, 127; and A.A. JUST, Jr., *Luke*, II, 625, n. 3. In addition to L.T. Johnson's aforementioned citations, see also the use of the terms, "high" (ὑψηλός) and "abomination" (βδέλυγμα), in 1Kgs 11,5.7, with reference to idol worship; the latter term's connection with divorce (see ἐξαποστέλλω), in Mal 2,11.16, in the context of idolatrous love; and the expression, "abomination before" (βδέλυγμα ἐνώπιον: Luke 16,15), in Prov 11,1, as a reference to "balances of deception", i.e., deceptive or false scales suggesting dishonest money dealings! Generally, the Law condemns fraudulent business practices as an abomination. See, e.g., Deut 25,13–16;

Thus, as shown also in the following parable (Luke 16,19–31), "wealth is not necessarily a sign of righteousness"[91], for the latter requires both faithfulness to the law and generosity to the poor (see Luke 16,10–12.17)[92]. Whenever it is used without regard for the law or the poor, then, money becomes an abominable idol, desecrating the heart of man as if it were a desolation set up in God's holy temple[93].

Moreover, in the light of the previous verses (vv. 13–14), Jesus' words about God's knowledge of the human "heart" (καρδία) may be here not only an intimation of Jesus' own divine identity, but also a hint pointing towards the Šᵉma' (see, e.g., Deut 6,5 and Luke 10,27)[94].

Already, the saying on the incompatibility of serving God and mammon, with which the previous narrative segment of the chapter culminates (vv. 1b–13), introduces discreetly the fundamental notion of "loving" God contained in the Šᵉma' (see ἀγαπήσεις: Luke 16,13 and Deut 6,5). The opening words of the primary segment (vv. 14–31) in which the meaning of Luke 16,16 is produced confirm the possibility of this allusion: the Pharisees are presented as "listening" (see ἤκουον: Luke 16,14a; and ἄκουε: Deut 6,4) and holding up their nose in derision of Jesus while simultaneously holding on to money, in direct contrast to Jesus' previous words (v. 13)[95]. At the end of the section (see vv. 29.31),

---

Lev 19,35–36; Prov 20,10.23; and, esp., Mic 6,10–12. See also P.S. CAMERON, *Violence*, 152.197, ns. 107.109; G. ROSSÉ, *Luca*, 631, n. 49; and F. BOVON, *Luc*, III, 89. Finally, in Mic 6,12, the Hebrew term used to indicate the negative deceitful character of the violence filling the hearts of the rich is חָמָס. As we have already noted (see Chap. IV, p. 218), the latter is never translated by the LXX with βία. In Mic 6,12, it is rendered with, "impiety" (ἀσέβεια), which for Micah indicates bribes and idolatrous love of money. See, e.g., Mic 1,5–7; and 3,8–11. See also S.P. CARBONE – G. RIZZI, *Il libro di Michea*, 174–179. Finally, a few Gk. mss. read "unrighteousness" (ἀδικίας) in lieu of "impiety" (ἀσέβεια). See also the *Vg.* (*iniquitatem*); and the critical apparatus, in J. ZIEGLER, ed., *Duodecim prophetae*, 222.

[91] C.H. TALBERT, *Reading Luke*, 156.

[92] See, e.g., Deut 6,25; 24,13; Tob 1,3; 2,14; 4,5–7; 12,8; 13,6; Ps 33(32),5; Prov 11,23–25; 14,31; 17,5; 19,17; 21,26; and 29,7. See also C.H. TALBERT, *Reading Luke*, 156–157.

[93] See, e.g., Dan 9,27; 11,31; 12,11; 1Macc 1,54; Matt 24,15; Mark 13,14; Luke 6,45; and 12,34. As G. Rossé (*Luca*, 628) points out, "Dio e mammona [...] sono presentati come due avversari in concorrenza. La lotta tuttavia non si svolge direttamente tra Dio e mammona. L'incompatibilità si situa nel *cuore* dell'uomo. È il cuore, cioè l'uomo nelle sue scelte fondamentali, che non deve compromettersi, essere diviso".

[94] For the biblical notion of God, as the "knower of hearts" (καρδιογνώστης), see, e.g., 1Sam 2,3; 16,7; 1Kgs 8,39; 1Chr 28,9; Jer 17,10; and, esp., Acts 1,24; and 15,8. For Jesus' own knowledge, see, e.g., Luke 2,35; 5,22; 6,8; 9,47; and 24,38. See also G. ROSSÉ, *Luca*, 631, n. 47. Other possible allusions to the Šᵉma' shall be noted as we move on with the analysis of the following sayings. For a list of authors who suggest such a broad reference, see Chap. I, p. 13, n. 83.

[95] See the use of the imperfect tenses of ἤκουον and ἐξεμυκτήριζον, and that of the present participle, in φιλάργυροι ὑπάρχοντες.

Abraham, the father of faith, echoes the importance of "listening" to the Law and the prophets, thus creating an *inclusio* around the whole segment, with a likely reference to both Jesus' divinity and the commandment of life[96].

Indeed, as shown by K.H. Tan, the Jewish profession of faith was employed theologically by the early Church to refer to Jesus' divine identity, in the context of a discussion concerning monotheism and idolatry with those members coming from the Judaic matrix[97]. In this sense, it is worth noting that, in contrast to taking upon one's shoulders the yoke of the kingdom of God, by sincerely reciting the *Š*eᵉ*maʿ* and loving God with all one's strength and/or mammon, the Jewish tradition associates the person who neglects the laws relating to generosity, and alms-giving to the poor, with an idolater who "breaks off from him the yoke of Heaven"[98] and has no share in the world to come[99]. Based on a hermeneutic method known as *notarikon* (Gk. νοταρικόν; Heb. נוטריקון), which may some-times consist of "breaking up a word into various components"[100], the term, "wickedness" (בליעל), in Deut 15,9, is interpreted here to mean "without" (בלי) "yoke" (על)[101]. As suggested by the context (see Deut 15,7–11), a person may be reluctant to lend to the poor, especially as the sabbatical year of remission of debts approaches (see Deut 15,1–6), mainly because of fear of losing one's loan altogether[102]. The invitation in the text, then, is not to entertain such

---

[96] See, e.g., Matt 5,17–20; 17,3.5; 22,40; Mark 9,4.7; 12,28–34; Luke 9,30.35; 10,25–28; 16,16–17.29.31; 24,27.44; John 1,45; 5,46–47; 13,34; Acts 3,22.35.37; 13,15.30.33; 28,23; Rom 13,8–10; Gal 5,14; and Jas 2,8.

[97] See K.H. TAN, "The Shema", 181–206.

[98] C.H. TALBERT, *Reading Luke*, 157.

[99] See, e.g., SifDev on Deut 13,14 (ed. L. FINKELSTEIN, 154); SifDev on Deut 15,9 (ed. *Ibid.*, 176); MTann on Deut 13,14 (ed. D.Z. HOFFMANN, II, 66); tPe 4.19–21 (ed. K.H. RENGSTORF, 80–81); LeqT on Deut 13,14 (ed. A.M. SILBERMANN – M. ROSENBAUM, 73); and mSan 10,4. See also Deut 15,4.7–11; P. BLACKMAN, *Mishnayoth*, IV, 289; J. NEUSNER – R.S. SARASON, ed., *The Tosefta*, 73–74; and E. CORTÉS – T. MARTÍNEZ, *Sifre*, I, 215.246.

[100] M.V. FOX, "Notarikon", *EJ*, XV, 315.

[101] See, e.g., BDB, "בְּלִי", 115; *Ibid.*, "בְּלִיַּעַל", 116; *Ibid.*, "עֹל", 760; and S. LIEBERMAN, *Hellenism*, 69–70. For the use of the *nôṭarîqôn* and the other rabbinic hermeneutic methods of biblical exegesis, see, e.g., J. LUZÁRRAGA, "Principios hermenéuticos", 177–193 (esp. 191); and W.S. TOWNER, "Hermeneutical Systems", 101–135 (esp. 127–128). For the NT allusion to and use of the rabbinic idiom, "to take upon oneself the yoke of the kingdom", see, e.g., Matt 11,29–30; and Mark 10,15. See also G. DALMAN, *The Words*, 96–97; and J. MARCUS, "Entering", 672–673. As the latter (*Ibid.*, 672, n. 50) points out, "Proselytes to Judaism were said to take upon themselves the yoke of the kingdom (Resh Lakish [ca. 250], *Tanḥuma, lech lecha* section 6, cited in Str-B, I, 176), and there is also a rabbinic tradition that compares the new proselyte to a newly born child (R. Jose [ca. 150], bYev 48b; cited by G.F. MOORE, *Judaism*, I, 335)".

[102] Since the Hebrew text lends itself to a wordplay on the name for the god, "Baal" (בעל), and the verb, "to profit" (יעל), the person harboring this wicked thought is identified further with an idolater. See, e.g., BDB, "בַּעַל", 127; and *Ibid.*, "יָעַל", 418.

a "wicked thought in your heart" (דבר עם־לבבך בליעל: Deut 15,9), by under-
taking this kind of greedy calculation, for God will bless with further prosperity
those who lend to the poor (see Deut 15,10; and Prov 19,17).

Of course, as we have already mentioned, being righteous in terms of generosity
and almsgiving entails a sense of faith and foresight that extend beyond those
of this world (see Luke 16,1b–8ab)[103]. It is not by chance that the corresponding
saying, in v. 8b, urges the readers to go beyond the wisdom of the world and
pass to faith, by engaging in generous acts of mercy or almsgiving, in view
of one's eternal destiny[104]. Also in v. 15b, then, Luke may wish to bring about
an analogous change in the reader's mind. In fact, the LXX renders the faith-
related terminology (see, e.g., אמן, אמונה, or אמת) not only with words, such as,
"truth" (ἀλήθεια) or "faith filled trust" (πίστις), but also with "righteousness"
(δικαιοσύνη)[105]. If Jesus calls here the Pharisees, "those who justify"
(δικαιοῦντες) themselves in the sight of men (v. 15b), it is most likely so as to
persuade them (and through them the Lucan readers as well) to place their "faith"
(אמונה) or "trust" (אמת) in the "one" (אחד: Deut 6,4) God, to the exclusion of all
idols, worldly wealth (ממונא, ממון) included[106].

---

[103] See, esp., Chap. III, pp. 134–143.157–158.

[104] See Chap. III, p. 157, fig. 2.

[105] See, e.g., Gen 15,6; 24,27.48–49; 32,11; 47,29; Exod 18,21; 34,6; Deut 13,14; 32,4;
Josh 2,14; 24,14; Pss 15(14),2; 31(30),5(6); 36(35),5(6); 40(39),10(11); Prov 3,3; 16,6;
Isa 1,21.26; 11,5; 25,1; 38,18–19; 39,8; 59,4; Jer 5,1.3; 28,9; 32,41; 33,6; Dan 8,12; 9,13;
etc. See also M. GRILLI, *L'impotenza*, 18.

[106] See, e.g., Pss 49(48),6(7); 52(51),7(9); and 62(61),10(11), whereby the hearers are
warned not to trust in wealth or the abundance of their riches. From an etymological
perspective, "mammon" (ממון) derives from the same Semitic root as "faith" (אמונה) or "trust"
(אמת), that is, √אמן, and most likely means, "that in which one puts one's trust". See, e.g.,
J.A. FITZMYER, *Luke*, II, 1109; G. ROSSÉ, *Luca*, 624, n. 20; and M. GRILLI, *Matteo*, 360–
361.364. For the danger of turning one's possessions into an idol against the first commandment, see, e.g., C.E.B. CRANFIELD, "Riches", 308–310.313. This pragmatic reading fits well
also with the subtle movement occurring in the whole narrative sequence (Luke 14,25–
17,10), from the language of justice to that of faith. On the one hand, see, e.g., "righteous"
(δίκαιοι: Luke 15,7); the attitude of the elder son, who has never neglected any command
(see οὐδέποτε ἐντολήν σου παρῆλθον: Luke 15,29); "unrighteousness" (ἀδικία: Luke 16,8a.9);
"unrighteous" (ἄδικος: Luke 16,10[2x].11); and "justifiers" (δικαιοῦντες: Luke 16,15b).
On the other hand, see, e.g., "faithful" (πιστός: Luke 16,10[2x].11.12); "true" (ἀληθινός:
Luke 16,11); "to entrust" (πιστεύω: Luke 16,11); "to be persuaded" (πείθεσθαι: Luke 16,31);
and "faith" (πίστις: Luke 17,5.6). See also R. MEYNET, *Luke*, 549.569–571.

2. Verse 16:

"The Law and the prophets until John; since then the kingdom of God is preached [as good news], and everyone gains entrance into it [by force of mammon]"[107].

At long last, this translation of the Greek text supersedes our preliminary neutral rendering of the verse. By way of recapitulation, let us consider the hermeneutic choices and answers which have thus far emerged from our study and how they apply to and shine through this final translation.

a) 16ab: "The Law and the Prophets" – "Kingdom of God" Relationship

As G.W. Klingsporn rightly notes, the first question we must ask ourselves with regard to the Lucan verse concerns the relationship between "the law and the prophets" (v. 16a) and the preaching of the βασιλεία of God as a good news (v. 16b). The second one has to do with the very meaning of the phrase, "and every-one gains entrance into it" (v. 16c)[108].

At the beginning of our study, we pointed out how one of the main semantic problems in Luke 16,16 concerns the exact meaning of the βασιλεία envisioned in this NT saying[109]. What does this lexeme mean here? G. Dalman maintains that, whenever it pertains to God, the Hebrew or Aramaic parallels (מלכות and מלכותא, respectively) are always dynamic (vs. static or local), in the sense that they indicate his kingly rule or kingship, never "the territory [or area] governed by him"[110]. Indeed, for H. Windisch no expression even closely matches the NT idea of one's entry into the kingdom of God, either in the OT or Jewish literature[111].

However, we concur with S. Aalen in considering that the βασιλεία of God, in Luke 16,16, is rather to be thought of as a confined area, and should thus be translated as "kingdom", as opposed to the kingly rule, power, or dominion[112]. As J. Marcus suggests, Jesus' sayings about the entrance into the kingdom of God

---

[107] "Ὁ νόμος καὶ οἱ προφῆται μέχρι Ἰωάννου· ἀπὸ τότε ἡ βασιλεία τοῦ θεοῦ εὐαγγελίζεται καὶ πᾶς εἰς αὐτὴν βιάζεται" (Luke 16,16). For the textual critical analysis and preliminary translation of the verse, see Chap. I, pp. 2–4.

[108] See G.W. KLINGSPORN, *The Law*, 389.

[109] See Chap. I, p. 10.

[110] G. DALMAN, *The Words*, 94.

[111] H. WINDISCH, "Die Sprüche", 163–192. See, e.g., G. DALMAN, *The Words*, 116.

[112] See S. AALEN, "'Reign' and 'House'", 231. In his attempt to argue against Dalman, the author goes too far, maintaining that the βασιλεία of God carries always a local sense in the Gospels, and that Jesus stands consciously in contrast with the OT Jewish usage of the term. See, e.g., *Ibid.*, 216–218.220–240. On the contrary, N. Eubank ("Storing up Treasure", 88–89) has recently illustrated how Heaven may have been conceived, already in the Second Temple period, "as a space where God's will is done ([Matt] 6,10) and where one should store one's treasure" with God. See also Deut 28,12; J.T. PENNINGTON, *Heaven*, 44–64. 253–278; and D.C. ALLISON, *Constructing Jesus*, 164–204.

can be interpreted in the light of both the people's entry into the land of Canaan (on the condition of obedience to God's commandments) and the liturgical ceremonies of entry into the Temple, with God the king going before his people[113]. In this sense, Jesus is like a king (see ὁ βασιλεύς: Luke 19,38), followed by "all" (πᾶς) those who enter the kingdom of God with him, through βία (see Luke 16,16c)[114]. Who these people are and what the latter lexeme involves in this verse shall become obvious in the next paragraph.

---

[113] See, e.g., Deut 4,1; 6,17–18; 16,20; Pss 15(14),1–5; 24(23),3–10; and 68(67),24–28(25–29). Thus, O. Keel (*The Symbolism*, 172) remarks: "In Ps 24,7, the temple gates are designated *pthy 'wlm*, 'gates of eternity' (RSV: 'ancient doors') [...] the term [...] might imply that the gates (of Heaven), to which the temple gates give visible form, have been located at this place from time immemorial (as at Bethel)". Jewish tradition identifies the stone placed by Jacob at his head as the foundation stone of the Jerusalem Temple. See, e.g., Gen 28,11.17–19.22; BerR 68,12; and 69,7. In Ps 15(14),5, one of the qualities of character necessary for one to be granted access to the Lord's Temple is generosity with money and assistance to the poor, in full compliance with the laws, rules, and regulations forbidding usury or interest. See, e.g., Exod 22,25(24); Lev 25,35–38; Deut 23,19–20(20–21); and Ezek 18,7–8.13.17–18. See also J. MARCUS, "Entering", 666–668. The author (*Ibid.*, 667) ventures then to argue in favor of a dynamic NT conception of the kingdom, which implies "a human entrance into (= participation in) God's manifestation of his kingly power". However, because of the NT local description of the kingdom in terms of a land or house, such an effort may not be necessary. See, e.g., *Ibid.*, 674; *Ibid.*, 675, n. 60; and Chap. IV, p. 204, n. 238. It is "à l'égard du Temple" that, according to M. Gourgues ("Jésus et la violence", 146), Jesus can be still considered somehow "sujet de violence".

[114] Luke is the only synoptic evangelist who gives Jesus the explicit title, "king" (βασιλεύς), as the latter enters triumphantly into Jerusalem (cf. Matt 21,19; Mark 11,9; and Luke 19,38; cf., also, John 12,13). See also Ps 118(117),26; Luke 1,32; 2,14; and 7,19. The idea of entering a kingdom behind its king is also visible in Luke 23,42–43. See, esp., "whenever you go into your kingdom" (ὅταν ἔλθῃς εἰς τὴν βασιλείαν σου: v. 42) and "you will be in Paradise with me" (μετ' ἐμοῦ ἔσῃ ἐν τῷ παραδείσῳ: v. 43). Thus, J.A. Fitzmyer (*Luke*, II, 1510–1511) remarks: "The noun *paradeisos* occurs further in the NT in 2Cor 12,4 and Rev 2,7 [...] It came into the Greek language from Old Persian (*pairidaêza*, 'enclosed space, precinct'). It is attested in Greek from the time of Xenophon (*Anab.* 1.2,7; 2.4,14; *Cyrop.* 1.3,14) in the sense of an 'enclosed park, garden'. It turns up likewise in Hebrew as *pardēs* (Cant 4,13; Qoh 2,5; Neh 2,8), meaning 'a treed park' [...] From its use in Genesis, it developed in time an eschatological nuance, a *place* [emphasis added] of expected bliss (e.g., Ezek 31,8), and even more specifically as the mythical *place or abode* [emphasis added] of the righteous after death (TLevi XVIII.10–11; PsSol 14,3; 1En XVII–XIX; LX.8; LXI.12). The last sense could be what is intended in this Lucan passage". In turn, S. Aalen ("'Reign' and 'House'", 217.231) rightly acknowledges: "Of course, there is the possibility that Jesus is the viceroy of God as the supreme king [...] Another highly important passage, when speaking of the kingdom of God, is Matt 11,12 = Luke 16,16 [...] The kingdom is here [Luke 16,16] clearly thought of as a house, or a similar confined area [...] the same interpretation is [...] very well possible in Matthew too". Finally, the author (*Ibid.*, 234) observes how, also in the Targumim, "the word ביח [...] is rendered as מלכו". This is true, esp. as regards the Messianic king. See, e.g., MT and TJ on 1Sam 2,35; 25,28; 2Sam 7,11–16.27; 1Kgs 2,24; 11,38; and 1Chr 17,10.25. See also E. VAN STAALDUINE-SULMAN, *The Targum*, 227–228.443.526–529.533.

As far as the first question is concerned, a number of commentators understand the relationship between "the law and the prophets" and the good news of the kingdom (v. 16ab) in terms of promise and fulfillment, wherein the former is superseded and so transformed by the latter[115]. However, we rather agree here with those who interpret this relationship in terms of two successive stages in the economy of divine revelation and salvation, each of which reveals the same will of the "one" God (see Deut 6,4) to a different audience: while before John "the law and the prophets" represent the message of God's revelation directly to the chosen people of Israel alone, after him the preaching of the kingdom extends that same message to everyone[116].

The relationship between these two stages is already foreshadowed in the Lucan Infancy Narrative, through the comparison between John the Baptist and Jesus[117]. Although a few of the same events narrated in the introductory chapters of Luke's Gospel are present also in Matthew's account, Luke's Infancy Narrative twines Jesus' story around that of John (see Luke 1,5–25.26–56; 1,57–80; and 2,1–52) in such a way as to present both characters as agents of God's saving purpose and history[118]. Although John the Baptist marks the point of transition between these

---

[115] See, e.g., S. SCHULZ, *Q*, 114–116; R. BANKS, *Jesus*, 215–218; I.H. MARSHALL, *Luke*, 627; R.A. GUELICH, *The Sermon*, 165; C.L. BLOMBERG, "The Law", 60–61; and G.W. KLINGSPORN, *The Law*, 389–390.

[116] See, e.g., Luke 3,6.10.12.14; 4,25–27; 7,4–5.9; 24,47; Acts 2,5; 10,35; and 15,13–21. See also J.S. JERVELL, "The Law", 21–36; E. FRANKLIN, *Christ the Lord*, 85–87.128; *Ibid.*, 200, n. 40; C.J.A. HICKLING, "A Tract", 262; H.L. EGELKRAUT, *Jesus' Mission*, 116–120; G.W. KLINGSPORN, *The Law*, 376–379.390–392.405; and C.H. TALBERT, *Reading Luke*, 161–173. As S. Sandmel (*A Jewish Understanding*, 183) remarks, the mention of the five brothers in Luke 16,29 might also be interpreted as an allusion to the Jews, who "have Moses and the prophets" and should thus listen to them.

[117] See, e.g., H. CONZELMANN, *The Theology*, 12–27.118; and J.A. FITZMYER, *Luke*, I, 170–171.181–185.310. Thus, C. Pellegrino (*Maria*, 309, n. 208) rightly summarizes it: "la relazione tra Legge-Profeti e Regno di Dio (Lc 16,16) è stata introdotta in Lc 1–2 dalla σύγκρισις Giovanni/Gesù, nel cui ambito si delinea la σύγκρισις Zaccaria-Elisabetta/Maria". See also *Ibid.*, 319. For the association between John the Baptist and Jesus as both contributing to the justification of wisdom, in Luke 7,35 (cf. Matt 11,19), see, e.g., D.A. CARSON, "Do the Prophets", 188–189.

[118] Cf., e.g., Matt 1,2–17 and Luke 3,23–38; Matt 1,18–25 and Luke 2,1–7; Matt 2,1–12 and Luke 2,8–20; and Matt 2,22–23 and Luke 2,39–40. See also K. ALAND, ed., *Synopsis*, 1–11. 341; and J.A. FITZMYER, *Luke*, I, 304–313 (esp. 306–308). As opposed to Mark (1,2–8) and John (1,19–28), Matthew (1,18–2,23) and Luke (1,5–2,52) do not begin their Gospel narrations with John the Baptist's preaching or ministry, but with stories about John's and Jesus' births and early years. More precisely, after a short prologue (Matt 1,1) and a preliminary genealogy (Matt 1,2–17), Matthew presents the figure of Jesus through a series of five episodes (Matt 1,18–25; 2,1–12.13–15.16–18.19–23), each of which is structured around the fulfilment of an OT prophetic quotation (see Matt 1,23; 2,6.15.18.23) occurring either at the climax or end of the story. In Luke, however, the prologue (1,1–4) is followed immediately by a series of stories about the births (1,5–2,7) and lives (2,8–52) of baby John and Jesus, which are composed of seven dramatic episodes (1,5–25.26–38.39–56.57–80; 2,1–21.22–40.41–52), closely intertwined to form three narrative cycles. Revolving around three main characters

two stages, he belongs already to the time of the Gospel preaching[119]. His greatness is due to the fact that he is chosen precisely to introduce Jesus and his own greatness[120]. Indeed, in Luke's Gospel the second stage in the economy of revelation does begin with John's appearance and ministry (see Luke 1–2; 3,1–7; and Acts 1,22). The evangelist portrays John as preaching the good news (see Luke 1,17; and 3,18), while addressing not only the people of Israel, but also the Gentiles (see Luke 3,10–14)[121]. Thus, G.W. Klingsporn rightly observes:

As a transitional figure between "the law and the prophets" and the preaching of the kingdom, John represents for Luke the continuity between Israel and Jesus[122].

Consequently, although periods and stages of God's revelation may shift from older to newer, "the law and the prophets" are neither superseded nor abolished (see Luke 16,17), since "the old", that is, the original "purpose of God" (Luke 7,30)

(Zechariah, Mary, and Simeon), each of these cycles begins with God's initiative and, moving from promise to fulfillment, ends with a praise response (1,46–55.68–79; and 2,29–32). See, esp., J.B. GREEN, *Luke*, 48.

[119] Whether the temporal expression, "until John" (μέχρι Ἰωάννου: Luke 16,16a), is to be viewed in an inclusive or exclusive sense, that is, whether in Luke's view the Baptist belongs to the period of "the law and the prophets" or to that of the proclamation of the good news of the kingdom, has been the subject of considerable debate among scholars for many years. A number of interpreters have argued in favour of an inclusive sense, placing John within the former stage. See, e.g., H. CONZELMANN, *The Theology*, 20–27; E.E. ELLIS, *Luke*, 202–203; and S. SCHULZ, *Q*, 264–265. However, we side here with those who associate the Lucan John with Jesus' proclamation of the Gospel. See, e.g., E. PERCY, *Die Botschaft*, 198–199; D. DAUBE, *The New Testament*, 285–286; E. BAMMEL, "Is Luke 16,16–18", 103; P.S. MINEAR, "Luke's Use", 111–130; W. WINK, *John*, 18–21.51–57; W.G. KÜMMEL, "'Das Gesetz'", 410–415; I.H. MARSHALL, *Luke*, 628–629; J.A. FITZMYER, *Luke*, I, 183–185; G.W. KLINGSPORN, *The Law*, 393–395; J. NOLLAND, *Luke*, II, 822; G. ROSSÉ, *Luca*, 634, n. 65; and A.A. JUST, Jr., *Luke*, II, 626.

[120] See, e.g., D.A. CARSON, "Do the Prophets", 181–183; and C.S. KEENER, *Matthew*, 337–339. Thus, the latter (*Ibid.*, 338) rightly points out: "Jewish people usually viewed the era of the prophets as ending with Malachi".

[121] As G.W. Klingsporn (*The Law*, 397) notes, "Luke's Gospel suggests that John's preaching of repentance not only helps inaugurate the kingdom of God but also reveals the universality of the kingdom, because John's message is addressed to *all* people". Although a few scholars (see, e.g., J.A. FITZMYER, *Luke*, I, 470; and J. NOLLAND, *Luke*, I, 150) identify the soldiers mentioned in Luke 3,14 as Jewish mercenaries or temple guards, A. Kyrychenko (*The Roman Army*, 144) is probably right: "There is no indication in the text that the tax collectors or the soldiers were Jewish [...] The wider context [...] seems to indicate the presence of Gentiles. Building on the prophecy of Simeon concerning a 'light of revelation for the Gentiles' (2,32), John quotes Isaiah 40, making the point that 'all flesh', Gentiles included, will see 'the salvation of God' (3,6)". See also *Ibid.*, 143–145; and J.-N. ALETTI, *Il racconto*, 150. For the Rabbinic classification of the Gentiles as "birds of the air" (see Ezek 17,23; 31,6; Dan 4,12.21; Luke 13,19; Acts 10,12; and 11,6) and "violent people" (*'annās*), see, e.g., bAZ 10b; A.M. HUNTER, "Interpreting the Parables", 168, n. 2; S.T. LACHS, *A Rabbinic Commentary*, 158; and Chap. IV, pp. 202–203 and p. 246, n. 523.

[122] G.W. KLINGSPORN, *The Law*, 395.

for the salvation of his people and all mankind, "is good" (Luke 5,39b), and every scribe who has been instructed in the kingdom of Heaven can take from his storehouse both the old and the new, as required by the circumstances (see Matt 13,52)[123]. In fact, according to an ancient Jewish tradition, when God gave the Law at Sinai, he initially offered it to all the nations (הגוים)[124]. But, after they rejected God's revelation, God turned to Israel and gave this precious gift to them, which they promptly accepted (cf. Exod 24,7)[125]. On the word of Luke 16,16a, then, this stage lasted up to John the Baptist. Starting with him, God communicated his "new" revelation to all the nations, just as at Sinai; however, consistent with the Lucan reversal theme, it was now disclosed first to Israel and, only after their partial rejection, also to the Gentiles[126]. As J. Dupont and J.-N. Aletti remark, in Luke-Acts the divine plan of salvation manifested by the Law and the prophets encompasses all humanity, both Jews and non-Jews, even when it is the rejection of one that fosters the evangelization of the other[127]. John the Baptist, thus, functions as the turning point between these two stages, just like the lens of an eye or a scope (see figure # 3).

---

[123] See, esp., R.S. GOOD, "Jesus", 19–20.32. As the author (*Ibid.*, 36) points out, "what may be regarded in it [Jesus' ministry] as new is, in Luke's understanding, the recovery of the old, its application to the present, and the promise of its total fulfilment in the future; for 'the old is good'". A propos of the Law, BemR on Num 7,19 (ed. A.K. WÜNSCHE, 326) compares the Torah to wine. Also, Cyril of Alexandria (*Hom. Pasc.*, XXVI.3 [*PG* 77, 925c]) explains the relationship between old and new through the analogy of the painter, who does not wipe out the previous strokes by which he disposed the colors, but simply spreads them, to make the images clearer. For Luke's notion of a fundamental divine purpose or will for the salvation of humankind, see, e.g., Luke 7,30; Acts 2,23; 4,28; 5,38–39; 13,36; 15,13–18; 20,24–27; and 22,14–15. See also C.H. TALBERT, *Reading Luke*, 164–169; and J.A. FITZMYER, *Luke*, I, 179–181.

[124] See, e.g., MekhY on Exod 19,2 (ed. J.Z. LAUTERBACH, I, 293–295); SifDev 343 (ed. L. FINKELSTEIN, 395–397); PesR 30.4 (ed. M. FRIEDMANN, 158a–160b); and TanB on Gen 17,2 (ed. J.T. TOWNSEND, I, 82). See also G.F. MOORE, *Judaism*, I, 277; and C.H. TALBERT, *Reading Luke*, 171.

[125] According to the rabbinic interpretation of Exod 24,7, the fact that the "doing" precedes the "listening" (see נעשה ונשמע) indicates the wisdom, zeal, faith, and devotion of the people's answer before God's gift of the Law and expresses their readiness to freely and willingly serve the Lord. See, e.g., MekhSh on Exod 24,7 (ed. W.D. NELSON, 373–374); SifDev 6,5.32 (ed. L. FINKELSTEIN, 73a); and bShab 88a. See also E. MUNK, *The Call of the Torah*, II, 351–353.

[126] See, e.g., Luke 1,68; 2,32; 3,6; 7,17; 13,29; 14,15.23; 19,44; 21,24; 24,47; Acts 1,8; 2,1–11.16–17.36.39; 4,12.27; 8,27.37; 9,15; 10,22.35.45; 11,1.15–19; 13,44–48; 14,16.27; 15,1–3.7–9.11–17; 17,17; 18,6; 26,17.20.22–23; 28,24–28; and Rom 1,16; 10,5–11,36. See also E. HAENCHEN, *The Acts*, 101; G. SCHNEIDER, *Die Apostelgeschichte*, I, 246–247; C.H. TALBERT, *Reading Luke*, 161–173 (esp. 169.172–173); C.K. BARRETT, *The Acts*, I, 49–56; J.A. FITZMYER, *The Acts*, 59–60.301–302.517–522; J.-N. ALETTI, *Il racconto*, 146–180; and D. MARGUERAT, *Les Actes*, 73–74.

[127] See J. DUPONT, *Nouvelles études*, 310; and J.-N. ALETTI, *Il racconto*, 169–170. Thus, the latter (*Ibid.*, 170) writes: "Come dice J. Dupont, il rifiuto degli ebrei e la missione ai pagani non si spiegano l'uno con l'altra, 'ma l'uno e l'altra a partire dal disegno di Dio manifestato dai profeti', anche se, concretamente, è il rifiuto degli ebrei a favorire l'evangelizzazione dei pagani".

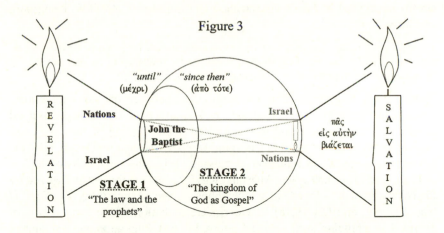

Figure 3

Therefore, as also vv. 17–18 show, the validity and authority of "the law and the prophets" is not supplanted by the Gospel, but upheld and extended[128]. The juxtaposition of the sayings in Luke 16,16–18 indicates the continuity between God's past revelation to Israel and the preaching of the good news of the kingdom to all[129]. Moreover, just as the figure of John (v. 16), so the ongoing validity of the law (v. 17) is a mark of continuation between these two stages of divine revelation[130]. The very mention of John in the dictum is thus an expression of the continuity between Israel and Jesus, but also a sign of the inclusive character of God's kingdom,

---

[128] See, e.g., G.W. KLINGSPORN, *The Law*, 392–393. For instance, the author (*Ibid.*, 393) points out: "Luke thus expresses his view that Christianity is not a new or disruptive movement but one in natural continuity with the law and the prophets and the Jewish past". Similarly, S. Sandmel (*A Jewish Understanding*, 182) had already noted: "Luke is telling us that the climax in the history of revelation has come through Christ, but that the old is by no means annulled. These passages [i.e., Luke 16,16–17], which are joined together in Luke, demonstrating the continuity of the Gospel with what has gone before, do appear in Matthew, but they are widely separated from each other [cf. Matt 5,17–18; and 11,12–13], and appear in contexts that give different meanings". See also Mark 2,22; Matt 9,17; and Luke 5,37–39 (NB: the proverb, "The old is good", in Luke 5,39b, is found in no parallel); R.S. GOOD, "Jesus", 19–36; and G.W. KLINGSPORN, *The Law*, 206–208.225–257.433. The point made by these scholars is that Christianity is not viewed as something completely new by Luke, but as the continuation of something old and, as M.J. Cook ("Anti-Judaism", 133) states, "that something old (Judaism) is something very good indeed".

[129] For instance, M. Pamment ("Singleness", 76) rightly points out that the saying in Luke 16,16a could be interpreted to mean that the law and the prophets were valid until John the Baptist's appearance, "only [...] if it is separated from Luke 16,17". See, e.g., G.W. KLINGSPORN, *The Law*, 407. For the meaning of "law" (νόμος) as equivalent of both "Torah" and "Gospel", see, e.g., HD. HUMMEL, *The Word*, 62–63; and A.A. JUST, Jr., *Luke*, II, 627. Thus, the latter (*Ibid.*, 627, n. 11) adds: "Examples where νόμος means 'Gospel' in this broad sense may include Jas 1,25; 2,8–12; and 4,11".

[130] See G.W. KLINGSPORN, *The Law*, 395–396.

already anticipated in John's proclamation and ministry[131]. As G.W. Klingsporn concludes,

The message of the kingdom does not bring an end to the law and the prophets. On the contrary, says Luke, Jesus' preaching of the kingdom completes the revelation of the past and upholds the message of the prophets and the continuing validity of the law[132].

Finally, a key to understanding the relationship between the two expressions, "the law and the prophets" (v. 16a) and "the kingdom of God is preached as good news" (v. 16b), can be found in the attested understanding of the love commandment, as both contained in and enlightened by the Satt on Deut 6,5. If "the law and the prophets" (ὁ νόμος καὶ οἱ προφῆται) signifies the totality of the law of Israel (see πάντα τὸν νόμον Μωυσῆ: 2Kgs 23,25), then this is summarized by the commandment to love God and neighbor connected with the *Šᵉmaʿ Yiśrāʾēl* (see Deut 6,5; and Lev 19,18)[133]. The sincere recitation of the latter is in turn regarded as a binding legal oath and referred to as taking upon one's shoulders the yoke of "the kingdom of God" (ἡ βασιλέια τοῦ θεου)[134].

Thus, as Table VI indicates, "the law and the prophets" point forward to the "kingdom of God" (1 → 4), just as the "violent" entrance into "it" refers back to them (4 ← 7), via the love commandment and the right use of one's strength or mammon (according to the Satt on Deut 6,5). What distinguishes them, however, is illustrated by the remaining syntagmas: from "John" onwards (2 → 3) there is an additional good news, which consists in that the kingdom of God is now being offered to "everyone" (5 → 6)[135]. In fact, while "the law and the prophets" were *de facto* revealed solely to the people of Israel, and thus only they were given the possibility to "enter" the "kingdom of God" (1 → 4 → 7), since John and the preaching of the kingdom as good news (3 → 4 → 5), the scope of that divine

---

[131] See, e.g., G.W. KLINGSPORN, *The Law*, 406–407.

[132] G.W. KLINGSPORN, *The Law*, 398. See also E. FRANKLIN, *Christ the Lord*, 85–87.128.190–191. As C.S. Keener (*Matthew*, 338) observes, also in the Jewish oral tradition, the law and the prophets pointed forward to the coming of the messianic kingdom "(bBer 34b; San 99a; Shab 63a; earlier attested in Acts 3,24)". Thus, W.D. Davies (*Paul*, 72) points out: "When the Rabbis taught, moreover, that the Messiah when he came would bring a new Law, they thought of that Law as new not in the sense that it would be contrary to the Law of Moses but that it would explain it more fully". See, e.g., BerR 98.9; QohR 11.1; BHM 3.27; and 6.47. See also R. PATAI, *The Messiah Texts*, 247–257.

[133] See, esp., Chap. IV, p. 239, n. 480.

[134] The idea implies recognizing God as king and Lord of one's life, as well as total obedience to His laws or commandments. See, e.g., Str-B, I, 173–178; and E. JÜNGEL, *Paulus und Jesus*, 177. For the yoke of the law or kingdom, see, e.g., P. DI LUCCIO, *The Quelle*, 91, n. 142; and C.S. KEENER, *Matthew*, 348, n. 36.

[135] Thus, G.W. Klingsporn (*The Law*, 402) remarks: "Luke's πᾶς ... βιάζεται is an expression of his characteristic emphasis on the universality of the Gospel". See also A. VON HARNACK, "Zwei Worte", 947–949.955; J.M. CREED, *Luke*, 207; and Chap. II, pp. 56–60.88 (esp. 56).

revelation granting access to God's kingdom has become universal (6 → 7). The commandment to love God with all one's strength or mammon has been made known to the Gentiles as well, thus leaving open the possibility of them taking upon themselves the same yoke as the people of Israel, that is, that of the "kingdom of God" (4).

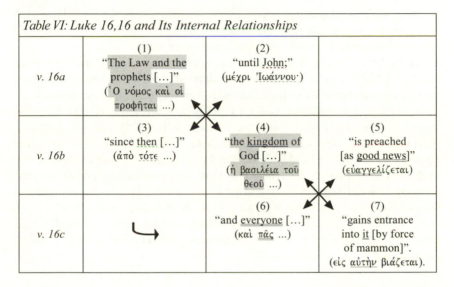

Table VI: Luke 16,16 and Its Internal Relationships

	(1) "The Law and the prophets [...]" ('Ο νόμος καὶ οἱ προφῆται ...)	(2) "until John;" (μέχρι Ἰωάννου·)	
v. 16a			
v. 16b	(3) "since then [...]" (ἀπὸ τότε ...)	(4) "the kingdom of God [...]" (ἡ βασιλέια τοῦ θεοῦ ...)	(5) "is preached [as good news]" (εὐαγγελίζεται)
v. 16c		(6) "and everyone [...]" (καὶ πᾶς ...)	(7) "gains entrance into it [by force of mammon]". (εἰς αὐτὴν βιάζεται).

Such a progressive openness of God's revelation, from Israel to Gentiles, and from both of them to everybody, is already visible in the slight change in con-vergence signified by the substantives, "Law" (Torah), "prophets", and "kingdom of God" (1 → 4). Although the former has been treasured jealously in Jewish tradition as a marriage contract (כתובה) between God and Israel, with Moses being the paranymph, since the very beginning of the revelation at Sinai, this was so that Israel might be a light to the nations and that the nations may feel attracted by such a light (see, e.g., Deut 4,1–2.6)[136]. Thus, the missionary message to the Gentiles begins already in the Law, but develops mostly in and

---

[136] See, e.g., MekhY on Exod 19,17; TgCant on Cant 1,2; ShirR 1.2; ShemR 46.1; D. DAUBE, *The New Testament*, 293–294; A. SERRA, *Miryam*, 167–181.206–209; and K. AMBROSE, *Jew Among Jews*, 172–173. As D. Daube (*Ibid.*, 293) notes, in Jewish Greek literature, "the two great qualities of the Law, permanence and attractiveness for all, are eulogized side by side", and thus Luke's emphasis on everyone's use of βία to enter the kingdom and its association with the Law may express both his own universalistic tendency and Hellenistic Jewish influence. See, e.g., G.W. KLINGSPORN, *The Law*, 406, n. 115. One way in which Israel can be a light and source of blessings to the nations is through shrewdness in matters of riches (Luke 16,1b–8a) and care for the poor (Luke 16,19–31). See, e.g., Gen 12,1–3; 27,28–29; 30,27.30.37–43; 39,4–5; 41,33–39; 1Kgs 3,12–13; 4,29–31.34; 10,4–7.23–24; Prov 14,24; Isa 58,7–8.10; and Ezek 28,4.

through the prophets[137]. John the Baptist's and Jesus' ministry, as well as the proclamation of the good news of the kingdom, are then to be read in the wake of this movement and mission[138].

b) 16c: The Meaning of the Phrase, "and everyone gains entrance into it"

As far as the second question is concerned, the meaning of the βία-related verb in v. 16c in connection with the kingdom of God, which the pronoun "it" (αὐτήν) represents, is clearly the major crux of the verse.

As we have already mentioned in the course of our study, the verb lends itself to a number of different interpretations apropos of its either middle or passive form and positive or negative understanding. Generally, upon consideration of the verb in isolation, both are equally possible. However, based on the results of our analysis of both the context (Chap. III) and the language (Chap. IV) connected with it, we side here with the opinion of the clear majority of scholars who decide on the Lucan deponent middle form of the verb[139]. Also, based on the oldest and most long-established positive understanding of the saying (Chap. II) and the aforementioned key to the comprehension of the verse (see Table VI), we choose to read βιάζεσθαι in Luke 16,16 in the sense of a specific good news relating to the kingdom of God, which entails the universality of the latter's outreach, "beginning from [...] John" (Acts 1,22)[140].

---

[137] See, e.g., Gen 12,1–3; 22,18; 26,4; 28,14; Lev 19,33–34; Deut 31,12; Isa 11,9–12; 19,19–25; 25,6–7; 42,6; 49,6.8; 51,4–6; 53,3–7; 60,1–3; 66,18–23; Jer 3,17; 33,9; Joel 2,28; Amos 9,11–12; Jonah 4,1–11; Mic 4,1–5; Zech 2,11; 8,13.20–23; and 14,16–19. See also 1Kgs 8,41–43; 10,1.6–10; 2Kgs 5,1–19; Pss 22(21),26–28(27–29); 47(46),1–2(2–3); 66(65),4; 67(66),3(4).5(6); 86(85),9; 100(99),1; 117(116),1; and W.C. KAISER, Jr., *Mission*, 7–82.

[138] For the prophetic role of Jesus and John in Luke-Acts, see, e.g., Luke 1,17.76; 3,3–6; 4,24; 7,16.26–28.39; 13,33–34; 24,19; Acts 3,22–23; and 7,37. See also P.S. MINEAR, *To Heal*, 102–147; L.T. JOHNSON, *The Literary Function*, 38–126; J.A. FITZMYER, *Luke*, I, 463–475; J. NOLLAND, *Luke*, I, 196–197; M.L. STRAUSS, *The Davidic Messiah*, 222.227–230; and J.-N. ALETTI, *Il racconto*, 106–111.169–170.

[139] Starting with the exegesis of the Church Fathers and up to now, the vast majority of interpreters understands βιάζεται, in Luke 16,16, as middle. See, e.g., J.M. CREED, *Luke*, 207; F.W. DANKER, "Luke 16,16", 233; G.B. CAIRD, *Luke*, 189; I.H. MARSHALL, *Luke*, 629–630; P.S. CAMERON, *Violence*, 21.82; J.A. FITZMYER, *Luke*, II, 1117; G.W. KLINGSPORN, *The Law*, 402; and Chap. II, p. 61, n. 316.

[140] As G.W. Klingsporn (*The Law*, 402, n. 103) notes, "The Lucan context favors construing the term βιάζεται *in bonam partem*". In fact, Luke connects the concepts of "the kingdom of God" (ἡ βασιλέια τοῦ θεου) and "violence" (εἰς αὐτὴν βιάζεται) directly with that of the "preaching of the Good News" (εὐαγγελίζεται), thus emphasizing the distinctive positive character of the stage of God's revelation "from" (ἀπό: see Luke 16,16b and Acts 1,22) John onwards.

From the Baptist onward, the commandment to love God and neighbor, on which "the law and the prophets" hang, is offered to everyone as a way to gain entrance into the kingdom of God and thus inherit eternal life[141]. The Satt connected with the *Šᵉmaʿ Yiśrāʾēl* and Deut 6,5, which up to then was handed down in the context of synagogue liturgies accessible only to Jewish faithful, is now extended to all: "everyone" (πᾶς) can enter the divine kingly space by means of a specific nuance of βία, featuring a positive kind of force related to mammon, which actualizes one's love for God with all one's strength. The 1ˢᵗ c. educated Greek ear (most likely, the primary and predominant audience addressed by Luke in his writings), would be familiar with the nuances of the βία-related lexemes associated with wealth and property. Based on the LXX and the papyrological usage of this terminology, the same thing may be assumed to be true at the level of both the religious Judeo-Christian and Gentile strata of Luke's public. The meaning of v. 16c is thus definitely positive: entering or taking possession of God's heavenly property in terms of the legal principle of *usucapio* or *ḥazaqah*, by means of some physical "βίαιος" act, such as, almsgiving, is thus possible not only for the members of the chosen people, but also for the Gentile Christian faithful to whom Luke writes[142].

As we have already noted, in Luke's community, the danger of money-mammon represents an issue which the evangelist does address, over and over again[143]. From the immediate context of Luke 16,16, it is clear that Jesus' intended primary audience of the saying is the money-loving Pharisees (see Luke 16,14–15a). However, Jesus' disciples seem to be still present (see Luke 15,1–3; 16,1a.9a; and 17,1a). The word of admonishment that is addressed directly to the former group is thus given indirectly also to the latter and, more generally, to all those who "listen" to Jesus (see "listen to him": Luke 9,35 and 15,1; see also 16,14.29.31)[144]. In fact, the whole admonishment

---

[141] See, e.g., Matt 22,36–40; Mark 12,28–34; Luke 10,25–28; 18,18.20.22; Rom 13,9; Gal 5,14; and Jas 2,8.

[142] See, e.g., Acts 10,1–4.12.22.28.31.34–37.43–45; and 11,1.15–18. See also B. COHEN, *Jewish and Roman Law*, 291; and S. LLEWELYN, "The Introduction", 161–164. In this sense, as S. Cox ("Spiritual Forces", 259) remarks, the association between John and Jesus can be made also in terms of their love of God "with all their heart and soul and strength", or mammon. For a list of authors in favor of the identification of Jesus and/or John the Baptist with the βιασταί, see Chap. II, p. 77, n. 465. For the notion of the Gentiles as "violent" (*ʾannās*), see, esp., Chap. IV, p. 246, n. 523.

[143] See Chap. V, p. 251, n. 18.

[144] Thus, G. Rossé (*Luca*, 630) is right to wonder: "se l'argomento del capitolo riguarda l'uso della ricchezza, cosa stanno a fare al centro della composizione i vv. 16–18 sulla Legge?". The answer comes when we read these verses in the context of the *Šᵉmaʿ* and its shared targumic tradition on loving God with all one's possessions. It is no coincidence that, as to v. 14, the author himself (*Ibid.*, 630) notes: "Secondo la sua abitudine, Luca stesso compone questa introduzione che serve da transizione, ispirandosi all'affermazione di Gesù

to the Pharisees (see Luke 16,15b–31) is related to Jesus' previous teaching to the disciples (see ἤκουον δὲ ταῦτα πάντα: Luke 16,14a; see also Luke 16,1–13) and serves to reinforce it.

Therefore, by warning the Pharisees of the consequences of being lovers of money and not using their material possessions for the poor, Jesus has the disciples know as well what can happen whenever anyone tries to serve the "mammon-god". Telling the Pharisees of the need to listen to "the law and the prophets" (see Luke 16,16a.29.31) or, if you like, the beginning of the $\check{S}^e$*ma' Yiśrā'ēl* and the Satt connected with it, especially as far as the concept of "strength/mammon" is concerned, Jesus sets likewise before their eyes the reality of things[145]. While these Jews (Pharisees) are showing a lack of zeal or interest in taking possession of the "immovable" property of God's kingdom through almsgiving and *ḥazaqah*, mostly because of their greed, with the coming of John the Baptist and the preaching of the Gospel the way of entering the kingdom is being revealed to all. Everyone is being given access to the first and greatest commandment and, accordingly, can now take the kingdom's yoke and enter into it through almsgiving, *usucapio* and βία, whether Jew or Gentile.

As evinced by the religious and pagan literature cited in the previous section of our study, the temporal dimension of the expressions (μέχρι, ἀπό, and τότε) used in Luke 16,16ab, the close association of the verse with other sayings on juridical matters (see "law" and "divorce": vv. 17–18), as well as the eschatological and economical perspective of the chapter as a whole, concur in underlining that the violence needed to gain entrance into the kingdom of God consists in its "acquisition by force or more particularly by *usucapio*"[146]. Hence, by uttering the saying contained in Luke 16,16, Jesus intends to encourage his mixed-audience, whether by way of admonition (*via negativa*, as to Pharisees: see vv. 14–15a) or teaching (*via positiva*, as to disciples: see v. 1a), to respond to the good news of the kingdom and live the $\check{S}^e$*ma'* (see, esp., the framing occurrences of ἀκούειν around vv. 14 and 31), by loving God

---

del v. 13: Dio e mammona sono incompatibili". Then, on the subject of the verb, ἀκούειν, he (*Ibid.*, 630, n. 43) adds: "è volentieri usato da Luca come legame (Lc 2,18 ecc.)". Our suggestion is that, the verb may function here not only as a "link", but also as an indirect allusion to the $\check{S}^e$*ma'*, which as a corner stone of the Law (see Deut 6,5 and 2Kgs 23,25) the Pharisees boasted of knowing and observing.

[145] For instance, G.W. Klingsporn (*The Law*, 376) points out: "The saying in v. 16 is a simple statement of fact. Until John the law and the prophets performed their task in expressing the will of God. Since John the kingdom of God has been preached and people have responded to it". For the Lucan view that the law remains valid in conjunction with the proclamation of the kingdom, see also J.S. JERVELL, "The Law", 28–29 (esp., ns. 31.35); ID., *Luke and the People*, 137–147; E. FRANKLIN, *Christ the Lord*, 85–87.128; *Ibid.*, 200, n. 40; H.L. EGELKRAUT, *Jesus' Mission*, 116–120; and G.W. KLINGSPORN, *The Law*, 376–378.

[146] S.R. LLEWELYN, "Forcible Acquisition", 156. See, esp., Chap. III, pp. 108–111.155–161; and Chap. IV, pp. 188–204.

with all their strength or mammon through uninterrupted acts of almsgiving –
that is to say, "with fair certainty [...] the ideal way of handling possessions"[147] –
so as to acquire the right to own a certain "parcel of land" in the kingdom of God[148].

As L.T. Johnson argues, in Luke-Acts the language of the proper use
of possessions through almsgiving expresses the way one responds to the
"good news" (εὐαγγέλιον) of the kingdom of God:

> Luke introduces the positive use of possessions as a sign of response to the gift of the
> kingdom. It has two movements: separation from possessions and the bestowal of them
> on others [...] if a man's heart is centered on his earthly possessions, he will be incapable
> of responding to God's visitation; if his heart is centered on the kingdom, he will give away
> his possessions and find his treasure with God. In both responses, the disposition of posses-
> sions is a sign of the response of the heart to God[149].

However, in view of the relationship between the "the kingdom of God" and
"the law and the prophets" analyzed above (see v. 16ab), the same thing can be
said, not only about the second stage in the revelation of God's universal plan
of salvation (i.e., that of preaching the good news of the kingdom of God), but
also about the first one (i.e., that of the law and the prophets until John): the
positive use of possessions is also a sign of faithful response to the message
of the Torah[150]. Both stages, in fact, concern the same original "purpose
of God" (Luke 7,30), that is, the salvation of all peoples, whether Jews
or Gentiles[151]. The way "everyone" (πᾶς) responds to the free and personal dis-
closure of God's love and kingdom expresses itself in one's relationship with
money or possessions and their use[152].

---

[147] L.T. JOHNSON, *The Literary Function*, 10.

[148] Thus, C. Stratton ("Pressure", 418) writes: "Jesus is obviously contrasting the dis-
interestedness of the Pharisees and the self-righteous, needing no salvation, with those who
have energetically pressed to enter the kingdom under the Baptist's influence [...] It may be
paraphrased, 'Know, you followers of the esteem of men, that the law of God does not
change [...] that law [...] of which my words are a commentary. There are some now who
are following the ways of God and are pressing into the kingdom to which the Law points.
You had better follow!'". Also, at one with J.-M. Lagrange, D.J. Ireland (*Stewardship*, 132)
suggests that "the response to the preaching of the kingdom Jesus has in mind in v. 16
includes using 'worldly wealth to gain friends for yourselves (v. 9)'". See, e.g., J.-M. LA-
GRANGE, *Luc*, 440.

[149] L.T. JOHNSON, *The Literary Function*, 155. Also M. Grilli (*Matteo*, 361) concurs with
this idea: "Il retto uso dei beni", he writes "significa accoglienza del regno (cfr. Lc 18,24–25)".

[150] Thus, M. Grilli (*Matteo*, 349) remarks: "L'uso dei beni, in effetti, è un segnale di
fedeltà o infedeltà alla *Torah* [emphasis added]". In turn, J.S. Jervell (*Luke and the People*,
150) points out: "Almsgiving is important for Luke, and only for him among the New
Testament writers, as a sign of true adherence to the *law* [emphasis added] (11,41; 12,33;
Acts 9,36; 10,2.4.31; 24,17)". See also G.W. KLINGSPORN, *The Law*, 326, n. 130.

[151] See, e.g., Chap. V, p. 277, fig. 3.

[152] For instance, L.T. Johnson (*The Literary Function*, 158) asserts: "Luke's understanding
of possessions is such that they can stand as a symbol of the state of a man's heart before God".

Specifically, by reminding both Pharisees (directly) and disciples (indirectly) of the original purpose of God's revelation to Israel and their election "as the missionary people of God"[153] (see Luke 15,1–3; and 16,1a.14–15a), Luke 16,16 may be both a pragmatic (direct) reminder to the few Lucan Judeo-Christian readers of their own mission and vocation as a light to the nations and a (indirect) call to his mainly non-Jewish audience to be grateful for the opportunity granted to them to enter the kingdom of God and so take advantage of it by their right use of mammon and βία[154]. Indeed, as M. Grilli observes, the chiastic structure of the chapter, and the presence of two opposite groups of people in its audience, do question the minds of both ethnic categories of readers as to their fidelity to the Law, especially in the matter of one's use of riches[155].

Moreover, as we have seen in the second section of our study, the saying in Luke 16,16 receives further light from that in Luke 16,9[156]. Its teaching is addressed directly to disciples (see vv. 1a.9a), with whom all followers of Jesus identify themselves, whether they belong to the Lucan community or the Church in general[157]. By drawing their attention to the authority of Christ as its speaker, the expression, "And I tell you" (Καὶ ἐγὼ ὑμῖν λέγω: v. 9a), introduces already some earnest requests and solicits an answer on their part: since mammon must be used to befriend the poor and gain possession of eternal dwellings, Christians are called to love God with all their heart, soul, mind and,

---

[153] R.S. GOOD, "Jesus", 36.

[154] The general assumption behind the "pragmatic" reading of a text is that this is intended to be effective in the mind of the reader and to bring about a certain kind of reaction. It is quite possible that Luke 16,16 may wish to elicit gratitude, which can then induce detachment from and generosity with money. As L.T. Johnson (*The Literary Function*, 155.170) has evinced, Luke tends to employ the language about the positive use of possessions as a sign of "the inner response of men to God's Visitation" and "to the gift of the kingdom". See, e.g., *Ibid.*, 144–158. Finally, as J.-N. Aletti (*Il racconto*, 149) notes, it is significant that even Simeon's declaration, that the nations will share in God's salvation, occurs "nella lode" (see Luke 3,6). See also *Ibid.*, 146–150.

[155] Thus, M. GRILLI (*Matteo*, 349) writes: "L'esame del contesto comporta già una prima annotazione di carattere comunicativo e pragmatico. L'uso del chiasmo presenta ai lettori un insegnamento replicato, ma con disposizione e interlocutori diversi. La co-presenza dei discepoli e dei farisei mette a confronto due modi di essere fedeli alla Legge (cf. 16,16–18.29–31). L'uso dei beni, in effetti, è un segnale di fedeltà o infedeltà alla Torah, a cui fa riferimento sia Israele – nelle sue diverse articolazioni – sia il seguace di Cristo. In fondo si tratta proprio di questo: ai discepoli di Gesù viene presentato un atteggiamento dei farisei che costituisce un modello negativo. Il confronto provoca una presa di distanza: la fedeltà alla Legge va compresa altrimenti, anche nel caso dell'uso dei beni".

[156] See, e.g., Chap. III, p. 157, fig. 2.

[157] See, e.g., Acts 9,1; and M. GRILLI, *Matteo*, 352.

most of all, strength or mammon, and thus use βία to gain entrance into the kingdom of God[158].

Finally, Luke's community consists of members coming from varied social strata, which differ both socially and economically[159]. The encouragement is then for them *all* not only to make sure that there are no materially poor people among them (see Deut 15,4; and Acts 4,34)[160], but also to "be of one heart and soul" (Acts 4,32), especially in relation to prayer and the use of property, just as the understanding of Deut 6,4–5 in traditional Jewish writings suggests[161]. In fact, the absence of poverty is a divine blessing that is only granted on the condition of "listening" to the law and the prophets (see רק אם־שׁמוֹא תשׁמע: Deut 15,5; and Luke 16,16a.29.31) and, therefore, the good news of the kingdom. Thus, what is asked of the Lucan community is not so much a matter of wilful, ascetic or "monastic" poverty[162], as it is rather one of freedom and shrewdness in the use of riches, in view of one's entry into the kingdom as a call to fidelity to the love commandment and a consequence of it, in both its vertical and horizontal dimensions[163]. For without the *Šᵉma' Yiśrā'ēl*, which

---

[158] See Luke 10,27–28; and Satt on Deut 6,5. See also Luke 12,33; and 16,4.9.19–31. On the conative function of this and other speech acts, see, e.g., M. YAGUELLO, *Language*, 10–12; M. GRILLI, *L'impotenza*, 16–20; and ID., *Matteo*, 355–357.

[159] See, e.g., Acts 6,1; and M. GRILLI, *Matteo*, 339.

[160] In this sense, it is worth noting how, to avoid any misunderstanding, Luke leaves out the reference to Deut 15,11 concerning the indefinite permanence of the poor among God's people. See, e.g., Matt 26,11; Mark 14,7; and John 12,8.

[161] See, esp., the answer of Jacob's sons ("all together", "as one" and "wholeheartedly"), in CN (כחדה בלבה שלמה), TJI (כחדא בליבא שלים), and TJII (כולהון כחדא) on Deut 6,4; and P. DI LUCCIO, *The Quelle*, 205.213.274–275. Such an expression stands in stark contrast to idolatry. See, e.g., TJ on 1Kgs 18,21.37; TgPs on 44,19; and F.G. VOLTAGGIO, *La oración*, 311–313. See also Luke 8,3; Acts 2,42–47; and 4,32–35. To add emphasis, the latter account is then followed immediately by the positive example of Barnabas (see Acts 4,36–37) and, as an *exemplum contrarium*, the negative one of Ananias and Sapphira (cf. Acts 5,1–11). Another hint to the *Šᵉma'* could be seen also in the Lucan remark about the women's contribution (see Luke 8,3), occurring as it does between the emphatic mention of Jesus' proclamation of the kingdom of God (see κηρύσσων καὶ εὐαγγελιζόμενος τὴν βασιλείαν τοῦ θεοῦ: Luke 8,1; and, also, v. 10) and Jesus' call "to listen" (in the parable of the Sower, in Luke 8,4–15, ἀκούειν occurs 7x: vv. 8[2x].10.12.13.14.15).

[162] As expressed in Luke 14,33 (see ἀποτάσσεται), what is required of a disciple of Christ is that he or she may be "detached from" (ἀπὸ-τάσσεται) possessions, for God will provide abundantly for those who seek his kingdom (see, e.g., Luke 10,4; 12,31–32; and 22,35–36). Thus, M. Grilli (*Matteo*, 365) is right: "Da tutti Luca esige una liberalità senza restrizioni, indice di un distacco effettivo e non solo affettivo". As J. Philippe (*Searching*, 39) points out, however, "the Lord asks [...] an attitude of detachment at the level of the heart, a disposition to give Him everything. But He doesn't necessarily 'take' everything".

[163] Only in the Lucan account are the two quotations of Deut 6,5a and Lev 19,18b joined closely together into one single act of love (see ἀγαπᾶν: 4x in Mark 12,28–33; 2x in Matt 22,36–49; 1x in Luke 10,25–28) with no distinction between first and second.

solicits faith and trust in God in the perspective of his kingdom, mammon threatens to claim the place of the only One who is worthy of them[164].

3. Verse 17:

"But it is easier for Heaven and earth to pass by than for one stroke of a letter of the Law to fall"[165].

Following immediately after the statement of fact of v. 16, this assertion of the permanence of the divine Law is at times considered by some authors as being, "at the very least, unexpected"[166]. As we have just argued, however, if "the law and the prophets" (v. 16a) are not relics of a bygone era, supplanted by the newness of the kingdom of God and its revelation, then the contiguity of the two sayings is not as stunning as it may seem. The coordinating particle δέ, used to connect this verse to the previous one, may indicate contrast, disjunction, or distinction, although it can also express simple narrative progression or continuation of a discourse[167]. Indeed, considering the point made by v. 16, its adversative function seems quite appropriate here[168]. For instance, G.W. Klingsporn paraphrases the logical contrast between the two clauses as follows:

---

[164] Thus, M. Grilli (*Matteo*, 360) comments: "La radice *'aman*, da cui *mammona*, appartiene al vocabolario della fede. Si tratta di una radice che in ebraico significa *avere fiducia, rimanere* e definisce essenzialmente Dio, perché solo Dio è *Colui che è degno di fiducia, Colui che rimane*".

[165] "εὐκοπώτερον δέ ἐστιν τὸν οὐρανὸν καὶ τὴν γῆν παρελθεῖν ἢ τοῦ νόμου μίαν κεραίαν πεσεῖν" (Luke 16,17). The only textual variant worth mentioning is that which sees a replacement of the final verb, "to fall" (πεσεῖν), with, "to pass by" (παρελθεῖν), in (W) Codex Freerianus (or Washingtonius) and (a) Codex Vercellensis. By repeating the verb of the first phrase, this reading is basically a harmonization with Matt 5,18, which serves to strengthen the expressive effect of the parallelism between the two members of the sentence.

[166] G. ROSSÉ, *Luca*, 634. For instance, F.C. Grant ("Where Form Criticism", 18) considers v. 17, to be "in striking contradiction to both [vv.] 16 and 18", and so attributes the insertion of vv. 16–18 to "the work of some early owner or copyist [...] Luke was too good a literary artist, to say the least, to leave these glaring contradictions and inconsistencies unresolved". Obviously, we cannot agree more with F.C. Grant on the importance of stressing Luke's own artistry; however, we totally disagree with the interpretation he proposes as to the incoherence of the proximate context.

[167] See, e.g., Thayer, "δέ", 125; BDAG, "δέ", 213; and Wallace, 657–658.670–674.

[168] Thus, A.A. Just, Jr. (*Luke*, II, 623) notes: "δέ [...] is adversative, showing that 16,17 stands in contrast to 16,16".

The kingdom of God is open to every kind of person and all sorts of people are entering it (v. 16); but (δέ) this does not mean that God's law is relaxed or abolished, for the law has abiding validity[169].

The comparison between "the law" (ὁ νόμος) and "Heaven and earth" (ὁ οὐρανὸς καὶ ἡ γῆ) further supports such a reading of the verse[170]. The point of the assertion, then, is that the law in its totality, up to and including its most insignificant detail, is intended to last or remain unchanged indefinitely, even more than the relative transitory nature of the created order[171].

Hence, there is no need to force the interpretation of this saying, regarding it as Jesus' ironic statement against the conservative casuistry of the scribes[172]. Jesus is simply inserting "all the things" (ταῦτα πάντα: v. 14a) which he has been teaching so far (see Luke 14,25–16,16), especially as concerns the use of possessions and the entry into the kingdom of God (see Luke 16,1b–16),

---

[169] G.W. KLINGSPORN, *The Law*, 408. As I.H. Marshall (*Luke*, 630) comments, "Luke understands the saying literally: the law has lost none of its validity despite the coming of the kingdom".

[170] Among the authors interpreting the saying as an affirmation of the enduring validity of the law, see, e.g., G.F. MOORE, *Judaism*, I, 269–270; W.G. KÜMMEL, "Jesus", 127; J.M. CREED, *Luke*, 207; R. BANKS, *Jesus*, 214; I.H. MARSHALL, *Luke*, 630; J.A. FITZMYER, *Luke*, II, 1118; G.W. KLINGSPORN, *The Law*, 407–414; and J. NOLLAND, *Luke*, II, 821. For instance, G.W. Klingsporn (*The Law*, 379) observes: "Post-exilic Jewish literature and later rabbinic literature contain frequent assertions of the perduring validity of the law [...] the most natural interpretation is to understand the saying in the plain Jewish sense of an affirmation of the enduring validity of Torah". See Bar 4,1; 2Esdr 9,37; Jub VI.14; Sir 24,9; and AgBer 75,2 (51a). See also, G.F. MOORE, *Judaism*, I, 269–270; and G.W. KLINGSPORN, *The Law*, 350–352.379–380.407.

[171] See, e.g., Deut 11,21; Job 14,12; Pss 102(101),25–27(26–28); 119(118),160; Isa 40,8; 51,6.13; 66,22; Jer 10,10–12; Bar 4,1; Luke 12,56; 21,33 (par. Matt 24,35; and Mark 13,31); Acts 14,15; 17,24; and 2Pet 3,2–13. See also I.H. MARSHALL, *Luke*, 630; S.G. WILSON, *Luke*, 44; J.A. FITZMYER, *Luke*, II, 1118; G.W. KLINGSPORN, *The Law*, 350–352.408–409; and Chap. III, p. 159, n. 408. The hyperbolic emphasis on the abiding validity of the law is expressed also in the parallel Matthean form of the saying, by the addition of, "not even an iota" (ἰῶτα ἕν: Matt 5,18). For a discussion on the meaning of the Matthean additional temporal ἕως clauses as restricting or redefining the validity of the law, see, esp., G.W. KLINGSPORN, *The Law*, 411–412. In contrast to such a possible qualification, the author (*Ibid.*, 413) notes: "it is significant that Luke's version of the saying implies no temporal limits and attaches no qualifiers to the statement about the law. Luke 16,17 simply declares the eternal validity of the law". See also J. NOLLAND, *Luke*, II, 822. Other authors, however, underline rather the Semitic character of the Matthean ἕως clauses and their value as simple comparatives. See, e.g., J. DUPONT, *Les Béatitudes*, I, 116, n. 2; and G. ROSSÉ, *Luca*, 635, n. 68.

[172] See, e.g., T.W. MANSON, "The Sayings", 427; and G.B. CAIRD, *Luke*, 190. See also G.W. KLINGSPORN, *The Law*, 409, n. 125; and G. ROSSÉ, *Luca*, 635, n. 69.

within the framework of orthodoxy and faithfulness to the law, over against the ridicule of the Pharisees[173].

Additionally, the comprehension of v. 17 is improved considerably when its saying is allowed to "dialogue", as if it were, with the corresponding one, in vv. 10–12[174]. By virtue of its main pragmatic effect, the dictum in vv. 10–12 urges the readers directly (as disciples) to make a "faith-filled" (πιστός) use of mammon, namely, the least valuable thing which God has entrusted to them, in view of "true" eternal riches (see τὸ ἀληθινόν)[175]. If that is the case, and in the light of the overall pattern matching these verses with v. 17, then the latter may rather wish to appeal to the readers' devout reasoning indirectly (as Pharisees), urging them to submit to the "law" (νόμος) concerning interest-free almsgiving and charity to the poor (see, e.g., 4Macc 2,8), so that they too may be able to master this strong passion of their heart, which is the "love of money" (φιλαργυρίας)[176].

Finally, it is worth noting that the opening expression of the verse, "it is easier" (εὐκοπώτερον), occurs elsewhere in the NT only in two passages belonging to the triple Gospel tradition, in the context of either the forgiveness of sins or the rich man's entry into the kingdom of God[177]. Recent studies suggest that, at least for the Marcan form of these passages, there may already

---

[173] Thus, J.A. Fitzmyer (*Luke*, II, 1116) remarks: "It [the saying in v. 17] is used by Luke with hyperbole to stress rhetorically the continuity of Jesus' kingdom-preaching with the manifestation of God's will in the law of old. The former is but the logical and legitimate outgrowth of the latter [...] the continuing or abiding validity of the law will be stressed in Jesus' words at the end of the coming parable, 'If they listen not to Moses and the prophets...' [Luke 16,31]".

[174] See, e.g., Chap. III, p. 157, fig. 2.

[175] Thus, J. Nolland (*Luke*, II, 807) observes: "τὸ ἀληθινόν (lit. 'the true') is best rendered 'that which is of true value' [...] Presumably the ownership of the mammon of the world is here assumed to be God's. The riches that one has in one's own name cannot be very different from the 'treasure kept in heaven' of 12,33 (cf. 'your treasure' in v. 34)". See also *Ibid.*, II, 806–808.

[176] Thus, C.H. Talbert (*Reading Luke*, 158) remarks: "Verse 17 (cf. Matt 5,18) affirms the continuing validity of the law (cf. Acts 20,27–28). In this context doubtless the evangelist is thinking of the law that teaches about the care of the poor [...] the law is still in force, in particular that law dealing with the treatment of the poor". See also J.-M. LAGRANGE, *Luc*, 440; W.F. ARNDT, *Luke*, 360–361; R. BANKS, *Jesus*, 218; J.T. MARSHALL, *Luke*, 627; C.H. TALBERT, *Reading Luke*, 156–158; L. SABOURIN, *Luke*, 298; J.A. FITZMYER, *Luke*, II, 1116; D.J. IRELAND, *Stewardship*, 132–133 (esp., ns. 82–83); A.A. JUST, Jr., *Luke*, II, 623–624; and Chap. IV, pp. 213–216.

[177] See Matt 9,5; 19,24; Mark 2,9; 10,25; Luke 5,23; and 18,25. Among the authors who draw attention to the importance and syntax of the expression in the understanding of Luke 16,16–18, see, e.g., E. HIRSCH, *Die Worlagen*, 65–68. See also P.S. CAMERON, *Violence*, 138; F. BOVON, *Luc*, III, 92; and Chap. III, p. 153, n. 386.

exist some allusion to the $\check{S}^e ma^c$[178]. Almsgiving and love of God with all one's strength or mammon grant access to God's kingdom, not only in virtue of the legal right of *usucapio*, then, but also by the removal of every sinful hindrance (see, esp., Tob 12,9; Prov 16,6; and Sir 3,30)!

4. Verse 18:

"Anyone who dismisses his wife and marries another commits adultery, and he who marries one [who has been and still is] dismissed by [her] husband commits adultery"[179].

Although a few scholars see here an illustrative example of the "law" mentioned in the preceding verse, for a number of them the saying in v. 18 merely challenges the authority of Moses and the law on divorce and thus contradicts directly the assertion just made of its continuing validity[180]. Indeed, Jewish custom and Mosaic law did allow divorce and presuppose appropriate procedures, as well as the practice of remarriage (see Deut 24,1–4). Failing to recognize any logical relationship with its proximate context, these authors interpret the saying as an overt challenge or even an abrogation of the authority of the Jewish law and practice[181]. The Lucan Jesus would be here condemning

---

[178] See, e.g., J. MARCUS, "Authority", 197–198; F. MANNS, "Le Shema Israël", 111–112; C.A. EVANS, *Mark*, 97–99; G. KEERANKERI, *The Love Commandment*, 99–101; K.H. TAN, "The Shema", 200–204; E. WAALER, *The Shema*, 227–230; D. FORTUNA, *Il Figlio dell'ascolto*, 15, n. 35; and *Ibid*, 257–259.377.

[179] "πᾶς ὁ ἀπολύων τὴν γυναῖκα αὐτοῦ καὶ γαμῶν ἑτέραν μοιχεύει, καὶ ὁ ἀπολελυμένην ἀπὸ ἀνδρὸς γαμῶν μοιχεύει" (Luke 16,18). The only textual variants worth mentioning are those (in K M Π U 565 1346) which, without affecting the meaning, replace one or both occurrences of the active form of the verb, "to commit adultery" (μοιχεύει), with its passive (μοιχᾶται), thus harmonizing with both the Marcan and Matthean versions of the saying (see Mark 10,11.12 and Matt 5,32; 19,9). Whereas the latter use primarily μοιχάω (only in Matt 5,32, μοιχεύω occurs in conjunction with μοιχάω), Luke prefers to use twice the same verb (μοιχεύω), perhaps as a more direct reference to the law of Moses (see, esp., Luke 16,16.17.29.31) and the sixth commandment in particular (see Exod 20,13; Deut 5,17; Sir 23,23; Matt 5,27–28; 19,18; Mark 10,19; Luke 18,20; Rom 13,9; and Jas 2,11). See also the addition of the pronominal adjective, "everyone" (πᾶς), in several important mss. (e.g., א A E N P W Δ Θ Λ Π Ψ Ω $f^{1.13}$ 565 1424 1582 etc.), after the second καί. Its repetition strengthens the expressive effect of the parallelism between the two members of the sentence.

[180] Thus, J.A. Fitzmyer (*Luke*, II, 1119) remarks: "It is scarcely to be understood as an example of the 'law', since it goes beyond it in imposing a prohibition not contained in it". However, in view of some Qumran documents, it is not a radical break with all contemporary Jewish traditions either. See, e.g., J.A. FITZMYER, "The Matthean Divorce Texts", 213–223. For v. 18 as an illustrative example of v. 17, see, e.g., D. KOSCH, *Die Gottesherrschaft*, 61; J. SCHRÖTER, "Erwägungen", 452; and J. VERHEYDEN, "The Violators", 409, n. 47.

[181] For instance, J.A. Fitzmyer (*Luke*, II, 1119) comments: "The third saying in this Lucan editorial unit seems to move to an entirely different topic – even less related to the general

both divorcees' remarriage and divorce as such, without even feeling the need to mention the creation account as an authoritative foundation for his assertion (see Gen 1,27; 2,24; Mark 10,2–12; and Matt 19,3–12)[182].

Most of these authors, however, treat the saying in isolation, taking no account of the logical sequence of thought linking vv. 15b–18 together or with vv. 8b–13, as well as their relation to Luke 16 as a coherent narrative and thematic whole[183]. We have already dwelt at length on the function of these verses in the concentric structure of the chapter (Chap. III), and have also mentioned several scholars who see how v. 18 fits well within the thematic thread of the chapter because of the Jewish understanding of marriage[184]. Additionally, it must be noted here that the Lucan form of this verse differs from that of Mark, in that it presents only the man's perspective[185]. In other words, the prohibition is formulated merely from the viewpoint of the man,

---

theme of chap. 16 than the sayings on the law in the two preceding verses – viz. the prohibition of divorce (16,18)".

[182] See, esp., D.R. CATCHPOLE, "The Synoptic Divorce Material", 112.121; and S.G. WILSON, *Luke*, 45. For a list of texts dealing with the source, form, and redaction critical issues of the synoptic divorce material (i.e., Matt 5,31–32; 19,3–9; Mark 10,2–12; and Luke 16,18), see, e.g., J.A. FITZMYER, "The Matthean Divorce Texts", 197–226; and G.W. KLINGSPORN, *The Law*, 416, n. 139. See also 1Cor 7,10–11.

[183] Thus, G.W. Klingsporn (*The Law*, 415–416) rightly observes: "When isolated from its difficult Lucan context and examined in conjunction with other synoptic divorce material, it is understandable that the saying in Luke 16,18 could lead to the conclusions of Catchpole and Wilson". Moreover, M.-L. Rigato ("'Mosè ed i Profeti'", 155) remarks: "Lc 16,18 [...] è invece del tutto pertinente quando lo si comprenda nell'ottica del lettore/uditore *cristiano*, sia di provenienza dai giudei che dalle genti".

[184] See, e.g., Chap. II, p. 87, ns. 531–532; and Chap. III, pp. 160–161 (esp., n. 412). For instance, G. Rossé (*Luca*, 636) points out: "Il *loghion*, di stile giuridico, è da capirsi sullo sfondo dell'usanza sanzionata dalla Legge di Mosè per la quale l'acquisto di una moglie è una questione di contratto e di proprietà (importanza dell'aspetto finanziario) a vantaggio del marito: quest'ultimo ha la Legge dalla sua parte e possiede quindi il diritto di dare il libello di ripudio (Deut 24,1); egli può frequentare altre donne (se non sono già mogli di israeliti), mentre la donna sposata viene penalizzata per ogni infedeltà".

[185] The feminine perspective, present in Mark 10,12 (cf., also, 1Cor 7,10–11), is absent in Luke 16,18, as well as in Matt 5,32 and 19,9. Compared to the Matthean texts, however, Luke may be emphasizing the masculine perspective even further. See, e.g., "man, husband" (ἀνήρ: Luke 16,18). Thus, J.A. Fitzmyer ("The Matthean Divorce Texts", 201) remarks: "In its present Lucan form the saying is not only a prohibition of divorce but a judgment about a husband's marriage after the divorce [...] The Lucan form of the saying differs from the Pauline in that the subsequent marriage mentioned is that of the man, whereas in 1Cor 7 it is the woman's subsequent marriage". In turn, G. Rossé (*Luca*, 636) observes: "Mentre in Matteo il primo marito viene colpevolizzato appena ripudia la moglie perché la mette in condizione di risposarsi e quindi di commettere adulterio, in Luca l'uomo viene direttamente accusato di adulterio".

which essentially compares a wife to merchandise[186]. Thus, if Jesus' admonition to the Pharisees is about the proper use of money and the laws attached to that, as we maintain it is, then v. 18 is connected not only with the attached sayings (vv. 15b–17) but also with the rest of the chapter (see Luke 16,1–31).

Moreover, against the opinion that the verse denies the continuous validity of the Mosaic law expressed in the immediate context, the following considerations remain valid. As a matter of fact, consistent with the masculine legal perspective, women were "essentially objects of marriage"[187]. The law allowed only the man to write a certificate of dismissal (see Deut 24,1) and divorce his wife, and any pretext could be valued good enough to dismiss her and find another (see Matt 19,3)[188]. However, Luke's omission both of any clear reference to Deut 24,1 and of the whole episode of the divorce controversy (cf. Mark 10,2–12, esp., v. 4; and Matt 19,3–12, esp., v. 7) argues against any emphasis of his on the rejection of the Mosaic law. Moreover, unlike Matt 5,32 and 19,9, Luke follows Mark 10,11–12 in admitting no exceptions: a man cannot be a husband to two wives, just as a slave cannot serve two masters (cf. Luke 16,13)[189]!

Besides, can one really say that such a "radical" hermeneutic stance is in contradiction with "the law and the prophets until John" (Luke 16,16a)? A biblical tradition considered divorce already a hateful and impious act in God's eyes, bearing a resemblance to faithlessness towards God as a consequence

---

[186] As J.A. Fitzmyer ("The Matthean Divorce Texts", 202) explains: "the prohibition is cast completely from the OT or Jewish point of view, commenting on the action of the husband who would divorce his wife and marry again (or who would marry a divorced woman). Underlying it are the notions of the wife as the chattel of the husband, implied in such passages as Jer 6,12, Gen 31,15, Num 30,10–14, and of the OT allowance of divorce to the husband (Deut 24,1–4)". See also ID., *Luke*, II, 1120.

[187] U. LUZ, *Matthew*, I, 251.

[188] As A. Serra (*Miryam*, 37) notes, in Jewish and biblical tradition, "Dare il libello di ripudio compete ordinariamente all'uomo". See, e.g., *Ibid.*, 37–41. The Mishnah (mGit 9.10) reports a rabbinic debate concerning the legal grounds for divorce. While the school of Hillel permitted divorce for almost any reason, that of Shammai was much stricter, allowing it only in the case of sexual immorality. A similar hermeneutic discussion transpires in the Matthean formulation of the divorce texts. See, e.g., the addition, "for any reason" (κατὰ πᾶσαν αἰτίαν: Matt 19,3; cf. Mark 10,2), and the mention of one exception, "sexual immorality" (πορνεία: Matt 5,32 and 19,9). See also FLAVIUS JOSEPHUS, *A.J.*, XV.259–260 (ed. H.ST.J. THACKERAY – *al.*, VIII, 122–123); and J.A. FITZMYER, "The Matthean Divorce Texts", 207.214.223.

[189] See, e.g., 1Cor 7,10–11; J.A. FITZMYER, *Luke*, II, 1120; and Chap. III, p. 157, fig. 2. If this is so, there may even be a certain irony at work here on the part of Luke. The "husband" was generally viewed as "master, lord, or owner" (בַּעַל) of his wife (N.B.: the same Heb. term can designate a deity!), and the action of "marrying" a woman, as "ruling over" (בָּעַל) her. The connection of v. 18 with v. 13 could thus suggest the view of a husband as being rather the servant of his wife! See, e.g., *HALOT*, "בעל", I, 142–144.

of idolatry (cf. Mal 2,16)[190]. The Essenes at Qumran prohibited both polygamy and divorce equally (see, e.g., 11QT 57,17–19 and CD 4,21–5,6), based on the idea that both a multitude of wives and an abundance of riches could turn the king's heart away from the fear of God and his laws (see Deut 17,17–20)[191]. The significance given by the Lucan Jesus to the danger of greed and profuse possessions, in the context of one's entry into the kingdom of God, may thus go hand in hand with marriage laws and his firm prohibition against divorce and polygamy[192].

Finally, rather than contradicting the Mosaic law (see Deut 24,1), Jesus is doing here something which goes far beyond even just affirming its continuity! The "language" the Lucan Jesus is using is perfectly consonant with that of the Pharisees, and in a certain sense he is bearding the lion in his den[193]. Consistent with the general tendency of the Pharisees themselves, he is taking the law which prohibited priests from marrying divorced women and, up until then, was applied only to such a restricted class of people (see, e.g., Lev 21,1.7.10.13–14; and Ezek 44,22), and in line with Luke 16,16 (see πᾶς), is extending it to the point of embracing everybody[194]. Indeed, Jesus seems to place himself not only in con-

---

[190] See, e.g., U. LUZ, *Matthew*, I, 252. For the hermeneutic discussion of Mal 2,16 in the context of an exhortation against faithlessness and idolatry, see, e.g., M.A. SHIELDS, "Syncretism", 68–86 (esp., 81–86).

[191] See, e.g., J.A. FITZMYER, "The Matthean Divorce Texts", 213–223; ID., *Luke*, II, 1121; and U. LUZ, *Matthew*, I, 252, n. 17. The text of Deut 17,17 associates directly the increased number of wives to the accumulation of silver and gold: both can cause the heart "to turn away" (סור). As an allusion to Deut 17,17b, some fragments of the Damascus Document (CD 4,16) mention "unchastity" (הזנות) and "wealth" (ההון) as two of the three nets Belial uses to ensnare Israel. Finally, the additional comment of the TJI on Deut 17,17, "lest his heart be lifted up greatly and he rebel against the God of Heaven" (דלא יתרורם ליביה לחדא וימרד באלקא שמיא), seems to recall Jesus' words in Luke 16,15 (see, esp., καρδίας and ὑψηλόν). For the aforementioned Aramaic texts, see, e.g., H. NÖLDEKE, *Targum Jonathan*, 331; E.G. CLARKE, ed., *Targum Pseudo-Jonathan: Deuteronomy*, 51; F. GARCÍA MARTÍNEZ – E.J.C. TIGCHELAAR, ed., *The Dead Sea Scrolls*, I, 556; and *Ibid.*, II, 1278.

[192] See, e.g., Luke 12,15.31–32; 16,8.14.16; and 20,34. Thus, C. Pellegrino (*Maria*, 301–302) remarks: "Rilevante per la nostra indagine è il caso di Lc 16,8 – senza paralleli – dove Gesù contrappone i 'figli di questo tempo' ai 'figli della luce'; qui il sintagma οἱ υἱοὶ τοῦ αἰῶνος τούτου è identico a Lc 20,34 e qualifica coloro che sono condizionati dalle dinamiche terrene di tipo economico. In altre parole, l'essere οἱ υἱοὶ τοῦ αἰῶνος τούτου è caratterizzato in Lc 16,8 con l'astuzia economica, mentre in Lc 20,34 con la prassi matrimoniale; la prospettiva di entrambe le locuzioni è escatologica". See also Luke 16,18 and the emphatic preeminent position given by Luke to the commandment, "you shall not commit adultery", in Luke 18,20a, as compared to Exod 20,13–14; Deut 5,17–18; Matt 19,18; and Mark 10,19. See, e.g., *Ibid.*, 289, n. 171.

[193] For instance, F.C. Grant ("Where Form Criticism", 17) observes: "As a matter of fact, vv. 10–13 all set forth [already] good Pharisaic doctrine! So does v. 9: 'Make for yourselves friends by means of the unrighteous mammon' (see Strack-Billerbeck)".

[194] See, e.g., A. DETTWILER, "The Source Q", 59–60. Against this interpretation, J. Nolland (*Luke*, II, 820) argues: "the Lev 21,7 restriction has no real connection with issues either of divorce

tinuity with "the law" but, by conforming to the hermeneutic attitude shown by Ezekiel, also with "the prophets" themselves (see Luke 16,16a). In fact, just as Ezekiel extended this prohibition from the high priest alone to all priests, so Jesus extends it further, from all priests to all people[195].

In other words, in line with the contextual theme of one's use of property and the conflict with the Pharisees' love for money introduced in v. 14, Luke 16,18 may well express Jesus' own critique of the Pharisaic (male and materialistically oriented) conception of marriage and their desire to possess. Far from contradicting the Mosaic law, it represents rather its universal extension to all people (see πᾶς: Luke 16,16) and is an invitation to Luke's readers to be loving faithful husbands to no "other" (see ἑτέραν: Luke 16,18) wife, just as they are to be servants of no "other" (see ἕτερον: Luke 16,13) God[196].

---

or adultery". However, see, e.g., C.F. KEIL – F. DELITZSCH, *Commentary*, IX, 315; G.A. COOKE, *Ezekiel*, 485–486; A. ISAKSSON, *Marriage*, 147; J.A. FITZMYER, *Luke*, II, 1121; M. KLINGHARDT, *Gesetz*, 28; B.A. LEVINE, *Leviticus*, 143–144; J. MILGROM, *Leviticus*, II, 1804–1821; T.M. WILLIS, *Leviticus*, 178–181; and C. PELLEGRINO, *Maria*, 139–141.199.210.289. Nor is Jesus trying here to "ritualizzare l'esistenza dei suoi seguaci", as G. Rossé (*Luca*, 637, n. 78) objects. On the contrary, as J. Nolland (*Ibid.*, II, 820) acknowledges, Jesus' words must be read within "the tendency in Judaism (especially in Pharisaism) to laicize, and therefore apply [a law] to all", whether it is a priestly or "royal" legal text. Perhaps, an analogous example of the Pharisaic propensity to "laicization" may concern the ritual practice of hand washing. See, e.g., Exod 30,17–21; 40,12.30–32; Pss 26(25),6; 73(72),13; Mark 7,1–5; and Luke 11,37–38. See also J. NEUSNER, *The Rabbinic Traditions*, III, 286–300; ID., *From Politics*, 82–90.143–154 (esp., 83); W. LANE, *Mark*, 245–247; S.G. WILSON, *Luke*, 42; and G.W. KLINGSPORN, *The Law*, 193.196–197.312–314.

[195] Could this be so because of the biblical notion of Israel being "a royal priesthood and a holy nation"? See, e.g., Exod 19,5–6; 23,22 (LXX); Deut 7,6; 14,2; Isa 61,6; 62,12; 1Pet 2,5.9; Rev 1,6; and 5,10. Already, commenting on Exod 12,6b ("all the multitude shall sacrifice"), Philo (*QE*. I.10 [ed. F.H. COLSON – *al.*, II, 18–19]) notes that on the day of the Passover festival all people act as priests, offering sacrifice, because "the Savior and Liberator [ὁ σωτὴρ καὶ ἐλευθεροποιός] deemed them (all) equally worthy of sharing in the priesthood [...] He thought it just and fitting that before choosing the particular priests [τοὺς κατὰ μέρος ἱερεῖς] He should grant [χαρίσασθαι] priesthood to the whole nation in order that [...] the nation might be an archetypal example [παράδειγμα ἀρχέτυπον] to the temple-wardens [τοῖς νεωκοροίς, i.e., the Levites] and priests and those who exercise the high-priesthood [τῇ ἀρχιερωσύνῃ] in carrying out the sacred rites". See, also, PHILO, *Spec.* II.27.145 (ed. *Ibid.*, VII, 394–395); and ID., *Mos.* II.224 (ed. *Ibid.*, VI, 560–561). However, for some the radicalization of the Torah-observance goes back to the *Q* community. See, e.g., S. SCHULZ, "Die Bedeutung", 138–139; C.M. TUCKETT, *Q*, 408; J. VERHEYDEN, "The Violators", 410; and S.J. JOSEPH, "For Heaven", 174.177–178.

[196] Thus, G.W. Klingsporn (*The Law*, 377–378) rightly concludes: "Verse 18 is therefore demonstrative of the positive extension and application of the law rather than any abrogation of the law in Jesus' teaching. This [...] approach [...] interprets vv. 16–18 [...] as an expression of the enduring validity of the law in the teaching of Jesus and therefore as an indication by Luke of the continuity between Israel, Jesus and the church". See also W. GRUNDMANN, *Lukas*, 324; F. HAUCK, *Lukas*, 206; and G. ROSSÉ, *Luca*, 637–638.

By way of summary, G.W. Klingsporn recapitulates the message of the second set of saying thus:

Verses 16–18 are Jesus' assertion, over against the hypocrisy and ridicule of the Pharisees (vv. 14–15), that in his own proclamation and opening of the kingdom (v. 16) the law remains valid (v. 17). It is the Pharisees themselves who may one day discover that they have failed to recognize and properly respond to the law and the prophets (vv. 29.31) and the proclamation of the kingdom (vv. 19–31)[197].

E. Conclusion

What strength is thus needed to enter the kingdom of God? By which kind of violence does Heaven allow itself to be overwhelmed and won? With a moving declaration and great artistic intuition, Durante di Alighiero degli Alighieri, or simply known as Dante (1245–1321), does not hesitate to offer his inspiring poetic answer: it is the strength of fervent love and living hope together which alone conquers the kingdom of Heaven[198]!

As we have shown in the course of this study, exegesis and theology go hand in hand by relying upon the foundation stone of the text at one's disposal. Based on the clues provided by our previous synchronic and diachronic analytic findings, we have good reasons to believe that the saying in Luke 16,16, as it occurs in its present canonical form, is logically associated to its contextual unit in a positive fashion, which entails primarily the subject of possessions or money and their proper use in the hope of entering the "house-kingdom" of God.

Indeed, the parabolic frame of the chapter (Luke 16,1b–8a.19–31), the resonance prompted by the two concatenated sets of sayings sandwiched within it

---

[197] G.W. KLINGSPORN, *The Law*, 385. Overall, the author (*Ibid.*, 386) views Luke 16,16–18 "as an apologia on the part of Jesus in which he asserts that in his own preaching of the kingdom the authority of the Mosaic law remains valid and unchanged. Jesus contends throughout Luke 16, however, that while the law remains unchanged, the Pharisees' understanding of and response to the divine will must change. This interpretation of 16,16–18 is reinforced by the references to 'Moses and the prophets' in 16,29.31, for these references appear also to affirm the continuing validity of the law as a means of regulating conduct and calling people to respond to God".

[198] Thus, Dante (*Paradiso* XX.94–99 [ed. R. & J. HOLLANDER, 548–549]) writes: "*Regnum celorum* vïolenza pate da caldo amore e da viva speranza, che vince la divina volontate: non a guisa che l'omo a l'om sobranza, ma vince lei perché vuole esser vinta, e, vinta, vince con sua beninanza". By locating his paraphrase of the "violent passage" in Paradise (vs. Hell or Purgatory), as a solemn explanation for the salvation of two "Gentiles" (Trajan and Ripheus) by the divine eagle, the poet underlines his positive understanding of the Matthean saying in the light of Luke's universal scope. The theological virtues of love and hope, inspiring St. Gregory the Great's prayers, shall "bend" God's will to grant these unbaptized people a place in Paradise. See, e.g., N. FOSCA, "Il canto XX", 209–266 (esp. 246–251). As the author (*Ibid.*, 261) remarks, "il Cielo è aperto a tutti coloro che hanno desiderio e forza di conquistarlo".

(Luke 16,8b–13.15b–18), and the idea of the Pharisees' love of money (φιλαργυρία) placed strategically at the midpoint of the concentric arrangement (Luke 16,14), are distinctive features of conscious artistry and narrative intentionality on the part of Luke, linking βιάζεται (Luke 16,16) and νόμος (Luke 16,17) with μαμωνᾶς (Luke 16,9.10–12) and "that which belongs to another" (τὸ ἀλλότριον: Luke 16,12). Drawing upon a property-related semantic nuance of the βία-related verb, which was likely known to his predominantly Gentile Christian readers, chances are that Luke has fittingly placed the saying into the specific context of Luke 16 to emphasize the nonhostile use of "violence" needed to gain possession of an area in that kingdom, which properly belongs to God alone. Consistent with both Judaism and Hellenism, the idea of its forcible acquisition has been merged with the legal notion of *usucapio* (חזקה), the importance of "listening" (שמע), the language of faith (see, e.g., אמן, אמונה, אמת, or ממונא), and the concepts of love (אהבה) and strength (מאד) in the Satt on Deut 6,5, to convey a universal and eternal good news.

The hope of love itself is at the centre of God's revelation. "You shall love the Lord your God with all your heart [...] soul and [...] strength" (Deut 6,5). All the law and the prophets witness to this epitome of divine gospel and purpose. It is God's gracious will that all be given a place in his kingdom (see Luke 12,32). No molten calf, abomination, or love of mammon is to hinder the right response of the heart to the news of this gift. Heaven is willingly open to all, whether Jews or Gentiles, and all can now respond to the good news of its kingdom to gain entrance into it, by force of a shrewd, lawful, trustful, abundant, and continuous act of charity or almsgiving.

Chapter 6

Conclusion

A. The Advantageous Interpretation
of an Unneeded Omission

Sometimes, one may happen to come across sentences, which have the power to astonish and nurture us, simply because of their remarkable combination of brevity, boldness, and brilliance, wherein a few seemingly conflicting terms or recondite concepts can conceal so profound and diverse meanings as to turn themselves into just as many starting points for reflection and growth. The saying in Luke 16,16 may be categorized very well as one such sentence[1].

It is thus really a pity that this interesting and important verse in Luke is omitted from the Psalter and the current lectionary cycle of the Catholic Church, both for Sunday and Weekday Eucharistic Celebrations[2]. Indeed, as the Pontifical Biblical Commission has recently pointed out, scriptural texts do at times pose major challenges to interpretation, especially when these seem to promote or justify immoral behaviors, unjust social conditions, or sentiments of hatred and violence, which "can scandalize and disorient Christians"[3]. It is then reasonable to expect that some of these passages would be prudently left out from books dedicated to public liturgy and community prayer[4].

---

[1] For instance, in the introduction to his extensive research on the subject, P.S. Cameron (*Violence*, 1) asserts: "The difficulty which the 'Stürmerspruch' presents is notorious and the questions raised are legion. The meaning of almost every word [...] is disputed".

[2] The Lectionary contains only the following related accounts: Luke 16,1–8 (1x: Friday, 31st Week in Ordinary Time, Years I–II, # 489); Luke 16,9–15 (1x: Saturday, 31st Week in Ordinary Time, Years I–II, # 490); Luke 16,1–13 or 16,10–13 (1x: 25th Sunday in Ordinary Time, Year C, # 135); Luke 16,19–31 (2x: 26th Sunday in Ordinary Time, Year C, # 138; and Thursday, 2nd Week of Lent, Years I–II, # 233); Luke 17,1–6 (1x: Monday, 32nd Week in Ordinary Time, Years I–II, # 491); Luke 17,5–10 (1x: 27th Sunday in Ordinary Time, Year C, # 141); and Matt 11,11–15 (1x: Thursday, 2nd Week of Advent, Years I–II, # 184). For the Scripture indexes of the Sunday and Weekday Lectionary readings, see, respectively, *Lect.*, I, 854–855; and *Ibid.*, II, 914.917. For the index of biblical readings of the Psalter, see, e.g., *Lit.*, I, 1702.

[3] PONTIFICAL BIBLICAL COMMISSION, *The Inspiration and Truth*, § 124.

[4] This is certainly the case for Pss 137(136),9 ("Blessed the one who seizes your children and smashes them against the rock") and 143(142),12 ("And in your steadfast love utterly destroy my enemies and exterminate all those who attack my soul, for I am your servant"),

However, the choice of expunging biblical texts from religious worship may in the end produce the unwanted effect of creating doubts concerning both their adequacy for one's growth in faith and the sacred character of their inspiration and inerrancy[5]. If nonetheless, as upheld by the Church's Magisterium, all the canonical books of Sacred Scripture and their human authors are wholly and entirely inspired by God to convey in all their parts and without error the truth necessary for our salvation, then there is no reason for shying away from the interpretative challenges presented by their literal sense[6]. Indeed, as affirmed by Pope Benedict XVI, in his post-synodal Apostolic exhortation on the Word of God:

it would be a mistake to neglect those passages of Scripture that strike us as problematic. Rather, we should be aware that the correct interpretation of these passages requires a degree of expertise, acquired through a training that interprets the texts in their historical-literary context and within the Christian perspective which has as its ultimate hermeneutical key "the Gospel and the new commandment of Jesus Christ brought about in the paschal mystery". I encourage scholars and pastors to help all the faithful to approach these passages through an interpretation which enables their meaning to emerge in the light of the mystery of Christ[7].

---

as shown by the occurrences only of Pss 137(136),1–6 and 143(142),1–11 in the Psalter (see the Evening Prayer of Tuesday, Week IV; and the Night Prayer of Tuesday or the Morning Prayer of Thursday, Week IV, respectively) as well as the Lectionary (see the Responsorial Psalm of the 4th Sunday of Lent, Year B, # 32). While respecting this decision, the Pontifical Biblical Commission (*The Inspiration and Truth*, § 128) gives some indications to "allow believers [...] to make the entire patrimony of Israel's prayer their own". See *Ibid.*, §§ 128–131. Due to the hermeneutic crux of its βία-based term, it is likely that Luke 16,16 has likewise been omitted to prevent analogous scandals or misunderstandings from coming into existence in the first place.

[5] Thus, the Pontifical Biblical Commission (*The Inspiration and Truth*, § 125) observes: "One of the major obstacles to the reception of the Bible as inspired Word is the presence, especially in the Old Testament, of repeated cases of violence and cruelty, in many cases commanded by God; in many others, the object of prayers addressed to the Lord; in others still, directly attributed to him by the sacred author. The discomfort of the contemporary reader should not be minimized. It has, in fact, led some to assume a disapproving attitude toward some Old Testament texts, considered outdated and inadequate to nurture faith. The Catholic hierarchy was aware of the pastoral implications of the problem, deciding that entire biblical passages are not read in the public liturgy while systematically omitting those verses which would be offensive to Christian sensibilities. One could improperly deduce from this that a part of Sacred Scripture does not enjoy the charism of inspiration, since it would not be 'useful for teaching, for reproof, correction, and for training in righteousness' (2Tim 3,16)".

[6] See, e.g., 2Tim 3,15–16; and 2Pet 1,20–21. See also *DV*, §§ 11–13; R.E. BROWN, "Hermeneutics", 606–619; *CCC*, §§ 105–119; and PONTIFICAL BIBLICAL COMMISSION, *The Inspiration and Truth*, §§ 5–10.50–65.137–150.

[7] J. RATZINGER, BENEDICT XVI, *Verbum Domini*, § 42. The need to confront these ostensible contradictions with serious historical-scientific investigation has been reiterated by the Pontifical Biblical Commission (*The Inspiration and Truth*, § 105): "if inspiration encompasses the Old and New Testaments in their entirety, 'with all their parts' ([*DV*,] n. 11), we cannot eliminate any passage from the narrative; the exegete must strive to find

It is precisely with reference to the paschal mystery of Christ, his Gospel, and the Love Commandment, that our interpretation can help all the faithful to approach the saying in Luke 16,16 profitably. Then, far from having undesirable pastoral effects and being offensive to, or even scandalous for Christian sensibilities, it can be a source of growth for the current articulation of the life, faith, and practice of the Church.

Specifically, the aim of this general conclusion is to display the way in which the meaning of this NT verse remains relevant today, with the prospect of supplying an adequate stimulus to its reinstatement in the Church's public worship, as well as opening up further research perspectives. For the sake of clarity and the benefit of a general overview of the twists and turns of this study, we shall conclude our hermeneutic journey by subdividing this closing chapter as follows. After a brief summary of the major negative developments in the modern exegesis of the saying, as a partial explanation for the afore-mentioned omission, and following a short presentation of the conclusions of our study of the verse, as a contribution to the impasse about its positive meaning in the selected context of Luke 16, we shall bring out the need to retrieve the patristic interpretations of this saying. Attention shall be given especially to their relevance in current theological reflection, for the purpose of understanding better the relationship between asceticism and charity, as a way of life and a source of blessings, demanding a continuous eschatological-questioning attitude based on personal real-life experiences.

B. "Violence" and "Kingdom of God": Problem or Good News?

Throughout the centuries, and especially in the past decades, this obscure and challenging saying of Jesus has increasingly gained the attention of a countless number of biblical scholars and theologians. One of the most intriguing and perplexing issues, which has progressively fueled interest in the biblical verse, and currently appears either to generate confusion or constitute a hindrance to its sound comprehension, is the peculiar correlation between "violence" and "kingdom of God": can these two biblical-theological concepts converge peace-

---

the significance of every phrase in the context of the narrative as a whole by means of the various methods listed in the Pontifical Biblical Commission's document *The Interpretation of the Bible in the Church* (cf. *EB* 1259–60). Although a diachronic study of the texts is indispensable to understand the different reinterpretations of an oracle or an original narrative, the true sense of a passage is its final form, accepted into the canon of the Church". See also *Ibid.*, §§ 135–136.145–150.

fully as universal good news, or are we stuck with a problem between "irre-concilable opposites"[8]?

In his doctoral thesis entitled *Violence and the Kingdom. The Interpretation of Matthew 11,12*, P.S. Cameron employs the latter expression in concurring with the hermeneutic position held by A. Karlstadt, a German Christian theologian (1480–1541) who, in 1521, in Wittenberg – and thus, at the very dawning of the Protestant Reformation – heralded an unfriendly reading of this NT saying quite standard in the 20th c., in contrast to what up to then had been the interpreters' rather conciliating view on the subject[9]. Indeed, as remarked by some commentators, he was the first and, for few centuries, the only person to interpret the concept of force intrinsic to the βία-lexeme, "as evil and hostile to God"[10], and thus also "the first to challenge"[11] the patristic interpretations.

Starting with the writings of the Apostolic Fathers, and all the way up to Karlstadt's tractate, in fact, these two concepts were received unanimously *in bonam partem*, in a noncontradictory peaceful fashion. Specifically, the saying was interpreted to mean that the kingdom of God can be attained by means of a commendable, thievish, and heavenly violence, directed concur-rently at God and oneself, through either fasting, prayer, or almsgiving, and often associated with the virtue of faith and the force of love[12]. Giving alms in particular, renouncing not only one's material possessions, but even one's inner desire or affection for them, was for all "violent agents" (βιασταί) the privileged way to fight against greed and idolatry, raise one's eyes in faith to Heaven, foster one's ascetic attitude of love towards God and neighbor, and acquire, so to say, one's legal right to inherit the kingdom[13].

Such a continuous positive understanding, defining the first 1500 years of the reception of the saying, was then maintained and kept uninterrupted, with the exception of a few instances, also through the Reformation, the Enlightenment, and the Romantic period. Only in the 1800s did the irrecon-cilability between "violence" and "kingdom of God" begin to be seriously felt and the *in malam partem* interpretation of the saying was increasingly proposed with reference to sociopolitical or "physical violence" (physische Gewalt)[14] suffered at the hands of some hostile historical movement (e.g., Zealots, Baptists, Qumran's *'ārîṣîm*, Jewish religious authorities, Scribes and Pharisees,

---

[8] P.S. CAMERON, *Violence*, 34. See, e.g., Cf. R. DEVILLE – P. GRELOT, "Royaume", *VTB*, cols. 1142–1150; and, esp., X. LÉON-DUFOUR, "Violence", *VTB*, cols. 1360–1366.

[9] See, e.g., Chap. II, pp. 20–62, esp. 46–48.

[10] U. LUZ, *Matthew*, II, 144.

[11] P.S. CAMERON, *Violence*, 34. See also *Ibid.*, 29–30.46.

[12] See, esp., Chap. II, pp. 20–29.33–34.

[13] See, esp., Chap. II, pp. 25–29.35–36.43–45.

[14] A. SCHWEIZER, "Ob in der Stelle", 99.

Herod Antipas, or the devil himself)[15]. In other words, being ever more identified with the early Church in a state of persecution, the kingdom of God came to be considered as paradoxically vulnerable to being breached, undermined, and eventually robbed by all kinds of evil Stormers (cf. Matt 11,12bc)[16]. In the end, the earlier universally edifying explanation of the Gospel saying by the Fathers was pushed off the exegetical stage as either obsolete or too ascetic, and its universal message of good tidings was reduced to mere human explanations entirely consistent with man's world and history, and applicable only to a few intended people.

From those years on, moreover, as the scholarly desire to break off with traditional and long-standing solutions gradually increased, new suggestive lines of inquiry developed and different understandings of the βία-lexeme proliferated. Conjectural emendations and reconstructions of the original text, as well as fresh investigations of the Semitic background, historical milieu, and narrative context, emerged. Yet, as innovative and provocative as they were, the multiplicity of these new approaches, with their numberless arguments and solutions, was ultimately unable to achieve broad consensus. Indeed, if we wished to visually condense the divergent interpretations characterizing the modern history of this verse into an intriguing vignette, we could easily compare it to a contorted speleothem or helictite, that is, a curious twisted and torn form of stalactite, growing naturally on cave walls, ceilings, or underwater, branching or spiraling in any direction, often in fishtail, antler-like, and corkscrew forms, and seemingly defying gravity[17]. Despite all the efforts and the widespread scientific interest shown in their respective research fields, neither of these very enigmatic and fascinating subjects has yet met with a "satisfactory"[18] detailed explanation, capable of fostering the scholarly consensus-building process as to their specific existence and significance[19].

---

[15] See, esp., Chap. II, pp. 47–54.73–81.

[16] Against the use of this paradoxical language, see, esp., A. VON HARNACK, "Zwei Worte", 953. See also P.S. CAMERON, *Violence*, 78.

[17] See, e.g., C. HILL – P. FORTI, *Cave Minerals*, 76–81; and J. ROWLING, "Cataloguing Helictites" [accessed on-line: 25.04.2017], http://www.speleonics.com. au/jills/pastpapers/ helicat/. For a powerful and evocative image of such an intriguing vignette, see a copy of the painting entitled, *The Enigmatic "Helixthography" of Luke 16,16's Interpretation* (available online at: https://www.mohrsiebeck.com/9783161568596), made specially for the occasion of my doctoral defense by a dear friend and colleague of mine, Fr. Jorge Aviles, to whom I am particularly grateful.

[18] M.W. BATES, "Cryptic Codes", 74.

[19] Thus, L.C. Huff ("Artificial Helictites", 641) observes: "There has been much theorizing on their [i.e., the helictites'] formation, but, as yet, little uniformity of opinion has been reached". For the early history of research on the topic, see e.g., *Ibid.*, 647–649. In turn, R.E. Janssen ("Pickle Helictites", 345) remarks: "The growth of helictites in caverns is an intriguing subject of recent investigation among geologists". Despite the progress

Accordingly, in spite of the major developments in modern exegesis, the scientific research over the interpretation of the saying contained in our verse remains deadlocked over numerous issues[20]. Indeed, the rejection of the older positive interpretations of the Fathers and the proliferation of different negative understandings of its βία-lexeme have actually spawned a wide lack of consensus among exegetes about its very meaning. It is then likely that Luke 16,16 was omitted from the Church's liturgical texts as a consequence thereof, as well as for its apparent meaning. It is our hope that the material proposed in this exegetical and theological investigation will have served one day as a catalyst for further research and so contributed to reaching the necessary degree of agreement on the meaning of what remains a wonderfully complex and at once concise dictum, a *crux interpretum* in modern scholarship, otherwise known as the "violence passage"[21].

C. A "Violence of Love" for a Treasure in Heaven vs. a "Love of Violence" for a Treasure on Earth

Unfortunately, obscure and difficult Bible passages, such as ours, do lend themselves to arbitrary hostile applications[22]. Hence, even if some well-known Popes do mention our saying in their magisterial teachings, as an *in bonam partem* reference to the salutary counterforce of prayer and penance, against the forceful enemies of the soul[23], its current omission from the lectionary cycle

---

in current scientific research, however, G.K. Smith ("Helictites", 14) notes: "the debate over the helictites will continue to be a fascinating subject for years to come". Recently, N. Tisato and other scientists ("Microbial Mediation", 1) confirm: "their genesis remains [still] equivocal".

[20] See, e.g., Chap. I, pp. 8–11; and Chap. II, pp. 46–81.

[21] W. STENGER, "βιάζομαι, βιαστής", *EDNT*, I, 216.

[22] In a recent document approved by the Congregation for the Doctrine of the Faith, the International Theological Commission (*DTU*, § 26) mentions some problematic OT accounts, which can give the impression of a God who commands or loves violence: e.g., "the flood" (see Gen 6,5–8,22, esp. 6,6–7.11–13); the destruction of "Sodom and Gomorrah" (see Gen 19,1–38, esp. 19,13.24–25); the death of the Egyptians and "their firstborns" (see, e.g., Exod 11,1–12,51; 14,1–31, esp. 12,12.29–30 and 14,27–28); and the "wipeout of armies and cities" (see, e.g., Deut 7,1–2; 20,16–18; Num 21,1–3; Josh 6,20–21; 8,18–26; Ps 136[135],10–20). See also PONTIFICAL BIBLICAL COMMISSION, *The Inspiration and Truth*, §§ 124–134.

[23] See, e.g., G.A. RONCALLI, JOHN XXIII, *Paenitentiam Agere*, § 10; and K.J. WOJTYŁA, JOHN PAUL II, *Redemptor Hominis*, § 11. Thus, in a homily addressed to the University students of Rome during a Eucharist celebrated at St. Peter's Basilica (Thursday, Dec 11, 1986, §§ 3–4), the latter mentions also the positive "violence" of the saints, calls Jesus "the most holy violent one of all times", and underscores his power to "awaken from the ashes of our conscience that 'violent' which is in us, again able to 'conquer the kingdom of Heaven'". Ten years later (Thursday, Dec 12, 1996, § 1), on a similar occasion, he speaks also of "those who

makes it apparent that, at the pastoral level, the problem of Luke 16,16 continues to be felt by the Church Hierarchy.

As we saw in the course of our review, owing to the ongoing uncertainty about its meaning, there has been no lack of interpreters suggesting that the saying was initially meant even to encourage Jesus' Zealotic followers to have recourse to destructive violence for the sake of the kingdom[24]. Indeed, history teaches us that, along with some OT passages, other Gospel accounts, such as John 2,13–25, have occasionally been used to warrant brutal violence and killing[25]. Evidently, this is no exclusive reference to Christian Crusaders, but also to people as well as emperors and dictators of different religious traditions and civilizations, today as much as yesterday. Drawing from similar allegedly inspired texts, and in the wake of the famous Zealots, too often many "pious" men conceive themselves as divine instruments chosen to bring about God's kingdom on earth, socially, politically, and economically, even at the cost of vicious acts of ferocity and massacre. To avoid the risk of instrumentalizing again these challenging religious texts for interests extraneous to their inspired truth, the International Theological Commission has thus affirmed recently:

"*The final say* on the truth of the mystery of God in man's history must be left to the *power of love*. The biblical believer knows that in summing up his faith thus, he cannot go wrong, even when he is not capable of deciphering punctually words and signs [...] The *love of power*, after all, has never been God's *first word* [...] Jesus' enigmatic saying about the kingdom [...] in which one enters through an 'act of force' (cf. Matt 11,12), warns us that love continues to be exposed to violence [...] genuine love is not to be confused with the lack of courage, nor indicated as irresponsible naïveté, totally unaware of the dialectic between Spirit and strength [...] The dialectic [...] is a serious, high-profile drama, within the logic of God's love"[26].

In line with the aforementioned statement, and consistent with P. Beauchamp's writings, our findings encourage us to see a vehement "sweetness" (*douceur*) in βία, which ultimately originates in a combination of force and love[27]. It is only through the "power" or "violence of love" (*violence de l'amour*) and "of the Spirit" (*de l'Esprit*) – as opposed to the "love of violence" or "power" – that, in the words of the International Theological Commission, this "enigmatic saying" in Luke 16,16 can be "deciphered" as endorsing an "act of force" for

---

follow Christ [...] not without 'violence' against one's own passions and forces of evil", as of "peaceful 'men of violence' who conquer the kingdom for themselves, for others, for the world". See also ID., "Discorso al clero", at Latina's Cathedral (Sunday, Sept 29, 1991), § 3.

[24] See, e.g., Chap. II, p. 53, ns. 243–244.

[25] See, e.g., Chap. II, p. 46, n. 175; and *Ibid.*, p. 82, n. 507.

[26] *DTU*, §§ 28–29.31–32.

[27] See, e.g., P. BEAUCHAMP, *Le récit*, 267; ID., *Testament biblique*, 175–176; P. BEAUCHAMP – D. VASSE, *La violence*, 48–52; and A. WÉNIN, "De la douceur", 23–40 (esp. 37–39).

the sake of the kingdom of God[28]. Taking into due account the outcome of our investigation, it is our conviction that the latter endeavour consists in nothing else than in an "act of charity".

As evidenced by our study, the saying is connected with the primary theme of the chapter, namely, the right use of riches in view of one's future entry into the house-kingdom of God, and thus needs to be interpreted accordingly. Specifically, Luke 16,1–31 follows a concentric arrangement revolving around a mid-turning point on the subject of the love of money (v. 14), and is structured in such a way as to suggest a correspondence of the verb βιάζομαι (v. 16) with the term μαμωνᾶς (v. 9)[29]. In fact, there exists an overlooked or forgotten semantic nuance of the βία-based verb which associates it directly with wealth and property. It is this specific undertone that allows us to consider the "violence" contained in Luke 16,16 primarily in terms of money, strength, and love[30].

Used in different circumstances to express the general idea of "power" (δύναμις) or "strength" (ἰσχύς), βία is often utilized, just like βίος, not only in relation to the notion of "life", but also that of "livelihood" (i.e., those means by which life itself is supported), and frequently associated with the concepts of "riches" (πλοῦτος) or "abundance" (כביר, מאד, or πλῆθος), in the context of one's lawful acquisition of someone else's property, by means of the legal principle of *usucapio*[31]. In fact, contrary to what one may expect, in the earliest Greek literary sources the verb βιάζεσθαι is originally devoid of any moral connotation and etymologically related to a natural force of life or instinct for self-preservation (cf., e.g., βία/*vis* and βίος/*vita*)[32]. As our papyrological survey indicates, the verb is later applied also to forceful entry into a house, road, city, or parcel of land, frequently without the knowledge of their lawful owners or agreement with them[33]. In spite of the too often misused combination

---

[28] As we have seen, Luke is definitely aware of a positive meaning of βία, since he applies the latter also to the Holy Spirit. Cf., e.g., Acts 2,2.4; and Chap. IV, p. 246, n. 518. In fact, apart from their ambiguous meaning in the "violence passage" itself, the βία-related terms are never patently used in the Gospels to describe the violence carried out against Jesus, John, or their disciples, nor do they possess merely negative connotations in Luke's writings. The same can be said also concerning the non-exclusively negative nuances of the verb "to seize" (ἁρπάζειν), in Matt 11,12c. For instance, P.S. Cameron (*Violence*, 130) remarks: "ἁρπάζειν is used on four separate occasions in the New Testament of being caught up by the Spirit or by God or into heaven, which can scarcely be considered *in malam partem*". See, e.g., Acts 8,39; 2Cor 12,2.4; 1Thess 4,17; and Rev 12,5. See also P.S. CAMERON, *Violence*, 130, n. 234.

[29] See, e.g., Chap. III, pp. 89–164 (esp. 90–116.155–161).

[30] See, e.g., Chap. IV, pp. 166–245.

[31] See, e.g., Chap. IV, pp. 166–239.

[32] See, esp., Chap. IV, pp. 166–171.

[33] See, e.g., *Pap. Magd.* 1.17–18 (ed. P. JOUGUET – *al.*, II, 58); *Ibid.*, 27.2–4 (ed. O. GUÉRAUD, II, 171); *Pap. Tebt.* 779.4–7 (ed. B.P. GRENFELL – *al.*, III, 212–213); *Ibid.*, 804.9 (ed. *Ibid.*, III, 258); *Pap. Lond.* 45.29–32 (ed. F.G. KENYON – H.I. BELL, I, 36); *Pap. Taur.* 2.26–28 (ed. U. WILCKEN, II, 48); *Ibid.* 1.1.29–1.2.31 (ed. *Ibid.*, II, 62);

of these terms, it is likewise apparent that the LXX never uses βία to translate the Hebrew term for sinful violence (חמס)[34]. Quite the reverse, despite the intrinsic ambivalence of the term, the Greco-Jewish writings produced at the turn of the Common Era present the latter as a valuable force, suitable for choosing justice over greed, and comparable to the use of all of one's strength or all of the means at one's disposal (see, e.g., 4Macc 2,8; and PHILO, *Spec.* II.3.9)[35].

Lastly, a peculiar and rather significant connection between the notions of "kingdom" (מלכות), "strength" (ἰσχύς), "life" (נפש), "love" (אהבה), and "mammon" (ממון), emerges as soon as we take into account the Satt on Deut 6,5 and their related rabbinical writings[36]. Accordingly, many of the strategic "signals for comprehension"[37] scattered in the narrative context of Luke 16,16 (see, e.g., the recurrent notions of listening, loving, and trusting) receive a remarkable amount of light[38]. Being the only NT author that actually makes use of the βία-based terms, above and beyond the occurrences of βιάζεται in Matt 11,12 and Luke 16,16, it is very likely that Luke has drawn on his knowledge of the Greek verb's economic "shades of meaning"[39], and placed the saying in such a context, in order to refer to a non-hostile use of force, consistent with the legal notion of acquisition by *usucapio*, or ḥazaqah (חזקה), and the more religious one of the love of God with all one's "muchness" (מאד), can be used to take possession of the immovable property of God's kingdom[40].

In this sense, the occurrence of the verb βιάζεσθαι in Luke 16,16 implies in all probability the lawful "seizing" (see ἁρπάζειν: Matt 11,12c) of such a divine space, without asking for "the consent of God"[41] (i.e., its lawful owner), as well as the uninterrupted "use" of this space (see *usus-capere*) through constant acts of charity or almsgiving (i.e., the best means of transferring funds from earth to Heaven)[42]. In turn, the βιασταί represent likely "all" (πᾶς) those who,

---

Pap. Par. 15.1.18 (ed. *Ibid.*, II, 52); etc. See also R. TAUBENSCHLAG, *The Law*, 443–444; C. SPICQ, "βιάζομαι", *TLNT*, I, 288; S.R. LLEWELYN, "Forcible Acquisition", 130–147; and Chap. IV, pp. 188–204 (esp. 189–196).

[34] See, e.g., Chap. IV, pp. 205–220 (esp. 218).

[35] See, e.g., C.L. BRENTON, *The Septuagint*, 229; H. ANDERSON, "4 Maccabees", 531–543.546; and G. GIURISATO, "Come Luca", 462. See also Gen 33,11.21; Judg 14,15; 2Kgs 5,16.23; Prov 22,22; and Chap. IV, pp. 213–216.226.

[36] See, e.g., Chap. IV, pp. 205–239 (esp. 233–239).

[37] D. MARGUERAT – Y. BOURQUIN, *How to Read*, 145.

[38] See, esp., Chap. IV, p. 239.

[39] P.S. CAMERON, *Violence*, 142.

[40] See, e.g., S.R. LLEWELYN, "The Introduction", 152.156; D.C. ALLISON, Jr., *Constructing Jesus*, 171–179; D. FORTUNA, *Il Figlio dell'ascolto*, 102, n. 13; and Chap. IV, pp. 188–189.199–204.241–246.

[41] S.R. LLEWELYN, "The Traditionsgeschichte", 348.

[42] See, esp., F. D'AGOSTINO, *BIA*, 1–126; C. SPICQ, "βιάζομαι", *TLNT*, I, 288; S.R. LLEWELYN, "Forcible Acquisition", 130–162; ID., "The Introduction", 154–167; A. TOSATO, *Vangelo*, 307–457; G.A. ANDERSON, "Faith", 29–34; and N. EUBANK, "Storing up Treasure", 77–92.

investing, so to say, into Heaven, as a result of their eschatological outlook of faith, turn out "to stand" or "come up" in God's kingdom by loving him to the extreme (see βία-στῆναι), namely, with all their abundance or strength (see the Satt on Deut 6,5). By means of a specific nuance of βία, their love is therefore actualized into a positive violence, which is related not only to mammon, but also to the legal notion of *usucapio* (see, e.g., the comparable use of the temporal expressions in Luke 16,16 and the legal proceedings of Hermias)[43].

All in all, the solution proposed in our study warrants a new look at the teachings on violence, kingdom, and riches, surrounding Luke 16,16. Far from encouraging undesirable pastoral implications, it rather substantiates the validity of the traditional and long-running positive interpretation of the Fathers, particularly with regard to the "violent" power of almsgiving. Indeed, Luke has probably wished to underscore through this saying the universal and positive aspect of entry into the kingdom of God as a perpetual good news for all peoples, Jews and Gentiles alike. By engaging his intended readers in generous acts of charity or almsgiving in view of their eternal destiny, he has likewise addressed the specific issue of the danger that an improper use of riches constitutes for all, inasmuch as it can be a hindrance to the right response of the heart before the gift of the kingdom of God. The invitation for the Lucan readers, but then, by extension, also for all subsequent Christian believers, is therefore to respond to the good news of the kingdom and live the Š^ema' (see, esp., the framing occurrences of ἀκούειν around vv. 14 and 31), by placing their "faith" (אמונה) or "trust" (אמת) in the *one* God (see Deut 6,4; and Luke 16,13), to the exclusion of all idols, worldly wealth (ממון) included, and by loving God with all their hearts (see Luke 16,15b), life (see βίος), and, most of all, their strength (see βία)[44].

---

[43] See, esp., Chap. IV, pp. 192–193.199–204.245–246; and Chap. V, pp. 280–286.

[44] See, esp., Chap. V, pp. 281–286. Already several studies have suggested the possibility of an enlightening relationship between the Jewish prayer of the Š^ema' and some NT passages, by drawing attention to the specific historical-exegetical Jewish understanding of that prayer, just as we have explored it in the linguistic and semantic section of our study. See, e.g., C.F. EVANS, "Central Section", 37–53; B. GERHARDSSON, *The Good Samaritan*; ID., "The Parable of the Sower", 165–193; ID., "Du judéochristianisme", 23–36; ID., "The Shema in Early Christianity", 275–293; ID., *The Shema in the New Testament*, 31–38; ID., *The Testing*; M. MCNAMARA, *Targum*, 65–68.189–194; J.T. FORESTELL, *Targumic Traditions*, 87.88.91; F. MANNS, *La Preghiera*, 140–149; ID., "Le Shema Israël", 107–117; J. MARCUS, "Authority", 196–211; K.H. TAN, "The Shema", 181–206; E. WAALER, *The Shema*, 49–122.206–446; P. DI LUCCIO, *The Quelle*, 191–217.206; and D. FORTUNA, *Il Figlio dell'ascolto*, 232–429. Thus, far from being the relic of a bygone era (as J. Jeremias implies), there exists a cluster of significant Gospel traditions that refer implicitly to the Š^ema' as a template for Christological reflection. Cf. J. JEREMIAS, *The Prayers of Jesus*, 66–81; and K.H. TAN, "The Shema", 181–206. As far as Lucan studies go, in particular, M. Miyoshi has already seen possible allusions to it, both in the structure of Luke 10–13 and the parable of the Good Samaritan (Luke 10,25–37), which seems to work as a commentary (*māšāl*) to both Deut 6,5 and Lev 19,18. See M. MIYOSHI, "Das jüdische Gebet Š^ema'", 70–

Thus, against A. Karlstadt's or P.S. Cameron's stance, it is apparent that "violence" and "kingdom of God" can and, indeed, do meet as universal good news. Contrary to a Zealotic and destructive "love of violence" for the sake of a treasure on this earth, "force" and "love" converge sweetly and peacefully into what can be called "the violence of love" for the benefit of a heavenly treasure. Paraphrasing the words of the International Theological Commission cited above, such an "exposure" of love to the βία-related language may be said to unfold in human history, inasmuch as the God of love is "forced", so to say, to grant the right of a heavenly abode in his kingly property lawfully, to all those who perform deeds of charity.

That is also why the initial basic intuition of the Fathers ought not to be easily passed over. In fact, owing most probably to their knowledge of Greek and their sensibility to the jurisprudential language, their interpretation of the saying took for granted a couple of significant nuances of this verb, which over time became increasingly vague and then, eventually, got lost somewhere along the road. Because of wrong turns in the modern study of this verse, nearly all of the patristic reflections on it were thus neglected. For this reason and on account of their relevance today, it is important that we recover those perceptions by devoting our attention to what this saying really reveals about the ascetical life of every Christian, and see likewise how the Church can benefit from an interior liberation from excessive attachment to material wealth and possessions.

D. The "Strong Tones" of Asceticism and Charity: Their Theological Relevance Today

Based on the traditions of earlier writers and written for Christians aspiring to live the Gospel to the full after the pattern of Christ himself, the monastic rule of one of the patron saints of Europe reads thus:

And if we wish to dwell in the tabernacle of His kingdom, we shall by no means reach it unless we run thither by our good deeds [...] if we fulfil those duties, we shall be heirs of

---

123 (esp. 87.115). See also C.A. KIMBALL, *Jesus' Exposition*, 133–135; F. MANNS, "Le Shema Israël", 112–113; M. LÓPEZ BARRIO, *El tema del "Agape"*, 119; E. WAALER, *The Shema*, 222, n. 72; and M. CRIMELLA, *Marta*, 59–133. This study of ours would then be a further example in the same direction. As such, it may also constitute a matter of interest for the Jewish-Christian dialogue. A further line of research could be perhaps to investigate the possibility of a relationship between the two stages of God's revelation within the original plan of the universal salvation of mankind and the Jewish eschatological tradition of the two Messiahs, i.e., the Son of Joseph (or Ephraim) and the Son of David. See, e.g., bSan 94a; *Ibid.*, 98ab; *Ibid.*, 99a; bSuk 52a; G. SMITH, "The Returning King", 1–7; and R.L. EISEN-BERG, *What the Rabbis Said*, 189–196.

the kingdom of Heaven. Our hearts, therefore, and our bodies must be made ready to fight under the holy obedience of His commands[45].

Fighting under Pharisaic obedience to the Mosaic law and filled with ardent zeal for the coming of God's kingdom, members of the 1st century Jewish movement known as "Zealots" (ζηλωταί) strove likewise after similar objectives, and were ready even to suffer to such ends[46]. Today, like yesterday, religious fundamentalists make identical or analogous claims. However, the wars these men fight, and the violence they advocate, are a different thing altogether. In fact, in reference to the excerpt above, everything always and solely depends on what one intends, for God's "commands", and what measures are taken to accomplish them. Thus, if Zealots and fundamentalists endorse violence for the sake of a socio-political economic freedom, by force of arms and with a sanctimonious fervor, saints fight violently for an ascetic liberty, by having recourse to spiritual weapons under the emblem of love. The question which violent followers and faithful fighters of every age should then answer is the same as that which Pilate once asked the crowd: "Whom do you want me to release for you, (Jesus) Barabbas or Jesus who is called Christ?" (Matt 27,17)[47].

---

[45] "*In cujus regni tabernaculo si volumus habitare, nisi illuc bonis actibus currendo, minime pervenitur* [...] *si compleamus habitatoris officium, erimus hæredes regni cælorum. Ergo preparanda sunt corda et corpora nostra sanctæ præceptorum obedientiæ militanda*" (BENEDICT OF NURSIA, *Reg. mon.* [ed. D.O. HUNTER BLAIR, 6–11]).

[46] As Thayer ("ζηλωτής", 271) observes, the term ζηλωτής indicates, "*one burning with zeal*; *a zealot* [...] From the time of the Maccabees there existed among the Jews a class of men, called *Zealots*, who rigorously adhered to the Mosaic law and endeavored even by resorting to violence, after the example of Phinehas (Num 25,11; ζηλωτὴς Φινεές 4Macc 18,12), to prevent religion from being violated by others; but in the latter days of the Jewish commonwealth, they used their holy zeal as a pretext for the basest crimes, FLAVIUS JOSEPHUS, *B.J.*, IV.3.9; IV.5.1; IV.6.3; VII.8.1. To this class perhaps Simon the apostle had belonged, and hence got the surname ὁ ζηλωτής: Luke 6,15; Acts 1,13". See also 2Macc 4,2; Acts 21,20; 22,3; 1Cor 14,12; Gal 1,14; Tit 2,14; and 1Pet 3,13.

[47] Over and above the Aramaic meaning of the name, "Barabbas" (Βαραββᾶς, lit., "son of a father/teacher"), the inclusion of, "Jesus" ('Ιησοῦν), immediately before that, in a number of textual witnesses (e.g., Θ *f*¹ 700 *pc* sy^s), highlights further the irony of the choice offered between the two characters and that of the ideal of violence which they symbolically stand for. See, e.g., Matt 7,14.21; 26,52.55; 27,16.38; Mark 14,48; 15,7.27; Luke 13,24.28; 22,52; 23,19.25; and John 18,11.40. See also H.H. HIRSCHBERG, "Simon Bariona", 171–191; R. MARCUS, "A Note", 281; K.H. RENGSTORF, "λῃστής", *TDNT*, IV, 257–262 (esp. 257–259); and *CCC*, §§ 596–598. Thus, the Holy Father, Pope Benedict XVI (*Spe Salvi*, § 4) states: "Christianity did not bring a message of social revolution like that of the ill-fated Spartacus, whose struggle led to so much bloodshed. Jesus was not Spartacus, he was not engaged in a fight for political liberation like Barabbas or Bar-Kochba. Jesus, who himself died on the Cross, brought something totally different". Consistent with the meaning of his name (ישׁוע, "Yahweh's salvation") Jesus Christ did bring us salvation, but through the cross, rather than through the sword (see, e.g., Matt 26,52; and John 18,11).

In other words, as the International Theological Commission points out, it is true that the stories of love between the believer and God are generally marked by "strong tones" or a spirited "profile"[48]; nevertheless, at the core of our faith and at the heart of our personal stories with God is the obedience to no commandment other than that of life and love: "Hear, O Israel: the Lord our God is one Lord, and you shall love the Lord your God with all your heart, and with all your soul, and with all your might" (Deut 6,4–5). Thus, Pope Benedict XVI writes:

In acknowledging the centrality of love, Christian faith has retained the core of Israel's faith, while at the same time giving it new depth and breadth. The pious Jew prayed daily the words of the *Book of Deuteronomy* which expressed the heart of his existence [...] Jesus united into a single precept this commandment of love for God and the commandment of love for neighbour found in the *Book of Leviticus*: "You shall love your neighbour as yourself" (19,18; cf. Mark 12,29–31). Since God has first loved us (cf. 1John 4,10), love is now no longer a mere "command"; it is the response to the gift of love with which God draws near to us. In a world where the name of God is sometimes associated with vengeance or even a duty of hatred and violence, this message is both timely and significant[49].

This is why we must retrieve the patristic interpretations of our saying and acknowledge, in the words of C.A. Hall, how "Christian living in later ages can still drink profitably from the well of patristic exegesis"[50]. Indeed, as the author continues,

reading the Fathers can be surprisingly relevant for the contemporary Christian because the Fathers tend to grasp facets of the gospel that modern sensibilities too often overlook. They hear music in Scripture to which we remain tone-deaf. They frequently emphasize truths that contemporary Christians dearly need to remember [...] The Fathers hear and see where we tend to be deaf and blind[51].

As we have observed in the course of our study, drawing inspiration from Biblical and Jewish traditions, the Church Fathers did see the whole of human life here on earth as violent warfare, but only against enemies, such as the flesh, the world, and the devil, and by means of mere ascetic spiritual weapons, such as prayer, fasting, and almsgiving[52]. Indeed, the context of Luke 16 does make clear that we should live our lives "violently", but then again only as a mindful preparation for death and the afterlife (see, esp., Luke 16,2–3.9.16.22–31). It is true: one may object that Sacred Scripture attests how God's very "soul hates

---

[48] See, e.g., *DTU*, § 32.

[49] J. RATZINGER, BENEDICT XVI, *Deus Caritas Est*, § 1.

[50] C.A. HALL, *Reading Scripture*, 35.

[51] C.A. HALL, *Reading Scripture*, 38.41.

[52] See, e.g., Exod 34,28; 1Kgs 19,8; Matt 3,4; 4,2; 5,28; 8,20; 19,11–12.21.23–30; Mark 1,13; Luke 8,3; 9,58–62; 14,33; 16,13; Acts 3,6; 4,32; 1Cor 9,24–27; 2Cor 10,3–6; Eph 6,10–20; and Jas 4,4. See also Chap. II, pp. 20–36.

the lover of violence" (Ps 10[11],5b)[53], and accordingly, "the violent ones shall not inherit the kingdom of God" (1Cor 6,9)[54]. However, as the Fathers did emphasize in their interpretations of the saying, not all βιασταί are necessarily iniquitous (ἄδικοι), just as not all βία is essentially immoral (ἀδικία). Indeed, if the exertion of "force" (vim)[55], which the verb βιάζομαι basically implies, is not contrary to human dignity and freedom, but contributes to make a person all the more human and free, then, this "violence of love" can be thought of as a just force of freedom and life: freedom from the enslaving "abomination" (βδέλυγμα: Luke 16,15) of the idolatry of money, and life arising as a result of "justice" (δικαιοσύνη), in the Jewish sense of ṣᵉdāqāh (צדקה)[56]. In fact, just as a new human "life" (βίος) is the fruit of two people's "love" (ἀγάπη), so those "means of subsistence" (βίοι) that the poor receive in the form of "alms" are the fruit of someone else's "charity" (caritas)!

Moreover, in the NT, the kingdom of God is also promised to "those who love" (ἀγαπῶσιν) God and neighbor (see Jas 2,5.8), and related to the concept of ḥayil (see Mark 9,1; and 1Cor 4,20), which, in a way akin to βία/βίος, can mean not only "power", "force", "strength", but also "abundance", "resources", "possessions" and "wealth"[57]. In other words, it is very likely that the violence

---

[53] In both MT (ואהב חמס שנאה נפשו) and TgPs (ורחמי חטופין סנאת נפשיה) on Ps 11,5b, the suffixed form, "his very soul/being/self" (נפשו), is attributed to God as the seat of his feelings and passions. The LXX (ὁ δὲ ἀγαπῶν ἀδικίαν μισεῖ τὴν ἑαυτοῦ ψυχήν) and Vg. (qui autem diligit iniquitatem odit animam suam), instead, take the term נפש as the object (vs. subject) of the verb "to hate" (שׂנא), translating the Semitic word for "violence" (חמס and חטוף) with "iniquity" (ἀδικία and iniquitas). See also Gen 6,13; and Isa 1,14.

[54] "ἄδικοι θεοῦ βασιλείαν οὐ κληρονομήσουσιν" (1Cor 6,9). By "violent ones", we are here purposefully alluding to the aforementioned association between "violence" (חמס or חטוף) and "iniquity" (ἀδικία or iniquitas), which clearly differs from βία (vis).

[55] See, e.g., the Vg. on Matt 11,12b and Luke 16,16c. See also CCLEE, "vis", 1638.

[56] Thus, R.L. Eisenberg (What the Rabbis Said, 68–69) remarks: "The Rabbis continually stressed the importance of tzedakah (charity). Literally meaning 'righteousness', tzedakah is a duty rather than merely a generous act toward the poor [...] The Rabbis believed that tzedakah promotes 'peace and good understanding between Israel and their Father in Heaven' and thus 'brings the redemption nearer' (bBB 10a), atones for sins (bBB 9a), delivers from death (bBB 10a) [...] can lengthen one's life (bRHSh 18a) and be rewarded in the world to come (bBB 11a). Conversely, 'Anyone who shuts his eyes to [a request for] charity is like one who worships idols [i.e., because he worships money]' (bKet 68a; bBB 10a)". See, e.g., Tob 12,9; 14,11; Prov 16,6; Sir 3,30; Ezek 33,13–15; Matt 5,20; 6,33; 13,44–46; 19,23–24; Mark 10,23–25; Luke 12,31; 18,11.22.24–25; and Acts 10,2.22.31.35; 11,18. See also Jastrow, "צְדָקָה", II, 1263–1264; and HALOT, "צְדָקָה", II, 1006.

[57] See, e.g., BDB, "חַיִל", 298–299; C.P. WEBER, "חַיִל", TWOT, I, 271–272; and Sokoloff, "ܚܝܠܐ", 447–448. The Syriac translation of Mark 9,1 and 1Cor 4,20 renders the Greek expression, "with power" (ἐν δυνάμει), with bᵉḥayilā (ܒܚܝܠܐ). The same Syriac term, ḥayil (ܚܝܠܐ), is also used to translate the Greek word, "strength" (ἰσχύς), both in Mark 12,30.33 and Luke 10,27a, namely, the only two Synoptic texts that refer directly to the mᵉ'ōd (מאד) of Deut 6,5 (vs. Matt 22,37). See, also, OSG, II, 489; and the marginal

required to enter the kingdom of God and strongly recommended by the saying contained in Luke 16,16 involves a force directed towards one's "pouch" or "pocket", so to say, which, as Pope Francis loves to repeat, is also the favourite door used by the devil to enter our lives[58]! Insofar as that makes the person who exerts it ultimately freer, more contented, and loving, "the violence of love" may also be thought of, as stated by the Church Fathers, as a "happy" (*beata*)[59] and "beautiful violence" (βία καλή)[60] performed through almsgiving, for the purpose of a "beautiful robbery: that of Heaven" (ἁρπαγή καλή· ἡ τῶν οὐρανῶν)[61]! Finally, to avoid any Pelagian tone and reliance on human efforts alone, the conquest of the kingdom of God may very well be attributed to the work of the Holy Spirit within us (see Acts 2,2.4), a Spirit of "life" (βίος) and "strength" (βία)[62].

By way of summary and for the sake of clarity, the Greek text of Luke 16,16 can therefore be translated and explained as follows:

"The Law and the prophets until John; since then the kingdom of God is preached [as good news], and everyone gains entrance into it [by force of mammon]"[63].

In other words, "the Law and the prophets" – summed up in the commandment to love God and neighbor, and intended to provide for humanity the right direction towards the fullness of life in God[64] – until John were only

---

gloss, חיליכון ("with [all] your *ḥayil*"), in CNI on Deut 6,5. Finally, with regard to the love commandment, W.C. Kaiser ("מְאֹד", *TWOT*, I, 487) notes: "the NT struggles to express the depth of the word *mᵉ'ōd*".

[58] See, e.g., J.M. BERGOGLIO, FRANCIS, "In Heaven's Stock Exchange", 2; ID., "Who Are We to Cause Division?", 10; ID., "A Life of Testimony", 7; and ID., "An Economy of Communion", 4. Analogous considerations apply also to the public context. Thus, V. Gaetan ("'Industry of Death'", [accessed on-line: 06.05.2017], http://www.ncregister.com/daily-news/industry-of-death-pope-francis-on-arms-dealers-and-causes-of-world-war-iii) reports: "Faced with cataclysmic violence in the Middle East, which he terms a 'piecemeal' World War III, Pope Francis has not shied away from suggesting a major cause of deadly international conflict: financial interest. To audiences ranging from Italian schoolchildren to the U.S. Congress, the Holy Father says arms merchants are the profiteers fueling war".

[59] AMBROSE OF MILAN, *Serm.* II.3 (*PL* 17, 627c). See also MAXIMUS OF TURIN, *Serm. temp.* LXI.4 (ed. A. MUTZENBECHER, 247; and *PL* 57, 534c); and Chap. II, p. 32.

[60] CLEMENT OF ALEXANDRIA, *Quis div.* XXI (ed. G.W. BUTTERWORTH, 314). See, e.g., JOHN DAMASCENE, *Parall.* (*PG* 95, 1264b; *PG* 96, 181a.401d); and Chap. II, pp. 21.28–29. See also Luke 18,23; 19,6.8; and 2Cor 9,7.

[61] JOHN CHRYSOSTOM, *Hom. 1 Cor* XL.4 (*PG* 61, 352δ).

[62] See, e.g., Isa 11,2; Mic 3,8; Luke 1,17; 4,14; John 6,63; Acts 1,8; 10,38; Rom 1,4; 8,2.6; 15,13.19; 1Cor 2,4; 5,4; 2Cor 3,6; Gal 6,8; Eph 3,16; 1Thess 1,5; and 2Tim 1,7.

[63] "Ὁ νόμος καὶ οἱ προφῆται μέχρι Ἰωάννου· ἀπὸ τότε ἡ βασιλέια τοῦ θεοῦ εὐαγγελίζεται καὶ πᾶς εἰς αὐτὴν βιάζεται" (Luke 16,16).

[64] See, esp., 2Kgs 23,25. The Hebrew term for "Law" (תורה, i.e., Torah) derives from the Hiphil of the verbal root ירה, meaning "to point out, direct". Thus, the Law implies primarily a direction and was originally meant by God as a guidance, to restore his people's

within the reach of the people of Israel; from John onward (see Acts 1,22), however, their core message and interpretation was made known in clear and understandable terms for everyone. Through the proclamation of the kingdom of God, all peoples, whether Jews or Gentiles, can now respond to the good news of this revelation by their positive use of mammon and so inherit eternal life (see Luke 10,25–28). The divine kingly space is thus made accessible not only to the members of the chosen people, but also to the Gentile Christian faithful to whom Luke predominantly writes. "Everyone" (πᾶς) can gain entrance to the kingdom of God by means of a specific nuance of βία, which featuring a shrewd kind of force related to money and pointing to the "βίαιος" act of alms-giving, actualizes one's love for God with all one's "strength" (ἰσχύς) in terms of the legal principle of *usucapio* or *ḥazaqah*[65].

These conclusions can hopefully open up further research perspectives and offer a precious contribution to the impasse about the positive meaning of the saying, not only in the selected context of Luke 16, but also within "the Gospel and the new commandment of Jesus Christ brought about in the paschal mystery"[66]. Indeed, as Pope Francis has stated during his recent pastoral visit to Egypt, "the only fanaticism [estremismo] believers can have is that of charity!"[67]. For as Peter Chrysologus writes,

Love does not reflect; it is unreasonable and knows no moderation. Love refuses to be consoled when its goal proves impossible, despises all hindrances to the attainment of its object. Love [...] thus follows its own promptings[68].

It is in Jesus Christ that God himself has in fact "shown love in the extreme"[69], overturning the criteria of power and riches, which too often rule our human relations, and showing us a better way to the kingdom of God: that of charity. As a result, the message of Luke 16,16 is very relevant, also because it challenges the life, faith, and practice of all Christian faithful indiscriminately, urging them to use their wealth and possessions shrewdly and teleologically, as a response to the good

---

lives and revive their strength. See, e.g., Lev 18,5; 26,1–46; Deut 30,15–20; Neh 9,29; Pss 16(15),10(11); 19(18),7(8); 119(118),25.28.37.77.93.105; and Ezek 20,11.13.21. See also BDB, "תּוֹרָה", 435.

[65] See, e.g., the way in which Aquila uses the term ἰσχύς to translate the Hebrew noun חָזְקָה (see Jonah 3,8; and Dan 11,2), meaning both "strength" and "wealth", but which, with a different vocalization (חֲזָקָה), can also refer to the aforementioned technical term for *usucapio*. See, e.g., BDB, "חָזְקָה", 305; *Ibid.*, "חֲזָקָה", 306; F. FIELD, *Origenis Hexaplorum*, II, 929.986; J. REIDER – N. TURNER, *An Index*, 120; and Chap. IV, p. 207.

[66] J. RATZINGER, BENEDICT XVI, *Verbum Domini*, § 42.

[67] J.M. BERGOGLIO, FRANCIS, "The Fanaticism of Charity", 14.

[68] *Lit.*, I, 236. "*Amor ignorat judicium, ratione caret, modum nescit. Amor non accipit de impossibilitate solatium, non recipit de difficultate remedium. Amor [...] ideo vadit quo ducitur*" (PETER CHRYSOLOGUS, *Serm.* CXLVII [*PL* 52, 595c]).

[69] K.J. WOJTYŁA, JOHN PAUL II, *Mane Nobiscum Domine*, § 28.

news of the kingdom of God which "draws near to us"[70], and for the twofold purpose of the forgiveness of their sins and their legitimate entrance into Heaven.

More precisely, the theological implications of the saying in Luke 16,16
spur us all to ask ourselves: Which one is the God in whom we, as both
Church community and individuals, really place our trust today[71]? Currently,
in many North American dioceses, special collections after Communion –
commonly known as "second collections" – are becoming more and more the
norm before the end of Mass, whereas in Germany all officially registered
Catholics are being obliged to pay a membership tax, on their annual income
tax bill, called "Church tax" (Kirchensteuer), upon penalty of their exclusion
from sacramental and community life, which is comparable to a *de facto*
excommunication[72]. Reflecting on the Gospel of the temptations of Jesus
according to Luke, Pope Benedict XVI stressed the importance of asking
ourselves "a fundamental question: What really counts in my life?"[73]. As
C.A. Hall remarks, it is a matter of fact that these days, more than ever before,
we are constantly tempted "to live in two worlds – the kingdom of this world
and the kingdom of God"[74]. For this reason, independently from the vow of
poverty and the call to religious life, freedom or detachment from money and
material possessions is a call which concerns all true disciples in the crowds,
yesterday as well as today, whether one belongs to the ordained diocesan
ministry or the laity[75].

For how many Christians live today in this world as if Heaven did not
exist? Love of money has the power to take away discernment, and with it

---

[70] J. RATZINGER, BENEDICT XVI, *Deus Caritas Est*, § 1.

[71] As we have already seen, from an etymological perspective, "mammon" (ממון) derives
from the same Semitic root as "faith" (אמונה) or "trust" (אמת), that is, √אמן, and most likely
means, "that in which one puts one's trust". See, e.g., J.A. FITZMYER, *Luke*, II, 1109;
G. ROSSÉ, *Luca*, 624, n. 20; M. GRILLI, *Matteo*, 360–361; and Chap. III, p. 100, n. 75. As
the latter (*Ibid.*, 364) remarks: "È interessante e paradossale che sull'emblema del
capitalismo mondiale sia scritto proprio 'in God *'aman*', cioè *in God we trust*! Appunto:
dobbiamo tornare a chiederci chi è il Dio nel quale noi – come credenti – poniamo fiducia.
Sottoporci come Chiesa a questo vaglio è fondamentale".

[72] Thus, in his address to the German Bishops, during their recent *ad Limina* visit
(Nov 20, 2015), Pope Francis has drawn attention to "a very strong decrease in attendance
at Sunday Mass, as well as in the sacramental life", speaking of "an erosion of the Catholic
faith in Germany", mainly because of "the trend towards increasing institutionalization [...]
a sort of new Pelagianism, which leads us to put faith in administrative structures and perfect
organizations. Excessive centralization, rather than proving helpful, complicates both the
Church's life and her missionary dynamic".

[73] J. RATZINGER, BENEDICT XVI, "General Audience" (13 February, 2013), 2.

[74] C.A. HALL, *Reading Scripture*, 34.

[75] For instance, a lay person, such as, K. Argüello (*Anotaciones*, 4.33) notes: "Tienes
que aprender a desprenderte cíclicamente de todo, para ser más libre y más feliz [...] tu
opinión, tu casa, tus cosas, tu dinero [...] Dalo todo, cada minuto, y serás libre".

also the gaze of faith and the longing for eternal dwellings[76]. Blinded by the allurement of riches and power, we can squander our lives or substances, failing to see the Lazarus laid at our gate and losing sight of our eternal destiny. Like the five brothers in the parable (see Luke 16,27–31), we can turn a deaf ear to scripture and miss the chance to repent, while still in this world and time. The settling of accounts nevertheless will not delay (see Luke 16,2). In fact, however long our earthly life may be, sooner or later it will end. Rich and poor alike, all eventually die, because our existence on this earth is of its nature oriented eschatologically. Really, how many of us live with this glance of faith, as to invest our money, time, and talents, constantly into Heaven? To this effect, Luke 16,16 has still got something to tell us. Without βία, our "means of subsistence" have the potential to turn not only into our very "lives" (βίοι), but also into our "masters" or "lords" (κύριοι)! Luke is clear: neither does life consist in the abundance of possessions, nor can a servant love simultaneously two masters (see Luke 12,15; and 16,13)! Indeed, as Chiara Corbella Petrillo was fond of saying, it is absolutely true: "possession is the opposite of love"[77]!

In this sense, only "the violence of love" can give real meaning to our existence. As V.E. Frankl himself experienced and acknowledged in Nazi death-camps, the true essence of man, "the ultimate and the highest goal to which man can aspire"[78], even when this has lost him everything he has to live, is nothing else but to love. Looking at the existential void of our consumeristic society, the Austrian neurologist and psychiatrist observes:

The truth is that as the struggle for survival has subsided, the question has emerged: survival for what? Even more people today have the means to live but no meaning to live for[79].

---

[76] See, e.g., Chap. III, p. 161, n. 414.

[77] S. TROISI – C. PACCINI, Siamo nati, 153. More precisely, Chiara (Ibid., 153) writes: "Qualsiasi cosa farai avrà senso solo se la vedrai in funzione della vita eterna. Se starai amando veramente te ne accorgerai dal fatto che nulla t'appartiene veramente perché tutto è un dono. Come dice S. Francesco: il contrario dell'amore è il possesso!". To use the aforenoted expression of Pope John Paul II (see Conclusion, p. 341, n. 23), Chiara could be referred to as a "violent" saint of our time. After writing these words as a sort of testament to her son, in view of his first birthday, she left this world detached from all her possessions (see Luke 14,26.33), loving to the point of welcoming a new life, even when that meant not to undergo the medical treatment which could have saved her.

[78] V.E. FRANKL, Man's Search, 38.

[79] V.E. FRANKL, The Unheard Cry, 21. In citing the author, A. Pattakos (Prisoners, 82–83) remarks: "In America, we live surrounded by more material wealth than any other society in the world. Yet we are restless, unhappy, disconnected, both from others and from our inner lives. Our suicide rates for young people are increasing [...] In the face of material abundance, our inner emptiness, or 'existential vacuum' in Frankl's words, has become ever more pressing".

Indeed, it is truly significant that Frankl would come to this most eloquent of insights precisely while enduring the horrendous material and affective vacuum in one of those concentration camps:

A thought transfixed me: for the first time in my life I saw the truth as it is set into song by so many poets, proclaimed as the final wisdom by so many thinkers [...] I grasped the meaning of the greatest secret that human poetry and human thought and belief have to impart: *The salvation of man is through love and in love*. I understood how a man who has nothing left in this world still may know bliss, be it only for a brief moment, in the contemplation of his beloved[80].

Such a profound grasp of the truth, such an awareness and a blessing, is thus granted to the poor, the afflicted ones; it is to such as these that the "good news of the kingdom" (εὐαγγέλιον τῆς βασιλείας) is announced[81]! These poor are yet identified with the disciples, "as a class of followers"[82] rather than a social state of being, that is, inasmuch as they have experienced, at least once in their lives, what it means to leave everything to follow Christ and totally trust in him[83]. According to our interpretation, by transferring one's possessions into God's own kingly property, without necessarily asking, so to say, for his lawful consent, Luke 16,16 suggests that anyone may legitimately *violate* and take hold of a place in his kingdom, granted that this transfer be nonstop: this, too, may be a good news of the kingdom brought "to the poor" (πτωχοῖς)[84]! After all, already in the OT, God is said to have always planned and prepared such a "hereditary property" (נחלה) "for the poor" (לעני)[85].

The call to discipleship, however, is not so much for all to be poor in the strict economic sense of the term, as rather to seek first the kingdom of God and experience the blessedness of God's copious providence[86]. Being detached

---

[80] V.E. FRANKL, *Man's Search*, 38.

[81] See, e.g., Luke 4,18; 6,20–23; 7,22; and 16,16.

[82] G.T. MEADORS, "The 'Poor'", 310. The idea of their group association with Jesus is stressed also by the expression, "because of [ἕνεκα] the Son of Man" (Luke 6,22).

[83] See, e.g., Luke 4,18; 5,11; 6,20; 14,33; and 16,16b.

[84] See, e.g., Isa 61,1; Mark 10,21; Matt 4,23; 5,3; 9,35; 11,5; 24,14; Luke 4,18.43; 6,20.24; 8,1; 14,13.21; 16,16.22; 18,22; 19,8; 21,2–4; and Acts 8,12. Of all beatitudes, only in Luke 6,20 ("Blessed are you who are poor, for *yours* [emphasis added] is the kingdom of God!") the Lucan Jesus uses the possessive pronoun, "yours" (ὑμέτερος), in an emphatic position and with reference to the kingdom of God. Its sole other occurrence in Luke's Gospel is in Luke 16,12. Here again, Jesus addresses the disciples (see Luke 16,1a.9a) and tells them that they will receive "that which is their own" (τὸ ὑμέτερον), on the condition that they are found faithful in their dealings with what belongs to someone else, that is, mammon (see Luke 16,11). Thus, it is possible that Luke 16,12 alludes to the kingdom of God meant for the disciples, provided they use their wealth shrewdly, as an investment in such a direction.

[85] See, esp., Ps 68[67],10[11].18[19]; Luke 12,31–32; and 14,13.21.

[86] See, esp., Luke 12,31; and 18,29–30. See also Chap. V, p. 285, n. 162.

from *all* one's possessions (see Luke 14,33) and selling *all* to have a treasure in Heaven (see Luke 12,21.33–34; 16,9.16; and 18,22) are attitudes and conducts that relate to "everyone" (πᾶς), without exception (see Luke 21,2–4), insofar as they are equivalent to loving God with *all* of one's strength or mammon (see the Satt on Deut 6,5). As such, they are also the expression and profession of an adult faith and a sign of the right response of the heart before the gift of the kingdom of God and its good news[87]. Welcoming the good news or listening to it generates faith and gratitude, and these can in turn bring about detachment from money and generosity with it[88].

Almsgiving, in this sense, is neither an end in itself, nor a philanthropic exercise, but a means to set one's heart wholly on God (see Luke 12,33–34), "a sign of true adherence to the law"[89] and "the ideal way of handling possessions"[90], which entails a sense of faith and foresight that extend beyond those of this world. Moreover, it is not a question of one sporadic act, for that would allow one's heart to get attached to mammon again! The legal principle of *usucapio* or *ḥazaqah*, with which Luke 16,16 appears to be consistent, requires an uninterrupted (vs. one-off) use of someone else's property, which is to correspond to the Christian's constant attitude of "giving", modelled after the well-established selfish habit of the shrewd steward's "wasteful" eschatological character (see Luke 16,1b–8a)[91].

In other words, all disciples of Christ are called to answer the love of God for them with a limitless amount of love, which is reflected in their full detachment (see Luke 14,33) from material possessions (see "You shall love [...] with *all* [emphasis added] your strength": Deut 6,5). This ascetic attitude allows them to "give" alms to "everyone" (παντί: Luke 6,30; cf. Matt 5,42) who asks of them, in imitation of God himself[92]. We could say, therefore, that discipleship is a matter of "spiritual childhood"[93], that is, a total, confident,

---

[87] Thus, F. Bovon (*L'œuvre de Luc*, 233) observes: "Luc fait de l'argent un pierre de touche de la foi". See, esp., Luke 14,25.33. See also Luke 16,13.

[88] See, e.g., Rom 10,17; Col 2,6–7; and Heb 12,28. See also L.T. JOHNSON, *The Literary Function*, 144–158 (esp. 155); and Chap. V, pp. 283–284 (esp. ns. 148–149.154).

[89] J.S. JERVELL, *Luke and the People*, 150.

[90] L.T. JOHNSON, *The Literary Function*, 10.

[91] See, e.g., Chap. III, pp. 134–143.

[92] See, e.g., Matt 7,2.8a; Mark 4,24; Luke 6,38; and 11,10a. Thus, in his commentary on Luke 6,30, G. Rossé (*Luca*, 224) remarks: "Dà a chi[-unque] ti chiede! È un appello all'amore senza misura. Il motivo di tale comportamento non è da ricercarsi nel disprezzo dei beni terreni, ma nella *volontà* [emphasis added] di mettere al centro della propria esistenza il principio del dono di sé".

[93] As G. Ricciardi ("The Popes", [accessed on-line: 06.05.2017], http://www.30giorni.it/articoli_id_907_l3.htm) points out, this expression was used by Pope Benedict XV, on August 14, 1921, as he proclaimed the Decree on the heroic virtues of Teresa of Lisieux: "for the first time, a Pope used the expression 'spiritual childhood' in reference to the

and filial abandonment into the hands of God, as exemplified, for instance, by Tabitha, who "was full of good deeds [πλήρης ἔργων ἀγαθῶν] and acts of charity [ἐλεημοσυνῶν], which she was continually doing [ἐποίει]" (Acts 9,36), as well as Cornelius, who "was continually giving [ποιῶν] many alms [ἐλεημοσύνας πολλάς] to the people" (Acts 10,2).

Finally, translating "violence" into love for God with *all* our strength or mammon does not mean obviously that all access into God's kingdom can be reduced to ṣ^eḏāqāh. *Not everything* said in the Gospels concerning the entrance into the kingdom can in fact be condensed into *almsgiving*. Loving God with all one's strength is only one of the concrete ways by which we can love God with all our heart (see Deut 6,5). The way to enter the kingdom is rather the love commanded in the *Š^ema*ʿ. Other sayings regarding the entrance into God's kingdom may be about loving God also with all one's life and mind[94]. This is not to say, however, that the "locked door" of Luke 16,16 and its hermeneutic impasse may not be opened with the "key" of charity and almsgiving. On the contrary, to paraphrase Pope Francis' recent words in Egypt and on the word of Luke 16,16, we can say that the only violence the Christian can have is that called forth by the *Š^ema*ʿ, namely, "the violence of love", for both God and neighbor (see Luke 10,27), such that, by the power of the Holy Spirit, one can gratefully respond to the kerygma of the kingdom and renounce worldly possessions for the purpose of an eternal dwelling in Heaven.

In the light of all the foregoing considerations, therefore, violent detachment of the self from material goods and generous sharing of wealth with those in need are still essential, today as yesterday. Unfortunately, in "post-Enlightenment" theology, the Patristic heritage is often rejected and forgotten because of a skeptical rationalism, which turns a deaf ear to whatever is in tune with authority, tradition, and asceticism[95]. However, at the end of this exegetical and theological investigation, we believe we have good reasons for applying John of Salisbury's renowned metaphor not only to prophets and

---

'doctrine' of the saint of Lisieux: 'Spiritual childhood', said the Pope 'is formed by trust in God and by blind abandonment into his hands [...] We hope that the secret of the sanctity of Sister Teresa of the Child Jesus remains hidden to no one".

[94] For instance, the necessity of suffering tribulations and persecutions in order to enter the kingdom (see Acts 14,22) could fit into loving God with all one's life, whereas the requirement of being like children (see Luke 18,16), may refer to loving God with all one's mind, in the sense that a child is expected to obey and trust his father's guidance (vs. his own reasoning), accepting the unfolding of his will in the concrete events of his history, with gratitude and praise (see Pss 8,2; and 131[130],2). This too may constitute another possible line of research.

[95] See, esp., C.A. HALL, *Reading Scripture*, 19–42.

evangelists, but also to these early colossi of our faith and their perspicacious interpretation of the saying, and as such we firmly state:

"we are almost like dwarfs sitting [astride] on giants' shoulders, so that we can see more [things] and much farther than they, however not because of the acuity of our own sight, or the height of our own body, but because we are brought higher and lifted up [by them] to gigantic heights"[96].

---

[96] "*nos esse quasi nanos gigantum umeris insidentes, ut possimus plura eis et remotiora videre, non utique proprii visus acumine, aut eminentia corporis, sed quia in altum subvehimur et extollimur magnitudine gigantea*" (JOHN OF SALISBURY, *Metal.* III.4 [ed. J.B. HALL, 116]). This metaphor has since then been cited by several distinguished Jewish and Christian researchers throughout history, and often in the field of astrophysics and science (e.g., I. Newton and S. Hawking). See, e.g., H.W. TURNBULL – *al.*, ed., *The Correspondence*, I, 416; S.Z. LEIMAN, "From the pages", 90–94; and S. HOWKING, ed., *On the Shoulders*. However, as R. Cantalamessa (*Sulle spalle*, 7) rightly remarks, "essa non è nata nell'ambito della scienza, bensì della teologia". Its artistic expression in statues and images of not a few medieval gothic churches (e.g., the stained glass rose window of Chartres' Cathedral) interprets these giants as being both the prophets with their Law and the evangelists with their Gospels. Nothing yet prevents us from thinking of them also as the Church Fathers with their Interpretation of the saying contained in Luke 16,16.

Bibliography

AALEN, S., "'Reign' and 'House' in the Kingdom of God in the Gospels", *NTS* 8.3 (1962) 215–240.

AICHELE, G., "Jesus' Violence", in T. PIPPIN – G. AICHELE, ed., *Violence, Utopia, and the Kingdom of God. Fantasy and Ideology in the Bible*, London / New York NY, 1998, 72–91.

ALAND, K., ed., *Synopsis Quattuor Evangeliorum. Locis parallelis Evangeliorum apocryphorum et partum adhibitis*, Stuttgart 1963, 1988[13].

–, ed., *Synopsis of the Four Gospels. Greek – English Edition of the Synopsis Quattuor Evangeliorum. On the basis of the Greek Text of Nestle-Aland 27th Edition and Greek New Testament 4th Revised Edition. The English Text is the Second Edition of the Revised Standard Version*, Stuttgart 2007[13].

ALETTI, J.-N., *L'arte di raccontare Gesù Cristo. La scrittura narrativa del vangelo di Luca*, BiBi(B) 7, Brescia 1991; Fr. orig., *L'art de raconteur Jésus Christ. L'écriture narrative de l'Évangile de Luc*, Paris 1989.

–, *Il racconto come teologia. Studio narrativo del terzo Vangelo e del libro degli Atti degli Apostoli*, CBi, Roma 1996, Bologna 2009[2].

ALEXIS-BAKER, A., "Violence, Nonviolence and the Temple Incident in John 2,13–15", *BInterp* 20 (2012) 73–96.

ALLEN, W.C., *A Critical and Exegetical Commentary on the Gospel According to St. Matthew*, ICC, Edinburg 1907[2].

ALLISON, D.C., *Constructing Jesus. Memory, Imagination, and History*, Grand Rapids MI, 2010.

ALMQUIST, H., *Plutarch und das Neue Testament. Ein Beitrag zum Corpus Hellenisticum Novi Testamenti*, ASNU 15, Upsala 1946.

ALTER, R., *The Art of Biblical Narrative*, New York NY, 1981, repr. 2011.

AMBROSE, K., *Jew Among Jews. Rehabilitating Paul*, Eugene OR, 2015.

ANDERSON, G.A., *Sin. A History*, New Haven CT, 2009.

–, "Faith and Finance", *FiTh* 193 (2009) 29–34.

–, "The Evolution of Sin", *ChrTo* 54.3 (2010) 30–33.

–, "Is Purgatory Biblical?", *FiTh* 217 (2011) 39–44.

–, "Giving to be Forgiven. Alms in the Bible", *CCen* 130.18 (2013) 26–33.

ANDERSON, H., "4 Maccabees (First Century A.D.). A New Translation and Introduction", in J.H. CHARLESWORTH, ed., *The Old Testament Pseudepigrapha*, II, Garden City NY, 1985, 531–564.

ARGÜELLO, K., *Anotaciones (1988–2014)*, Madrid 2016.

ARNALDEZ, R. – al., ed., *Les oeuvres de Philon d'Alexandrie. Publiées sous le patronage de l'université de Lyon*, I–XXXVI, Paris 1961–1988.

ARNDT, W.F., *Bible Commentary. The Gospel According to St. Luke*, St. Louis MO, 1956.

ATSMA, A.J., "BIA" [access: 17.02.2016], http://www.theoi.com/Daimon/Bia. html.

AUBINEAU, M., ed., *Grégoire de Nysse. Traité de la virginité. Introduction, texte critique, traduction commentaire et index*, SC 119, Paris 1966.

–, ed., *Les homélies festales d'Hésychius de Jérusalem*, I. *Les homélies i–xv*, SHG 59, Brussels 1978.

AUJAC, G. – LASERRE, F., ed., *Strabon. Géographie. Introduction. Texte établi et traduit*, I–IX, CUFr, Paris 1969–1981.

AUNE, D.E., *The New Testament in Its Literary Environment*, Cambridge 1987, Philadephia PA, 1989.

AUSTIN, M.R., "The Hypocritical Son", *EvQ* 57 (1985) 307–315.

BAILEY, K.E., *Poet & Peasant and Through Peasant Eyes. A Literary-Cultural Approach to the Parables of Luke*, Grand Rapids MI, 1976, repr. 1983.

BAIRD, J.A., *Audience Criticism and the Historical Jesus*, NTLi, Philadelphia PA, 1969.

BALL, M., "The Parables of the Unjust Steward and the Rich Man and Lazarus", *ET* 106.11 (1995) 329–330.

BALLA, I., *Ben Sira on Family, Gender and Sexuality*, DCLS 8, Berlin / New York NY, 2011.

BALOT, R.K., *A Genealogy of "Greed" in Classical Athens*, diss., Princeton 1998.

VON BALTHASAR, H.U., *Origène. Esprit et feu*, I–II, Paris 1958–1960.

BAMMEL, E., "Is Luke 16,16–18 of Baptist's Provenience?", *HThR* 51.2 (1958) 101–106.

–, "Any Deyathiqi Partially Cancelled is Completely Cancelled", *JSSt* 5.4 (1960) 355–358.

BANDINI, M. – DORION, L.-A., ed., *Xénophon. Mémorables*, I.1, CUFr, Paris 2000.

BANKS, R., *Jesus and the Law in the Synoptic Tradition*, SNTS.MS 28, Cambridge 1975.

BARCLAY, W., *The Gospel of Luke*, DSBS, Louisville KY, 1953, 1975[2].

BARDY, G., ed., *Eusèbe de Césarée. Histoire ecclésiastique. Texte grec, traduction et annotation*, I–IV, SC 31, 41, 55, 73, Paris 1952, 1955, 1958, 1960.

BARDY, G. – LEFEVRE, F.G., ed., *Hippolyte. Commentaire sur Daniel*, SC 14, Paris 1947.

BAREILLE, J., ed., *Oeuvres complètes de Saint Jean Chrysostome d'après toutes les éditions faites jusqu'a ce jour*, I–XXI, Paris 1865–1878.

BARNARD, L.W., *St. Justin Martyr. The First and Second Apologies. Translated with Introduction and Notes*, ACW 56, New York NY / Mahwah NJ, 1997.

BARNETT, P.W., "Who Were the 'Biastai' (Mt 11,12–13)?", *RTR* 36.3 (1977) 65–70.

BARRETT, C.K., *A Critical and Exegetical Commentary on the Acts of the Apostles*, I–II, ICC, Edinburgh 1994–1998, London / New York NY, 2004.

BARTELINK, G.J.M., ed., *Callinicos. Vie d'Hypatios*, SC 177, Paris 1971.

BARTH, M., "The Dishonest Steward and His Lord. Reflections on Luke 16,1–13", in D.Y. HADIDIAN, ed., *From Faith To Faith*, Fs. D.G. Miller, PTh.MS 31, Pittsburg PA, 1979, 65–73.

BATE, H.N., ed., *The Sibylline Oracles. Books III–V*, TED, London / New York NY, 1918.

BATES, M.W., "Cryptic Codes and a Violent King: a New Proposal for Matthew 11,12 and Luke 16,16–18", *CBQ* 75.1 (2013) 74–93.

BATIFFOL, P., ed., *Le Livre de la Prière d'Aseneth*, StPatr 1, Paris 1889, 1–115.

BATTEN, L.W., *A Critical and Exegetical Commentary on the Books of Ezra and Nehemiah*, ICC, New York NY, 1913.

BAUER, B., *Kritik der evangelischen Geschichte der Synoptiker*, I–II, Leipzig 1841, 1846[2].

BAUER, F.C., *Kritische Untersuchungen über die kanonischen Evangelien. Ihr Verhältniss zu einander. Ihren Charakter und Ursprung*, Tübingen 1847.

BEASLEY-MURRAY, G.R., *Jesus and the Kingdom of God*, Grand Rapids MI, 1986.

BEAUCHAMP, P., *Le récit, la lettre et le corps. Essais bibliques*, CFi 114, Paris 1982, 1992[2].

–, *Testament biblique. Recueil d'articles parus dans Études*, Paris 2001.

BEAUCHAMP, P. – VASSE, D., *La violence dans la Bible*, CEv 76, Paris 1991.

BEAVIS, M.A., "Ancient Slavery as an Interpretive Context for the New Testament Servant Parables with Special Reference to the Unjust Steward (Luke 16,1–8)", *JBL* 111.1 (1992) 37–54.

BEDNARZ, T., "Status Disputes and Disparate Dicta: Humor Rhetoric in Luke 16,14–18", *BInterp* 21.3 (2013) 377–415.

BEEKES, R.S.P. – DE VAAN, M., *Comparative Indo-European Linguistics. An Introduction*, Amsterdam / Philadelphia PA, 1995, 2011[2].

BEENTJES, P.C., *The Book of Ben Sira in Hebrew. A Text Edition of All Extant Hebrew Manuscripts and a Synopsis of all Parallel Hebrew Ben Sira Texts*, VT.S 68, Leiden / New York NY / Köln 1997.

BEKKER, I. – *al.*, ed., *Diodori Bibliotheca Historica*, I–V, BSGRT, Lipsiae 1888–1906.

BELLINI, E. – MASCHIO, G., ed., *Ireneo di Lione. Contro le eresie e gli altri scritti*, Già 320, Milano / Como 1979, 1997[2].

BENDINELLI, G., ed., *Origene. Commento a Matteo. Series*, I–II, OpOr 11.5–6, Roma 2004, 2006.

BENSLY, R.L., ed., *The Fourth Book of Maccabees and Kindred in Syriac. First Edited on Manuscript Authority*, Cambridge 1895.

BENVENISTE, É., *Le vocabulaire des institutions indo-européennes*, I–II, Paris 1969.

BENZ, E. – KLOSTERMANN, E., ed., *Matthäuserklärung*, I. *Die griechisch erhaltenen Tomoi*, GCS 40, Leipzig 1935.

VAN DER BERG, R.M., ed., *Proclus' Hymns. Essays, Translations, Commentary*, PhAnt 90, Leiden 2001.

BERGERET, J., *La violence fondamentale. L'inépuisable Œdipe*, Paris 1984, repr. 2014.

–, "Toxicomanies et prevention primaire", *DAD* 25.2 (1990) 187–192.

–, "Adolescence. The Croassroads of Violence", *JAHe* 13.5 (1992) 418–419.

–, *La violence et la vie. La face cachée de l'œdipe*, BiScP, Paris 1994.

–, *Sigmund Freud. Suite et poursuite*, Psych., Paris 2009.

BERGOGLIO, J.M., FRANCIS, "In Heaven's Stock Exchange" (Morning Meditation, in the Chapel of the *Domus Sanctae Marthae*: 19 June, 2015), in *L'Osservatore Romano. Weekly ed. in English* (26 June, 2015), Vatican City, n. 26.

–, "Who Are We to Cause Division?" (Address at the Meeting with the Members of the Renewal in the Holy Spirit, in St. Peter's Square: 3 July, 2015), in *L'Osservatore Romano*, Weekly ed. in English (31 July, 2015), Vatican City, n. 31.

–, "Address of His Holiness Pope Francis to the Bishops of the Episcopal Conference of the Federal Republic of Germany on Their *ad Limina* Visit. Friday, 20 November, 2015", [On-line edition: access 12.07. 2017], https://w2.vatican.va/content/francesco/en/speeches/2015/november/documents/papa-francesco_20151120_adlimina-rep-fed-germania.html.

–, "A Life of Testimony" (Address at a Refresher Seminar for Bishops of Mission Territories, in the Consistory Hall: 9 September, 2016), in *L'Osservatore Romano*, Weekly ed. in English (16 September, 2016), Vatican City, n. 37.

–, "An Economy of Communion" (Address at the Public Audience to the Focolare Movement, in the Paul VI Hall: 4 February, 2017), in *L'Osservatore Romano*, Weekly ed. in English (10 February, 2017), Vatican City, n. 6.

–, "The Fanaticism of Charity" (Mass with the Catholic Community, in the Air Defense Stadium of Cairo: 29 April, 2017), in *L'Osservatore Romano. Weekly ed. in English* (5 May, 2017), Vatican City, n. 18.

BERLIN, A. – BRETTLER, M.Z., ed., *The Jewish Study Bible*, New York NY, 2004.

BERNADICOU, P.J., "The Spirituality of Luke's Travel Narrative", *RfR* 36 (1977) 455–466.

BERTHELOT, K., "Zeal for God and Divine Law in Philo and the Dead Sea Scrolls", *SPhA* 19 (2007) 113–129.

BETZ, O., "Jesu Heiliger Krieg", *NovT* 2.2 (1957) 116–136.

–, "The Eschatological Interpretation of the Sinai-Tradition in Qumran and in the New Testament", *RdQ* 6.1 (1967) 89–107.

BEWER, J.A., *A Critical and Exegetical Commentary on Jonah*, ICC, New York NY, 1912.

BEYENKA, M.M., *Saint Ambrose. Letters*, FaCh 26, Washington DC, 1954, repr. 1967.

BEZA, T., *Annotationes maiores in Novum D.N. Jesu Christi Testamentum*, I–II, Geneva 1556, 1594[2].

BIRD, N., *The Distribution of Indo-European Root Morphemes (A Checklist for Philologists)*, Wiesbaden 1982.

BIRKS, M.J., "St. Matthew 11,12", *ET* 22.9 (1911) 425–426.

BISSELL, E.C., ed., *The Apocrypha of the Old Testament. With Historical Introductions, a Revised Translation, and Notes Critical and Explanatory*, LCHS 15, New York NY, 1880.

BIVIN, D. – BLIZZARD, R.B., Jr., *Understanding the Difficult Words of Jesus. New Insights from a Hebraic Perspective*, Austin TX 1984.

BLACK, M., *An Aramaic Approach to the Gospels and Acts*, Oxford 1946, 1967[3], repr. 1979.

–, "The Kingdom of God has come", *ET* 63.9 (1952) 289–290.

–, ed., *Liber Enoch. Apocalypsis Henochi Graece*, PVTG 3, Leiden 1970.

–, *The Book of Enoch or I Enoch. A New English Edition with Commentary and Textual Notes*, SVTP 7, Leiden 1985.

BLACKMAN, P., ed., *Mishnayoth*, I–VI, London 1951–1956.

BLANC, C., *Origène. Commentaire sur Saint Jean. Texte grec avant-propos, traduction et notes*, II, SC 157, Paris 1970.

BLEEK, F., *Synoptische Erklärung der drei ersten Evangelien*, I–II, Leipzig 1862.

BLOCH, R., "Note méthologique pour l'étude de la literature rabbinique", *RSR* 43 (1955) 194–227.

–, "Bia", BNP, II, 621.

BLOMBERG, C.L., "Midrash, Chiasmus, and the Outline of Luke's Central Section," in R.T. FRANCE – D. WENHAM, ed., *Gospel Perspectives*, III, Sheffield 1983, 217–261.

–, "The Law in Luke-Acts", *JSNT* 22 (1984) 53–80.

–, "When is a Parallel Really a Parallel? A Test Case: The Lucan Parables", *WThJ* 46.1 (1984) 78–103.

–, *Interpreting the Parables*, Downers Grove IL, 1990.

–, *Neither Poverty Nor Riches. A Biblical Theology of Possessions*, NSBT 7, Leicester 1999.

BOBICHON, P., ed., *Justin Martyr. Dialogue avec Tryphon. Édition critique*, I–II, Par. 47.1–2, Fribourg 2003.

BOCCACCIO, P. – BERARDI, G., ed., *Ecclesiasticus. Textus Hebraeus secundum fragmenta reperta*, VTM, Roma 1986.

BOCK, D.L., *Luke*, I–II, BECNT 3a–b, Grand Rapids MI, 1994–1996.

–, "The Parable of the Rich Man and Lazarus and the Ethics of Jesus", *SWJT* 40.1 (1997) 63–72.

–, *A Theology of Luke and Acts. Biblical Theology of the New Testament*, Grand Rapids MI, 2012.

BOESE, H., ed., *Anonymi Glosa Psalmorum ex traditione seniorum*, I–II, AGLB 22, 25, Freiburg 1992, 1994.

BOISMARD, M.E. – LAMOUILLE, A., ed., *Synopsis graeca quattuor Evangeliorum*, Leuven / Paris 1986.

BOKSER, B.M., "Talmudic Form Criticism", *JJS* 31 (1980) 46–60.

BOLAND, A., "Royaume de Dieu et royauté du Christ", *DSp* 13 (1988) 1026–1097.

BOLIN, A., *Du bon usage des richesses. Etude exégétique et narrative de la parabole du gestionnaire avisé (Lc 16.1–13)*, diss., Collonges-sous-Salève 2012.

BOLIN, T.M., *Freedom Beyond Forgiveness. The Book of Jonah Re-Examined*, JSOT.S 236, Sheffield 1997.

BONATO, A., "Il regno di Dio negli scritti di S. Ambrogio e di S. Agostino", *DSBP* 58 (2011) 206–343.

BONNARD, I.É., ed., *Jérôme. Commentaire sur saint Matthieu. Texte latin, introduction, traduction et notes*, I–II, SC 242, 259, Paris 1977, 1979.

DE BOOR, C., ed., *Georgii monachi chronicon*, I–II, BSGRT, Lipsiae 1904, 1978.

BORGEN, P. – FUGLSETH, K. – SKARSTEN, R., *The Philo Index. A Complete Greek Word Index to the Writings of Philo of Alexandria. Lemmatised & Computer-Generated*, UniSt 25, Dragvoll 1997.

BORRET, M., ed., *Origène. Homélies sur le Lévitique. Texte latin, traduction et notes*, I–II, SC 286–287, Paris 1981.

BOTTE, B., ed., *Ambroise de Milan. Des sacrements. Des mystères. Explication du Symbole. Texte établi, traduit et annoté*, SC 25, Paris 1961.

BOVON, F., *L'œuvre de Luc. Études d'exégèse et de théologie*, LeDiv 130, Paris 1987.

–, *L'Évangile selon Saint Luc. I. 1,1–9,50. II. 9,51–14,35. III. 15,1–19,27. IV. 19,28–24,53*, CNT 3a–d, Genève 1991, 1996, 2001, 2009.

–, *Luke the Theologian. Fifty-five Years of Research (1950–2005)*, Waco TX, 2005[2].

BOWRA, C.M., *Greek Lyric Poetry. From Alcman to Simonides*, Oxford 1936, 1961[2].

BRANDON, S.G.F., *Jesus and the Zealots. A Study of the Political Factor in Primitive Christianity*, Manchester 1967.

BRANDT, W., "Matthäus c. 11,12", *ZNW* 11 (1910) 247–248.

BRANSCOMB, B.H., *Jesus and the Law of Moses*, New York NY, 1930.

BRAUMANN, G., "'Dem Himmelreich wird Gewalt angetan' (Mt 11:12 par.)", *ZNW* 52.1–2 (1961) 104–109.

BRENTON, C.L., *The Septuagint Version of the Old Testament and Apocrypha with an English Translation and with Various Readings and Critical Notes*, London / New York NY, 1900.

BRETSCHER, P.G., "The Parable of the Unjust Steward. A New Approach to Luke 16,1–9", *CTM* 22 (1951) 756–762.

BREWER, D.I., "Review Article. The Use of Rabbinic Sources in Gospel Studies", *TynB* 50.2 (1999) 281–298.

BRIDGES, C.B. – WHEELER, R.E., "The Evil Eye in the Sermon on the Mount", *SCJ* 4 (2001) 69–79.

BRIGGS, C.A. – BRIGGS, E.G., *A Critical and Exegetical Commentary on the Book of Psalms*, I–II, ICC, Edinburgh 1907.

BRIXHE, C., *Phonétique et phonologie du Grec ancien. I. Quelques grandes questions*, BCILL 82, Louvain 1996.

BROWN, R.E., "Hermeneutics", in R.E. BROWN – J.A. FITZMYER – R.E. MURPHY, ed., *The Jerome Biblical Commentary*, II, Englewood Cliffs NJ, 1968, 605–623.

BROWNE, R.W., ed., *The Nicomachean Ethics of Aristotle. Translated, with Notes, Original and Selected; An Analytical Introduction; and Questions for the Use of Students*, BCL, London 1871.

BRUCE, A.B., *The Parabolic Teaching of Christ. A Systematic and Critical Study of the Parables of Our Lord*, London 1882, New York NY, 1892[3].

BRUCE, F.F., *The Acts of the Apostles. The Greek Text with Introduction and Commentary*, London 1951, Grand Rapids MI, 1990[3].

BRUEHLER, B.B., "Reweaving the Texture of Luke 16,14–18", *JBPR* 5 (2013) 49–67.

BRYEN, A.Z., "Visibility and Violence in Petitions from Roman Egypt", *GRBS* 48 (2008) 181–200.

–, *Violence in Roman Egypt. A Study in Legal Interpretation*, Philadelphia PA, 2013.

BUCER, M., *Enarrationes Perpetuae. In Sacra Quatuor Evangelia*, Argentorati 1530.

BÜCHLER, A., *Studies in Sin and Atonement in the Rabbinic Literature of the First Century*, PJC 11, London 1928.

BULTMANN, R., *The History of the Synoptic Tradition*, Oxford 1963, 1968[2]; Ger. orig., *Die Geschichte der Synoptischen Tradition*, Göttingen 1931.

BURKETT, D.R., *Rethinking the Gospel Sources*, I–II, New York NY, 2004; Atlanta GA, 2009.

BURKITT, F.C., "PHARES, PEREZ, and Matthew 11,12", *JThS* 30.3 (1929) 254–258.

BURNET, J., ed., *Platonis Opera*, I–V, SCBO, Oxonii 1962–1985.

–, ed., *The Ethics of Aristotle. Edited with an Introduction and Notes*, London 1900.

BUSSINO, S., *The Greek Additions in the Book of Ben Sira. Translated from the Italian by Michael Tait*, AnBib 203, Rome 2013.

BUTCHART, A. – MIKTON, C., ed., *Global Status Report on Violence Prevention*, WHO, Geneva 2014.

BUTTERWORTH, G.W., ed., *Clement of Alexandria Exhortation to the Greeks, The Rich Man's Salvation, To the Newly Baptized*, LCL 92, London / Cambridge MA, 1919, repr. 1979.

BYRNE, B.J., *The Hospitality of God. A Reading of Luke's Gospel*, Collegeville MN, 2000.

CACITTI, R., "'Ad caelestes thesauros'. L'esegesi della pericope del 'giovane ricco' nella parenesi di Cipriano di Cartagine", *Aevum* 65 (1991) 151–169; 67 (1993) 129–171.

CADBURY, H.J., "The Tradition", in F.J.F. JACKSON – K. LAKE, ed., *The Beginnings of Christianity. The Acts of the Apostles*, II.1, London 1922, 209–264.

–, *The Making of Luke-Acts*, Peabody MA, 1927, 1958[2], repr. 1999.

–, "The Kingdom of God and Ourselves", *CCen* 67 (1950) 172–173.

–, "The Single Eye", *HThR* 47.2 (1954) 69–74.

CAIRD, G.B., *The Gospel of St. Luke*, PNTC, New York NY, 1963, repr. 1985.

CALMET, A., *Commentaire littéral sur tous les livres de l'Ancien et du Nouveau Testament*, I–XXVI, Paris 1707–1716.

CALVIN, J., *Commentaries on the Twelve Minor Prophets*, I–V, Edinburg 1846–1849.

–, *Commentarius in Harmoniam Evangelicam*, in G. BAUM – E. CUNITZ – E. REUSS, ed., *Ioannis Calvini. Opera quae supersunt omnia*, XLV, CR, Brunsvigae 1891, 2–830; Eng. trans., *A Harmony of the Gospels. Matthew, Mark and Luke*, I–III, CCS, Grand Rapids MI, 1972, 1979–1980.

CAMERON, A. – HALL, S.G., *Eusebius. Life of Constantine. Introduction, Translation, and Commentary*, CAHS, Oxford 1999.

CAMERON, P.S., *Violence and the Kingdom. The Interpretation of Matthew 11,12*, ANTJ 5, Frankfurt am Main 1984, 1988[2].

–, *Ibid.* [review of K.A. BARTA, *CBQ* 48.1 (1986) 133–135].

–, "J'accuse", *SJRS* 11.2 (1990) 107–112.

–, "The Making of a Heretic", *The Age. Opinion-Analysis*, Melbourne 1993, 14.

–, *Necessary Heresies. Alternatives to Fundamentalism*, Marrickville NSW, 1993.

–, *Heretic. The True Story of an Australian Convicted of Heresy*, Sidney 1994.

CAMPBELL, D.A., ed., *Greek Lyric with an English Translation*, I–V, LCL, London / Cambridge MA, 1982–1993.

CAMPS, G.M. – UBACH, B.M., "Un sentido bíblico de ἄδικος, ἀδικία y la interpretación de Lc 16,1–13", *EstBib* 25 (1966) 75–82.

CANTALAMESSA, R., *Sulle spalle dei giganti. Le grandi verità della fede meditate e vissute con i Padri della Chiesa*, Cinesello Balsamo MI, 2014.

CARBONE, S.P. – RIZZI, G., *Il libro di Michea. Secondo il testo ebraico Masoretico. Secondo la versione greca della LXX. Secondo la parafrasi aramaica targumica*, Bologna 1996.

CARREGA, G.L., *La Vetus Syra del Vangelo di Luca. Trasmissione e ricezione del testo*, Roma 2013.

CARRIÈRE, J., ed., *Théognis. Poèmes élégiaques. Texte établi, traduit et commenté*, CUFr, Paris 1948, repr. 1975.

CARSON, D.A., "Do the Prophets and the Law Quit Prophesying before John? A Note on Matthew 11,13", in C.A. EVANS – W.R. STEGNER, ed., *The Gospels and the Scriptures of Israel*, JSNT.S 104, Sheffield 1994, 179–194.

CATCHPOLE, D.R., "The Synoptic Divorce Material as a Traditio-Historical Problem", *BJRL* 57.1 (1974) 92–127.

–, "On Doing Violence to the Kingdom", *JTSA* 25 (1978) 50–61.

–, *The Quest for Q*, Edinburgh 1993.

CAUSSE, J.-D., "La violence archaïque et le paradoxe du sacrifice aux dieux obscurs", in J.-D. CAUSSE – É. CUVILLIER – A. WENIN, ed., *Divine violence. Approche exégétique et anthropologique*, LiBi, Paris 2011, 67–98; It. trans., "La violenza arcaica e il paradosso del sacrificio agli dèi oscuri", in J.-D. CAUSSE – É. CUVILLIER – A. WÉNIN, ed., *Violenza divina. Un problema esegetico e antropologico*, Bologna 2012, 53–77.

CERESA GASTALDO, A., ed., *Massimo Confessore. Capitoli sulla carità. Editi criticamente con introduzione, versione e note*, VSen 3, Roma 1963.

CERVANTES GABARRÓN, J., ed., *Sinopsis bilingüe de los tres primeros Evangelios con los paralelos del Evangelio de Juan*, InEsB 4, Estella 1999.

CHALK, H.H.O., "*APETH and BIA* in Euripides' *Herakles*", *SPJHS* 82 (1962) 7–18.

CHAMBERLAIN, W.D., "Till the Son of Man Be Come", *Interp.* 7.1 (1953) 3–13.

CHAMBERS, M., ed., *Aristoteles. Athenaion politeia*, BSGRT, Leipzig 1986.

CHAMBRY, É., ed, *Ésope. Fables. Texte établi et traduit*, CUFr, Paris 1927.

CHARLES, R.H., ed., *The Book of Jubilees or the Little Genesis. Translated from the Editor's Ethiopic Text and Edited, with Introduction, Notes, and Indices*, London 1902.

–, *The Apocrypha and Pseudepigrapha of the Old Testament in English. With Introductions and Critical and Explanatory Notes to the Several Books*, I–II, Oxford 1913.

CHARLESWORTH, J.H., ed., *The History of the Rechabites. The Greek Recension*, SBL.PS 10, Chico CA, 1982.

–, ed., *The Old Testament Pseudepigrapha*, I–II, Garden City NY, 1983–1985.

–, *The Old Testament Pseudepigrapha & the New Testament*, Harrisburg PA, 1985, repr. 1998.

–, "In the Crucible. The Pseudepigrapha as Biblical Interpretation", in J.H. CHARLESWORTH – C.A. EVANS, ed., *The Pseudepigrapha and Early Biblical Interpretation*, JSPE.S 14, SSEJC 2, Sheffield 1993, 20–43.

CHASE, F.H., *The Lord's Prayer in the Early Church*, Cambridge 1981.

CHATELET, F., "Remarques sur le concept de violence (ou non)", *EPh* 23.1 (1968) 31–38.

CHEONG, C.-S.A., *A Dialogic Reading of The Steward Parable (Luke 16,1–9)*, StBL 28, New York NY, 2001.

CHILDERS, J.W. – KIRAZ, G.A., ed., *The Syriac Peshiṭta Bible with English Translation. Luke*, AntiB, Piscataway NJ, 2013.

CHILTON, B.D., "The Violent Kingdom. Redactions and Traditions in Luke 16,16/ Matt 11,12.13", in *God in Strength. Jesus' Announcement of the Kingdom*, SNTU.B 1, Freistadt 1979, 203–230.

CLARK, K.W., *The Gentile Bias and Other Essays*, NT.S 54, Leiden 1980.

CLARKE, E.G., ed., *Targum Pseudo-Jonathan: Deuteronomy. Translated, with Notes*, ArBib 5B, Edinburgh 1998.

CLINES, D.J.A., *The Esther Scroll. The Story of the Story*, JSOT.S 30, Sheffield 1984.

COHEN, B., *Jewish and Roman Law. A Comparative Study*, I, New York NY, 1966.

COHEN, D., *Theft in Athenian Law*, MBPF 74, Munich 1983.

COHOON, J.W. – *al.*, ed., *Dio Chrysostom with an English Translation*, I–V, LCL, London / Cambridge MA, 1932–1964.

COLLART, P. – JOUGUET, P., "Un papyrus ptolémaïque provenant de Deir el-Bahari", *EtPap* 2 (1933) 23–40.

COLSON, F.H. – *al.*, ed., *Philo with an English Translation*, I–XII, LCL, London / Cambridge MA, 1929–1963, repr. 1981–1999.

COMBRINK, H.J.B., "A Social-Scientific Perspective on the Parable of the 'Unjust' Steward (Luke 16,1–8a)", *Neotest.* 30.2 (1996) 281–306.

COMMISSION FOR RELIGIOUS RELATIONS WITH THE JEWS, *Notes on the Correct Way to Present the Jews and Judaism in Preaching and Catechesis of the Roman Catholic Church*, Vatican City 1985.

CONRAD, M.J., "פרץ", *TDOT*, XII, 104–110.

CONZELMANN, H., *Die Mitte der Zeit. Studien zur Theologie des Lukas*, BHTh 17, Tübingen 1954; Eng. trans., *The Theology of St. Luke*, London 1960.

COOK, M.J., "Anti-Judaism in the New Testament", *USQR* 38 (1983) 125–137.

COOKE, G.A., *A Critical and Exegetical Commentary on the Book of Ezekiel*, ICC, Edinburgh 1936.

CORNTHWAITE, C.J., *Torah in the Diaspora. A Comparative Study of Philo and 4 Maccabees*, diss., London ON, 2013.

CORTÉS, E., *Los Discursos de Adiós de Gen 49 a Jn 13–17. Pistas para la historia de un género literario en la antigua literatura judía*, Barcelona 1976.

CORTÉS, E. – MARTÍNEZ, T., *Sifre Deuteronomio. Comentario tannaítico al libro del Deuteronomio*, I–II, CSPac 40.60, Barcelona 1989–1997.

CORTÉS, J.B. – GATTI, F.M., "On the Meaning of Luke 16,16", *JBL* 106.2 (1987) 247–259.

COSENTINO, A., "The Testament of Solomon", *JQR* 11 (1898) 1–45.

–, ed., *Testamento di Salomone*, CTePa 230, Roma 2013.

COURTONNE, Y., ed., *Saint Basile. Homélies sur la richesse. Edition Critique et Exégétique. Thèse présentée à la Faculté des Lettres de l'Université de Paris*, Paris 1935.

–, ed., *Saint Basile. Lettres*, I–III, Paris 1957–1966.

COX, S., "Spiritual Forces. St. Matt 11,12", *Exp.* 3 (1876) 252–264.

CRANFIELD, C.E.B., "Riches and the Kingdom of God. St. Mark 10,17–31", *SJTh* 4.3 (1951) 302–313.

CRAWFORD, H.T., *A Critical and Exegetical Commentary on the Book of Proverbs*, ICC, New York NY, 1916.

CREED, J.M., *The Gospel According to St. Luke. The Greek Text with Introduction, Notes, and Indices*, London 1930.

CRIMELLA, M., *Marta, Marta! Quattro esempi di "triangolo drammatico" nel "grande viaggio di Luca"*, StRic, Assisi 2009.

CROISET, M., ed., *Démosthène. Harangues. Texte établi et traduit*, I–II, CUFr, Paris 1924–1946.

DE CROM, D., "The *Letter of Aristeas* and the Authority of the Septuagint", *JSPE* 17.2 (2008) 141–160.

CROSS, F.M. – *al.*, ed., *Qumran Cave 4. XII. 1–2 Samuel*, DJD 17, Oxford 2005.

CROSSAN, J.D., "The Parable of the Wicked Husbandmen", *JBL* 90.4 (1971) 451–465.

–, "Servant Parables of Jesus", *Semeia* 1 (1974) 17–62.

CROUZEL, H., *L'Église primitive face au divorce. Du premier au cinquième siècle*, Paris 1971.

CROUZEL, H. – FOURNIER, F. – PÉRICHON, P., ed., *Origène. Homélies sur Saint Luc. Texte latin et fragments grecs. Introduction, traduction et notes*, SC 87, Paris 1962.

CULMANN, O., *The State in the New Testament*, London 1957.

CUVILLIER, É., "Jésus aux prises avec la violence dans l'Évangile de Matthieu", *ETR* 74.3 (1999) 335–349.

D'AGOSTINO, F., *BIA. Violenza e giustizia nella filosofia e nella letteratura della Grecia antica. Sondaggi lessicali*, UnCAT 100, Milano 1983.

DAHLMANN, W., *'H βία im Recht der Papyri*, diss., Köln 1968.

DAIN, A. – MAZON, P., ed., *Sophocle. Texte établi et traduit*, I–III, CUFr, Paris 1955–1960.

DAL COVOLO, E., "Il Regno di Dio in alcune testimonianze del secondo secolo. Appunti per la storia di un concetto neotestamentario", *RivBib* 27 (1979) 313–324.

–, "'Regno di Dio' nel Dialogo di Giustino con Trifone Giudeo", *Aug.* 28 (1988) 111–123.

–, "Escatologia e apocalittica nei primi secoli cristiani. Il regno di Dio e la sua attesa negli Apologisti greci del II secolo", *Sal.* 62 (2000) 625–643.

DALE, A.M., ed., *Euripides. Helen. Edited with Introduction and Commentary*, Oxford 1967, repr. 1971.

DALMAN, G., *Die Worte Jesu. Mit Berücksichtigung des nachkanonischen jüdischen Schrifttums und der aramäistischen Sprache erörtert*, Leipzig 1898, 1930[2]; Eng. trans., *The Words of Jesus: Considered in the Light of Post-Biblical Jewish Writings and the Aramaic Language*, Edinburgh 1902, repr. 1909.

DALY, K.N., *Greek and Roman Mythology A to Z*, New York NY, 1992, 2009[3].

DANIELI, M.I., ed., *Origene. Commento al Vangelo di Matteo*, I–III, CTePa 145, 151, 157, Roma 1998, 1999, 2001.

DANKER, F.W., "Luke 16,16 – An Opposition Logion", *JBL* 77.3 (1958) 231–243.

DAUBE, D., *The New Testament and Rabbinic Judaism*, JPe, London 1956, repr. 1984.

–, "The Linguistics of Suicide", *PPAf* 1.4 (1972) 387–437.

DAVIES, W.D., *Paul and Rabbinic Judaism. Some Rabbinic Elements in Pauline Theology*, Philadelphia PA, 1980.

DAVIES, W.D. – ALLISON, D.C., Jr., *A Critical and Exegetical Commentary on the Gospel According to Saint Matthew*, I–III, ICC, London / New York NY, 1988–1997, repr. 2004.

DAWSON, C., ed., *Medieval Essays*, New York NY, 1954.

DEISSMANN, G.A., *Neue Bibelstudien. Sprachgeschichtliche Beiträge, zumeist aus den Papyri und Inschriften zur Erklärung des Neuen Testaments*, Marburg 1897; Eng. trans., DEISSMANN, G.A. – GRIEVE, A., *Bible Studies. Contributions Chiefly from Papyri and Inscriptions to the History of the Language, the Literature, and the Religion of Hellenistic Judaism and Primitive Christianity*, Edimburgh 1903.

DEKKERS, E., *Clavis Patrum Latinorum. Qua in Corpus Christianorum edendum optimas quasque scriptorum recensiones a Tertulliano ad Bedam*, CChr.SL, Steenbrugis 1951, 1995[3].

DEL GRANDE, C., *Hybris. Colpa e castigo nell'espressione poetica e letteraria degli scrittori della Grecia antica da Omero a Cleante*, Napoli 1947.

DELITZSCH, F., *Biblical Commentary on the Book of Job*, II, CFTL 11, Edinburgh 1872.

–, *Die vier Evangelien ins Hebräische übersetzt von Franz Delitzsch (1877–1890–1902)*, THEv 4, Turnhout 1984.

DELLING, G., "τάσσω", *TDNT*, VIII, 27–48.

DE MARIA, W., *Deadly Disclosures. Whistleblowing and the Ethical Meltdown of Australia*, Adelaide 1999.

DENAUX, A., "Het lucaanse reisverhaal (Lc. 9,51–19,44)", *CBG* 14 (1968) 214–242; 15 (1969) 464–501.

–, "The Delineation of the Lukan Travel Narrative within the overall Structure of the Gospel of Luke", in C. FOCANT, ed., *The Synoptic Gospels. Source Criticism and the New Literary Criticism*, BEThL 110, Leuven 1993, 359–392.

–, ed., *Studies in the Gospel of Luke. Structure, Language and Theology*, TThS 4, Berlin 2010.

DENNERT, B.C., "A Survey of the Interpretative History of the Parable of the Dishonest Steward (Luke 16,1–9)", in P. WALTERS, ed., *From Judaism to Christianity. Tradition and Transition*, Fs. T.H. Tobin, NT.S 136, Leiden 2010, 145–152.

DERRETT, J.D.M., "Fresh Light on St. Luke 16". I. "The Parable of the Unjust Steward". II. "Dives and Lazarus and the Preceding Sayings", *NTS* 7.3–4 (1961) 198–219.364–380.

–, *Law in the New Testament*, London 1970.

–, *Jesus' Audience. The Social and Psychological Environment in which He Worked. Prolegomena to a Restatement of the Teaching of Jesus*, London 1973.

DESCOURTIEUX, P, ed., *Hilaire de Poitiers. Commentaires sur les Psaumes. Texte critique du CCL 61 (J. Doignon). Introduction, traduction, notes et index*, I–II, SC 515, 565, Paris 2008, 2014.

DE SILVA, D.A., "The Parable of the Prudent Steward and Its Lucan Context", *CrTR* 6.2 (1993) 255–268.

DETTWILER, A., "The Source Q and the Torah", in M. TAIT – P. OAKES, ed., *The Torah in the New Testament. Papers Delivered at the Manchester-Lausanne Seminar of June 2008*, LNTS 401, London / New York NY, 2009, 32–64.

DEVILLE, R. – GRELOT, P., "Royaume", *VTB*, cols. 1142–1150.

DE WAARD, J., "Translation Techniques Used by the Greek Translators on Amos", *Bib* 59.3 (1978) 339–350.

DEWICK, E.C., *Primitive Christian Eschatology. The Hulsean Prize Essay for 1908*, Cambridge 1912.

DIBELIUS, F., "Der Spruch vom gezwungenen Himmelreich", *ThStKr* 86 (1913) 285–288.

DIBELIUS, M., *Die urchristliche Überlieferung von Johannes dem Täufer*, FRLANT 15, Göttingen 1911.

DIELS, H. – KRANZ, W., ed., *Die Fragmente der Vorsokratiker. Griechisch und Deutsch*, I–III, Berlin 1952–1954.

DÍEZ MACHO, A., ed., *Neophyti 1. Targum Palestinense. Ms de la biblioteca Vaticana*, I–VI, CSIC.TE 7–13, Madrid / Barcelona 1968–1979.

DI LUCCIO, P., *The Quelle and the Targums. Righteousness in the Sermon on the Mount/ Plain*, AnBib 175, Rome 2009.

–, "La giustizia del Battista, i miracoli di Gesù e le proibizioni dei *targumim*. A proposito della storia della formazione di una tradizione della fonte Q (*Lc* 7,18–30)", in P. GAMBERINI, ed., *Giovanni Battista: un profeta e tre religioni*, OiChr 12, Trapani 2011, 25–48.

DINDORF, W., ed., *Athanasii Alexandrini praecepta ad Antiochum*, Lipsiae 1857.

DI STEFANO, E., *Ornamento e architettura. L'estetica funzionalistica di Louis H. Sullivan*, AestP 89, Palermo 2010.

DITTENBERGER, G., ed., *Sylloge. Inscriptionum Graecarum*, I–IV, Lipsiae 1883–1898, 1915–1924³.

DODD, C.H., *The Parables of the Kingdom*, London 1935, 1936³.

DOIGNON, J., ed., *Hilaire de Poitiers. Sur Matthieu*, I–II, SC 254, 258, Paris 1978, 1979.

DONAHUE, J.R., *The Gospel in Parable. Metaphor, Narrative, and Theology in the Synoptic Gospels*, Philadelphia PA, 1988.

DOROTHY, C.V., *The Books of Esther. Structure, Genre and Textual Integrity*, JSOT.S 187, Sheffield 1997.

DOWDEN, K., *European Paganism. The Realities of Cult from Antiquity to the Middle Ages*, New York NY, 2000.

DOYLE, R., "Matthew 11,12 – A Challenge to the Evangelist's Community", *Coll.* 18.1 (1985) 20–30.

DOYLE, R.E., "ΌΛΒΟΣ, ΚΌΡΟΣ, ΎΒΡΙΣ and ΆΤΗ from Hesiod to Aeschylus", *Traditio* 26 (1970) 293–303.

DRAZIN, I., ed., *Targum Onkelos to Numbers. An English Translation of the Text with Analysis and Commentary (Based on the A. Sperber and A. Berliner Editions)*, Denver CO, 1998.

DRURY, J., *Tradition and Design in Luke's Gospel. A Study in Early Christian Historiography*, London 1976.

DUNCAN, J. – DERRETT, J.D.M., *Law in the New Testament*, Eugene OR, 1970.

DUNN, J.D.G. – ROGERSON, J.W., ed., *Eerdmans Commentary on the Bible*, Grand Rapids MI / Cambridge 2003.

DU PLESSIS, I.J., "Reading Luke 12,35–48 as Part of the Travel Narrative", *Neotest.* 22.2 (1988) 217–234.

–, "Philanthropy or Sarcasm? Another Look at the Parable of the Dishonest Manager (Luke 16,1–13)", *Neotest.* 24.1 (1990) 1–20.

DUPONT, J., *Les Béatitudes. III. Les Évangélistes*, EtB, Paris 1973.

–, "L'exemple de l'intendant débrouillard (Lc 16,1–13)", *ASeign* 56 (1974) 67–78.

–, *Nouvelles études sur les Actes des Apôtres*, LeDiv 118, Paris 1984.

DURKIN, J., "A Cultural Reading of Luke 16,1–9", *JTAK* 31.2 (2007) 7–20.

EASTMAN, S., "The Evil Eye and the Curse of the Law. Galatians 3,1 Revisited", *JSNT* 83 (2001) 69–87.

EASTON, B.S., *The Gospel According to St. Luke. A Critical and Exegetical Commentary*, Edimburgh 1926.

ECKERMANN, J.C.R., *Erklärung aller dunkeln Stellen des Neuen Testamentes. Theils in einem zusammenhängenden Commentar über einzelne Bücher. Theils in einer treuen Ueber-setzung, mit eingeschalteten Erklärungen in einer treuen Ueberfetzung*, I–III, Kiel 1806–1808.

EDMONDS, J.M., ed., *Elegy and Iambus. Being the Remains of All the Greek Elegiac and Iambic Poets. From Callinus to Crates with the Anacreontea. Newly Edited and Translated*, I–II, LCL 258–259, London / Cambridge MA, 1931, repr. 1979–1982.

EDWARDS, R.A., *A Theology of Q. Eschatology, Prophecy, and Wisdom*, Philadelphia PA, 1976.

–, "Matthew's Use of Q in Chapter Eleven", in J. DELOBEL, ed., *Logia. Les paroles de Jésus – The Sayings of Jesus*, Fs. J. Coppens, BEThL 59, Leuven 1982, 257–275.

EGELKRAUT, H.L., *Jesus' Mission to Jerusalem. A Redaction Critical Study of the Travel Narrative in the Gospel of Luke, Luke 9,51–19,48*, EHS.T 80, Frankfurt 1976.

EHRMAN, B.D. – PLEŠE, Z., ed., *The Apocryphal Gospels. Texts and Translations*, New York NY, 2011.

EISENBERG, R.L., *What the Rabbis Said. 250 Topics from the Talmud*, Santa Barbara CA, 2010.

ELLIOTT, J.H., "The Evil Eye and the Sermon on the Mount. Contours of a Pervasive Belief in Social Scientific Perspective", *BInterp* 2.1 (1994) 51–84.

ELLIOTT, J.K., *A Synopsis of the Apocryphal Nativity and Infancy Narratives*, NTTS 34, Leiden / Boston MA, 2006.

ELLIS, E.E., *The Gospel of Luke*, NCBC, Grand Rapids MI / London, 1966, repr. 1983.

EMERY, P.-Y., ed., *Bernard de Clairvaux. Éloge de la nouvelle chevalerie. Vie de saint Malachie. Épitaphe, Hymne, Lettres. Introductions, traductions, notes et index*, SC 367, Paris 1990.

ENGLANDER, E.K., *Understanding Violence*, Mahwah NJ, 2003[2].

ERNST, J., *Das Evangelium nach Lukas*, RNT 3, Regensburg 1977; It. trans., *Il Vangelo secondo Luca*, I–II, Brescia 1985.

ÉTAIX, R., ed., *Gregorius Magnus. Homiliae in Evangelia*, CChr.SL 141, Turnholti 1999.

EUBANK, N., "Storing up Treasure with God in the Heavens. Celestial Investments in Matthew 6,1–21", *CBQ* 76 (2014) 77–92.

EVANS, C.A., "Luke and the Rewritten Bible. Aspects of Lukan Hagiography", in J.H. CHARLESWORTH – C.A. EVANS, ed., *The Pseudepigrapha and Early Biblical Interpretation*, JSPE.S 14, SSEJC 2, Sheffield 1993, 170–201.

–, *Mark 8,21–16,20*, WBC 34b, Nashville TN, 2001.

–, "The Pseudepigrapha and the Problem of Background 'Parallels' in the Study of the Acts of the Apostles", in G.S. OEGEMA – J.H. CHARLESWORTH, ed., *The Pseudepigrapha and Christian Origins. Essays from the Studiorum Novi Testamenti Societas*, JCTC 4, London / New York NY, 2008, 139–150.

EVANS, C.F., "The Central Section of St. Luke's Gospel", in D.E. NINEHAM, ed., *Studies in the Gospel*, Fs. R.H. Lightfoot, Oxford 1955, 37–53.

EVANS, E., ed., *Tertullian's Tract on the Prayer. The Latin Text with Critical Notes, an English Translation, an Introduction, and Explanatory Observations*, London 1953.

FANNING, B.M., *Verbal Aspect in New Testament Greek*, OTM, Oxford, 1990.

FARAONE, C.A. – RIFE, J.L., "A Greek Curse against a Thief from the Koutsongila Cemetery at Roman Kenchreai", *ZPE* 160 (2007) 141–157.

FARNES, A.T., "A New Interpretation of Luke's Prodigal Manager (Luke 16,1–8a)", *ASPub* [On-line edition: access 12.11.2015] 65 (2011) 1–24, http://scholarsarchive.byu.edu/studentpub/65.

FARRELL, H.K., "The Structure and Theology of Luke's Central Section", *TrinJ* 7 (1986) 33–54.

FATOUROS, G., ed., *Theodori Studitae Epistulae*, I–II, CFHB.B 31, Berlin / New York NY, 1992.

FAUSTI, S., *Una comunità legge il Vangelo di Luca*, CLPB, Bologna 1994.

FELDMAN, L.H., *Jew and Gentile in the Ancient World. Attitudes and Interactions from Alexander to Justinian*, Princeton NJ, 1993.

FEUILLET, A., "La parabole du mauvais riche et du pauvre Lazare (Lc 16,19–31) antithèse de la parabole de l'intendant astucieux (Lc 16,1–9)", *NRTh* 101 (1979) 212–223.

FIELD, F., *Origenis Hexaplorum. Quae supersunt, sive, Veterum interpretum Graecorum in totum Vetus Testamentum fragmenta. Post Flaminium Nobilium, Drusium, et Montefalconium, adhibita etiam versione syro-hexaplari, concinnavit, enmandavit, et multis partibus auxit*, I–II, Oxonii 1875, Hildesheim 1964.

FINKELSTEIN, L., ed., *Siphre ad Deuteronomium. H.S. Horovitzii schedis usus cum variis lectionibus et adnotationibus*, CTan 3.3, Berolini 1939, repr. New York NY, 1969.

FISHER, N.R.E., *Hybris. A Study in the Values of Honour and Shame in Ancient Greece*, Warminster 1992.

FITZMYER, J.A., "The Story of the Dishonest Manager (Luke 16,1–13)", *TS* 25.1 (1964) 23–42.

–, "The Matthean Divorce Texts and Some New Palestinian Evidence", *TS* 37.2 (1976) 197–226.

–, *The Gospel According to Luke. Introduction, Translation and Notes*, I–II, AncB 28, Garden City NY, 1981–1985; Span. trans., *El Evangelio segun Lucas. Traduccion y commentarios*, I–IV, Madrid 1987.

–, *The Biblical Commission's Document "The Interpretation of the Bible in the Church". Text and Commentary*, SubBi 18, Rome 1995.

–, *The Acts of the Apostles. A New Translation with Introduction and Commentary*, AncYB 31, New York NY, 1998, repr. 2008.

FLACELIERE, R., ed., *Dialogue sur l'amour (Eroticos). Texte et traduction avec une introduction et des notes*, AULy 21, Paris 1953.

FLEDDERMANN, H.T., *Q. A Reconstruction and Commentary*, BiTS 1, Leuven / Paris / Dudley MA, 2005.

FLETCHER, D.R., "The Riddle of the Unjust Steward. Is Irony the Key?", *JBL* 82.1 (1963) 15–30.

FLUSSER, D., *Jesus in Selbstzeugnissen und Bilddokumenten*, RoMo, Hamburg 1968; Eng. trans., FLUSSER, D. – NOTLEY, R.S., ed., *The Sage from Galilee. Rediscovering Jesus' Genius*, Cambridge / Grand Rapids MI, 2007[4].

–, "'The Book of Mysteries' and a Synagogal Prayer", in *Knesset Israel. Literature and Life in the Synagogue*, Fs. E. Fleischer, Jerusalem 1994.

FOCANT, C., "Tromper le Mamon d'iniquité (Lc 16,1–13)", in F. REFOULE, ed., *À cause de l'Évangile. Ètudes sur les Synoptiques et les Actes*, Fs. J. Dupont, LeDiv 123, Paris 1985, 547–569.

FOLEY, M., "*Peitho* and *Bia*. The Force of Language", *Sympl.* 20.1–2 (2012) 173–181.

FORESTELL, J.T., *Targumic Traditions and the New Testament. An Annotated Bibliography with a New Testament Index*, SBL.AS 4, Chico CA, 1979.

FORTIN, J.R., "Saint Anselm on the Kingdom of Heaven: A Model of Right Order", *SAJ* 6.1 (2008) 1–10.

FORTUNA, D., *Il Figlio dell'ascolto. L'autocomprensione del Gesù storico alla luce dello Shema' Yisra'el*, Cinesello Balsamo MI, 2012.

FOSCA, N., "Il canto XX del *Paradiso*. Giustizia e predestinazione", *SDan* 79 (2014) 209–266.

FOSTER, P., "Matthew's Use of 'Jewish' Traditions from Q", in M. TIWALD, ed., *Kein Jota wird vergehen. Das Gesetzesverständnis der Logienquelle vor dem Hintergrund frühjüdischer Theologie*, BWANT 200, Stuttgart 2013, 179–201.

FOSTER, R., "Why on Earth Use 'Kingdom of Heaven'? Matthew's Terminology Revisited", *NTS* 48.4 (2002) 487–499.

FOURGOUS, D., "L'invention des armes en Grèce ancienne", *ASNP* 3.6 (1976) 1123–1164.

FOX, M.V., "Notarikon", *EJ*, XV, 314–315.

FRANKL, V.E., *Man's Search for Meaning. Young Readers Edition*, Boston MA, 1959, repr. 2017.

–, *The Unheard Cry for Meaning. Psychotherapy and Humanism*, New York NY, 1978.

FRANKLIN, E., *Christ the Lord. A Study in the Purpose and Theology of Luke-Acts*, London 1975.

FRIDRICHSEN, A., "Neutestamentliche Wortforschung. Zu Matt 11,11–15", *ThZ* 2 (1946) 470–471.

FRIEDMANN, M., ed., *Pesikta Rabbati. Midrasch für den Fest-Cyclus und die ausgezeichneten Sabbathe. Kritisch bearbeitet, commentirt, durch neue handschriftliche Haggadas vermehrt, mit Bibel- und Personen- Indices*, Wien 1880.

FRÖHLICH, W., ed., *The Letters of Saint Anselm of Canterbury*, I. *Letters 1–147*, CistSS 96, Kalamazoo MI, 1990.

FUCHS, É., "L'Évangile et l'argent. La parabole de l'intendant intelligent", *BCPE* 30.2 (1978) 3–14 = in ID., *L'exigence et le don. Un parcours éthique (1978–1997)*, ChEth 35, Genève 2000, 189–200.

–, *L'éthique chrétienne. Du Nouveau Testament aux défis contemporains*, ChEth 40, Genève 2003.

FUNK, R.W., "Structure in the Narrative Parables of Jesus", *Semeia* 2 (1974) 51–73.

GÄCHTER, P., "The Parable of the Dishonest Steward after Oriental Conceptions", *CBQ* 12.2 (1950) 121–131.

GAETAN, V., "'Industry of Death': Pope Francis on Arms Dealers and Causes of World War III", *NCR* [On-line edition: access 06.05.2017], February 9, 2016, http://www.nc register.com/daily-news/industry-of-death-pope-francis-on-arms-dealers-and-causes-of-world-war-iii.

GALLAY, P., ed., *Grégoire de Nazianze. Lettres théologiques. Introduction, texte critique, traduction et notes*, SC 208, Paris 1974.

GARCIA MARTINEZ, F. – TIGCHELAAR, E.J.C., ed., *The Dead Sea Scrolls. Study Edition (Transcriptions)*, Leiden / Boston / Köln, 1997–1998.

GARCÍA VALDÉS, M., ed., *De Iside et Osiride. Introducción, texto crítico, traducción y commentario*, TeCom 13, Pisa 1995.

GARGANO, G.I., *Il sapore dei Padri della Chiesa nell'esegesi biblica. Introduzione a una lettura sapienziale della Scrittura*, Cinesello Balsamo MI, 2009.

GEFFCKEN, J., ed., *Die Oracula Sibyllina*, GCS 8, Leipzig 1902.

GEORGE, A., "Tradition et rédaction chez Luc. La construction du troisième Évangile", *EThL* 43.1 (1967) 100–129.

GERHARDSSON, B., *The Good Samaritan – The Good Shepherd?*, CoNT 16, Lund 1958.

–, "The Parable of the Sower and Its Interpretation", *NTS* 14 (1967–1968) 165–193.

–, "Jésus livré et abandonné d'après la passion selon S. Matthieu", *RB* 76 (1969) 206–227.

–, "Du judéochristianisme à Jésus par le Shema", *RSR* 60 (1972) 23–36.

–, "The Shema in Early Christianity", in F. VAN SEGBROEK – *al.*, ed., *The Four Gospels 1992*, Fs. F. Neirynck, Leuven 1992, 275–293.

–, *The Shema in the New Testament. Deut 6,4–5 in Significant Passages*, Lund 1996.

–, *The Testing of God's Son (Matt 4,1–11 & Par.). An Analysis of an Early Christian Midrash*, CB.NT 2.1, Lund 1996.

GERNET, L. – BIZOS, M., ed., *Lysias. Discours. Texte établi et traduit*, I–II, CUFr, Paris 1926–1943.

GFRÖRER, A.F., *Geschichte des Urchristenthums*, I–III, Stuttgart 1838, 91–98.

GIBSON, J.C.L., *Genesis*, I–II, DSBS, Edinburgh / Louisville KY, 1981–1982.

GIL, M., "Land Ownership in Palestine under Roman Rule", *RIDA* 17 (1970) 11–53.

GILLMAN, J., *Possessions and the Life of Faith. A Reading of Luke-Acts*, ZS.NT, Collegeville MN, 1991.

GIURISATO, G., "Come Luca struttura il viaggio e le altre parti del suo Vangelo. Una composizione paradigmatica: 12,13–34.35–48; 16,1–18.19–31", *RivBib* 46 (1998) 419–484.

GNILKA, J., *Das Matthäusevangelium. Kommentar und Einleitungsfragen*, I–II, HThK 1, Freiburg / Basel / Wien 1986–1988.

GODET, F., *A Commentary on the Gospel of St. Luke*, I–II, CFTL 45–46, Edinburgh 1875, 1893[5].

GOGUEL, M., *Au seuil de l'Évangile. Jean-Baptiste*, BH, Paris 1928.

GOOD, R.S., "Jesus, Protagonist of the Old, in Luke 5,33–39", *NovT* 25.1 (1983) 19–36.

GOODACRE, M.S., "A Monopoly on Marcan Priority? Fallacies at the Heart of Q", in *Society of Biblical Literature. Seminar Papers. Annual Meeting 2000*, SBL.SPS 39, Atlanta GA, 2000, 583–622.

GOODRICH, J.K., "Voluntary Debt Remission and the Parable of the Unjust Steward (Luke 16,1–13)", *JBL* 131.3 (2012) 547–566.

GORDON, G.J., *World Biblical Commentary*, II, Dallas TX, 1994.

GOULDER, M.D., "The Chiastic Structure of the Lucan Journey", in F.L. CROSS, ed., *Studia Evangelica*, II, TU 87, Berlin 1964, 195–202.

–, "Is Q a Juggernaut?", *JBL* 115.4 (1996) 667–681.

GOURGUES, M., "Jésus et la violence", *ScEs* 31.2 (1979) 125–146.

–, *Les Paraboles de Luc. D'amont en aval*, ScBi.E 3, Paris / Montréal QC, 1997.

GOWLER, D.B., *Host, Guest, Enemy, and Friend. Portraits of the Pharisees in Luke and Acts*, ESEC 2, New York NY, 1991.

–, "'At His Gate Lay a Poor Man': A Dialogic Reading of Luke 16,19–31", *PRSt* 32.3 (2005) 249–265.

GRADL, H.-G., "Von den Kosten des Reichtums. Die Beispielerzählung vom reichen Mann und armen Lazarus (Lk 16,19–31) textpragmatisch gelesen", *MThZ* 56 (2005) 305–317.

GRANT, F.C., "Where Form Criticism and Textual Criticism Overlap", *JBL* 59.1 (1940) 11–21.

–, *The Gospels. Their Origin and Growth,* New York NY, 1957.

GRANT, J. – O'NEILL, F.W.S., "The Unjust Steward", *ET* 16.5 (1905) 239–240.

GRASSO, S., *Luca. Traduzione e commento*, ComBib, Roma 1999.

GRAY, G.B., *A Critical and Exegetical Commentary on Numbers*, ICC, New York NY, 1903, repr. 1951.

GRAY, K., *Elements of Land Law*, London 1987, 1999².

GREEN, J.B., *The Gospel of Luke*, NICNT, Grand Rapids MI, 1997.

GREENE, M.D., "The Parable of the Unjust Steward as Question and Challenge", *ET* 112.3 (2000) 83–87.

GRENFELL, B.P. – al., ed., *The Tebtunis Papyri*, I–IV, UCP.GRA 1–4, London / New York NY, 1902–1976.

–, ed., *The Oxyrhynchos Papyri*, I–LXXX, London, 1898–2014.

GRILLI, M., *L'impotenza che salva. Il mistero della croce in Mc 8,27–10,52. Lettura in chiave comunicativa*, StBi 58, Frascati RM, 2009.

–, *Matteo, Marco, Luca e gli Atti degli Apostoli*, Frascati RM, 2015.

GROSSFELD, B., ed., *The Targum Onqelos to Deuteronomy. Translated, with Apparatus and Notes*, ArBib 9, Edinburgh 1988.

–, *The Two Targums of Esther. Translated, with Apparatus and Notes*, ArBib 18, Edinburgh 1991.

GRUNDMANN, W., *Das Evanglium nach Lukas*, ThHK 3, Berlin 1934, 1961².

GUCCIONE, A., "Il cielo è dei violenti? Religione e violenza. La pericope di Matt 11,12", *Stud.* 4 (2008) 489–504.

GUELICH, R.A., *The Sermon on the Mount. A Foundation for Understanding*, Waco TX, 1982.

GUÉRAUD, O., ed., *ΕΝΤΕΥΞΕΙΣ: Requêtes et plaintes adressées au Roi d'Égypte au IIIe siècle avant J.-C.*, I–II, PSREP.T 1, Le Caire 1931–1932.

GULICK, C.B., ed., *Athenaeus. The Deipnosophists*, I–VII, LCL, London / Cambridge MA, 1967–1980.

GUY, J.-C., ed., *Les apophtegmes des pères. Collection systématique*, I–III, SC 387, 474, 498, Paris 1993, 2003, 2005.

GWATKIN, H.M., *Selections from Early Writers. Illustrative of Church History to the Time of Constatine*, London 1893.

HADJADJ, F., *Et les violents s'en emparent. Coups de grâce*, Saint-Victor-de-Morestel 1999.

HAENCHEN, E., *The Acts of the Apostles. A Commentary*, Philadelphia PA, 1971; Ger. orig., *Die Apostelgeschichte*, KEK 3.5, Göttingen 1965¹⁴.

HÄFNER, G., "Gewalt gegen die Basileia? Zum Problem der Auslegung des 'Stürmerspruches' Mt 11,12", *ZNW* 83.1–2 (1992) 21–51.

HAHN, J., "Violence", BNP, XV, 439–447.

HALL, C.A., *Reading Scripture with the Church Fathers*, Downers Grove IL, 1998.

HALL, J.B., ed., *Ioannis Saresberiensis. Metalogicon*, CChr.CM 98, Turnholti 1991.

HARD, R., *The Routledge Handbook of Greek Mythology. Based on H.J. Rose's Handbook of Greek Mythology*, London / New York NY, 2004.

HARDER, G., "σπουδάζω, σπουδή, σπουδαῖος", *TDNT*, VII, 559–568.

HARMON, A.M., ed., *Lucian with an English Translation*, I–VIII, LCL, London / Cambridge MA, 1913–1962, repr. 1968–1979.

VON HARNACK, A., *Das Wesen des Christentums. Sechzehn Vorlesungen vor Studierenden aller Facultäten im Wintersemester 1899/1900 an der Universität Berlin gehalten*, Leipzig 1900, 1908²; Eng. trans., *What is Christianity? Lectures Delivered in the University of Berlin during the Winter-Term 1889/1990*, New York NY / London 1901, 1908².

–, "Zwei Worte Jesu. Matth. 6,13 = Luk. 11,4; Matth. 11,12f. = Luk. 16,16", *SPAW* (1907) 942–957.

–, *The Sayings of Jesus. The Second Source of St. Matthew and St. Luke*, CThL 23, London 1908.

–, *Marcion. Das Evangelium vom Fremden Gott. Eine Monographie zur Geschichte der Grundlegung der katholischen Kirche*, TU 45, Leipzig 1921, 1924².

HARRIS, H.A., "Where Love and Reason Fail: Fundamentalist and Liberal Intolerance Examined with Reference to Peter Cameron's Heresy Trial", *StMR* 164 (1996) 2–9.

HARRIS, R.L., "חָמַס", *TWOT*, I, 297.

HATCH, E. – REDPATH, H.A., *A Concordance to the Septuagint and the Other Greek Versions of the Old Testament (Including the Apocryphal Books)*, I–III, Oxford 1897–1906, repr. Graz 1954.

HATCHER, K.M., "In Gold We Trust. The Parable of the Rich Man and Lazarus (Luke 16,19–31)", *RExp* 109.2 (2012) 277–283.

HAUCK, F., *Das Evangelium des Lukas. Synoptiker II*, ThHK.TP 3, Leipzig 1934.

–, "μαμωνᾶς", *TDNT*, IV, 388–390.

HAYS, C.M., *Luke's Wealth Ethics. A Study in Their Coherence and Character*, WUNT 275, Tübingen 2010.

HEIKEL, I.A., ed., *Eusebius Werke. I. Über das Leben Constantins. Constantins Rede an die heilige Versammlung. Tricennatsrede an Constantin*, GCS 7, Leipzig 1902.

HEIL, C., *Lukas und Q. Studien zur lukanischen Redaktion des Spruch-evangeliums Q*, BZNW 111, Berlin / New York NY, 2003.

HEINIMANN, F., *Nomos und Physis. Herkunft und Bedeutung einer Antithese im griechischen Denken des 5. Jahrhunderts*, Darmstadt 1945, repr. 1965.

HELDT, P., "New Testament Apocrypha", in D.E. AUNE, ed., *The Blackwell Companion to the New Testament*, BCRe, Malden MA, 2010, 652–675.

HENGEL, M., *Die Zeloten. Untersuchungen zur jüdischen Freiheitsbewegung in der Zeit von Herodes I. bis 70 n. Chr.*, AGJU 1, Leiden 1961, 1976².

–, *Gewalt und Gewaltlosigkeit. Zur "politischen Theologie" in neutestamentlicher Zeit*, CwH 118, Stuttgart 1971.

HENNECKE, E. – SCHNEEMELCHER, W., ed., *New Testament Apocrypha*, I–II, Philadelphia PA, 1963–1964; Ger. orig., *Neutestamentliche Apocryphen*, Tübingen 1959–1964.

VAN HENTEN, J.W. – AVEMARIE, F., ed., *Martyrdom and Noble Death. Selected Texts from Graeco-Roman, Jewish and Christian Antiquity*, London / New York NY, 2002.

HESSE, F.H., *Das Muratori'sche Fragment. Neu untersucht und erklärt*, Giefsen 1873.

HICKLING, C.J.A., "A Tract on Jesus and the Pharisees. A Conjecture on the Redaction of Luke 15 and 16", *HeyJ* 16.3 (1975) 253–265.

HIERS, R.H., "Friends by Unrighteous Mammon. The Eschatological Proletariat (Luke 16,9)", *JAAR* 38.1 (1970) 30–36.

–, *The Kingdom of God in the Synoptic Tradition*, UFHM 33, Gainesville FL, 1970.

HILBERG, I., ed., *Sancti Eusebii Hieronymi. Epistulae*, I–IV, CSEL 54, 55, 56.1–2, Vindobonae 1996.

HILGENFELD, A., *Die Evangelien nach ihrer Entstehung und geschichtlichen Bedeutung*, Leipzig 1854.

HILL, C. – FORTI, P., *Cave Minerals of the World*, Huntsville AL, 1976, 1997².

HILL, D., *The Gospel of Matthew*, NCB, London 1972.

HIRSCH, E., *Die Worlagen des Lukas und das Sondergut des Mattäus*, FrE 2, Tübingen 1941.

HIRSCHBERG, H.H., "Simon Bariona and the Ebionites", *JBL* 61.3 (1942) 171–191.

HIRZEL, R., *Themis, Dike und Verwandtes. Ein Beitrag zur Geschichte der Rechtsidee bei den Griechen*, Leipzig 1907.

HOBART, W.K., *The Medical Language of St. Luke. A Proof from Internal Evidence that "The Gospel According to St. Luke" and "The Acts of the Apostles" Were Written by the Same Person, and that the Writer was a Medical Man*, DUP.S, Dublin 1882.

HOBBS, T.R., *2 Kings*, WBC 13, Dallas TX, 1985.

HOCK, R.F., "Lazarus and Micyllus. Greco-Roman backgrounds to Luke 16,19–31", *JBL* 106.3 (1987) 447–463.

HOFFMANN, D.Z., ed., *Midrasch Tannaïm zum Deuteronomium. Aus der in der Königlichen Bibliothek zu Berlin befindlichen Handschrift des "Midrasch haggadol" gesammelt und mit Anmerkungen versehen nebst mehreren Beilagen*, II, Berlin 1909.

HOFFMANN, P., *Studien zur Theologie der Logienquelle*, NTA.NF 8, Münster 1972, 1982³.

HOLDEN, H.A., ed., *Plutarch's Life of Themistocles. With Introduction, Critical and Explanatory Notes, Indices and Map*, ClS, London / New York NY, 1881, 1892³.

HOLLADAY, W.L., *Jeremiah 1. A Commentary on the Book of the Prophet Jeremiah*, I, Hermeneia, Philadelphia PA, 1986.

HOLLANDER, R. & J., ed., *Dante Alighieri. Paradiso. A Verse Translation, Introduction and Notes*, New York NY, 2007, repr. 2008.

HOLTZMANN, H.J., *Die Synoptiker*, HC 1, Tübigen / Leipzig 1889, 1901³.

HOOLEY, B.A. – MASON, A.J., "Some Thoughts on the Parable of the Unjust Steward (Luke 16,1–9)", *AusBR* 6 (1958) 47–59.

HORSLEY, R.A., "Ethics and Exegesis: 'Love Your Enemies' and the Doctrine of Non-Violence", *JAAR* 54.1 (1986) 3–31.

VAN DER HORST, P.W., ed., *The Sentences of Pseudo-Phocylides. With Introduction and Commentary*, SVTP 4, Leiden 1978.

HORT, F.J.A., *Judaistic Christianity*, Cambridge 1894.

HOWKING, S., ed., *On the Shoulders of Giants. The Great Works of Physics and Astronomy*, London 2002.

HOYT, T., Jr., *The Poor in Luke-Acts*, diss., Durham NC, 1974.

HROBON, B., *Ethical Dimension of Cult in the Book of Isaiah*, BZAW 418, Berlin / New York NY, 2010.

HÜBNER, H., *Das Gesetz in der synoptischen Tradition. Studien zur These einer progressiven Qumranisierung und Judaisierung innerhalb der synoptischen Tradition*, Göttingen 1973, 1986².

HUDE, K., ed., *Xenophon. Memorabilia*, BSGRT, Stutgardiae 1985.

HUFF, L.C., "Artificial Helictites and Gypsum Flowers", *JGeo* 48.6 (1940) 641–659.

HULTGREN, A.J., *Jesus and His Adversaries. The Form and Function of the Conflict Stories in the Synoptic Tradition*, Minneapolis MN, 1979.

HULTGREN, S.J., "The Apostolic Church's Influence on the Order of Sayings in the Double Tradition. Part II, Luke's Travel Narrative", *ZNW* 100.2 (2009) 199–222.

HUMMEL, H.D., *The Word Becoming Flesh. An Introduction to the Origin, Purpose and Meaning of the Old Testament*, St. Luis MO, 1979.

HUNT, A.S. – EDGAR, C.C. – PAGE, D.L., ed., *Select Papyri with an English Translation*, I–III, LCL, London / Cambridge MA, 1932–1950.

HUNTER, A.M., "Interpreting the Parables. II, The Gospel in Parables", *Interp.* 14.2 (1960) 167–185.

HUNTER BLAIR, D.O., ed., *The Rule of Saint Benedict with an English Translation and Explanatory Notes*, London / Edinburgh, 1888, 1907[2].

IHSSEN, B.L., *They Who Give from Evil. The Response of the Eastern Church to Money-lending in the Early Christian Era*, Cambridge 2012, repr. 2013.

IMMISCH, O., ed., *Aristotelis Politica*, BSGRT, Lipsiae 1909.

IRELAND, D.J., "A History of Recent Interpretation of the Parable of the Unjust Steward (Luke 16,1–13)", *WThJ* 51 (1989) 293–318.

–, *Stewardship and the Kingdom of God. An Historical, Exegetical, and Contextual Study of the Parable of the Unjust Steward in Luke 16,1–13*, NT.S 70, Leiden / Köln / New York NY, 1992.

–, *Ibid.* [review of C.L. BLOMBERG, *WThJ* 55.2 (1993) 351–352].

–, *Ibid.* [review of W.S. KURZ, *CBQ* 56.1 (1994) 140–141].

–, *Ibid.* [review of P.-É. LANGEVIN, *ScEs* 46.1 (1994) 111].

ISAKSSON, A., *Marriage and Ministry in the New Temple*, ASNU 24, Lund 1965.

JACKSON, F.J.F. – LAKE, K., ed., *The Beginnings of Christianity. The Acts of the Apostles*, I–V, London 1920–1933.

JAEGER, W., ed., *Aristotelis, Metaphysica. Recognovit brevique adnotatione critica instruxit*, SCBO, Oxonii 1957.

JAEGER, W. – *al.*, ed., *Gregorii Nysseni Opera Ascetica*, in W. JAEGER, ed., *Gregorii Nysseni Opera*, VIII.1, ISCH, Leiden 1952.

JAMES, M.R., *Apocrypha Anecdota. A Collection of Thirteen Apocryphal Books and Fragments*, TaS 2.3, Cambridge 1893.

JANSSEN, R.E., "Pickle Helictites", *ScMon* 58.5 (1944) 345–347.

JANZEN, J.G., *Abraham and All the Families of the Earth. A Commentary on the Book of Genesis 12–50*, ITC, Edinburgh / Grand Rapids MI, 1993.

JAUBERT, A., ed., *Clément de Rome. Épître aux Corinthiens*, SC 167, Paris 1971, repr. 2000.

JELLAMO, A., *Il cammino di Dike. L'idea di giustizia da Omero a Eschilo*, Roma 2005.

–, "Alle radici del principio *suumcuique tribuere*", *Hypn.* 23 (2009) 245–257.

JEREMIAS, J., *The Parables of Jesus*, NTLi, London 1954, New York NY, 1963; Ger. orig., *Die Gleichnisse Jesu*, AThANT 11, Zürich 1947, Göttingen 1962[6].

–, *The Prayers of Jesus*, SBT 6, London 1967.

JERVELL, J.S., "The Law in Luke-Acts", *HThR* 64 (1971) 21–36.

–, *Luke and the People of God. A New Look at Luke-Acts*, Minneapolis MN, 1972, repr. Eugene OR, 2002.

JOHNSON, L.T., *The Literary Function of Possessions in Luke-Acts*, SBL.DS 39, Missoula MT, 1977.

JOLY, R., *Hermas. Le Pasteur. Introduction, texte critique, traductione et notes*, SC 53, Paris 1958, 1968[2].

JONES, W.H.S., ed., *Pausanias. Description of Greece. With and English Translation*, I–IV, LCL, London / Cambridge MA, 1918–1935, repr. 1961–1964.

DE JONGE, M. – *al.*, ed., *The Testaments of the Tewlve Patriarchs. A Critical Edition of the Greek Text*, PVTG 1, Leiden 1978.

JÖRDENS, A., "Griechische Briefe aus Ägypten", *TUAT.NF* 3 (2006) 399–420.

JOSEPH, S.J., "'For Heaven and Earth to Pass Away?'. Reexamining Q 16,16–18, Eschatology, and the Law", *ZNW* 105.2 (2014) 169–188.

JOUGUET, P., ed., *Papyrus de Théadelphie*, Paris 1911.

JOUGUET, P. – *al.*, ed., *Papyrus grecs*, I–IV, IPUL, Paris 1907–1928.

JOÜON, P., "Imparfaits de 'continuation' dans la Lettre d'Aristée et dans les Evangiles", *RSR* 28 (1938) 93–96.

JÜLICHER, A., *Die Gleichnisreden Jesu*, I–II, Tübingen 1898, 1910².

JUNG, C.G. – KERÉNYI, K., ed., *Essays on a Science of Mythology. The Myths of the Divine Child and the Divine Maiden*, New York NY, 1949, repr. 1963; Ger. orig., *Einführung in das Wesen der Mythologie. Das göttliche Kind. Das göttliche Mädchen*, Zürich 1940, 1951⁴.

JÜNGEL, E., *Paulus und Jesus. Eine Untersuchung zur Präzisierung der Frage nach dem Ursprung der Christologie*, HUTh 2, Tübingen 1962, 1964²; It. trans., *Paolo e Gesù. Alle origini della cristologia*, BT 13, Brescia 1978.

JUST, A.A., Jr., *Luke. A Theological Exposition of Sacred Scripture*, I–II, ConCom, St. Louis MO, 1996–1997.

KAISER, W.C., "מָאֹר", *TWOT*, I, 487.

–, Jr., *Mission in the Old Testament. Israel as a Light to the Nations*, Grand Rapids MI, 2000.

KANT, I., *Religion Within the Boundary of Pure Reason*, Edinburgh 1838; Ger. orig., *Religion innerhalb der Grenzen der blossen Vernunft*, Königsberg 1793.

KARLSTADT, A., *Berichtung dyesser red: Das reich gotis leydet gewaldt, und die gewaldtige nhemen oder rauben das selbig*, Wittemberg 1521.

KARRIS, R.J., "Poor and Rich: The Lukan *Sitz im Leben*", in C.H. TALBERT, ed., *Perspectives on Luke-Acts*, Danville VA, 1978, 112–125.

KÄSEMANN, E., "Das Problem des historichen Jesus", *ZThK* 51 (1954) 125–153 = *Exegetische Versuche und Besinnungen*, I, Göttingen 1960, 187–214; Eng. trans., "The Problem of the Historical Jesus", in *Essays on New Testament Themes*, SBT 41, London 1964, 15–47.

KEEL, O., *The Symbolism of the Biblical World. Ancient Near Eastern Iconography and the Book of Psalms*, New York NY, 1978, repr. 1997; Ger. orig., *Die Welt der altorientalischen Bildsymbolik und das Alte Testament. Am Beispiel der Psalmen*, Köln 1972.

KEENER, C.S., *The Gospel of Matthew. A Socio-Rhetorical Commentary*, Cambridge / Grand Rapids MI, 2009.

KEERANKERI, G., *The Love Commandment in Mark. An Exegetico-Theological Study of Mark 12,28–34*, AnBib 150, Rome 2003.

KEHINDE, S.F., "'The Violent Kingdom' in Matthew 11,12 and Its Implications for Contemporary Christians", *OJTh* 12 (2007) 99–106.

KEIL, C.F. – DELITZSCH, F., *Commentary on the Old Testament*, I–X, Grand Rapids MI, 1866–1891, repr. 1980.

KENNEDY, G.A., *Greek Rhetoric under Christian Emperors*, HRh 3, Princeton NJ, 1983.

–, *Invention and Method. Two Rhetorical Treatises from the Hermogenic Corpus*, SBL.W 15, Atlanta GA, 2005.

KENYON, F.G. – BELL, H.I., ed., *Greek Papyri in the British Museum. Catalogue, with Texts*, I–V, London 1893–1917, Milan 1973.

KILGALLEN, J.J., "Luke 15 and 16. A Connection", *Bib.* 73 (1992) 369–376.

–, "The Purpose of Luke's Divorce Text (16,18)", *Bib.* 76 (1995) 229–238.

–, *Twenty Parables of Jesus in the Gospel of Luke*, SubBi 32, Roma 2008.

KIMBALL, C.A., *Jesus' Exposition of the Old Testament in Luke's Gospel*, JSNT.S 94, Sheffield 1994.

KIRK, G.S., ed., *Heraclitus. The Cosmic Fragments*, New York NY, 1954, repr. 2010.

KISHIK, D., "Life and Violence", *Tel.* 150 (2010) 143–149.

–, *The Power of Life. Agamben and the Coming Politics (To Imagine a Form of Life, II)*, Stanford CA, 2012.

KITZ, A.M., "Undivided Inheritance and Lot Casting in the Book of Joshua", *JBL* 119.4 (2000) 601–618.

KLEIN, H., *Das Lukasevangelium*, KEK 1.3, Göttingen 2006.

KLIJN, A.F.J., *Jewish-Christian Gospel Traditions*, SVigChr 17, Leiden 1992.

KLINGHARDT, M., *Gesetz und Volk Gottes. Das lukanische Verständnis des Gesetzes nach Herkunft, Funktion und seinem Ort in der Geschichte des Urchristentums*, WUNT 32, Tübingen 1988.

–, *Das älteste Evangelium und die Entstehung der kanonischen Evangelien*, I–II, TANZ 60.1–2, Tübingen 2015.

KLINGSPORN, G.W., *The Law in the Gospel of Luke*, diss., Ann Arbor MI, 1985.

KLOPPENBORG, J.S., "The Dishonoured Master (Luke 16,1–8a)", *Bib.* 70.4 (1989) 474–495.

–, "*Nomos* and *Ethos* in Q", in H.D. BETZ – al., ed., *Gospel Origins and Christian Beginnings*, Fs. J.M. Robinson, Sonoma 1990, 35–48.

–, *Q, the Earliest Gospel. An Introduction to the Original Stories and Sayings of Jesus*, Louisville KY, 2008.

KLOSTERMANN, E., *Das Lukasevangelium*, HNT 5, Tübingen 1919, 1975[3].

KNIGHTS, C.H., "The Rechabites Revisited. The History of the Rechabites Twenty-Five Years On", *JSPE* 23.4 (2014) 307–320.

KNOX, W.L., *The Sources of the Synoptic Gospels*, I–II, Cambridge 1953–1957.

KOESTER, H., "Apocryphal and Canonical Gospels", *HThR* 73.1–2 (1980) 105–130.

VAN KOETSVELD, C.E., *Die Gleichnisse des Evangeliums als Hausbuch für die christliche Familie*, Leipzig 1904.

KÖGEL, J., "Zum Gleichnis vom ungerechten Haushälter, Bemerkungen zu Luk. 16,1–13", *BFCT* 18 (1914) 581–612.

KOSCH, D., *Die Gottesherrschaft im Zeichen des Widerspruchs: traditions und redaktionsgeschichtliche Untersuchung von Lk 16,16 // Mt 11,12f bei Jesus, Q und Lukas*, EHS.T 257, Bern / Frankfurt / New York NY, 1985.

–, *Die eschatologische Tora des Menschensohnes. Untersuchungen zur Rezeption der Stellung Jesu zur Tora in Q*, NTOA 12, Freiburg / Göttingen 1989.

KOSMALA, H., "The Parable of the Unjust Steward in the Light of Qumran", *ASTI* 3 (1964) 114–121.

KRÄMER, M., *Das Rätsel der Parabel vom ungerechten Verwalter. Lk 16,1–13. Auslegungsgeschichte – Umfang – Sinn. Eine Diskussion der Probleme und Lösungsvorschläge der Verwalterparabel von den Vätern bis heute*, Zürich 1972.

KREMER, J., "Der arme Lazarus. Lazarus, der Freund Jesu. Beobachtungen zur Beziehung zwischen Lk 16,19–31 und Joh 11,1–46", in F. REFOULÉ, ed., *À cause de l'Évangile. Études sur les Synoptiques et les Actes*, Fs. J. Dupont, LeDiv 123, Paris 1985, 571–584.

KRETZER, A., *Die Herrschaft der Himmel und die Söhne des Reiches. Eine redaktionsgeschichtliche Untersuchung zum Basileiabegriff und Basileiaverständnis im Matthäusevangelium*, SBM 10, Würzburg 1971.

KRUG, E.G. – al., ed., *World Report on Violence and Health*, WHO, Geneva 2002.

KRÜGER, R., "Lucas 16,1–13. La opción decisiva: por la ley de Dios o por la ley del capital", *CuTe(BA)* 15.1–2 (1996) 97–112.

KUHN, G., *Das muratorische Fragment. Über die Bücher des neuen Testaments. Mit Einleitung und Erklärung*, Zürich 1892.

KÜMMEL, W.G., "Jesus und der jüdische Traditionsgedanke", *ZNW* 33.2 (1934) 105–130.

–, "'Das Gesetz und die Propheten gehen bis Johannes' – Lukas 16,16 im Zusammenhang der heilsgeschichtlichen Theologie der Lukasschriften", in O. BOECHER – K. HAAKER, ed., *Verborum Veritas*, Fs. G. Stählin, Wuppertal 1970, 89–102 = in G. BRAUMANN, ed., *Das Lukas-Evangelium*, Darmstadt 1974, 398–415.

KURZ, W.S., "Narrative Approaches to Luke-Acts", *Bib.* 68.2 (1987) 195–220.

–, *Reading Luke-Acts. Dynamics of Biblical Narrative*, Westminster / Louisville KY, 1993.

KUTSCH, E., "הוֹן", *TDOT*, III, 364–368.

KVALBEIN, H., "Jesus and the Poor. Two Texts and a Tentative Conclusion", *Themelios* 12.3 (1987) 80–87.

KWON, Y.-G., "Forgiveness, Faith, and the Lordship of Jesus. A Contextual Reading of Luke 17,1–10", *KENTS* 11.3 (2012) 613–642 = in S.B CHOI – J.K. HWANG – M.J. LEE, ed., *Fire in My Soul. Essays on Pauline Soteriology and the Gospels*, Fs. S. Kim, Eugene OR, 2014, 184–213.

KYRYCHENKO, A., *The Roman Army and the Expansion of the Gospel. The Role of the Centurion in Luke-Acts*, BZNW 203, Berlin / Boston MA, 2014.

LACHS, S.T., *A Rabbinic Commentary on the New Testament. The Gospels of Matthew, Mark, and Luke*, Hoboken NJ, 1987.

DE LACY, P.H. – *al.*, ed., *Plutarch's Moralia*, I–XV, LCL, London / Cambridge MA, 1962–2004.

LADD, G.E., *The Presence of the Future. The Eschatology in Biblical Realism*, London 1974, repr. New York NY, 2002.

LAGRANGE, J.-M., *Évangile selon Saint Luc*, EtB, Paris 1921, 1948[8].

–, *Évangile selon Saint Matthieu*, EtB, Paris 1923.

LAISTNER, M.L.W., *Expositio Actuum Apostolorum et retractatio. Bedae Venerabilis*, CChr.SL 121, Turnholti 1983.

LAKE, K., *The Apostolic Fathers with an English Translation*, I–II, LCL, London / Cambridge MA, 1959.

LAKE, K. – *al.*, ed., *Eusebius. The Ecclesiastical History with an English Translation*, I–II, LCL 54, London / Cambridge / New York NY, 1926, 1932.

LANDRY, D. – MAY, B., "Honour Restored. New Light on the Parable of the Prudent Steward (Luke 16,1–8a)", *JBL* 119.2 (2000) 287–309.

LANE, W., *The Gosepl According to Mark*, NICNT 2, Grand Rapids MI, 1974.

LANGE, J.P., *Das Evangelium nach Matthäus*, THBW, Bielefeld 1857.

LANGHORNE, J. – LANGHORNE, W., ed., *Plutarch's Lives. Translated from the Original Greek, with Notes Critical and Historical, and a Life of Plutarch*, I–VI, London 1809.

LAUTERBACH, J.Z., ed., *Mekhilta de-Rabbi Ishmael. A Critical Edition Based on the Manuscripts and Early Editions, with an English Translation, Introduction, and Notes*, I–III, Philadelphia PA, 1933–1935, 2004[2].

LAVEE, M., "Rabbinic Literature and the History of Judaism in Late Antiquity. Challenges, Methodologies and New Approaches", in M. GOODMAN – P. ALEXANDER, ed., *Rabbinic Texts and the History of Late-Roman Palestine*, PBA 165, Oxford 2010, 319–351.

LAVERGNE, C., *Évangile selon Saint Luc*, EtB, Paris 1932.

LEANEY, A.R.C., *A Commentary on the Gospel According to St. Luke*, BNTC, London 1958, 1966[2].

LECLERCQ, J., "L'idée de la royauté du Christ dans l'œuvre de S. Justin", *ATh* 6 (1946) 84–95.

–, *L'idée de la royauté du Christ au Moyen Âge*, UnSa 32, Paris 1959.

LECLERCQ, J. – ROCHAIS, H., ed., *Sancti Bernardi Opera*, I–VIII, Romae 1966–1977.

LEE, W., *The Conclusion of the New Testament. Messages 205–220*, Anaheim CA, 1988.

LEGRAND, PH.-E., ed., *Hérodote. Histoires. Texte établi et traduit*, I–X, CUFr, Paris 1946–1954.

LEHTIPUU, O., "Characterization and Persuasion. The Rich Man and the Poor Man in Luke 16,19–31", in D. RHOADS – K. SYREENI, ed., *Characterization in the Gospels. Reconceiving Narrative Criticism*, JSNT.S 184, Sheffield 1999, 73–105.

–, *The Afterlife Imagery in Luke's Story of the Rich Man and Lazarus*, NT.S 123, Boston MA, 2007.

LEIMAN, S.Z., "From the pages of Tradition. Dwarfs on the Shoulders of Giants", *Trad.* 27.3 (1993) 90–94.

LEON-DUFOUR, X., "Violence", *VTB*, cols. 1360–1366.

LE SAINT, W.P., *Tertullian. Treatises on Penance and on Purity*, ACW 8, London / Westminister MD, 1959.

LEVERTOFF, P.P. – GOUDGE, H.L., *The Gospel According to St. Matthew*, in C. GORE – H.L. GOUDGE – A. GUILLAUME, ed., *A New Commentary on Holy Scripture. Including the Apocrypha*, London 1928, repr. 1929, 124–207.

LEVEY, S.H., ed., *The Targum of Ezekiel. Translated, with a Critical Introduction, Apparatus, and Notes*, ArBib 13, Edinburgh 1987.

LEVINE, B.A., *Leviticus. The Traditional Hebrew Text with the New JPS Translation*, JPSTC, Philadelphia PA, 1989.

LIBERMAN, G., *Alcée. Fragments. Texte établi, traduit et annoté*, I–II, CUFr, Paris 1999.

LIEBERMAN, S., ed., *Midrash Devarim Rabba*, Jerusalem 1940, 1974³.

–, *Hellenism in Jewish Palestine. Studies in the Literary Transmission Beliefs and Manners of Palestine in the I Century B.C.E. – IV Century C.E.*, New York NY, 1950.

LIEBREICH, L.J., "Notes on Greek Version of Symmachus", *JBL* 63.4 (1944) 397–403.

LIETZMANN, H., *Das muratorische Fragment und die monarchianischen Prologue zu den Evangelien*, KIT 1, Bonn 1902.

LIGHTFOOT, J., *A Commentary on the New Testament from the Talmud and Hebraica*, I–IV, Oxford 1859, Grand Rapids MI, 2003⁴.

LIGHTFOOT, J.B., *S. Clement of Rome. The Two Epistles to the Corinthians. A Revised Text with Introduction and Notes*, I–II, London 1869–1877.

–, ed., *The Apostolic Fathers*, I–III, London 1989.

LINKE, W., "Anioł (ἄγγελος) w LXX Hi. Rozwój teologii czy języka religijnego?", *WST* 20.1 (2007) 75–94.

–, "'Gwałt' a królowanie Boga. Studium logionu o Janie Chrzcicielu i Królestwie Bożym (Mt 11,12–13; Łk 16,16)", *WST* 24.2 (2011) 91–112.

LIPSIUS, H., *Das attische Recht und Rechtsverfahren mit Benutzung des Attischen Processes*, I–II, Leipzig 1905–1908.

LLEWELYN, S.R., "The Traditionsgeschichte of Matt 11,12–13, par. Luke 16,16", *NovT* 36.4 (1994) 330–349.

–, "Forcible Acquisition and the Meaning of Matt 11,12", in NDIEC 7, Sydney 1994, 130–162.

–, "The Introduction of Ḥazaqah into Jewish Law", *JSJ* 27.2 (1996) 154–167.

LOBEL, E. – PAGE, D., ed., *Poetarum lesbiorum fragmenta*, Oxford 1955.

LOISY, A.F., *Les Èvangiles synoptiques. Traduction et commentaire*, I–II, Ceffonds 1907–1908.

LOMMATZSCH, C.H.E., – al, ed., *Origenis Opera omnia. Quae graece vel latine tantum extant et ejus nomine circumferuntur*, I–XXV, Berolini 1831–1848.

LÓPEZ BARRIO, M., *El tema del "Agape" en la Primera Carta de San Juan. Estudio de 1 Jn 4,7–21: una perspectiva antropológico-social*, TG.ST 114, Roma 2004.

LÖWITH, K., *Meaning in History*, Chicago IL, 1949.

LU, H., *Xenophon's Theory of Moral Education*, Newcastle upon Tyne 2015.

DE LUBAC, H., *Exégèse Mediévale. Les quatre sens de l'Écriture*, I–IV, 1959–1964.

LUPERINI, R., *La fine del postmoderno*, Idet. 3, Napoli 2005.

LUPIERI, E., *Giovanni Battista nelle tradizioni sinottiche*, StBi 82, Brescia 1988.

–, "Mammona iniquitatis. Can we make sense of the parable of the Dishonest Steward?", in P. WALTERS, ed., *From Judaism to Christianity. Tradition and Transition*, Fs. T.H. Tobin, NT.S 136, Leiden 2010, 131–144.

LUZ, U., *Das Evangelium nach Matthäus*, I–IV, EKK, Zurich / Neukirchen / Vluyn 1985–2002; Eng. trans., *Matthew. A Commentary*, I–III, Hermeneia, Minneapolis MN, 2001–2007.

LUZÁRRAGA, J., "Principios hermenéuticos de exegesis bíblica en el rabinismo primitivo", *EstBib* 30 (1971) 177–193.

LYGRE, J.G., "Of What Charges? (Luke 16,1–2)", *BTB* 32.1 (2002) 21–28.

LYONNET, S., *Il Nuovo Testamento alla luce dell'Antico (Lezioni tenute dall' autore alla VII Settimana Biblica del Clero, Napoli, luglio 1968)*, Brescia 1972.

MACLAREN, A., *Expositions of Holy Scripture. Luke*, I–II, Grand Rapids MI, 2009.

MACLEAN, S., "The 'Heretic' at God's Right Hand", in *The Age. Features*, Melbourne 1995.

MALINA, B.J. – ROHRBAUGH, R.L., *Social-Science Commentary on the Synoptic Gospels*, Minneapolis MN, 1992.

MANN, J., "Changes in the Divine Service of the Synagogue due to Religious Persecutions", *HUCA* 4 (1927) 241–302.

MANNS, F., *La preghiera d'Israele al tempo di Gesù*, StBi 28, Bologna 1996; Fr. orig., *La prière d'Israël à l'heure de Jésus*, Jérusalem 1986.

–, "Le Shema Israël, clé de lecture de quelques textes johanniques", in L. PADOVESE, ed., *Turchia: la Chiesa e la sua storia*. VIII. *Atti del V Simposio di Efeso su S. Giovanni apostolo*, Roma 1995, 107–117.

–, *Le judéo-christianisme, mémoire ou prophétie?*, ThH 112, Paris 2000.

–, "Il Regno di Dio nel giudaismo", *DSBP* 57 (2011) 141–162.

MANSON, S., ed., *Flavius Josephus. Translation and Commentary*, I–X, BrJP, Leiden / Köln / Boston MA, 1999–2016.

MANSON, T.W., "The Sayings of Jesus", in H.D.A. MAJOR – T.W. MANSON – C.J. WRIGHT, ed., *The Mission and Message of Jesus. An Exposition of the Gospels in the Light of Modern Research*, New York NY, 1938, 301–639.

–, *The Sayings of Jesus. As Recorded in the Gospels According to St. Matthew and St. Luke*, London 1949.

MANSON, W., *The Gospel of Luke*, MNTC, New York NY, 1930.

MARCOS, M., "'He Forced with Gentleness'. Emperor Julian's Attitude to Religious Coercion", *AnTard* 17 (2009) 191–204.

MARCOVICH, M., ed., *Iustini Martyris. Apologiae pro Christianis*, PTS 38, Berlin / New York NY, 1994.

MARCUS, J., "Entering into the Kingly Power of God", *JBL* 107.4 (1988) 663–675.

–, "Authority to Forgive Sins upon the Earth: The Shema in the Gospel of Mark", in C.A. EVANS – W.R. STEGNER, ed., *The Gospels and the Scriptures of Israel*, JSNT.S 104, Sheffield 1994, 196–211.

MARCUS, R., "A Note on Bariona", *JBL* 61.4 (1942) 281.

MARGUERAT, D., "L'évangile selon Luc", in *Introduction au Nouveau Testament. Son histoire, son écriture, sa théologie*, MoBi 41, Genève 2000, 83–104.

–, "Le règne, Jésus et la Loi (Q 16,16–18)", in C. COULOT – D. FRICKER, ed., *Le Jugement dans l'un et l'autre Testament* 2, Fs. J. Schlosser, LeDiv 198, Paris 2004, 113–127.

–, *Les Actes des Apôtres*, I–II, CNT 5, Genève 2007, 2015².

MARGUERAT, D. – BOURQUIN, Y., *How to Read Bible Stories. An Introduction to Narrative Criticism*, London 1999; Fr. orig., *Pour lire les récits bibliques*, Paris 1998.

MARGUERAT, D. – WÉNIN, A., *Sapori del racconto biblico. Una nuova guida a testi millenari*, EDP 4, Bologna 2013; Fr. orig., *Saveurs du récit biblique. Un nouveau guide pour des textes millénaires*, Genève / Paris 2012.

MARKON, I.D., ed., *Commentarius in Librum Duodecim Prophetarum, quem composuit Daniel Al-Kumissi (Saec. IX)*, Jerusalem 1957.

MARROU, H.-I., ed., *À Diognète. Introduction, édition critique, traduction et commentaire*, SC 33, Paris 1951.

MARSHALL, I.H., *Luke. Historian and Theologian*, Exeter 1970.

–, *The Gospel of Luke. A Commentary on the Greek Text*, NIGTC, Grand Rapids MI, 1978.

–, "The Hope of a New Age: the Kingdom of God in the New Testament", *Themelios* 11.1 (1985) 5–15 = in *Jesus the Saviour. Studies in New Testament Theology*, Downers Grove IL / London 1990, 213–238.

MARSHALL, J.T., "Aussercanonische Paralleltexte zu den Evangelien", *CritR* 6 (1896) 45–54.

MARTELLI, F., "Reazione antiagostiniana nelle *Historiae* di Orosio?", *RSAnt* 12 (1982) 217–239.

MARTIN, J., *Antike rhetorik. Technik und Methode*, HAW 2.3, München 1974.

MARTIN, V. – KASSER, R., ed., *Papyrus Bodmer XIV. Evangile de Luc chap. 3–24*, Cologny / Genève 1961.

MARULLI, L., "'And How Much Do You Owe...? Take Your Bill, Sit Down Quickly, and Write...' (Luke 16,5–6)", *TynB* 63.2 (2012) 199–216.

MARZULLO, B., *Studi di poesia eolica*, Firenze 1958.

MATERA, F.J., *Passion Narratives and Gospel Theologies. Interpreting the Synoptics Through Their Passion Stories*, Eugene OR, 1986, repr. 2001.

–, "Jesus' Journey to Jerusalem (Luke 9,51–19,46). A Conflict with Israel", *JSNT* 51 (1993) 57–77.

MATHEWSON, D., "The Parable of the Unjust Steward (Luke 16,1–13). A Reexamination of the Traditional View in Light of Recent Challenges", *JETS* 38.1 (1995) 29–39.

MATHIEU, G. – BREMOND, É., ed., *Isocrate. Discours. Texte établi et traduit*, I–IV, CUFr, Paris 1928–1962.

MAZON, P., ed. *Eschyle. Texte établi et traduit*, I–II, CUFr, Paris 1920–1925.

MCARTHUR, H.K., "The Origin of the 'Q' Symbol", *ET* 88.4 (1977) 119–120.

MCCOWN, C.C., ed., *The Testament of Solomon. Edited from Manuscripts at Mount Athos, Bologna, Holkham Hall, Jerusalem, London, Milan, Paris and Vienna*, UNT 9, Leipzig 1922.

MCKANE, W., *A Critical and Exegetical Commentary on Jeremiah*, I, ICC, Edinburgh 1986, repr. 1999.

MCKAY, K.L., "Aspect in Imperatival Constructions in the New Testament Greek", *NovT* 27 (1985) 201–226.

MCNAMARA, M., *Targum and Testament Revisited. Aramaic Paraphrases of the Hebrew Bible: A Light on the New Testament*, Grand Rapids MI, 1972, 2010[2].

–, ed., *Targum Neofity 1: Deuteronomy. Translated, with Apparatus and Notes*, ArBib 5A, Edinburgh 1997.

MEADORS, G.T., "The 'Poor' in the Beatitudes of Matthew and Luke", *GTJ* 6.2 (1985) 305–314.

MEIER, J.P., *Law and History in Matthew's Gospel. A Redactional Study of Matt 5,17–48*, AnBib 71, Rome 1976.

–, *The Vision of Matthew. Christ, Church, and Morality in the First Gospel*, Eugene OR, 1991.

–, *A Marginal Jew. Rethinking the Historical Jesus*, ABRL, New York NY, 2001.

MELANCHTHON, P., *Annotationes in Euangelium Matthaei*, in C.G. BRETSCHNEIDER, ed., *Philippi Melanthonis. Opera quae supersunt omnia*, XIV, Halis Saxonum 1847, 530–1042.

MENOUD, P.-H., "Le sens du verbe dans Lc 16,16", in A. DESCAMPS – A. DE HALLEUX, ed., *Melanges Bibliques,* Fs. B. Rigaux, Gembloux 1970, 207–212 = in P.-H. MENOUD – J.-L. LEUBA – O. CULLMANN, ed., *Jésus-Christ et la foi. Recherches néotestamentaires*, Neuchâtel / Paris 1975, 125–130.

MÉRIDIER, L. – al., ed., *Euripide. Texte établi et traduit*, I–VIII, CUFr, Paris 1925–2003.

MERK, A., ed., *Novum Testamentum graece et latine*, SPIB 65, Romae 1933, 1984[10].

MERKLEIN, H.M., *Die Gottesherrschaft als Handlungsprinzip. Untersuchung zur Ethik Jesu*, FzB 34, Würzburg 1978, 1981[2].

MERRILL, E.H., *Deuteronomy*, NAC 4, Nashville TN, 1994.

MERX, A., *Die vier kanonischen Evangelien nach ihrem ältesten bekannten texte. Uebersetzung und erläuterung der syrischen im Sinaikloster gefundenen palimpsest-handschrift*, I–IV, Berlin 1897–1911.

METZGER, J.A., *Consumption and Wealth in Luke's Travel Narrative*, BIS 88, Leiden / Boston MA, 2007.

MEYER, A., *Jesu Muttersprache. Das galiläische Aramäisch in seiner Bedeutung für die Erklärung der Reden Jesu und der Evangelien überhaupt*, Freiburg / Leipzig 1896.

MEYNET, R., *L'Évangile de Luc*, RhSem 1, Paris 2005; Eng. trans., *Luke. The Gospel of the Children of Israel*, RBS 4, Rome / Miami FL, 2015.

MICAELLI, C. – MUNIER, C., *Tertullien. La pudicité*, I–II, SC 394–395, Paris 1993.

MICHAEL, J.H., "A Conjecture on Matthew 11,12", *HThR* 14.4 (1921) 375–377.

MICHAELIS, W., *Der Herr verzieht nicht die Verheissung. Die Aussagen Jesu über die Nähe des Jüngsten Tages*, Bern 1942.

–, "σκηνή", *TDNT*, VII, 368–394.

MILGROM, J., *Leviticus. A New Translation with Introduction and Commentary*, I–III, AncB 3ab, New York NY, 1991, 2000, 2001.

MILLER, J.W., *Proverbs*, BCBC, Scottdale PA / Waterloo ON, 2004.

MINEAR, P.S., "Luke's Use of the Birth Stories", in L.E. KECK – J.L. MARTYN, ed., *Studies in Luke-Acts. Essays Presented in Honor of Paul Schubert*, Nashville TN, 1966, 111–130.

–, *To Heal and to Reveal. The Prophetic Vocation According to Luke*, New York NY, 1976.

MIYOSHI, M., "Das jüdische Gebet Šᵉmaʿ und die Abfolge der Traditionsstücke in Lk 10–13", *AJBI* 7 (1981), 70–123.

MOELLER, T.G., *Youth Aggression and Violence. A Psychological Approach*, Mahwah NJ, 2001.

MOESSNER, D.P., "Suffering, Intercession and Eschatological Atonement. An Uncommon Common View in the Testament of Moses and in Luke-Acts", in J.H. CHARLESWORTH – C.A. EVANS, ed., *The Pseudepigrapha and Early Biblical Interpretation*, JSPE.S 14, SSEJC 2, Sheffield 1993, 202–227.

MOFFATT, J., *The Theology of the Gospels*, ST, New York NY, 1913, 1920[2].

MONAT, P., "L'exégèse de la parabole de 'L'Intendant infidèle', du IIᵉ au XVIIIᵉ siècle", *REAug* 38 (1992) 89–123.

MONTGOMERY, J.A., *A Critical and Exegetical Commentary on the Book of Daniel*, ICC, Edinburgh 1927, repr. 1959.

–, *A Critical and Exegetical Commentary on the Books of Kings*, ICC, Edinburgh 1951, repr. 1960.

MONTGOMERY BOICE, J., *Genesis. An Expositional Commentary*, II, Grand Rapids MI, 1985, repr. 1998.

MOORE, F.J., "The Parable of the Unjust Steward", *AThR* 47.1 (1965) 103–105.

MOORE, G.F., *Judaism in the First Centuries of the Christian Era. The Age of the Tannaim*, I–III, Cambridge 1927–1930.

MOORE, S.D. – ANDERSON, J.C., "Taking it Like a Man. Masculinity in 4 Maccabees", *JBL* 117.2 (1998) 249–273.

MOORE, W.E., "ΒΙΑΖΩ, ΑΡΠΑΖΩ, and Cognates in Josephus", *NTS* 21.4 (1974–1975) 519–543.

MORESCHINI, C. – BRAUN, R., ed., *Tertullien. Contre Marcion*, IV, SC 456, Paris 2001.

MORGENTHALER, R., *Die lukanische Geschichtsschreibung als Zeugnis. Gestalt und Gehalt der Kunst des Lukas*, I–II, AThANT 14–15, Zürich 1949.

MORIN, G., ed., *Sancti Caesarii Arelatensis. Sermones. Nunc primum in unum collecti et ad leges artis criticae ex innumeris mss. recogniti*, I–II, CChr.SL 103–104, Turnholti 1953.

–, ed., *Commentarioli in Psalmos*, in *S. Hieronymi Presbyteri Opera*, I.1, CChr.SL 72, Turnholti 1959, 163–245.

MORRIS, L., *The Gospel According to St. Luke. An Introduction and Commentary*, TNTC, Grand Rapids MI, 1974.

MOSS, C.R., "Blurred Vision and Ethical Confusion. The Rhetorical Function of Matthew 6,22–23", *CBQ* 73 (2011) 757–776.

MOXNES, H., *Economy of the Kingdom. Social Conflict and Economic Relations in Luke's Gospel*, OBTh 23, Philadelphia PA, 1988.

MUELLER, M.M., *Saint Caesarius of Arles. Sermons*, I, FaCh 31, Washington DC, 1956, repr. 2004.

MULLEN, B. – JOHNSON, C., *The Psychology of Consumer Behaviour*, Hillsdale NJ, 1990.

MUNK, E., *The Call of the Torah. An Anthology of Interpretation and Commentary on the Five Books of Moses*, I–V, Brooklyn NY, 2001.

MUNTEANU, D.L., *Tragic Pathos. Pity and Fear in Greek Philosophy and Tragedy*, Cambridge 2012.

MURPHY, R.E., *Proverbs*, WBC 22, Nashville TN, 1998.

MURRAY, A.T., ed., *Homer. The Odyssey with an English Translation*, I–II, LCL 104–105, London / Cambridge MA, 1919, repr. 1980–1984.

MURRAY, A.T. – WYATT, W.F., ed., *Homer. The Iliad with an English Translation*, I–II, LCL 170–171, London / Cambridge MA, 1924–1925, 1999².

MURRAY, G., "The Unjust Steward", *ET* 15.7 (1904) 307–310.

MUTZENBECHER, A., ed., *Maximi Episcopi Taurinensis. Sermones*, CChr.SL 23, Turnholti 1962.

NAGY, G., *The Best of the Achaeans. Concepts of the Hero in Archaic Greek Poetry*, Baltimore MD, 1979.

NALPATHILCHIRA, J., *"Everything is Ready: Come to the Marriage Banquet". The Parable of the Invitation to the Royal Marriage Banquet (Matt 22,1–14) in the Context of Matthew's Gospel*, AnBib 196, Rome 2012.

NAUCK, A. – SNELL, B., ed., *Tragicorum Graecorum fragmenta. Supplementum continens nova fragmenta euripidea et adespota apud scriptores veteres reperta*, Hildesheim 1889, repr. 1964.

NAVARRE, O. – *al.*, ed., *Démosthène. Plaidoyers politiques*, I–IV, CUFr, Paris 1947–1959.

NELSON, W.D., ed., *Mekhilta de-Rabbi Shimon bar Yohai. Translated into English with Critical Introduction and Annotation*, Philadelphia PA, 2006.

NEUFELD, E., "The Prohibition against Loans at Interest in the Old Testament", *HUCA* 26 (1955) 355–412.

NEUHÄUSLER, E., *Anspruch und Antwort Gottes. Zur Lehre von den Weisungen innerhalb der synoptischen Jesusverkündigung*, Düsseldorf 1962.

NEUSNER, J., *The Rabbinic Traditions About the Pharisees Before 70*, I–III, Leiden 1971.

–, *From Politics to Piety. The Emergence of Pharisaic Judaism*, Englewood Cliffs NJ, 1973.

–, *The Talmud of the Land of Israel. A Preliminary Translation and Explanation*, I–XXXV, ChiStHJ, Chicago IL, 1983–1994.

–, ed., *Sifre to Deuteronomy. An Analytical Translation*, I–II, BJS 98.101, Atlanta GA, 1987.

–, "Comparing Sources: Mishnah/Tosefta and Gospel", in *Jewish Law from Moses to the Mishnah. The Hiram College Lectures on Religion for 1999 and Other Papers*, SFSHJ 187, Atlanta GA, 1998, 119–135.

–, *The Theology of the Halakhah*, Leiden 2001.

NEUSNER, J. – SARASON, R.S., ed., *The Tosefta. Translated from the Hebrew. First Division. Zeraim (The Order of Agriculture)*, Hoboken NJ, 1986.

NEVEU, M.J., "Apologues, by Carlo Lodoli", *JAEd* 64.1 (2010) 57–64.

NICACCI, A., "Dall'aoristo all'imperfetto o dal primo piano allo sfondo. Un paragone tra sintassi greca e sintassi ebraica", *SBFLA* 42 (1992) 85–108.

NICACCI, A. – PAZZINI, M. – TADIELLO, R., *Il libro di Giona. Analisi del testo ebraico e del racconto*, SBFA, Gerusalemme 2004; repr. Milano 2013.

NIESE, B., ed., *Flavii Iosephi Opera*, I–VII, Berolini 1887–1895.

NIKOLOPOULOS, P.G., ed., *Αἱ εἰς τὸν Ἰωάννην τὸν Χρυσόστομον ἐσφαλμένως ἀποδιδόμεναι ἐπιστολαί*, Athens 1973.

NIKOLSKY, R., "The *History of the Rechabites* and the Jeremiah Literature", *JSP* 13.2 (2002) 185–207.

NIR, R., "'It is not Right for a Man who Worships God to Repay His Neighbor Evil for Evil': Christian Ethics in *Joseph and Aseneth* 22–29 (Chapters 22–29)", *JHScr* 13.5 (2013) 1–29.

NITZSCH, C.I., *System der Christlichen Lehre für academische Vorlesungen*, Bonn 1829.

NOËL, F., *The Travel Narrative in the Gospel of Luke. Interpretation of Lk 9,51–19,28*, CBRA 5, Brussel 2004.

NÖLDEKE, H., *Targum Jonathan ben Uzziel on the Pentateuch*, Berlin 1903.

NOLLAND, J., *Luke*, I–III, WBC 35a–c, Dallas TX, 1989–1993.

NÖSGEN, K.F., *Die Evangelien nach Matthäus, Markus und Lukas*, Nördlingen 1886.

NOTLEY, R.S., "The Kingdom of Heaven Forcefully Advances", in C.A. EVANS, ed., *The Interpretation of Scripture in Early Judaism and Christianity. Studies in Language and Tradition*, JSPE.S 33, Sheffield 2000, 279–311.

OEGEMA, G.S., "The Pseudepigrapha and the Narrative in Luke-Acts", in G.S. OEGEMA – J.H. CHARLESWORTH, ed., *The Pseudepigrapha and Christian Origins. Essays from the Studiorum Novi Testamenti Societas*, JCTC 4, London / New York NY, 2008, 151–165.

OESTERLEY, W.O.E., *The Gospel Parables in the Light of their Jewish Background*, SPCK, London, 1936, repr. 1938.

Ó FEARGHAIL, F., *The Introduction to Luke-Acts. A Study of the Role of Luke 1,1–4.44 in the Composition of Luke's Two-Volume Work*, AnBib 126, Rome 1991.

OLDFATHER, W.A., ed., *Epictetus. The Discourses as Reported by Arrian, the Manual, and Fragments, with an English Translation*, I–II, LCL 131.218, London / Cambridge MA, 1925–1928, repr. 1978–1979.

OLIVAR, A., ed., *Sancti Petri Chrysologi. Collectio Sermonum*, I–III, CChr.SL 24a–b, Turnholti 1975, 1981–1982.

OLSHAUSEN, H., *Biblischer Commentar über sämmtliche Schriften des Neuen Testaments. Zunächst für Prediger und Studirende*, I–VII, Königsberg 1837–1853; Eng. trans., *Biblical Commentary on the New Testament*, I–VI, New York NY, 1858–1860.

OMANSON, R.L., *A Textual Guide to the Greek New Testament*, Stuttgart 2006.

VAN OOSTERZEE, J.J., *Das Evangelium nach Lukas. Theologisch-homiletisch bearbeitet*, THBW, Bielefeld 1859, 1861[2]; Eng. trans., *The Gospel According to Luke. An Exegetical and Doctrinal Commentary*, LCHS, Edinburg 1862–1863, 1872[6].

O'TOOLE, R.F., *The Unity of Luke's Theology. An Analysis of Luke-Acts*, Wilmington 1984.

–, "Theophilus", *ABD*, VI, 511–512.

OTTO, R., *The Kingdom of God and the Son of Man. A Study in the History of Religion*, London 1938, repr. 1943; Ger. orig., *Das Reich Gottes und Menschensohn. Ein religionsgeschichtlicher Versuch*, München 1934.

OUAKNIN, M.-A., *Le Dieci Parole. Il Decalogo riletto e commentato dai Maestri ebrei antichi e moderni*, Milano 2001[4]; Fr. orig., *Le Dix Commandements*, Paris 1999.

PAFFENROTH, K., *The Story of Jesus According to L*, JSNT.S 147, Sheffield 1997.

PAGE, D., *Sappho and Alcaeus. An Introduction to the Study of Ancient Lesbian Poetry*, Oxford 1955, repr. 1987.

PALARDY, W.B., *Saint Peter Chrysologous. Selected Sermons*, II–III, FaCh 109–110, Washington DC, 2004–2005.

PALIARD, C., *Lire l'écriture, écouter la Parole. La parabole de l'économe infidèle*, LiBi 53, Paris 1980.

PALLIS, A., *Notes on St. Luke and the Acts*, London 1928.

PAMMENT, M., "Singleness and Matthew's Attitude to the Torah", *JSNT* 17.5 (1983) 73–86.

PANIMOLLE, F., "Il Regno di Dio nei Vangeli e negli Atti degli apostoli", *DSBP* 57 (2011) 163–224.

PARROTT, D.M., "The Dishonest Steward (Luke 16,1–8a) and Luke's Special Parable Collection", *NTS* 37.4 (1991) 499–515.

VAN PARYS, M., "L'Église et le Royaume de Dieu. Quelques témoignages des Pères de l'Église", *Iren.* 76 (2003) 47–63.

PATAI, R., *The Messiah Texts. Jewish Legends of Three Thousand Years*, Detroit MI, 1988.

PATER, C.A., *Karlstadt as the Father of the Baptist Movements. The Emergence of Lay Protestantism*, Toronto 1984.

PATILLON, M., *La théorie du discours chez Hermogène le rhéteur. Essai sur les structures linguistiques de la rhétorique ancienne*, CEA 117, Paris 1988.

PATON, L.B., *A Critical and Exegetical Commentary on the Book of Esther*, ICC, Edinburgh 1908, repr. 1951.

PATTAKOS, A., *Prisoners of Our Thoughts. Viktor Frankl's Principles for Discovering Meaning in Life and Work*, San Francisco CA, 2004, 2008[2].

PAUL, G., "The Unjust Steward and the Interpretation of Luke 16,9", *Theol.* 61 (1958) 189–193.

PAUL, L., *Die Vorstellungen vom Messias und vom Gottesreich bei den Synoptikern*, Bonn 1895.

PAUL, S.M. – CROSS, F.M., *Amos. A Commentary on the Book of Amos*, Hermeneia, Minneapolis MN, 1991.

PAX, E., "Der Reiche und der arme Lazarus. Eine Milieustudie", *SBFLA* 25 (1975) 254–268.

PEARSON, A.C., ed., *The Fragments of Sophocles. With Additional Notes from the Papers of Sir R.C. Jebb and Dr. W.G. Headlam*, I–III, Cambridge 1917.

PÉDECH, P. – *al.*, ed., *Polybe. Histoires. Texte établi et traduit*, I–X, CUFr, Paris 1961–1995.

PELAND, G., "Le thème biblique du Règne chez saint Hilaire de Poitiers", *Gr.* 60 (1979) 639–674.

PELLEGRINO, C., *Maria di Nazaret, Profezia del Regno. Un approccio narrativo a Lc 1,34*, AnBib 206, Roma 2014.

PENNA, R., "Appunti sul come e perché il Nuovo Testamento si rapporta all'Antico", *Bib.* 81 (2000) 95–104.

PENNINGTON, J.T., *Heaven and Earth in the Gospel of Matthew*, NT.S 126, Leiden / Boston MA, 2007.

PERCY, E., *Die Botschaft Jesu. Eine Traditionskritische und Exegetische Untersuchung*, LUÂ 49.5, Lund 1953.

PERRIN, N., *The Kingdom of God in the Teaching of Jesus*, NTLi, London 1963.

–, "The Evangelist as Author: Reflections on Method in the Study and Interpretation of the Synoptic Gospels and Acts", *BR* 17.1 (1972) 5–18.

–, *Jesus and the Language of the Kingdom. Symbol and Metaphor in New Testament Interpretation*, Philadelphia PA, 1976.

PERRY, A.M., "A Judeo-Christian Source in Luke", *JBL* 49.2 (1930) 181–194.

PERSON, R.F., Jr., *In Conversation with Jonah. Conversation Analysis, Literary Criticism, and the Book of Jonah*, JSOT.S 220, Sheffield 1996.

PERVO, R.I., *Acts. A Commentary*, Hermeneia, Minneapolis MN, 2009.

PETREQUIN, J.E., ed., *Chirurgie d'Hippocrate*, I–II, Paris 1877–1878.

PFIEIDERER, O., *The Development of Rational Theology in Germany since Kant. And Ist Progress in Great Britain*, New York NY, 1890, repr. 2013.

PHILIPPE, J., *Searching for and Maintaining Peace. A Small Treatise on Peace of Heart*, New York NY, 2002.

PHILLIPS, J.B., *The Gospels. Translated into Modern English*, New York NY, 1952.

PHILLIPS, T.E., "Revisiting Philo: Discussions of Wealth and Poverty in Philo's Ethical Discourse", *JNTS* 83 (2001) 111–121.

PICHERY, E., ed., *Jean Cassien. Conférences. Introduction, texte Latin, traduction et notes*, I–III, SC 42, 54, 64, Paris 1955, 1958, 1959.

PICKAR, C.H., "The Unjust Steward (Luke 16,1–9)", *CBQ* 1.3 (1939) 250–253.

PIETERSMA, A. – WRIGHT, B.G., ed., *A New English Translation of the Septuagint and the Other Greek Translations Traditionally Included under That Title*, Oxford / New York NY, 2007.

PIPER, R.A., "Social Background and Thematic Structure in Luke 16", in F. VAN SEGBROECK – al., ed., *The Four Gospels 1992*, Fs. F. Neirynck, II, BEThL 100.2, Leuven 1992, 1637–1662.

PISANI, V., *L'etimologia. Storia – Questioni – Metodo*, Torino 1947.

–, *Manuale storico della lingua greca*, StGL 11, Brescia 1947, 1973².

–, *Glottologia indoeuropea. Manuale di grammatica comparata delle lingue indoeuropee, con speciale riguardo del greco e del latino*, Torino 1949, 1998⁴.

–, *Le lingue indoeuropee*, StGL 5, Brescia 1971.

PLUMMER, A., *A Critical and Exegetical Commentary on the Gospel According to St. Luke*, ICC, New York NY, 1920.

POCOCK, E., *A Commentary on the Prophecy of Micah*, in L. TWELLS, ed., *The Theological Works of the Learned Dr. Pocock*, I, London 1740.

POIRIER, M., ed., *Cyprien de Carthage. La Bienfaisance et les Aumônes*, SC 440, Paris 1999.

POLAG, A., *Fragmenta Q. Textheft zur Logienquelle*, Neukirchen / Vluyn 1979.

PONTIFICAL BIBLICAL COMMISSION, *The Jewish People and their Sacred Scriptures in the Christian Bible*, Vatican City 2002; Fr. trans., ID., *Le people juif e ses Saintes Écritures dans la Bible chrétienne*, EV 20, Bologna 2004, 506–834.

–, *The Inspiration and Truth of Sacred Scripture. The Word That Comes from God and Speaks of God for the Salvation of the World*, Collegeville MN, 2014; It. orig., *Ispirazione e verità della Sacra Scrittura. La parola che viene da Dio e parla di Dio per salvare il mondo*, Città del Vaticano 2014.

POPPI, A., *Sinossi dei quattro vangeli. Introduzione e commento*, II, Padova 1990.

–, ed., *Nuova Sinossi dei quattro Vangeli. Greco – Italiano*, I. *Testo*, Padova 2006.

PORRELLO, M.S., "Omicidio tra vendetta privata e punizione", *D&Q* 8 (2008) 139–165.

PORTER, S.E., "The Parable of the Unjust Steward (Luke 16,1–13). Irony is the Key", in D.J.A. CLINES – S.E. FOWL – S.E. PORTER, ed., *The Bible in Three Dimensions. Essays in Celebration of Fourty Years of Biblical Studies in the University of Sheffield*, JSOT.S 87, Sheffield 1990, 127–153.

POWELL, M.A., *What Are They Saying About Luke?*, New York NY, 1989.

PRANTL, C., ed., *Aristotelis de coelo et de generatione et corruptione*, BSGRT, Lipsiae 1881.

PREISKER, H., "Lukas 16,1–7", *ThLZ* 74 (1949) 85–92.

–, "ἔπαινος", *TDNT*, II, 586–588.

PRINCIPE, S., "Chi era Luca?", *Henoch* 21 (1999) 131–146.

PRINZIVALLI, E., "Il millenarismo in Oriente da Metodio ad Apollinare", ASEs 15 (1998) 138–151.

PROPP, W.H.C., *Exodus 1–18. A New Translation with Introduction and Commentary*, AncB 2, New York NY, 1999.

RABE, H., ed., *Hermogenis opera*, RhG 6, Lipsiae 1913.

RACE, W.H., ed., *Pindar. Odes. Fragments. Edited and Translated*, I–II, LCL 56.485, London / Cambridge MA, 1997.

RACKHAM, H., ed., *Aristotle. The Nichomachean Ethics with an English Translation*, XIX, LCL 73, London / Cambridge MA, 1926, repr. 1982.

RADERMAKERS, J. – BOSSUYT, P., *Jésus Parole de la Grâce selon Saint Luc*, Bruxelles 1981; It. trans., *Lettura pastorale del Vangelo di Luca*, Bologna 1983.

RADL, W., *Paulus und Jesus im lukanischen Doppelwerk. Untersuchung zu Parallelmotiven im Lukasevangelium und in der Apostelgeschichte*, EHS.T 49, Bern / Frankfurt 1975.

RALPH, B., "The Kingdom of Heaven Suffereth Violence", *ET* 28.9 (1917) 427.

RAMELLI, I.L.E., "Luke 16,16: The Good News of God's Kingdom is Proclaimed and Everyone is Forced into it", *JBL* 127.4 (2008) 737–758.

RAMSEY, B., *John Cassian. The Conferences*, ACW 57, New York NY / Mahwah NJ, 1997.

RAPPAPORT, U., "*Defining* the Letter of Aristeas *Again*", *JSPE* 21.3 (2012) 285–303.

RATZINGER, J., BENEDICT XVI, *Das Heil der Menchen – Innerweltlich und christlich*, in F. SCHULLER, ed., *Grundsatzreden aus fünf Jahrzehnten*, Regensburg 2005.

–, *Deus Caritas Est. Encyclical Letter of the Supreme Pontiff Benedict XVI to the Bishops, Priests, and Deacons, Men and Women Religious, and all the Lay Faithful on Christian Love*, Vatican City 2006; Lat. orig., "Litterae encyclicae *Deus caritas est*", *AAS* 98 (2006) 217–252.

–, *Spe Salvi. Encyclical Letter of the Supreme Pontiff Benedict XVI to the Bishops, Priests, and Deacons, Men and Women Religious, and all the Lay Faithful on Christian Hope*, Vatican City 2007; Lat. orig., "Litterae encyclicae *Spe salvi*", *AAS* 99 (2007) 985–1027.

–, *Jesus of Nazareth*. I. *From the Baptism in the Jordan to the Transfiguration*, New York NY, 2007.

–, *Post-Synodal Apostolic Exhortation Verbum Domini of the Holy Father Benedict XVI to the Bishops, Clergy, Consacrated Persons and the Lay Faithful on the Word of God in the Life and Mission of the Church*, Vatican City 2010.

–, "General Audience, in the Paul VI Adience Hall: Wednesday, 13 February, 2013", [Online edition: access 13.07.2017], http://w2.vatican.va/content/benedict-xvi/en/audiences/2013/documents/hf_ben-xvi_aud_20130213.pdf.

RAVASI, G., *Il libro dei Salmi. Commento e attualizzazione*, II, CLPB, Bologna 1985, 2002[9].

REDDIT, P.L., "The Concept of Nomos in Fourth Maccabees", *CBQ* 45.2 (1983) 249–270.

REGNAULT, L. – DE PREVILLE, J., ed., *Dorothée de Gaza. Œuvres Spirituelles. Introduction, texte grec, traduction et notes*, SC 92, Paris 1963.

REICKE, B.I., *Lukasevangeliet*, Stockholm 1962; Eng. trans., *The Gospel of Luke*, Richmond VA, 1964.

REIDER, J. – TURNER, N., *An Index to Aquila. Greek – Hebrew. Hebrew – Greek. Latin – Hebrew. With the Syriac and Armenian Evidence*, VT.S 12, Leiden 1966.

REIFFERSCHEID, A. – WISSOWA, G., ed., *De Ieiunio adversus Psychicos*, in *Quinti Septimi Florentis Tertulliani. Opera*, II.29, CChr.SL 2, Turnholti 1954, 1255–1277.

RENGSTORF, K.H., *Das Evangelium nach Lukas*, NTD 3, Göttingen 1936, 1958[8]; It. trans., *Il Vangelo secondo Luca*, NT 3, Brescia 1980.

–, "ἑταῖρος", *TDNT*, II, 699–701.

–, "λῃστής", *TDNT*, IV, 257–262.

–, ed., *Die Tosefta. Text. Seder I: Zeraim*, Stuttgart 1983.

VAN RENSBURG, J.J.J., "A Syntactical Reading of Luke 12,35–48", *Neotest.* 22.2 (1988) 415–438.

RESCH, A., *Aussercanonische Paralleltexte zu den Evangelien*, I–IV, TU 10, Leipzig 1893–1897.

RESCH, G., *Das Aposteldecret nach seiner ausserkanonischen Textgestalt*, TU 28.3, Leipzig 1905.

RESSEGUIE, J.L., "Point of View in the Central Section of Luke (9,51–19,44)", *JETS* 25.1 (1982) 41–47.

–, *Narrative Criticism of the New Testament. An Introduction*, Grand Rapids MI, 2005.

RICCIARDI, G., "The Popes and Little Teresa of the Child Jesus", *30Days* [On-line edition: access 06.05.2017] 5 (2003), http://www.30giorni.it/articoli_id_907_l3.htm.

RIGATO, M.-L., "'Mosè e i Profeti' in Chiave Cristiana: un pronunciamento e un midrash (Lc 16,16–18+19–31)", *RivBib* 45 (1997) 143–177.

–, "Luca originario Giudeo, forse di stirpe Levitica, seguace dei 'testimoni oculari' (Lc 1,2–3). Una rilettura delle fonti più antiche con riscontri nell'opera di Luca", in G. LEONARDI – F.G.B. TROLESE, ed., *San Luca evangelista testimone della fede che unisce. Atti del Congresso internazionale. Padova, 16–21 Ottobre 2000*, I, FRSEP 28, Padova 2002, 391–422.

RINCK, W.G., "Über Matth. 11,12; 21,31: eine exegetische und eine kritische Bemerkung gegen Prof. Schweizer in Zürich", *ThStKr* 13 (1840) 1020–1021.

RINDOŠ, J., "The Place of John the Baptist within Luke's Sacred History", in L. DE SANTOS – S. GRASSO, ed., *"Perché stessero con Lui"*, Fs. K. Stock, AnBib 180, Roma 2010, 269–286.

RITZ, H.-J., "βίος, βιωτικός", *EDNT*, I, 219.

ROBERTS, W.R., ed., *Demetrius on Style. The Greek Text of Demetrius De Elocutione. Edited after the Paris Manuscript, with Introduction, Translation, Facsimiles, etc.*, Cambridge 1902.

ROBINSON, J.M. – HOFFMANN, P. – KLOPPENBORG, J.S., ed., *The Critical Edition of Q: Synopsis Including the Gospels of Matthew and Luke, Mark and Thomas with English, German, and French Translations of Q and Thomas*, Hermeneia, Minneapolis MN, 2000.

ROBINSON, W.C., Jr., "The Theological Context for Interpreting Luke's Travel Narrative (9,51ff.)", *JBL* 79.1 (1960) 20–31.

ROGERS, B.B., ed., *Aristophanes with the English Translation*, I–III, LCL, London / Cambridge MA, 1924–1930.

RÖMER, T., "Des meurtres et des guerres. Le Dieu de la Bible hébraïque aime-t-il la violence?", in D. MARGUERAT, ed., *Dieu est-il violent ?*, Paris 2008, 35–57.

RONCALLI, G.A., JOHN XXIII, *Paenitentiam Agere. Encyclical Letter of Pope John XXIII on the Need for the Practice of Interior and Exterior Penance*, Vatican City 1962; Lat. orig., "Litterae encyclicae *Paenitentiam agere*", *AAS* 54 (1962) 481–491.

ROOKER, M., *The Ten Commandments. Ethics for the Twenty-First Century*, Nashville TN, 2010.

RORDORF, W. – TUILIER, A., ed., *La Doctrine des douze apôtres (Didachè). Introduction, texte critique, traduction, notes, appendice et index*, SC 248, Paris 1978.

ROSS, W.D., ed., *Aristotelis. Physica. Recognovit brevique adnotatione critica instruxit*, SCBO, Oxonii 1950, repr. 1985.

–, ed., *Aristotelis. Ars Rhetorica. Recognovit brevique adnotatione critica instruxit*, SCBO, Oxonii 1959.

ROSSANO, P., ed., *Vangelo secondo Luca*, Milano 1984.

ROSSÉ, G., *Il Vangelo di Luca. Commento esegetico e teologico*, Roma 1992, 2012[5].

ROUSSEAU, A. – al., ed., *Irénée de Lyon. Contre les hérésies. Livre IV. Édition critique d'après les versions arménienne et latine*, II, SC 100, Paris 1965.

–, ed., *Irénée de Lyon. Contre les hérésies. Livre V. Édition critique d'après les versions arménienne et latine*, I–II, SC 152, Paris 1969.

–, ed., *Irénée de Lyon. Contre les hérésies. Livre III. Édition critique*, I–II, SC 210–211, Paris 1974.

ROUSSEL, P., ed. *Isée. Discours. Texte établi et traduit*, CUFr, Paris 1922.

ROWLING, J., "Cataloguing Helictites and Other Capillary-Controlled Speleothems", December 2000 [access: 25.04.2017], http://www.speleonics.com.au/jills/pastpapers/helicat/.

DE RUBEIS, B.M., ed., *Summa contra Gentiles. Divi Thomae Aquitanis. Angelici et v. ecclesiae doctoris ordinis praedicatorum. Quatuor tributa libris. De veritate catholicae fidei. Editio regens Partenopeia. Volumen unicum complectens lib. 1. 2. 3. et 4. nec non dissertationem praeviam*, Neapoli 1846.

RUPP, G., "Andrew Karlstadt and Reformation Puritanism", *JThS.NS* 10.2 (1959) 308–326.

–, *Patterns of Reformation*, London / Philadelphia PA, 1969.

RYKWERT, J., "Lodoli on Function and Representation", *ArcR* 160 (1976) 21–26.

RZACH, A., ed., *ΧΡΗΣΜΟΙ ΣΙΒΥΛΛΙΑΚΟΙ. Oracula Sibyllina*, Pragae / Vindobonae / Lipsiae 1891.

SABOURIN, L., *The Gospel According to St. Matthew. Preliminary Notions*, Rome 1970.

–, *The Gospel According to St. Luke. Introduction and Commentary*, Bandra 1984.

SALDARINI, A.J., "Form Criticism of Rabbinic Literature", *JBL* 96 (1977) 257–274.

SÁNCHEZ CARO, J.M. – HERRERA GARCÍA, R.M. – DELGADO JARA, M.I., ed., *Alfonso de Madrigal, el Tostado. Introducción al Evangelio según San Mateo. Edición bilingüe. Texto, traducción, introducción y notas*, FD 3, Ávila / Salamanca 2008.

SANDERS, E.P., *Judaism: Practice and Belief, 63 BCE – 66 CE*, London 1992.

–, "Common Judaism and the Synagogue in the First Century", in S. FINE, ed., *Jews, Christians, and Polytheists in the Ancient Synagogue. Cultural Interaction during the Greco-Roman Period*, BHJS, London 1999, repr. New York NY, 2005, 1–15.

SANDERS, J.A., "Introduction: Why the Pseudepigrapha?", in J.H. CHARLESWORTH – C.A. EVANS, ed., *The Pseudepigrapha and Early Biblical Interpretation*, JSPE.S 14, SSEJC 2, Sheffield 1993, 13–19.

SANDMEL, S., *A Jewish Understanding of the New Testament*, Cincinnati OH, 1956.

DE SANTOS OTERO, A., *Los Evangelios Apócrifos. Estudios introductorios y versión de los textos originales*, BAC.EE, Madrid 2001, repr. 2005.

SASSON, J.M., *Jonah. A New Translation with Introduction, Commentary, and Interpretation*, London / New Haven CT, 2008.

SCARPAT, G., *Quarto Libro dei Maccabei. Testo, traduzione, introduzione e commento*, Bib.TS 9, Brescia 2006.

SCARPI, P., ed., *Apollodoro. I miti Greci (Biblioteca)*, SGEL, Milano 1996.

SCHARBERT, J., "זוּר", *TDOT*, IV, 46–51.

SCHELLENBERG, R.S., "Which Master? Whose Steward? Metalepsis and Lordship in the Parable of the Prudent Steward (Luke 16,1–13)", *JSNT* 30.3 (2008) 263–288.

VON SCHLATTER, A., *Der Evangelist Matthäus. Seine Sprache, sein Ziel, seine Selbständigkeit. Ein Kommentar zum ersten Evangelium*, Stuttgart 1929, 1963[6].

–, *Die Evangelien nach Markus und Lukas*, EzNT, Stuttgart 1954.

–, *Johannes der Täufer. Herausgegeben von Wilhelm Michaelis*, Basel 1956.

SCHLEIERMACHER, F.E.D., *Über die Schriften des Lukas. Ein kritischer Versuch*, I, Berlin 1817.

SCHLOSSER, J., "Le Règne aux mains des 'violents'", in *Le règne de Dieu dans les dits de Jésus*, II, EtB, Paris 1980, 509–539.

SCHMID, J., *Das Evangelium nach Lukas*, RNT 3, Regensburg 1941, 1955[3]; Span. trans., *El Evangelio según San Lucas*, BHer.SE 94, Barcelona 1968, 1981[3].

–, *Das Evangelium nach Matthäus*, RNT 1, Regensburg 1948, 1965[5]; It. trans., *L'Evangelo secondo Matteo*, NTComm 1, Brescia 1976[4].

–, *Sinossi dei tre primi Evangeli. Con i passi paralleli di Giovanni*, Brescia 1970; Ger. orig., *Synopse der drei ersten Evangelien. Mit Beifügung der Johannes-Parallelen*, Regensburg 1968.

SCHMIDT, T.E., "Hostility to Wealth in Philo of Alexandria", *JSNT* 19.6 (1983) 85–97.

SCHMITT, F.S., ed., *Sancti Anselmi Cantuariensis archiepiscopi. Opera ommnia*, I–VI, Seckau / Roma / Edinburg 1938–1961.

SCHNACKENBURG, R., *Règne et Royaume de Dieu. Essai de théologie biblique*, EtT 2, Paris 1965; Ger. orig., *Gottes Herrschaft und Reich. Eine biblisch-theologische Studie*, Freiburg 1959.

SCHNECKENBURGER, M., *Beiträge zur Einleitung ins Neue Testament und zur Erklärung seiner schwierigen Stellen*, Stuttgart 1832.

SCHNEIDER, G., *Die Apostelgeschichte*, I–II, HThK 5, Freiburg / Basel / Wien 1980–1982; It. trans., SOFFRITTI, O., ed., *Gli Atti degli Apostoli. Testo greco e traduzione*, I–II, CTNT 5, Brescia 1985–1986.

SCHNIDER, F. – STENGER, W., "Die offene Tür und die unüberschreitbare Kluft. Struktur-analytische Überlegungen zum Gleichnis vom reichen Mann und armen Lazarus (Lk 16,19–31)", *NTS* 25.3 (1979) 273–283.

SCHNIEWIND, J., *Das Evangelium nach Matthäus*, Göttingen 1936, 1984[13].

SCHOLANDER, H., "Zu Mt. 11,12", *ZNW* 13 (1912) 172–175.

SCHOTTROFF, L., *Die Gleichnisse Jesu*, Gütersloh 2005; It. trans., *Le parabole di Gesù*, InTr 32, Brescia 2007.

SCHRENK, G., "βιάζομαι, βιαστής", *TDNT*, I, 609–614.

SCHRÖTER, J., "Erwägungen zum Gesetzesverständnis in Q anhand von Q 16,16–18", in C.M. TUCKETT, ed., *The Scriptures in the Gospels*, BEThL 131, Leuven 1997, 441–457.

SCHULZ, D., *Über die Parabel vom Verwalter. Lukas 16,1ff. Ein Versuch*, Breslau 1821.

SCHULZ, S., "Die Bedeutung des Markus für die Theologiegeschichte des Urchristentums", in F.L. CROSS, ed., *Studia Evangelica*, II, TU 87, Berlin 1964, 135–145.

–, *Q. Die Spruchquelle der Evangelisten*, Zürich 1972.

SCHUMACHER, R.D., "Saving Like a Fool and Spending Like It Isn't Yours. Reading the Parable of the Unjust Steward (Luke 16,1–8a) in Light of the Parable of the Rich Fool (Luke 12,16–20)", *RExp* 109.2 (2012) 269–276.

SCHÜRMANN, H., " '*Wer daher eines dieser geringsten Gebote auflöst...*'. *Wo fand Matthäus das Logion Matt 5,19*", *BZ* 4 (1960) 238–250 = *Traditionsgeschichtliche Untersuchungen zu den synoptischen Evangelien. Beiträge*, KBANT, Düsseldorf 1968, 126–136.

–, "Das Zeugnis der Redenquelle für die Basileai-Verkündigung Jesu", in J. DELOBEL, ed., *Logia. Les paroles de Jésus – The Sayings of Jesus*, Fs. J. Coppens, BEThL 59, Leuven 1982, 121–200.

SCHWARZ, G., "... lobte den betrügerischen Verwalter? (Lukas 16,8a)", *BZ* 18 (1974) 94–95.

SCHWEITZER, A., *Das Messianitäts – und Leidensgeheimnis. Eine Skizze des Lebens Jesu*, Tübingen 1901, 1956[3]; Eng. trans., *The Mystery of the Kingdom of God. The Secret of Jesus' Messiahship and Passion*, New York NY, 1914.

–, *The Quest of the Historical Jesus. A Critical Study of Its Progress from Reimarus to Wede*, London 1910, 1911[2]; Ger. orig., *Von Reimarus zu Wrede: eine Geschichte der Leben-Jesu-Forschung*, Tübingen 1906.

–, *Reich Gottes und Christentum*, Tübingen 1967.

SCHWEIZER, A., "Ob in der Stelle Matth. 11,12 ein Lob oder ein Tadel erhalten sei?", *ThStKr* 9 (1836) 90–122.

SCOTT, B.B., "A Master's Praise. Luke 16,1–8a", *Bib.* 64.2 (1983) 173–188.

SCOTT, E.F., "'The Kingdom of Heaven suffereth violence'. An Exposition of Matt 11,12–13", *BiWo* 30.6 (1907) 460–463.

–, *The Kingdom and the Messiah*, Edinburgh 1911.

SECCOMBE, D.P., *Possessions and the Poor in Luke-Acts*, SNTU.B 6, Linz 1983.

SEGRE, C., _Avviamento all'analisi del testo letterario_, EiPB 165, Torino 1985.

SELLEW, P., "Interior Monologue as a Narrative Device in the Parables of Luke", _JBL_ 111.2 (1992) 239–253.

SELLIN, G., "Komposition, Quellen und Funktion des lukanischen Reiseberichtes (Lk 9,52–19,28)", _NovT_ 20.2 (1978) 100–135.

SEMBRANO, L., "Il Regno di Dio nel Primo Testamento", _DSBP_ 57 (2011) 19–140.

SENIOR, D., _Matthew_, ANTC, Nashville TN, 1998.

SERRA, A., _Miryam. Figlia di Sion. La Donna di Nazaret e il femminile a partire dal giudaismo antico_, MdN 6, Milano 1997.

SHELLARD, B., _New Light on Luke. Its Purpose, Sources and Literary Context_, JSNT.S 215, London / New York NY, 2002, repr. 2004.

SHEROUSE, A.P., "The One Percent and the Gospel of Luke", _RExp_ 110.2 (2013) 285–293.

SHIELDS, M.A., "Syncretism and Divorce in Malachi 2,10–16", _ZAW_ 111(1999) 68–86.

SHINAN, A., _The Embroidered Targum. The Aggadah in Targum Pseudo-Jonathan of the Pentateuch_, Jerusalem 1992.

SIDER, R.J., _Andreas Bodenstein von Karlstadt. The Development of His Thought, 1515–1525_, SMRT 11, Leiden 1974.

SIGAL, P., "Early Christian and Rabbinic Liturgical Affinities", _NTS_ 30 (1984) 63–90.

–, _The Halakhah of Jesus of Nazareth According to the Gospel of Matthew_, SBL 18, Atlanta GA, 2007.

SIJPESTEIJN, P.J., ed., _The Wisconsin Papyri_. I., PLB 16, Leiden 1967; II., SAEp 11, Zutphen 1977.

SILBERMANN, A.M. – ROSENBAUM, M., ed., _Chumash with Targum Onkelos, Haphtaroth and Rashi's Commentary. Translated into English and Annotated. Devarim_, Jerusalem 1934.

SILVA, M., _Biblical Words and Their Meaning. An Introduction to Lexical Semantics_, Grand Rapids MI, 1983, 1994².

DESILVA, D.A., _4 Maccabees_, GAP, Sheffield 1998.

–, "The Sinaiticus Text of 4 Maccabees", _CBQ_ 68.1 (2006) 47–62.

–, "The Human Ideal, the Problem of Evil, and Moral Responsibility in 4 Maccabees", _BBR_ 23.1 (2013) 57–77.

SIMON, E., "Bia et Kratos", LIMC, III.1, 114–115.

SIMONETTI, M. – _al._, ed., _Sancti Cypriani Episcopi Opera_, I–III.4, CChr.SL 3, Turnholti 1972–2004.

SINTENIS, C., ed., _Plutarchi. Vitae Parallelae_, I–V, BSGRT, Lipsiae 1881–1902.

SKEHAN, P.W. – DI LELLA, A.A., _The Wisdom of Ben Sira. A New Translation with Notes, Introduction and Commentary_, AncYB 39, New York NY, 1974, repr. 2008.

SLINGS, S.R., ed., _Platonis Rempublicam. Recognovit brevique adnotatione critica instruxit_, SCBO, Oxonii 2003.

SMELIK, W.F., _The Targum of Judges_, OTS 36, Leiden 1995.

SMITH, C.F., ed., _Thucydides_, I–IV, LCL, London / Cambridge MA, 1975–1980.

SMITH, G., "The Returning King: The 'Two Messiahs' in Zechariah", _IMJP_ 15.5 (2004) 1–7.

SMITH, G.K., "Helictites – What are They?", _ACav_ 143 (1998) 14.

SMITH, H.W., ed., _Aeschylus with an English Translation_, I–II, LCL, London / Cambridge MA, 1956–1957.

SMITH, J.P., ed., _A Compendious Syriac Dictionary. Founded upon the Thesaurus Syriacus of R. Payne Smith_, Oxford 1903.

SMITH, W., ed., _Dictionary of Greek and Roman Biography and Mythology_, I–III, Boston MA, 1867.

SNELL, B. – MAEHLER, H., ed., *Pindari Carmina cum fragmenti*, I–IV, BSGRT, Lipsiae 1955–1975, repr. 1989.

SNODGRASS, K.R, *Stories with Intent. A Comprehensive Guide to the Parables of Jesus*, Grand Rapids MI, 2008.

SNOY, T., "Approche littéraire de Luc 16", *FV* 72.3 (1973) 39–68.

SOLMSEN, F. – *al.*, ed., *Hesiodi Theogonia. Opera et Dies Scutum. Fragmenta selecta*, Oxoni 1970, 1990³.

SPARKS, H.F.D., ed., *The Apocryphal Old Testament*, New York NY, 1984.

SPENCE, H.D.M. – EXELL, J.S., ed., *The Gospel According to St. Luke*, I–II, PulC, Bellingham WA, 2004.

SPENGEL, L., ed., *Rhetores Graeci*, I–III, Lipsiae 1853–1856, 1894.

SPICQ, C., *Agapè dans le Nouveau Testament. Analyse des textes*, I–III, EtB, Paris 1958–1959.

–, *Théologie morale du Nouveau Testament*, I–II, EtB, Paris 1964, 1970⁴.

–, *Notes de lexicographie néo-testamentaire*, I–III, OBO 22, Fribourg / Göttingen 1978, repr. 1982 = *Lexique théologique du Nouveau Testament*, Paris / Fribourg 1991².

–, "βιάζομαι", *TLNT*, I, 287–291.

SPRAGUE, R.K., "Dissoi Logoi or Dialexeis. Two-Fold Arguments", *Mind* 77.306 (1968) 155–167.

VAN STAALDUINE-SULMAN, E., *The Targum of Samuel*, SAIS 1, Leiden / Köln / Boston MA, 2002.

STADTMÜLLER, H., ed., *Anthologia Graeca epigrammatum Palatina cum Planudea*, I–III, BSGRT, Lipsiae 1894–1899.

STÄHLIN, O., ed., *Clemens Alexandrinus. Opera*, I–IV, GCS 52, Leipzig 1905–1936, Berlin 1985⁴.

STANDAERT, B., "L'art de composer dans l'œuvre de Luc", in F. REFOULE, ed., *À cause de l'Évangile. Ètudes sur les Synoptiques et les Actes*, Fs. J. Dupont, LeDiv 123, Paris 1985, 323–347.

STANKO, E.A., ed., *The Meanings of Violence*, London / New York NY, 2003.

STEIN, R.H., *An Introduction to the Parables of Jesus*, Philadelphia PA, 1981.

–, *Luke*, NAC 24, Nashville TN, 1992.

STEIN, S., "The Laws on Interest in the Old Testament", *JThS* 4.2 (1953) 161–170.

STENGER, W., "βιάζομαι, βιαστής", *EDNT*, I, 216–219.

STIER, R., *Die Reden des Herrn Jesu. Andeutungen für gläubiges Verständnis derselben*, I–VI, Barmen 1843–1848.

STONE, M.E., ed., *Jewish Writings of the Second Temple Period. Apocrypha, Pseudepigrapha, Qumran Sectarian Writings, Philo, Josephus*, CRI 2.2, Assen / Philadelphia PA, 1984.

STORY, J.L., "Twin Parables of Stewardship in Luke 16", *AThI* 2.1 (2009) 105–120.

STRATTON, C., "Pressure for the Kingdom. An Exposition", *Interp.* 8.4 (1954) 414–421.

STRAUSS, M.L., *The Davidic Messiah in Luke-Acts. The Promise and its Fulfillment in Lukan Christology*, JSNT.S 110, Sheffield 1995.

STRECKER, G., *Der Weg der Gerechtigkeit. Untersuchung zur Theologie des Matthäus*, FRLANT 82, Göttingen 1962.

STREETER, B.H., *The Four Gospels. A Study of Origins treating of the Manuscript Tradition, Sources, Authorship, & Dates*, Eugene OR, 1924, repr. 2008.

STUART, D., *Hosea-Jonah*, WBC 31, Dallas TX, 1987.

SUBILIA, V., *Il Regno di Dio. Interpretazioni nel corso dei secoli*, SSNStT 15, Torino 1993.

SULLIVAN, L.H., "The Tall Office Building Artistically Considered", *LipM* (March 1896) 403–409.

SUSEMIHL, F., ed., *Aristotelis quae feruntur Magna Moralia*, BSGR, Lipsiae 1883.

–, ed., *Aristotelis quae feruntur Oeconomica*, BSGR, Lipsiae 1887.

SWEET, D., "'Noble Sweat'. *Paideia* in the Gymnasium and the Torture Chamber of 4 Maccabees", *Glossolalia* 4.2 (2012) 11–23.

SYNOD OF BISHOPS (XII ORDINARY GENERAL ASSEMBLY), "*Instrumentum Laboris*. The Word of God in the Life and Mission of the Church", in *L'Osservatore Romano. Weekly ed. in English. Special Insert. Document* (25 June, 2008), Vatican City, n. 26.

TALBERT, C.H., "Lucan Patterns (Luke 10,21–18,30 as Chiasmus)", in *Literary Patterns, Theological Themes, and the Genre of Luke-Acts*, SBL.MS 20, Missoula MT, 1974, 51–56.

–, *Reading Luke. A Literary and Theological Commentary on the Third Gospel*, RNTS, New York NY, 1982, repr. Macon GA, 2002.

–, "Between Text and Sermon: Matthew 11,2–24", *Interp.* 64.4 (2010) 406–408.

TAN, K.H., "The Shema and Early Christianity", *TynB* 52.9 (2008) 181–206.

TANGHE, V., "Abraham, son fils et son envoyé (Luc 16,19–31)", *RB* 91.4 (1984) 557–577.

TANNEHILL, R.C., *The Narrative Unity of Luke-Acts. A Literary Interpretation*, I–II, Philadelphia PA / Minneapolis MN, 1986–1990.

–, *Luke*, ANTC, Nashville TN, 1996.

TARTAGLIA, L., ed., *Eusebio di Cesarea. Sulla vita di Costantino. Introduzione, traduzione e note*, QKoin 8, Napoli 1984.

TAUBENSCHLAG, R., "Periods and Terms in Graeco-Roman Egypt", in *Atti del Congresso Internazionale di Diritto Romano e di Storia del Diritto*, III, Verona 1948, 353–366 = in *Opera Minora*, II, Warsaw 1959, 171–187.

–, *The Law of Greco-Roman Egypt in the Light of the Papyri*, Warsaw 1955, Milan 1972².

TAUBERSCHMIDT, G., *Secondary Parallelism. A Study of Translation Technique in LXX Proverbs*, SBL.AB 15, Atlanta GA, 2004.

TAYLOR, V., *Behind the Third Gospel. A Study of the Proto-Luke Hypothesis*, Oxford 1926.

–, "The Order of Q", *JThS* 4.1 (1953) 27–31.

TERRY, M.S., ed., *The Sibylline Oracle. Translated from the Greek into English Blank Verse*, New York NY / Cincinnati OH, 1899.

THACKERAY, H.ST.J., ed., *The Letter of Aristeas. Translated into English with an Introduction and Notes*, London / New York NY, 1904.

THACKERAY, H.ST.J. – *al.*, ed., *Josephus with an English Translation*, I–X, LCL, London / Cambridge MA, 1926–1981.

THACKSTON, W.M., *Introduction to Syriac. An Elementary Grammar with Readings from Syriac Literature*, Bethesda MD, 1999.

THEIßEN, G., "Jünger als Gewalttäter (Mt 11,12f; Lk 16,16): der Stürmerspruch als Selbststigmatisierung einer Minorität", in D. HELLHOLM – H. MOXNES – T.K. SEIM – F.S.J. JERVELL, ed., *Mighty Minorities? Minorities in Early Christianity – Positions and Strategies*, Fs. J. Jervell, StTh 49.1, Oslo / Copenhagen / Stockholm / Boston MA, 1995, 183–200 = in A. MERTZ, ed., *Jesus als historische Gestalt. Beiträge zur Jesusforschung* 60, Fs. G. Theißen, FRLANT 202, Göttingen 2003, 153–168.

THIERING, B.E., "Are the 'Violent Men' False Teachers?", *NovT* 21.4 (1979) 293–297.

TISATO, N. – *al.*, "Microbial Mediation of Complex Subterranean Mineral Structures", *SciRep* 5 (2015) 1–9.

VON TISCHENDORF, C., ed., *Evangelia Apocrypha. Adhibitis plurimis codicibus graecis et latinis maximam partem nunc primum consultis atque ineditorum copia insignibus*, Lipsiae 1853.

–, ed., *Apocalypses Apocryphae. Mosis, Esdrae, Pauli, Iohannis, item Mariae Dormitio. Additis Evangeliorum et Actuum Apocryphorum Supplementis*, Lipsiae 1866.

TISSOT, G., ed., *Ambroise de Milan. Traité sur l'Évangile de S. Luc*, I–II, SC 45, 52, Paris 1956, 1958.

TOPEL, L.J., "On the Injustice of the Unjust Steward. Luke 16,1–13", *CBQ* 37.2 (1975) 216–227.

TORREY, C.C., *The Four Gospels. A New Translation*, London / New York NY, 1933.

–, *Our Translated Gospels. Some of the Evidence*, London 1936.

TOSATO, A., *Vangelo e ricchezza. Nuove prospettive esegetiche*, Pol. 46, Catanzaro 2002.

TOSTATUS, A., *Commentariorum in Euangelium Matthaei. Pars Tertia*, Venetiis 1596.

TOWNER, W.S., "Hermeneutical Systems of Hillel and the Tannaim. A Fresh Look", *HUCA* 53 (1982) 101–135.

TOWNSEND, J.T., ed., *Midrash Tanḥuma. Translated into English with Introduction, Indices, and Brief Notes (S. Buber Recension)*, I–III, Hoboken NJ, 1989–2003.

TRAPÉ, A. – PICCOLOMINI, P.R., ed., *Opera Omnia di Sant'Agostino. Edizione bilingue*, I–XLIV.3, NBAg 1–3, Roma 1965–2009.

TREDENNICK, H. – *al.*, ed., *Aristotle with an English Translation*, I–XXIII, LCL, London / Cambridge MA, 1926–1970, repr. 1971–1995.

TREVISAN, P., ed., *S. Giovanni Climaco. Scala Paradisi*, I–II, CPS.G 8–9, Torino 1941.

TRITES, A.A. – W.J. LARKIN, *The Gospel of Luke and Acts*, CoBC 12, Carol Stream IL, 2006.

TROCMÉ, E., *Jésus de Nazareth. Vu par les témoins de sa vie*, BT(N), Neuchâtel 1971; It. trans., *Gesù di Nazaret. Visto dai testimoni della sua vita*, Brescia 1975.

TROISI, S. – PACCINI, C., *Siamo nati e non moriremo mai più. Storia di Chiara Corbella Petrillo*, Assisi 2013.

TROXEL, R.L., *LXX-Isaiah as Translation and Interpretation. The Strategies of the Translator of the Septuagint of Isaiah*, JSJ.S 124, Leiden – Boston MA, 2008.

TROXLE, J.A., Jr., *Doing Justice to the Unjust Steward. An Exegetical Examination of Luke 16,1–13 and its Context*, diss., Ann Arbor MI, 2003.

TSUMURA, D.T., *The First Book of Samuel*, NICOT, Grand Rapids MI, 2007.

TUCKER, W.D., Jr, *Jonah. A Handbook on the Hebrew Text*, Waco TX, 2006.

TUCKETT, C.M., *Q and the History of Early Christianity. Studies on Q*, Edinburgh 1996.

–, "The Current State of the Synoptic Problem", in P. FOSTER – *al.*, ed., *New Studies in the Synoptic Problem. Oxford Conference, April 2008*, Fs. C.M. Tuckett, BEThL 239, Leuven / Paris / Walpole MA, 2011, 9–50.

TURNBULL, H.W. – *al.*, ed., *The Correspondence of Isaac Newton*, I–VII, Cambridge 1959–1977.

TYSON, J.B., "Conflict as a Literary Theme in the Gospel of Luke", in W.R. FARMER, ed., *New Synoptic Studies. The Cambridge Conference and Beyond*, Macon GA, 1983, 303–327.

UDOH, F., "The Tale of an Unrighteous Slave (Luke 16,1–8[13])", *JBL* 128.2 (2009) 311–335.

UEBERSCHAER, F., *Weisheit aus der Begegnung. Bildung nach dem Buch Ben Sira*, BZAW 379, Berlin / New York NY, 2007.

ULUHOGIAN, G., *Basilio di Cesarea. Il Libro delle Domande (Le Regole)*, XIX–XX, CSCO.Ar 536–537, Louvain 1993–1994.

URBACH, E.E., *The Sages. Their Concepts and Beliefs*, I, Jerusalem 1975.

VANDERKAM, J.C., ed., *The Book of Jubilees. A Critical Text*, I–II, CSCO.Ae 510–511, Louvain 1989.

–, "Recent Scolarship on the Book of Jubilees", *CBRe* 6.3 (2008) 405–431.

VAN HECK, A., ed., *De beneficentia (vulgo De pauperibus amandi I)*, in G. HEIL – A. VAN HECK – E. GEBHARDT – A. SPIRA, ed., *Gregorii Nysseni Opera. IX. Sermones. Pars I*, ISCH, Leiden 1967, 91–108.

–, ed., *In illud quatenus uni ex his fecistis mihi fecistis (vulgo De pauperibus amandis II)*, in G. HEIL – A. VAN HECK – E. GEBHARDT – A. SPIRA, ed., *Gregorii Nysseni Opera. IX. Sermones. Pars I*, ISCH, Leiden 1967, 109–127.

VAUCHER, M., "Un couple infernal. Vie et violence", *Choisir* (2007) 13–16.

–, "Vie, violence… La haine, voie de transformation de la violence", in D. MARGUERAT, ed., *Dieu est-il violent?*, Paris 2008, 13–33.

VAUCHES, A., *La spiritualité du Moyen Âge occidental (VIIIᵉ–XIIIᵉ siècles)*, S.Hist 19, Paris 1975.

VERHEYDEN, J., "The Violators of the Kingdom of God: Struggling with Q Polemics in Q 16,16–18", in H.W. HOLLANDER – J. TROMP – R. BUITENWERF, ed., *Jesus, Paul, and Early Christianity*, Fs. H.J. de Jonge, NT.S 130, Leiden / Boston MA, 2008, 397–415.

VERMES, G., "Jewish Literature and New Testament Exegesis: Reflections on Methodology", *JJS* 33 (1982) 362–376.

VERNANT, J.-P., *Myth and Thought among the Greeks*, London 1983; Fr. orig., *Mythe et pensée chez les Grecs*, Paris 1965.

–, *Mythe et société en grèce ancienne*, TaAp, Paris 1974.

VIA, D.O., Jr., *The Parables. Their Literary and Existential Dimension*, Philadelphia PA, 1967.

–, "Parable and Example Story. A Literary-Structuralist Approach", *Semeia* 1 (1974) 105–133.

VINCE, J.H. – DEWITT, N.W. – MURRAY, A.T., ed., *Demosthenes with an English Translation*, I–VII, LCL, London / Cambridge MA, 1926–1949, repr. 1962–1984.

VIVIANO, B.T., *The Kingdom of God in History*, GNS 27, Wilmington DE, 1988; Fr. trans., ID., *Le Royaume de Dieu dans l'histoire*, LiBi 96, Paris 1992.

VOGELS, W., "Having and Longing. A Semiotic Analysis of Luke 16,19–31", *EeT* 20.1 (1989) 27–46.

VOLTAGGIO, F.G., *La oración de los padres y las madres de Israel. Investigación en el Targum del Pentateuco. La Antigua tradición judía y los orígenes del cristianismo*, BiMi 33, Estella (Navarra) 2010.

VOLZ, P., *Jüdische Eschatologie von Daniel bis Akiba*, Tübingen / Leipzig 1903.

VRIEZEN, T.C. – VAN DER WOUDE, A.S., *Ancient Israelite and Early Jewish Literature*, Leiden / Boston MA, 2005.

WAALER, E., *The Shema and the First Commandment in First Corinthians. An Intertextual Approach to Paul's Re-reading of Deuteronomy*, WUNT 253, Tübingen 2008.

WAGNER, M., *Saint Basil. Ascetical Works*, FaCh 9, Washington DC, 1950, repr. 1970.

WALTERS, P., *The Assumed Authorial Unity of Luke and Acts. A Reassessment of the Evidence*, SNTS.MS 145, Cambridge 2008.

WARMINGTON, E.H., ed., *Remains of Old Latin*, I–IV, LCL, London / Cambridge MA, 1935–1940, repr. 1961–1979.

WAY, A.S., ed., *Euripides. With and English Translation*, I–IV, LCL, London / Cambridge MA, 1912, repr. 1958–1959.

WAYMENT, T.A., *The Text of the New Testament Apocrypha (100–400 CE)*, London / New York NY, 2013.

WEAVER, D.J., "'Suffering Violence' and the Kingdom of Heaven (Matt 11,12): A Matthean Manual for Life in a Time of War", *HTS* 67.1 (2011) 1–12.

WEBER, C.P., "חַיִל", *TWOT*, I, 271–272.

WEBER, F., *Jüdische Theologie auf Grund des Talmud und verwandter Schriften*, Leipzig 1880, 1897².

WEISS, B., *Das Matthäus-Evangelium*, KEK 1.1, Göttingen 1832, 1898⁹.

WEISS, J., *Die Predigt Jesu vom Reiche Gottes*, Göttingen 1892, 1900²; Eng. trans., HIERS, R.H. – HOLLAND, D.L., ed., *Jesus' Proclamation of the Kingdom of God*, LJeS, Philadelphia PA, 1971.

WEISSE, C.H., ed., *Die evangelische Geschichte. Kritisch und philosophisch*, I–II, Leipzig 1838.

WELLHAUSEN, J., *Das Evangelium Matthaei*, Berlin 1904, 1914².

WENDLAND, P., ed., *Aristeae ad Philocratem epistula. Cum ceteris de origine versionis LXX interpretum testimoniis*, Lipsiae 1900.

WENHAM, D. – *al.*, ed., *Exploring the New Testament*, I–II, Downers Grove IL, 2001–2002.

WENHAM, G.W., *Genesis*, I–II, WBC 1–2, Dallas TX, 1987–1994.

WENHAM, J., "The Identification of Luke", *EvQ* 63.1 (1991) 3–44.

WÉNIN, A., "De la douceur première à la douceur conquise sur la mort. Violence, loi et justice dans les écrits de Paul Beauchamp", *Théophilyon* 17.1 (2012) 23–40.

WERNER, M., *Die Entstehung des christlichen Dogmas*, Bern 1941.

WEST, M.L., ed., *Iambi et elegi Graeci. Ante Alexandrum cantati*, I–II, Oxonii 1971–1972, repr. 1989–1992.

DE WETTE, W.M.L., *Kurze Erklärung des Evangeliums Matthäi*, KEHNT 1.1, Leipzig 1836.

WHITE, D.S., *Patriarch Photius of Constantinople*, Brookline MA, 1981.

WHITE, E. – GERARD, H., ed., *Hesiod. The Homeric Hymns and Homerica with an English Translation*, LCL 57, London / Cambridge MA, 1914, repr. 1970.

WHYBRAY, R.N., *Wealth and Poverty in the Book of Proverbs*, JSOT.S 99, Sheffield 1990.

WIEFEL, W., *Das Evanglium nach Lukas*, ThHK 3, Berlin 1988.

WILCKEN, U., ed., *Urkunden der Ptolemäerzeit (ältere Funde)*, I–II, Berlin 1927–1957.

WILKINSON, G., ed., *Aristotelis Ethicorum Nicomacheorum libri decem. Codicum mss. collatione recogniti, et notis illustrati*, Oxonii 1809³.

WILLIAMS, F.E., "Is Almsgiving the Point of the 'Unjust Steward'?", *JBL* 83.3 (1964) 293–297.

WILLIAMSON, H.G.M., *Ezra, Nehemiah*, WBC 16, Dallas TX, 1985.

WILLIS, J.T., "The Juxtaposition of Synonymous and Chiastic Parallelism in Tricola in O.T. Hebrew Psalm Poetry", *VT* 29 (1979) 465–480.

WILLIS, T.M., *Leviticus*, AOTC, Nashville TN, 2009.

WILSON, S.G., *Luke and the Law*, SNTS.MS 50, Cambridge MA, 1983.

WILSON, W.T., *The Sentences of Pseudo-Phocylides*, CEJL, Berlin 2005.

–, *Philo of Alexandria. On Virtues. Introduction, Translation, and Commentary*, PhAl.CS 3, Leiden / Boston MA, 2011.

WINDISCH, H., "Die Sprüche vom Eingehen in das Reich Gottes", *ZNW* 27.2 (1928) 163–192.

WINK, W., *John the Baptist in the Gospel Tradition*, SNTS.MS 7, Cambridge 1968.

WINSTON, D., *The Wisdom of Solomon. A New Translation with Introduction and Commentary*, AncYB 43, New York NY, 1974, repr. 2008.

WITHERUP, R.D., *101 Questions and Answers on Paul*, New York NY / Mahwah NJ, 2003.

WOJTYŁA, K.J., JOHN PAUL II, *Redemptor Hominis. Encyclical Letter of the Supreme Pontiff John Paul II to his Venerable Brothers in the Episcopate, the Priests, the Religious Families, the Sons and Daughters of the Church, and to All Men and Women of Good Will, at the Beginning of His Papal Ministry*, Vatican City 1979; Lat. orig., "Litterae encyclicae *Paenitentiam agere*", *AAS* 71 (1979) 257–324.

–, "Celebrazione Eucaristica per gli universitari romani. Omelia di Giovanni Paolo II, Giovedì, 11 dicembre 1986" [On-line edition: access 08.05.2017], https://w2.vatican.va/content/john-paul-ii/it/homilies/1986/documents/hf_jp-ii_hom_19861211_universitari-romani.html.

–, "Homily of His Holiness John Paul II, During the Mass for University Students and Professors. St. Peter's Basilica. Thursday, 12 December 1996" [On-line edition: access 08.05.2017], https://w2.vatican.va/content/john-paul-ii/en/homilies/1996/documents/hf_jp-ii_hom_19961212.html.

WOJTYŁA, K.J., JOHN PAUL II, "Discorso al clero, ai religiosi e alle religiose. Cattedrale di Latina – Domenica, 29 Settembre 1991. Visita pastorale a Latina" [On-line edition: access 08.05.2017], http://w2.vatican.va/content/john-paul-ii/it/speeches/1991/september/ documents/hf_jp-ii_spe_19910929_clero-religiosi.html.

–, *Mane Nobiscum Domine. Apostolic Letter of the Holy Father John Paul II to the Bishops, Clergy and Faithful, for the Year of the Eucharist*, Vatican City 2004; Lat. orig., "Epistulae Apostolicae *Mane nobiscum Domine*", *AAS* 97 (2005) 337–352.

WOLF, E., *Griechisches Rechtsdenken*, I–IV, Frankfurt am Main 1950–1970.

WOODINGTON, J.D., "Charity and Deliverance from Death in the Accounts of Tabitha and Cornelius", *CBQ* 79.4 (2017) 634–650.

WRIGHT, B.G., "The Letter of Aristeas and the Question of Septuagint Origins Redux", *JAJud* 2 (2011) 303–325.

WRIGHT, F.A., ed., *Select Letters of St. Jerome*, LCL 262, London / Cambridge MA, 1933, repr. 1980.

WRIGHT, R.B., ed., *The Psalms of Solomon. A Critical Edition of the Greek Text*, JCTC 1, London / New York NY, 2007.

WRIGHT, S.E., "Parables on Poverty and Riches (Luke 12,13–21; 16,1–13; 16,19–31)", in R.N. LONGENECKER, ed., *The Challenge of Jesus' Parables*, Grand Rapids MI, 2000, 217–239.

WÜNSCHE, A.K., ed., *Der Midrasch Bemidbar Rabba. Das ist die allegorische Auslegung des vierten Buches Mose*, BRab 4.1, Leipzig 1885.

YAGUELLO, M., *Language Through the Looking Glass. Exploring Language and Linguistics*, New York NY, 1998.

YORK, A.D., "The Dating of Targumic Literature", *JSJ* 5 (1974) 49–62.

YOUNG, B.H., *Jesus the Jewish Theologian*, Peabody MA, 1995.

ZAHN, T., *Das Evangelium des Matthäus*, KNT 1, Leipzig 1903, 1922[4].

–, *Das Evangelium des Lukas*, KNT 3, Leipzig 1913.

ZELZER, M. – FALLER, O., ed., *Sancti Ambrosi Opera*, X.1–4, CSEL 82, Vindobonae 1968–1996.

ZEOLLA, G.F., ed., *Analytical-Literal Translation of the Old Testament (Septuagint)*, IV, Denver 2014.

ZIEGLER, J., ed., *Duodecim prophetae*, SVTG 13, Göttingen 1943.

–, ed., *Sapientia Iesu Filii Sirach*, SVTG 12.2, Göttingen 1980.

ZIMMERLI, W., *Ezekiel 2. A Commentary on the Book of the Prophet Ezekiel*, II, Hermeneia, Philadelphia PA, 1983.

ZINCONE, S., "Regno di Dio nei Padri dei primi secoli", *DSBP* 58 (2011) 25–75.

ZINGERLE, A., ed., *Sancti Hilarii Episcopi Pictaviensis. Tractatus super Psalmos*, CSEL 22, Vindobonae 1891.

ZVI, E.B., *Signs of Jonah. Reading and Rereading in Ancient Yehud*, JSOT.S 367, London / New York NY, 2003.

ZYRO, F.F., "Erklärung von Matth. 11,12", *ThStKr* 33 (1860) 398–410.

–, "Neue Auslegung der Stelle Matth. 11,12", *ThStKr* 46 (1873) 663–704.

Index of References

Old Testament

Old Testament Pseudepigrapha

New Testament

New Testament Apocrypha

Qumran Texts

Ancient Papyri

Ancient Authors

Patristic and Medieval Works

Rabbinic Literature

Church Documents

Index of Authors Cited

Index of Subjects

Wissenschaftliche Untersuchungen zum Neuen Testament

Edited by Jörg Frey (Zürich)

Associate Editors:

Markus Bockmuehl (Oxford) · James A. Kelhoffer (Uppsala)
Tobias Nicklas (Regensburg) · Janet Spittler (Charlottesville, VA)
J. Ross Wagner (Durham, NC)

WUNT I is an international series dealing with the entire field of early Christianity and its Jewish and Graeco-Roman environment. Its historical-philological profile and interdisciplinary outlook, which its long-term editor Martin Hengel was instrumental in establishing, is maintained by an international team of editors representing a wide range of the traditions and themes of New Testament scholarship. The sole criteria for acceptance to the series are the scholarly quality and lasting merit of the work being submitted. Apart from the specialist monographs of experienced researchers, some of which may be habilitations, *WUNT I* features collections of essays by renowned scholars, source material collections and editions as well as conference proceedings in the form of a handbook on themes central to the discipline.

WUNT II complements the first series by offering a publishing platform in paperback for outstanding writing by up-and-coming young researchers. Dissertations and monographs are presented alongside innovative conference volumes on fundamental themes of New Testament research. Like Series I, it is marked by a historical-philological character and an international orientation that transcends exegetical schools and subject boundaries. The academic quality of Series II is overseen by the same team of editors.

WUNT I:
ISSN: 0512-1604
Suggested citation: WUNT I
All available volumes can be found at
www.mohrsiebeck.com/wunt1

WUNT II:
ISSN: 0340-9570
Suggested citation: WUNT II
All available volumes can be found
at *www.mohrsiebeck.com/wunt2*

Mohr Siebeck
www.mohrsiebeck.com